Introducing Language

D1471460

Introducing Language in Use, second edition provides a lively and accessible introduction to the study of language and linguistics. Drawing on a vast range of data and examples of language in its many forms, this book provides students with the tools they need to analyse real language in diverse contexts.

The second edition of this best-selling textbook has been fully revised and updated with entirely new chapters on phonology and sociolinguistics, two separate chapters on syntax and grammar, completely rewritten chapters on multilingualism, psycholinguistics and world Englishes, and a greater focus on corpus linguistics.

Introducing Language in Use:

- covers all the core areas and topics of language study, including semiotics, communication, grammar, phonetics, phonology, words, semantics, variety in language, history of English, world Englishes, multilingualism, psycholinguistics, sociolinguistics, language acquisition, conversation analysis, pragmatics and politeness
- adopts a 'how to' approach, encouraging students to apply their knowledge as they learn it
- draws on examples of language from around the world in forms ranging from conversation to advertising and text messaging, always giving precedence to real language in use
- includes activities throughout the text and an extensive glossary of terms.

The book is supported by a companion website offering a wealth of additional resources including commentaries on the activities in the book, suggested further reading and references, links to useful websites, more texts to analyse, additional web activities, 'fun with language' exercises, discussion questions and an additional 'Language in Education' chapter.

This is an essential coursebook for all introductory courses in English language, communication and linguistics.

Visit the companion website at www.routledge.com/cw/merrison.

Andrew John Merrison is a senior lecturer in linguistics at York St John University. He has taught at the Universities of Durham, Edinburgh, York, and at Queen Margaret College, Edinburgh.

Aileen Bloomer is a Fellow in Linguistics at York St John University. She has also worked in Warwick, Germany, Vietnam and China.

Patrick Griffiths (1942–2012) was a professor of English at Beppu University Japan and had previously taught at the University of the South Pacific, the University of York (UK) and York St John University.

Christopher J. Hall is Reader in Applied Linguistics at York St John University. He taught previously at the University of the Americas in Puebla, Mexico.

Praise for this edition:

'Across an extended range of topics and examples, this new edition builds on proven strengths of the first: it is accessible, up-to-date, and rich in exemplification and follow-up activities. What makes the new edition particularly useful as prescribed course reading is the easy movement it achieves from introductory concepts and description through to practical analysis of what the volume is then most eloquent about: language in use.'

Professor Alan Durant, *Middlesex University, UK*

'*Introducing Language in Use* provides a comprehensive and practical introduction to the study of language and communication. It guides students in a step-by-step fashion into doing analyses of language at different levels: phonology, morphology, syntax, semantics and pragmatics. Not only structural aspects are discussed, but also language acquisition and its use in different contexts and for different purposes. This second edition goes deeper than the first one by adding and updating several chapters and it can be recommended as course book to students of linguistics and English, as well as to anyone interested in human language.'

Professor Gisela Håkansson, *Lund University, Sweden*

'*Introducing Language in Use* (second edition) is an ideal course book for students or anyone beginning to study linguistics and languages. It provides a comprehensive and thorough overview of the traditional core subjects of linguistics (phonetics/phonology, syntax and morphology) and describes recent developments in English and all its global variations. It also includes fascinating material on language and the mind.'

Dr Irina Moore, *University of Wolverhampton, UK*

'This comprehensive introduction to the main topics in language study is an excellent addition to the field. The style is accessible, lively and engaging. Plenty of exercises and examples make it particularly useful for both teachers and general readers.'

Dr Elizabeth Holt, *University of Huddersfield, UK*

'This book is perfect for teaching the basics of linguistics to undergraduate students on all types of English programmes, especially to classes where backgrounds can be very different. It covers all the main branches of linguistics and presents language as a behaviour that always occurs in a social context. It offers a wide range of examples and activities that students can perform in groups as homework or when in class, thus helping to shape seminars around students' questions and needs. The style is very student-friendly, constant cross-referencing and very detailed reminders and headers help students revise, and an interdisciplinary approach is always supported. It is much more than a textbook and a great teaching tool.'

Dr Arianna Maiorani, *Loughborough University, UK*

'*Introducing Language in Use* is an intelligent, lively, well-paced and well-written textbook that will capture and hold students' attention and challenge them with a battery of engaging questions and meaningful activities. Its tone is explanatory without being patronizing and it neither overdoes the jargon nor shies away from introducing technically more difficult concepts. It is good at incorporating external readings and supplementary information and balances easily on the tightrope between entertaining and educating. Thoroughly recommended for undergraduate students.'

Professor Barbara Fennell, *University of Aberdeen, UK*

'Introducing Language in Use provides a comprehensive introduction to several core fields of linguistic enquiry. The inclusion of real-world examples, and the walk-through analyses which accompany them, make this text a practical introduction to language analysis, suitable not only for students of linguistics, but also for emerging clinicians who need to develop core knowledge of language and speech.'

Ms Colleen Holt, University of Melbourne, Australia

'An enjoyable, accessible and up-to-date introduction to linguistics which moves away from orthodox prescriptions of "correct" language use and digs into the complexities of human communication. The wealth of practical activities presented is essential for a thorough understanding of concepts and paradigms.'

Dr Eva Codó, Autonomous University of Barcelona, Spain

'Introducing Language in Use is a comprehensive, easy-to-follow guide to linguistics, navigating every aspect of language-related inquiry, from grammar and meaning to cognition and social interaction. It is organized in a clear fashion, and written in plain English that makes obtuse linguistic concepts eminently accessible to a wide audience.'

Professor Bao Zhiming, National University of Singapore

Introducing Language in Use

A Coursebook

SECOND EDITION

Andrew John Merrison,
Aileen Bloomer, Patrick Griffiths
and Christopher J. Hall

Routledge
Taylor & Francis Group

LONDON AND NEW YORK

First published 2005
by Routledge

This second edition published 2014
by Routledge
2 Park Square, Milton Park, Abingdon, Oxon OX14 4RN

and by Routledge
711 Third Avenue, New York, NY 10017

Routledge is an imprint of the Taylor & Francis Group, an informa business

© 2014 Andrew John Merrison, Aileen Bloomer, Patrick Griffiths and Christopher J. Hall
The right of the authors to be identified as authors of this work has been asserted by them in accordance with sections 77 and 78 of the Copyright, Designs and Patents Act 1988.

British Library Cataloguing in Publication Data
A catalogue record for this book is available from the British Library

Library of Congress Cataloging-in-Publication Data Bloomer, Aileen, 1947-
Introducing language in use: a coursebook / Andrew John Merrison, Aileen Bloomer, Patrick Griffiths and Christopher J. Hall. — Second Edition / Merrison, Andrew.
pages cm
Previous edition was authored by Bloomer, Aileen.
1. Language and languages—Textbooks. 2. Linguistics—Textbooks. I. Title.
P107.B59 2013
410.71—dc23

2013015357

ISBN: 978–0–415–58305–3 (hbk)
ISBN: 978–0–415–58338–1 (pbk)
ISBN: 978–1–315–88431–8 (ebk)

Typeset in Joanna
by RefineCatch Limited, Bungay, Suffolk

To the memory of

Patrick Griffiths

linguist, teacher, gentleman, friend

Contents

Figures

Tables

Texts

Preface to the Second Edition

We noted that a lot happened to us during the writing of the first edition: we could say the same about the period of writing the second edition. Saddest of all was the death of our co-author, Patrick Griffiths, to whom we dedicate this second edition. He was the best of colleagues, a good friend to us and to so many other people and simply a good and gentle man. May this second edition be a worthy tribute to his scholarship.

From the beginning of working on the second edition, we welcomed a new author to the ILU team. All three original authors were delighted when Chris Hall agreed to join us in our adventure and exploration.

Comments from many users of the book led to some of the changes in this edition: phonetics is now in two chapters and there is a new chapter on phonology, the original chapter on syntax and grammar has been divided to form two chapters on syntax and on grammar respectively, and there is a new chapter on sociolinguistics to respond to requests for some more theory. All the chapters have been updated in terms of reading and reference material and most chapters have at least some new data to work on – the sources of language in use are undoubtedly infinite. Chapter 14 has been completely rewritten. Chapters 16 and 18 are substantially changed from the first edition. As in the first edition, a final chapter contains yet more language in use for you to analyse – in the second edition, this chapter and the data are presented on the companion website rather than in the print edition.

Acknowledgements

We thank Patrick's family for allowing us to use and develop the materials he had already produced in preparation for this second edition. Without that, our task would have been so much greater.

We also thank

- colleagues at York St John University for their support, especially those in the Department of Languages and Linguistics and in the Language and Identities in InterAction (LIdIA) Research Unit
- the publishers' reviewers for their always helpful comments
- staff at Routledge for their patience and practical support
- all our students for everything they have taught us.

Deserving of our especial thanks are Kaspar Forrest, Peter Gray, Chloe Langford, Harriet Palmann, Cathi Poole and Daniel Schmidtke.

Andrew Merrison thanks Sally, Ben and Joe for repeatedly tolerating the apparently interminable absence of him qua husband and father over recent years. He promises to do more washing up and build more Lego very, very soon.

Chris Hall thanks Juan Galindo, Patrick Smith and Rachel Wicaksono.

And like last time, we thank each other for so much: for the debates about linguistics and truth, about life, the universe and everything, for the support each gave to all when the going got tough and last but not least for the sheer fun we have had in writing this second edition. We hope that our continuing enthusiasm for language and matters linguistic shines through the following pages and encourages you not just to share in our perpetual sense of wonder at this extraordinary phenomenon of language in use but also to explore its intricacies and complexities.

We remain ever indebted to those we acknowledged in the first edition – their names are in print there and we hope they understand that we remain very appreciative of their support.

The authors and publisher would like to acknowledge and thank all of the reviewers who provided valuable feedback throughout the writing process. They include:

Professor David Bradley, La Trobe University, Australia
Dr Stephanie Brewster, University of Wolverhampton, UK
Professor Alan Durant, Middlesex University, UK
Professor Barbara Fennell, University of Aberdeen, UK
Professor Gisela Håkansson, Lund University, Sweden
Dr Liz Holt, University of Huddersfield, UK
Dr Arianna Maiorani, Loughborough University, UK
Dr Oliver Mason, formerly of the University of Birmingham, UK
Dr Irina Moore, University of Wolverhampton, UK

Permissions

- Figure 1.3 'Semiotics' from Crystal, D. *The Encyclopedia of Language* (3rd edn) Cambridge University Press, p. 423. © Cambridge University Press 2010, reproduced with permission.
- Table 1.1 'Similarities in modern languages'; Table 1.2 'Numbers in ancient languages'; and Table 1.3 'Similarities in ancient languages', from Barber, C. 1993. *The English Language: A Historical Introduction.* © Cambridge University Press 1993, reproduced with permission.
- 'A League of Our Own' by Jason Burt, from the *Independent* Sports online 4 March 2003. © the Independent 2003. Reproduced with permission.
- Table 5.1 'Frequency of Use' from *Word Frequencies in Present Day British Speech and Writing* by Leech *et al.*, published by Pearson Limited, copyright Pearson Education Limited 2001. Reproduced with permission.
- Figure 8.2 'Fairclough's model of discourse' from Fairclough, N. (2001) *Language and Power*, Harlow: Pearson Education. Reproduced with permission.
- Text 8.1 'Creative Deception' from Pilling, A. (2001) 'A Story from Cameroon', *New Internationalist Calendar*, Market Harborough: New Internationalist. Reproduced with permission.
- Text 8.4 'Get comfortable not knowing' from the book *Don't Sweat the Small Stuff and It's All Small Stuff* by Richard Carlson Ph.D.© 1997 Richard Carlson Ph.D. Used by permission of Hyperion.
- Text 8.5 'Lily O'Brien's Italian collection'. Reproduced with permission.
- Text 8.6 PM calls for a republic: published in the *Guardian* 18 August 2010 p. 11 © Guardian News and Media Ltd 2013. Reproduced with permission.
- Text 8.7 From *Coram Boy* by Jamila Gavin (London: Egmont, 2000) reprinted with permission of David Higham.
- Text 8.8 Future tense: published in the *Guardian* 30 August 2010 p. 11 © Guardian News and Media Ltd 2013. Reproduced with permission.
- Text 8.9 Claudy bombing: published in the *Guardian* 30 August 2010 p. 11 © Guardian News and Media Ltd 2013. Reproduced with permission.
- Text 8.11 'Heaven Scent', reproduced by kind permission of Lever Faberge and Ogilvy & Mather.
- Text 8.12 *More!* Magazine advertisement, 1997, reproduced by permission of *More!*/ Bauer Media.
- Text 8.13 *Hamlet* at Kennington from Tagholm, R. (1996) *Poems Not on the Underground: A Parody*, Moreton-in-Marsh: Windsurf Press, p. 16. ©Roger Tagholm 1996. Reprinted by permission of Orion Publishing Group.
- Text 8.14 'English as a foreign language' by John Mullan from G2, Shortcuts, the *Guardian*, 4 March 2003. © Guardian News and Media Ltd 2003. Reproduced with permission.

- Table 13.2 and Figure 13.3 from Nikolas Coupland and Adam Jaworski, *Sociolinguistics*, published 1997, Macmillan Press. Reproduced with permission of Palgrave Macmillan.
- Figure 14.1: Numskulls comic strip. From: http://imageshack.us/photo/my-images /356/3120202414c4195e8a4bss2.jpg/ © DC Thomson & Co. Ltd. 2013. Reproduced with permission.
- Quotes and reproduction of Figure 16.3 'Language use in a bilingual family': from pp. 303–4 of the following: LINC Coordinators (1992) Language in the National Curriculum: Materials for Professional Development. Nottingham: Department of English Studies, University of Nottingham. Reproduced by kind permission of the University of Nottingham.
- Figure 17.3 Middle English dialect boundaries from Crystal, D. *The Encyclopedia of Language* (2nd edn), 2003 Cambridge University Press, p. 50. © Cambridge University Press 1995, 2003, reproduced with permission.
- Figure 17.4 Old English dialect boundaries from Crystal, D. *The Encyclopedia of Language* (2nd edn), 2003 Cambridge University Press, p. 50. © Cambridge University Press 1995, 2003, reproduced with permission.

Every effort has been made to trace copyright holders and obtain their permission for use of copyright material. The publisher apologises for any errors or omissions in the above list and would be grateful if notified of any corrections that should be incorporated in future reprints or editions of this book.

Symbols and Abbreviations

In general, we follow standard linguistic conventions:

Focus

Lx   indicates that the writer is referring to Line x in a chunk of language data

→   indicates that the particular nugget of language under discussion is to be found in the line against which the arrow occurs.

Unacceptability

*   before an example indicates that the example is ungrammatical

!   before an example indicates that the example is seriously wrong semantically

?   before an example indicates that the example is odd semantically.

Bracketing

[ ]   Phonetic symbols appear inside square brackets, e.g. [ɹ]

/ /   Phonemic symbols appear between slash brackets, e.g. /r/

{ }   Morphemes are enclosed in curly (also known as *brace*) brackets { }, e.g. {-ing}

< >   Letters appear inside angle brackets, e.g. <e>.

Examples might make the bracketing clearer:

	In written language	In spoken language
What leaders do	<lead>	[lid]
A heavy metal	<lead>	[lɛd]
What leaders did	<led>	[lɛd]

In the word *leaders* there are three morphemes: {lead}, {-er} and {-s}.

In syntactic analysis:

| | single vertical straight brackets indicate phrase boundaries

‖   ‖ double vertical straight lines indicate clause boundaries

⦀   ⦀ triple vertical straight lines indicate clause complex boundaries.

For all orthographic conventions for transcribing talk-in-interaction, see Chapter 2.

Using the book

→	indicates a cross-reference to another section in the book
→ R.x	indicates a reference to a paper in Griffiths, P., Merrison, A. J. and Bloomer, A. (2010), *Introducing Language in Use: A Reader*, Abingdon: Routledge
→ W.x	indicates a reference to a website. The URLs are all provided on the website associated with *Introducing Language in Use* and can be found at www.routledge.com/cw/merrison
🔑	indicates that a commentary on the activity can be found on the companion website at www.routledge.com/cw/merrison. If there is no commentary on the activity, there will be no 🔑 in the box.

Prologue

The essence of language is human activity – activity on the part of one individual to make himself understood by another, and activity on the part of that other to understand what was in the mind of the first. These two individuals, the producer and the recipient of language, or as we may more conveniently call them, the speaker and the hearer, and their relations to one another, should never be lost sight of if we want to understand the nature of language, and of that part of language which is dealt with in grammar. But in former times this was often overlooked, and words and forms were often treated as if they were things or natural objects with an existence of their own – a conception which may have been to a great extent fostered through a too exclusive preoccupation with written or printed words, but which is fundamentally false, as will easily be seen with a little reflexion.

Otto Jespersen

Read Me!

INTRODUCTION

This book is an introduction to how **language** is used in infinitely intriguing ways and how even detailed analysis of these areas can be fun and fascinating. We focus unashamedly on language. However, while it is a particularly important part of **communication**, we unreservedly accept that the **context** (linguistic and non-linguistic) within which language is used is crucial for understanding how it is being used and what meaning is being expressed. We also recognize that language use is problematical – it is not as simple as many would like to believe. Recently a UK newspaper had as a headline on an inside page:

> Green Giant Vegetable Champion

and if all you do is look at the words, then ambiguity abounds. Can a vegetable be a champion? Is it a giant vegetable or a giant champion? What is green (the giant, the vegetable or the champion)? To be fair to the newspaper, they partly resolved the ambiguity by printing the first two words in one colour and the last two words in another (colour itself can be communicative, of course) but then the reader is left with the concept of a green giant (is the language being used literally or metaphorically, or even commercially?) and a vegetable champion. While this may seem strange, in the world of horticultural competitions vegetables can be champions but in this article, the newspaper focused on the gentleman who had grown the champion vegetable (in this event, a cabbage).

This is a book which describes language in use and shows how that language can be analysed. It is not a **prescriptive** book full of rules that you should obey, nor a dictionary telling you what **words** mean. It will not tell you how you should pronounce words. It will not tell you how to talk to your boss or your friends. It will not tell you how many words your child must understand by the age of one year nor how your brain should process language. It will not tell you whether it is right that English is a (the?) world language. Nor will it necessarily accept the idea that there is such a thing as *the* English language.

We adopt a functional approach to language and language analysis, an approach that starts with data from language in use rather than abstract theories. A function is a use to which something is put. Language is used for many purposes, which perhaps all have in common that meaning is conveyed. Meaning depends on context, as in the following two conversations.

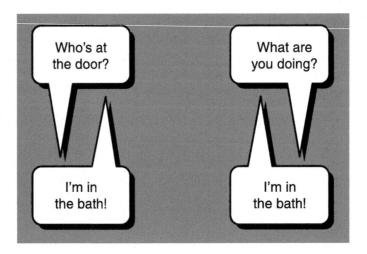

Exactly the same words are used to answer a question but one (which?) is simply providing information whilst the other is arguably explaining why s/he cannot go to the door to find out who is there. Speakers (and writers) make (normally subconscious) choices about what language to use (how to say and how to sequence the words they select) in relation to their audience, their topic of conversation and the context of their **utterance**.

HOW DO WE THINK ABOUT LANGUAGE?

Many people think of language in terms of bricks (the sounds and words) and mortar (the grammar) in the creation of a building or wall (the linguistic **text**). We asked our linguistics students how they thought about language and language analysis and they produced some very creative responses.

One said, 'language is like a new box of rubber bands – they are all messed up together and it is very hard to pull one single band out to use' and explained that there were so many aspects to language that, while recognizing the interconnectedness, you need to be clear about which aspect of language you are analysing at any one time.

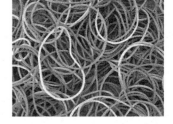

Another said, 'analysing language was like climbing a mountain – just as you get to what you think is the summit, there is another peak on the horizon for you to consider ... but that is what makes it fun' and so recognized that while it can seem hard-going at times to understand the basics, there is a clear pay-off later.

A third student said, 'it's a bit like being in a very large swimming pool – everything is very easy on the surface but you know – or think you know – that there is a lot going on underneath'. This view recognizes very clearly the ability to use language to achieve our aims with the recognition that there are dangers in the deep waters and that using language sometimes goes wrong.

Another expanded this image to claim that 'it's more like bobbing around on the wide ocean where there are no landmarks to help you and you know that there are dangers lurking beneath the surface but somehow you make sense of it all'.

When we reported such comments to our colleagues, one of them replied that language analysis was all a bit like sex – infinitely creative and only any fun when you are doing it.

We certainly believe that the best way to learn about language and about how to analyse it is to do it rather than simply be told how to do it and such an approach is at the heart of every chapter in this book.

But how do we think about language? Do any of these images help? Is language like a jigsaw such that all you have to do is get the right pieces in the right place and the picture is complete? Or does the image of cogwheels better allow for the dynamic nature of language and its ability to change constantly? Of course, cogwheels might suggest that language only moves in circles rather than in any particular direction! Are humans the only animals capable of using language? In the same way that the scientists are looking to see if there has ever been life on Mars, is there a comparable language question of 'is there language out there'? Language in use normally needs at least two people, for sure, but are they always cooperating and do they share the same goals when doing so? Is language sometimes used as a disguise?

What are the building blocks of language? An individual sound or an individual letter can be meaningless on its own but in combination with other symbols the meanings can be very significant. For any language, there is a finite number of words in its vocabulary, a countable number of sounds and a restricted set of rules for combining sounds and words to create comprehensible utterances. If the resources of any language are finite, as it appears, how extraordinary that language in use appears to allow us to express novel and unique utterances to an apparently infinite extent.

How, then, is language to be analysed? In this book, we take the approach that the best starting point is to look at and listen to language in use and then analysis can begin to explain how the resources of the language are being exploited. There are clearly different approaches to analysis that are possible – the functional approach here considers the different forms of language in use, within given contexts, to express given meanings. Because of our emphasis on language in use, as far as possible the language extracts used for presentation or analysis are authentic pieces of language. Only where absolutely necessary have we created language samples to demonstrate a particular point.

WHY IS LANGUAGE WORTH STUDYING?

 Some people want to argue that our ability to use language is actually the essence of what makes us human and that it marks us out from the other animals. For that reason alone, language in use is well worth studying, but there are other reasons. We use language to convey information to each other, to ask about opinions or interpretations, to express our feelings to each other. Sometimes it is very easy to say what we mean and sometimes we find that we have said something that we did not intend. Sometimes we find that we are saying two things at the same time, in the same way that optical illusions can represent two things at once. Surely, the more the workings of language are understood, the more sensitive we are likely to be to the multiple meanings that language is used to convey. Knowledge of linguistics provides endless fascination for later thought – scientists need labs but linguists just need ears and eyes.

However, there are other, more instrumental, reasons for studying language and having a detailed knowledge of how the system works. There are many areas of work where a particularly detailed knowledge of how language works is very important.

- The professions of teaching and medicine use language to educate, to nurse, to explain and to reassure, and specifically within these groups:
  - teachers of additional languages use linguistic descriptions of languages to help learners learn more effectively;
  - speech and language therapists use their insights into language to help people who find using language problematic in a variety of ways.
- Broadcast and print journalists use language to tell us what is going on in our world and many people choose which TV channel to watch or which newspaper to read by the way the language is used to present events. Other parts of the media in advertising and marketing use language in conjunction with visual images to persuade us that we really do want and need that stuff.
- A company's staff are its greatest asset, so there are financial reasons for having Human Resources managers who know how language is used in dealing with people.
- Some workers use language to talk about language: lexicographers (dictionary writers), editors, publishers, academics in universities.
- Actors use the insights of language analysis to achieve plausible renditions of accents for roles that they are playing; dramatists create dialogue that can be seen as realistic; novelists and poets craft their language with enormous care to enhance their readers' artistic experience.
- Legislative and criminal justice systems use language very precisely to frame and debate laws, and to decide innocence or guilt. Increasingly, forensic linguists are brought in as expert witnesses for the prosecution or for the defence.

Anyone who can justifiably claim that they have a detailed understanding of how language can be used to achieve specific aims has to be of interest to an employer. Writing this section led us to wonder yet again whether there are any human endeavours where a sound knowledge of how language works is not applicable – we still cannot think of many. Even a Trappist monk who has taken a vow of silence prays to his God – in silence, perhaps, but still (probably) using language.

HOW TO USE THIS BOOK

What is in each chapter?

Each chapter has been written so that it can be read fairly independently of the others, but frequent cross-referencing (indicated by this symbol ➜) indicates how one area of language analysis might impinge on many others at the same time. The cross-referencing also shows how the chapters link in sequences other than the order in which they are presented in the book – sequences which you will find explained later in this section where we suggest alternative routes through the material. In each chapter, you will also find cross-references to texts in a sister volume to this book, *Introducing Language in Use: A Reader* (shown by the symbols ➜ R). We have referred the reader to the internet either by providing references in the conventional fashion or by using the symbol (➜ W). Conventional references are just that; references indicated by (➜W) are generally used for websites that allow you to find more examples, more detail, more tools for language analysis, or just more fun uses of language. A list of these websites can be found on the companion website at www.routledge.com/cw/merrison. On this website you will also find all the academic references for each chapter. Unusually, we have not kept the references with each chapter but they are available – as they always should be for any piece of academic writing: in this case they are on the website with the suggestions for further reading and the commentaries on the activities.

Each chapter contains activities which you should carry out. Students very often learn better through an active approach to the material and we recommend very strongly that you should have a go at each of the activities. Most of the activities have a commentary (indicated by the symbol ⌼ at the beginning of the activity) with solutions to problems presented for analysis, or possible responses to more general issues raised. Please do read the commentaries which you will find on the companion website (www.routledge. com/cw/merrison) after you have tried to do the activity – occasionally they include additional material on the topic that does not appear elsewhere in the chapter and therefore sometimes need to be read in order to follow what comes next.

Some chapters are likely to be easier to read than others. Some present the more technical concepts that you need for analysing language in use, making precise statements about it and understanding the work of professional linguists. Other chapters show you how to apply that core knowledge. Because of the nature of the topic, yet other chapters concentrate more on conceptualizing language than analysing it, and so are more theoretical than others. This is clarified later in this introduction where we show you different possible ways to access the material.

Each chapter suggests further reading and you will find this on the companion website at www.routledge.com/cw/merrison. We do not expect for one minute that a student will read all the suggestions that we offer. Your tutor can offer guidance on which ones are most appropriate for your programme of study. If you are studying independently, then a visit to a library and browsing some of the titles will show you which ones best suit your purposes.

Many chapters suggest that you use a good dictionary. It is not our place to prescribe which dictionary you should use – though the Oxford English Dictionary or Webster's would certainly be good starting points and both are available either in print or online. Whichever dictionary you choose to use, we would recommend that:

- The bigger the version of the dictionary, the better. Small dictionaries are unlikely to contain enough detail for the work you will be doing.
- The newer the dictionary, the better. It will then contain the most recent usages of different words.
- If you want to use a dictionary based on a corpus of English usage, Collins COBUILD is well worth considering.

All chapters follow conventional bracketing and notation systems which are listed on page xviii.

Most of the time, the data that we use is just language stuff that we happened to have. We did not sit down and invent the language samples to prove the point we wanted to make, nor did we rush round looking for particular examples to make our points – the language was there, all around us, and we simply adopted it as useful to our purposes. You can do the same, if you start looking and listening actively to what is going on around you.

We have put some extra texts into a virtual Chapter 19 to give you more samples of language on which to hone your analytical skills. We recognise that many of the examples we use in the textbook are of UK or US English origin so Chapter 19 includes examples from other varieties of English and from other languages. Chapter 19 is only available on the website associated with this book at www.routledge.com/cw/merrison.

All chapters necessarily introduce some technical linguistic terms and by the end of the book you will have a large **metalinguistic** tool-bag (language terms to talk about language). Many of these terms are in **bold type** to indicate that they are used in more than one chapter and that they appear in the glossary. This is useful if you come across a term (for example in a chapter where an explanation is not provided) and are uncertain of its meaning. The purpose of the glossary is to help your memory, not to teach you the item in the first place.

MOVING FROM ONE CHAPTER TO ANOTHER

As with any journey (and learning about something or simply reading a book can be seen as a metaphorical journey), there are different means of transport and different routes that can be taken. Imagine travelling from a country town to the capital city. How many routes are there? How many different modes of travel could you choose? In the same way, there are different routes through this book and we outline some of those here. You may come up with another route, though, that we have not thought of. If it is right for you, then that is all that matters.

A straight line

This linear route will lead the reader from the wide issues of language and communication (➜ 1) to consideration of language in its most frequent manifestation of talk (➜ 2), hence starting from an aspect of language use with which all will be very familiar, even if some (tutors?) think it an unconventional place to start the analysis of language. When we talk, we are aiming to achieve our purposes in that talk (➜ 3) and we aim to achieve that purpose as effectively and as appropriately as possible (➜ 4). To achieve those purposes,

we need to use words (➜ 5) with their associated meanings (➜ 6) and we combine those words according to the rules of **syntax** (➜ 7) and **grammar** (➜ 8). To speak a language we need some knowledge of the **phonetic** system of that language (➜ 9, 10) and of its sound system or **phonology** (➜ 11). From that perspective, there is then a clear link to the topic of **accent** and **dialect** and other individual and group variation in use of language (➜ 12, 13). Using a language means activating the knowledge we have of it stored in our minds/brains (➜ 14), and that knowledge is acquired in infancy for one's first language(s), or later in life for a second language (➜ 15); many people are multilingual, knowing and using more than one language (➜ 16). What is certain is that patterns of language use change over time (➜ 17) and that the relatively recent phenomenon of English as a world language (➜ 18) has implications for everyone, not just for speakers of English. In the first edition we addressed the issues for education of the global spread of the English language. This chapter is now available on the website associated with this second edition at www.routledge.com/cw/merrison.

We think that this is the most likely route through the book that students will choose to take.

However, tutors might wish to deal with the topics in a different order from the order that we might choose. There are other routes through the material and we suggest some here.

A topic-based route

For all their independence of each other and interdependence on each other, the chapters can be grouped in different ways. After this introduction, Chapter 1 sets the scene for the whole book. Thereafter the following thematic threads might be explored as follows:

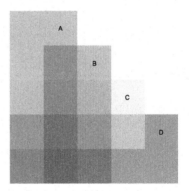

- discourse in Chapters 2, 3, 4 and 8
- core areas of linguistics in Chapters 5, 6, 7, 8, 9, 10, 11
- psycholinguistic and language acquisition issues in Chapters 14, 15, 16
- sociolinguistic issues in Chapters 12, 13, 17 and 18

and then Chapter 19 will provide texts for further practice.

These topics could, of course, be addressed in any order, not necessarily the order in which they are listed here.

A traditional route

A relatively traditional route through the material might initially consider the core areas of linguistics before moving on to the applications. The chapters might therefore be considered in the following order:

1　Chapter 1 to contextualize language within the area of communication

2　core areas of linguistics in Chapters 5, 6, 7, 8, 9, 10 and 11

3   discourse in Chapters 2, 3, 4 and 8
4   sociolinguistic variety in Chapters 12, 13, 17, 18
5   psycholinguistic issues in Chapters 14, 15, 16.

A less conventional route

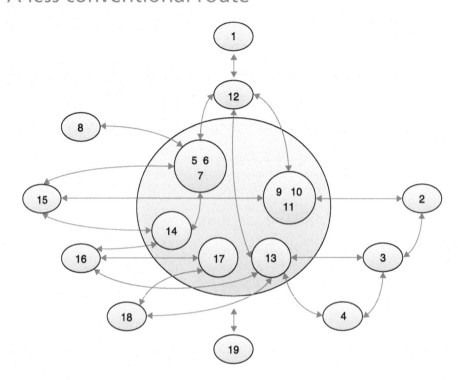

On this route, it is argued that for each peripheral area of linguistics, there is at least one related core area of study (or that each core area of study has at least one closely related application). The authors might prefer to move from language in use to the core areas but recognize that readers will have their own preferences in this matter.

Chapter 1 sets the scene for all that follows (or provides a summarizing conclusion to what has been read) and then:

● words, semantics, syntax and grammar form a basis for work on varieties of language and, in addition, psycholinguistics
● phonetics and phonology form a basis for work on varieties of language as well for work on conversation analysis
● psycholinguistics forms a basis for work on language acquisition and on multilingualism
● a sense of the history of the language can support work on multilingualism and on world Englishes
● sociolinguistics can support work on pragmatics and on social issues relating to power and politeness in language use, multilingualism, and world Englishes.

Arguably, this list of grouped chapters could be read from top to bottom or from bottom to top.

A serendipitous route

Of course, you could just stick a pin in to the table of contents and take that chapter as the first one to read and then repeat the process until you have read all the chapters – or read as many as you want to read.

Wherever you start and whatever route you take through the material, all we can hope now is that you continue reading, that you enjoy learning about language and that you become ever more fascinated by this amazingly complex phenomenon of language in use.

Chapter 1
Language, Communication and Semiotics

Key Ideas in this Chapter

- Even though language and communication are considered by many people to be the same thing, there are significant differences between the two concepts.

- Semiotics is communication by signs – language may be one sign system but human beings communicate with each other in many other ways as well.

- There are many non-linguistic means of communication.

- The culture of a given society affects the way in which that society communicates within itself and with other cultures or societies.

- Animals communicate with each other but none use a linguistic system to do so.

- The similarities between modern languages are evidence for positing language families.

- The genealogy of language shows how modern languages derive from ancient languages but we will almost certainly never know the absolute origins of human language.

1.1 INTRODUCTION

Consider this situation and decide why you think the teacher is suspicious.

> A child in a school playground is asked by a teacher whether he kicked a ball against a window. He answers 'No', but simultaneously rubs his chin. His friends smile whilst the teacher looks on, suspiciously.

Your response will almost certainly have considered what the child said in relation to the whole situation: in other words you will have considered aspects of **language** use in **context**. That context includes what the child did as well as what other people did and you might have wondered whether rubbing the chin communicated anything. Many people feel reasonably comfortable in arguing that language and **communication** do not have the same meaning. However, many would be less confident if they were asked to specify the difference between the two. What do you think is the difference in meaning and use of the two terms? Activity 1.1 should help you clarify your thoughts.

Activity 1.1 0—π

Do you think that the participants in each of the scenarios below are using language? Why (not)? Are some communicating but not using language? Discuss your opinions with others if possible.

1   A shop trader in India converses with a customer in English. He shakes his head from side-to-side when agreeing to a sale price.
2   A woman notices an attractive man entering the room and simultaneously blushes.
3   A child of South Asian background in a UK school is being reprimanded by a teacher. The child is looking at the floor and the teacher becomes increasingly annoyed, finally demanding, 'Look at me when I'm talking to you!'.
4   Gordon, aged 65, had a stroke and his ability to express himself through speech has been impaired. He vocalizes 'yes' and 'no' quite clearly and uses lots of exaggerated hand, arm and facial movements. However, his attempt to ask where a new helper at his support group comes from is met with the offer of a cup of coffee.
5   Annie, aged 87, speaks fluently. In fact, it is hard to get a word in edgeways. To see her, through her sitting room window, talking to her daughter, anyone would think they were having a real heart-to-heart. Inside the room, though, Annie's daughter has little idea of what her mother is talking about. Annie's speech consists of largely unconnected phrases and clichés.
6   In a research centre, a chimpanzee uses American Sign Language (as used by people who are deaf) to sign 'food' to one of her human carers, and is given some.
7   A tout at a racetrack is using hand signals to indicate betting odds.
8   On receiving a call that some prospective buyers for their house are on their way, Alicia and James put on a pot of freshly ground coffee.
9   In Kenya, a vervet monkey spies a leopard nearby and vocalizes. Immediately, the vervet monkey's group runs up trees onto the thinner branches, thus avoiding the danger as the leopard can't follow them there.
10 Ben and Emma correspond by email and texting. They have never met and yet feel they know each other well, even though Ben lives in the USA and Emma in Australia.

Most people will probably accept that something is being communicated in each of these scenarios. However, the nature of the communication is different in each. It is clear that the extent to which language is being used varies from one scenario to another. Some people mistakenly think that *communication* is just another word for *language*, or vice versa. In this book we argue that, although there are non-language based means of communication, language is rather special and that the context within which language is used can affect or even determine the way(s) in which it is used.

1.2 LANGUAGE AND COMMUNICATON

Crystal and Varley (1993: 4) state that 'Communication is the sending and receiving of messages. It refers to any message, not just the highly structured symbolic messages of language'. For them, communication is a broader concept than language, and language is included *within* what is meant by communication: still a widely accepted view.

Jakobson's model of linguistic communication (Figure 1.1) is widely known and represents six major components of verbal communication.

In his model, which is sometimes known as a **code model**, a message giver (the addresser) transmits a message to a receiver (the addressee). The message must be such that it can be put into words (the **code**). There must be a point of contact linking the addresser and the addressee: there will be a psychological link between them as well as a physical contact whether that be face-to-face or at a distance. The importance of context in shaping or determining the form of the message has already been noted. Jakobson's model is helpful but it does not capture the circularity of much communication: during the same communication event, the same individual is repeatedly both addresser and addressee.

Such circularity is more clearly shown in the model of communication (Figure 1.2) presented by Osgood and Schramm (in McQuail and Windahl 1993) which shows how the participants in the communication process, the interpreters, are both encoders and decoders of the different messages.

Whilst this model clearly shows the to-ing and fro-ing (➜ 1.4 reciprocity) of communication, it may not work quite so well as an illustration of the processes involved in reading a poem, for example, where the reader (as message decoder and interpreter) gives no immediate or direct feedback to the poet (as message encoder). Similarly, the model may not so usefully represent the communication involved in viewing a painting or a sculpture or in listening to a symphony. Communication is usually a multi-party phenomenon (at least two parties are involved) but this is not always obviously the case. Who is the addressee of the diary writer recording their responses to events, for example? Who is the addressee of a portrait photographer or a landscape artist? Who is the addressee of a to-do list written by the very person who has to carry out the tasks on the list? Such communicative events as these cannot easily be captured in a two-dimensional model on paper.

Verbal is often used these days as a synonym for *oral* as in verbal warnings preceding written warnings in disciplinary procedures. Here we are using it to mean communication with *words*.

If there is always an addresser and an addressee, what is going on when people talk to themselves? This used to be regarded as a sign of incipient mental instability. How might it be viewed in more modern times?

Communication – like language – is far from straightforward. Sometimes A says something to B but really wants C to (over)hear. Political statements or speeches sometimes work in this way.

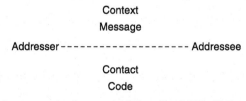

Context

Message

Addresser ------------------- Addressee

Contact

Code

Figure 1.1 Jakobson's communication model (Chandler 2007: 181)

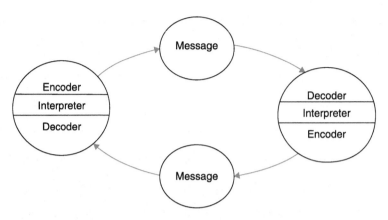

Figure 1.2 Osgood and Schramm's communication model (McQuail and Windahl 1993: 19)

To help you consider further the complexity of communication using language, before you read any further, do Activity 1.2.

Activity 1.2 showed how people can use different types of communication and how hard it can be deliberately to present conflicting messages. Most of the time the systems work together to present a consistent message but it is sometimes possible that our body language can contradict what we are saying.

Many people consider language capable of expressing *any* message a human might wish to send but there is an opposing view that, however impressive language may be, it is not capable of expressing *every* message that a human might wish to convey. On the day after the bombings in March 2004 in Madrid, *The Guardian*, a UK daily newspaper, reported on the:

> biggest mass protest in Spanish history. At first, the worst thing was the silence. The loudest, most raucous city in Europe … was suddenly mute. 'There are no words to describe this' was the answer from the cleaners at the station, the Italian woman at the bus-stop. Language had failed everyone.

Maybe silence could better 'express' people's feelings and if so there is a valid question about the communicative significance of silence (➔ 2), whether that silence be during a conversation or during a concert. Why is there a two-minute silence at the annual Remembrance Day ceremonies in the UK and, often, and not just in the UK, a national silence in the aftermath of a shocking (sometimes a terrorist) tragedy? Sometimes silence is ritualized as in these examples and sometimes it emerges unexpectedly but nonetheless, one might argue, with communicative purpose.

1.3 LINGUISTIC COMMUNICATION AND SEMIOTICS

Simply put, semiotics or semiology is 'the study of signs' (Chandler 2007: 1) and almost anything can become a semiotic sign: what colour clothes you wear or how you speak, what food you eat or how fast you walk. Each of these behaviours can be interpreted as transmitting some message, whether intentionally or unintentionally. As you read the

---

Proverbially, *speech is silver, silence is golden* and for centuries silence has been seen as good. Trappist monks and Quakers would presumably agree. In 1952, John Cage composed 'Four minutes thirty-three seconds' – of silence with a pianist sitting at the piano not hitting a single key. What might be being communicated – and how?

Even unintended signs can be interpreted (➔ Activity 1.2) – a doctor will interpret (and perhaps use in diagnosis) such non-intentional and non-controllable behaviours as sneezing or sweating.

Activity 1.2 🔑

If possible, work in a group with two other people and be prepared to relax and lose your inhibitions! If you are working on your own, imagine carrying out the role plays and work out what you think the issues might be.

Photocopy the following list of role plays and then cut them up into slips of paper with one activity per slip. RP5a and RP5b must necessarily be done together but should be treated as separate activities at this stage. Divide the slips of paper between the members of the group, without reading them first. The person holding each slip of paper is responsible for following the instructions on the slip. Take turns 'acting out' the role play with a partner, in line with your instructions. Each role play requires two participants so, in each group, one person should take the role of observer and should make notes on what happens and how it happens.

Role plays

RP1. Talk about how shy you are, but use very confident body language.

RP2. Talk about your family. When you talk, move your mouth *very* expressively but try to keep the rest of your body very still.

RP3. Talk about your favourite film to a specific partner. Maintain *intense* eye contact with them all the time.

RP4. Without saying a word, use *only* the *usual* everyday gestures, movements and facial expressions which you would normally employ alongside talking to convey the message to a partner that you have been upset by something they said yesterday.

RP5a. Your role is to explain to the selection panel the reasons why you think you are suitable for the job as a … (agree on the particular job with whoever who has RP5b).

RP5b. You are on a selection panel interviewing for a … (agree on the particular job with whoever has RP5a but do not give them any of the other information which is on your slip of paper).

All you may say to the candidate is 'Yes, continue' or, in answer to a question, something on the lines of 'We will come back to that later'. Keep perfectly still and give no gestural feedback at all to the applicant as they are talking to you.

RP6. Talk about your most scary experience but keep your body and head *absolutely* still.

RP7. Without saying a word, use *only* the *usual* everyday gestures, movements and facial expressions which you would normally employ alongside talking to convey the message to a tutor that you haven't completed your coursework assignment on time.

If you are working in groups, listen to the observations from each observer and see what common features there are in the points they make. If you are working on your own, you will have your own ideas to compare with the commentary.

commentary on Activity 1.2, you will have noted comments about social norms and cultural understandings of particular behaviour as well as recognition that different cultures might interpret the same behaviour in a different way. The fact that the behaviours are (or can be) interpreted means that they have some semiotic significance.

At the heart of semiotics lie notions of a sign and a symbolic system. In communication, signs are organized into systems within which each sign has a conventional meaning (➔ 6). In other words, each sign has become associated with a meaning (a 'conventional meaning') which can be transferred or re-used from one context to another. Traffic lights represent a very simple symbolic system: in the UK, red means 'stop', red+amber means 'get ready to move', green means 'go', amber means 'prepare to stop' and next comes red so you are back to the beginning of the sequence. Each light (or combination of lights) has an agreed meaning within its own system though the sequence and meaning of the symbols can vary from one culture (or country, in the case of traffic lights) to another: use a search engine to check the meanings of each light in two separate traffic systems, say France and the UK or the US (where amber is called yellow). These meanings are so clear that the traffic light system, or aspects of it, can be used as a metaphor in other contexts (for example, in business conversations you might hear somebody say 'We got the green light on that project'). There are different relationships between the sign (sometimes called the *signifier*) and the **referent** (sometimes called the *signified*). Traffic lights are SYMBOLIC signs in that there is no intrinsic reason why the colour green should mean *go* and the colour red *stop*. It is a cultural consensus. Portraits and diagrams are ICONIC signs in that they represent more closely the referent to which they refer. Smoke is an INDEXICAL sign of fire in that it indicates its referent (rather than being symbolic or iconic) in the same way as egg-timers indicate time. You might like to consider the communicative value of different ring-tones on mobile phones or of different fonts (why is this book printed in Joanna and not in **comic sans**, HERCULANUM or *Zapfino*?). Some modern computers offer collections of fonts labelled, for example, *fun*, *traditional* or *web*: who decides which fonts go into these categories and on what grounds? Much work on semiotics stems from linguistics but a semiotic approach can be taken to any sign system, whether it be dance, food, clothes, colour, music, soap operas or fairy tales (➔ R1.4, R4.7).

Crystal (2010: 423) provides a very useful diagrammatic summary of semiotics and different forms of linguistic and non-linguistic communication which is reproduced in Figure 1.3.

The diagram first subdivides along the lines of the five senses which are used to send and receive messages: auditory–vocal (hearing/sound-based); visual (sight-based); tactile (touch-based); olfactory (smell-based); and gustatory (taste-based). These are often termed the **modes** or channels of communication.

Each mode is then subdivided further into more specific manifestations, some of which are language-based (linguistic), others of which are not. The linguistic manifestations are listed here:

> Linguistic behaviour is intentional – we choose what words to use. What about non-linguistic communication manifestations and semiotic codes – to what extent are these intentional?

- *Speech*: via the auditory–vocal channel. (Morse code – a system for conveying linguistic messages – can be transmitted by sound, though usually by machine rather than by use of the vocal tract.)
- Visually-based *sign language*: where this "replaces" speech. In these cases the sign language has the capacity to express the same complex and highly structured messages as speech, as in deaf sign languages, semaphore (the use of flag positions to represent letters) and Morse code (when light is transmitted).

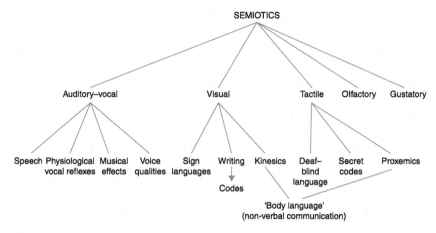

Figure 1.3 Semiotics (Crystal 2010: 423)

- *Writing* (visually-based) and writing-related codes: such as those produced by the World War II Enigma machines to send out secret messages about military movements.
- *Deaf–blind language systems* (tactile mode): for example, the writing system Braille relies on touch for reading letters. Some deaf–blind systems make use of touch to spell out messages on the hand of the receiver such as the Deafblind Manual Alphabet (➔ W1.1).

One way of understanding why these systems are considered to be linguistic is to ask yourself whether a message on any topic could be conveyed using each of them. Language-based manifestations have special characteristics: they are capable of conveying highly complex and detailed messages, providing the language (or code) used is known by all communicating parties. It might take a long time to send a given message using some of the linguistic manifestations, such as semaphore or Morse code, but it is quite possible to communicate in detail about past and future events as well as about here and not-here through these manifestations. The non-linguistic manifestations cannot normally be used to send complex messages. The remaining manifestations within the diagram are not usually considered to be linguistic or language-based, though they do represent ways in which other types of message can be communicated. Activity 1.3 should help to clarify the distinction.

So it would seem that the term *body language*, so often used in everyday conversation, is a misnomer. Facial expression, bodily gesture, patterns of touch or embrace and the communicative use of body odour (e.g. perfume, aftershave) are not strictly language. A term much preferred by communication specialists is **non-verbal communication** (NVC). It is used especially of KINESIC (facial expression, bodily gesture) and PROXEMIC (physical proximity) behaviour. Note that the term *verbal*, as used in this field, must mean 'language' or 'linguistic' and definitely not 'spoken' or 'oral'.

Some gestures and facial expressions are designed to fill a role which could be occupied by speech (or language). For example, police directing traffic will use a combination of gesture, posture and bodily orientation, possibly combined with facial expression. This could be replaced by language, but the officer's gestures, being conveyed and received by the visual mode, are more efficient in communicating simple messages to drivers in

Activity 1.3 0—ᵣ

Consider the following questions:

1   Could you communicate a simple message about meeting someone at 3 o'clock tomorrow (➔ 3) using only the olfactory (smell) or gustatory (taste) modes or channels?

2   Could you communicate that same message using only voice quality (➔ 2)? All you actually say is 'ah' but you can produce that vowel in whatever way you like: you could try shouting, whispering or squeaking.

3   Could you signal that your guinea-pig died last Tuesday using only physiological-vocal reflexes (such as coughing or snoring)?

4   Could you discuss the price of potatoes using facial expression and bodily gesture only?

5   Could you ask the bank manager for a loan using proxemic behaviours (e.g. patterns of touch, physical distancing) only?

6   Could a member of a Masonic Lodge inform another Mason of the state of his wife's health, simply through a Masonic handshake?

Physical proximity relates to the notion of personal space – another frequently used expression. We are all very aware of when somebody stands too close to us for our comfort though not theirs. There are cultural norms in this as in so many other behaviours.

enclosed vehicles in a noisy environment than sound-based verbal instructions might be. Other examples of NVC which are designed to substitute for language include the visual signalling which commonly takes place on the world's stock exchanges or racecourses, or the simple 'thumbs up' sign, now used in many parts of the world to mean something like *yes, OK, good* or *agreed*. However, even from these few examples, it can once again be noted that only relatively simple messages tend to be conveyed by such NVC.

Other NVC operates as part of an auxiliary system, to add emphasis or support to language. Examples of this include the unconscious hand gestures most of us make when speaking. Morris (1978) has attempted to classify such auxiliary NVC both within and across cultures. In terms of hand gestures used to accompany speech, he notes gestures such as the:

- precision gesture – the hand appears to grip a small object between thumb and forefinger at the same time as a very specific point is made
- baton gesture – the hand appears to beat in time with the speech and to emphasize points being made
- hand chop – a decisive gesture, as though attempting to cut through an argument to the essential features
- palm down – a palliative gesture, though quite a dominant one, as though addressing inferiors.

Morris (1978) demonstrates how non-verbal behaviour can be very deeply embedded. In Japanese culture, how deeply one bows to one's interlocutor during face-to-face interaction is very significant and there are recordings of Japanese people bowing when speaking on the telephone, when there is usually no expectation of sending any visual message, though the use of webcams might be making this behaviour less remarkable. Some non-verbal behaviour is intentionally communicative (e.g. nodding or winking) whilst other NVC (e.g. blinking or wheeziness) is unintentionally communicative or 'informative' in the way Lyons (1977: 33) uses the term when he says that 'a signal is informative if (regardless of the intentions of the sender) it makes the receiver aware of something of which he was not previously aware'. Did non-linguistic signals precede language? When acquiring a mother tongue (➔ 15), children use gestures to express meanings before using words and language. In the evolution of communication and language, it appears that human beings could express meanings through the use of pictographs tens of thousands of years before writing was systematized.

In the light of this information, you might like to consider again the points made by the observers of each role play in Activity 1.2. To what extent can the information and the terminology that has just been introduced be used to describe what happened in the role plays?

Some people maintain that every conscious and intentional (so unintended activities such as sneezing are not included) human activity involves language at some stage because language is inextricably bound to human thought processes and therefore to "intending". If this is true, then an artist will think through the process of painting using words and a musician will work out his/her composition using words. However, many would fiercely play down or even deny the involvement of language in artistic expression; for them, artistic modes such as dance, music, sculpture, fine art or photography express messages which sometimes can't be conveyed in words and these messages are created without any language-based thought processes. Before considering the experience of Josie Beszant (➔W1.2), a professional artist and once a student of linguistics, you might like to wonder whether you think that there are any intentional human activities that do not involve language and to discuss your thoughts on this with somebody else.

One day in a linguistics class on **grammar**, Josie was suddenly struck both by the interconnectedness of the components of human communication systems and by their different qualities and capabilities in conveying messages. Josie notes how the experience gave her 'inspiration for new paintings and quite a new way of working'. The result was a series of paintings, each one with an English word somewhere in the painting. The next Activities, 1.4a and 1.4b, are perhaps more reflective and less analytical than others in this book but lead you to consider the relationship between language and other, some might say more abstract, methods of communication used by human beings. If nothing else, the activities will provide food for thought – food for the brain if not for the body!

Some people argue that it is our ability to use language (not our ability to communicate – other animals can do that as you will see later in this chapter) that makes human beings different from all other animals.

Activity 1.4a

Two of Josie's paintings, 'safe' and 'thought', appear in Figure 1.4 and you can find the colour versions of these on the website associated with this book together with two other paintings.

How do you interpret the images? Remember to think about colour, shape and form as well as the use of words in the paintings. Ask other people about their interpretations and compare their opinions with yours. Do you each take different meanings or messages from the paintings or do you all have very similar opinions?

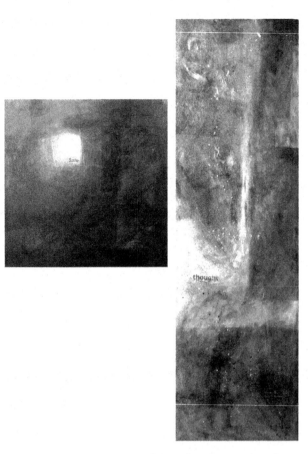

Figure 1.4 'safe' and 'thought'. We are grateful to Josie Beszant for allowing us to reproduce in black and white her paintings, 'safe' and 'thought'. You should be able to see the original colours on the website associated with this book at W1.3

Activity 1.4b

We asked Josie to reflect on what had happened and to consider how this realization had affected her painting. Read what she wrote and then consider the questions below.

My paintings have previously fallen into the category of illustrations. They have been developed from a series of sketches and inspired by stories and the life around me. This new departure meant that I was painting instinctually, not starting with a sketch but with colour ... After colour came textural layers and glazes and a feeling that I was painting a concept. The word or words on the painting came last in the process and I don't know how they were chosen, just that they were right for the image. One of the questions that kept recurring was 'Can a word say it all?' with the answer being a definite 'no'. The paintings are about what words can tell us, how each individual's perception of reality is unique and how we use words to try to bridge the gap between our realities. The paintings are also about the nuances, the word associations and the differences in meaning that can arise from simple words.

Were you surprised to hear that the words came to Josie last in the process of creating the images? What do you think are the implications of her last two sentences? In what way do you think a musician might make comments similar to Josie's comments about the process of composing?

1.4 HUMAN AND ANIMAL COMMUNICATION

Dr Dolittle is perhaps not the only person who has dreamt of talking to the animals or who has wondered what animals might be able to tell us if only we and they could talk to each other. Much of the research so far into animal communication has been based on trying to teach animals to use human language. Washoe, a chimpanzee, was raised by the psychologists Beatrix and Allen Gardner, and was taught to use American Sign Language (ASL) signs to communicate with them. This choice of language was the result of earlier work with other chimpanzees, Viki and Gua, as a result of which it had become clear that chimpanzees, like other primates, are not able to produce the sounds of human language. Crystal (2010: 422) reports that Washoe 'had only 2 signs after 6 months of training' and that 'it took her just over four years to acquire 132 ASL signs, many of which bore striking similarities to the general word meanings observed in child language acquisition' (➜ 15).

Ann and David Premack chose to use coloured plastic shapes to encourage Sarah, another chimpanzee, to communicate with them. The different colours and shapes represented different actions or objects and Sarah manipulated these to express meanings. Some of these meanings could be in 'complex structures such as *If Sarah put red on green, Mary give Sarah chocolate*' (Yule 2010: 18).

The excitement from such projects about what chimps could do was tempered by the work of Herbert Terrace with the chimp, Nim Chimpsky, when Terrace demonstrated by using a freeze-frame video technique that Nim could be seen copying what his trainer had just done, thereby showing that he was imitating and apparently not using language in a creative way. Creativity is one of the essential design features of language enumerated by Charles Hockett, an American linguist whose work will be briefly summarized later in this chapter. The website YouTube has clips showing some of the work with animals – key in 'animal communication' and be discriminating about which clips you observe. Some clips are of the serious research which was carried out – others are much less serious and yet others are critical of the research.

Research on the extent to which animals can communicate using some form of human language does begin to indicate what human language is, by showing what the animals can't achieve in comparison to humans. From this research and from research into children's acquisition of language (➜ 15, R4.3), possible insights can be gained into the

Whilst we can work out what the animals might be communicating to their human companions, it is much harder to know what they might be saying to each other though the research into vervet monkeys perhaps gives some idea (➜ W1.4)

Whilst such an approach to research may appear very negative by focusing on what the animals cannot do, it can be very productive – as can be the research into psycholinguistics from analysing what effects brain-damage, from whatever cause, has on the individual's ability to (continue to) use language (➜ 14).

development of human language from its earliest beginnings. A Darwinian evolutionary perspective would argue that animal communication is in certain ways similar to early human communication and that, therefore, the more we can learn about animal communication, the greater our understanding of the development of human language from its earliest beginnings will be. However, Chomsky (2002: 148) claims that 'it seems to be absurd to regard [language] as an offshoot of non-human primate calls', a view which supports the argument that language is a unique characteristic of human beings. Pinker (1994: 18) argues that 'language is not a cultural artifact that we learn the way we learn to tell time' but that it is rather:

> a complex, specialized skill, which develops in the child spontaneously, without conscious effort or formal instruction, is deployed without awareness of its underlying logic, is qualitatively the same in every individual, and is distinct from more general abilities to process information or behave intelligently.

and therefore he prefers to talk about the language 'instinct'.

Clearly, there are different opinions to consider. The two major theories are either that human language developed after and alongside other communication systems (sometimes called the discontinuity theory) or that human language developed out of other communication systems (the continuity theory). Will we ever really know which is right?

Charles Hockett proposed certain features which he claimed differentiate language from other animal communication systems and they are summarized here (Yule 2010: 11ff. provides a similar summary). As was shown in the models of communication at the beginning of this chapter, language is:

- RECIPROCAL in that the sender of the message can also be the receiver of a message even within a single interaction. Some might want to argue that speech, or use of the auditory–vocal channel, is a defining feature of language but experience suggests that that cannot be right: sign languages used by deaf communities demonstrate all the core features of language listed below.
- SPECIALIZED in that it is mostly used for a particular purpose.
- NON-DIRECTIONAL in that usually you do not need to see the speaker in order to pick up an oral linguistic signal which fades rapidly.
- REFLEXIVE in that it can be used metalinguistically (➜ 7) to reflect on itself and how it is used.

In addition:

- DISPLACEMENT allows us to discuss the not-now and the not-here. This allows us to talk about events from our past and about our future plans, and about places that we have and have never visited.
- ARBITRARINESS allows for the lack of any intrinsic link between the linguistic form (the linguistic sign) and its referent or meaning. It relies on symbolic rather than iconic signs. Our four-footed best friend is called *dog* in English, *Hund* in German, *chien* in French and *gou* in Chinese – if there were a logical link between form and meaning, we would expect greater similarities between such labels. (Other examples of

Ferdinand de Saussure was one of the first linguists to introduce the notion of the *linguistic sign* which he saw as the basic unit of communication (R➜ 3.6).

arbitrariness can be found in Chapter 5.) Onomatopoeic terms perhaps show some link between form and meaning but even then one has to accept that cats say *miaow* in English, *meu meu* in Bengali, *niaou* in Greek and *(n)ya-ong* in Korean (➔ W1.5). Given this, if onomatopoeic terms really do represent the sound, we must think that cats (or other animals) in different countries vocalize differently. What do you think? There are various pages on the web that will provide information – key 'animal sounds' or 'what do animals say in other languages?' into a search engine or visit Derek Abbot's animal noise page (➔ W1.6) as a starter.

- PRODUCTIVITY (or CREATIVITY) allows us to produce novel **utterances** whenever we need to (➔ 14). Of course, there are a lot of formulaic utterances that each individual repeats regularly, such as greetings, leave-takings and apologizing. Most individuals have their preferred forms (which greeting do you use most often – do you say *hello* or *hi*, for example?) though they are quite capable of using other forms in the repertoire. But such utterances as 'I love spinach – it's got a flexible decimal point, you know' or 'the kids were endearing in their bluntness as they threw a brick through my window' or 'I bet you're glad you've got hair' are clearly not formulaic and are most unlikely to be heard again other than as quotations of the original utterance. Each utterance was heard by at least one of the authors in everyday conversation.

- Without CULTURAL TRANSMISSION, language will not be passed from one generation to the next. A child in a linguistically impoverished environment will not acquire language to the same extent as a child towards whom language is constantly being directed (➔ 15) and a child in a non-linguistic environment will not acquire language at all. The most frequently quoted example is that of Genie (Yule 2010: chapter12) who was discovered at the age of 13 with virtually no language as a result of the appalling conditions in which she had been raised with no linguistic input at all. She did later develop some ability in language and, indeed, went through many of the same early stages of language acquisition as have been observed in much younger children, but her tragic childhood experiences show how there has to be some language input for a child to acquire language.

- DISCRETENESS relates to the fact that the individual sounds of a language may not appear to be so very distinct from each other and yet these differences are significant. Make a long *s*-sound and then make a long *sh*-sound. Now alternate these two sounds without any gap between them. They are very similar sounds (differing only in place of articulation ➔ 9, 10) but in English they are significantly different, as is shown by the English **minimal pairs** (➔ 11) *lease* and *leash* or *so* and *show*. The sounds are not significantly different in Finnish: on the day that a Finnish friend of one of the authors became a British citizen, she announced 'Now I am Britiss'.

- DUALITY reflects the fact that in terms of speech production, there are two levels of patterning. Each language has its own discrete sounds (**phonemes** ➔ 11) but these phonemes do not individually carry any meaning. The sounds need to be combined in different ways to make meaningful **morphemes** and **words** (➔ 5) as, for example, in the words *pot* and *top* which contain the same individual sounds but where the different order of sounds create very different meanings.

Whilst these distinguishing features of human language are widely accepted, there are differing ways of conceptualizing language. Pinker talks about the 'language instinct' (as above). Chomsky has explored the idea that the human capacity for language might be innate and attempts to specify what it is that the native speaker–hearer of a given language knows – what is stored in their brain about language (their COMPETENCE). He is less interested in the socially constrained issues of how they use language (their PERFORMANCE). He has explored the universal properties of language as opposed to limiting his research to individual languages. Halliday (➔ R2.3) views language more as a social behaviour than as a body of mentally-represented knowledge and it is this perspective that we adopt in *Introducing Language in Use*.

1.5 LANGUAGE FAMILIES

It was noted in the characteristics of language summarized above that there is an arbitrary relationship between the linguistic sign and its referent. However, in some cases, there are clear similarities from one language to another and a speaker of English who is trying to learn German will have noted such similarities as German *Vater* and English father, German *Mutter* and English mother, just as a Spanish speaker learning French will notice the similarities between Spanish *padre* and French *père* and between Spanish *madre* and French *mère*. The examples can be replicated with other languages and with other lexical items, such as those listed by Barber, Beal and Shaw *et al.* (2009: 58) from which the examples in Table 1.1 are taken.

Kinship metaphor is a useful way to discuss these relationships between languages – but nobody would want to take it much further than direct relations – there are no 'second cousins five times removed' in language family trees. You need a lot of evidence to support such a claim as well.

When they exist, similarities between languages such as those in Table 1.1 are interesting and can be helpful to language learners (➔ 15.6). However, unhelpfully, there are also 'false friends' between languages, such as English *sensible*, which is not translated by French *sensible*, as the latter means 'sensitive' and the English meaning is translated by the French word 'raisonnable'. The existence of similarities supports a claim that some languages are closely linked or related to one another (they have many similarities) and others are more distantly connected with fewer similarities. From here it is but a short step to start talking metaphorically about language families. We have noted that there are similarities between modern languages. Philologists who study the history of language have also noted similarities between ancient languages and claim that these can be used to argue that many modern languages have a common ancestry.

Consider Barber *et al.*'s (2009: 62) revealing comparison of the numbers 1–10 in Old English, classical Latin, classical Greek, Sanskrit (an ancient language of northern India), Gothic (an extinct language spoken by the Goths and of which only one fourth century text, a translation of the Bible, remains). Their tabular format is reproduced in Table 1.2 which you need to study for Activity 1.5.

Table 1.1 Similarities in modern languages

English	German	Swedish
stone	Stein	sten
bone	Bein	ben
oak	Eiche	ek
goat	Geiss	get
one	ein	en

Table 1.2 Numbers in ancient languages

	Latin	Greek	Sanskrit	Gothic	Old English
1	unus	heis	eka	ains	ân
2	duo	duo	dvau	twai	twêgen, twâ
3	três	treis	trayas	–	þrîe
4	quattuor	tettares	catvâras	fidwor	fêower
5	quînque	pente	panca	fimf	fîf
6	sex	hex	sat	saihs	siex
7	septem	hepta	sapta	sibun	seofon
8	octô	oktô	astau	ahtau	eahta
9	novem	ennea	nava	niun	nigon
10	decem	deka	dasa	taihun	tîen

Table 1.3 Similarities in ancient languages

Modern English	Old English	Gothic	Latin	Greek	Sanskrit
father	fæder	fadar	pater	pater	pitar
nephew	nefa	–	nepos	–	napât
far	feor	fairra	–	perâ	paras
full	full	fulls	plênus	plêrês	pûrna
feather	feþer	–	penna	pteron	patra
skin	fell	fill	pellis	pella	–

Activity 1.5 🔑

Look at Table 1.2 and identify any regularities or patterns that you can across the columns.

Barber *et al.* (2009: 63) show how there are other similarities across these ancient languages, reinforcing the claim that they are related. Greek and Sanskrit use <p> in the number *five* where Gothic and Old English use <f> and this similarity is maintained in words other than numbers. Table 1.3 reproduces some of the evidence (with slightly different formatting from the original).

It is true that the correspondences between words might not be exact across the entire language systems but this evidence and similar evidence from syntax and phonology is sufficiently strong to allow Barber *et al.* (2009: 63) to assert confidently that 'it is certain that these languages are related' and that they have a common ancestor. The name given to this ancestor language is Indo-European and it is thought that it was spoken 'around

6,000 years ago, probably somewhere in eastern Europe, possibly in southern Russia, by a group of people who rode horses and had wheeled vehicles, agriculture and domesticated animals' (Trask 1995: 114). Crystal (2010: 308) provides a family tree for Indo-European which is particularly useful in that it shows the surprisingly wide geographical distribution of the languages in that family.

However, human language is much older than this. The difficulties of exploring such ancient languages are enormous, not least because of the lack of evidence. Proto-Nostratic is postulated as 'a very remote ancestor' (Trask 1995: 114) of Indo-European and of other language families but the 'Nostratic hypothesis is still deeply controversial' (Trask 1995: 114). Maybe we will never know how old human language really is and where it really comes from, though that should not stop us from trying to explore a phenomenon that some would argue is central to what makes us human in the first place.

1.6 SUMMARY

This chapter has addressed the relationship between language, communication and semiotics, noting that different cultures also have an effect on the way language is used within that community/society. It has shown how human language differs from animal communication systems and how attempts to teach animals to use language have been only partially successful. It has briefly addressed some of the links between different languages, both modern and ancient, and has also considered the possible origins of human language.

1.7 FURTHER ACTIVITIES

Activity 1.6

Identify as many modes of communication (linguistic or otherwise) as you can for, say, a fairy story such as *Snow White* or *Cinderella*. What are the advantages and disadvantages of each mode for the story telling?

Activity 1.7

Think about the communication value of flowers, or of colour, or of music. Some concrete questions might help.

- How would you react if somebody gave you dandelions or roses, lilies or hyacinths – and does it matter whether you imagine that they give you a bouquet or a bunch?
- What colour(s) would you choose to paint your bedroom, your office or your living room and why? What is the effect or communicative value of different colours?

- What music do you think appropriate for different events? You might like to think about a graduation ceremony, a funeral, a wedding or a birthday party. Might the age of the central person/people affect your decision and if so, how?

In each case, as you answer the question, explain your answer to yourself. If possible, ask other people the same questions and compare your response with theirs.

In the light of material presented in this chapter, consider to what extent you think it makes sense to talk of the language of flowers, the language of colour and the language of music. You will be able to find further information on all of these areas on the internet.

COMMENTARY ON ACTIVITIES

⚲ Remember that this symbol indicates that there is a commentary on the activity that you can find on the companion website at www.routledge.com/cw/merrison.

FURTHER READING and REFERENCES

Suggestions for further reading on the topics discussed in this chapter can be found on the companion website (www.routledge.com/cw/merrison).

Any piece of academic writing must always provide a list of publications to which reference has been made. Unusually and very unconventionally, this information is provided on the companion website (www.routledge.com/cw/merrison). Always ask your tutor about how you are to present references for any piece of work that you submit.

Chapter 2
Conversation Analysis: Talk-in-Interaction

Key Ideas in this Chapter

- Conversation isn't random, it is highly organized.

- Speakers design their talk for their hearers/listeners.

- The immediacy of conversation means any problems can be resolved very quickly.

- Transcribing talk allows for the identification of organizational patterns in conversation.

- Distinct organizational patterns are found in talk: turn-taking, silence and the sequencing of turns into paired (and longer) units.

2.1 INTRODUCTION

Have you ever been in a situation in which one speaker effectively dominated a conversation? Even if you have not, do you recognize any of the following clichés in English which relate to this very scenario?

- He's a right chatterbox.
- She can talk for England.
- He can talk 'til the cows come home.
- She could talk the hind legs off a donkey.
- He never lets me get a word in edgeways.

Let us suppose that we heard someone make such a remark about someone. How might a linguist begin to verify the legitimacy, and study the implications of, say, 'He never lets me get a word in edgeways'? Among other things, the answer to such a question will involve an understanding of the organization of taking turns at talk, and that is what this chapter is designed to provide: an understanding of the organization of turn-taking in spontaneous talk-in-interaction.

Although there are exceptions, many syntacticians (linguists interested in **grammar**) would have you believe that the most important aspects of the theory of language are essentially aspects of the theory of sentences. Of course, sentence-sized chunks are an important part of language: they are discrete, very well organized and much fun to model theoretically ($\rightarrow$ 7). But that doesn't mean that sentence-sized chunks are the *only* part of language which is discrete, very well organized and much fun to model theoretically. Let us dispel a myth: talk-in-interaction (henceforth 'talk') is *also* incredibly well structured, and while we are perhaps not yet able to publish 'grammars of talk', there are many regularities which conversation analysis (CA) has uncovered since its birth in the mid-1960s.

This chapter therefore offers another view of the linguistic horizon by giving an introduction to some of the techniques and insights provided by CA with the aim of demonstrating 'how talk is organized'. What you should learn from this chapter and its related activities is outlined below:

- some conventions for making detailed written records of talk
- talk is organized on a turn-by-turn basis whereby generally one speaker speaks at a time and overlaps (when they occur) are typically resolved quickly
- organization in sequences (sequential organization) is important; we need to give a careful, detailed description/analysis of turns, their components and their sequential placement in the ongoing talk
- speakers design their talk for their recipient(s)
- each turn at talk provides the speaker with the opportunity to display to their **interlocutor** what they have made of their interlocutor's preceding turn (this provides a resource for analysts as well as for participants: we can make claims about what participants are doing with their talk by looking to see how it is treated by their interlocutor in next-turn position – i.e. our analysis is warranted by showing participant orientation to the talk/interactional task being analysed)

- everything gets into talk for a reason and conversation analysts ask 'what interactional task is this bit of talk addressed to/trying to accomplish?'
- CA's basic method is to look in detail at what people are doing at a particular point in interaction – what they are saying, what they are not saying, how they are saying something in a particular way, with particular sounds (**phonetics**), particular word order (**syntax**), particular choices of words (**lexical choice**) – in order to work out what this 'doing' might be a solution for (wording based on ten Have, 2007: 16)
- in other words, conversation analysts continually ask of their data: 'WHY THAT NOW?'.

2.2 ANALYSING TALK: CONVERSATION ANALYSIS OR DISCOURSE ANALYSIS?

This chapter is concerned with the analysis of spoken interaction (talk). Because spoken interaction is often known as *discourse*, you will find a lot of literature under the heading of 'discourse analysis'. The main title of this chapter, however, is 'conversation analysis'. So what's the difference between discourse analysis and conversation analysis? Very simply, discourse analysts tend to adopt a deductive methodology (reasoning from the general to the specific), focusing on rules for producing well-formed units of language larger than the sentence (➜ 8). Conversation analysts, on the other hand, tend to adopt an *inductive* methodology (reasoning from the particular to the general), being interested in the general patterns of how talk-in-interaction is organized. Another potential difference stems from the ambiguity of the word *discourse*. Since 'discourse' can be used to refer to *any* continuous stretch of language use larger than a sentence, it can also be (and often is) used in relation to written language. Traditionally, however, conversation analysis (CA) has only ever applied to the study of spoken language. (That said, one of the authors has recently been to at least one CA data session which analysed the interaction in an online forum, so even this strict focus on spoken language is beginning to shift.) While the contributions to be made from discourse analysis are not to be denied, only techniques and insights provided by CA are addressed in this particular chapter. (For further discussion of discourse analysis, see Chapter 8.)

Finally, the subtitle of this chapter ('talk-in-interaction') should be explained. While CA was originally concerned solely with *conversational* interaction, more recently other (often institutional) styles of talk have been analysed using CA principles: for example, courtroom interaction, interviews, medical consultations, political speeches, radio phone-in shows, speech and language therapy sessions, stand-up comedy, task-oriented interaction, and so on. For this reason, many writers and analysts prefer to speak of analysing 'talk-in-interaction', rather than the more specific (and apparently more restrictive) term 'conversation'.

2.2.1 Conversation analysis

CA is an academic discipline which was developed by Harvey Sacks, a sociologist working at the University of California, in the mid-1960s. The sociologists who followed Sacks (including Emanuel Schegloff and Gail Jefferson and many, many others since) are often called ethnomethodologists. They believe that the proper object of the study of language use is the set of techniques – or methods – that actual participants use in constructing and interpreting the actions inherent in actual talk. Hence *ethnomethodology*: the study of 'ethnic' (participants' own) methods. Although 'pure' CA has its home in sociology, in this chapter we will be looking at it through the eyes of a linguist.

Followers of CA are firm believers in data-driven theories. They believe that the analyst must not come to the data with pre-defined ideas about what goes on but rather must wait for the data to yield the patterns that the participants themselves orient to in talk. The focus of CA is on the (sometimes very mundane-looking) characteristics of spoken interaction. Just some of the many issues that have been investigated include: turn-taking, repair mechanisms, agreements, disagreements, openings, closings, compliments and various issues relating to institutionalized talk. In this chapter, however, we can concentrate on only a few aspects. So what should be covered and what left out? Following Sacks (1984: 27), the way that this dilemma will be dealt with will be to pick a bit of data that we just 'happen to have' and use it to demonstrate how talk is an organized phenomenon.

In order to conduct any rigorous study, the analyst needs some body of evidence to observe. For the analyst of talk, that means finding instances of talk in order to make observations. But human ears and brains are not particularly efficient when it comes to accurately remembering all that goes on in the fast flow of speech. If you don't believe this, try Activity 2.1.

Activity 2.1

Without warning, ask someone to repeat what you just said. If it was anything much more complicated than a minimally simple single sentence, then it is doubtful that they will be able to give you a verbatim repetition. Sure, they may *paraphrase* what you said reasonably enough, but that won't do for analytic purposes. And even if they *are* able to give an accurate repetition of the words you used, they are certainly much less likely to be able to recreate your pauses and **intonation** pattern with much accuracy. To fully check their (in)ability to do this, you may prefer to play them a bit of conversation that you have access to on video (on YouTube, for example).

2.3 TRANSCRIPTION

So how do conversation analysts avoid relying on their less-than-perfect memories? Well, to start with, they enlist the aid of audio (and often video) recordings of the interactions they are interested in. But even recordings have their problems, and at least in the first instance, it is sometimes easier to *see* what is going on in talk than hear it. Thus, in almost all cases, analysts also choose to work from a detailed written record of what is on tape (or more often these days on an MP3, WAV or video file). It is called a **transcript** or transcription of the interaction.

Typically, transcriptions end up looking a bit like a script for a play, with abbreviated character names down the left hand margin and what they say to the right of the names – as in Extract 2.1, which is a transcript of a telephone conversation (now fairly well known in the CA world) between participants who we have anonymised as Justine (Just) and Chester (Ches). It was collected in the early 1970s by a student of Anita Pomerantz who has generously given permission for its inclusion here. This version was transcribed by Gail Jefferson. The extract is used here because of its fame. A sound recording of this conversation is available on the companion website for you to listen to.

It was Gail Jefferson who transcribed the infamous Nixon Watergate tapes.

Syracuse is a city in the state of New York, USA.

Extract 2.1: Trip to Syracuse

```
01  Just:   Hullo:,
02             (0.3)
03  Ches:   hHello is eh::m:: (0.2) .hh-.hh Justine there?
04  Just:   Ya::h, this is Justi:[ne,
05  Ches:                        [.hh Oh hi this's Chester
06          about th'trip teh Syracuse?
07  Just:   Ye:a:h, Hi (k-ch)
08  Ches:   Hi howuh you doin.
09  Just:   Goo::[d,
10  Ches:        [hhhe:h heh .hhhh I wuz uh:m: (.) .hh I wen'
11          ah:- (0.3) I spoke teh the gi:r- I spoke tih Sarah.
12  (Ches): (.hhhh)/(0.4)
13  Ches:   And u:m:: (.) ih wz rea:lly ba:d because she
14          decided of a:ll weekends fuh this one tih go awa:y
15             (0.6)
16  Just:   Wha:t¿
17             (0.4)
18  Ches:   She decidih tih go away this weekend.
19  Just:   Yea:h,
20  Ches:   .hhhh=
21  (Ile):  =.kh[h
22  Ches:       [So tha:[:t
23  (Ile):            [k-khhh
24  Ches:   Yihknow I really don't have a place tuh sta:y.
25  Just:   .hh Oh:::::.hh
26             (0.2)
27  Just:   .hhh So yih not g'nna go up this weeken'¿
28  ( ):    (hhh)/(0.2)
29  Ches:   Nu::h I don't think so.
30  Just:   How about the following weekend.
31             (0.8)
32  Ches:   .hh Dat's the vacation isn'it?
33  Just:   .hhhhh Oh:. .hh ALright so:- no ha:ssle,
34             (.)
```

```
35  Just:   S[o-
36  Ches:    [Ye:h,
37  Just:   Yihkno:w::
38  ( ):    .hhh
39  Just:   So we'll make it fer another ti:me then.
40                 (0.5)
41  Just:   Yihknow jis let me know when yer g'nna go:.
42  Ches:   .hh Sure .hh
43  Just:   yihknow that- that's awl, whenever you have
44          intentions'v going .hh let me know.
45  Ches:   Ri:ght.
46  Just:   Oka::y?
47  Ches:   Okay,=
48  Just:   =Thanks inneh- e- than:ks: anyway Chester,
49  Ches:   Ri:ght.
50  Just:   Oka:y?
51  Ches:   Oka[y,
52  Just:      [Ta:ke keyuh
53  Ches:   Speak tih you [(    )
54  Just:                 [Bye: bye
55  Ches:   Bye,
```

Of course, this extract has a lot of 'stuff' in it that wouldn't be found in a play script. For example there are stray square brackets (as in lines 4 and 5, 9 and 10), odd punctuation (such as the commas at the ends of lines 1, 4, 9), line numbers in the left hand margin, numbers in parentheses and unconventional spellings. In the next section these conventions will be explained.

2.3.1 Transcription conventions

First and foremost, it is important always to remember that any transcription is only a representation of talk; it is not the data – it is just a re-presentation of the data, a fixing of the data in written form to act as an aide-memoire for the analyst to be able to more easily 'see' what's going on in the interaction. It also acts as a way of enabling readers of printed documents (such as book chapters or journal articles) to get a sense of what the data must have sounded like. For both these reasons, CA transcripts are often very detailed and they regularly employ a range of conventions designed to (as best as possible) re-present various subtleties in the talk (such as overlap, silence, speed, intonation, volume, pitch, emphasis, etc.).

While there are many ways of representing talk in a written form, the transcription conventions used in CA are usually based on the system developed by Gail Jefferson (another good reason for picking the Syracuse data). It is very important to note, however, that not every researcher uses every convention, that some writers use some of the symbols differently, and that some occasionally feel the need to invent their own notation symbols. However, whatever system an author chooses, they should always provide a listing of their conventions so that their readers can interpret the transcripts. Below we will see examples of many of these conventions with (where possible) examples from 'Syracuse'. (Don't worry if there are no examples in 'Syracuse' – there will be plenty in Activity 2.2.)

Overlapping turns

See chapter 8 for discussion
of the writing of guidelines.

| 1 | [| When there is already someone speaking, a single left bracket [marks the start of overlapped talk. The transcripts are formatted so that when overlaps occur, the overlapping contribution is arranged on the page directly below the relevant part of the already on-going contribution. For example: lines 35–36 and 51–52. |
| 2 |] | The offset (end) of all overlapped contributions is usually shown by a right bracket at the appropriate points in the turns of both participants. Overlaps are very brief in 'Syracuse' and Jefferson has chosen not to mark the offsets. This highlights a very important point about transcription: while recognized guidelines exist, that is all they are – guidelines. That is why, as mentioned above, you will often find transcriptions using different symbols or possibly even using symbols differently. However, as long as any departures from the norm are explicitly noted, there should be few problems. |

A useful convention for *multi-party* talk was developed by Karen Brown, one of our students. She distinguished the offsets of multiple overlaps in a turn by appending the closing brackets with a number in parentheses. For example, when](17) is used in a pair of **utterances** it indicates the 17th offset of simultaneous talk in the transcript. As](17) will appear twice, it clearly shows which utterances finish where.

Turns which start simultaneously

| 3 | [[| When there is no current speaker, onset of simultaneous contributions from both participants is sometimes marked using double left brackets. |

Latched contributions

| 4 | = | An utterance that immediately follows the preceding utterance without a gap is said to be a latched utterance. It is transcribed with a pair of = signs: one at the end of the preceding stretch of talk and one immediately prior to the onset of the latched utterance. For example: lines 47–48. |

Pauses

| 5 | (.) | A micro pause of less than 0.2 seconds. For example: lines 10 and 13. |
| 6 | (0.0) | Longer pauses are timed to the nearest tenth of a second and are put within parentheses, so (3.1) represents a silence of 3.1 seconds. For example: lines 2, 3 and 11. |

Where silences cannot be attributed to a speaker, the pause is marked on its own line. For example: lines 2, 15, 17.

If you are transcribing but don't have access to a stopwatch, it might be useful to know that speaking at a normal speed (➜ 14) produces approximately five syllables per second (hence 1 syllable = 0.2 seconds). Hence amateur photographers developing film, sky divers waiting to pull their rip cords and Ross Geller from the sitcom *Friends* (final series where he (mis)times his spray-on tan) often use 'Mississippi' as a counting tool: 'one Mississippi' = 5 syllables = 1 second.

7	+	Pauses may be transcribed with + signs if overlap needs marking (though the need for this is rare). Each + represents a pause of approximately 0.1 seconds in length.
8	((pause))	Long, untimed pauses are marked by ((pause)). These are rarely found because if a silence is long enough to be noticeable, it is long enough to be timed.

Characteristics of delivery

9	> <	Talk delivered at a faster rate than surrounding talk is transcribed within angled brackets pointing inwards (or >> << for *much* faster talk).
10	< >	Talk delivered at a slower rate than surrounding talk is transcribed within angled brackets pointing outwards (or << >> for *much* slower talk).
11	-	Indicates the utterance is cut off mid-flow. In terms of phonetics, this often involves **glottal** closure (➜ 9). It is a very powerful device for maintaining a turn. For example: lines 11, 43, 48.
12	:	Elongation of the preceding sound. The more colons, the longer the sound. For example: lines 1, 3, 4 and a really long stretch in line 25.
13	?	Gradual rising intonation. While a ? at the end of a unit of talk might often co-occur with a syntactic question (as in lines 3, 32, 46), it is important to note that it doesn't necessarily mean that the utterance in question is, in fact, a syntactic question. For example, the utterance in lines 5 and 6 is clearly a statement, and yet Jefferson has used a ? to indicate that the pitch gradually rises towards the end. This highlights the point that traditional punctuation marks are not used for punctuation, but rather as an attempt to represent *intonation*.

Because this non-question, high rising terminal (HRT) intonation is a feature of Australian speech, it is sometimes known as Australian Question Intonation (or AQI) (➜ 12).

14	.	Gradual falling intonation. While a . might often co-occur with a statement (as in lines 11, 18, 24), it is important to note that it doesn't necessarily mean that. For example, the utterance in line 8 is clearly a question (marked by the word *how*), and yet Jefferson has used a . to indicate that the pitch gradually falls towards the end. A similar example can be found in line 30.

15	,	Fall–rise intonation. This intonation pattern is often found in an unfinished turn-in-progress. For example in line 4, the first comma after 'Ya::h' apparently indicates that Justine has not finished her turn. Again, the intonation represented by a comma does not necessarily mean that a turn is in progress, as indicated by the comma at the end of Justine's turn in line 4.
16	!	More animated intonation (often rise–fall).
17	…	Utterance 'trails off'.

Abnormal volume and pitch

18	° °	Text surrounded by degree signs is quieter than the surrounding talk. We distinguish four levels of quietness: °quiet°, °°very quiet°°, °°°exceedingly quiet°°°, and °°°°virtually inaudible°°°°.
19	CAPITALS	Louder than the normal surrounding talk. (This convention is often adopted in emails where capitalization can be interpreted as SHOUTING!) For example: line 33 where the first syllable of 'alright' is transcribed as being louder. There are several other capital letters throughout 'Syracuse', but they are always isolated and don't represent loudness. For example, some transcribers use initial capital letters at the beginning of utterances – and some don't; some use them for proper names (like *Justine*, *Chester*, *Syracuse*, *Sarah*) – and some don't; but nearly all transcribers (fickle as they are) tend to maintain a capital letter for the first person **pronoun**, 'I'.
20	↑ ↑	Notably higher shift in pitch for the text between the upward pointing arrows.
21	↓ ↓	Notably lower shift in pitch from the surrounding talk.
22	<u>underlining</u>	Other emphasis/**stress** (sometimes indicated by *italics*). For example: lines 1, 3, 4, 5 – indeed, virtually <u>every</u> line seems to have some emphasis!

Non-verbal activity

23	h	Audible outbreath (number of hs corresponds to length of breath). For example: lines 3 (before 'Hello'), 23, 28.
24	.h	Audible inbreath (number of hs corresponds to length of breath). For example: lines 3, 5, 10. For obvious reasons audible inbreath occurs most often utterance-initially.
25	ha/heh	Syllable of laughter. For example: line 10 (twice). Using cha indicates laughter involving some degree of friction.
26	((cough))	Representations of non-verbal behaviour are transcribed within double parentheses.
27	.pt	Represents the noise that lips make as they open at the beginning of an utterance (in fact there is often also a flavour of alveolar click ➜ 9).

Transcription doubt

28   ( )   Parentheses indicate talk that cannot be accurately transcribed. Any transcription within the parentheses indicates merely a *possible* hearing. (An X within the parentheses can be used to represent a syllable. Some authors may use Xs (or some other symbol) for syllables but without parentheses.) For example: in line 12 there is doubt as to whether the speaker is Chester (though he is the most likely) and also doubt as to whether it is an inbreath or a silence of 0.4 seconds. A similar example occurs on line 28 with an outbreath (though here, the speaker is completely indeterminable). A final example occurs on line 53 where Jefferson hears Chester saying *something* while Justine overlaps with 'Bye: bye' but she cannot offer even a best guess as to what.

Other conventions

29   odd spelling   Non-conventional spelling is often used to more closely represent the actual pronunciation of words. Examples occur on most lines in 'Syracuse'.

30   anonymity   Where appropriate, personal details (such as names, addresses, telephone numbers, bank account details, etc.) are usually anonymized with alternative words of a similar syllable structure.

31   line numbers   Transcript lines are numbered (not necessarily individually) in the left hand margin.

32   ➜   When analysing data, lines of particular interest can be indicated using an arrow in the left margin. We will see examples later in the chapter.

33   courier font   CA transcripts are often typed in Courier font. This is because Courier is what is called a non-proportionally spaced font. In other words, every character in Courier is the same width (so an <i> takes up the same space as a <w>). In this way, transcripts can be relatively easily aligned without the need for using tabs.

2.4 TASK-ORIENTED DATA

Soon, Extract 2.2 will be used to illustrate what Sacks (1984: 27) calls 'a bunch of observations' about the orderedness of talk. However, because the content of this data might initially seem a little odd, some prior explanation will be useful. The recording is of a pair of participants (PK and DN) engaged in a task that was designed to elicit natural, yet restricted dialogue. The task in question is known as the 'Map Task' (see Anderson *et al.* 1991). It has been widely used to support the study of spontaneous speech and **communication** of normally developing children, neurotypical adults, sleep-deprived soldiers, aphasic adults (➜ 14), visually impaired adults, and children with speech and language disorders. It has also been used to investigate professionally interpreted interactions between monolingual British Sign Language users and monolingual English speakers.

In this task, two dialogue partners each have a schematic map drawn on a large sheet of paper (see Figure 2.1). The task involves one participant (designated the Information Giver (IG)) describing the pre-drawn route on his map to the other participant (the Information Follower (IF)), whose map has no route. The IG's ultimate aim is to get the IF to successfully draw the route. The participants sit opposite each other at a table with a barrier built between them so that neither can see the other's map.

Although both IG and IF have copies of the basic map, differences exist between the two – specifically, the IG has three landmarks which are absent from the IF's map, which in turn has three landmarks that are not on the IG's. Thus, in total, there are six 'problem' points to be discovered *en route*. In the pair of maps in Figure 2.1, the three IG-specific landmarks are *cat*, *flower* and *kennel*; the IF-specific features are *flamingo*, *well* and *dog*. The reason for the existence of these landmark mismatches is to set up a genuine information gap between the participants.

The participants are made aware that there may be discrepancies. They are also told that there is no time constraint. So while the data in Extract 2.2 is clearly not conversational, it is unscripted, natural and, most certainly, talk-in-interaction. It is therefore valid and most useful for our current purposes.

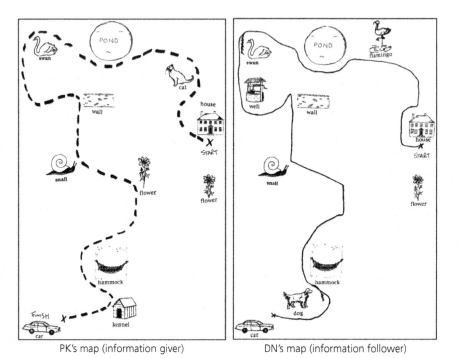

PK's map (information giver)   DN's map (information follower)

Figure 2.1 Maps for Extract 2.2

Activity 2.2

Now you have seen examples of various transcription symbols, find examples of these conventions in Extract 2.2

All are present except: (7) +, (8) ((pause)) and (32) ➜.

Extract 2.2: Map task data (PK & DN)

You should be able to listen to this interaction at www.routledge.com/cw/merrison.

```
01   PK   .pt First na[me?]
     DN                [Right.] Okay ((eyebrow flash))
     PK   First name again?
     DN   Dale.
05   PK   ↓Dale.↓ (.) Right Dale. (1.0) To the right of your
          map roughly approximately,
     DN   °Aha°
     PK   say seven inches down or eight inches down,
     DN   [[>°Yeah°<]
10   PK   [[°°have you°°] have you got a ↑starting↑ mark.
     DN   Yeah I've got a- a starting mark
          and it's just below a house.
     PK   It's just below the house=
     DN   =°Aha°
15   PK   Okay. (1.3) ((cough)) °.pt° If I was moving from
          (0.9) to the left o' the house and coming upwards,
          before you start drawing,
     DN   °Mm°
     PK   is there an obstruction above it?
20   DN   (1.2) Er (.) right at the top of the map there's
          a flamingo,
     PK   At the very top?=
     DN   =Yeah
     PK   Is there anything below that=
25   DN   =>There's nothing< directly below it °at all.°=
     PK   =°.pt°=There's nothing below it.
     DN   [[°°No.°°]
     PK   [[Okay] So (.) imagine r:oughly about (.) <an inch
          and a half above the house.>
30   DN   °°°.pt°°°=Yeah=
     PK   =You know the the the the the the left hand chimney
     DN   °°°.pt°°° Aha.
     PK   And I want you take a (1.3) ((cough)) roughly (3.2)
          a route from the 'X' right?
```

```
35   DN   °°°.pt°°°=°Yeah°
     PK   just past - just passing the lower edge of the house
          left hand side o' the house,=
     DN   =°Yeah°
     PK   Bring it round in a circle,
40   DN   °°°.pt°°°=°Yeah°
     PK   Okay? Until you stop roughly above the w-
          does it say ↑house above↑ your house.
     DN   (.) °↑Yeah↑°
     PK   Well okay bring it round in a circle and you stop
45        just about an inch which above the letter 'h' okay?
     DN   (0.8) >Oh d'you say there's another house.<
     PK   °Hmm?°
     DN   >Did you say there was another house<
     PK   >No no it's just the one hou- [no X] - =
50   DN                                [°Right°]
     PK   =is< is er has it has it got the word 'house'
          on it?
     DN   °°.pt°°=Yeah
     PK   ↓°Well°↓ (.) just above the 'h' you should -
55        come from your start and draw your route,
     DN   Yeah
     PK   round in a circle. Come round i- out by about (.)
          an inch from the end of the ↑house↑
     DN   Yeah
60   PK   nice circle round (.) until you stop (.) roughly
          about- a- about an inch above (.) the letter 'house'
          - the letter 'h' (1.1) °where it says 'house'. Okay?°
     DN   Okay yeah.
     PK   Now [you stop there.]
65   DN       [Right >what by the left<] chimney (X)
     PK   Hmm?
     DN   Near the left chimney
     PK   °°.pt°°=(.hh) No jus: above the left chimney
          [>but it's above<] the left chimney=
70   DN   [°°Yeah°°]
     PK   =you'd be stopping somewhere roughly about an inch
          and a half °°off. Okay?°°
     DN   °Okay°
     PK   °Okay?° So you stop there. (0.9) Now (.) bring your
75        route approximately up about another ↑inch↑ in a-
          er roughly an inch an' a half in from the edge o' yer
          map, going north.
     DN   °Yeah.° Straight up
     PK   °Straight ↑up↑ Ok[ay?°]
80   DN                   [Okay]
```

```
      PK   Right. (0.8) Now (1.3) you should be approximately
           roughly (0.9) what say three and a half inches
           from the top o' your (.) map?
      DN   °Aha yeah° °°I'm [a bit more maybe°°]
 85   PK                   [°Okay?] That's good.°
           (1.2) Now °°°.pt°°° before we start circling down-
           round to your left,
      DN   °°Mmm.°°
      PK   is there any other obstructions: say roughly about the
 90        middle of <your map(h)?> °°°.pt°°°=Er near the head.
      DN   Er °°°.pt°°° (1.9) on the left of the flamingo, (.)
           I've got a pond.=
      PK   =°That's it that's what we're looking for.°
      DN   °°Yeah°°
 95   PK   .pt=Okay? (.) Right. (0.9) Now where you've stopped
           (.) on your route,
      DN   °.pt=Aha°
      PK   Right?
      DN   ((small nod))
100   PK   I want you to circl:e up and round to your left, °(.h)°
           until you c- is there a small mark (.) a- underneath
           where it says 'pond'.=
      DN   °°.pt°° (.) Er no.
      PK   There's not.=
105   DN   =°°Er no°°=
      PK   =You know underneath - underneath the word 'pond'
           there's not a- a wee mark=
      DN   =>>Oh is like a<< wa:ve.
      PK   Like a wee wave.=
110   DN   =°Yeah°=
      PK   =↑°Yes°↑=
      DN   =>So there's thr[ee-<] there's THREE waves altogether.
      PK                   [Three]
      DN   [[<°There's the one wave.°>]
115   PK   [[There's three waves aye] it's it's like
           (.) it's like the moon
           [you know two eye- two eyebrows and a …
           ((nod)) Okay!]
      DN   [°Yeah ((nod)) yeah. Got it. Yeah. (.) Aha° ((no]ds))
120   PK   °(.h)° Right (1.0) now with you coming from >the< right
           hand side o' your map,
      DN   °Yeah°=
      PK   =Okay? °(.h)° I want you to go up in your circle
           very gently and start moving to the left .hhh
125        and the the head o' your circle should be equal
           w- with (.) that small wave which is approximately
           say (0.8) three eighths (0.9) from the bottom o'
           the pond upwards?
```

```
       DN   .pt=Aha yeah.=
 130   PK   =Okay. So: (.) whe- where you left off (.) above
            the word house
       DN   Yeah
       PK   (0.7) circle up, okay?
       DN   Yeah
 135   PK   And round [to your le]ft (.) very gently
       DN             [>°relative to°<]
       DN   °Yeah.°
       PK   Okay? [[°And-°]
       DN   [[>Under the] flamingo<
 140   PK   (1.0) ((cough)) Well you're below the you'll be f
            [below] the falingo [you're] er flamingo. Okay?
       DN   [>°Below it°<]       [°Yeah°]
       PK   And head towards the word (.) towards 'pond' the the
            pond. Okay?=
 145   DN   =°Yeah°
       PK   °.pt° And the the head o' your circle should be equal:
            (.) with the wave. Okay?
       DN   °°°.pt°°°=°Okay yeah°
       PK   °Okay?° °°°.pt°°°=And start to dip down, (.)
 150        under the pond and pass it by quarter of an inch.
       DN   °Yeah°
       PK   (.) Okay? Come right round under the pond
            [>until you're about<]=
       DN   [°°Yeah?°°]
 155   PK   =(.) quarter o' an inch (.) circling under the pond.
            Okay?
       DN   °↑Yeah↑°=
       PK   =°°°.pt°°°=And when you get to the - as you start (.)
            to the er the: to get parallel with the circle wi'
 160        pond on the left hand side o' the pond,
       DN   °Yeah°=
       PK   =S'like to move up, (.) stop there. Okay?
       DN   °Okay.°
```

2.5 SO HOW *IS* TALK ORGANIZED?

Remember that the aim of this chapter is to demonstrate *how talk is organized* and so the question is, where to start. CA's rightful answer is always 'the data', and now that you have some appreciation of the tools for transcribing spoken interaction, we can begin to consider the dialogue between PK and DN. However, before starting to investigate the transcription of the data, we will reiterate a point that was made above: Extract 2.2 is a transcription of the data – it is not the data itself. The data is the talk that was produced in the original interaction. The transcript is merely a *representation* (= re-presentation) of that data. While transcribers should always endeavour to represent the data as faithfully as possible (for readers may never have access to the original recordings – hence the level of detail put into transcriptions), it is important to recognize the limitations of translating one medium (talk) into another (the written record of that talk). Thus, while Extract 2.2 is often referred to as 'the data', that should always be read as shorthand for 'the transcript of the data'.

2.5.1 Turns

Even the very briefest glance at conversational data will uncover some basic observable facts and in their seminal paper on 'A simplest systematics for the organization of turn-taking for conversation', Sacks *et al.* (1974: 700f.) noted that the following observations seem to be worth trying to explain:

- speaker change occurs (people take turns)
- generally only one participant speaks at a time
- when overlap occurs it is usually brief
- the order and distribution of turns is not fixed in advance but varies within and between conversations
- the size or length of speaker turns varies from one turn to the next
- turns (or **turn constructional units**) can be composed of: a single lexical item (**word**); **phrases**; clauses; full sentences
- what participants say in their turns, or what actions they perform with their turns, is not restricted or specified in advance.

In order to account for these observable facts, Sacks *et al.* (1974) proposed a set of rules which operate on a *turn-by-turn basis*. It is assumed that a speaker initially gets just one unit of talk (turn constructional unit or TCU). At the end of a TCU is what is called a **transition relevance place** or TRP and it is at these predictable (*projectable*) TRPs that speaker change can occur.

Sacks *et al.*'s rules operate at TRPs. In these rules (wording here is based on Levinson 1983: 298), C stands for 'current speaker' and N for 'next speaker':

Rule 1

(a)   If C selects N in current turn, then at the first TRP after N-selection, C must stop speaking, and N must speak next. C may select N by a number of means, for example by using N's name, by looking at N or by asking N a question.

(b)   If C does not select N, then any other party may self-select, with the first to speak gaining rights to the next turn (though *rights* are not the same as a *guarantee*).

(c)   If C has not selected N, and no other party self-selects (under option (b)), then C may (but need not) continue speaking (i.e. claim rights to a further TCU).

Rule 2 – applies at all subsequent TRPs

When Rule (1c) has been applied by C, at the next TRP Rules 1 (a)–(c) apply again until speaker change is achieved.

These rules predict that:

(1)   only one speaker will generally be speaking at any time (because each speaker will
        wait either until they are selected or until a legitimate opportunity arises where they
        may select themselves)
(2)   overlaps may occur where there are competing next speakers (as allowed by 1b)
(3)   overlaps may occur at misprojected TRPs. In other words N starts to speak where
        they (wrongly) anticipated a TRP but where C had not actually yet completed their
        current TCU.

Activity 2.3 ⊙⊤

Find examples of evidence for each of these three predictions in the data
(Extract 2.2).

Overlap or interruption?

Thus far, **overlap** has simply been seen as a case of where more than one speaker speaks
simultaneously. For some purposes, however (for example when analysing issues such as
agreement, conflict, control, dominance or power), it can be useful to distinguish two
specific types of simultaneous talk.

A very basic distinction can be made as follows: overlap does not violate the current
speaker's turn – often because it occurs near a possible TRP; **interruption**, on the other
hand, does violate the current speaker's turn – it is an attempt to take the floor from the
current speaker while they are still producing their TCU. (For a finer distinction, see
Hutchby and Wooffitt 2008: 54ff.)

Activity 2.4 ⊙⊤

Find more examples of simultaneous talk in the data and decide whether they count
as overlap or interruption.

2.5.2 The sounds of silence

Inter-turn silence

In addition to accounting for the brevity of simultaneous talk, Sacks et al.'s (1974)
rules allow three different types of inter-turn silence (silence between turns) to be
distinguished:

- lapses (due to the non-application of Rule 1)
- gaps (before the application of 1b or 1c)
- attributable silences (after the application of Rule 1a).

Activity 2.5 0—

Find examples of different types of silence in the data.

Intra-turn silence

Silence is not only found between turns. It also occurs within them.

Activity 2.6 0—

Find examples of intra-turn (within-turn) silence in the data. When you have found an example, consider (a) why it is allowed to exist (in other words, why the other speaker doesn't start talking) and (b) what it might exist for (in other words, think about 'what interactional task it is trying to accomplish').

2.5.3 Sequences of turns

Having dealt briefly with how talk is organized into turn-sized chunks, in this section we turn our attention to larger chunks of organization – in other words, *sequences* of turns.

Adjacency pairs

When anyone says anything (so long as they are not the very first person to talk in the interaction), it will usually be assumed that their utterance is pertinent, relevant, fitted and somehow *related* to the immediately prior utterance. Or, as Sacks (1995, vol. 2: 559) puts it:

> there is only one generic place where you need not include information as to which utterance you're intending to relate an utterance to, and that is if you are in next position to an utterance. Which is to say that for adjacently placed utterances, where a next intends to relate to a last, no other means than positioning is [*sic*] necessary in order to locate which utterance you're intending to deal with.

This notion of immediate relevance (cf. Grice's third maxim ➔ 3) leads onto the idea that utterances can be tied to one another in pairs by what Sacks (1995, vol. 1: 150) called 'tying rules'. Later these utterance pairs became known as **adjacency pairs**. Adjacency pairs are sequences of two communicative actions (usually, though not exclusively, performed by utterances) that are:

- (usually) produced by different speakers
- (usually) adjacent to one another
- ordered as a first part and a second part
- categorized (or *typed*) so that any given first part requires a particular type of second (from a limited range).

In Table 2.1 there are some examples of paired utterance types.

Table 2.1 Examples of possible adjacency pairs

	Part 1	Part 2
1	**Greeting** Hello!	**Greeting** Hi!
2	**Check** What's your name again?	**Clarification** John Doe.
3	**Question** So why were you late today?	**Answer** I've already told you!
4	**Apology** I do apologise.	**Acceptance** Please – don't mention it.
5	**Compliment** That shirt really suits you!	**Thanks** Thank you.
6	**Opinion** Beethoven's fifth symphony is wonderful.	**Agreement** Yes – it's absolutely perfect!
7	**Blame** It's all your fault we were late.	**Denial** No it isn't.
8	**Offer** Can I help you?	**Acceptance** Thank you very much!
9	**Assertion** I would like to do a linguistics degree here.	**Acknowledgement** Oh *would* you?
10	**Request** Can you lend me $5?	**Acceptance** Certainly – not a problem!
11	**Instruction** Say the password!	**Compliance** I have only postage stamps left.

While each time only one instance of a second part has been given, other types are, of course, quite possible and reasonable (e.g. we can ignore greetings, refuse to answer questions, disagree with opinions, decline offers and so on).

Activity 2.7 🔑

1   With a friend, say the pairs in Table 2.1 out loud. How do they sound?
2   Now try them again starting from 1 but with your friend starting from 2. So the pairs go 1–2, 2–3, 3–4 etc. Stop when your friend has done number 11. How do they sound?
3   Now try once more but while you start at 1, your friend should start at 3 (so 1–3, 2–4, 3–5 …). Stop when your friend has done number 11. How do they sound?

Activity 2.8 🔑

Find examples of pairs in Extract 2.2 that are adjacent.

Insertion sequences

Of course, adjacency pairs need not be strictly adjacent as several sub-goals might first have to be initiated and resolved in order to get the top level task done.

Activity 2.9

In Example 2 there are four question–response pairs. In the right hand margin, mark the questions (Q1–Q4) and their respective responses (R1–R4) to see which pairs are actually *adjacent*.

Example 2: Mair's Deli

Archie:	Can I have a sandwich to take away please?
Eric:	What would you like?
Archie:	What would you recommend?
Eric:	Are you a vegetarian?
Archie:	Yes.
Eric:	Well the vegetarian cajun pâté is good.
Archie:	Okay I'll have one of those then!
Eric:	Right, that'll be £3.20 please.

You should read the commentary on this activity on the companion website before continuing.

> ### Activity 2.10 ⊶
>
> Find examples of pairs which are not adjacent because of insertion sequences in Extract 2.2.

So, because not all paired parts are necessarily adjacent, what is needed is a weakening of the criterion of strict adjacency to a notion known as *conditional relevance*: on the production of a first part, some second part becomes both relevant and expectable. Furthermore, if a second part is not produced it will be seen to be absent, and anything that is not a second part in next position will be seen to be some preliminary to doing the second part. In short, the first part of an adjacency pair sets up specific expectations which have to be attended to. This helps explain why the very first turns at talk in Extract 2.2 are neither a simple adjacency pair, nor a pair with an insertion sequence. For convenience those lines are repeated in Extract 2.2a.

Extract 2.2a

```
01     PK     .pt First na[me?]
02     DN                  [Right.] Okay ((eyebrow flash))
03     PK     First name again?
04     DN     Dale.
05     PK     ↓Dale.↓ (.) Right Dale. (1.0)
```

In L1, PK begins the dialogue with the first part of a pair: he asks his partner his name. According to our story so far, what should then follow is a fitting second part to that query. Instead, DN does something which seems to function as a signal that he is ready to begin the task. But whatever L2 is, it is clearly possible to claim that it *isn't* a response to L1: 'Okay' is not Dale's first name! ('Right' has not been analysed as part of a possible response to L1 as it is quite unlikely that a reply could have been produced by DN *before* PK had finished his query). It seems, then, that DN has simply not heard PK's utterance (and hence, going back to the promise of commentary in Activity 2.4, it makes very little sense to class it as interruptive).

From this very small piece of analysis it should be clear that it is very important to consider not only the words spoken, but also their precise sequential placement with respect to other words spoken.

At the beginning of this chapter it was noted that each turn at talk provides the speaker with the opportunity to display to their interlocutor what they have made of their interlocutor's preceding turn. Because of this, claims can be made about what participants are doing with their talk by looking to see how it is treated by their interlocutor in next-turn position – i.e. the analysis is warranted by showing participant orientation to the talk being analysed. It is therefore (initially) PK's third turn response to DN that justifies the analytic claim that L2 isn't a response to L1 *because that is the way PK treats it*. From L3 it is clear that PK takes DN's utterance as not offering his first name – because if it was, that would make asking for it again in L3 irrelevant and inappropriate. (Of course in L4 there is also the subsequent evidence from DN himself that his name is not 'Okay'.)

This is noteworthy, not because it is remarkable that PK recognizes that 'Okay' is not his partner's first name, but rather because he does not interpret it as *some preliminary to doing an appropriate second part*. In other words, PK treats L2 as in no way relevant to his first pair part query in L1: he apparently realizes that DN isn't shunning him – he just didn't hear the question.

What is yet more interesting in this sequence is that it provides us with evidence that the adjacency pair is indeed a strong organizing principle in talk-in-interaction. Because PK recognizes that an appropriate second part is truly and *totally* absent and because the organizational power of the adjacency pair is so strong, PK goes in pursuit of a fitting second pair part by redoing his query. (For further discussions of response pursuit see Pomerantz 1984.)

Chaining

Before this chapter ends, another reason why it was important to mention adjacency pairs should be discussed – namely that adjacency pairs are linked into the system of turn-taking by the following rule:

Adjacency pair rule
On the finished production of a first part of some pair, Current speaker must subsequently stop speaking to give Next an opportunity to produce some second part to the same pair.

Because of this rule, adjacency pairs are an extremely useful device for selecting potential next speakers. It is not just through the more obvious question–response pair type that Current speaker can select Next, but rather by using any first pair part of any type. And that – using one of Sacks' favourite words – is neat (in all senses of the word). What's even neater is that combined with this, the 'tying' strength of the adjacency pair (as we saw briefly in PK's pursuit of DN's name) can be responsible for preventing talk from grinding to a halt (even when in some cases we might like it to).

Many (if not most) utterances can potentially be analysed as belonging to some type of adjacency pair – even the very first utterance in an interaction can demand some appropriate second part. If the second speaker on dutiful completion of their second part then appends a new first pair part, that will generate the need for further talk. If the first speaker responds in a similar way we no longer have just a pair of utterances, nor even just two pairs of utterances but rather the beginnings of a conversation.

This process is known as CHAINING and a very simple example of this happened when Angelo (who lives at number 3) popped out to the shops to buy some milk. On the way, he noticed a neighbour (who lives at number 25) coming towards him. They know each other just sufficiently to say hello. Despite their lack of intimacy, however, politeness demanded a greeting, so Angelo tried to get away with a perfunctory 'Hi'. But his neighbour wasn't joining in in doing perfunctory indifference – he was doing being friendly:

Example 3: Neighbours passing in the street

Angelo:	Hi.	Part 1: *Greeting*
Neighbour:	Hello, (.)	Part 2: *Greeting*
	How are you.=	Part 1: *Well-being enquiry*
Angelo:	=I'm fine thanks,=	Part 2: *Response*
	=Are you?=	Part 1: *Well-being enquiry*
Neighbour:	=Yes thank you!	Part 2: *Response*

Ironically, because of the neighbour's friendly appendage of 'How are you', Angelo was compelled (after an initial response of 'I'm fine thanks') into returning the friendly social enquiry. But by this time they had already passed each other, so although they were doing the business of organized talk-in-interaction, it was hardly very *social* interaction – each of them was delivering their final utterance into mid air rather than face-to-face!

Activity 2.11 🔑

Find examples of chained utterances in the data. (Hint: you have already seen some.) You should note that separate first and second pair parts are not always needed. Sometimes a second pair part will simultaneously act as the first pair of a new sequence.

2.6 SUMMARY

This chapter has done at least two things. It has introduced you to many of the conventions needed for detailed transcription and it has given you a flavour of some of the fundamental aspects relating to turn-taking, namely: TCUs, TRPs, overlap, interruption, speaker selection, types of silence, adjacency pairs, insertion sequences and chaining. And this has been achieved by providing you with an extract of data in order for you to uncover for yourself part of the highly organized nature of talk-in-interaction.

2.7 FURTHER ACTIVITIES

Activity 2.12

Return to the 'Syracuse' data. Rummage around in it and see what you can come up with. While you're rooting around in the data you might like to think about some of the following specific questions:

1   What displays of understanding are done (and *how* are they done)?
2   What's the difference between 'Hi' and 'Hello'?
3   What evidence is there of talk which is specifically designed with the recipient in mind?
4   What does 'Oh' do in lines 5, 25 and 33?
5   What does 'What¿' do in L16? (The ¿ represents a slight rise in intonation.)
6   How does Chester treat (interpret) this 'What¿' in L16?
7   What are the consequences of Chester's choice of interpretation?
8   What's the purpose (upshot) of the call?
9   Who formulates (explicitly says out loud) the upshot?

10   How does the upshot get formulated?
11   What other options were possible for formulating the upshot?
12   What differences are there between Chester's positive responses and his negative responses?
13.   What's going on in lines 34–38?
14.   Why might Chester change from 'girl' to 'Sarah' in L11?
15.   How is the call terminated?
16.   What else is interesting?

Activity 2.13

Consider the following set of PK's silences in Extract 2.2. What interactional task (or tasks) might they be designed to accomplish? In thinking about this, you might like to consider the close proximity of the words: 'right', 'okay' and 'now' and the placement of these turns within the overall task.

05	PK	(.) Right Dale. (1.0)
15	PK	Okay. (1.3)
74	PK	(0.9) Now (.)
81	PK	Right. (0.8) Now (1.3)
95	PK	(.) Right. (0.9)
119	PK	Right (1.0)

COMMENTARY ON ACTIVITIES

⊶ Remember that this symbol indicates that there is a commentary on the activity that you can find on the companion website at www.routledge.com/cw/merrison.

FURTHER READING and REFERENCES

Suggestions for further reading on the topics discussed in this chapter can be found on the companion website (www.routledge.com/cw/merrison).

Any piece of academic writing must always provide a list of publications to which reference has been made. Unusually and very unconventionally, this information is provided on the companion website (www.routledge.com/cw/merrison). Always ask your tutor about how you are to present references for any piece of work that you submit.

Chapter 3
Pragmatics

Key Ideas in this Chapter

- Meaning is far from precise – ambiguity is more prevalent than we might initially think.

- Context (e.g. who said it? where? when?) is what helps us disambiguate multiple meanings.

- Issues of appropriacy, likelihood and relevance are also at play in interpreting meanings.

- Language is used for doing things and the branch of linguistics that first took this seriously is Speech Act Theory.

- Grice's theory of conversational organization was an initial attempt to explain how it is that language users can mean more than they actually say by relying on various inferences.

3.1 INTRODUCTION

(1)   Specially made to meet their growing needs

What does (1) mean? All that can be claimed with any great certainty is that something (as yet unspecified) is made specially in order to fulfil the (again unspecified) growing needs of some person(s). Not very illuminating really! That is until we return this snippet of language to some of its original context as in (1'):

(1')   SMA PROGRESS follow-on milk for older babies and toddlers
       Specially made to meet their growing needs

With this additional contextual knowledge the meaning of (1) becomes more transparent: the something (previously unspecified) is SMA PROGRESS follow-on milk for older babies and toddlers and therefore it can now be assumed that this milk is made specially in order to fulfil the growing needs of older babies and toddlers.

But that isn't the whole story: what do *Specially made* and *growing needs* mean? Does 'Specially made' mean that SMA PROGRESS is 'bespoke' milk for this particular client group, or is it that the milk is made in an exceptional manner? Or both? And are the needs of the children expanding or is it rather that the milk is to suit the requirements of the children's growth? Or both? It is indeed possible that the writers intended all four meanings. Irrespective of the answers, these are questions for **pragmatics** which deals with analysing language in context.

If **semantics** is the study of meanings as stored in language, waiting to be put to use (➔ 6), then pragmatics focuses on how speakers and writers use their knowledge to convey meanings. In short, pragmatics studies how language is used in the interpretation of actual **utterances**. This means that people who study pragmatics are interested in *when* language is used, *where* it is used, *who* it is used by, *how* it is used, what it is used for, and, perhaps most importantly, *how it gets interpreted* as doing the things it is used for by the people who use it when they do so.

But how *do* speakers' intentions get interpreted by their audience? This chapter provides the beginnings of an answer to that question, and in doing so covers such topics as: **entailment, ambiguity, context, deixis** and **reference, direct** and **indirect speech acts, inferences** and **implicatures** and Grice's maxims of conversation. All these issues are used to show that a **code model** of language (whereby a speaker 'simply says the words' and a hearer 'simply decodes them' to get the intended message ➔ 1) is too simplistic to explain a great deal of actual language use.

An 'utterance' is a technical term for the physical production of any linguistic behaviour. It is not restricted only to spoken language but includes written text as well.

3.2 WHAT IS LANGUAGE USED *FOR*?

One reason (and some may say the *main* reason) for using language is obvious: language exists to say stuff about the world – to convey messages. And fortunately, for most of us at least, conveying messages with language is easy: we just have an idea, turn that thought into words (in the right order, of course), make various bits of our bodies move (lungs, **vocal cords**, tongue, lips ➔ 9, 10) and send the message out into the big wide world for someone to hear and (if they know the words and know about the **syntax** (or word order ➔ 7)) consequently understand. In this way, then, a lot of the time, encoding and decoding (i.e. using) language *really is that simple* and such a model of how language works is called a code model (➜ 1).

3.2.1 The code model

Let's look at some examples of the code model in action.

(2)   York is between Edinburgh and London.
(3)   London is between York and Edinburgh.
(4)   Edinburgh is between London and York.

  If we understand the words *and, between, Edinburgh, is, London, York* and if we know the way English syntax works, then we will know that only one of (2), (3) and (4) can be true (and, as it happens, that one is (2)). That's because *between* means that, given three **entities** (entities are people, things, places, events, times, tunes, ideas – indeed, whatever we can think and talk about), the first entity is located on some (potentially metaphorical) line or scale with the other two entities towards opposite ends. The concept of entities links with that of participant as outlined in Chapter 7.

3.2.2 Frege's principle

Not all languages rely on word order in the way that English does – some languages (e.g. German) rely on suffixes on words to indicate these syntactic relations.

What we have just discovered is that 'the interpretation of a sentence is a function of the interpretation of its parts and the syntactic relations holding between the parts' (Enç 1988: 240). This is known as Frege's principle. It is because of Frege's principle that we can understand that different processes are going on in (5) and (6) – because while the individual words are the same, the order is different and so the syntactic relations holding between those words are also different (in (5) Sally is the grammatical **Subject** and Ben the **Complement direct object** and in (6) it's the other way round ➜ 7, 14.4).

(5)   Sally changed Ben.
(6)   Ben changed Sally.

3.2.3 Entailment

Be careful not to confuse the term *proposition* with the word class label *preposition* (➜ 7).

So Frege's principle (*meaning = words + order*) does a lot of the work involved in understanding what people say. Another useful tool for getting at meaning is entailment. Entailments (➜ 6) are the conclusions (inferences) which are *guaranteed* to be true given the truth of an initial **proposition**. Thus, if we know that (7) is true (and we take the human, rather than spider meaning of *widow*), then we will automatically and unquestioningly know that (8)–(12) are also true:

(7)   Marjorie is a widow.
(8)   Marjorie is female.

(9)   Marjorie is alive.
(10)   Marjorie was at some time married.
(11)   The person who Marjorie was once married to is now dead.
(12)   Marjorie is at the current time not married.

We know that (8)–(12) must be true because if we try to cancel (deny) those inferences, something goes wrong (technically marked by the !) as shown in (8′)–(12′) – none of which can be *literally* true:

(8′)   ! Marjorie is a widow but she's not female.
(9′)   ! Marjorie is a widow but she's dead.
(10′)   ! Marjorie is a widow but she's never been married.
(11′)   ! Marjorie is a widow but her husband is still alive.
(12′)   ! Marjorie is a widow and she's married.

You may initially have doubts about (12) and (12′), but just think about Marjorie filling in an official document (say for a passport) and answering the marital status question. You might now agree that in order for Marjorie to tick the 'widow' box then she shouldn't be married, and if she ticks the 'married' box, then she is officially not a widow – she may have once been a widow but she is certainly not one anymore!

Together, Frege's principle and entailments will generate a lot of the meanings in people's utterances and with them we can decode (13)–(15) as most likely having the meanings set out in (16)–(18):

(13)   We saw her duck.
(14)   He told Damien Hirst to paint the walls with fluffy white lambs.
(15)   The scientist spotted the monkey with the telescope.
(16)   The speaker and the people the speaker is speaking on behalf of viewed a water fowl belonging to a pre-specified female person.
(17)   'Hey – Damien! Paint fluffy white lambs on the walls!'
(18)   By using a tubular monocular magnification device, a pre-specified person who is professionally engaged in scientific activity caught sight of a pre-specified primate.

3.2.4 Ambiguity

Activity 3.1 🔑

Look again at examples (13)–(15). Can you see any possible additional meanings other than (16)–(18) (in other words, can you spot how they could be ambiguous)?

So, given that many utterances are potentially ambiguous, if we used only the code model to work out what a message meant, then we would always have to allow all of the possible ambiguous interpretations for every single utterance and consequently we would never know which was the 'correct' version that the speaker had intended. But when we hear people talking we do not regularly find ourselves swamped by a baffling range of possible meanings, so clearly there must be some method for interpreters of messages to work out what the utterers of those messages must have intended and part of that method involves relying on the context of the utterance.

3.3 CONTEXT PART I: WHO? WHERE? WHEN?

In conveying messages about the world, we have to do two things: we have to refer to entities and we have to say something about those entities. In this section, let us concentrate on referring to an entity, which involves providing enough detail for the listener to successfully pick out whatever the speaker is referring to, as in (19):

(19)   Can I have one of the chocolate bars that are on the bottom shelf to the left of the Snickers and underneath the Mars bars?

As the typical linguistic act is speaking – where the speaker and listener(s) are usually face-to-face in the same place (at the same time) – generally, much can be understood just in relation to:

- the speaker and listener
- where they are in the location
- where other things in the location are relative to them
- the moment of speech/time of utterance.

Face-to-face, in a restricted location, speakers can use a minimal amount of description and yet still unambiguously pick out what's being spoken about by using expressions that make crucial use of the location of entities relative to speaker and hearer. Such expressions are called ➜ deictic and the act of using them is called DEIXIS. Deixis (equivalent to verbal pointing ➜ 8) comes in three major types:

- person deixis
  (e.g. I, me, mine, my, you, your, yours, verb endings in some languages)
- time deixis
  (e.g. then, yesterday, now, in five minutes, verb tenses)
- place deixis
  (e.g. this, that, here, there, above, behind, left, right, come, go).

Consequently, a little boy was able to stand at the counter in a shop, point and say (20):

(20)   Can I have one of those?

and the shopkeeper knew (because she was there, could follow his pointing and implicitly knew about deixis) that what he wanted was a Milky Way chocolate bar (which just happened to be on the bottom shelf to the left of the Snickers and underneath the Mars bars). Example (21) involves all three types of deictic expression:

(21)   I'll meet you here tomorrow at 3 o'clock and I'll give you one.

Without a good deal of contextual information, this utterance is extremely vague: who is *I*? who is *you*? where is *here*? when is *tomorrow*? *what* will be given? and is that 3*am* or 3*pm*?

Unless we know who the speaker and hearer(s) are (say, Andrew and Aileen), where they are (say, in Andrew's office in York), when the conversation is taking place (say, 6 December 2012), and what the topic of conversation is (say, Andrew's latest draft of this chapter), then we will not be able to uncover the intended message which is made explicit in (22):

(22)   I, Andrew, will meet you, Aileen, in my office in York at 3 o'clock on 7 December
        2012 and give you a copy of the latest draft of my pragmatics chapter.

3.3 CONTEXT PART II: APPROPRIACY, LIKELIHOOD AND RELEVANCE

Assuming that the listener can work out which entities the speaker is referring to, how can context help disambiguate what is said about those entities? Above, we left unanswered how it is that we know whether the 3 o'clock in (21) is 3*am* or 3*pm*. What disambiguates this is knowledge of the way the world generally operates: because we don't expect academics to be in their offices in the wee small hours of the morning we are led to the pm interpretation and so we get (23) as the full explicit intended meaning behind (21):

(23)   I, Andrew, will meet you, Aileen, in my office in York at 3 o'clock *in the afternoon* on
        7 December 2012 and give you a copy of the latest draft of my pragmatics chapter.

In this way then, by drawing on general knowledge of appropriate and relevant ways the world can work, on seeing (24) on a leaflet advertising admission to a theme park, no-one will immediately worry about how they would cope as a parent, nor wonder which orphanage donated all the children to be given away!

(24)　　Special Offer: free child with every full paying adult.

It is partly the context of knowing that the topic is about theme park admission that leads people to conclude that it is not a free *child*, but rather a free *child's admission* that is being offered. But perhaps equally important is their contextual knowledge of how the world works which helps to disambiguate the message – because they know that while it would clearly be 'special', giving away children is usually neither (a) legal, nor (b) much of an enticement to visit entertainment attractions!

By relying on knowledge of the way the world generally operates and on the context of the utterance – by taking into consideration who made the utterance, who they were speaking to, where and when they uttered it and what the topic of conversation was – a lot of the time all but one of the theoretically possible meanings become either inappropriate or irrelevant (which is why many of the suggested answers to Activity 3.1 may have seemed very contrived). Thus, by taking into account the context, we are very often able to work out both uniquely and correctly what was intended by an utterance, and that (together with Frege's principle) is how information gets conveyed – but of course, not all utterances are simply concerned with conveying information, as we shall see in the next section.

3.4 SPEECH ACTS

When a speaker or writer produces a **declarative** sentence (see Table 3.1 and ➔ 7) they undertake a certain responsibility, or commitment, to the hearer that a particular state of affairs, or situation, exists in the world. When utterances work like this, they are called acts of assertion and this is what was happening in (24) – it was being asserted that if an adult were to pay full price, then (the admission for) a child would be free. Some more examples of assertions (statements which could be checked for their truthfulness) might include:

(25)　　York beat Manchester Utd 4–3 on aggregate in the Coca-Cola Cup.
(26)　　Theeree's something eextreemeely wrong with thee <EE> keey on my computeer keeyboard.
(27)　　If you don't understand this chapter you might find Grundy (2008) useful.
(28)　　There's a wasp in your ear.
(29)　　There's a piece of fish on the table.

However, many messages aren't just about making (asserting) descriptions about the way the world is in order to convey information. For example, while (24) did indeed *assert* the existence of a special offer (and so *informs* the readers of that special offer), it was simultaneously doing much more than that – it was also *advertising* the theme park, *offering* a free child's admission and, with that, *attempting to persuade* (*entice*) the reader to visit. And each of these doings (advertising, offering, enticing) was being done with words alone.

Now clearly we can perform actions by physically doing something. For example, it can be argued that we can:

- make a bid of £500 at an auction by nodding
- congratulate someone by giving them a pat on the back (or a hug or a kiss or a hand-shake)
- acknowledge a £12,000 loan by smiling and taking the cheque.

But we can also perform (do) the above acts by speaking/writing, as in (30)–(32):

(30)   I *bid* five hundred pounds.

(31)   I *congratulate* you.

(32)   We the undersigned, <FULL NAME> and <FULL NAME>, hereinafter referred to as 'the borrowers', both residing at <FULL ADDRESS> … Edinburgh in the region of Lothian Scotland hereby *acknowledge* that we have received a loan of twelve thousand pounds sterling from Sheila Ena <SURNAME> of <FULL ADDRESS> … Peterborough in the county of Cambridge England, hereinafter referred to as 'the lender'.

When our words perform some action – whether in speech, as in (30) and (31), or in writing, as in (32) – we say that they are performing a **speech act** and each of the three examples above both *describes* some speech act (*congratulating, bidding, acknowledging*) and simul-taneously *performs* that act. These types of utterance are called performatives.

Certain special **verbs** can make the utterance of a sentence performative; these are called performative verbs and many sentences use these performative verbs as an essential part of some act such that *without* them being uttered the act *cannot* be performed. This is very often the case in public ceremonies:

(33)   baptizing: I baptize you in the name of the Father, Son and Holy Spirit

(34)   marrying: I now pronounce you man and wife

(35)   sentencing: I sentence you to life imprisonment

(36)   naming ships: I name this ship *Titanic*.

3.4.1 Felicity conditions

Of course, in order for these acts to be performed legitimately (or felicitously) certain conditions have to be met. Austin (1975: 14f.) called these conditions the felicity condi-tions of a performative and, as in Austin, they are categorized below using capitalized Greek letters:

(A.1)   There must exist an accepted conventional procedure having a certain conven-tional effect: in the UK, a man simply saying to his wife 'I divorce you' any number of times won't count as a legal divorce, because simply saying 'I divorce you' is not, in the UK, the accepted conventional procedure.

(A.2)   Certain acts can only be done by certain people in certain places with certain props. You can't name a ship if it already has a name; or if you are not the desig-nated namer; nor without a bottle of champagne, a slipway and at least one witness.

(B.1)   The procedure must be done by all participants correctly. You have to say the right words. Thankfully, you can't marry someone by saying 'Please pass the mustard'.

For each Greek letter you need to read here, this is the way to say it (first the capital letter form and then the lower case letter form): alpha Α α; beta Β β; gamma Γ γ. Use a search engine to find the rest of the Greek or any other alphabet, if you are interested in letter forms.

(**B**.2)   The procedure must be done by all participants completely. If I say 'I bet you £5 you can't do a simultaneous voiced bilabial, alveolar uvular trill!' the bet is no good unless you say something to the effect of 'You're on!' – i.e. there must be satisfactory uptake.

(**Γ**.1)   Speakers should be sincere in their acts – they should have the appropriate thoughts or feelings (for example, someone who says *thank you* should in fact be grateful).

(**Γ**.2)   and their subsequent conduct should also be appropriate (for example, someone who makes a promise to do something – such as pay out on a bet – should subsequently fulfil that promise; and someone who advises should not subsequently chastise the person who acts on that advice).

If any one of these conditions is not met, then the act is said to be 'infelicitous' (or, as Austin also liked to call it, *unhappy*) – in other words, something can go wrong; exactly *what* might go wrong with the act depends on what type of condition is not met:

A.1–B.2 violations: misfires – the act is null and void

The first four conditions (sometimes called the 'necessary conditions' of a performative) state that:

- the act must be recognized by convention
- the person performing the act must have the authority to do so
- in certain cases, the occasion of the utterance must be right
- the act has to be executed correctly and completely.

If any one of these necessary conditions is not met, the act could 'misfire' and not count as the act that was intended.

Γ1–Γ2 violations: abuses – the act is hollow

Γ.1 and Γ.2 are sometimes called the 'sincerity conditions' of a performative. These are the conditions of the situation (in which the utterance is made) that must be fulfilled if the act is to be carried out sincerely.

If the person performing the act does so insincerely (i.e. without the appropriate beliefs/feelings or by not carrying out certain actions) their act will *not* be null and void but they may be judged guilty of an 'abuse' (NB: sincerity may often be overridden by politeness ➔ 4).

The various infelicities are schematically summarized in Figure 3.1.

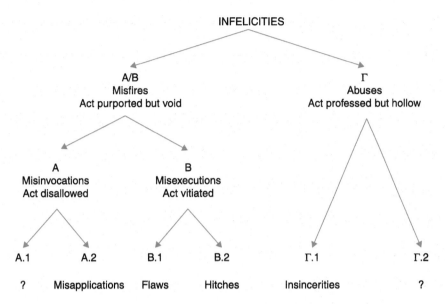

Figure 3.1 Types of speech act infelicity (based on Austin 1975: 18)

3.4.2 Explicit and implicit performatives

Performative utterances generally use sentences which have:

- first person subjects
- active simple present tensed verbs (➜ 7)
- one of a special set of performative verbs (that allow the use of *hereby*).

In this way, then, you could perform (if somewhat awkwardly) the act of warning someone that a car is approaching by explicitly using the performative verb *warn* in the simple present tense with a first person subject as in (37):

(37)   I (hereby) warn you that a car is approaching.

But you don't *necessarily* need the performative verb to be in the simple present tense with a first person subject to make an utterance do (perform) something. You could equally well warn someone that a car is approaching by uttering (38) in which there is a *second person* singular subject and a *non-active* (**passive** ➜ 7) **verb (group)**:

(38)   You are (hereby) warned that a car is approaching.

But you don't even *necessarily* need a performative verb. You can warn someone that a car is approaching by uttering (39) in which there is an implicit warning and a non-performative verb (hence the oddity/ungrammaticalness of *hereby* in (39')):

(39)   There is a car approaching!
(39')   *There hereby is a car approaching!

Using a * in front of an example indicates that the example is considered to be ungrammatical.

Furthermore, you can even completely do without either a subject or a verb. You can implicitly (and perhaps most appropriately) warn someone that a car is approaching by shouting (40):

(40)   Car!

It seems that simply by uttering words we can perform various actions (e.g. warnings) and furthermore these actions can be done either explicitly or implicitly. It seems some new definitions are needed:

- EXPLICIT PERFORMATIVE: a performative utterance that uses a performative verb
- PRIMARY PERFORMATIVE: a non-explicit performative (i.e. an utterance which tries to *do* something but without using a special performative verb)
- CONSTATIVE: a non-performative assertion (i.e. an utterance which is not trying to *do* anything other than make a simple statement).

3.4.3 A closer look at constatives

Activity 3.2 O⊷

Earlier we said that while (24) did indeed *assert* the existence of a special offer, it was simultaneously *advertising* the theme park and *offering* a free child's admission. Now reconsider examples (25)–(29) which were also used as examples of assertions (which we would now call *constatives*). Can you see any possible additional acts that these utterances might be performing over and above their obvious assertions? (Hint: try thinking of contexts in which they may be uttered.)

There is a commentary on the companion website which you should read before continuing.

By now, you should be getting the idea that given the right context, many utterances can perform many speech acts indeed – even those utterances which at first glance just look like declarative non-performative assertions. So it would seem that the original distinction we made between performatives and constatives is already becoming somewhat blurred. The performative–constative dichotomy was therefore eventually rejected in favour of a theory of speech acts in which just about all utterances can be thought of as actually *doing* something (see Austin 1975). For example, utterances can: *accuse, amuse, apologize, assert, boast, congratulate, console, demand, excuse, free, gloat, greet, hail, insult, jibe, kid, leer, mock, name, offer, persuade, please, promise, query, recommend, recriminate, scare, suggest, thank, urge, value, warn, yearn* …

Although there is not space here to go into any great detail, a flavour of the extended theory would be worthwhile. According to Austin, when we speak, we simultaneously perform several acts:

- PHONIC ACT: the act of making vocal sounds (➔ 9)
- LOCUTIONARY ACT: the communicative act of uttering a sentence (involving the acts of referring to certain objects in the world and saying stuff about them)

- ILLOCUTIONARY ACT: the act (defined by social convention) which is performed when making an utterance: e.g. accusing, apologizing, asserting, boasting, congratulating
- PERLOCUTIONARY ACT: the (not necessarily intentional) act of causing a certain effect on the hearer (and possibly others) e.g. amusing, persuading, pleasing, scaring.

The type of speech act that we have mainly been dealing with up until now (accusing, apologizing etc.) is what Austin finally called the **illocutionary act** (or occasionally the illocutionary *force* of the act). But now what we also have is the notion of the *perlocutionary act* (which is often useful in discussions of miscommunication). It is important to recognize the existence of this type of act because **communication** (➜ 1) is not a unilateral process – it always takes (at least) two!

Consider a speaker apologizing for some wrong doing, or congratulating their colleague on the recent birth of their son, or warning someone of an impending car/ wasp. People don't usually carry out these sorts of acts for the sake of it, but rather to produce certain perlocutionary effects: they apologize to receive forgiveness, they congratulate to make the hearer feel good, they warn to make the hearer take evasive action and so on. But before the hearer can do any of these things, they have to recognize that acts of apology, congratulation and warning have been done. In other words, there has to be what Austin calls illocutionary uptake, otherwise the initial act (no matter how well intentioned) will not be successful. Of course, simply recognizing and understanding the illocutionary force will not guarantee a successful perlocutionary effect – the hearer is always able to choose not to (re)act in the intended/ anticipated manner: so non-compliance is not always about miscommunication (as many parents will affirm).

As an example, consider the perhaps universal children's playground activity of something like (41):

(41)	Child 1: Watch out – there's a wasp!	(PSEUDO-WARNING)
	Child 2: Where?!	(QUERY)
	Child 1: Made you look, made you stare,	
	made you lose your underwear!	(TEASE)

If Child 2 is too often subject to these sorts of playful teases, they may eventually come to not recognize the intention behind (40) *Car!* and instead interpret it as a joke (or a simple assertion) rather than as a warning. Sadly, not achieving appropriate illocutionary uptake in your addressees can have serious consequences (hence the fable about the boy who cried wolf).

Fortunately, however, most of the time we do correctly recognize the intended force behind utterances – even though that force can be conveyed either explicitly or implicitly (as seen above) and either directly or indirectly (as will be seen in the next sections).

3.4.4 Direct speech acts

English has three major sentence (or **mood**) types: **declarative, interrogative** and **imperative** (➜ 7). Each of these has associated with it a typical act, as in Table 3.1.

Table 3.1 Sentence types and direct speech acts (in English)

Sentence Type (syntactic form)	Typical Linguistic Act (pragmatic function)
Declarative: Subject + Verb ... Interrogative: Verb + Subject ... Imperative: No overt Subject	Asserting Questioning Ordering/Requesting

The **direct illocution** of an utterance is the illocution most directly indicated by the literal meaning of what is uttered. In other words, when syntactic form and pragmatic function match, the effect is called a **direct speech act**, as in (42)–(44):

(42)   I like to play golf.
        (*Declarative* form functioning as an *assertion*)
(43)   Have you ever been lectured on pragmatics?
        (*Interrogative* form functioning as a *question*)
(44)   Promise me you won't laugh.
        (*Imperative* form functioning as an *order*)

3.4.5 Indirect speech acts

In everyday conversations, however, the majority of illocutions are, in fact, *indirect*. The **indirect illocution** of an utterance is any further illocution an utterance might have. In other words, when form and function *do not* match, we call the effect an **indirect speech act**, as in (45)–(47):

(45)   Context: At the ticket office of York railway station.
                          Traveller to sales clerk.
        Utterance: I'd like a day return to Sheffield please.
        Sentence type: Declarative
        Act: Ordering/Requesting:
                          Sell me a day return train ticket to Sheffield.

(46)   Context: At a nightclub. One friend to another.
        Utterance: Has he got a cute bum or what?
        Sentence type: Interrogative
        Act: Assertion:
                          He's got a cute bum!

(47)   Context: In a psychiatrist's office. Psychiatrist to client.
        Utterance: Tell me why you hate your father!
        Sentence type: Imperative
        Act: Question:
                          Why do you hate your father?

So because speech acts can be implicit and indirect, often what someone *means* is not actually what they *say*. Thus we must ask how it is that we seem to be able to work out the intended force of an illocution. The answer has a good deal to do with what background knowledge the hearer has – knowledge which helps determine what inferences (conclusions) and therefore what meanings it is reasonable to get from an utterance.

3.4.6 Useful knowledge

There are various types of knowledge that can be useful in interpreting what a speaker means with their utterance. These include knowledge of:

- the physical context of the situation
- the topic of conversation
- the participants in conversation
- the world (including culture, basic science, religion, current affairs …)
- how language works in principled ways.

Let us look at some examples:

Physical context

(48)   Can I have one of those?

Without being aware of the physical context of the situation, it would be impossible to tell both who *I* is, and also what *one of those* is.

Topic

(49)   Michael changed Ben.

Without knowing about the topic of conversation (and possibly also about the participants), it would be impossible to tell for sure whether Michael changed Ben's *character* or his *nappy*. Indeed, it might even be the case that Michael had a pet called Ben which he eventually got fed up with and so exchanged it for some other animal.

Participants

(50)   Dr Jones persuaded Mr Smythe that he should operate on him immediately.

Without knowledge of the participants it would be impossible to tell for sure who does the operating and who gets operated on. For example, consider the following two possible alternatives for participant roles (where the subscript letters indicate which entities co-refer):

(50a)   Rob Jones is a doctor in a hospital;
Tim Smythe is a patient of Dr Jones.
Dr Jones$_i$ persuaded Mr Smythe$_j$ that he$_i$ should operate on him$_j$ immediately.

(50b)   Rob Jones is a doctor in a hospital;
         Tim Smythe is a consultant surgeon.
         Dr Jones$_i$ persuaded Mr Smythe$_j$ that he$_j$ should operate on him$_{k/i}$ immediately.
         (The k subscript denotes that Smythe could sensibly operate on someone *other*
         than Jones.)

World

(51)   Marjorie: Would you like some chocolate?
         Joan: Is the Pope Catholic?

Without knowledge of the world (specifically the religion of the Pope), it would be
impossible to tell whether or not Joan wanted some chocolate.

3.5 LANGUAGE USE RELIES ON ASSUMPTIONS

One of the authors has
several mantras. One
of them is this: 'While
reality is clearly important,
what *really* matters is
people's *perceptions of
reality'.*

While knowledge of various aspects of the context can all clearly be involved in aiding the
interpretation of utterances, what actually counts as *relevant* context is potentially vast. According
to Sperber and Wilson (1995: 15f.), the context can be thought of as 'a subset of the hearer's
assumptions about the world' and furthermore, it is 'these assumptions, [...] rather than the
actual state of the world, that affect the interpretation of an utterance'. This can have serious
consequences for interpreting language in use. Let us use an example to illustrate.
     Let us assume:

Premise 1: $P \rightarrow Q$ (read as: 'if P, then Q')
                  which is logically equivalent to:
                  $\neg Q \rightarrow \neg P$ (read as: 'if not Q, then not P')

Now if we also *assume* Premise 2: $\neg Q$ (read as: 'not Q'), we are logically led to the conclusion: $\neg P$ (read as: 'not P'). Now let's use a worded example:

(52)   Marjorie: Will you have a piece of chocolate?
         Joan: If I eat chocolate I'll get fat.

Let P   = have (i.e. eat) a piece of chocolate
Let Q   = get fat

And, as before, let:

Premise 1: $P \rightarrow Q$ (which is equivalent to: $\neg Q \rightarrow \neg P$)
Premise 2: $\neg Q$
                        ───────
Conclusion: $\neg P$

If we assume that, like a lot of body-conscious individuals, Joan wants not to get fat
(i.e. if we assume Premise 2, not Q) then we will logically be led to conclude not P (i.e.
Joan will not eat the chocolate), and hence that Joan is *implicitly* declining Marjorie's offer,

which Marjorie should logically be able to work out. However, for Marjorie to reach this conclusion, *she* must also assume that Joan wants not to get fat (i.e. not Q). Any other assumption (e.g. Q) will not guarantee that she will understand Joan's response as a declination. While assuming that Joan *wants* to get fat (Q) is perhaps a little unusual, there is nothing absurd in the scenario where Joan is an actor who needs to put on weight for an up-coming role (or is a recovering anorexic, or is about to go on a polar expedition and needs to increase her fat reserves), and so it is of vital importance that both Joan and Marjorie share the same assumption – otherwise Marjorie will misinterpret Joan's response.

This has led Sperber and Wilson (1995: 18, emphasis added) to comment that 'the context in which an utterance is understood must be strictly limited to *mutual* knowledge; otherwise inference cannot function as an effective aspect of decoding'. Gazdar and Good put it a little more strongly, saying that 'comprehension can only be guaranteed by identical knowledge bases' but of course, if speakers and hearers shared exactly the same thoughts (had the same knowledge), that 'would render communication redundant' (1982: 100 footnote 7).

Clearly, none of us has exactly the same knowledge as anyone else, and consequently communication is indeed a necessary part of life. So the question we must ask now is, if we do not have identical knowledge bases, how do we ever manage to communicate anything which relies on inferences? H. Paul Grice proposed a solution.

3.6 GRICE'S THEORY OF CONVERSATIONAL ORGANIZATION

Grice was interested in how it is that we can imply something without actually saying it (as Joan implies a 'yes' in (51) and a 'no' in (52) despite not actually saying so). For him, the answer lay in the assumption that as rational communicators, we appear to take it for granted that an utterance should make sense in the given context (otherwise it would not be worth a speaker uttering it or a hearer processing it). He called this assumption the Cooperative Principle (CP) (Grice 1975: 45):

> **Make your conversational contribution such as is required, at the stage at which it occurs, by the accepted purpose or direction of the talk exchange in which you are engaged.**

To this overarching principle, he added four main maxims of conversation:

MAXIM OF QUANTITY

1   Make your contribution as informative as is required (for the current purposes of the exchange).
2   Do not make your contribution more informative than is required.

MAXIM OF QUALITY

1   Do not say what you believe to be false.
2   Do not say that for which you lack adequate evidence.

Sperber and Wilson (1995) have developed a theory of pragmatics (Relevance Theory) which claims that an assumption of relevance is really the only principle that is necessary.

MAXIM OF RELEVANCE

1   Be relevant.

MAXIM OF MANNER (be perspicuous)

1   Avoid obscurity of expression.
2   Avoid ambiguity.
3   Be brief (avoid unnecessary prolixity).
4   Be orderly.

In other words, Grice suggested that when we talk, we *assume* that all participants orient towards successful communication as a goal and in so doing it is assumed that they are all appropriately INFORMATIVE, TRUTHFUL, RELEVANT and CLEAR.

3.6.1 What can we do with these maxims?

We can ADHERE to them

(53)   Marjorie: I need to speak to Tommy – is he in this morning, Joan?
        Joan: Yes – he's in the kitchen.

Here we see Joan's response to Marjorie's question as being clear, relevant and (we assume) truthful. It is also adequately and appropriately informative (note that although Marjorie asked a yes–no question, a simple 'Yes' would have been an inadequate response because in order to speak to Tommy, Marjorie first needs to locate him). In short Joan is abiding by the CP and its attendant maxims. There are, however, occasions where speakers choose not to do so …

We can VIOLATE them because of a maxim clash

Some years ago when Alan was organizing a school reunion an ex-pupil (Bob) started talking about a fellow ex-pupil, Jay Walton. When it transpired that Jay wouldn't be attending, Bob said he would like to get in touch with him and so he asked where Jay lived:

(54)   Bob: Where does Jay live?
        Alan: Somewhere in the South of France.

Although Alan did not explicitly say so, if he was observing the CP (specifically trying to be as informative as appropriate for Bob's needs), he will have implied that he did not have any more specific information. The reasoning goes like this:

- There is no reason to suppose that Alan is deliberately shirking his conversational responsibilities and not observing the CP.
- Alan's answer is, as indeed he well knows, less informative than is required to meet Bob's needs – simply addressing a letter to 'Jay Walton, Somewhere in the South of France' is most unlikely to have been successful!

- This appears to be a violation of the maxim of quantity. (Make your contribution as informative as is required.)
- An explanation for this apparent violation might be that had Alan been *more* informative, he would have violated the maxim of quality. (Don't say what you don't have evidence for.)
- Therefore the implication is that Alan either does not know or can't remember which particular town in the South of France Jay lives in.

In British culture, it is considered more important not to tell untruths than to say what your interlocutor wants to hear. This is not necessarily the case for all cultures however.

We can *FLOUT* them (deliberately choose to not observe them)

On the whole, because we assume that participants in talk exchanges *do* adhere to these maxims, when a speaker appears to deliberately fail to observe any one of them (known as 'flouting' a maxim), a so-called conversational implicature obtains – since the hearer assumes that her interlocutor is observing the *overall* CP. In other words, in flouts, 'though some maxim is violated *at the level of what is said*, the hearer is entitled to assume that that maxim, or at least the overall Cooperative Principle, is observed *at the level of what is implicated*' (Grice 1975: 52, emphasis added).

Let's look at an example of how deliberately flouting the maxims leads to implied meanings.

(55)   Marjorie: Am I in need of a rather large gin and tonic after teaching pragmatics all afternoon!
        Joan: Well 'The Tap and Spile' is just along the road …

Considering only what Joan *says*, her response – even if truthful – seems to be rather obscure, bearing little relation to Marjorie's prior comment. It thus seems to be of little informative use to the thirsty pragmatics lecturer – Joan appears to be not adequately fulfilling her communicative role. However, if, rather than assuming she is being deliberately obtuse, it is assumed that Joan *is* following the CP and is indeed being informative, truthful, relevant and clear, then although she doesn't actually say so, Marjorie will be led to conclude that she is implying that 'The Tap and Spile' is a place which sells beverages (specifically, gin and tonic – in other words it isn't a coffee shop), that it will be open for the sale of such beverages and that the distance along the road which Marjorie would have to travel to get there is not unreasonable for the transport available. Since Joan will assume that Marjorie will assume that Joan is abiding by the CP and its maxims, Joan is able to imply all these things without actually saying them. And in this way, she is able to avoid an otherwise necessarily complex response such as in (55′):

(55′)   Marjorie: Am I in need of a rather large gin and tonic after teaching pragmatics all afternoon!
        Joan: Well 'The Tap and Spile' is a place which sells beverages – specifically, gin and tonic – that will be open for the sale of such beverages and the distance along the road which you would have to travel to get there is not unreasonable for the transport available.

Implicature certainly has its uses and the following examples provide yet further evidence of this fact.

Flouting the maxim of quantity

(56)   Interviewer: What did you think of Tony Blair as Prime Minister?
        Interviewee: He was always well dressed and he had a great smile.

Here, by not providing sufficient information relating to Blair's qualities as a statesman, the interviewee has clearly flouted the maxim of quantity. However, rather than assume that they are being deliberately uncooperative, we instead assume that because the words themselves are apparently in violation of the maxim, the speaker must be implying something appropriately informative. Hence we are led to the inference that they did not rate him as prime minister. Very importantly, this type of implied inference is not an entailment – it is not always necessarily true, and as such, it is possible for it to be denied: should the interviewer explicitly confront the interviewee with this conclusion, the latter could always legitimately say that that was not what they had *said*!

If we are to be appropriately informative in our talk exchanges, we should always actually inform. That may seem too obvious to be worth mentioning – a tautology (necessary truth) in fact. And yet there are many expressions which when considered only at the level of the words uttered are indeed tautologous:

(57)   Boys will be boys!
(58)   What will be will be!
(59)   It ain't over 'til it's over.
(60)   When it's over it's over.

All these expressions have the underlying format of 'If P, then P', and, as can be seen, irrespective of what the proposition P is, the expression must necessarily always be true (hence they are all tautologies). As such, none of them should be able to *say* anything we don't already know. And indeed, they don't – but they do *imply* things.

The final pair of examples illustrate this point rather neatly: while on the surface they appear to be saying *exactly* the same thing (if *over, then over*), they imply different meanings – (59) implies that 'there is *still hope*' while (60) implies '*all hope is gone*'.

Flouting the maxim of quality

Alternatively, we can convey meaning implicitly by flouting the maxim of quality. Example (61) comes from a breakfast TV show where, just before each advert break, a celebrity did a small piece to camera. It was aired before 8am.

(61)   I'm Rufus and I'm asleep at the moment.

Clearly Rufus was literally not telling the truth. This utterance therefore contravenes the maxim of quality. And yet, rather than think that he was not following the CP, we assume that Rufus must have been trying to imply something. Thus we conclude that what he must have meant is that while obviously awake at the time of *recording*, at the projected time of *transmission* he would be asleep and in this way he is able to display some subtle (non-obvious) humour.

It is this assumption of implicit truthfulness which allows us to understand many non-literal expressions as idiomatic.

(62)   Marjorie: He got out of bed on the wrong side this morning.

Whenever someone says (62), it is nearly always the case that they can have no adequate supporting evidence: how could they possibly know which side of the bed he got out of, or indeed which side counts as the wrong one? And yet, rather than assume that the speaker is ignoring the second submaxim of quality by *saying* something for which they lack adequate evidence, we instead assume that they must be being cooperative in what they are *implying* (here, the idiomatic meaning that 'he' is in a grouchy mood). Again, note that this implicature is not an entailment as the idiom conclusion ('he is grouchy') could subsequently be reasonably denied (technically known as **cancelled**) as shown in Marjorie's third and final utterance in (63):

(63)   Marjorie: Have you seen your dad yet today?
            Timmy: No.
            Marjorie: He got out of bed on the wrong side this morning.
            Timmy: Oh! Is he grouchy?
            Marjorie: No – the daft man got out of bed on my side and he's still wearing my slippers!

Flouting the maxim of relevance

(64)   Marjorie: Have you done your homework, Timmy?
            Timmy: What time's dinner?

Here, by changing the subject (by not being relevant), Timmy implies that he has not done his homework.

Flouting the maxim of manner

(65)   Marjorie: Has anyone taken the d-o-g for a w-a-l-k?

Although she is speaking in an obscure way, we wouldn't ordinarily assume that Marjorie is deliberately trying to be uncooperative. People often spell out (or otherwise avoid) words that should not, for some reason (often because they are taboo), be said out loud (such as the wizards in the Harry Potter books who cannot bring themselves to utter the name of the evil 'Lord Voldemort' and so instead use 'He Who Must Not Be Named' or 'You-Know-Who'). Thus we might infer that while the dog in (65) could perhaps understand the words *dog* and *walk*, it can't spell! Again, this is only an implicature, not an entailment – after all, Marjorie may often talk in this apparently odd way.

In case you are not convinced, consider the following examples where A, an **aphasic** individual (language impaired due to brain damage ➜ 14), has problems with word retrieval, and yet is able to spell out words well enough to make himself understood. Indeed, this is apparently such a useful strategy that his non-aphasic interlocutor (B) also adopts it in (67) to ask about the elephant:

(66) and (67) are extracts from Map Task dialogues. See 2.4 for details.

```
(66)   A:   Is - is there anything in between the I-G-L-O-O
            and the house - and the dog?
       B:   There's a noose.

(67)   A:   And (2.2) I wonder (if) I've got that right
            'cos we're no got a (1.4) hmm (1.9) and we're
            going to (2.0) a place that I (.) can't- can't
            say S-N-A-K-E?
       B:   (1.0) Snake?=
       A:   =Ye::s=
       B:   =I don't have a snake. Where is the snake?
       A:   Er (.) right north
       B:   (.hh) It's right north. Now do you have an
            elephant? (1.4) (.hh) Elephant (.) E-L-E->P-H-
            A-N-T?<=
       A:   =No
       B:   You don't have an elephant=
       A:   =No
       B:   OK. It's a bit confusing
```

3.7 SUMMARY

To interpret various speech acts we often need to go beyond literal meaning to get at speaker meaning. We often have to make inferences based on context. Not all these inferences will be entailments (and thus necessarily true in all circumstances). Some inferences will be implicatures that are generated because of a particular context.

When people use language, we assume they are being cooperative (in a Gricean sense) and are following Grice's maxims of conversation *viz.*: being informative, truthful, relevant and clear. We can adhere to these maxims; we can violate them because of a maxim clash; or we can flout (deliberately not observe) them to generate an implicature. Flouting a maxim will give rise to a conversational implicature since a speaker who might not appear to be observing the CP at the level of what is *said*, *can* be assumed to be observing the CP at the level of what is *implicated*. Importantly, while implicatures are inferences, they are not entailments, and can therefore be cancelled (denied).

What this chapter has shown, then, is that in order to fully understand language in use – in order to be able to properly interpret utterances – we often need to consider issues such as *when* that language is used, *where* it is used, *who* it is used by, and what it is used *for* and *how*. Furthermore, very often we cannot rely solely on the literal meaning and syntactic ordering of the words in order to understand the intended meaning of an utterance. Much language is potentially ambiguous and for interpretation to be successful, various types of contextual knowledge as well as vital inferential processes and an assumption of cooperative linguistic behaviour are all required.

In short, a code model of language (whereby a speaker 'simply says the words' and a hearer 'simply decodes them' to get the intended message) is *too* simplistic to explain a great deal of actual language use and it is the discipline of pragmatics which is responsible for providing better explanations of how language is used in the interpretation of utterances.

3.8 FURTHER ACTIVITY

Activity 3.3

What implicatures might be generated by (68)–(70)? What (if any) special contexts are required?

(68)   It's cold in here isn't it?!
(69)   Have you had a fight with a lawnmower?
(70)   Ben's crying!

COMMENTARY ON ACTIVITIES

☞ Remember that this symbol indicates that there is a commentary on the activity that you can find on the companion website at www.routledge.com/cw/ merrison

FURTHER READING and REFERENCES

Suggestions for further reading on the topics discussed in this chapter can be found on the companion website (www.routledge.com/cw/merrison).

Any piece of academic writing must always provide a list of publications to which reference has been made. Unusually and very unconventionally, this information is provided on the companion website (www.routledge.com/cw/merrison). Always ask your tutor about how you are to present references for any piece of work that you submit.

Chapter 4
Power and Politeness

Key Ideas in this Chapter

- Language in use is necessarily about language choice.

- Everything that is uttered indexes something.

- Interpersonal relationships between interlocutors affect the linguistic formulation of any utterance.

- Linguistic politeness is more complex than just saying 'please' and 'thank you'.

- Positive and negative politeness is considered in the terms used by Brown and Levinson.

- Why should we bother to be linguistically polite? Because it helps us to achieve our goals within the interaction.

4.1 INTRODUCTION

This chapter neatly links to Chapter 3 because in many respects, power and politeness are both areas pertinent to applied pragmatics. Furthermore, power and politeness necessarily involve the analysis of interactional data which is most often talk (➔ 2).

This chapter provides a brief introduction to power, **face**, and face threatening acts (FTAs) to show that linguistic behaviour is linked to social **context**.

4.2 SOCIAL AND PRAGMATIC CONSEQUENCES OF LINGUISTIC CHOICE

In Chapter 2 it is noted that conversation analysts should continually be asking of their data: 'WHY THAT NOW'? In fact, in this book we would argue that any linguist interested in studying *language in use* should ask the same question. We always have a choice of what we say or write and one of the linguist's tasks is to uncover what *choice X* achieves that *choice Y* doesn't. Often the choices that we make differ in their social and pragmatic consequences. Consider something as relatively mundane as asking someone to get you a drink:

Example 4.1: Getting a can of coke

The scene

It's break time in a long linguistics seminar. Because you have been talking a lot, you're thirsty and want a drink. But you are also too exhausted to walk to the vending machine along the corridor and down two flights of stairs.

Below are seven choices for explicitly asking someone to get you a can of Coke. Rank them from least polite to most polite.

The choices

(1)   Get me a Coke.
(2)   Get me a Coke, Andy!
(3)   You'll be a pal and get us a Coke won't you Andy?
(4)   Could you possibly get me a Coke from the machine please, Andy? I'll go next week.
(5)   If you're going to the machine, could you possibly get me a Coke while you're there please?
(6)   If you're going to the machine, would you possibly be so kind as to get me a Coke while you're there please?
(7)   I'm really sorry to ask, but if you're going to the machine, I'd be ever so grateful if you would possibly be so kind as to get me a Coke while you're there please.

A betting person might wager you had ranked these choices from (1)–(7), with (1) as the least polite and (7) as most polite. There are good reasons why you might have chosen this order and by the end of the chapter you should be able to work out why. But which of these choices would you actually use to ask someone to get you a can of Coke? The answer, hopefully, should be: 'It depends!'. More specifically, it would depend on who you are asking, how well you know them, how much power they have over you, how much effort it costs them to get the can of drink and perhaps even what benefits there might be for them if they get it. For example, you might use (1), (2) or (3) to your best friend, signalling the intimacy of your relationship (hence the friendliness of your request). On the other hand, you might choose (4) or (5) to a student in the class who you know less well. Finally, (6) and (7) are ways you just might ask your professor to get you the drink – (7) is almost certainly not a way to ask your best friend (they would think you were being sarcastic). Indeed, it is possibly so over the top that it verges on obsequiousness.

So in this chapter we will investigate perhaps the most fundamental aspect of all language in use: linguistic choice – why do people choose to use language the way they do? Our answer covers issues of power and politeness (though in reality, these two concepts are intricately interlinked).

4.3 POWER

There can be a very fine line between politeness and impoliteness: overpolite behaviour can be interpreted as impolite and apparently impolite behaviour can be treated as perfectly appropriate. It's all very complicated (but that's what makes it fascinating to study).

Power is defined and manifested very differently in varying contexts: political, academic, medical, legal, family ...

What, then, is power? While this is a simple question to ask, it is actually really difficult to answer. Thornborrow (2002: 5) even likens it to a 'conceptual can of worms'. It is therefore not a question we can give a full answer to here (for further discussion, see Thornborrow 2002, Mooney *et al.* 2011 or Fairclough 2001). For now let's consider two definitions, both of which feature the term 'control'. For Fairclough, power 'is to do with powerful participants *controlling and constraining the contributions of non-powerful participants*' (2001: 38f., original emphasis). Brown and Levinson's (1987: 77) version is slightly more comprehensive:

> P[ower ...] is the degree to which H[earer] can impose his own plans and his own self-evaluation [...] at the expense of S[peaker]'s plans and self-evaluation. In general there are two sources of P[ower ...] material control (over economic distribution and physical force) and metaphysical control (over the actions of others [...]).

What both of these definitions allow for is the fact that power is not absolute and immutable but rather is contingent upon contextual factors. For example, when you are in a tutorial, your professor has power over you, but if they came to you for salsa lessons, you would have power over them. Activity 4.1 involves an example that happened to one of the authors.

Activity 4.1 o—ᴛ

The scene

Abe (a linguist) telephones his sister. His 25-year-old (ex-marine) police officer nephew (who normally lives away from home) answers. After some initial pleasantries, Abe gets to the purpose of his call. (For transcription conventions, see 2.3.1.)

The exchange

		((telephone rings))
	Matt:	Hello?
	Abe:	Oh hi Matt. How're you doin'.
		How's that broken arm of yours.
05	Matt:	Oh it's okay thanks. (.) A bit itchy.
		((several turns omitted))
	Abe:	You've got SKY haven't you.
	Matt:	At home, (.) yes.
	Abe:	Does that mean you can get *CBeebies*?
10	Matt:	Hang on a minute mate, I'll just have a check.
		((long pause while Matt checks with his mum))
		Yes we can.
	Abe:	Can you do me a hu:::ge ↑fa↑vour.
	Matt:	Yeah?
15	Abe:	On *CBeebies* tonight,
	Matt:	Yeah?
	Abe:	At five to seven, *Newsround* is on.
	Matt:	Yeah?
	Abe:	Could you possibly record it for me?=I'm interested in the
20		<u>exact</u> wording of the West Indian Cricket Board's
		apology for the West Indies' abysmal performance in
		the first test. They put up a quote of the apology and I keep
		missing it on terrestrial TV. Could you write it down for me
		and call me back with it?
25	Matt:	Sure. No worries mate.
	Abe:	Thanks ever so much. I'll talk to you later.
	Matt:	Okay. Bye!
	Abe:	Bye.

NB *Newsround* is a news and current affairs programme shown on the *CBeebies* UK TV channel for young children.

The questions

(a) Who has what power in this interaction? Why?
(b) What evidence of power is there? Is it linguistic or non-linguistic?
(c) In what other possible scenarios (linguistic or otherwise) might there be a power differential between these participants? Why?

Activity 4.1 touched on some of the ways that interpersonal relations and situational contexts can determine who has what power to control the actions of others – in short, who can expect to get their own way. The same sort of themes can be applied to all interactions where people want to achieve various goals. The basic point is this: to be successful in achieving your goal(s) you have to go about interacting in just the right way. To use an extreme example, it would be irrational and most inappropriate to attempt to get an extension for a linguistics essay from your professor by saying 'Give me an extension, bitch!'. To achieve our aims, we have to interact in a way that meets our addressee's expectations of how we should interact in that particular context and that often involves using linguistic politeness.

4.4 POLITENESS

Although not the origin of the phrase, you might relate the saying 'mind your Ps and Qs' to 'mind your *pleases* and *thankyous*'.

Saying 'please' and 'thank you' is one way that very young children are initiated into linguistically/socially polite behaviour.

For linguists, as Cutting notes (2002: 44, original emphasis), politeness does 'not refer to the social rules of behaviour such as letting people go first through a door, or wiping your mouth on the serviette rather than on the back of your hand'. Nor is it simply a matter of saying *please* and *thank you*, though that is indeed part of it. So what is politeness? There are many definitions depending on who you read. Here is a collection ranging from the general to the more specific:

> 'politeness' is the term we use to describe the relationship between how something is said to an addressee and that addressee's judgement of how it should be said.
>
> (Grundy 2008: 202)

> [Politeness refers] to whatever means are employed to display consideration for one's addressee's feelings (or face), regardless of the social distance between the speaker and the addressee.
>
> (Green 1996: 151)

> 'politeness' will be used to refer to behaviour which actively expresses positive concern for others, as well as non-imposing distancing behaviour.
>
> (Holmes 1995: 5)

It is often claimed that 'face' is particularly important in China and other countries in the Far East. It should therefore not be surprising that Goffman recognizes the importance of the Chinese concept from the very beginning of his seminal paper 'On Face-Work'.

Holmes' version comes closest to paraphrasing the highly influential ideas of Brown and Levinson (1987, 2006) who propose a theory of politeness phenomena heavily based on Goffman's (1967) notion of face (as in the phrases 'to lose face' and 'to save face') and the related face threatening acts (FTAs). Although their model has been incredibly influential, there are certainly criticisms to be levelled at, and also theoretical alternatives to, Brown and Levinson's ideas (for just some examples, see discussions in Watts et al. 1992; Eelen 2001, Watts 2003 and Locher and Watts 2005). One of the main criticisms is that their approach to politeness phenomena appears to be rather focused on the speech acts (➔ 3) inherent in single utterances rather than taking a larger discourse view of language use (➔ 8). However, because it is invariably necessary to have an understanding of Brown and Levinson's theory in order to be able to properly understand alternative models, it is an overview of Brown and Levinson's contribution which is the main concern of this chapter.

Brown and Levinson (henceforth B&L) suggest that people have certain needs and that two of these are the need for freedom (autonomy) and the need to be valued (self-worth). And because these needs are fragile, they require careful tending by all participants involved.

While the following quotations are long, it is nevertheless useful to see how B&L (1987: 61) put it themselves:

> We make the following assumptions: that all competent adult members of a society have (and know each other to have):
>
> (i) 'face', the public self-image that every member wants to claim for himself, consisting in two related aspects:
>   (a) negative face [autonomy]: the basic claim to territories, personal preserves, rights to non-distraction – i.e. to freedom of action and freedom from imposition
>   (b) positive face [self-worth]: the positive consistent self-image or 'personality' (crucially including the desire that this self-image be accepted and approved of) claimed by interactants
> (ii) certain rational capacities, in particular consistent modes of reasoning from ends to the means that will achieve those ends.

B&L add a footnote to their comment about 'all competent adult members of a society'. The footnote says 'juvenile, mad, incapacitated persons partially excepted'.

A further assumption (1987: 61) which needs to be included is that:

> In general, people cooperate (and assume each other's cooperation) in maintaining face in interaction, such cooperation being based on the mutual vulnerability of face. That is, normally everyone's face depends on everyone else's being maintained, and since people can be expected to defend their faces if threatened, and in defending their own to threaten others' faces, it is in general in every participant's best interest to maintain each others' face, that is to act in ways that assure the other participants that the agent is heedful of the assumptions concerning face given under (i) above.

4.4.1 Face threatening acts

So when people interact, they run the risk of threatening (and damaging) the face of those involved. As B&L say (1987: 65):

> certain kinds of acts intrinsically threaten face, namely those acts that by their nature run contrary to the face wants of the addressee and/or the speaker. By 'act' we have in mind what is intended to be done by a verbal or non-verbal communication, just as one or more 'speech acts' can be assigned to an utterance.

When language is used to perform some action rather than simply describe the world, it is said to be performing a speech act (→ 3).

Because it is possible to distinguish between positive face (self-worth) and negative face (autonomy), we can distinguish the sorts of acts that threaten each type of face. This is done in the following sections which will be crucial for applying B&L's ideas to data.

The terms *positive face* and *negative face* are used in this chapter in line with B&L's usage even though these are actually potentially dangerous labels – it is often mistakenly assumed that 'positive' face is inherently *good*, and 'negative' face inherently *bad*. Clark's (1996) terms *self-worth* and *autonomy* avoid this possible confusion.

4.4.2 Threats to H's negative face

Closely following B&L (1987: 65f.), acts can threaten the hearer's (H's) negative face wants by indicating that the speaker (S) does not intend to avoid impeding H's freedom of action. For example:

1   acts that suggest that H will have to do some future act, A, and consequently put pressure on H to actually *do* (or refrain from doing) A:
    (a)   orders, requests
    (b)   suggestions, advice
    (c)   remindings
    (d)   threats, warnings, dares

2   acts that suggest some positive future act on the part of S towards H which consequently put pressure on H to accept (or reject) and might therefore lead to H incurring a debt:
    (a)   offers
    (b)   promises

For some cultures it is a social imperative on H to give the thing complimented on to S.

3   acts that suggest some desire on the part of S towards H or H's goods which may put pressure on H either to protect the object of S's desire or to give it to S:
    (a)   compliments, expressions of envy or admiration
    (b)   expressions of strong negative emotions toward H (e.g. hatred, anger, lust)

4.4.3 Threats to H's positive face

When S indicates that they do not care about or are indifferent to H's feelings, H's positive face wants can be threatened. For example (still closely following B&L 1987: 66f.):

1   acts that suggest that S has a negative opinion of some aspect(s) of H's positive face:
    (a)   expressions of disapproval, criticism, ridicule, complaints, reprimands, accusations, insults
    (b)   contradictions, disagreements, challenges

2   acts that suggest that S doesn't care about H's positive face:
    (a)   expressions of violent emotions
    (b)   irreverence, mention of taboo subjects
    (c)   bringing bad news about H or good news about S
    (d)   raising dangerously emotional or divisive topics
    (e)   blatant non-cooperation
    (f)   misuse of terms of address.

Just as acts can threaten the face of the Hearer, they can also threaten the face (negative and positive) of the Speaker. However, B&L treat these FTAs as less complicated by using a simple list (shown below) rather than a more complex system of categorization.

4.4.4 Threats to S's negative face

(a)   expressing thanks
(b)   accepting H's thanks or apology
(c)   excuses
(d)   accepting offers
(e)   ignoring H's *faux pas*
(f)   unwilling promises.

4.4.5 Threats to S's positive face

(a)   apologizing
(b)   accepting a compliment
(c)   breakdown of physical control over body
(d)   self-humiliation, self-contradiction, acting stupid
(e)   confessing, admitting guilt or responsibility
(f)   emotion leakage, non-control of laughter or tears.

4.4.6 Applying Brown and Levinson's ideas

If you have persevered this far through what must have seemed like an endless list, well done! Now comes the pay-off for your effort. Have a go at Activity 4.2.

Activity 4.2 🔑

The scene

A Friday night in 2003 in the UK. It was 9.30 pm and dark. Adam, a 38-year-old white male, was walking along the street in a black suit, white shirt and black bow tie. He was carrying a briefcase. 50 metres ahead was a petrol station. 150 metres ahead was a newsagents and tobacconists. Two young teenage girls were walking a few paces in front of him wearing shell suits (casual sportswear).

The exchange

01	Girl:	Here mate c'n ya go to the shop for us please=
	Adam:	=No.
03	Girl:	Why?
	Adam:	Because if you want *me* to go, it's for something illegal.
05	Girl:	It's only for a packet of *FAGS*!!

NB: In the UK, *fags* is a slang term for cigarettes (➜ 12)

4.4.7 Calculating face threat

It was noted earlier that being over polite could become impolite. In the same way, being too zealous in paying face can become in itself face-threatening.

By now it should have become clear that engaging in normal interaction (either as Speaker or Hearer) runs the risk of losing face. Consequently, interactants have to jointly cooperate to maintain face, making sure to pay face whenever an FTA must be performed to meet the current goal. And that assumes we somehow know when an act is indeed a face threatening one and, more specifically, it assumes that we somehow know how much face paying is appropriate. How we gauge the seriousness of potential face loss is addressed in B&L's (1987: 76) formula expressed (in slightly modified form) as:

$$W = D(H,S) + P(H,S) + Rx$$

Where:

W = weightiness of FTA x
$D(H,S)$ = social distance between H and S
$P(H,S)$ = power H has over S
R = the degree to which FTA x is considered an imposition

This rather daunting-looking formula really isn't that scary. It's just a concise way of saying that the degree (or 'weightiness') of face threat caused by a speaker's act, x, depends on three main variables:

(D)   DISTANCE: how close (relatively speaking) the speaker is in social terms to their hearer (the less socially equivalent they are, the more threatening the speaker's act will seem – cf. asking a favour of friends vs. strangers); *and*

(P)   POWER: how much power (relatively speaking) the hearer can legitimately exert over the speaker (the more powerful the hearer, the more threatening the speaker's act will seem – cf. professors asking favours of their students vs. students asking favours of their professors); *and*

(R)   RANK: how imposing (relatively speaking) the act x is considered to be in the given culture (the more imposing, the more threatening the speaker's act will seem – cf. asking for the time vs. asking to borrow someone's brand new car).

B&L note that any numbers used in this formula represent only relative values (hence the 'relatively speaking' in each of the above). Furthermore, they suggest (1987: 287 footnote 18) that values between 1 and 7 ('or so') may be adequate for each variable. On this assumption then, an act which scores 21/21 can be thought of as extremely face threatening indeed, while one that scores just 3/21 will be hardly threatening at all. While on the subject of relativism, we should always remember that different interactants may differ in their estimates of D, P and R.

Two further very important points still need to be made about B&L's weightiness formula. First, the degree of face threat depends upon the *combination* of D, P and R. In other words, for B&L, it doesn't matter whether a score of, say, 9 is made up of D=2 + P=3 + R=4, or D=4 + P=3 + R=2, or D=1 + P=1 + R=7, or … whatever. For B&L, a weightiness value of N is just a weightiness value of N and how N is actually made up is essentially irrelevant. Second (and more fundamental to B&L's theory) is the assumption that whenever an FTA must be performed to meet the current goal, the speaker should redress any face loss, paying compensatory face by using the most appropriate of five possible linguistic strategies.

Whether the supposed irrelevance of the make up of W_x should be accepted entirely without question is a matter well worth considering – but not one we can go into here, sadly.

4.5 COMPENSATORY LINGUISTIC STRATEGIES

(1) Do the FTA on record (explicitly) without redressive action, baldly (i.e. directly, concisely, clearly, and unambiguously – cf. Grice's maxims ➜ 3).

(2) Do the FTA on record (explicitly) with positive politeness as redress (discussed below).

(3) Do the FTA on record (explicitly) with negative politeness as redress (discussed below).

(4) Do the FTA off record (implicitly ➜ 3).

(5) Don't do the FTA at all (it just ain't worth it!).

Which strategy is chosen depends on the estimation of the weightiness of the face threat (*W*): with a low estimation of risk of face loss, a speaker should choose a low numbered strategy; with a higher estimation of risk of face loss, a speaker should choose a higher numbered one. If the estimated risk is extremely high, then a speaker may consider it socially and pragmatically more sensible to entirely forego achieving their current goal and hence not attempt the act in any form whatsoever (➜ 3, 13). These ranked options are set out in Figure 4.1 (based on B&L 1987: 69).

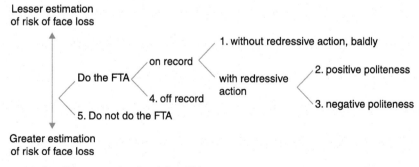

Figure 4.1 Possible strategies for doing FTAs

If we were to take B&L's values of '1 to 7 or so' to be 1–9 (for they do themselves (in their footnote 18) mention Miller's 'magical number 7 ± 2'), we would reap the advantage of being able to neatly categorize each estimated relative value for D, P and R as being *low* (1–3), *mid* (4–6) or *high* (7–9). A range of 1–9 would also conveniently allow for *W* to have values from 3–27, which would then conveniently sub-divide into five equal sub-ranges: sub-range 1 = *W* values of 3–7; sub-range 2 = *W* values of 8–12; sub-range 3 = *W* values of 13–17; sub-range 4 = *W* values of 18–22; and sub-range 5 = *W* values of 23–27. From there we could make a working hypothesis that a *W* value in any sub-range would correspond to the equivalent-numbered linguistic strategy.

While such equally divided ranges are certainly a theoretical possibility, it is important to note that B&L do not make such a strong claim. Rather, their assumptions simply predict that rational people 'will choose a higher-numbered strategy as the threat increases' (B&L 1987: 83). Exactly how the *W* values co-vary with the linguistic strategy numbers will always be an empirical matter and, of course, it will also be culture-specific.

Activity 4.3 looks more closely at these five possible strategies.

Activity 4.3 🔑

The scene

Some weeks ago, Arthur's fairly new neighbours, James and Hannah, had a window put into the attic of their house. He can only guess that this was in the bedroom of Megan (the teenage daughter of the house), for on the evening of the window's installation a 'young gentleman caller' spent a considerable time 'conversing' with her as she draped herself out of the new aperture. Having recently breathed sighs of relief at the relocation of the previous occupants (who had a teenage daughter to whom many vulgar male teenage youths seemed to be inexorably and permanently attracted), he had visions of the tone of the neighbourhood plummeting. So here was his very real dilemma. Given that he would much rather live in a 'nice' neighbourhood than in a street awash with malingering sexually charged teenagers shouting at the top of their voices all night long, his goal was to get this type of undesirable pubescent behaviour to cease. His dilemma was how to do so. Fortunately, being a linguist, he had B&L to provide possible solutions – he obviously had a choice of five possible strategies. He also had other linguists to discuss this with later!

The choices

He could have chosen to:

(8) do the FTA on record without redressive action, baldly 'Tell your daughter to stop lowering the tone of the neighbourhood by hanging out of the attic window and shouting to her boyfriend down at street level.'

(9) do the FTA on record with positive politeness redressive action 'Hey Jim, I bet you had something to say last night about Megan's boyfriend's less than high standards of social considerateness, didn't you?!'

(10) do the FTA on record with negative politeness redressive action 'I'm sorry to ask, but could you possibly ask your daughter to be a tad quieter in the evenings in future please? Thanks.'

(11) do the FTA off record 'Are you all enjoying the benefits of the new attic conversion?'

(12) not do the FTA at all

The questions

(a) Which option do you think he chose?
(b) Why? (Hint: think about possible values of D, P, R and hence, *W*.)
(c) What possible consequences might his choice have had?
(d) What possible consequences might each of the other four choices have had?

4.6 POLITENESS STRATEGIES

We have been discussing positive and negative politeness rather generally for some time. Now it is time to put some flesh on the bones of these terms. In other words, what counts as positive and negative politeness? In short, positive politeness (recognition of self-worth) is linguistic behaviour which signals that the speaker wants/needs/appreciates (at least some of) the same things as the hearer. Negative politeness (recognition of autonomy) is linguistic behaviour which signals that the speaker recognizes the hearer's fundamental right to unimpeded action. Using editorial brackets, we can now return to Holmes' (1995: 5) definition that we encountered earlier:

> 'politeness' will be used to refer to behaviour which actively expresses positive concern for others [positive politeness], as well as non-imposing distancing behaviour [negative politeness].

In the next two sections we provide more specific (though still general) examples of these types of behaviour.

4.6.1 Positive politeness strategies

The following list (taken from B&L 1987: 101–129) should begin to offer some ideas of ways of paying positive face. That B&L take 28 pages to do this while we use less than one should indicate that for anyone interested, there are plenty more details to be had than supplied here. While each example is numbered as in B&L, we have added a '+' to indicate these as positive politeness strategies. Note that the order of occurrence of these strategies does not reflect any degree of politeness.

Claim common ground

(+1)   Notice/attend to H's wants
(+2)   Exaggerate interest/approval/sympathy in/of/with H
(+3)   Intensify interest for H (use question tags; direct quotes; historic present)
(+4)   Use in-group identity markers (solidarity address forms; dialect; slang; contraction)
(+5)   Seek agreement (safe topics; repetition)
(+6)   Avoid disagreement (token agreement; pseudo-agreement; white lies)
(+7)   Presuppose/assert common ground (gossip; speak from H's point of view (use H's deictic centre); presuppose H's knowledge)
(+8)   Joke

Convey that S and H are cooperators

(+9)   Assert knowledge of H's wants
(+10)   Offer, promise
(+11)   Be optimistic (reduce degree of imposition)
(+12)   Include S and H in the activity
(+13)   Give (or ask for) reasons (why not ...?)
(+14)   Assume/assert reciprocity (you scratch my back ...)

Fulfil H's want for some X

(+15)   Give gifts to H (goods, sympathy, compliments ...)

4.6.2 Negative politeness strategies

The following list (taken from B&L 1987: 129–211) illustrates ways of paying negative face. Again, we are forced into brevity, reducing B&L's 82 pages to half a page. Also again, each example is numbered as in B&L, but with a '–' to indicate these as negative politeness strategies. The order of occurrence of strategies does not reflect any degree of politeness.

Be direct

(–1)   Be conventionally indirect

Don't presume/assume

(–2)   Question, hedge

Don't coerce H

(–3)   Be pessimistic
(–4)   Minimize imposition
(–5)   Give deference (humble yourself; treat H as superior)

Communicate S's want to not impinge on H

(−6)   Apologize
(−7)   Impersonalize S and H (avoid pronouns I and you)
(−8)   State the FTA as a general rule
(−9)   Nominalize

Redress other wants of H's

(−10)   Go on record as incurring a debt

And so, at last, we are in a position to apply these strategies to our set of 'Coke utterances' from Example 4.1 at the beginning of this chapter.

Activity 4.4 🔑

(a)   Return to Example 4.1 and work out which strategies are being used in each utterance. NB: you may well find more than one type of strategy in each.
(b)   Has this helped you understand why the utterances seem more polite as you go down the list?

There are three important points that still need making.

1   Although this account has mainly been concerned with various types of strategy for dealing with *on-record* FTAs, B&L also devote 16 pages to 15 ways of paying face off-record.

2   It must be made clear that being linguistically polite does not necessarily entail sincerity: there may actually be no common ground, no optimism, no intention of reciprocity, no deference, no regret at imposition and so on. All that matters, however, is the fact that someone *made the effort* to go through the motions of politeness and it is this effort that makes an act of linguistic politeness polite.

3   The examples in this chapter have presented a somewhat Anglo-centric view of linguistic politeness – cross-cultural differences are not only possible, they are to be expected!

4.7 SUMMARY

This chapter has investigated Brown and Levinson's theory of politeness in language use (incorporating a brief discussion of issues relating to power) and in doing so, has shown that linguistic behaviour is linked to social context. People always have a choice of what they say or write and it is the linguist's task to uncover how those choices differ in their social and pragmatic consequences – even in interactional tasks as socially diverse as asking someone to: (i) get a can of Coke, (ii) watch TV and write something down, (iii) buy cigarettes, or (iv) curb the behaviour of antisocial youngsters.

In short, the take-home message of this chapter is that by using redressive action in the form of appropriate linguistic politeness strategies, we are likely to be more successful in achieving the goals which our language use is employed to serve than if we paid no heed to our fellow humans' need for freedom (autonomy) and their need to be valued (self-worth).

4.8 FURTHER ACTIVITY

Activity 4.5

Using the ideas discussed in this chapter (with a particular emphasis on the social and pragmatic consequences of a speaker's various choices), provide analyses of the following data.

The scene

It's the beginning of a committee meeting. The chairperson has forgotten to bring paper.

The choices

(13)   Give me some paper.
(14)   Has anybody got a bit of paper I can have?
(15)   Has anybody got a little bit of paper I can have?
(16)   Has anybody got a little bit of paper I can borrow?

COMMENTARY ON ACTIVITIES

○━╈ Remember that this symbol indicates that there is a commentary on the activity that you can find on the companion website at www.routledge.com/cw/merrison.

FURTHER READING and REFERENCES

Suggestions for further reading on the topics discussed in this chapter can be found on the companion website (www.routledge.com/cw/merrison).

Any piece of academic writing must always provide a list of publications to which reference has been made. Unusually and very unconventionally, this information is provided on the companion website (www.routledge.com/cw/merrison). Always ask your tutor about how you are to present references for any piece of work that you submit.

Chapter 5
Words

Key Ideas in this Chapter

- Words are the fundamentally arbitrary union of a meaning and a form, but there is partial predictability from the internal structure that some words have.

- A vocabulary headword is a language resource, located in the minds of users of the language. It covers a collection of different manifestations of words in actual use.

- The study of words in corpora (big computer-searchable collections of texts) is interesting and informative.

- How occurrences of words in texts are grouped and related to vocabulary headwords is important.

- The distribution of grammatical (also called function words) words is different from the distribution of content words.

- A fairly small part of a person's vocabulary is used disproportionately often.

- We have ways of deriving new words from existing ones.

5.1 INTRODUCTION

Google Labs have digitized more than 5 million of the books that were printed between 1400 and 2008. End-to-end the computer files are billions of words long. The Google N-gram Viewer (➔ W5.1) is a specialist browser enabling anyone with access to the internet to begin exploring how words are used in those books. A language gains and loses words over time. The popularity of a word can change over time as can the way it is used (➔ 17).

Searching with the N-gram Viewer for particular words yield graphs showing variations in how often the words appeared in print over the centuries, or shorter periods of time that you can specify. A sample of what can easily be found out about the words *radio* and *wireless* will be discussed as an example.

The first non-temporary radio transmitting and receiving station was built in 1896 by the Marconi Wireless Telegraph Company. The company did not have *radio* in its name. Expressions like *wireless telegraphy*, *wireless telephony* and *wireless message* were used in talking about this venture and what it offered: communication 'without wires' being needed to link the sender and receiver. People were soon shortening these labels to just *wireless*. In grammatical terms (➔ 7) they were converting the adjective *wireless* into a noun *wireless* (more on this in Section 5.5.2). Marconi's invention involved *rays radiating* from the transmitter, and that yielded another label, *radio-telegraphy*, also soon shortened to *radio*. When the N-gram Viewer is asked to display how often the words *radio* and *wireless* were used in Google Lab's vast collection of English language books over the period 1880 to 2008 it generates a graph like the one shown in Figure 5.1.

Both words first appear at the end of the nineteenth century. The N-gram Viewer has links to examples of the instances it has counted. One such is the following, a report from the year 1900 of a speech made by a Colonel Temple about *wireless telegraphic communication*.

> In responding to the courteous invitation of the Committee of the Bengal Chamber of Commerce to address its members on the commercial value of wireless telegraphic communication with the Andamans and Nicobars, I feel some diffidence …

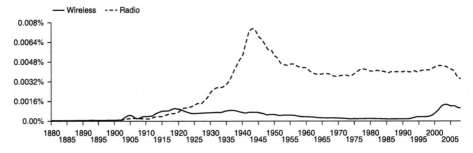

Figure 5.1 Google N-gram display of percentage frequency of use of *radio* and *wireless* in books between 1880 and 2008 (graph based on March 2011 output from http://ngrams.googlelabs.com/)

Radio leads in the early 1900s. However, a steady rise in the frequency of use of the word *wireless* in the books soon puts *wireless* back in front and it stays ahead until, as you can see in the graph, it is overtaken by *radio* around 1920. *Radio* has been the more frequently used word all the time since then, generally by a big margin. But an interesting development is evident in the bottom right-hand corner of Figure 5.1: there was an upswing in the frequency of use of *wireless* from the mid-1990s.

The N-gram Viewer is case sensitive, so the curve for *Radio* could be different from the one shown in Figure 5.1 for *radio*.

Activity 5.1 ⚷

Thinking of situations in which you might have heard or read the word *wireless* in the final few years of the last century and the first few years of the present century, can you suggest why its frequency of use increased over that period?

What do people know when they know a language? What do they know that enables them to act as language users? They know rules of syntax (➔ 7), conventions for use (➔ 3), a pronunciation system (➔ 9, 10) and, of course, lots of words: the vocabulary of the language.

A word is a like a knot joining some threads. Each word connects a meaning (➔ 6) to a pronunciation (➔ 9, 10), a spelling too for people who can read and write, and a word class − for example, noun, adjective, conjunction (➔ 7). Thus learning the word that is spelt <annoy> involves getting to know that it goes with the meaning 'make mildly angry' and the pronunciation [əˈnɔɪ], and fits into sentences as a verb. Vocabulary learning requires storage of many items in memory (➔ 14), and one aim of the present chapter is to look at how many words a language user needs (➔ 5.4). The quantity and the different kinds of words needed can be gauged from the occurrence of words in texts.

5.1.1 Structure and arbitrariness within words

Vocabulary involves more than just the remembering of items. When words are built up out of meaningful parts, there are recurring patterns (consider, for example, *football* or *handball*, made from *foot* or *hand* plus *ball*; or the making of the nouns *manager* and *teacher* by putting the suffix {-er} on to the verbs *manage* and *teach*). A short account of word-building is the final topic in this chapter, because it is needed as part of a framework for understanding what is being done when occurrences of words are either grouped together or treated as different.

Here is an example of how memorized items are distinct from assembly according to patterns (➔ 14.3). Assuming you agree that 5,280 is a bigger number than 4,840, how do you know that? You are not likely to have learnt it as a specific item: '5,280 is bigger than 4,840'. Presumably you learnt principles about numbers, and those principles can be used to compare any two numbers for size.

How about the label for one's head: the English word *head*? If you know the word, then it is surely something you learnt as a specific item. People who know French have, on the other hand, learnt specifically that that body part is called *tête*; and German speakers store in their memories the word *Kopf* for the same thing. That different languages can have different words for 'head' indicates that the connection between a word and its meaning can be a matter of arbitrary (unprincipled) convention (➜ 1). Neither *head* nor *Kopf* nor *tête* can be split into smaller parts that contribute separately to the meaning. Memorization is the only way to handle arbitrary conventions. A word like *fire-fighter*, on the other hand, has meaningful parts (*fire*, *fight* and {*-er*}) that give hints about the meaning of the whole word.

Activity 5.2 🔑

An *undertaker* is not a person who carries things into a cellar, nor someone who conducts tours to Australia. An undertaker (in the USA, a *mortician*) has the job of seeing to the arrangements for funerals.

Suggest what the following words *might* have meant on account of the meanings of their parts and say what they generally *do* mean in English.

- a *cooker*
- a *password*
- a *windbreak*
- an *egghead*
- to *overtake*

It might seem that the words in Activity 5.2 are a selection of weird ones that happen to have somewhat unpredictable meanings. Perhaps we would see principles at work in a more normal set of words – *hairbrush*, *makeover* and *downsize*, for example. However, even with these three (chosen pretty well at random) there are details that just have to be memorized:

- hairbrushes could have been made from hair, like a hair-shirt, but aren't; they are brushes for hair
- a makeover involves only appearance and styling; not just any remaking
- downsizing usually includes a reduction only in the number of employees (when talking about business) or a reduction in the number of rooms (when talking about accommodation and/or moving house).

5.2 TOKENS IN A TEXT OR CORPUS, HEADWORDS IN A VOCABULARY

A language has a large collection of words. Individual users of a language have a lot of those words in their heads, in readiness for use in comprehension and production (➜ 14). Then there are all the actual instances of words used. See Figure 5.2.

Every occurrence of a word in a text is called a (word) *token*. In Figure 5.2, in the fragment in the box, *radio* is a token and *radios* is a different token, even though they relate to the same headword RADIO from the English language or in the mind of a person who knows English. The fragment of text shown in the box contains 21 word tokens. We'll represent headwords in capital letters. They are vocabulary units in the system of English: RADIO is a distinct unit from SIGNAL. Two of the tokens in the text fragment shown in the box are

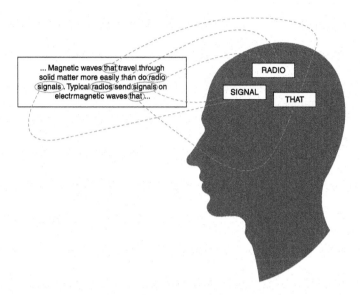

Figure 5.2 A text (from a magazine article, dated 2010), represented here by the fragment in the box, contains word tokens. These correspond to headwords in the vocabulary of a person (or a language)

waves. They are different tokens, one appears in second position and the other is second last in that fragment. However, they are manifestations of the same headword WAVE.

5.2.1 Corpus linguistics

A CORPUS (plural *corpora*) is a representative sample of texts (written or spoken, or including both). A **text** (➔ 8) is a sequence of connected utterances that have occurred in the course of genuine language use, whether written or spoken. The sequence is regarded as forming a whole. A text could be a recorded conversation, an SMS message, the epitaph on a grave, Shakespeare's tragic play *Hamlet*, a recipe for making fried rice, a lecture on vocabulary development, etc.

A corpus linguist is one whose work is focused or based on corpora. See McEnery and Wilson (2001). Corpus linguistics is a branch of linguistics that studies the facts of usage in collections of naturally-occurring examples of language use. Findings from corpus linguistics provide evidence for refining theories of language, theories of language use and language acquisition theories (➔ 15). Corpora also serve many practical purposes, for instance dictionary-making, computerized translation, and developing syllabuses for language learners.

Nowadays a corpus is almost always in computer-readable and searchable form and the total number of word tokens in the corpus will often be tens or hundreds of millions. Useful corpora will have tags on everything that they contain, making it possible to extract information about each item, such as the kind of text it occurred in, the social character-istics of its writer or speaker, each word token's word class (for example, whether a given occurrence of *radio* was as a noun or a verb), its semantic sense (for example whether a particular token of *sentence* meant 'construction made with words' or whether it meant 'judicial allocation of a penalty').

Remember that word classes e.g. nouns, verbs, prepositions, conjunctions etc. are discussed in detail in Chapter 7.

Relevant to this chapter is the fact that corpora have been used in many studies of the distribution of words in people's deployment of language, that is, in texts. Quantifying word usage requires decisions (see Activity 5.5: what is a word?) about what will be counted. If we want to know how long a chapter of a book is we could count pages. Newspaper articles were traditionally measured in column inches. The length of a speech could be given in minutes. But pages come in many sizes, columns in various widths and some people talk faster than others; and what if we want to compare the length of a written chapter with the length of a speech? The number of word tokens in a speech or chapter is one reasonable way of indicating length.

The Corpus of Contemporary American English (COCA) was assembled by Mark Davies, Professor of Corpus Linguistics at Brigham Young University. It is large, up-to-date, versatile and has good access facilities. As explained on the COCA website, it contains more than 450 million word tokens 'equally divided among spoken, fiction, popular magazines, newspapers, and academic texts. It includes 20 million word [tokens] each year from 1990–2012 … ', making it particularly suitable for investigating changes happening now in American English (➔ W5.2). There are corpora for other languages and other varieties of English (for a survey, see Xiao 2008).

Through the same website, it is easy to gain access to other corpora such as the British National Corpus (BNC), the Bank of English (BOE) or the Oxford English Corpus (OEC).

5.2.2 Vocabulary

To assess the size or variety of a person's **vocabulary** – the stock of words that they know – we count headwords. Consider the two tokens of the noun *waves* in the Figure 5.2 text fragment. Someone who can make reasonable sense of that text fragment must know – amongst many other things they would need to know – the headword WAVE (a noun). But that person should not be credited with another vocabulary item if it turns out they can also deal with tokens of that noun in the singular form, *wave*. Being able to deal with both plural *waves* and singular *wave* indicates knowledge of grammar, not an addition to vocabulary. Whether tokens of that noun headword are spelt with an initial capital letter or not *Wave*, *wave*, *Waves* or *waves*, or printed in a different font, it is still just testimony to knowledge of the same headword. For many purposes, the same noun headword WAVE covers spoken tokens /weɪv/ and /weɪvz/ too.

Arguably there is a different headword for the verb that is spelt in the same way. WAVE the verb is represented in print by the grammatically related set of verb tokens *wave*, *waves*, *waved* and *waving*. Usually the software used for searching through a corpus allows you to retrieve sets of related forms just from specifying the headword. The search that was done for the commentary on Activity 5.1, requested information about WIRELESS and the count was 4,972 tokens of *wireless* and 2 of *wirelesses*.

In Chapter 15 it is asserted that young children generally have a vocabulary of between 100 and 200 words at age one and a half years. That is based on counting the headwords that the child knows. Of course, evidence for knowledge of headwords comes from examining the word tokens that the child is able to understand and produce.

5.3 WORDS IN A TEXT

Activity 5.3 presents a text that will be studied quite closely in this chapter to illustrate some aspects of the distribution of words.

Activity 5.3 🗝

Part of a newspaper article on racism in football is reprinted below. Find all the word tokens in it that are closely linked to racism or football; also count how many times each of these topic-specific words occurs.

Here is a start: *racism* (2), *football* (1), *midfield* (1). The words *launched*, *his* and *currently* could be used in relation to many other topics besides racism and football, so they are not reasonable answers here.

The noughties

The Londoner Joel 'Jobi' McAnuff, 21, has recently launched his professional football career. He currently plays in midfield for Wimbledon.

'To be honest, there is not a lot of racism now on the terraces and any abuse you get from the fans does not tend to be about your colour. I have been subjected to racist abuse only once, five years ago when I was in the youth team. It was an FA Youth Cup game with a club notorious for its attitude. The spectators were shouting "black this and that", and directing abuse at the parents and away fans as well as the players. It even carried on after the game, which we won, which made them even more angry. We told the manager, who had witnessed it himself. But there wasn't an awful lot we could do.

The situation has undoubtedly improved enormously. An older black player at Wimbledon, Michael Thomas, told us what it was like in the 1980s with bananas being thrown and abuse. Back then it was definitely much harder to make it as a black player. If the racists had had their way then there would not have been any black players at all.

Despite my experiences, I still believe that not enough is being done to counter racism, especially by the authorities. Organisations such as Uefa and Fifa should be taking a stronger stance, especially in European games. Clubs who have a problem with racists should be penalised. It is as simple as that.'

(Source: Jason Burt, the *Independent*, 4 March 2003)

Including the two words in the heading *The noughties*, this text is 254 word tokens in length. (Near the end of the second paragraph, *wasn't* counts as two: *was* and *n't*.) Only a rather small proportion of the words in the text are ones with a close connection to racism or football. If the list given in the commentary is accepted, then only 39 are closely related to its topics. (The figure 39 comes from 4 tokens of *abuse* added to 4 tokens of *black*, and so on through the rest of the list in the commentary, ending with one each of *won*, *manager*, *Uefa* and *Fifa*.) Thirty-nine words out of 254 is just over 15 per cent. The remaining nearly 85 per cent of the 254 printed words are not closely linked with the text's two main topics.

Before looking at the nature of the other 85 per cent of the words, a technical term commonly used by corpus linguists is going to be introduced for a set of grammatically related forms that belong under a headword.

There are corpus linguistic methods for locating 'key' words in a text: ones that occur more often in a particular text than would be expected from their frequency in otherwise comparable texts. See Scott and Tribble (2006: Ch.4).

5.3.1 Headwords and lemmas

The noughties text has 254 tokens, but there are fewer headwords represented in it because some words are recycled: for instance WIMBLEDON is represented in the text by two tokens (one in the first paragraph and one in the third paragraph), the headword WITH is represented in the text by three tokens.

See chapter 14 to see how the term *lemma* is used in different contexts.

The text includes, in order of appearance, the following tokens: *The The the the the The the the the the The the the the the*. One way of summarizing those is to say that the text has 14 tokens of the headword THE. A LEMMA is the set of forms grouped together under a headword. The lemma of THE, insofar as can be seen from the text of Activity 5.3, is thus the set {*The, the*}; an initial capital does not change *the* into a distinct vocabulary word.

Of course, a capital letter can distinguish headwords. For example the lemma {*turkey, turkeys, turkey's, turkeys'*} relates to a poultry headword TURKEY$_P$ (subscripted P for poultry for present convenience only), but the lemma of TURKEY$_C$ (just for now, subscripted C for country) is {*Turkey, Turkey's*}.

In *The noughties* text, four tokens have the spelling *not* and one token is spelt *n't*. When the word *not* is tacked on to the end of a verb it takes the form *n't*; so it is reasonable to group *not* and *n't* together and say that there are five tokens in the text of the lemma {*not, n't*}, different forms of the headword NOT. The lemma is a list of the variants that corpus software needs to retrieve if it is to fit with our human language-using notion of different forms of the 'the same word'.

The form chosen from a lemma to be the headword is generally:

- the most basic one in the lemma, for example one lacking an **affix** (= prefix or suffix) in preference to ones that have the affix, so the verb form LAUNCH would probably be chosen as the headword from the lemma {launch, relaunch, launching, launched}
- the one that has the largest number of tokens, for example five of the eight tokens of {*a, an, An*} in the text are *a*, so A is a sensible choice for headword of this family
- the form that dictionary-makers usually choose to list alphabetically.

Activity 5.4 🔑

Here are some lists of word tokens from *The noughties* text. Choose an appropriate head-word for each list, count the tokens for that headword and write out summaries like: 'The lemma {*game, games*} under the headword GAME is represented by three tokens'.

- racist racists racists
- has have had has had had have have
- be is be been was was were was was being was been is being be be is
- does do done
- and and and and and and

Racist and its plural *racists* are clearly variants of the same word, but should they perhaps have been put into the same lemma as *racism*, which has two tokens in the text?

The meanings are different: a *racist* is a person, but *racism* is a condition of societies. *Racist* and *racism* are related, but the issue is whether the meaning relationship ('a X-ist is someone who upholds X-ism') is obvious enough to make one meaning predictable from the other. According to some **psycholinguists** separate storage in memory is not required for information that can be predicted from knowledge of patterns (➔ 14). Proficient speakers of English would generally make the connection. An intermediate-level learner of English as a foreign language, who does not know the relevant word-making patterns, might treat *racist* and *racism* as unrelated, i.e. separately-stored memory items. (This issue is revisited in Sections 5.4 and 5.5.1.)

5.3.2 Content words and grammatical words

Words that carry the content of our communications are called CONTENT WORDS. These are the words that connect language to the world outside of language: to the people, creatures, things, ideas, places, times, events, qualities, actions and relationships that we talk and write about. Content words are nouns, verbs, adjectives and adverbs (➔ 7). Many words in the sample text are content words: for instance the nouns *authorities* and *problem*, the verbs *shouting* and *penalized*, the adjectives *professional* and *notorious*, the adverbs *currently* and *enormously*. These are not as closely associated with the topics of *The noughties* as the words picked out in Activity 5.2, but they make important connections to the world that is being written about. Of course, words like *racists*, *racism* and *football*, which are closely connected to the text's topics, are also content words.

GRAMMATICAL WORDS, such as *the*, *it*, *do* and *with*, do not have links – close or distant – to topics; they are used in texts about anything and everything. Grammatical words carry some very general meanings and they link words into sentence structures. When content words and grammatical words are counted we find differences.

Of the 254 word tokens in the text of Activity 5.2, there are 146 tokens of grammatical words (57 per cent) and the remaining 108 tokens (43 per cent) are content words. Other texts might well have different proportions. However, when headwords are considered, there are usually more content words represented in a text than grammatical words: the tokens of content words in this text are from 87 different content headwords, but the tokens of grammatical words come under only 55 different headwords. Think about it: lots of grammatical word tokens (146) come under relatively few headwords (55). On average there should be more tokens for a given grammatical word than for a given content word. The following counts fit this expectation. They are for headwords that have at least three tokens each in *The noughties*.

Grammatical words (with number of tokens of each shown in brackets):

    BE (17)
    THE (14)
    HAVE (8)
    A (8)
    IT (7)
    AND (6)
    AS (6)
    NOT (5)
    IN (4)

Though *be* and *do* are verbs, they are grammatical words (see the next paragraph in the body of the chapter) rather than content words. Furthermore, some members of other word classes – especially prepositions – carry content, e.g. *above* and *below* are used to express different relations among things. Thus the distinction between content words and grammatical words is not as straightforward as suggested.

TO (4)
WE (4)
THERE (3)
DO (3)
I (3)
WITH (3)
AT (3).

Content words (numbers of tokens in brackets):
ABUSE (4)
BLACK (4)
PLAYER (4)
RACIST (3)
GAME (3).

Perhaps you counted five tokens of TO, rather than four. However, the tokens belong to two different headwords. In 'subjected to racist abuse' *to* is a preposition. The other four tokens represent a TO that goes in front of verbs (➔7).

Grammatical words tend to be recycled a lot. This is because there are fewer of them (a few hundred headwords only; see Nation 2001: 430–1) and they are needed regardless of what people are writing or talking about. How often tokens of a word appear in a text is the FREQUENCY (OF USE) of the word. In corpus linguistics frequency of use is commonly stated as number of tokens per million words of text.

A handy reference book on the frequency of use of words in written and spoken English (Leech *et al.* 2001) was based on the British National Corpus (➔ W5.3), totalling 100 million words. Its figures show very high frequencies for some grammatical words: for instance tokens representing the word family *be* averaged out at more than 40,000 times per million words of text and tokens of *the* more than 60,000 times per million. By contrast, the same book shows much lower frequencies for content words, e.g. the noun *abuse* had 37 tokens/million, the adjective *black* 226/million, and there were 138/million for *player*. There are tens of thousands of content headwords to choose from; so, on average, individual ones do not get used as frequently as a typical grammatical word.

A rank table – a sort of "league table" of popularity of words – in the Leech *et al.* word frequency book (2001: 120) shows that all of the top 50 most frequently used word forms in English are grammatical words and a large majority of the 50 next most frequently used are also grammatical words. The most frequently used content words are the verb form *said* (53rd in the ranking, with 2,087 tokens per million words of text) and the nouns *time* (1,542 per million) and *people* (1,241 per million).

Table 5.1 shows that there is a wide range of frequencies for both grammatical words and content words, from rarely used words (with one token or fewer per million words of text) to ones with tens of, hundreds of, or more than a thousand tokens per million words of text. However, it is only among grammatical words that we find families represented by tens of thousands of tokens per million words.

The frequencies in Table 5.1 are for headwords, e.g. 25,056 next to the headword A (the indefinite article) is the sum of 21,626 for *a* and 3,430 for *an*, and the total number of tokens of forms in the lemma {*prowl, prowls, prowling, prowled*} gives a rounded average for the headword PROWL of two tokens per million words of text. Some of the lemmas for headwords in the table have only one member, e.g. *about* and *real* are "one-member lemmas".

The distribution of labour amongst words is highly skewed. Relatively small numbers of words are used again and again, while others rest for a long time between appearances. There are plenty of words that are in some sense words of English but which get used so rarely as to be unknown to many users of the language. In their computer analysis of

Table 5.1 Frequency of use (in tokens per million words) of selected grammatical words
and content words (figures from Leech *et al.* 2001 and the associated website)

Grammatical words									
OF	29,391	SO	1,893	EVERY	401	ALBEIT	14	OUTWITH	1
A	25,056	ABOUT	1,524	SOMEONE+	187	OURS	17	ERE	1
Content words									
		SEE	1,920	BRING	439	SPARE	19	PROWL	2
		YEAR	1,639	REAL	227	FOREVER	18	BIGOT	1

100 million words of text, Leech *et al.* (2001: 8) found three-quarters of a million different forms (757,087 to be precise) and 52 per cent of these were represented by only one token each.

Three-quarters of a million is far more than the number of words that a speaker of English needs to store in memory. Many of the items included in this total were the names of big numbers, e.g. 1,040,325 (yes, it's a word (→ Text 7.1 and the analysis of numbers there)) and other words constructed for an occasion (e.g. *turquoise-striped*). Language users typically make up such words by rule rather than taking them from memory as prefabricated wholes. There were plenty of names too, including *John-go-to-bed-at-noon* (which seems to have occurred at least twice among the 100 million tokens analysed), technical words (e.g. *acetylsalicylic*), verbal mimes (such as *aaaaargh*) and many spelling variants.

5.4 HOW MANY WORDS DO INDIVIDUALS KNOW?

This is a hard question to answer. The usual approach is to test people on a selection of the large number of words that it is assumed they could potentially know. Then the percentage of words they know out of the selection is used to estimate the size of their vocabulary. Higher estimates are obtained with recognition tests than in tests requiring productive recall. Tricky decisions have to be made, for example concerning the grouping of items into lemmas and whether to exclude proper nouns (names of people, etc. → 7) from consideration. Paul Nation – an applied linguist – and his colleagues have undertaken detailed studies that offer some well-founded estimates.

Nation (2001: 9, 365) gives 20,000 word families as an approximate total for the vocabulary size of a young university graduate whose first language is English. (As will be explained later, a word family is an extended kind of lemma.) Because of the very large numbers of people, world-wide, who learn English as a foreign language (→ 15, 18), it is of practical interest to get some idea of the minimum number of words needed to use English for particular purposes. One focus of research has been the vocabulary needs of people who have English as a foreign language and wish to study for a university degree through the medium of English. If a native English-speaking student ends up with knowledge of the words grouped under something like 20,000 headwords, is that what a student with English as a foreign language has to aim for, or will fewer words suffice in English for Academic Purposes (EAP)?

The question can be approached by examining the distribution of words in the materials that undergraduates in an English-speaking university have to handle, starting with the books they are expected to read. Written texts usually have a richer selection of words than speech; so what the students meet in lectures and seminars is likely to be a subset of what is found in their books.

Nation (2001: 17) reports some quite surprising results. Knowledge of only the items grouped under the 1,000 most frequently used word families of English will allow EAP students to read nearly 74 per cent of the tokens they are likely to meet in academic texts, which is to say that they should, on average, be able to cope with eight of the words in a typical 11-word line in an academic textbook. Knowledge of the next 1,000 most frequently used word families would give them access to another 4.5 per cent of the word tokens in academic writing. Two thousand is far fewer than the 20,000 word families that native-speaking university students probably know.

With a vocabulary only one-tenth that of a native-speaker undergraduate, it is astonishing that nearly 80 per cent of the word tokens in an academic text become accessible. The diminishing return is striking too: the EAP learner gets a lot more access for learning the hardest-working 1,000 words than for learning the next 1,000 most frequent words. The first 1,000 includes almost all of the grammatical words, which (as noted in 5.3.2) are re-used a lot, as well as the most popular content words, e.g. *say, see, sell* and *people*. With the second 1,000, the learner has started into the great mass of content words, with each one generally having a relatively small chance of occurrence in a given text.

Remember that a headword is the head of a set of related forms (though some sets have only one member, like the conjunction *whether*). In the research done for the word frequency book of Leech *et al.* (2001) the verb BELIEVE headed a lemma of four verb forms *believe, believes, believing, believed*; a different headword, the noun BELIEF, headed the pair *belief* and *beliefs*; and DISBELIEF was a separate headword. However, in the first of the 1,000-word lists used by Nation (2001) the family headed by BELIEVE encompasses all seven of these word forms. The justification for grouping all of them together is that a grasp of relevant systematic relationships between words (for example the effect of the suffix {-ing} on a verb, or the effect of the prefix {dis-}) should enable someone who has learnt one of these words to work out the likely meanings of the others when they are encountered in text. It is for extended lemmas, such as {*believe, believes, believing, believed, belief, beliefs* and *disbelief* } that the term WORD FAMILY is used in this chapter. These different groupings under headwords opted for by different teams of researchers are both justifiable. The important thing is to know how items were grouped for a given corpus. (In 5.5.1, the basis for differentiating between a lemma and a word family will be sharpened up.)

In the research of Nation and his collaborators, the first 1,000 word families of English include 4,119 different word forms, and 3,708 word forms are grouped under the second 1,000 headwords. Thus the 20,000 headwords thought to be known by a first-language English-speaking graduate might subsume up to 80,000 word forms.

Figure 5.3 is a version of *The noughties* from Activity 5.3 showing tokens representing only the 1,000 most frequent word families of English. The number of tokens is 195, which is 77 per cent of the original 254. (This version of the text was produced using Paul Nation's vocabulary program *Range* (➔ W5.4).

Most readers of this stripped-down text are likely to recognize that race features in it, but it would take a lucky guess to tell that it is about football.

The next version of *The noughties* (Figure 5.4) – again prepared with the aid of Nation's *Range* program (➔ W5.4) – shows the tokens that should be recognizable to a person who

The _____

The _____ _____ '_____' _____ , 21, has recently _____ his _____ _____ _____ . He currently plays in _____ for _____ .

'To be _____ , there is not a _____ of _____ now on the _____ and any _____ you get from the _____ does not _____ to be about your colour. I have been subjected to _____ _____ only once, five years ago when I was in the youth _____ . It was an _____ Youth _____ game with a _____ _____ for its _____ . The _____ were _____ "black this and that", and directing _____ at the _____ and away _____ as well as the players. It even carried on after the game, which we won, which made them even more _____ . We told the _____ , who had _____ it himself. But there wasn't an _____ _____ we could do.

The situation has undoubtedly _____ _____ . An older black player at _____ , _____ _____ , told us what it was like in the 1980s with _____ being thrown and _____ . Back then it was _____ much harder to make it as a black player. If the _____ had had their way then there would not have been any black players at all.

_____ my experiences, I still believe that not enough is being done to _____ _____ , _____ by the _____ . Organisations such as _____ and _____ should be taking a stronger _____ , _____ in _____ games. _____ who have a problem with _____ should be _____ . It is as simple as that.'

Figure 5.3 Newspaper text (Jason Burt, *Independent* 4 March 2003) preserving word tokens representing only the 1,000 most frequent word families of English (_____represents a missing word) © 2005, Bloomer, Griffiths and Merrison

The _____

The _____ _____ '_____' _____ , 21, has recently _____ his _____ <u>football</u> _____ . He currently plays in _____ for _____ .

'To be <u>honest</u>, there is not a <u>lot</u> of _____ now on the _____ and any _____ you get from the <u>fans</u> does not <u>tend</u> to be about your colour. I have been subjected to _____ _____ only once, five years ago when I was in the youth _____ . It was an _____ Youth <u>Cup</u> game with a <u>club</u> _____ for its _____ . The _____ were <u>shouting</u> "black this and that", and directing _____ at the <u>parents</u> and away <u>fans</u> as well as the players. It even carried on after the game, which we won, which made them even more <u>angry</u>. We told the <u>manager</u>, who had <u>witnessed</u> it himself. But there wasn't an _____ <u>lot</u> we could do.

The situation has undoubtedly <u>improved</u> _____ . An older black player at _____ , _____ _____ , told us what it was like in the 1980s with _____ being thrown and _____ . Back then it was _____ much harder to make it as a black player. If the _____ had had their way then there would not have been any black players at all.

_____ my experiences, I still believe that not enough is being done to _____ _____ , <u>especially</u> by the _____ . Organisations such as _____ and _____ should be taking a stronger _____ , <u>especially</u> in _____ games. <u>Clubs</u> who have a problem with _____ should be _____ . It is as simple as that.'

Figure 5.4 Newspaper text (Jason Burt, *Independent* 4 March 2003) preserving word tokens representing only the 2,000 most frequently used English headwords (_____ represents a missing word) © 2005, Bloomer, Griffiths and Merrison

knows the top-ranked 2,000 word families of English. The 18 tokens (another 7 per cent of 254) representing headwords from the second thousand have been underlined.

Eighty-four per cent (77 + 7) is more than the 78 per cent coverage reported by Nation (2001: 17). However, his figure was for academic texts, which this is not. Even with 84 per cent of the words readable, however, the text still does not make full sense. If the names *Londoner, Joel 'Jobi' McAnuff, Wimbledon* and *Michael Thomas* had been left in, then it might help a reader to at least identify these as names, by their initial capital letters. Proper nouns were intentionally excluded from Nation's lists of the first and second thousand headwords of English, though both *Michael* and *Thomas* (not any of the others) occurred often enough to be in the top 2,000.

In books and talks on specialized subjects – bird-watching, mountain bikes, dance, chemistry, medicine, antiques – we find TECHNICAL WORDS, ones that tend to be used with relatively high frequency in texts in the particular topic area and which often have special meanings in the subject. Chung and Nation (2003) found that about 31 per cent of the tokens in an anatomy textbook were technical words (e.g. *organ* and *thorax*). In an applied linguistics textbook about 21 per cent of tokens were technical words such as *instruct* and *lexicon*. People tend to learn technical words as part of becoming acquainted with a particular subject.

Some technical words are used fairly frequently in textbooks of all kinds (e.g. *organ* and *instruct*, from among the four examples just given), but they tend to be used with even higher frequency when they have a special role in a technical text. They are also likely to have restricted meanings when used technically; for instance, *instruct* in an applied linguistics context is usually a label for what happens in language classes. Technical words like *thorax* and *lexicon* tend to appear in a limited range of texts, mainly in discourse from the technical field in question. The very fact of their occurrence sometimes signals 'this is technical talk/writing' (➜ 12). *The noughties* is not a piece of technical writing, but Activity 5.3 was something like an assessment of a text's technical words.

How many technical terms have to be learnt in mastering a subject? Chung and Nation (2003) report the technical vocabulary for the anatomy book as 4,270 items and that of the applied linguistics book as 835.

Knowledge of the top 2,000 word families of English can give an EAP learner access to well over 70 per cent of the word tokens in quite difficult material (84 per cent for the *noughties* text). This is why learner dictionaries like the *Collins Cobuild New Student's* (Sinclair *et al.*, 2002) mark the highest frequency words distinctively. Language learners will often have knowledge of technical words from their subject training and this can increase access to nearly 90 per cent of the tokens in a text. So a reader could handle almost nine out of ten word tokens in a technical text in a given subject by knowing the most common 2,000 general words of general English and somewhere between about 1,000 and 4,500 technical words. What about the 10 per cent or so of text tokens still not accounted for? Some of these will be names, some will be numbers. Having to look into a bilingual dictionary for one word out of every ten is perhaps not an intolerable burden. Furthermore, context alone might enable a reader to guess the meanings of some of these remaining words (➜ 3).

The last part of this unit is about how words are constructed and the extent to which the meanings of some words can be correctly guessed from recognizing the components and the way they have been put together: essentially, what linguists call MORPHOLOGY. This emphasizes the point that what can be worked out does not have to be stored in memory.

5.5 MORPHOLOGY

In commentary on a televised cricket match in August 2002, Simon Hughes spoke about Hoggard's *close-to-the-stumps-ness*. The expression *close-to-the-stumps-ness* is a word, of a kind called a PHRASAL WORD, because it has a whole phrase (➔ 7) *close to the stumps* packed inside it. We know it is a word because the morpheme {-ness} is a suffix that appears only on words, where it has the effect of making adjectives into abstract nouns, e.g. *good* + {-ness} ➔ *goodness*, *contradictory* + {-ness} ➔ *contradictoriness*. *Close*, the head of the phrase, is an adjective, which is why {-ness} can be put on the end.

Another phrasal word is *A4-and-a-bit-on-the-side*. This is in the British National Corpus (➔ W5.5). It occurred less often than once per million words. Will it or *close-to-the-stumps-ness* or *noughties* appear in dictionaries in the future? That depends on whether they catch on or not. Coining a word (making it up) is a different matter from the word passing into general use and becoming an item that users of the language store as part of their knowledge of the language. ACRONYMY is a widely-used strategy for coining a word from a phrase: a spelling is made from the initial letters of the phrase, which can then be pronounced, e.g. *SARS* for the illness 'severe acute respiratory syndrome' or NEET for 'not in education, employment or training'. In the *noughties* article, *Uefa* and *Fifa* are acronyms.

People cannot usually be expected to guess the meaning of a new acronym, so when newsreaders began using the word *SARS*, in 2003, they generally explained its meaning. Languages also have processes that transform existing words (➔ R2.1) more directly to produce ones with different meanings, as when *unsalaried* 'not receiving a salary' was formed from *salaried*, itself derived from the word *salary*. In such cases there is some basis for guessing at the meaning (although it is possible to be mistaken).

> A **morpheme** is the minimal unit of grammar (➔ 7) and meaning: morphemes are combined to form words (➔ Fig 7.1). Morphemes may be free and form words on their own (e.g. *sun, friend* or *happy*) or they may be bound morphemes (underlined in the following examples) and therefore unable to form words e.g. <u>un</u>happy, sun<u>ny</u> or happi<u>ly</u>. Now think about words like *uncouth* or *inept* in relation to free/bound morphemes.

5.5.1 Derivation *versus* inflection

Processes that derive (or have derived) a word with a predictable new meaning from an existing word are called DERIVATIONAL. Derivational processes may change word class, e.g. *salaried*, an adjective, is derived from a noun *salary*. But derivational processes do not always affect word class; for instance *unsalaried* is an adjective derived from an adjective. INFLECTIONAL RULES (➔ 7) are different. They never change word class. Instead of being used to make words with new meanings, inflectional rules produce the appropriate form of a word to suit different positions in sentences, e.g. the plural is the form of noun required to fit with plural determiners such as *these, those* or *both*.

Inflectional rules relate to the different members of a lemma, e.g. the lemma headed by the verb THROW includes the inflected forms *throws, threw, throwing* and *thrown*. The meaning differences that come from inflecting words are usually highly predictable; for instance changing any verb to past tense adds the meaning 'before now' and pluralizing a noun adds 'more than one' to the meaning. However, the meaning changes introduced in derivational processes can be quirky; for instance although *salaried* means 'receiving a salary' and the adjective *waged* means 'receiving a wage', *moneyed* (also spelt *monied*) means 'having a lot of money', rather than 'receiving money'.

Because of unpredictabilities in the meaning changes introduced by derivation, some researchers (e.g. Leech *et al.* 2001) choose not to accept them as uniting lemma items under a headword, while others (e.g. Nation 2001) feel that there is often sufficient predictability in familiar derivational processes to use them, in addition to inflectional relationships, for grouping items into families (a difference already discussed in Section 5.4).

5.5.2 Derivation by conversion and by compounding

English has **prefix** morphemes (e.g. {un-}, {re-}) and **suffix** morphemes (e.g. {-er}, {-ly}) for deriving words from existing words, adding meanings such as 'not' (as in u̲n̲happy), 'again' (e.g. r̲e̲run), 'one who does it' (e.g. teach̲e̲r̲), 'in a … way' (e.g. wild̲l̲y̲). However, CONVERSION is a derivational process that makes new words without any change to the form of the word; no suffixes or prefixes are used. COMPOUNDING is the making of a word by putting together a pair of existing words (e.g. *youth team*, in the text of Activity 5.3).

Growing up as speakers of English, children as young as two and a half years old are able to make new words according to patterns (Clark and Hecht 1982; ➜ 15). The earliest is the simplest: no change at all, just press a new duty on to an existing word, as when a child uses the word *broom* to mean 'sweep'. This is called CONVERSION: a form of one word class is converted into one of another word class. Using the noun *broom* as a verb is not conventional in adult English, but the process of conversion is widespread in the language, e.g. *to brush* means to 'clean or tidy with a brush'. The fact that English has two different headwords BROOM and SWEEP is an argument for regarding the noun *brush* and the verb *brush* as different types. We can see conversion from the verb *ask* to a noun form in *That's a big ask*.

At around the same age as the first instances of conversion, young children begin making COMPOUND WORDS (Clark 2003: 285). In a compound, two (or more) words are put together to make another word, as with the child word *blow-machine* meaning a 'machine that blows' (a *fan* in adult English). The child was using a pattern common in English, for example a *blow hole* (in rocks or on a whale) is 'a hole that blows'.

There is more to compounding than just putting words together. They have to be put into the correct sequence according to the rules of the language involved. If there was an English compound word *paper journal*, it would be some kind of journal, but the French expression *papier journal* does not denote a kind of journal or newspaper; it means 'newsprint', a kind of paper, the kind that newspapers are printed on. English compound words have two features that justify thinking of them as words in their own right. First, they often have idiosyncratic meanings. The words *windbreak*, *overtake*, *password* and *egghead* in Activity 5.2 are compounds and the point was made that their meanings are not entirely predictable. There are aspects of each that simply have to be learnt. This implies that compounds have to be stored as items in memory. Speaking specifically about English, Carstairs-McCarthy says that '[i]nterpretation of new compounds relies in practice less on strictly linguistic regularities than on context and general knowledge' (2002: 95).

English words tend to be pronounced with strong **stress** somewhere near the beginning, e.g. **con**sequence is pronounced with the stress on the first syllable (➜ 11). The same is true of many compounds, particularly those that are nouns, and stress on the first

The Japanese compound 手袋 *tebukuro* (literally 'hand bag') means 'glove', a reasonable enough label for bags that go on hands. But the (British) English compound *handbag* does not mean 'glove'.

English written usage is rather inconsistent on whether compounds appear as single words (e.g. *steamroller*), or with hyphens (e.g. *steam-roller*) or with internal spaces (e.g. *steam roller*): see Bauer (1998: 68–9).

component word is a useful way of recognizing spoken compounds in English. Examples are **un**dertaker, **news**print, **blow** hole, **le**tterbox, **steam**-roller.

Compounding makes words that can, in turn, be put into compounds. For instance, the text in Activity 5.3 contained the compound *FA Youth Cup game*. *Youth Cup* is a compound word, meaning 'trophy for young players'. The FA (the Football Association) is responsible for this particular Youth Cup; so, making a compound out of the words *FA* and *Youth Cup*, we can refer to it as the *FA Youth Cup*. To talk about a game played for the FA Youth Cup, we can make a more elaborate compound: *FA Youth Cup game*.

5.6 SUMMARY

Most words have unpredictable meanings and just have to be remembered. Corpus linguistics provides really interesting ways of studying the use of language, but care must be taken to understand how the software is grouping words in its searches. In the sentence 'If the racists had had their way then there would not have been any black players at all' there are two tokens of *had* and one token of *have*. Function (or grammatical) words, like *if* and *and*, are used in communications about anything. There is a limited number of them and some are used very often. Content words, e.g. *black* and *player*, link to what is spoken or written about. There are many content words, some having very low frequency of use. Knowledge of 2,000 high frequency word families and a couple of thousand relevant technical words can give access to nearly 90 per cent of the tokens in difficult written texts. New words are made by imaginative invention, but also systematically through derivational processes such as conversion and compounding.

5.7 FURTHER ACTIVITIES

Activity 5.5

Photocopy the version of *The noughties* text that retains tokens of only the most frequent 2,000 word families of English (Figure 5.4). Write *Londoner, Joel 'Jobi' McAnuff, Wimbledon, Michael Thomas, FA, Fifa* and *Uefa* into the appropriate gaps. Then ask a friend to read it and 'think aloud' while guessing what words should go into the remaining gaps. You should note down your friend's thoughts.

The least frequent ones amongst the missing words, according to Leech *et al.* (2001), are *notorious* (9 per million), *enormously* (8 per million), *penalised* (4 per million, including the version spelt with < z >) and *racist/s* (2 per million). Are tokens of these four harder to guess than the others? Anyone who correctly identifies *noughties* as the word missing from the heading should be congratulated on having uncanny insight!

Activity 5.6

It is not surprising that throughout this chapter, we have used the word *word* very often. But what is a word? Everybody thinks they know the answer to the question but when we set our students an essay (2,500 words) with the title 'What is a word?', they found the activity very challenging. What do you think a *word* is? Hall (2005 Part II) addresses this very issue – but do work out what you think the answer is (or might be) before you turn to others for their views.

COMMENTARY ON ACTIVITIES

○━┳ Remember that this symbol indicates that there is a commentary on the activity that you can find on the companion website at www.routledge.com/cw/merrison.

FURTHER READING and REFERENCES

Suggestions for further reading on the topics discussed in this chapter can be found on the companion website (www.routledge.com/cw/merrison).

Any piece of academic writing must always provide a list of publications to which reference has been made. Unusually and very unconventionally, this information is provided on the companion website (www.routledge.com/cw/merrison). Always ask your tutor about how you are to present references for any piece of work that you submit.

Chapter 6
Semantics

Key Ideas in this Chapter

- Words have meanings but to explain the meaning of a word, we frequently need to know the context in which the word is being used.

- Semantic knowledge tells us how to use a word; encyclopaedic knowledge tells us about the world, not about language.

- Logical relationships e.g. entailment, are used to determine the meaning of words.

- Semantic relationships are part of each language though the examples in this chapter are taken from the English language.

- The major semantic relationships involve words having similar/identical meanings (e.g. synonymy), words having opposite meanings (e.g. antonymy, converseness) and the relationship of part to whole (e.g. metonymy, meronymy).

6.1 INTRODUCTION

Chapter 3 introduces **pragmatics**, one part of the study of meaning. Chapter 6 is about semantics, the other essential component. When people know a language they have a powerful system – grammar plus vocabulary – for communicating meanings (➔ 1, R3.6). Semantics is the study of meanings as stored in language, waiting to be put to use. Pragmatics focuses on how speakers and writers actually use their language knowledge to convey meanings.

The story of how a young man from an alcohol-free family found himself paying for other people's drinks in a British pub illustrates the difference between semantics and pragmatics. Alan was not a linguist. He was training as a social worker. He knew English, so he knew the following items of semantic information implicitly (even if he wasn't all that sure about the terms **verb, noun phrase, pronoun** and **suffix**):

- the meaning of the verb *drink*
- that there are *drinks* called *beer, whisky, wine, lemonade*, etc.
- that the pronoun *you* is used to refer to the person(s) being spoken to
- that putting the suffix {-ing} on to an action verb and at the same time putting *are/is/am* in front of the verb indicates that the action is currently happening (➔ 7 progressive aspect)
- that *what*-questions ask for specific information, usually in the form of a noun phrase.

Alan had been brought up in a teetotal household. He had never been in a pub but felt that if he was going to be a social worker he had better learn something about them. He stepped into one, desperately hoping for inspiration on what to do next. To his relief, he recognized one of two men chatting at the bar. He decided to go and say hello, casually ask what they were drinking and then order the same for himself. Maybe they would even offer to buy him a drink and that way he could discover the routine involved in placing an order.

Alan walked across, smiled, greeted his acquaintance and, with a momentary look at the men's glasses, asked, 'What are you drinking?'. They were pleasantly surprised, waved over the barman and said, 'Our friend is getting us another round'. Alan asked for a lemonade for himself and paid for all three drinks!

Alan had the semantic knowledge needed to frame the question 'What are you drinking?' but in a British pub someone who says this is usually understood as offering to buy the next lot of drinks. The "offer" meaning arises from social knowledge and conventions about what is done in pubs, taken together with thoughts about why a speaker might pose that question in a pub. Semantically, 'What are you drinking?' is just a question, with the word *what* marking the object of the verb as missing information. The offer meaning is a context-dependent elaboration. Our pragmatic skill enables us to construct contextual meanings on top of semantic foundations.

In different contexts there are other sentences that can be used to offer to buy drinks and there are different uses that can be made of the sentence 'What are you drinking?' (for example, when an anxious carer sees a four-year-old or a ninety-four-year-old drinking something dubious). A full account of meaning in language requires both semantics and pragmatics (➔ R1.4). The present chapter is about semantics, the study of meaning in the abstract system of a language – important because the central characteristic of language is that it encodes meanings (➜1).

Chapter 5 mentions the obvious fact that words have meanings. Here, in Chapter 6, the focus is on the nature of word meanings and how they can be described. It should be noted, however, that syntax (➜ 7) also has a bearing on meaning, because arranging the same words differently can change meaning, e.g. *The boat is in the water* means something different from *The water is in the boat* (➜ 7). And a *flower garden* is not the same kind of thing as a *garden flower* (➜ 5 compound words).

The approach to semantics taken in this chapter (there are certainly other approaches but this approach fits well with our focus on language in use (➜ R2.3)) begins with this question: among the words and sentences of a language, what meanings are equivalent? Thinking about English, answers to that question would include the information that the verb *drink* means the same as *consume liquid*; and that a long-winded equivalent of *I'd like a drink* could be *I'd like some water or lemonade or coffee or milk or beer or whisky or* … .

Understanding what counts as a normal answer to 'What are you drinking?' depends on knowing the labels for different beverages that belong under the general noun *drink* (Grandy 1987: 261). Thus the semantic knowledge that 'lemonade is a drink', 'beer is a drink', 'X is a drink' are first steps in explaining what goes on when people ask and answer questions such as 'What are you drinking?'.

Linguists doing semantics attempt to account for meaning as stored in language systems. An important part of this is word meaning. It turns out that word meaning cannot adequately be studied by thinking of words in isolation. For instance, it could be irrelevant to answer the question 'What does *bear* mean?' by talking about 'giving birth to'. See Figure 6.1 (and also think about the ambiguity of words pronounced in isolation, like [naɪt] – *knight* or *night*). Semanticists find that they need to consider words in terms of how the words contribute to the meanings of sentences.

A componential semantic analysis (➜ 14.3.2) specifies meanings in relation to universal binary characteristics. Such characteristics as [+/– MALE], [+/– ADULT] and [+/– HUMAN] would allow for the meanings of *man, woman, boy, girl, ram* all to be at least in part established: *girl* would be [+HUMAN, –MALE, –ADULT] and *ram* [–HUMAN, +ADULT, +MALE].

Figure 6.1 'Knight/night on bear/bare mountain' (apologies to Mussorgsky)

6.1.1 Word meaning is found in sentences

Activity 6.1

Here are three questions as preparation for what comes next in the chapter, so please answer them before reading on. First-reaction answers will do.

- Are snakes animals?
- Are birds animals?
- Do the words *thief* and *robber* have exactly the same meaning?

There is no commentary on this activity. The purpose of the questions should become clear fairly soon.

Example (1) is a news story to illustrate some important starting points.

(1)   **Snakes stolen from zoo**
        BORDEAUX, France, AFP –
        Slick thieves stole two boa
        constrictors and a python from a
        zoo in southwest France, officials said.
            The robbers also stole five
        parrots, a cockatoo and four turtles
        in an overnight raid at the zoo in
        Pessac near Bordeaux.
            Police are questioning animal
        specialists in the region on the trail
        of the missing animals.
                    (*Fiji Times*, 15 July 1995)

Think about learners of English who are unsure about the meanings of some of the words in the report. Partial knowledge of word meanings can lead to confusion. The headline mentions *snakes*, and diligent learners who look up words in bilingual dictionaries would find that both *python* and *boa constrictor* – the first two creatures listed – are snakes; so why not guess that all the stolen creatures were snakes? It's not very likely, but it is just imaginable that someone with an insecure grasp on English could think that parrots, cockatoos and turtles are kinds of snakes, because that seems to fit the headline! Readers with a good knowledge of English do not even begin to make that sort of mistake because they have much more of an idea of which species labels come under the general term *snakes* and which don't. And the word *also*, before *stole* in the second paragraph, indicates that other things were stolen besides snakes.

6.1.2 Semantic knowledge versus encyclopaedic knowledge

Those aspects of meaning that depend directly on the vocabulary (➜ 5) and syntax (➜ 7) of a language are termed SEMANTIC KNOWLEDGE. Semantics is not an attempt to catalogue everything that humans know (ENCYCLOPAEDIC KNOWLEDGE). The difference between the knowledge of meaning that comes from knowing a language – English for example – and knowledge that is beyond semantics can be illustrated with the snake theft report (Example 1).

Zoologists say that pythons are different from boa constrictors, but many competent speakers of English who aren't snake specialists probably couldn't distinguish between the two. Some might even think that the two words label the same kind of snake. Ordinary speakers of English can learn some zoology by asking snake experts about the classification of snakes, but it can't seriously be claimed that this improves their knowledge about the English *language*. From a semantic point of view, people know most of what there is to know about the meanings of these two English words as long as they know that a *python* is a kind of *snake* and a *boa constrictor* is a kind of *snake*. They might or might not also know that a *python* is not a *boa constrictor* (and a *boa constrictor* is not a *python*).

Encyclopaedic knowledge of how to connect words to the world is shared out among the members of a speech community (➜ 1). Different people have different specialisms: embroidery, website designing, hydrology, biology, electronics, cooking, metallurgy, knitting, bicycle maintenance and so on. English semantic knowledge of the meanings of *boa constrictor* and *python* is not enough to identify and distinguish specimens of these snakes with certainty. Not being able to tell snakes apart could be an embarrassment for someone who works in a zoo, but it is not a sign of an imperfect grasp of English!

Note that different words do not always have different meanings. Languages have SYNONYMS (➜ 6.3.2), words with the same meaning. For example *wildebeest* and *gnu* are synonymous. In the newspaper story (Example 1) it is *and* in the phrase 'stole two boa constrictors and a python' that indicates absence of synonymy; in a different story the journalist could not sensibly write 'stole two wildebeest and a gnu … '.

As a rough and ready test, the distinction between semantic knowledge and encyclopaedic knowledge can be made by considering who could best help if you lack a particular piece of information. If the obvious best person to go and see would be a language teacher, then you are probably dealing with semantic knowledge. If some other specialist – an embroiderer, biologist, chemist or cook, for example – is the obvious best person to ask, then it is probably encyclopaedic knowledge.

> Semantic knowledge is part of what all competent users of a language know.

> Encyclopaedic knowledge is knowledge of the world outside of language.

> Words that have the same meaning are synonyms of each other.

Activity 6.2 🔑

State some items of semantic knowledge about the following words and some items of encyclopaedic knowledge about them: *shoes, footwear, clothing, boots, sandals, soles, heels.*

Please read the commentary on the companion website before you read any further.

The semantics of the words in Activity 6.2 (and therefore what you were thinking about as you completed the activity) are sketched in (2).

(2)

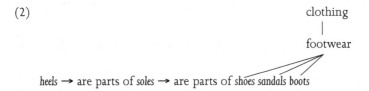

Diagrams like (2) will become familiar in the course of this chapter.

6.1.3 How to discover word meanings

Activity 6.1, near the beginning of this chapter, asked whether birds and snakes are animals and whether *thief* and *robber* have the same meaning. People might be inclined to answer 'Well, maybe' or 'It depends' or 'I'm not sure'. Some would feel that the way to handle that sort of question, if you are unsure, is to look up the words in a dictionary. That is a fairly reasonable thing to do, but you need to wonder how the dictionary makers know what answers to give.

The meaning of a word is discovered by observing how it is used in sentences. Looking at the newspaper report on Pessac Zoo's losses, it is clear that the reporter treated *robbers* and *thieves* as synonymous. The *The* in front of *robbers* signals that 'at this point in the article you already know something about these individuals' (➜ 8.3 on reference). Look back at Example (1). At the start of the second paragraph, how could the reader already know about the robbers? It must be that the journalist is referring to the same individuals as the ones called *thieves* in the first paragraph; so for current purposes in this report, *robbers* and *thieves* are taken as having the same meaning (even though in other contexts the writer might choose to distinguish between *robber* and *thief*, e.g. a robber might be a thief who uses violence.)

The final paragraph of the newspaper report sums up in terms of 'missing animals'; so here, the word *animals* is used as a general term covering *snakes*, *boa constrictors*, *pythons*, *parrots*, *cockatoos* and *turtles*.

The point of this section has been that knowledge of a language gives us good intuitions about the meanings of sentences, but our intuitions about the meanings of isolated words are generally less confident. Word meanings contribute to sentence meanings and we have ways of working out word meanings from seeing how they are used in sentences (➜ 7). This is often clear when one person asks another about the meaning of a word, for example when a child who is reading a book asks 'What does *portend* mean?', most adults would want to know the whole sentence before answering.

6.1.4 Chicken first or egg first?

Activity 6.3 🔑

Which seems better to you: attempting to explain the meaning of *thief* as 'one who steals', or explaining the meaning of *steal* as 'doing what a thief does'?

Explaining the meanings of words in terms of other words is a natural way to proceed. And when linguists are engaged in semantics they do it too. (*What means the same as what else?* is a fundamental question in semantics.)

Dictionary makers, whose job includes semantics, prefer to write their definitions using words that are more familiar than the word being defined. *Thief* should then be defined via *steal*, because *steal* (used, on average, 48 times per million words) is more frequent (word frequency ➔ 5) than the word *thief* (17 times per million words). (The figures for frequency of use are from Leech *et al.* 2001.)

The next section introduces a way of understanding how the meanings of words tie in with what we can be sure of when a given sentence is true. For instance, if it is news that some turtles have just been stolen then they must now be missing; and this follows from a connection in meaning between the words *steal* and *missing*.

Two adults (J and P) were talking to a 5-year-old who wondered what a florist is.
J responded with 'It's where you buy flowers'.
P said 'It's a flower shop'.
Both are explaining the meaning of *florist* by using other words.

6.2 ENTAILMENT

Any piece of furniture that is a *chair* must be a *seat*. If (3a) is true then (3b) must be true too – as long as we are talking about the same piece of furniture.

(3a)   That piece of furniture is a chair.
(3b)   That piece of furniture is a seat.
(3c)   !That piece of furniture is a chair, but it is not a seat.

The '!' on the front of an example indicates serious semantic anomaly.

Sentence (3c) is a contradiction: we know that all chairs are seats, but the clause *but it is not a seat* attempts to cancel that idea. An exclamation point (!) at the beginning of an example, like (3c), marks it as one that is seriously wrong semantically.

The inference that (3b) must be true whenever (3a) is true – provided the piece of furniture referred to is the same one – is an example of what is called *entailment* (➔ 3). A test for it is that, as in (3c), you get a contradiction from any attempt to cancel (deny) an entailment.

The sentences in (4) are another illustration of entailment. Sentence (4a) entails all three of (4b–d). Each of them must be true whenever (4a) is true.

(4a)   *It's a sandal.*
         entails:
(4b)   *It's an item of footwear.*
(4c)   *It's got a sole.*
(4d)   *Its upper part is ventilated.*

Look at it the other way round too. Unless something is footwear with a sole and a ventilated upper, it can't be a sandal; when any of (4b–d) aren't true, (4a) can't be true. Notice that the entailments (4b–d) are the sorts of sentences that could be used to explain the meaning of *sandal*. Thus entailments highlight essential aspects of the meanings of words in an entailing sentence, (4a) here; and that is why the concept of entailment is useful for doing semantics. If one sentence entails another, then both of the following conditions are met:

Entailment between two sentences guarantees we can infer that the second sentence is true whenever the first is true.

- when the first sentence is true the other sentence is also true
- when the second sentence – the entailed one – is false, the first sentence is false.

Informally, when one sentence entails another, we say that 'the second sentence follows from the first one'.

Take (4a) as the first sentence in the definition and (4b) as the second sentence. Anything that is a *sandal* has to be *footwear*; there is no way of dodging that. And – second bullet point, with (4b) as the second sentence – if something isn't footwear it is not going to stand a chance of counting as a *sandal*.

Activity 6.4 🔑

Try working through the definition again, but this time think of (4c) as the second sentence, while keeping (4a) as the first sentence.

Entailed sentences are necessary conditions for the truth of sentences that entail them: unless they are true the entailing sentence cannot be true. Entailment is associated with sentence meanings, but words make important contributions to the meanings of sentences, and that is going to be explored next.

6.2.1 Why use words in sentences?

When people tell us something, we generally do not just memorize what they say. Instead we draw inferences, conclusions like 'if that is so, then this, that and the other are going on'. Entailments are a semantic kind of inference. (A pragmatic sort of inference called **implicature** is introduced in Chapter 3.)

The point of using words in sentences and of making choices about which words to use is that different words can give a sentence different entailments, i.e. changing a word in a sentence can change the entailments of the sentence. And with different entailments, the sentence can lead listeners or readers to different inferences.

When (5a) is true then (5b) must be true.
(5a)   Sally has found Joe's shirt.
(5b)   Sally knows the whereabouts of Joe's shirt.

The fact that (5b) is not an entailment of *Sally has lost Joe's shirt* highlights the role of *found* in making (5b) available as an entailment for (5a). With *lost* in place of *found*, the sentence would entail, amongst other things, that *Sally does not know the whereabouts of Joe's shirt*. And some other sentences that can be made by replacing *found* or *lost* with another word would not give any firm information about Sally's knowledge of where the shirt is. For example neither *Sally has seen Joe's shirt* nor *Sally has washed Joe's shirt* guarantees the truth of either *Sally knows the whereabouts of Joe's shirt* or *Sally does not know the whereabouts of Joe's shirt*.

A semantic description of a word's meaning is an account of the entailment possibili-ties that become available when the word is used in sentences. The data come from intui-tive judgements about which sentences follow from which other sentences, which do not, and about what contradicts what. Some examples of judgements about data are

Semantics focuses on the entailment possibilities that words make available for sentences.

presented in (6). Sentences judged to be unproblematic are presented without any special marks. Exclamation marks at the beginning indicate sentences that are seriously problematic semantically, and question marks are put in front of ones that are semantically odd but not as peculiar as the ones with exclamations. The words *so* and *but* have been deliberately capitalized to draw attention to them. They are useful words to use in testing intuitions about entailments.

(6)   It's a sandal SO its upper is ventilated.
            She is a head teacher SO she is in charge of a school.
            It's a knife SO it has a blade.
            ?She is a head teacher SO she knows a foreign language.
            !Henry is a dog SO Henry is a vegetable. (contradiction)
            Henry is a dog SO Henry is not a mouse.
            ?Henry is a dog BUT Henry can bark.
            (It's not surprising that a dog can bark, which makes *but* inappropriate here.)
            !Henry is a dog BUT Henry is a vegetable. (contradiction)
            Henry is a dog SO Henry is an animal.
            !Martha has lost Henry SO she knows precisely where he is. (contradiction)

The difference between semantic knowledge and encyclopaedic knowledge has already been explained informally. Entailment makes it possible to firm up the distinction. The semantic knowledge associated with a word is no more and no less than the entailment possibilities that come from using the word in sentences. Entailments are necessary conditions for an entailing sentence to be true. And features of word meanings that influence necessary conditions for the truth of sentences must be regarded as important.

> A precondition for a sentence to stand a chance of being true is that its entailments are true.

Activity 6.5 ⚷

This activity is a double-check on some basic knowledge needed for understanding most of the rest of the chapter.

> (i)   She is swimming in the sea.
> (ii)   She is in the water.

(a)   Assuming that 'she' is the same person in both cases, then, talking about the same moment in time, we can be sure that sentence (ii) is true if sentence (i) is true. What is the technical term for this inference from (i) to (ii)?

(b)   Assuming that 'she' is the same person in both cases and that we are talking about the same moment in time, what could we conclude about the truth of sentence (i) when sentence (ii) is *false*?

(c)   Under the same assumptions, what could we conclude about (i) when sentence (ii) is *true*?

6.3 SEMANTIC RELATIONSHIPS

This chapter concentrates on meaning relationships between words. They are an impor-tant part of a full description of the meaning system of a language, because they affect the entailments that sentences can have. Seven different semantic relationships between words are going to be described and illustrated in sub-sections 6.3.1–6.3.7.

6.3.1 Hyponymy

This relationship can be thought of as meaning 'kind of' or 'type of'. It holds between, for example, *footwear* and *clothing* (*footwear* is one kind of *clothing*), or between *clothing* and *stuff* (*clothing* is one kind of *stuff*), as depicted in (7).

> Hyponymy holds between a hyponym, a word with a more specific meaning, and a less specific superordinate.

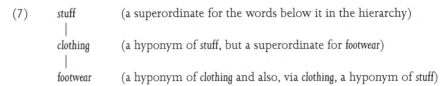

(7)   *stuff*   (a superordinate for the words below it in the hierarchy)
          |
        clothing   (a hyponym of *stuff*, but a superordinate for *footwear*)
          |
        footwear   (a hyponym of *clothing* and also, via *clothing*, a hyponym of *stuff*)

A SUPERORDINATE is a word with more general meaning than the specific terms under it. Words with more specific meanings under a superordinate are HYPONYMS of the super-ordinate. HYPONYMY is the relationship that holds between a hyponym and its superordinate(s). (Sometimes alternative (but equivalent) terms for these concepts may also be encountered: HYPERONYM (and sometimes without the <o>, HYPERNYM) instead of 'superordinate'; SUBORDINATE instead of 'hyponym'.)

The semantic relationship between *sprint* and *run* is hyponymy: *sprinting* is a particular kind of *running*, namely 'fast running'. This fact relates to entailment as follows: putting these two words, in turn, into a given slot in a sentence, like the slot represented by the underlining in *I saw you _____ to the library yesterday*, gives two sentences and one of them entails the other, but the entailment does not go back from the second sentence to the first. See (8a, b).

(8a)   *I saw you sprint to the library yesterday*
          entails *I saw you run to the library yesterday*.

         But

(8b)   *I saw you run to the library yesterday*
          does not entail *I saw you sprint to the library yesterday*.

Proof that (8a) is an entailment is seen in the contradictoriness of (9a): people can't sprint without running. If it is true that the speaker saw the addressee sprinting then it must be true that the speaker saw the addressee running.

(9a)   !I saw you sprint to the library yesterday, but you weren't running.
(9b)   I saw you run to the library yesterday, but you weren't sprinting.

Example (9b) is not contradictory, because, although someone who ran to the library might have sprinted, the person could, alternatively, just have jogged there. Because (9b) is not contradictory, 'does not entail' has been written between the two sentences in (8b). (Note: 'does not entail' means something different from 'entails … not'.) The entailment goes from a sentence containing *sprint* to a sentence with *run* in it, as noted in (8a), while (8b) records that there isn't an entailment in the reverse direction.

To summarize: hyponymy licenses one-way entailments between sentences that are identical except for substitution in one slot. There is a rule that is generally true: the sentence that gives the entailment (as in I *saw* you *sprint* …, in (8a)) is the one that contains the hyponym, and the entailed sentence (as in I *saw* you *run* in (8a)) contains the superordinate. (This rule does have exceptions, for instance entailment goes the other way round if the sentences are negative, but the matter is not discussed further in this book. (Hurford *et al.* 2007: 114–116 offer some more on this.))

> Hyponymy yields one-way entailment between sentences.

Hyponymy is a relationship that passes up through superordinates: if X is a hyponym of Y and Y is a hyponym of Z, then X is a hyponym of Z. This was illustrated in (7), which showed *footwear* as a hyponym of *clothing* and, via *clothing*, of the superordinate *stuff*. Another example is: *sprint* is a hyponym of *run*; and *run*, in turn, is a hyponym of *move*; so *sprint* is a hyponym of *move*. Evidence for this is that (10a) makes good sense but (10b) is contradictory.

(10a)   I saw you sprinting, so you were moving.
(10b   !Carl sprinted, but he did not move at all.

Figures 6.2 and 6.3 show sets of words linked by hyponymy. (The branches with *etc.* on them indicate that the diagrams are incomplete. For instance, *do (something)* has many other hyponyms, such as *make* and *hit*.)

The meanings given in single quotation marks for some of the words in Figures 6.2 and 6.3 demonstrate that the meaning of a superordinate is part of the meaning of its hyponyms. The meaning of a hyponym is that of the superordinate altered by a modifier. For example, the word *jog*, a hyponym of *run*, is equivalent in meaning to 'run slowly': the meaning of *run* – the superordinate term – plus a modifier, 'slowly'. Take *lawyer* as another

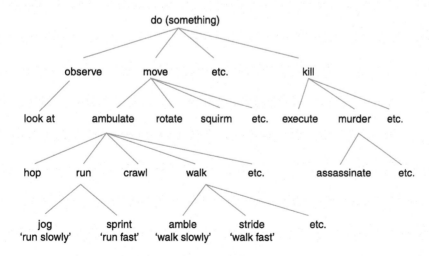

Figure 6.2 Some hyponyms of *do (something)*

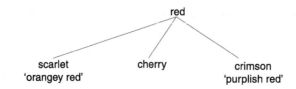

Figure 6.3 Some hyponyms of *red*

example. It is a hyponym of *professional* and means 'professional who gives advice on the law' (*who gives advice on the law* is a long modifier called a relative clause ➜ 7). Thus the words of a language can be seen as 'shorthand' expressions for more roundabout ways of saying things.

Hyponyms of a given superordinate are CO-HYPONYMS to each other, e.g. *amble*, *stride* and *march* are co-hyponyms under the superordinate *walk* (see Figure 6.2 and Activity 6.6).

A hyponym's meaning is the meaning of its superordinate modified in some way.

Activity 6.6

If the following verbs were added to those in Figure 6.2, where should they be positioned?

   fly, march, massacre, watch

Writing a brief meaning for each of the verbs, in the form of a superordinate word with an appropriate modifier, should make it clear where the words belong in the diagram.

6.3.2 Synonymy

In English, *amble* and *stroll* have the same meaning. Technically, they are synonyms; the relationship between them is SYNONYMY. This ensures that the two-way pattern of entailment shown in (11) holds for this pair of words. (Compare (11) with (8), where the entailment went in one direction only.)

Synonymy between words supports two-way entailment between sentences.

(11)   *They ambled round the square entails   They strolled round the square.*
        and
        They strolled round the square entails   They ambled round the square.

If there are two-way entailments between a pair of sentences, as in (11), and those sentences differ only by the replacement of one word, then the substituted words are synonyms.

Scarlet and *vermilion* are also synonymous, which allows (and can be diagnosed by) the same pattern of entailment, as shown in (12).

Paraphrase is a relationship of sameness of meaning between sentences (synonymy is the corresponding relationship between words).

(12)   *I painted my wheels vermilion entails   I painted my wheels scarlet.*
        and
        I painted my wheels scarlet entails   I painted my wheels vermilion.

A technical term for two-way entailment between sentences, as in (11) and (12), is *paraphrase*.

Some more synonym pairs in English are listed in (13).

(13)   leave/depart
        famous/renowned
        bucket/pail
        spotless/immaculate
        view/prospect (the nouns, not the verbs)
        begin/commence
        lorry/truck
        vermillion/scarlet

Entailment is based purely on truth conditions. Sociolinguistic differences of dialect and register (➜ 12) are irrelevant to synonymy defined in terms of entailment. *Trash*, *rubbish* and *garbage* are synonymous even though their use correlates with various social and geographical factors.

It is important to restrict the term 'synonymy' only to certain senses of words. For example, the noun *truck* can also mean the undercarriage of a skateboard where the wheels are attached. This sense of *truck* is clearly not synonymous with *lorry*.

One of the authors has noticed that meetings that used to *start* at a given time now *commence* at that time. If the words are synonyms, what might make speakers use one rather than the other? And do meetings *begin* these days or not?

Activity 6.7

Based on entailment and truth conditions, each of the following groups is internally synonymous:

i   *infant, child, kid*
ii   *begin, start, commence.*

From your experience, identify how social and geographical factors affect their use. You might like to consider prestige and non-prestige forms of the language (➜ 16) or formal and informal situations (➜ 12) as starting points.

Synonymy gives a language user the potential to construct paraphrases by mere substitution of one word for another. Converseness, the semantic relationship to be discussed next, requires substitution plus reordering of noun phrases before it will yield sentences equivalent in meaning.

6.3.3 Converseness

North (of) and *south (of)* are a converse pair. See (14).

(14)   Europe is north of Africa entails Africa is south of Europe.
        and
        Africa is south of Europe entails Europe is north of Africa.

As with synonymy, illustrated in (11) and (12), there is two-way entailment in (14): one sentence entails another and is itself entailed by the sentence that it entails (i.e. the

Converseness between a pair of words licenses paraphrase between sentences, after rearrangement of other parts of the sentences.

two sentences are paraphrases of each other). And, as with synonymy, words have been substituted: one sentence has *north* where the other has *south*. Unlike synonymy, the entailment pattern for converses involves an additional change: **noun phrases** are swapped around: one sentence starts with *Europe* and ends with *Africa*, but the other sentence names the two continents in the reverse of that order.

Pairs of adjective 'comparative forms' (such as *wider* ~ *narrower*, *more careful* ~ *less careful* (➔ 7)) are also converses, as shown in (15).

(15)   *The Amazon is wider than the Thames*
         entails *The Thames is narrower than the Amazon*

         and *The Thames is narrower than the Amazon*
         entails *The Amazon is wider than the Thames.*

6.3.4 Incompatibility among co-hyponyms

The relationship called *incompatibility* holds among all the hyponyms of a given superordinate (except for any that happen to be synonyms). Synonymy is sameness in meaning. Incompatibility is one kind of difference in meaning. (Other sorts of meaning difference are antonymy and complementarity, to be described later.) In Figure 6.4, *tree, bush* and *vine* are co-hyponyms. Calling them co-hyponyms signifies that they come under the same superordinate, *plant* in this case. Saying that the co-hyponyms are incompatible draws attention to them being different kinds of plant.

Sets of incompatible co-hyponyms in Figure 6.4 are: *mongoose, tiger* and *horse* (under the superordinate *animal*); *mongoose, tiger, horse* and *plant* (under the superordinate *thing*); *plant* and *animal* (under *thing*); and so on.

The relationship of incompatibility gives entailments from affirmative sentences to negative sentences, as shown in (16). As well as being negative, the negative sentences differ from the affirmative sentences by inter-substitution of members of a set of incompatible terms. (Look at Figure 6.4 if necessary.)

Incompatibility involves meaning differences among words that are similar because of sharing a superordinate. It licenses one-way entailments from affirmative sentences to negative ones.

(16)   *That's a horse*   entails   *That's not a tiger.*
         That's a horse   entails   *That's not a mongoose.*
         That's a horse   entails   *That's not a plant.*
         That's a horse   entails   *That's not a tree.*
         That plant is a tree   entails   *That plant is not a bush.*

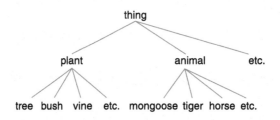

Figure 6.4 Some hyponyms of *thing*

However, it is not possible to switch sentences between the left-hand and right-hand columns in (16). Incompatibility does not license entailment from a negative sentence to a corresponding sentence with one of the other co-hyponyms. For instance, *That's not a tiger* does not entail *That's a horse*. The animal being spoken about could be a mongoose, or perhaps not even an animal. (*That's not a tiger, it's my stripy beach towel.*)

It might seem that everything is incompatible with everything else, but that is not so. While *run*, *walk* and *hop* are incompatible with each other, *run* is not incompatible with *sing*, nor with *think*, nor with *whistle*, nor with many other actions and states of affairs. See (17).

(17)   *Marcia was running at the moment when I saw her*
        entails *Marcia was not walking at the moment when I saw her.*
        And
        Marcia was running at the moment when I saw her
        entails *Marcia was not hopping at the moment when I saw her.*
        But
        Marcia was running at the moment when I saw her
        does not entail *Marcia was not whistling at the moment when I saw her.*
        Similarly
        Marcia was running at the moment when I saw her
        does not entail *Marcia was not tall at the moment when I saw her.*

The point is that incompatibility is not just any old difference in meaning. It is difference against a background of similarity (the similarity being given by the contribution to the meanings of the words from their shared superordinate). Look again at Figure 6.2: the higher up the 'tree' you go to find a shared superordinate, the less similarity of meaning there is: there is less similarity of meaning between *jog* and *murder* (words which share a 'linguistic great-grandparent' than between *jog* and *sprint* (which share a 'linguistic parent').

The metaphor of a family tree is widely used in linguistics for showing closer or more distant relationships e.g. language families (➜ 1).

6.3.5 Antonymy

The term *antonymy* is often used as a general purpose label for oppositeness in meaning, but here (following Lyons 1977) it is going to be restricted to oppositeness with the pattern of entailments shown in (18). All four lines of the pattern are required to establish that *hot* and *cold* are antonyms.

(18)   *The water is hot*   entails   *The water is not cold.*
        The water is cold   entails   *The water is not hot.*
        The water is not hot   does not entail   *The water is cold.*
        The water is not cold   does not entail   *The water is hot.*

When looking at the last two lines of (18), bear in mind that water that is *not hot* (or *not cold*) could be tepid, or lukewarm. This specific patterning of oppositeness is also often called GRADABLE ANTONYMY (see binary antonymy below).

Antonymy holds between pairs of words which, when substituted for each other in a sentence frame, give entailments only from affirmative to negative sentences (the first two lines of (18)), not in the reverse direction (the third and fourth lines in (18)). This makes antonymy a special case of incompatibility, namely incompatibility holding between pairs of terms rather than within larger sets, something that can be confirmed by comparing (16) and the associated discussion with (18).

In practice, members of antonym pairs usually have another characteristic too: they are gradable adjectives or adverbs. In English, gradability can be tested for by the possibility of modification with *very* and *more* or {*-er*} (➜ 7.3.1 comparative forms). Such modification is acceptable in (19a, b), but not in (19c–e). The conclusions about gradability are shown in brackets.

(19a)   very tight (*Tight* is gradable.)
(19b)   This light is very bright, but that one is brighter (*Bright* is gradable.)
(19c)   ?The lid is very shut (*Shut* is not gradable.)
(19d)   !This light is onner than that one ('Electrical' *on* is not gradable.)
(19e)   !The street lamp is even more on ('Electrical' *on* is not gradable.)

6.3.6 Complementarity

This relationship (also called BINARY ANTONYMY) is a non-gradable type of oppositeness. For complementarity, there are entailments both from affirmative sentences to the corresponding negative sentences (which is what ordinary antonymy allows) and from negative sentences to the corresponding affirmative sentences, which is where complementarity goes beyond the pattern shown for antonyms in (18). See (20) for the entailment pattern that establishes complementarity as the relationship between *on* and *off* (when talking about electrical appliances).

(20)   That light is on   entails   That light is not off.
         That light is off   entails   That light is not on.
         That light is not on   entails   That light is off.
         That light is not off   entails   That light is on.

Between them, a pair of complementaries occupies the whole of a dimension. The English language does not recognize middle ground between 'electrical' *on* and *off*, or – another complementary pair – between *pass* and *fail*; you either *pass* a test or you *fail* it. In (19d, e) it was shown that electrical *on* is not gradable, and it is generally the case that complementary adjectives are not gradable. This comes from the absence of middle ground between the members of a complementary pair.

Examples of complementaries are relatively hard to find. It seems that they have a tendency to give up some of the middle ground, and drift off into being (gradable) antonyms.

Activity 6.8

Compare the patterns in (18) and (20). Make sure you can see the differences between the entailments licensed by a pair of antonyms and those that come from using a pair of complementaries in sentences.

> ### Activity 6.9 🔑
>
> Giving reasons to support your decisions, say whether the relationship within each of the following pairs is converseness, incompatibility, antonymy or complementarity:
>
> faster/slower   right/wrong
> light/heavy   rise/fall
> sparrow/wren   cheap/expensive
> precede/follow   be stopping/be starting

6.3.7 Meronymy

MERONYMY relates 'parts of' to wholes. Figure 6.5 gives examples, using arrows to distinguish this relationship from hyponymy (shown in Figures 6.2–6.4).

A word X is a meronym of another word Y if sentences of both of the patterns in (21) are well-formed (Cruse 2000: 153).

Wholes have parts. Meronymy relates part labels (termed meronyms) to labels for their wholes.

(21a)   *An X (or Xes) is (/are) part of a Y.*
(21b)   *A Y has an X. (Or: A Y has Xs.)*

Examples are given in (22a, b). Because the first sentence in (22c) is semantically problematic, we can tell that *driver* is not a meronym of *truck*.

(22a)   A toe is part of a foot.
          A foot has toes.
(22b)   A cab is part of a truck.
          A truck has a cab.
(22c)   !A driver is part of a truck.
          A truck has a driver.

Unlike the other semantic relationships, meronymy has not been defined in this chapter in terms of an entailment pattern. However, meronymy does connect with entailment possibilities, as suggested in (23); so a proper definition in terms of entailment patterns should be feasible.

(23)   *The prongs are broken*   entails   *The fork is broken*
          (with reference to the same fork at the same point in time).
          My toe is injured   entails   *My foot is injured.*

          But
          The driver is ill does not entail *!The truck is ill.*
          (Therefore *driver* is not a meronym of *truck*.)

Note that meronymy is different from hyponymy: a *thigh* is part of a *leg*, not a kind of *leg*; a *handle* is part of a *fork*, not a kind of *fork*. And, in contrast: a *leg* is a kind of *limb*; a *fork* is a kind of *utensil*; etc.

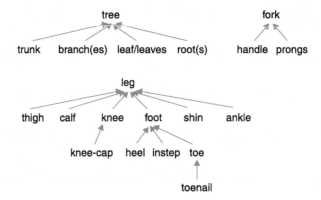

Figure 6.5 Some meronyms of *tree, fork* and *leg*

6.4 GLIMPSES BEYOND THIS INTRODUCTION

Content words are nouns, verbs, adjectives and adverbs.

Semantics is not without difficult issues but, to keep things short and – we hope – easier to understand, they have so far been ignored. The issue of words having multiple meanings will be briefly discussed ➔ 6.4.2.

Semantics has also been presented as if there was only one way of doing it (i.e. in terms of semantic relationships). And only **content word** (➔ 5) meanings have been dealt with. However, the meaning of a sentence arises from not only the content words in it but also from the structure of the sentence and the **function words** that are part of that structure (➔ 3.2.2 Frege's principle). Semantics is seriously incomplete without a treatment of the ways in which sentence meaning is composed out of content word meanings assembled in syntactic structures.

Function words are ones like *a, and, all*.

An important group of approaches to semantic research, known collectively as FORMAL SEMANTICS or LOGICAL SEMANTICS (see Further Reading on the companion website www. routledge.com/cw/merrison), has different priorities from those exemplified in the present chapter. Formal semantics has concentrated mainly on rigorously accounting for how syntactic construction affects meaning and this has necessarily involved study of the semantic properties of certain grammatical words, including markers of negation (such as *not*), conjunctions (*and, or, if … then*, etc.), quantifiers (like *some, all* and *every*) and modal auxiliaries (for example *must* and *may*). This is valuable and interesting work – an essential complement to what has been set out in this chapter – but it is also difficult. Some pointers are given in the Further Reading section to books that explain formal semantics.

6.4.1 Verb eventualities

The four kinds of eventuality (ACTIVITY, STATE, ACHIEVEMENT and ACCOMPLISHMENT) are different ways that sentences, partly because of the particular verbs in them, portray an event or situation.

Formal semantics has not generally been concerned with details of the meanings of content words (the kinds of words discussed in the earlier sections of this chapter), because the meanings of such words have usually been viewed by formal semanticists as intractable: mostly not constituted according to general principles and too prone to vary pragmatically with context of use. However, there is interesting systematic organization in a particular class of meanings rooted in verbs and adjectives. This has been of interest in formal semantics because it is systematic and because it appears in interactions with syntactic structure. It has several different labels but will be termed *eventuality* here (following Cann *et al.* 2009: 182). The person whose analysis originally drew attention to eventuality was a philosopher, Zeno Vendler, in an essay called 'Verbs and times' (1967). A brief introduction is presented now.

The examples in (24) illustrate the four kinds of EVENTUALITY, with Vendler's names for them.

(24a)   The branch is breaking.   ACTIVITY
(24b)   The branch is broken now.   STATE
(24c)   The branch broke.   ACHIEVEMENT
(24d)   The wind broke the branch.   ACCOMPLISHMENT

Activities and states (24a, b) portray continuing, homogeneous situations. The start and end of the breaking (24a) or the broken state (24b) is not in focus in these first two sentences, and nothing much changes during the periods spoken about in (24a, b). In contrast to this, achievements and accomplishments (24c, d) involve transitions from a starting situation − branch not broken − to a different ending − branch broken. The contrast between, on the one hand, activities and states and, on the other, achievements and accomplishments can be brought out by adding phrases that denote a length of time, as in (25). Sharp transitions do not very sensibly go with length of time specifications.

(25a)   ACTIVITY:
          The branch was breaking for hours.

(25b)   STATE:
          The branch hung broken for three days (before being tidied up).

(25c)   ACHIEVEMENT:
          ?The branch broke for hours.

(25d)   ACCOMPLISHMENT:
          ?The wind broke the branch for hours.

Even if a high-speed camera or careful observation shows otherwise, the English language treats achievements (24c, 25c) as if they were instantaneous, with no duration at all. Accomplishments (24d, 25d) are different, in that they represent an event as involving preliminary activity −which could have a long or short duration − that culminates in a change of state; the wind wrenches away at the branch and eventually the branch snaps. Furthermore, in activities, achievements and accomplishments (24a, c, d; 25a, c, d) there is dynamism: things are happening and changing. The points just made are summarized in Table 6.1.

Progressive aspect (*be* + Verb-*ing* (➔ 7)) indicates both durativity and dynamism, so it applies naturally only to activities and accomplishments, as shown in (26).

(26a)   activity: The branch was breaking for hours.
(26b)   state: ?The branch was being broken since the storm.
(26c)   achievement: (What happened?)
                               ?The branch was breaking at 11:07 p.m.
(26d)   accomplishment: The wind was breaking the branch
                               (so we propped it up with a ladder).

Table 6.1 Dynamism and durativity in the four eventualities

	having duration	lacking duration
having dynamism	ACTIVITIES ACCOMPLISHMENTS (have duration in the lead-in phase)	ACHIEVEMENTS
lacking dynamism	STATES	

A selection of other sentences is given in (27) to show that the pattern is not restricted to the verb *break*. It is general across many different verbs and adjectives. The point of using just one verb *break* in (24–26) was to highlight the fact that syntactic structure has a role in distinguishing between the four eventualities.

The usual positive aura of the words *achievement* and *accomplishment* is not relevant here, where the words are used as technical terms. The example *the dam burst* may be an achievement in this technical sense but the disastrous consequences would not lead the layman to regard it as an achievement in the sense that reaching the top of Everest might be so considered.

(27)   activities: The children are sleeping.
                               The army occupied the country.
        states: He was lucky.
                               They are insured.
        achievements: The dam burst.
                               The plane touched down.
        accomplishments: He ate up his dinner.
                               Sue ran to the finish.

Accomplishments are semantically a complex kind of eventuality, built up out of the other three. An accomplishment incorporates an activity that begins in one state and ends with the achievement of a switch into another state. For the accomplishment illustrated in the last sentence of (27): Sue is not at the finish(ing line); she engages in the activity of running; she reaches the finish (an achievement); and is then in the state of having finished (the race).

6.4.2 Polysemy and homonymy

Perhaps you noticed that the word *heel(s)* appeared in two contexts in this chapter, in Example (2) and in Figure 6.5. Three different familiar meanings of the English noun *heel* are listed in (28).

(28)   *heel*   'back part of foot' (as in Figure 6.5)
        heel   'back part of sole of shoe' (as in Example 2)
        heel   'part of sock around heel of foot'

When we can easily understand how the different meanings of a word are related, then that is polysemy. When the different meanings of a given form appear to be unrelated it is homonymy.

POLYSEMY is the technical term for cases like this, where a word has different meanings that are clearly related, according to the intuitions of present-day users of the language. It is to be distinguished from homonymy, cases where – again in the understanding of contemporary speakers – meanings that go with a given word-form are unrelated:

for example, *coach* meaning 'highway bus' or 'trainer/instructor'; *to lie* 'rest horizontally' or 'deliberately utter falsehoods'. Löbner (2002: 44) asserts that 'While homonymy is a rare and accidental phenomenon, polysemy is abundant. It is rather the rule than the exception.'

Homonymy is not a problem. The solution is to accept that unrelated words sometimes accidentally share the same form, as in the cases of *coach* and *lie*. But with polysemy the similarity is motivated, not accidental: given that *heel* is the label for the 'back part of the foot' (as it has been since Old English times (➔ 17) and given that a sock (when spread out) looks similar to a foot, we can see the reasonableness of *heel* metaphorically coming to be used for the back part of the sock. And given that the rear of the sole of a shoe functions adjacent to and supports the heel of the foot, it is understandable that a metonymic transfer of the label *heel* could take place. We might think that the range of meanings covered by a polysemic word should seem obvious to users within a given language: of course each of the pointers of a non-digital clock or watch should be called a *hand* (➔ 13 on the Sapir–Whorf hypothesis). Not so hasty – in French the word used is *aiguille* 'needle' and likewise for Japanese 針 *hari* 'needle' but in German it is *Zeiger* 'pointer'.

The two main lines of figurative thinking that, in the histories of languages, lead to polysemy are metaphor and metonymy and these will be addressed here only briefly. In metonymy, things that are related (including *parts* of things; ➔ meronymy in 6.3.7) can be used to convey meaning figuratively, e.g. because the executives in charge of companies generally wear suits (as opposed to, say, the workers on the factory floor who may wear overalls or other, more 'regular' clothing), *the suits are getting a pay rise* can refer to just the managers; similarly, soldiers have boots, so *boots on the ground* can be used to refer to the military occupying a territory; and the crew of a ship have hands, so *all hands on deck* can refer to all (and by extension, not just naval) personnel – not just the structures at the end of their arms!

METAPHOR (➔ 8, R2.6) is the non-literal use of language. Earlier in this chapter we talked about 'linguistic family trees', arguably a double metaphor. A *tree* is a large plant with a bark that grows in a forest and there are many kinds of trees e.g. oak, ash, banyan which all have fundamentally the same shape. A *family tree* is a metaphorical way of presenting kinship relations: the diagram that could be drawn of these relationships can look like a tree (though sometimes it looks as though it is growing upside down depending on whether the ancestors are at the bottom or the top of the diagram – different cultures draw these family trees in different ways). In linguistics, some diagrams can look like family trees and so linguists can talk about mother–daughter relationships or as we did earlier in this chapter about great-grand-parental relationships. Just as in family kinship, relations can be closer or more distant and that can have implications for the analysis. Language is regularly used metaphorically: life is viewed variously as a journey, as a battle or as a rich tapestry. In Chapter 1 we present some of the metaphors our students used to explain what language is for them.

If you are interested in metaphor, metonymy and historical semantics (the large topic of historical meaning changes), there are many interesting analyses to read about in Cognitive Semantics (see Further Reading on the companion website). Cognitive semanticists contend that linguistic semantic knowledge cannot consistently be distinguished from encyclopaedic knowledge. Seeing language as inseparably intertwined with all the rest of thought, it is natural that they should be interested in how thoughts about similarity (metaphor) and connections (metonymy) in the world as we live in it and perceive it can affect meanings.

6.5 SUMMARY

Semantics is the study of equivalences in the meaning systems of languages and this is what underlies the way we ordinarily explain the meanings of words using other words. Semantics does not include all our knowledge of the world. We have clear intuitions about the meanings of sentences, and the meaning of a word is found in the contributions it makes to sentence meaning. Substituting one word for another in a sentence can affect what the sentence entails. (Entailments are what must be true if a given sentence is true.) Semantic relationships, such as synonymy, converseness and antonymy hold between words, but they summarize patterns of entailment between sentences containing those words. At the end of the chapter the notion of eventualities was introduced: sentences, partly because of the verbs in them, portray events/situations in systematically different ways. The issue of words and word-forms having more than one meaning was broached too. Formal semantics and cognitive semantics were signposted.

6.6 FURTHER ACTIVITIES

Activity 6.10

! *The child shouted softly when she saw what had happened* is contradictory, because shout licenses an entailment to the effect that the utterance in question was loud, whereas *softly* supports an entailment that it was not loud. The contradictoriness of the example indicates that 'loudly' is part of the meaning of shout.

Test whether or not each of the following verbs, when used in sentences, licenses the sentences to entail what is shown in brackets on the right.

yell	(The utterance is loud.)
blare	(The sound is loud.)
bark	(The sound is loud.)
whisper	(The utterance is relatively quiet.)
amble	(The motion is slow.)
run	(The motion is fast.)

You need to make up sentences and then judge whether they are OK or problematic, e.g. *The dog barked softly; I was embarrassed when he whispered so loudly; They ambled rapidly to the other side of the park.*

Activity 6.11

Find ways of giving the meaning of each of the following in terms of an expression that includes the word *have*.

take, own, get, keep, borrow, give

Here is a start: X *takes* Y (from Z) means 'X causes X to have Y (and Z not to have Y)'.

COMMENTARY ON ACTIVITIES

○━┳ Remember that this symbol indicates that there is a commentary on the activity that you can find on the companion website at www.routledge.com/cw/merrison.

FURTHER READING and REFERENCES

Suggestions for further reading on the topics discussed in this chapter can be found on the companion website (www.routledge.com/cw/merrison).

Any piece of academic writing must always provide a list of publications to which reference has been made. Unusually and very unconventionally, this information is provided on the companion website (www.routledge.com/cw/merrison). Always ask your tutor about how you are to present references for any piece of work that you submit.

Chapter 7
Syntax: Word to Clause

Key Ideas in this Chapter

- The terms *syntax* and *grammar* are sometimes used as synonyms: in this book, we use *syntax* to cover the structure of phrases and clauses and we use *grammar* to cover larger chunks of text.

- Issues relating to syntax and grammar are not independent of questions of meaning.

- Technical terms are essential for accurate descriptions of linguistic phenomena and we present a lot of the necessary metalanguage.

- The analysis of word classes, of phrase structure and of clause structure is explained and activities offer opportunities for you to develop your own analytic skills.

7.1 INTRODUCTION

The authors found the following groups of words on a menu one evening. They all knew what each word meant but working out exactly what was on offer proved to be a completely different matter. See what you make of the menu items:

Apple glazed slow cooked outdoor reared pork belly with crackling spears

Char-grilled 21 day matured Wolds select sirloin steak with truffled butter

Warm 'Doreen's' black pudding salad

To make sense of any of these items on the menu it is not enough simply to understand the meaning of the individual words – you have to understand how the words fit together in sequence to create meaningful communication: was the apple glazed slowly or was the cooking slow? Was the cooking outdoor or were the pigs reared outdoors? Had the steak been chargrilled for 21 days or had the steak matured for 21 days? Was Doreen warm or was the salad or the black pudding warm? Once the syntactic structure of each menu item was understood, then we knew what we were being offered and whether we wanted to choose this item or not (and we noted that the vegetarians amongst us had a problem). If you can retrieve the meaning of an utterance, then you have *some* understanding (implicit if not explicit) of **syntax** or **grammar**. Whether your understanding is implicit or explicit is not important to your ability to understand the meaning but it is important to your ability to discuss issues of syntax and grammar. We presume that you are a student of linguistics and so we take it as unarguable that you need to be able to talk about matters linguistic in precise and appropriate terms, otherwise you would probably not be reading this book.

Every subject or topic has its own specific terminology and structures, and the subject of language is not different. Everybody can appreciate a beautiful garden whether they can name the flowers or not. Those who can name the shrubs and the flowers (whether with the technical Latin names or with the more everyday names) can have more detailed and more technical discussions, even more interesting discussions perhaps, as they can say things more concisely and more precisely. They can advise why certain plantings or arrangements of flowers work well together while other groupings are not so successful. Similarly, chemists who know the names of the chemicals and of the chemical processes which they are using in an experiment can talk more efficiently about the experiments they are carrying out, often reporting these experiments in the passive voice to remove the human element from the chemical processes: it is the process that is important not who individually carries out the specific tasks. The same thing applies to cooking where the use of the **imperative** in recipes instructs the reader on what to do next in order to create the dish of their choice. In the same way, we need specific language to talk about language (a *metalanguage*) and as far as syntax and grammar (➜ 8) are concerned, you will learn the major terms needed in these two chapters.

Metalanguage is language used to talk about language (like jargon/specialist vocabulary in other subject areas) so includes technical terms such as *noun, clause, text, phoneme, lexeme, mean length of utterance*.

Activity 7.1

Each of us knows the technical language of subjects in which we are particularly interested. For each of two areas of interest to you,

(a)   list at least ten lexical items which are specific to or which have a specialized meaning in that area
(b)   list some of the features of language use linked with that area.

Technical terms from language and linguistics can be found throughout this book so here are two other areas as examples: *Bell-ringing/campanology*:

(a)   sally, tail end, bob, single, doubles, caters, triples, change, four to three, look to, treble's going, she's gone.
(b)   Imperatives are used by the conductor (e.g. *Go plain bob doubles, Stand*) and no other ringer in the band says anything while the ringing is taking place.

UK law:

(a)   case, brief, jury, trial, magistrate, defence, prosecution, complainant, appellant, argue, 'Your Honour', crown court, counsel, solicitor.
(b)   Open (e.g. *What happened next?*) and closed (e.g. *Did you have a clear view of the defendant?*) questions are used frequently in the presentation of evidence by both defence and prosecution as well as persuasive language (e.g. *you will see that* ...; *it is clear that* ...) in the summing up of the case to the jury.

Whatever language you normally use to manage your everyday life, the fact that you are reading this book (and we hope understanding what you are reading!) means that you must understand how to make sense of (or decode) the structures of the English language. That you could work out what might be on offer at the restaurant (whether you like such food or not) means that you can work out relatively complex structures as well. It does not necessarily mean that you have a vocabulary or a language to talk about the syntactic structure of English. By the end of this chapter, you will have increased your metalinguistic abilities in relation to English syntax and grammar.

While it can be argued that simply being able to analyse clauses does not greatly help us understand language in use, we would argue that it is an essential skill for being able to recognize patterns of language in use (you will find that patterns of use can be discovered in almost all texts as a result of careful analysis) and hence for being able to make valid, evidence-based comments about language in use in a whole range of contexts – look in other chapters in this book to find examples. Like all skills, the ability needs to be learnt and learning a skill takes time, effort and practice. However, the more you practise and learn, the easier it will become to recognize the patterns of language in use without having to write down all the detail every time. And once you can recognize the patterns in language in use, you will be able to make valid and justified comments about the chunk of language that you are considering at any given time.

7.2 SYNTAX AND GRAMMAR

Many people use syntax and grammar as virtual synonyms. Traditionally, *grammar* has been used quite broadly to cover any aspect of the structure of the language including semantics (➜ 6) and phonology (➜ 10). *Syntax* is more narrowly defined as the structure of sentences, **clauses** and **phrases**.

As with all subjects, there are different ways of approaching the subject under discussion and grammar or syntax is no different. Simply (or perhaps not so simply) the change of term from *grammar* to *syntax* shows how different people consider the matter. *Grammar* was used to refer to all structural aspects of language especially the relationship between semantics (➜ 6) and grammatical structure and there were considerable debates about that relationship: does the meaning one wishes to express determine (or at the very least influence) the structure one uses to express it or does the structure determine (or at the very least influence) what we are able to say? The Sapir–Whorf hypothesis (➜ 13) relates to these questions and is addressed briefly later in this section.

Traditionally *grammar* considered issues of morphology (➜ 5) and sentence structure and it has a long history both in terms of time (from the time of the ancient Greeks, Indians and Romans) and place in that in medieval times the Chinese, the Jews and the Arabs all did work on their own languages and on the languages of others. Progress was relatively slow, however, and largely based on parsing (the analysis of sentences in their component parts).

Our focus in this book is on language in use, on language in a social context and so we choose to adopt a functional approach (as originally outlined by Michael Halliday) which analyses language use in relation to what people want to say about the world around them (➜ R2.3). In introducing such a model of language analysis, Halliday (1994: 106) asserts that language 'enables human beings to build a mental picture of reality, to make sense of what goes on around and inside them' and he continues that 'the clause plays a central role, because it embodies a general principle for modelling experience – namely, the principle that reality is made up of processes'. In Halliday's view, humans experience reality as a sequence of 'goings-on' and he uses the term 'processes' to talk about these experiences. He argues that people recognize that things happen, that they think and feel, and that they generalize from their experiences to make statements or to ask questions, to exclaim or to give instructions in relation to the world around them. He recognizes three major types of process:

1   material processes – events which occur in the external world around us
2   mental processes – events which occur in the inner world of our minds
3   relational processes – states which exist in the world around us

He claims that all languages are structured to allow people to discuss and report their experience of the world and that there is a link between people's understanding of their world and their language use. In other words, the meanings that people want to express affect the linguistic choices that people make in expressing those meanings.

Before moving into more detail on syntactic analysis and explaining some of the technical terms (the *metalanguage*), you might like to reflect on the following questions which arise from the points just made. If each language has its own grammatical system which relates to its semantic and phonological system, then any acquirer/learner of a language

(➔ 15) has to learn not just the words and sounds of that language, but also its structure and how the language expresses meaning. And remember that most young children are competent users of these systems by the age of five years.

However, if the structure of a language is so closely related to the language users' experience of the world and if it is true that language users carve up the world according to the syntax of their language, there is a question about how far use of a language influences (or to put it more strongly, determines) our perception of the world around us – the fundamental question addressed in the Sapir–Whorf hypothesis. When learning another language, does the second language learner have to learn to understand the world in a different way? In other words, can you learn a second language without learning how that language is used to represent the world? Do different languages, therefore, because they have different linguistic systems, represent different world views? And does second language users' use of a given language affect the way in which that language might develop? Think of the way in which English is currently used throughout the world by both native speakers and non-native speakers of English (➔ 18). These apparently simple questions will provide much food for background thought as you develop your skills in linguistic analysis.

Issues of meaning are directly addressed in other chapters (➔ 3, 5, 6) so the focus in this chapter is on syntax, on the ordering of words within phrases and clauses and how those clauses then combine to form sentences. Sentences combine to form larger chunks of text and we deal with that in Chapter 8. Our preference for a functional approach to language relates to our focus of analysing language in use rather than language as a purely symbolic system.

Syntactic analysis can be approached from a bird's eye view or from a worm's eye view. The bird's eye view of grammar would start with a large chunk of text and pull it apart to see how it is constructed. It would start at the top of the **hierarchy of rank** (Figure 7.1) and work down through the layers. The worm's eye view of grammar would start at the bottom of the hierarchy and gradually build up to the text. This chapter will begin by looking at word classes (for information about morphemes ➔ 5) and show how words combine to form phrases and clauses in sentences which form text – in other words, we are starting from the worm's eye view.

In diagram form, the hierarchy of rank can be seen in Figure 7.1 and the brackets indicate how to read the hierarchy. So we can read from top to bottom of the hierarchy and say that a text (whether written or spoken) consists of one or more sentences, each sentence consists of one or more clauses, each clause of one or more phrases, each phrase of one or more words, each word of one or more morphemes and each morpheme of one or more phonemes. Alternatively we can read from the bottom to the top of the hierarchy and say that one or more phonemes combine to form a morpheme, one or more morphemes combine to form a word, one or more words combine to form a phrase, one or more phrases combine to form a clause, one or more clauses combine to form a sentence and one or more sentences combine to form a text. A text could consist of a single sentence which consists of a single clause which consists of a single phrase which consists of a single word which consists of a single morpheme: for example, *Stop!* (a warning sign), *Wait* (a carer to a child or distracted adult or even to a dog), *No!* (a teacher to a child) or *Pencil* (a teacher to a young child in school to ensure the correct writing implement is used).

Given that there are certain basics on which everyone can agree for the most part (though the fine detail of a theoretical analysis and categorization might differ between

The Sapir–Whorf hypothesis (➔ 13) appears in a strong form (that our language determines our view of the world) and in a weaker form (that our language influences our world view). Currently, most linguists will accept the weaker version (➔ R 3.5; ➔ 1, 13)

A simple sentence contains one single clause – examples might be *Chris worked very hard yesterday* or *Andrew will not see all his family this weekend.*

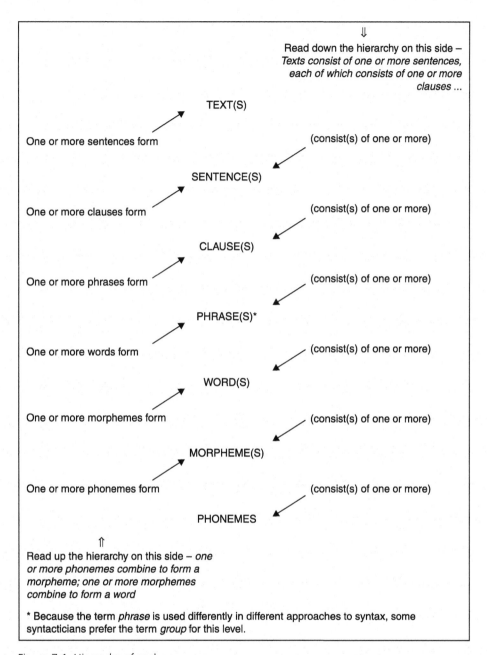

⇓
Read down the hierarchy on this side –
Texts consist of one or more sentences,
each of which consists of one or more
clauses ...

TEXT(S)

One or more sentences form

(consist(s) of one or more)

SENTENCE(S)

One or more clauses form

(consist(s) of one or more)

CLAUSE(S)

One or more phrases form

(consist(s) of one or more)

PHRASE(S)*

One or more words form

(consist(s) of one or more)

WORD(S)

One or more morphemes form

(consist(s) of one or more)

MORPHEME(S)

One or more phonemes form

(consist(s) of one or more)

PHONEMES

⇑
Read up the hierarchy on this side – *one*
or more phonemes combine to form a
morpheme; one or more morphemes
combine to form a word

* Because the term *phrase* is used differently in different approaches to syntax, some
syntacticians prefer the term *group* for this level.

Figure 7.1 Hierarchy of rank

analysts) and since our focus is on analysing language in use, we shall look at small
samples of language – short texts – and see what we can say about the units that form the
text. In this chapter we shall go no further than looking at what units form clauses
(or simple sentences). For more information on how a longer text might be constructed,
you will need to look at Chapter 8.

7.3 WORD CLASSES

It is clear that for all the words in any language there are rules of some kind that determine which ones can go where and in what order – though speakers/writers do have considerable flexibility in how creative they can be. The first sentence in Text 7.1 is quite easy to read but if the words were in a different order – say – *answer be easy need not questions simple to –* it would not make much sense to an English reader. In English, word order is important: there is a significant difference in meaning between these invented examples (just work out who paid each time) with the same words in a different order each time:

(1)   Aileen bought Patrick, Andrew and Chris a drink.
(2)   Andrew bought Chris, Patrick and Aileen a drink.
(3)   Chris bought Andrew, Aileen and Patrick a drink.
(4)   Patrick bought Aileen, Chris and Andrew a drink.

There are two groups of word classes: open classes of words and closed classes of words. Open classes are those within which speakers create new words as they need to while closed classes, covering words like *the* and *to*, are part of the grammatical framework and do not often get added to. As people invented more things, new words were needed to label them (*helicopter, television, bytes*). Some new labels were originally the name of the producer of the product (e.g. Hoover) and then were generalized to mean the whole class of goods in that category. Indeed, *hoover* is now used as a verb whatever make of machine the individual might be using. New words added to the Oxford English Dictionary (OED) in 2010 include for example, LBD (acronym for *little black dress* and the fact that the acronym goes into the dictionary might make you want to wonder what a *word* is ➔ 5), *frenemy, bromance, exit strategy* and *vuvuzela*, as well as labels for new ways of behaving (e.g. *catastrophize, overthink, defriend* or *unfriend*) or for descriptions (e.g. *matchy-matchy*).

> OMG, LOL and other examples from text speak are almost treated as words these days. Will they ever appear in dictionaries?

In the newspapers, during the period of working on this second edition, we have noticed *austerians* and *celebrification*; the former in relation to those espousing austerity in the financial circumstances of the time and the latter in discussing the process of making celebrities out of anybody and everybody. At a meeting, somebody commented that archaeology was being 'heritagized' and the linguists present were sidetracked for a while reflecting on this (apparently – and to them) new coinage. Only time will tell if these and similar neologisms will become more permanent or remain transient.

Syntacticians (specialists in the study of syntax) use the traditional word class labels of **noun, verb, adjective, adverb, pronoun, preposition** and **conjunction** but add newer terms like **determiner** to complete the list. The older notional definitions on the lines of *a noun is a naming word, a verb is a doing word* and *an adjective is a describing word* are not particularly helpful as the basis of a rigorous, detailed and (hopefully) objective linguistic analysis. Do all verbs 'do' an action and do all verbs cover the doing of things? What about verbs like *seem* and *be*? Are they 'doing'? In the phrase *a gravel path*, does 'gravel' not describe the path even though the word *gravel* is a noun not an adjective?

There are four open classes of words: noun, verb, adjective and adverb. These four classes are often called the **content word** classes: they carry the bulk of the content of what the speaker wishes to refer to. The other word categories – including pronoun, preposition, determiner and conjunction – are closed categories, often called the group of **function**

words or **grammatical words**. A sentence with words only from these word classes would not provide much information for the hearer/reader. There have been few, if any, newly coined words in these closed categories over the centuries though there have been attempts recently to find a gender neutral pronoun to indicate he+she. Many people have challenged the fairness of using *he* to include females and hence apparently new pronoun forms such as *s/he* or *he/she* have appeared but it is noticeable that whilst these may appear in written text, there are few examples occurring easily in speech. Another response to the dilemma, is to use *they/their* as in an example like 'Every child must be able to tie their shoelaces before they start school'.

Read Text 7.1 before you read any further as some of the examples in the following discussion will come from that text (that piece of language in use) and from other texts that will be introduced later.

Text 7.1 The Collatz-Syracuse-Ulam problem (Stewart 2009: 26)

	Simple questions need not be easy to answer. Here's a famous example.
2	You can explore it with pencil or paper, or a calculator, but what it does in general baffles even the world's greatest mathematicians. They think they
4	know the answer, but no one can prove it. It goes like this.
	• Think of a number. Now apply the following rules over and over again:
6	• If the number is even divide it by 2.
	• If the number is odd, multiply it by 3 and add 1.
8	
	What happens?
10	I thought of 11. This is odd, so the next number is $3 \times 11 + 1 = 34$. That's even, so I divide by 2 to get 17. This is odd, and leads to 52. After
12	that the numbers go 26, 13, 40, 20, 10, 5, 16, 8, 4, 2, 1. From there we get 4, 2, 1, 4, 2, 1 indefinitely. So usually we add a third rule:
14	• If you reach 1, stop. In 1937, Lothar Collatz asked whether this procedure always reaches 1, no
16	matter what number you start with. More than seventy years later, we still don't know the answer.

7.3.1 Open classes

Nouns

The noun class is probably one of the largest in English. There are three subsets. Nouns can be sub-classified as count nouns, non-count nouns (called mass nouns by some) and proper nouns. Count nouns can be singular (e.g. *example, calculator, number*) or plural (e.g. *questions, mathematicians, rules*) and the regular plural inflection in English is to add {*-s*} to the end of the

If you make *paper* plural, it is not really the substance *paper* that you are counting but rather the number of sheets or of reams of paper. Similarly, you can count pounds or kilos of rice or gallons/litres of petrol or oil, bars of soap or sacks of manure but the substances themselves, *rice, petrol, oil, soap* and *manure* cannot themselves be counted. There is variability in this for speakers of international varieties of English where you might hear *some informations* or *softwares* (➔ 18, R2.7).

word. Not all plurals are regular. What is the plural of the words *man, goose, foot,* and *mouse*? Some words do not mark the plural but we know we can count sheep or fish so they must be able to function as plurals even if there is no plural **morpheme** added to the word stem. Non-count nouns (e.g. *paper* in Text 7.1 or *pork* from the menu items at the beginning of this chapter) cannot be counted so the noun cannot be made plural. The final subset within this word class is that of proper noun of which there are three examples in Text 7.1: *Collatz, Syracuse* and *Ulam*. Proper nouns name something unique, for example, an individual person or a people, a place or a river etc.: e.g. *Alex, Spanish, York, Buckingham Palace, India, Thames.* In English, a proper noun (but not the other kinds of nouns) is written with a capital letter wherever it appears in a sentence. In German, all nouns are always written with a capital letter.

Activity 7.2 ⚷

Read Text 7.2 and identify all the nouns in the first paragraph. Be as precise as you can – specify each in terms of singular, plural, count or non-count (sometimes called mass nouns) nouns, proper nouns.

Text 7.2 St William of York – his life and death

[…]

A treasurer of York Minster, William was elected to the archbishopric in
2   1141. However, his close connections to both the Norman and English royal
houses clouded his triumph with accusations of corruption. Although his
4   position was consecrated in 1143 he was deposed by Pope Eugenius III.
[…]
6   William was sent into exile until 1153 when three of his main opponents
[…] all died. William quickly petitioned the new pope for his pallium of
8   office.
William was finally consecrated as archbishop in Winchester in late 1153-
10   54. He returned to York in triumph. A great crowd assembled on Ouse
bridge to greet him. The bridge collapsed under the weight of the crowd,
12   many of whom fell into the waters beneath. William blessed the crowd and
nobody was hurt – his only lifetime miracle.
14   After his first mass and celebratory feast William fell ill and died a week
later. Osbert, the Archdeacon, a long-standing opponent of William, was
16   accused of poisoning the chalice. Although the matter went to court, it was
never resolved.
18   […]
THE ST WILLIAM WINDOW OF YORK MINSTER – A BRIEF
20   HISTORY
[…]
22   The window was created in about 1414/15, during a national period of
revival of the cult of St William. This revival of a hitherto largely ignored

24   local saint was mainly attributable to the efforts of staunchly Lancastrian
      clergy. They hoped to distract the populace from the growing cult of
26   Archbishop Scrope, executed in 1405 for open rebellion against Henry IV,
      but allowed to be buried in the Minster.
28   [...]
      The window was the gift of Beatrice, the Dowager Lady Ros. Five donor
30   panels depicting members of her family form the bottom row of the
      window. Beatrice died in 1415 having out-lived her husband and two of her
32   five sons. The Ros of Helmsley family were long-standing benefactors and
      their heraldry appears throughout the Minster.
34   The high quality of the painting suggests that the window was the work of
      the workshop of John Thornton of Coventry. Thornton was the master
36   glazier responsible for the Great East Window, 1405–1408.

Verbs

In Standard English (➔ 12), all main or **lexical verbs** (**auxiliary verbs** will be considered later in this chapter) have five forms (see Table 7.1). A **finite** form of the verb shows tense and in English verbs there is only a past tense form or a present tense form for a verb even though it is perfectly possibly to talk about past time, present time and future time. A **non-finite** form does not indicate tense. Past tense forms (Column C) all refer to completed actions in the past. The present tense forms in Column B must have the third person singular (*he/she/it*) as grammatical subject as in *it baffles, she goes, he is*. With first or second person subject and with third person plural (see Table 7.2), the present tense form looks like the base form as in Column A. The use of the non-finite forms (as in Column D and Column E) will be explained later in this chapter.

Some technical labels are just plain confusing. The {-ing} form is traditionally called the present participle but it can be used with past tense (as well as present tense) auxiliary verbs as in *I am/was swimming*. The {-en} form is traditionally called the past participle but it can be used with present tense (as well as past tense) auxiliary verbs as in *He has/had spoken*.

Activity 7.3 🔑

Verbs such as *prove, need, apply* and *answer* are called regular verbs. Verbs such as *think, be, eat* and *drive* are called irregular. Look at the different verb forms for each verb in Table 7.1 and decide what justifies the label *irregular*.

Table 7.1 Verb forms

	A	B	C	D	E
From Text 7.1	*finite* if used as present tense OR *non-finite* if used with a finite auxiliary (➔ 7.4.5)	*finite forms* (indicate tense)		*non-finite forms* (do not indicate tense)	
		Present tense	Past tense	The {-*ing*} form	The {-*en*} form
	need answer be think prove go apply get	needs answers is thinks proves goes applies gets	needed answered was thought proved went applied got	needing answering being thinking proving going applying getting	needed answered been thought proved gone applied got (UK) gotten (US)
and some more examples not in Text 7.1	take eat drive put sit	takes eats drives puts sits	took ate drove put sat	taking eating driving putting sitting	taken eaten driven put sat

Activity 7.4

Quickly copy out the framework of Table 7.1 with just the column headings filled in. Choose a short article in a newspaper or a paragraph from a longer one, identify the verbs in the article and work out the five forms of each verb. If you have problems with any of them, check out the answers in a good dictionary (➔ Read Me!).

Verbs can be TRANSITIVE or INTRANSITIVE in English. For current purposes, we can say that intransitive verbs relate to processes (in the Hallidayan sense ➔ 7.2) with only one obligatory participant e.g. _The children_ are sleeping, _The dog_ died or _Everyone_ sneezed. Transitive verbs relate to processes with two obligatory participants e.g. _Liz_ cleaned _the cooker_, _Anne_ wrote _the letter_ or more than two as in the examples _Giles_ gave _his children a treat_ or _Vernon_ put _the dinner_ _in the oven_. (In the latter example, the meaning of *put* requires that somebody puts something (or somebody) in a particular place. You cannot say simply *_Vernon put the dinner._)

Adjectives

In English, adjectives appear before nouns in noun phrases (see next section) and in Text 7.1 you will have found *simple, easy, famous* just in the first line. Adjectives also appear in position Y in structures like 'X is/was Y' as in Text 7.1 *the number is even* or *the number is odd*. Many adjectives also admit comparison and then the **suffixes** {-er} and {-est} can be added as in *great, greater, greatest*. Some adjectives form the comparative and superlative forms by using the intensifying adverbs *more* and *most* as in *more famous* (comparative form) and *most famous* (superlative form). Some adjectives have irregular forms as, for example, the adjective *good* has the comparative form *better* and the superlative form *best*. Not all adjectives can be graded or compared – something is either unique or it is not and you cannot really be more or less alive or superb (➔ 6) though you will hear people saying 'It was quite unique' or 'That was absolutely superb' as well as the metaphorical use of somebody claiming to 'feel more dead than alive'. Sports commentary at the 2012 Olympic Games provided plenty of examples of such uses.

English has absorbed not only words from other languages over the centuries (➔ 17) but also structures. In German, all comparatives/superlatives are formed by adding a suffix; in French all are formed by using intensifying adverbs.

Activity 7.5

Read a front-page article in a recent newspaper (preferably not a tabloid). Identify all the adjectives. For each adjective work out the comparative and superlative form of the adjective. Then create your own text using the comparative or superlative forms of half of the adjectives that you found.

Adverbs

Many adverbs end with the suffix {-ly} (e.g. *finally, stunningly, badly* or *creatively*) but not all do (e.g. *well, fast, more, very*). Not all words that end in -ly are adverbs: *apply* in Text 7.1 is a verb as are *rely* and *multiply; lovely, frilly, ghastly* and *sly* are adjectives and *butterfly* is a noun as are *belly, gully* and *jelly*.

You should read Text 7.2 *St William of York* again before reading about the functions of adverbs.

Adverbs have three major functions:

(a)   they describe actions or modify verbs in which context they tend to give information about time, place and manner as in these examples from Text 7.2: *William quickly petitioned, William was finally consecrated*,

(b)   they can modify adjectives as in these examples from Text 7.2: *largely ignored local saint* and *staunchly Lancastrian clergy*,

(c)   they can modify other adverbs as in, for example, *more staunchly, very fast*.

Like adjectives, adverbs can also be compared but adverbs appear in different structures in English. The comparative and superlative forms of adverbs are formed in the same way as they are formed in adjectives: examples might be *Tom plays the guitar more frequently than Adam but Adam can do karate more effectively than Tom: Kate and Richard can swim faster than both the boys*.

> ## Activity 7.6
>
> Think of people you know, work out who can do what better than others. Write out sentences about them and underline the adverbs. An example might be:
>
> Chris can ride a bike _well_ but Andrew rides _more confidently_ and Patrick always rode _the most carefully._

7.3.2 Closed classes

Pronouns

It would be logical to think that pronouns should stand in place of nouns. This is true, but they also stand in place of noun phrases/groups (see later in this chapter). In Text 7.1, it is clear that *you* refers to the reader, *they* refers back in the text to *the world's greatest mathematicians* and it refers back to the number. Personal pronouns differ according to number (singular or plural) and relation to speaker (see Table 7.2) and are inflected for case, which means that there are different forms of the pronoun depending on the syntactic function of the pronoun in the sentence. In other languages (e.g. German, Latin) all nouns, not just pronouns, are inflected for case. These inflections, or inflectional morphemes, are added to the word for syntactic reasons. They do not change the word class of the word to which they are added as derivational morphemes do (➔ 5.5.2), nor do they change the meaning of the word.

As well as the personal pronouns shown in Table 7.2, there are also reflexive pronouns (e.g. *myself, yourself*) and demonstrative pronouns (e.g. *this, that, these, those*). The use of reflexive pronouns seems to be changing currently. Traditionally, reflexive pronouns are used in examples such as I *saw myself in the mirror* or they are used for emphasis as in *Jake did that himself*. While still used in these traditional ways, recently heard examples include *Can you send it to myself, please?* or *I'll phone yourself* compared with Standard English *Can you send it to me, please?* or *I'll phone you*.

The *case* system in grammar allows suffixes to be added to nouns to show the role that the noun (or noun phrase) will take in a clause/sentence. In Old English (➔ 17), all nouns were inflected for case. In Modern English the only case ending still used is the genitive case with the suffix *'s/s'* added to show (usually) possession as in *Doreen's black pudding salad, the child's shoe* or *the authors' intentions*. However, the genitive case does not always indicate possession: *the cow's milk* (would be glossed as milk from the cow) and a *women's university* (glossed as a university for women).

Determiners

Determiners indicate the range of **reference** of a noun and examples can be found in Text 7.1. *A* and *the* each appear several times and once you know that they are labelled indefinite article and definite article respectively, then you should be able to start analysing how they are used: *a famous example* indicates that this problem is but one of many; *the world's greatest mathematicians* indicates that there is only one world (as far as we know!); *the answer* indicates that there is only one definite answer to the problem. Using the definite article *the* tells the addressee/receiver that there is a specific **referent** (the answer to the problem, or the only world we know of) whereas using the indefinite article *a/an* means the speaker could be referring to any example. How does the speaker decide whether to use *a* or *an*?

Text 7.3 Passport out of here (Keyes 2005: 49)

Activity 7.7 🔑

Think about the difference in meaning between these two examples:

(a)   Can I have a pen, please?
(b)   Can I have the pen, please?

Table 7.2 Personal pronouns: number and case

Number	Singular			Plural		
Person	**subject case**	**object case**	**possessive case**	**subject case**	**object case**	**possessive case**
1st person (refers to speaker)	I	me	mine	we	us	ours
2nd person (refers to hearer)	you	you	yours	you	you	yours
3rd person (neither speaker nor hearer)	he she it	him her it	his hers its	they	them	theirs

The more technical label for subject case is *nominative*, for object case *accusative* and for possessive case *genitive*.

Many people want to label *my, your, his, her, our* and *their* as pronouns but it will be clear that these words behave much more like determiners than pronouns: like determiners, they have to come before a noun as in *his close* connections, *her five sons* and *their heraldry* (Text 7.2), *my mouth, my passport* (Text 7.3); unlike pronouns they cannot stand on their own in place of a noun phrase as in *This is my and that is your.

Text 7.3 Passport out of here (Keyes 2005: 49)

Many years ago I was living in London and about to visit New York for
2   the first time. My sister had moved there four months previously, and I was
going to spend Christmas with her. Three nights before the off I began to
4   pack and when I looked in my 'official things' drawer for my passport, there
it was – gone! Except it couldn't be. It had sat in that drawer since I'd last

6   needed it, on a trip to Greece the previous summer. I rummaged through bills
     and stuff expecting it to appear and when it didn't I took the entire
8   contents out and systematically went through each item one by one – nada.
     My mouth went a little dry, my heart-rate increased, but I told myself that it
10   was there, I just couldn't see it – hadn't my mother always told me that I
     couldn't find the water in the river?
12   But unless it had gone invisible it simply Was Not There and with sweaty
     hands I began to tear my room apart, going through every pocket of every
14   item of clothing in my wardrobe, looking in old rucksacks and handbags,
     pulling books out of my bookcase, and although I stumbled across a handful
16   of sandy drachmas and half a bag of inexplicably abandoned Maltesers (still
     edible, quite nice actually), there was no passport. Then I launched an attack
18   on the rest of the flat and late into the night I finally had to admit the
     inadmissible: my passport wasn't here. At this stage I was almost
20   whimpering with terror; although my ticket to New York had put a huge
     dent in my meagre finances, it was non-changeable and non-refundable. If I
22   hadn't a passport in two days' time I wouldn't be going.

What is the difference in meanings?

Prepositions

Prepositions often indicate meanings related to time and place and it is interesting to note that the same prepositions can be used in relation to each: *at the corner of the street* and *at ten o'clock this evening*; *in a week* and *in the city*. Each preposition has only one form and most of them consist of only one word though there are multi-word prepositions such as *next to, because of* or *in spite of* to name a few. Examples in Text 7.1 include *with, in, of* and *by*; in Text 7.2 *with, into, to*; in Text 7.3 *for, before, through*. Other examples would include *under, after, between* and *on behalf of*.

Activity 7.8 ⚓

Identify all the prepositions in Texts 7.1, 7.2 (part 1) and 7.3. For each, try to specify the meaning of the preposition and then use a good dictionary (➜ Read Me!) to see how your conclusion compares with what the dictionary states.

If you *blow up* the balloons how is the meaning different from *blowing up* the building as in a terrorist act? Which of these two events is legal because *break in* means something different in each example: *somebody broke in the house last night* or *I broke in my new trainers over the last few days*? What about all the possibilities with the verb *turn: off, down, up, over*? Or the verb *get*?

Prepositions occur before noun phrases as shown in the last paragraphs but they can also appear in verb groups. The permitted constructions become very complex but you might like to think about the difference between *to look up a word / to look a word up in the dictionary* (where the same meaning is expressed when the word *up* appears in either of the two possible places) or *to look up the street* (where *up* can only appear in one place for the meaning to be retained – if you move *up* then the meaning changes).

Conjunctions

Conjunctions are words which join or link two words, phrases or clauses and there are two main groups: COORDINATING CONJUNCTIONS and SUBORDINATING CONJUNCTIONS.

The coordinating conjunctions in English are *and*, *but* and *or* and the same structure normally appears on either side of the coordinating conjunction. In Text 7.1, *pencil and paper* shows the coordinating conjunction *and* linking two nouns which in turn are then offered jointly as an alternative to using a calculator by the use of the coordinating conjunction *or*. In the sentence *They think they know the answer, but no one can prove it* the coordinating conjunction but links two clauses (clauses will be discussed later in this chapter) inside the sentence as also in Text 7.2 *William blessed the crowd and nobody was hurt*.

Subordinating conjunctions (which are underlined in these examples) normally link a subordinate clause into a main clause. In Text 7.1, <u>If</u> *the number is even/odd*, the subordinating conjunction if (with the clause it belongs to) provides a condition which determines the action to be taken. Concession is shown in the subordinate clause in Text 7.2 <u>Although</u> *the matter went to court, it was never resolved*. An example from Text 7.3 is <u>when</u> *I looked [...] in my drawer [...], there it was – gone!* indicates how the information in the first clause relates in time to the information in the second part of the sentence.

7.4 PHRASES

According to the hierarchy of rank (see Figure 7.1), words combine to form phrases – a term which in linguistics has a clear definition and structure, unlike the more general use of the word. There are five major types of phrase in English: all phrases must have one obligatory element and it is that element which controls the phrase.

Three phrases have a very similar structure based on the notion of headword and modifier. These three are the noun phrase (NP), the adjective phrase (AdjP) and the adverb phrase (AdvP). Each phrase must have a headword: a noun is the headword of an NP, an adjective the headword of an AdjP and an adverb the headword of an AdvP. The headword of any of these phrases can be modified: premodifiers come before the headword and postmodifiers after the headword. Sections 7.4.1, 7.4.3 and 7.4.4 provide more information and examples.

The prepositional phrase (PP) is easily recognized: the obligatory element is a preposition and its structure is preposition + noun phrase. From Text 7.1, *pencil or paper* is a coordinated NP; *with pencil and paper* a PP. From Text 7.2, *the archbishopric is* a NP; *to the archbishopric* a PP. From Text 7.3, *her* is a NP, *with her* is a PP. There are many other examples in these three and all other texts. PPs are discussed further in section 7.4.2.

> Remember that a phrase can consist of a single word, therefore a NP can consist of a single word and that word can be a noun or a pronoun.

The fifth unit at this level in the hierarchy of rank is the verb group (VG) which has as its obligatory element a verb. Functional syntacticians use the term verb group (VG) not the term verb phrase and this will be discussed further in 7.4.5. You should be aware that the term *verb phrase* might have different definitions in different approaches to grammar.

Table 7.3 Noun phrase (NP) structure

		premodification (modification before the headword)		HEADWORD	postmodification (modification after the headword)
likely syntactic classes		determiner numeral	adjectives nouns	noun	qualifier PP relative clause
Examples	(5) (6) (7) (8) (9) (10)	the some	crisp, white slushy good snowball dirty, slushy	snow snow snow snow snow snow	in the garden which lies on city pavements

7.4.1 Noun phrases

The NP structure should be clear from the invented examples in Table 7.3 – invented to show as many possible structures as we can. Example (5) shows a single word NP with the headword *snow*. If there is a determiner (e.g. *the, some*) as in (6) and (9), then the determiner will be the first word in the phrase. Adjectives (e.g. *crisp, white, slushy*) as in (6) and (7) and nouns (e.g. *snowball*) as in (8) can be used to premodify the head noun. In the postmodification slot, there is often a PP as in (9) (e.g. *in the garden, on city pavements*) or there can be a **relative clause** as in (10) (*which lies on city pavements*) – a structure that will be addressed in section 7.6.2. Table 7.3 shows one way of presenting the structure of an NP: in a box diagram. The structure of each NP is now shown in tree diagram form. The two different diagrams show exactly the same structural information – only the presentation is different.

(5)   *snow*

(6)   *the crisp white snow*

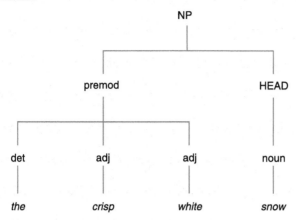

(7)   *slushy snow*

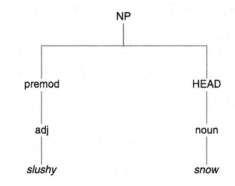

(8)   *good snowball snow*

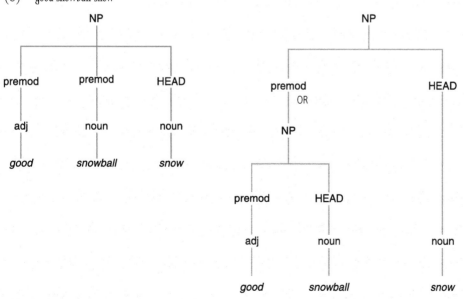

(9)   *some snow in the garden*

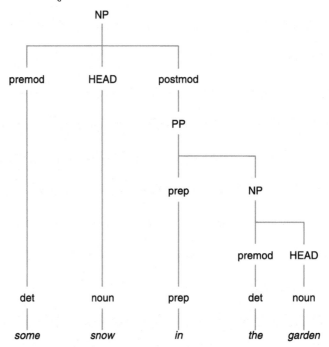

(10) *dirty slushy snow which lies on city pavements*

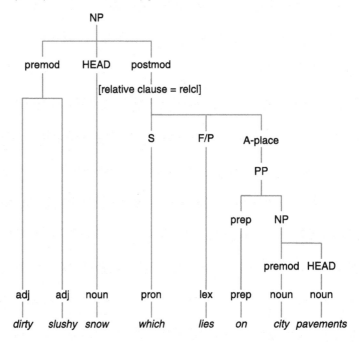

> ## ACTIVITY 7.9 🔑
>
> Look at Text 7.1 and identify all the NPs. For each NP that you identify, specify the structure in the same way as it is explained in Table 7.3 or, if you prefer, draw tree diagrams to show the structure.

NP structure can be ambiguous and the ambiguities can be entertaining as you spot them around the place (➜ 3 Example 24). Ones that the authors heard or saw around York at the time of writing include:

Fake finger injury: which is fake – the finger or the injury?

Fresh strawberries and cream: what is fresh – only the strawberries or both the strawberries and the cream?

The tree diagrams used here (Figure 7.2) show the two possible structures and therefore the two possible meanings of the NP of *fake finger injury*.

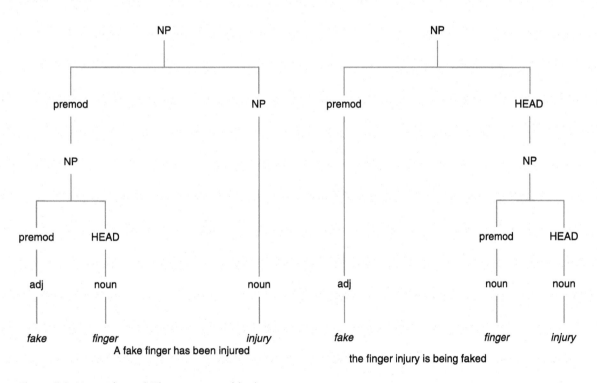

Figure 7.2 Noun phrase (NP) structure: ambiguity

> ### ACTIVITY 7.10 🔑
>
> Draw tree diagrams to show the possible meanings for *fresh strawberries and cream*.

> ### ACTIVITY 7.11 🔑
>
> Look again at the items on the menu at the beginning of this chapter. Each is a NP. For each, identify the headword, then any premodification items and then any post-modification. Remember that inside each NP, there might be other 'smaller' NPs.

A noun phrase can be replaced by a pronoun. Speakers and writers choose when to use nouns and when to use pronouns depending on how much information they think the addressee/receiver already knows and how much needs to be made explicit (➜ 3). This will be discussed later in this chapter but the point can be exemplified in the following text.

None of the authors felt comfortable with the example Here's it but all were comfortable with Here's one. What do you think?

If we were to replace each NP in the first three sentences in Text 7.1 with a pronoun, it would read as follows:

(11)   They need not be easy to answer. Here's it. You can explore it with them, or it, but what it does in general is baffle even them.

At the beginning of a text, as here, using pronouns is not helpful to the receiver of the message. Later in a text, they can be very useful, as in, for example, Text 7.2 where William's full name is repeated sometimes but on many occasions *he, him* or *his* are used to refer to him and to save tedious repetition of his name.

7.4.2 Preposition phrases

Post-positions occur in some languages, e.g. Latin, Chinese or Turkish.

Remember that each phrase must have one obligatory element and that determines the name of the phrase. Therefore, in a prepositional phrase, there must be a preposition. In English prepositions come before (pre-pose) NPs so the structure of a PP is prep + NP. In Text 7.1 *with pencil and paper* and *like this* are clearly PPs. From the same text, you can argue that *a calculator* is really a kind of reduced PP – the preposition has been omitted because of elision (➜ 8.3) as a result of the coordination of *with pencil and paper, or (with) a calculator*. The numbers are all nouns so the phrases *by 2* and *by 3* are also PPs. In Text 7.3, *sweaty hands* is a NP, with *sweaty hands* a PP as is in *old rucksacks and handbags, At this stage* and in *two days' time*.

7.4.3 Adjective phrases

You will recall that these have the same basic structure as NPs (modifier + HEAD) but in an AdjP of course the head word must be an adjective. Text 7.2 provides some examples. *Mainly attributable* and *staunchly Lancastrian* are both adjective phrases with premodification: the attribution cannot be entirely attributed to the efforts of the clergy and those clergy were not just Lancastrian but were very staunch or strong in the Lancastrian tendencies. Text 7.3 provides more examples: *still edible* and *quite nice*.

7.4.4 Adverb phrases

The same structure of modifier + HEAD requires an adverb as the head word in these phrases. Some created examples would make the point both very quickly and quite clearly but since there are now two examples in this sentence of AdvPs (*very quickly* and *quite clearly*) we do not need to make up any others. The two AdvPs have the same structure so one tree diagram (➜ Figure 7.3) will show how the structure works.

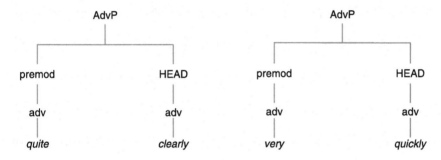

Figure 7.3 Adverb phrase structure

7.4.5 Verb group (VG)

The verb group is the most complex of all the group structures in English and has the greatest effect on clause structure (to be discussed later in this chapter ➜ 7.5).

Remember that a phrase (or group in the case of verbs) can consist of one or more words. Therefore, with examples taken from the texts in this chapter, the VG can consist of a single lexical (or main) verb (e.g. *think, know, consecrate, accuse, depict, live, see, launch, whimper*) or there can be more than one word in which case there will be auxiliary verbs before the lexical verb (e.g. *can explore, can prove, was elected, had moved, couldn't be, hadn't* [...] *told, wouldn't be going*). These verb groups (whether one word or more than one word) are finite because they show tense: *can* is the present tense, *had, could, would* all in the past. In a finite verb group in English, the first word in the group always carries tense.

Non-finite verb groups do not show tense; finite verb groups do. Table 7.1 will help you with this distinction but examples are always helpful. These examples (12 and 13 below) are largely taken from the texts in this chapter: a few are invented for the purpose but are typical of so many utterances heard every day.

(12)   non-finite VGs include
    (a)   V+ing forms as single-word VG
               e.g. <u>going</u> through every pocket (Text 7.3)
               <u>pulling</u> books out of my bookcase (Text 7.3)
    (b)   V+en forms as single word VG
               e.g. Once <u>bitten,</u> twice shy
               When <u>cooked</u>, remove from pan and serve.
    (c)   Imperative forms
    e.g.   <u>Divide</u> it by 2 (Text 7.1).
               stop. (Text 7.1)
    (d)   infinitives:
    e.g.   <u>To be</u>, or not <u>to be.</u>
               Better <u>to travel</u> hopefully than <u>to arrive.</u>
(13)   finite VGs include
    (a)   those in the present tense
               It <u>goes</u> like this (Text 7.1)
               Here<u>'s</u> a famous example (Text 7.1).
               They <u>think</u> they <u>know</u> the answer (Text 7.1)
               The high quality of the painting <u>suggests</u> (Text 7.2)
    (b)   those in the past tense
               I <u>thought</u> of 11 (Text 7.1)
               The bridge <u>collapsed</u> (Text 7.2)
               it <u>couldn</u>'t be (Text 7.3)
               <u>hadn</u>'t my mother always told me … ? (Text 7.3)
               I <u>was</u> whimpering with terror (Text 7.3)
               I <u>wouldn</u>'t be going. (Text 7.3)

Remember that there are only two tenses in the English language – present tense and past tense – to talk about past, present and future events. Although there are clearly ways in which we can use English to talk about future time, this is not the same as there being a future tense in the structure of English. How do you talk about your plans for this evening or for the coming weekend? Do Activity 7.12 to help you be clear about this.

ACTIVITY 7.12 🔑

Think about your plans for the future whether it be the coming weekend, your upcoming summer holidays or your life plan. Rather than just writing a list of targets in note form for yourself (e.g. shopping, summer in France, professor by age 45), imagine that you are writing a personal statement for someone else to read and so write in full sentences.

When there is more than one word in a VG, we say that there is an auxiliary verb and a lexical verb. We cannot use the same terminology of modifier and head as we did when discussing other types of phrases as the relationship between the elements in a VG are different from the relationships in NPs, AdjPs and AdvPs. This also explains why we talk about verb groups and not verb phrases (though other approaches to syntax and grammar will use the term *verb phrase*).

There can be more than one auxiliary in a VG and there are two main types of auxiliaries in English: primary auxiliaries and modal auxiliaries.

At the end of this brief consideration of primary auxiliaries and modal auxiliaries, we will consider how auxiliaries and tense combine within a VG.

Primary auxiliary verbs: do, have and be

The auxiliary *do* has three main uses in English:

(a) It can be used to make the negative form of a lexical verb.
(b) It can be used to form the interrogative (the question form) if there is no other auxiliary in the VG.
(c) It can be used to form a tag question if there is no other auxiliary in the VG.

To make the negative, *do* combines with the base form of the verb as in Text 7.1 *we still don't know the answer* and in Text 7.3 *when it didn't (appear)*. In Modern English we no longer say 'we know not the answer' or 'it appeared not' though such structures were certainly possible in older forms of English (→ Chapter 17). In the example from Text 7.1 (*we don't know the answer*) the auxiliary is in the present tense and in that from Text 7.3 (*it didn't appear*) it is in the past tense. In any finite VG the first element in the group carries tense so you would never find *it did not appeared* in a grammatical Modern English utterance.

Remember that an asterisk is used in linguistics to indicate an ill-formed formulation.

When *do* is used to form questions it comes at the beginning of the VG as in these examples which all relate in some way to Texts 7.1, 7.2 and 7.3:

(14) Did you use pencil and paper or a calculator?
(15) Do we know the answer yet?
(16) How did his royal connections cloud his triumph?
(17) Why did the bridge collapse?
(18) When did you look in the 'official things' drawer?
(19) Where do you keep your passport?

ACTIVITY 7.13

Read the first lines of Kipling's *I keep six honest serving men* from *The Elephant's Child*:

I keep six honest serving-men
(They taught me all I knew);
Their names are What and Why and When
And How and Where and Who.

Make at least two questions for each 'honest serving man' using the auxiliary *do* which relate to one the three texts we have been using in this chapter. Some examples might help:

> (20) Why are simple questions not always easy to answer?
> (21) When did William fall ill?
> (22) What did her mother mean about the river and the water?

Tag questions are more complicated in English than in many other languages. In French, whatever the tense and the polarity you simply add *n'est-ce pas?* and in German *nicht wahr?* Maybe the now often used *innit* is leading to a similar simplification.

There is variability in tag questions in international forms of English, where they often have simple forms as in other languages (→ 18).

Adding a tag question is one way of converting a **declarative** statement into an **interrogative** one. Consider the sentence in Text 7.2 *William was elected to the archbishopric in 1143.* The VG is *was elected* so to add a tag question to this sentence, use the auxiliary from the VG, reverse the polarity (i.e. if it is positive in the declarative clause, make it negative and vice versa) and add a pronoun that refers back to the subject (see later in this chapter) so you add *wasn't he?* In Text 7.3, find the sentence *Except it couldn't be* and add a tag question to that: use the modal verb from the VG, reverse the polarity, add a pronoun to refer back to the subject and so you end up with *Except it couldn't be, could it?*. In any clause where there is no auxiliary in the VG, you have to use *do* as an auxiliary in the tag. In Text 7.2, find the part of the sentence *three of his main opponents all died.* The VG consists of one word only – *died* – and so you have to provide the auxiliary for the tag and the tag has to be in the same tense as the verb in the original VG under discussion (in this case, past tense) to produce a tag question thus: *Three of his main opponents all died, didn't they?*.

ACTIVITY 7.14 0—╥

Add tag questions to the following clauses (drawn from the three texts in this chapter):

(a) They think they know the answer.
(b) No one can prove it.
(c) I thought of 11.
(d) Nobody was hurt.
(e) It had sat in that drawer.
(f) I rummaged through the bills.

The auxiliary verb *have* (in either present or past tense) is used to create the perfective aspect of the verb when it is combined with {-en} (or the past participle) form of a verb. Trask (1997: 21) defines aspect as being 'the way in which an action or a situation is distributed in time'. Look at the first paragraph of Text 7.3. There are two examples of VGs with auxiliary *have*: *my sister had moved there* and *it had sat there*. Ask yourself the question 'when did my sister move to New York in relation to the time of writing?'. The answer is four months before. Even without the NP *four months previously* the reader knows that the sister's move to New York predates the state of being about to visit New York because of the use of the perfective aspect with the auxiliary *had*. This would have been understood by a reader even if the text had read 'My sister had moved there and I was going to spend Christmas with her'. In other words, the use of the perfective aspect helps a reader/hearer to understand the order of events even if there is no explicit use of time adverbials (more on these later in this chapter). Similarly, we can discuss the use of 'It had sat in that drawer': the writer knows that she used the passport on her last visit to Greece and in the intervening period of time from that visit to the then present time (the time of looking for the passport) the passport had been in the drawer. Why writers might choose to present events of a narrative in non-chronological order will be considered in Chapter 8.

The observant reader will have noticed in Line 10 in the previous paragraph an apparent use of the perfective which does not appear to be linked to sequence of events. True. The relevant sentence is *This would have been understood by a reader even if the text had read …* and the importance here is that we were discussing conditions – in this case the interestingly named *impossible condition*. The published text is as it appears in Text 7.3 so it is impossible that it could appear, as suggested above, without the adverbial and so the different forms of the verbs indicate the impossibility of that condition. There are conditional sentences in Text 7.1 but these are quite possible conditions: *If the number is even, divide it by 2* and *If the number is odd, divide it by 3 and add 1*. Hence the verbs are in the present tense in the conditional clause (the clause that begins with *if*), which is followed by the imperative form of the following verbs: both the condition and the resulting action are quite possible and hence the different uses of tense.

ACTIVITY 7.15 🔑

List the events in the first paragraph of Text 7.3 in chronological order of occurrence, which may or may not be the order in which the events are narrated in the text.

The auxiliary verb *be* is used in two ways: to form the progressive aspect of the lexical verb or to form the passive voice of the lexical verb. Let us consider progressive aspect first: the auxiliary *be* is combined with the {-ing} form of the main (lexical) verb. Look at Text 7.3 for a clear example of this: *I was living in London*. Progressive aspect often indicates a state of affairs that was current and incomplete at the time of another action – in this case where the author was living at the time of the proposed visit to New York. The living in London was not completed: if it had been then it might have been formulated as *I lived in London before I went to New York* (and in this sentence you have just had another example of an impossible condition with the use of auxiliary *had*).

The second use of auxiliary *be* is in the passive voice when *be* combines with the {V-en} form of the verb. Voice is a two-part system within the English language that allows the message-giver (➜ 1) to choose how much information to give and how to provide it. Consider these two sentences which are obviously linked in terms of meaning:

(23)   Anne spoke the words clearly.
(24)   The words were spoken clearly.

Sentence (23) is in the active voice with the speaker (in this case, basically it is the person performing the action, the 'do-er') clearly named and in subject position (➜ 7.5.1); sentence (24) is in the passive voice and the actor or the 'do-er' (in this sentence, the speaker) is not named and another participant in the process appears in subject position.

Look at Text 7.2 where there are many examples of the passive voice: *William was elected* [...] *his position was consecrated* [...] *he was deposed* [...] *William was sent* [...]. In each example the reader is not told who carried out the action (who elected him? who consecrated his position? who deposed him? who sent him?) and perhaps this does not matter in this narration of historical events. The important focus for the narrative is that the events occurred – the election, the consecration, the deposing and the sending all happened. Narrators have a variety of ways of relating the events and this use of the passive voice is but one of the options at their disposal (➜ 8).

ACTIVITY 7.16 ⚓

From the second part of Text 7.2, identify at least two uses of the passive voice. Why do you think the writer has chosen this form rather than the active voice?

ACTIVITY 7.17 ⚓

Consider this sentence from a letter received recently:
The toilets have been refurbished and the lighting will be improved before the nights draw in.

Identify two examples of the passive voice and one of perfective aspect.

One problem is recognizing whether *do, be* or *have* are being used as primary auxiliary verb or as lexical verb in any given verb group. Consider the following examples, invented to illustrate the difficulty. The auxiliary use has been underlined in each example:

(25) <u>Did</u> you do the washing-up?
(26) What <u>are</u> you having for tea?
(27) I <u>have</u> done my homework.
(28) They <u>don</u>'t have cakes in the window today.
(29) <u>Have</u> you ever been to Paris?
(30) I <u>am</u> not being difficult.

Modal auxiliary verbs

Modal auxiliaries allow for a range of meanings to be expressed. Obligation can be expressed through the use of the modals *must, should* or *ought to* (think of the writing of national laws or of rules for a society, or of the guidelines as to how you should present your work for assessment); permission can be sought and granted through the use of *can, could* or *may* (think of how you ask permission to leave a seminar, to open a window); and possibility or prediction through the use the modal auxiliaries *will, may, might, could* (think of the language of horoscopes or the weather forecast). In conditional sentences, such as

Table 7.4 Auxiliary verbs: tense

	Present tense	**Past tense**
primary auxiliaries	am, is, are do, does have, has	was, were did had
modal auxiliaries	can may must, have (to) shall will *(no present tense form)*	could might had (to) should would ought to

What is the difference between *must* and *have to*? Is there any difference between *You must eat five portions of vegetables every day* and *You have to eat five portions of vegetables every* day? For some people there will be a difference, for others not.

Now consider the negative forms such as *You must not run riot* and *You don't have to run riot*. Most people will see a difference in the meaning. There is no past tense form of *must* – *had to* fills that gap.

'I would not do that if I were you' the modal *would* appears and *shall* is still used in offers, such as 'Shall I open the door for you?'.

Auxiliaries and tense

If the auxiliary is the first verb in a finite VG then the auxiliary will carry the tense marker for the VG. So, odd as it may seem in relation to how you will find the auxiliaries are used, it might be helpful to have an indication of which forms are in which tense (remember that there are only two tenses in English). Table 7.4 shows this.

7.5 SIMPLE CLAUSES

Working up the hierarchy of rank (Figure 7.1), the next level is that of the clause. A clause is part of a sentence that looks in many ways like a sentence itself: in other words, perhaps, a clause is a sentence inside a sentence. A sentence must contain a finite verb group: a clause within a sentence may be finite or non-finite (remember that the opposite to *finite* in linguistic terminology is *non-finite* not *infinite*).

Sentences are perhaps easier to recognize than clauses – at least in writing. A flippant, structurally unhelpful but perhaps-useful-for-beginners definition of a sentence is that it begins with a capital letter and ends with a full stop: this works in writing but not in speech (think about it!) and so clauses are much more use for analysis of speech than sentences. They are also, despite the complexities, often easier to analyse which is another good reason for basing an analysis on the clause rather than the sentence.

We will address simple structures first. From Text 7.2, we will consider the sentence *William blessed the crowd and nobody was hurt – his only lifetime miracle*. If, for the moment, we ignore the final NP *his only lifetime miracle*, this one sentence contains two clauses: *William blessed the crowd and nobody was hurt*. The two clauses are linked together (con-joined) with the coordinating conjunction *and*. Each clause could, in fact, be written as a sentence and the text could be presented as two sentences like this:

Defining the concept of *sentence* is problematic. Look in various linguistic reference books to see how each one defines a sentence: there will be a lot of variation and a lot of opinion rather than fact. For each definition that you find, work out in what way the definition is limited and does not fit some of the usages that we find in English language in use.

William blessed the crowd. Nobody was hurt.

Each clause expresses a simple proposition. Each clause is declarative – each makes a statement. Each clause is finite (which tense? Yes – past tense) and centres on the VG, a comment that merits further discussion. Without the VG, there would not be a sentence but rather a collection of NPs: *William, the crowd, nobody*. When you take out the VG, you take out the central part of the proposition, which is the event, or the believing or the knowing (➜ 7.2.2). So perhaps a more meaningful definition of a clause and therefore of a sentence is that a clause expresses a single proposition and that a sentence consists of one or more clauses (*cf.* Figure 7.1) and therefore can express one or more propositions. To identify a clause therefore, it is crucial to be able to identify the VG and the elements which 'hang' on that VG. We will consider the various parts of a clause in a moment but first let us consider the first two sentences in Text 7.2. Each sentence has one VG and therefore each sentence has one clause. Sentence 3 has two VGs (*was consecrated* and *was deposed*) and therefore this sentence has two clauses. Sentence 4 has two VGs (*was sent, died*) and therefore has two clauses. Sentence 5 has one VG (*petitioned*) and therefore one clause.

> Be careful not to confuse *proposition* which is a term from philosophy used to indicate a single unit of meaning (e.g. *It's cold today* or *The dog ate the bone*) and *preposition* which is a word class (e.g. *on, under,* or *by*).

ACTIVITY 7.18 0—⊤

Read the rest of Text 7.2 and identify how many clauses there are in each sentence.

Clauses can be declarative (normally declaring something or making a statement), interrogative (questioning) or imperative (instructing) and these terms relate to what is called the MOOD of the clause (➜3.4). Any text may have (any number of) examples of all three moods. The first two sentences in this paragraph are in declarative mood (as are so many sentences in this book). Text 7.1 has several imperative clauses: e.g. *think of a number, apply the rule over and over again* and *divide it by 2* to give just 3 examples. If you look at Text 7.4 *Conversation during a quiet shift*, you will find some interrogative clauses: *So what part of Yorkshire are you from?* and *Didn't you used to come and buy cabbages off my Dad?* which contains two interrogative clauses as there are two VGs. You will also see how the author has managed to indicate questioning by punctuation without using the VG to make the interrogative explicit: e.g. *Whereabouts?* or *Oh, landed gentry, then?* as well as a similar approach to a declarative clause where the punctuation indicates questioning purpose despite the declarative form in *You lived in York?*.

Text 7.4 Conversation during a quiet shift (Pannett 2008: 207)

	It was a quiet shift, which suited me fine. The longer I spent with this
2	particular WPC the better.
	'So what part of Yorkshire are you from?' I asked as I dawdled back towards
4	Pickering.
	'I was born a Yorkie.'
6	'Oh aye?'
	'Yep, the old Fulford Maternity Hospital.'

8   I was born there too, but I thought <u>it would sound daft</u> if <u>I told her that</u>.
     'Now a Designer Outlet or something,' I said.
10   'Something like that.'
     'And <u>you lived in York</u>?'
12   'No, <u>I was a country girl</u>. Still am at heart.'
     'Whereabouts?' 'Huby. You know it?'
14   I laughed aloud. 'That's amazing.'
     'Well, someone has to live there.'
16   'No, I mean … I am <u>from Crayke</u>.'
     Ann slapped the dashboard. 'I knew <u>I recognised your name</u>. <u>Didn't you use</u>
18   <u>to come and buy cabbages off my Dad</u>?'
     'Now that does take me back. No, <u>that wasn't me</u>. <u>It'd be my brother</u>. He
20   was starting out in fruit and veg deliveries. Traded in the old Viva and got a
     Bedford van. <u>Right old rattle-trap</u>. And you say <u>he bought stuff off your</u>
22   <u>Dad</u>?'
     'Aye, spuds, caulies, all that. <u>We had a small farm</u>.'
24   'Oh, landed gentry, eh?'
     'Oh yes indeed. We had a paddock too.'

7.5.1 Subject (of the clause)

You will recall from section 7.2 above that all syntacticians and grammarians from classical times onwards have generally accepted the idea that a clause can be analysed into its component parts and that initially a clause can be divided into two parts: the subject and the rest of the clause (sometimes called the predicate but in generative grammar referred to as the verb phrase which is why we use the term VG to avoid confusion and to remain consistent with functional grammar labelling). In an active sentence the subject is the doer of the verb (in a passive sentence it is never the do-er of the verb – one of the ways of determining the **voice** of the clause).

There are several ways (or tests) to identify the subject of a clause. We discuss three.

Test 1: Find the verb group of the clause (essentially we would imagine that you did this in Activity 7.18 when you worked out how many clauses there are in each sentence in Text 7.2) and ask the question 'who/what <u>verbs</u>?'. In the single-clause sentence in Text 7.1 You can explore it with pencil and paper, or a calculator, you can find the verb group (can explore), you ask the question Who/What can explore? and the answer is you. Therefore, you is the grammatical subject of the clause (= sentence in this case). In Text 7.2 in the sentence Osbert, the Archdeacon, a long-standing opponent of William, was accused of poisoning the chalice – find the VG (was accused), ask Who/what was accused? and the answer is Osbert, the Archdeacon a long-standing opponent of William.

Test 2: Add a tag question to a declarative clause and the pronoun in the tag question always refers back to the subject of that declarative clause. Add a tag question to You can explore it with pencil and paper, or a calculator and you end up with You can explore it with pencil and paper, or a calculator, can't you?: the pronoun in the tag question

The very long subject in the sentence from Text 7.2 actually demonstrates the phenomenon of NPs in apposition. Usually you find two NPs in apposition but in this sentence (unusually) there are three: *Osbert + the Archdeacon + a long-standing opponent of William*. Because the NPs are in apposition (i.e. they form three ways of referring to the same person, in this case) they are all part of the subject of the clause.

always refers back to the subject of the declarative clause therefore You is the subject of the declarative clause.

Test 3: Subject–verb agreement can be useful in examples where the verb form changes according to the singular or plural nature of the subject of the clause. This is often the case in passive clauses, for example

The doctor <u>was</u> asked about the victims (the doctor is the subject)

The nurses <u>were</u> asked about the victims (the nurses is the subject).

Activity 7.19 ⚏

Use whichever test you prefer (or better still, practise using all of them) to determine the grammatical subject of all the finite clauses in the first three paragraphs in Text 7.2.

Our initial division of the clause is into two parts: subject and predicate (or 'the rest of the clause'). What goes into the predicate largely depends on the verb as it is the verb which determines which elements are needed in a clause – technically put, it is the verb which determines the COMPLEMENTATION (the completion) that is needed in the clause.

Some clauses contain verbs which do not need any further complementation. These verbs will be intransitive and will be naming processes with only one participant such as to *go*, (Text 7.1), to *die*, to *fall*, (Text 7.2) to *whimper* (Text 7.3), or others such as *sigh, pounce, sleep*. If we put these into simple single-claused sentences (here invented for the purpose of demonstration) we might create items such as:

(31)   Tom has fallen
(32)   Adam had slept
(33)   Emily was singing
(34)   Sophie is flying
(35)   Jake was swimming.

So, to return to our simple intransitive clauses, the analysis of each of them is the same. In traditional/classical analysis, the two parts of the clause are called the subject and the predicate and the division of the clause is as shown in Table 7.5.

Table 7.5 Clause structure: subject, predicate

	SUBJECT	PREDICATE
31	Tom	has fallen
32	Adam	had slept
33	Emily	was singing
34	Sophie	is flying
35	Jake	was swimming

7.5.2 Finite and predicator

The term *subject* has already been explained. The predicate is divided into two parts – the **Finite** and the **Predicator**. The Finite is the part of the VG which carries tense. In our short, created-for-the-purpose clauses with intransitive verbs, each VG consists of two verbs: an auxiliary verb (which is both finite and the Finite) and the lexical verb or the Predicator (P). Despite the different propositions and the different tenses, the clauses all have the same structure, as shown in Table 7.6.

If there is only a single word in the VG, say in a clause such as *Jonathan laughed* then the analysis would look like Table 7.7 with F/P indicating that the Finite and the Predicator are fused into a single verb/word.

There can only ever be one Finite in a VG. There can be more than one auxiliary verb as a very forced example shows: *your assignment grades will have been being considered by several examiners*. This example has four auxiliaries (*will have been being*) but only the first auxiliary (*will*) is the finite. The lexical verb is *considered*.

Table 7.6 Clause structure: subject + finite + predicator (S F P)

These rows show the *clauses being analysed.*	31	Tom	has	fallen
	32	Adam	had	slept
	33	Emily	was	sighing
	34	Sophie	is	flying
	35	Jake	was	swimming
This row shows the elements of *clause structure.*		S Subject	F Finite	P Predicator
This row shows which type of *phrase is used in each element of* *clause structure. Note that the VG is* *divided into aux(iliary) + lex(ical).*		NP	VG	
			aux	lex

Table 7.7 Clause structure: subject + finite/predicator (S F/P)

This row shows the clause *being analysed.*	Jonathan	laughed	
This row shows the elements *of clause structure. The* *notation F/P shows that F and* *P are merged into one word.*	S Subject	F/P	
		Finite	Predicator
This row shows which type of *phrase is used in each element* *of clause structure.*	NP	VG	
		lex	

7.5.3 Complements

Transitive verbs must be complemented (or completed) to make sense: there must be something that comes after them in the clause. Transitive verbs usually express processes with two or more obligatory participants. Therefore, a complement is obligatory with transitive verbs. There are three different types of complement and which type is used depends on the verb and the meaning being expressed. We discuss each type in turn and we encourage you to resist the temptation to rush over the detail.

Complement direct object (Cdo)

The first type of complementation is with what is called a complement direct object. This is found in clauses reporting two-participant processes such as:

(36)   *You can explore it* (from Text 7.1 where the two participants in the process are *you* and *it*).
(37)   *Apply the following rules* (from Text 7.1 where in an imperative clause the two participants in the process are *the following rules* and the unnamed reader/hearer or the implicit *you* who is to carry out the instruction).
(38)   *Divide it* (from Text 7.1 where in an imperative clause the two participants in the process are *it* and the unnamed reader/hearer or the implicit *you* who is to carry out the instruction).
(39)   *William blessed the crowd* (from Text 7.2 where the two participants in the process are *William* and *the crowd* (the latter participant involving more than one person)).

The question test for Cdo would be generically *who/what does subject verb?* and the answer will give you the Cdo. For example in (36) if you ask *What can you* (= subject of the clause) *explore?*, the answer is *it* and therefore the NP *it* is functioning as Cdo in this clause. In (39) if you ask *Who/what does William* (= subject of the clause) *bless?* the answer is *the crowd* and therefore the NP *the crowd* is functioning as Cdo in this clause.

Table 7.8 might look complicated but it shows you how each of these examples would be analysed and how that analysis might be presented in box format.

Table 7.8 Clause structure: subject + finite + predicator + complement direct object + complement direct object (S F P Cdo)

These rows show the clauses being analysed.	(36)	You	can explore	it
	(37)		Apply	the following rules
	(38)		Divide	it
	(39)	William	blessed	the crowd
This row shows the elements of clause structure.		(36) S	(36) F P	(36) Cdo
			(37) P	(37) Cdo
			(38) P	(38) Cdo
		(39) S	(39) F/P	(39) Cdo
		S(ubject)	F(inite) and P(redicator)	C(omplement) d(irect) o(bject)
This row shows which phrase type is used in each element of clause structure and the structure of that phrase.		NP (36) pron (37) (38) (39) N prop	VG	NP (36) pron (37) det + adj + n (38) pron (39) det + n

Complement indirect object (Cio)

Three participant processes can be typified by thinking of the process of giving where the three participants are the *donor*, the *gift* itself and the *recipient*. Surprisingly (or perhaps not – think about the kinds of texts we have been considering) there are few examples of this construction in any of the three texts that we have been studying so far. However, in Text 7.3 you can find

(40)   I told myself that it was here.

and if you were to read to the end of the short story from which Text 7.3 is taken, you can find the following examples – all containing a complement indirect object (for the recipient):

(41)   I told my boss the whole terrible story.
(42)   We will organise you a new passport.
(43)   They gave me my pristine new passport.

In a simple declarative statement, the donor will usually be the subject, the gift will be the direct object (Cdo) and the recipient will be the indirect object (Cio). Table 7.9 shows the analysis.

Table 7.9 Clause structure: subject + finite + predicator + complement indirect object + complement direct object (S F P Cio Cdo)

These rows show the clauses being analysed.	(40) (41) (42) (43)	I I We They	told told will organise gave	myself my boss you me	that it was here the whole story a new passport my pristine new passport.
This row shows the elements of clause structure.		S	(40) F/P (41) F/P (42) F P (43) F/P	Cio	Cdo
This row shows which type of phrase is used in each element of clause structure and the structure of that phrase.		NP	VG	NP (40) pron (41) det + n (42) pron (43) pron	NP (40) clause* (41) det + adj + n (42) det + adj + n (43) det + adj + adj + n

*clauses inside other clauses will be addressed in section 7.6.3

These two famous examples look very similar in structure:
(i) Peter is easy to please (ii) Peter is eager to please.
The underlying structure is very different as you will work out when you consider who is pleasing who. In (i) Peter is being pleased whereas in (ii) he is doing the pleasing. Another example that what looks straightforward in language is not always so.

Intensive complement (Cint)

The third and final type of complement is called an intensive complement (Cint). In terms of meaning, this structure realizes single participant processes where an attribute or quality of the participant is being provided. We can consider these extracts:

(44)   *the number is even* (from Text 7.1)
(45)   *the number is odd* (from Text 7.1).
(46)   *The Ros of Helmsley family were long-standing benefactors* (from Text 7.2)
(47)   *it was non-changeable and non-refundable* (from Text 7.3).

All the examples talk about a single participant and the purpose of the clause is to provide further information about each. In a similar format to that used before, the structure of the clause can be shown in a box diagram as in Table 7.10.

Table 7.10 Clause structure: subject + finite + predicator + complement intensive (S F P Cint)

These rows show the clauses being analysed.	(44) (45) (46) (47)	the number the number the Ros family it	is is were was	even odd long-standing benefactors non-changeable and non-refundable.
This row shows the elements of clause structure.		S	(44) F/P* (45) F/P* (46) F/P* (47) F/P*	Cint
This row shows which type of phrase is used in each element of clause structure and the structure of that phrase.		NP (44) det + n (45) det + n (46) det + mod + n (47) pron	VG	(44) AdjP (45) AdjP (46) NP (47) AdjP

* Strictly speaking these would be analysed as just F in rigorous functional analysis, for reasons too complex to go into here.

7.5.4 Adjuncts

The final element for analysis in clause structure is that of ADJUNCT – an *optional* element (as opposed to those elements discussed so far which are obligatory (depending on the meaning being expressed and therefore the central verb in the clause)).

Adjuncts give information about time, place, manner, reason, cause, effect, agency, result and similar meanings. However, information about time and place might not always be an Adjunct in clause structure. Consider the NP *the next day* in these two examples:

(48)   He arrived the next day.
(49)   He enjoyed the next day.

In (48), *the next day* is functioning here as an adjunct because the NP tells you when the action happened (= when he arrived) and could be omitted and still leave a grammatical clause *He arrived*. In contrast, in (49), you only know that he enjoyed something (= the next day) and there is no indication of time or of any of the other meanings often expressed in adjunct position in clause structure. In (49), therefore, *the next day* is functioning as Cdo (the NP answers the question *what did he enjoy?*).

There are several examples of adjuncts in the texts we have been analysing in this chapter such as the examples here where the adjuncts have been underlined for clarity:

(50)   you can explore it <u>with pencil and paper, or a calculator</u> (Text 7.1)
(51)   apply the following rules <u>over and over again</u> (Text 7.1)
(52)   his position was consecrated <u>in 1143</u> (Text 7.2)
(53)   he was deposed <u>by Pope Eugenius III</u> (Text 7.2)
(54)   many of whom fell <u>into the river</u> (Text 7.2)
(55)   (he) died <u>a week later</u> (Text 7.2)
(56)   the matter went <u>to court</u> (Text 7.2)

Table 7.11 shows the analysis and also shows the adjunctival meaning. Please don't be scared of what looks like a complicated table! Just work your way through it carefully.

A Middle English (➔ 17) intransitive use of the verb *enjoy* appears to be being revived: where people used to say *enjoy the wedding* (or whatever event was to be enjoyed) you can often hear simply *enjoy* nowadays.

Table 7.11 Clause structure: subject + finite + predicator + complement + adjunct (S F P C A)

These rows show the clauses being analysed.	(50)	you	can explore	it	with pencil and paper or a calculator
	(51)		apply	the following rules	over and over again
	(52)	his position	was consecrated		in 1143
	(53)	he	was deposed		by Pope Eugenius III
	(54)	many of whom	fell		into the river
	(55)	he	died		a week later
	(56)	the matter	went		to court
This row shows the elements of clause structure.		S	(50) F P (51) F/P (52) F P (53) F P (54) F/P (55) F/P (56) F/P	(50) Cdo (51) Cdo	(50) A (instrument) (51) A (time) (52) A (time) (53) A (agent) (54) A (place) (55) A (time) (56) A (place)

(Continued)

Table 7.11 continued

This row shows which type of phrase is used in each element of clause structure.		NP	VG	(50) NP (51) NP	(50) PP (51) AdvP (52) PP (53) PP (54) PP (55) NP (56) PP

The numbers (which are nouns) must be Cdo as *4,2,1,4,2,1* answer the question for Cdo *What does subject* (we) *verb* (get)?

Whilst it might seem obvious that AdvPs should be used to make adjuncts, this is not always the case: NPs and PPs can often fulfil this function in a clause, as in (48).

Whilst there is usually at most only one of each of S, VG, Cdo, Cio or Cint in each clause there can often be more than one adjunct in any given clause. Consider the following clause (from Text 7.1):

(57)   From there we get 4, 2, 1, 4, 2, 1, indefinitely.

The first two words in the clause, the PP *from there*, and the final word in the clause, the AdvP *indefinitely* both function as adjuncts. In terms of S F P C A, the analysis of this clause is A S F/P Cdo A.

Activity 7.20 🔑

Read Text 7.4 and then

1   Analyse the <u>single-underlined</u> clauses in terms of S F P C A. You can choose whether you use box diagrams or tree diagrams to show the structure.
2   Analyse the <u>double-underlined</u> phrases in terms of premodifier, HEAD and postmodifier. Again, you can choose whether to use box diagrams or tree diagrams.

7.6 NOT SO SIMPLE CLAUSES

It is very clear that not all clauses are simple clauses like the ones that have been analysed so far in this chapter. Some clauses can become very complex through a range of linguistic processes and structures. Recursion and relative clauses were mentioned earlier in the chapter and a little more detail is provided here. We will also consider where a clause might be put into a clause at the level of S F P C A.

7.6.1 Recursion

While this term is used more often in generative grammar, it is a useful concept as it occurs very often in English (as well as in other languages). According to the hierarchy of rank (Figure 7.1), words combine to form phrases but as was discussed earlier, NPs can contain post-modifying PPs as in NPs such as *the man in the moon* and *the Houses of Parliament.* So the NP contains a PP – in other words one phrase is inside another phrase. Tree diagrams make this clear (Figures 7.4 and 7.5).

Similar examples occur in other types of phrase as in the invented example *quite clearly upset* where an AdvP premodifies an adjective in an AdjP (as shown in Figure 7.6).

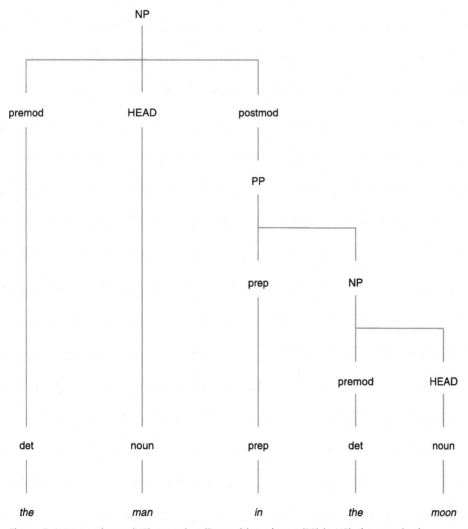

Figure 7.4 Noun phrase (NP) recursion (Preposition phrase (PP) in NP) *the man in the moon*

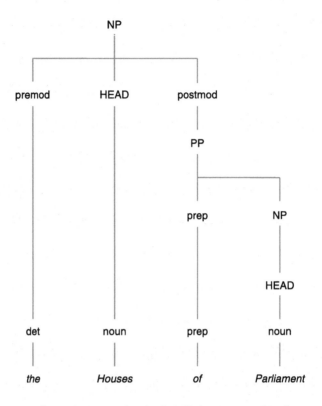

Figure 7.5 Noun phrase (NP) recursion (PP in NP) *the Houses of Parliament*

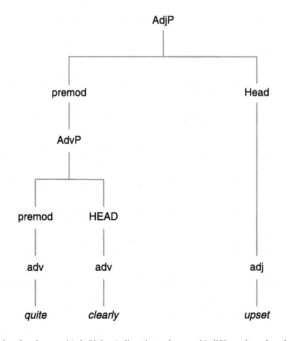

Figure 7.6 Adverb phrase (AdvP) in Adjective phrase (AdjP) *quite clearly upset*

> ## Activity 7.21 0—ᴛ
>
> Draw tree diagrams to show the structure of the following phrases:
>
> 1   From Text 7.2 – the NP *a long-standing opponent of William* and the PP *during a national period of revival of the cult of St William.*
> 2   From Text 7.3 – the NP *Three nights before the off* and the PP *through every pocket of every item of clothing in my wardrobe.*
> 3   There are no examples of recursion in Text 7.1. Can you suggest why this might be?

7.6.2 Relative clauses (a clause inside a noun phrase)

Not only can a phrase appear within a phrase but a clause can also, in certain contexts, appear within a phrase. Clauses which appear in the post-modification part of a NP are called RELATIVE CLAUSES. This does go against the hierarchy of rank (Figure 7.1) as it has so far been presented but it is certainly possible – and indeed it is quite a common construction in English and many other languages.

Relative clauses are clauses which post-modify the headword in noun phrases.

Text 7.5 from *Yes Prime Minister* has a large number of relative clauses in a comparatively short space of text (in the final paragraph of the excerpt in Text 7.5). This foreshadows matters that will be addressed in Chapter 8 – how linguistic patterning can be used in a text and in this particular text it is for comic effect. Read Text 7.5 first and then consider the following comments.

Text 7.5 'The British press according to Jim Hacker' (from *Yes Prime Minister*) (Lynn and Jay 1987)

	Bernard tried to comfort me. 'Prime Minister, I must say that I think you
2	worry too much about what the papers say.' I smiled at him. How little he
	knows. 'Bernard,' I said with a weary smile, 'I *have* to worry about them,
4	especially with the Party Conference looming.....'
	But Humphrey was unflappable. 'Let's not worry about it until there's
6	something more than a rumour. May I show you the Cabinet Agenda?'
	'Please. Humphrey,' I said. 'The papers are far more important.'
8	'With respect, Prime Minister,' replied Humphrey, impertinently, riled by
	my refusal to look at his silly agenda, 'they are not. The only way to
10	understand newspapers is to remember that they pander to their readers'
	prejudices.'
12	Humphrey knows nothing about newspapers. He's a Civil Servant. I'm a
	politician, I know all about them. I have to. They can make or break me. I
14	know exactly who reads them. *The Times* is read by the people who run the
	country. The *Daily Mirror* is read by the people who think they run the
16	country. The *Guardian* is read by the people who think they ought to run the
	country. The *Morning Star* is read by the people who think the country

18   ought to be run by another country. The *Independent* is read by people who
       don't know who is running the country but are sure they're doing it all
20   wrong. The *Daily Mail* is read by the wives of the people who run the
       country. The *Financial Times* is read by the people who own the country.
22   The *Daily Express* is read by the people who think the country ought to be
       run as it used to be run. The *Daily Telegraph* is read by the people who still
24   think it is their country. And the *Sun's* readers don't care who runs the
       country as long as she has big tits.

In an abbreviated way of showing how relative clauses work, each sentence has been re-presented here and the relative clause has been (following the conventions used in functional grammar) put inside double square brackets thus [[…]]. The headword of each NP containing a relative clause (which post-modifies the head noun in a NP, remember) is the word *people* and each relative clause begins with the RELATIVE PRONOUN *who*.

(57)   The *Times* is read by the people [[who run the country]].
(58)   The *Daily Mirror* is read by the people [[who think they run the country]].
(59)   The *Guardian* is read by the people [[who think they ought to run the country]].
(60)   The *Morning Star* is read by the people [[who think the country ought to be run by another country]].
(61)   The *Independent* is read by people [[who don't know who is running the country but are sure they're doing it all wrong]].
(62)   The *Daily Mail* is read by the wives of the people [[who run the country]].
(63)   The *FT* is read by the people [[who own the country]].
(64)   The *Daily Express* is read by the people [[who think the country ought to be run as it used to be run]].
(65)   The *Daily Telegraph* is read by the people [[who still think it is their country]].
(66)   And the *Sun's* readers don't care who runs the country providing she has big tits.

Figure 7.7 shows a tree diagram of the first of these sentences (57) and shows clearly how the relative clause fits inside the NP structure of which it is part. The tree diagram shows the same information in relation to the relative clause as the double brackets in (57) above. It also shows the clause structure: S F P C A. You will notice (if you read Figure 7.7 very carefully) that the label VG has not been put into the tree diagram as it was in the box diagrams (→ 7.5): F and P always form a VG *in some format* but it is the sheer multiplicity of possible formats that make it very difficult to put the label VG into a tree diagram – so we avoid the problem in this way.

Some of the relative clauses in Text 7.5 contain yet other clauses inside the relative clause itself but this phenomenon will be addressed later in section 7.6.4. The relative clauses in Text 7.5 all have the relative pronoun *who* in subject position within the relative clause. This is not always the case as, for example, in the NP *the house that Jack built*, the relative pronoun is *that*. Example (67) shows the relative clause by using brackets:

(67)   the house [[that Jack built]]

and Figure 7.8 shows the same structure in a tree diagram.

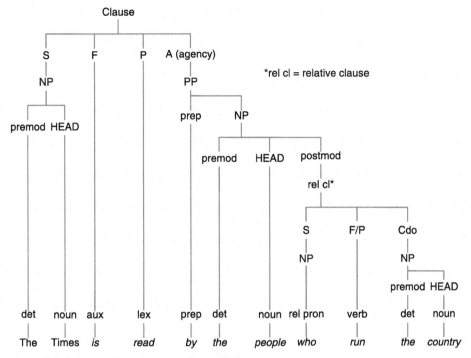

Figure 7.7 Relative clause in noun phrase (NP)

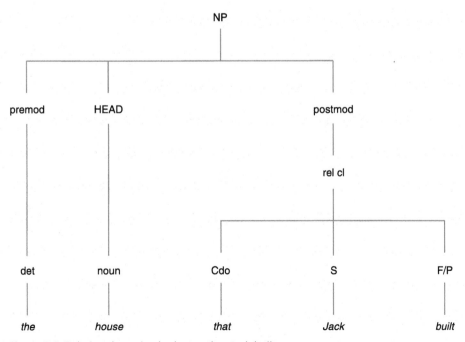

Figure 7.8 Relative clause in *the house that Jack built*

It should also now be clear how the double square brackets on the text relate to the clause boundaries as they are shown in the tree diagrams – two ways of representing exactly the same linguistic phenomenon. You can choose which way of representing syntactic structure you prefer (though your tutor may have their own views on this, of course).

In Text 7.5, notice how the syntactic pattern within the relative clauses becomes ever more complicated until a final much simpler clause delivers the punchline – and uses a completely different syntactic structure so to do.

7.6.3 Existential clauses

In section 7.5.1, we encountered problems when trying to find the syntactic subject of an existential clause. Consider the following clauses:

(68)   It simply was not there. (Text 7.3)
(69)   my passport wasn't here (Text 7.3)

In both these examples the adverbs *there* and *here* fit into an adjunct slot indicating place and the clauses can be analysed thus:

(68)   S A F/P A
(69)   S F/P A

Now consider the following clauses:

(70)   Here is a famous example (Text 7.1)
(71)   There is a tractor in the field.
(72)   There are some cowpats in the field.
(73)   There weren't any people by the tractor.
(74)   Wasn't there a driver with the tractor?

In 7.5.1, we considered three tests to enable us to find the subject of a clause, one of which involved asking the question *What verb(s)?* To work out an analysis for existential clauses, we need to address meaning. In (71, 72 and 73), it is arguable that the word *there* does not have its more usual meaning of *in that place*. This can be demonstrated by rewording (71) as *A tractor is in the field* and (72) as *Some cowpats are in the field*. In these reformulations, *there* is redundant: we know precisely where the tractor and the cowpats are because we are explicitly informed. In (71) and (72) *there* simply works as a place holder and is a form of empty subject: we could not say only **is a tractor in the field* as that would appear as an interrogative and for some reason the speaker/writer has chosen not to formulate the meaning as *a tractor is in the field*. There are various ways to annotate this and we recommend this version:

(S)	F	S	A(place)
There	is	a tractor	in the field

Examples (73) and (74) show the same existential clause structure in a negative clause (73) and an interrogative (74) clause.

7.6.4 Clauses in clauses

Examples of clauses inside clauses can also be found in Text 7.5.
I know exactly [[who reads them]].

(57)   *The Times* is read by the people [[who run the country]].
(58)   The *Daily Mirror* is read by the people [[who think [[they run the country]]]].
(59)   The *Guardian* is read by the people [[who think [[they ought to run the country]]]].
(60)   The *Morning Star* is read by the people [[who think [[the country ought to be run by another country]]]].
(61)   The *Independent* is read by people [[who don't know [[who is running the country]] but [[are sure [[they're doing it all wrong]]]].
(64)   The *Daily Express* is read by the people [[who think [[the country ought to be run [[as it used to be run]]]]]].
(65)   The *Daily Telegraph* is read by the people [[who still think [[it is their country]]]].
(66)   And the *Sun's* readers don't care [[who runs the country]] | |providing she has big tits| |.

The square bracketing shows how one clause nestles inside another in the place where you would expect to find a phrase. A brief explanation will clarify the analysis. In the introductory sentence, the subject is I, the verb group is the lexical verb *know*, *exactly* functions here as an adjunct and the clause *who reads them* functions as Cdo in that it gives information about what I know. Sentence (57) has a relative clause (➔ 7.6.2). Sentence (58) contains a relative clause *who think they run the country* which modifies the head word *people* in the NP and that relative clause itself contains a clause at Cdo *they run the country*. The rankshifted clause is shown by the brackets in (58) and by a tree diagram in Figure 7.9.

Bloor and Bloor (2013) use square brackets to indicate when a clause fits into a phrase structure and use double vertical lines to indicate a clause (inside a clause) boundary as is the case in (66). They use triple vertical lines to indicate a clause complex (more than one clause) – so (66) could be shown thus:

(66) |||And the *Sun's* readers don't care [[who runs the country]] ||providing she has big tits |||

where the triple vertical lines around the whole sentence indicate a clause cluster, the double vertical lines indicate a clause boundary inside that cluster and the double square brackets indicate a rankshifted clause inside phrase structure.

Perhaps for an introduction, syntactic life has become complicated enough. Chapter 8 will look at how clauses (with all the variation possible in their construction) can be used creatively to form text – the highest level in the hierarchy of rank.

Remember that you ask *what does Subject verb?* to find the Cdo and here the answer is *they run the country* which is a clause rather than the NP that you would expect e.g. they think great thoughts.

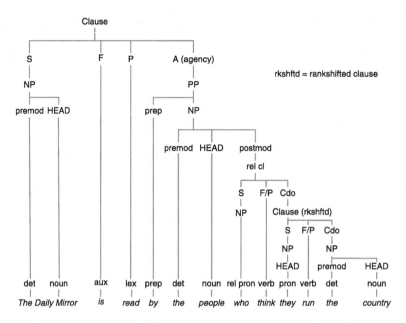

Figure 7.9 Rankshifted clause inside relative clause. Clauses which appear in a position where you would usually anticipate finding a phrase are called RANKSHIFTED CLAUSES

7.7 SUMMARY

In this chapter, you have seen how a simple clause can be constructed by choosing which words to use in which grammatical pattern and how the words themselves can impose a grammatical pattern. You have learnt some metalanguage to discuss your analyses. You have learnt some annotation to show how you have chosen to analyse the text in question (a bit like showing your workings in maths problems). You have learnt how to analyse individual phrases and clauses in terms of meaning and in terms of the syntax necessary to express that meaning. You have also – we hope – recognized the potential for creating very precise nuanced meaning by making careful selections from the syntactic options available to you as a user of language. Chapter 8 develops this by considering how individual sentences can be combined to form longer texts which are coherent and meaningful.

7.8 FURTHER ACTIVITY

Text 7.6 *Everybody, Somebody, Anybody and Nobody*

> This is a story about four people named Everybody, Somebody, Anybody
> and Nobody. There was an important job to be done and Everybody was
> sure that Somebody would do it. Anybody could have done it, but Nobody
> did it. Somebody got angry about that, because it was Everybody's job.
> Everybody thought Anybody could do it, but Nobody realized that
> Everybody wouldn't do it. It ended up that Everybody blamed Somebody
> when Nobody did what Anybody could have done.

Activity 7.22 ⚷

Read Text 7.6 and then carry out the following tasks.

(a) Identify the word classes of each word in Sentence (1) and (2). The names of the characters are syntactically interesting – using a good dictionary (➜ Read Me) may help you work out why.

(b) Identify the semantic processes in each clause in each sentence.

(c) Identify the verbs and verb groups in sentences (3) and (6), including aspect and tense.

(d) How many clauses are there in each of sentences (4), (5) and (6)?

(e) Analyse both clauses in sentence (4) – remember that *because* is a subordinating conjunction.

(f) Analyse the clause structure of sentences (5) and (6) which become increasingly complex.

> Remember that non-count nouns are also called mass nouns.

COMMENTARY ON ACTIVITIES

⚷ Remember that this symbol indicates that there is a commentary on the activity that you can find on the companion website at www.routledge.com/cw/merrison.

FURTHER READING and REFERENCES

Suggestions for further reading on the topics discussed in this chapter can be found on the companion website (www.routledge.com/cw/merrison).

Any piece of academic writing must always provide a list of publications to which reference has been made. Unusually and very unconventionally, this information is provided on the companion website (www.routledge.com/cw/merrison). Always ask your tutor about how you are to present references for any piece of work that you submit.

Chapter 8
Grammar: Clause to Text

Key Ideas in this Chapter

- What makes a text a text – why do not all sequences of sentences make a text?

- Who and what are texts for?

- How can a text be analysed? Some initial questions are offered to provide a starting point for budding discourse analysts.

8.1 INTRODUCTION

Before you read any further in this chapter, stop and think about your current knowledge of syntax and grammar. It is perfectly possible to understand texts without being able to analyse explicitly in detail how the language is being used – we all do that all the time. It is quite possible to analyse texts and show how they are constructed and therefore how they work as texts without any technical language but it is a lot easier if you have a language to talk about language (otherwise known as a **metalanguage**). You will find this chapter much easier to understand if you

- are reasonably confident about recognizing word classes
- can see (and explain) how individual words (or lexical items) combine to form phrases
- understand how phrases combine to form clauses and sentences.

Do Activity 8.1 before you go any further just to check that you are comfortable with these points.

Activity 8.1 🔑

Reread the first sentence of this introduction and then:

(a)   identify the word class of each word in the sentence
(b)   identify the phrases in the sentence
(c)   identify the clauses in the sentence
(d)   analyse the clauses (preferably in terms of S F P C A which is the functional system we use in this book and which is explained in Chapter 7).

S F P C A = **S**ubject **F**inite **P**redicator **C**omplement **A**djunct

---

If nothing else, this activity shows just how complex an easy-to-understand sentence can be to analyse.

If Activity 8.1 was scary, then perhaps it would be sensible to work carefully through the material covered in Chapter 7 before reading any further in this chapter. If Activity 8.1 seemed OK, you should now look at the **hierarchy of rank** (Figure 7.1) to make sure that you understand this principle. If Figure 7.1 is problematic, then perhaps it would again be sensible to check your understanding of the material presented in Chapter 7 before reading any more of this chapter.

But we will now presume that you are reasonably confident about basic syntax and are ready to take on the greater challenge (but perhaps also the greater fun) of seeing how all the elements combine to form clauses that can indeed become very complicated even in apparently simple texts. We start by considering complex clauses and sentences within texts. Then we can consider what makes a text a text and what other elements might be needed to complete a text (illustrations, for example ➜ 1).

8.2 COMPLEX CLAUSES AND SENTENCES

The hierarchy of rank (Figure 7.1) shows how smaller chunks of language combine to form larger units. Clearly, clauses can be combined to form sentences and this is evident in the text that forms this chapter and this whole book as well as in the individual texts chosen as data to demonstrate specific aspects of language in use. In this chapter, we provide a range of texts for analysis. The texts chosen here, as elsewhere, allow us to demonstrate certain points of analysis but importantly the vast majority are from language in use around us in our daily lives – very few (if any) have been written for the purpose of inclusion in this book (and where that is the case we make it very clear and provide the reasons for so doing).

Text 8.1 'Creative Deception'

CREATIVE DECEPTION

When the world was still very new the sun and the moon were equals and shone
2   with the same brightness. They were good friends and often went round together.
But one day everything changed.
4
They had decided to take their families bathing in the river. The sun took this family
6   out of sight, round a bend, so that they could get ready for their swim in private.
(In those days everybody was very polite.)
8
'I'll jump first,' said the sun as he went off. 'You'll know I'm in the water when it
10   starts to boil.'

12   But as soon as the sun was out of sight he ordered his children to cut down
branches from the trees. 'Set fire to them,' he said, 'and throw them into the river.
14   So they did.

16   The minute the moon saw the water bubbling and boiling, he jumped in. As he
swam about, clouds of steam swirled around his head. It was very hot 18 indeed.

20   When he climbed out again the moon discovered he had turned very pale. He
was frosty and cold and his brilliance was only a shadow of what it had been
22   before.

24   The sun mocked him. 'Now I will always be brighter than you,' he jeered. 'We didn't
go swimming at all!' It was a very cruel trick and the moon decided there and
26   then that he would have his revenge.

28   Time passed and a great famine came upon the earth. Every day people were dying.
The moon saw his chance to get his own back on the sun. But he hid his anger and paid
30   the sun a visit.

32   'We must kill our children,' he said, 'if we are to survive. There are too many
people to feed. Some must be sacrificed. I shall take my family upstream where
34   you once bathed in the river, and I shall kill them all. When you see the water running
with blood you will know that they are dead. Then you must start 36 killing yours.'

---

38 The sun agreed and when he saw that the river had turned red he killed every
    member of his family and threw their bodies into the water. But the moon
40 had done something very cruel. He had not killed his family at all. He had
    merely told his children to throw handfuls of red clay into the river, to make it
42 look like blood.

44 The sun, who had had so many wives and children, was now alone. And he is still
    alone, shining up there in the sky in great majesty. The moon is much less bright,
46 but he still has a family. These are the crowds of stars that shine with him, night after
    night.

Source: A Story from Cameroon retold by Ann Pilling and
taken from the *New Internationalist Calendar* 2001.

In the first paragraph of Text 8.1 'Creative Deception', some of the clauses are linked with coordinating **conjunctions** (*and, but, or*) to form compound clauses – sentences which contain coordinated clauses. The conjunctions are labelled *ccj* and the coordinated clauses are simply numbered in the order in which they appear in the sentence as shown in Table 8.1.

Other examples can be found in Text 8.1 on L21, L25, L29, L45–46, the latter example showing the clauses coordinated with *but*.

The combination of clauses within a written sentence or within a spoken **utterance** can become very complex, and speakers of English do not always realize the complexity of the structures they are using. In Text 8.1 L9–10, the sun says, 'You'll know I'm in the water when it starts to boil'. There are four distinct verb groups, so there are four clauses. The first two clauses can be dealt with first. In the process of *knowing* (➜ 7.2), there are two participants: the knower and the known or in other words, the knower knows something. That something, which in SFPCA would be analysed as complement direct object (Cdo) and normally realized by a noun phrase (NP), is in this example still Cdo in clause structure but it is realized by a clause and so it is enclosed in double square brackets to make clear that it is a RANKSHIFTED clause (a clause found inside another clause where you would normally expect to find a noun phrase). A similar phenomenon occurs later in the sentence: *to boil* must be the obligatory Cdo for the previous verb *start* and it must be obligatory because the VG *to boil* cannot simply be omitted from the sentence. If it were omitted, the sentence would

Table 8.1 Coordinated clauses

L1–2	The sun and the moon	were	equals	and	shone	with the same brightness		
	S	F	Cint	ccj	F/P	A(manner)		
	Clause 1				Clause 2			
L2	They	were	good friends	and	often	went	round	together
	S	F	Cint	ccj	A(time)	F/P	A(manner)	A(manner)
	Clause 1				Clause 2			

sound incomplete. This analysis of the sentence – with each rankshifted clause enclosed in double square brackets – is shown here:

> You'll know [[I'm in the water]] ‖ when it starts [[to boil]].

The final (non-rankshifted) clause in this sentence tells the moon *when* he will know that the sun is in the water (*when it starts to boil*), and therefore it is functioning in the same way as any other adjunct, giving, in this example, information about time. It is a subordinate clause because it cannot stand on its own as a sentence. Subordinate clauses are marked with double vertical lines. Triple vertical lines are used to indicate the boundaries of the entire clause complex. In written text, the clause complex boundary is co-terminous with the sentence boundary but when spoken language is being analysed there are no full stops to help us recognize the boundaries. The full analysis of this sentence, therefore, would look like this:

> ‖‖You'll know [[that I'm in the water]] ‖ when it starts [[to boil]] ‖‖

or in the now familiar box diagram (Table 8.2) or tree diagram (Figure 8.1) it looks like this:

Table 8.2 Complex clause structure 'Creative Deception'

L6	You	'll know	[[that	I	'm	in the water]]	when	it	starts	[[to boil]]
			[[	S	F	A(place)]]		S	F/P	[[Cdo]]
	S	F P	Cdo				A (time)			

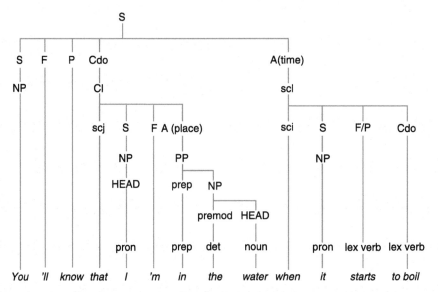

Figure 8.1 Complex clause structure 'Creative Deception'

Texts can, of course, be of very different lengths (➜ 7) and contain a mixture of simple and complex clauses. 'Creative Deception' is a simple story (though its philosophical message could be seen as quite important) but its language is a mixture of simple and complex clauses and sentences. Some texts – perhaps much shorter and even regarded as clichés – can look very simple but can be **ambiguous** – an ambiguity that can be the base for humour. Look at Text 8.2 *Flying pigs can be exciting*.

Text 8.2 Flying pigs can be exciting

Activity 8.2 ⚷

This clause *Flying pigs can be exciting* is ambiguous. The ambiguity is located in the subject slot of the main clause and is explained thus:

> either the {-*ing*} form of the verb is premodifying the noun so the clause is talking about pigs which fly or the subject is realized by a rankshifted clause and it is the action of flying pigs (similar to flying a kite, perhaps) which is exciting.

Draw out the diagrams (use brackets, box format or tree format – whichever you prefer) to show the structure appropriate to each of the two meanings and therefore to show the structural ambiguity which provides the humour.

The example used widely in linguistics discussions is *Flying planes can be dangerous*.

8.3 WHAT MAKES A TEXT A TEXT?

All the lower ranks in the hierarchy of rank (Figure 7.1) combine in so many different ways to create texts – but what is a text? Text grammar is not as tightly constrained as sentence or clause grammar and a writer has more choices available but the sentences which form a text are still going to be linked together in some way. It is hard to argue that the sentences in Text 8.3, each quite grammatical and meaningful on its own, form a coherent, cohesive and meaningful text. If these were the first sentences in any text that you were starting to read, you would wonder what might be coming next.

Text 8.3 Is this a text?

> We went to the furniture shop and looked at chairs. You sentenced the criminal to four years in prison. Zoë liked the dolls very much.

There are ways of linking sentences to create texts and to make clear to the reader the meaning of the whole discourse as well as the meaning of the individual sentences. Before you read any further, read any (or all) of the texts in Chapter 7 or in this chapter. It should be quite clear that the individual sentences in any of these texts are somehow linked together in a way that those in Text 8.3 are not. In terms of a functional approach to grammar, the textual function of language is being exploited, a function which Bloor and Bloor (2013: 13) characterize as 'the use of language to organize the text itself'.

Texts as narratives

Telling stories is sometimes used to mean telling a lie or an untruth – perhaps that is what fiction really is. Very often fictions have a purpose as in moral tales such as Text 8.1 and Text 8.4 and other parables and fables. The police and the courts spend a lot of time determining the truth of the stories they are being told.

There is no doubt that many of these texts are structured as narratives: they tell a story. In this chapter, examples might be Text 8.1 and Text 8.4 though the context of their story telling differs from one text to the next. In Chapter 7, Text 7.2 tells a story from history with precise dates to set the time of the story and Text 7.6 tells a very short story. Text 7.3 tells a story within a story (similar to an episode in a soap opera on TV) as does Text 7.4. What about Text 7.1 and Text 7.5? Neither tells a story but both are coherent texts – and indeed extracts from longer texts.

It can be argued that a great deal of language use relates to the telling of stories: telling our friends what we (or other people) have been up to recently or predicting what we think might happen at some point in the future. What is often referred to as 'wandering down memory lane' is really telling a story of family history – history itself is a narrative and historians choose what to put into that narrative (➜ 17, R2.5).

Labov (1999: 227, 234) presents an overall structure of narrative that is more detailed than the rather simplistic 'beginning', 'middle' and 'end'. He suggests that the following stages can be found in most narratives (though not necessarily in this order) and he provides indicative or 'underlying questions' to help identify each stage:

Abstract	what is this about?
Orientation	who? when? where? what?
Complicating Action	then what happened?
Evaluation	so what?
Result or *Resolution*	what finally happened?
Coda	closure of the narrative.

Text 8.4 'Get comfortable not knowing'

GET COMFORTABLE NOT KNOWING

There once was a village that had among its people a very wise old man. The villagers trusted this man to provide them with answers to their questions and concerns.

One day a farmer from the village went to the wise man and said in a frantic tone, 'Wise man, help me. A horrible thing has happened. My ox has died and I have no animal to help me plow my field! Isn't this the worst thing that could have possibly happened?' The wise old man replied 'Maybe so, maybe not.' The man hurried back to the village and reported to his neighbors. that the wise man had gone mad. Surely this *was* the worst thing that could have happened. Why couldn't he see this?

The very next day, however, a strong, young horse was seen near the man's farm. Because the man had no ox to rely on, he had the idea to catch the horse to replace his ox – and he did. How joyful the farmer was. Plowing the field had never been easier. He went back to the wise man to apologize. 'You were right, wise man. Losing my ox wasn't the worst thing that could have happened. It was a blessing in disguise! I never would have captured my new horse had that not happened. You must agree that this is the *best* thing that could have happened.' The wise man replied once again, 'Maybe so, maybe not.' Not again, thought the farmer. Surely the wise man had gone mad now.

But, once again, the farmer did not know what was to happen. A few days later the farmer's son was riding the horse and was thrown off. He broke his leg and would not be able to help with the crop. Oh no, thought the man. Now we will starve to death. Once again, the farmer went to the wise man. This time he said, 'How did you know that capturing my horse was not a good thing? You were right again. My son is injured and won't be able to help with the crop. This time I'm sure that this is the *worst* thing that could possibly have happened. You must agree this time.' But, just as he had done before, the wise man calmly looked at the farmer and in a compassionate tone replied once again, 'Maybe so, maybe not.' Enraged that the wise man could be so ignorant, the farmer stormed back to the village.

The next day troops arrived to take every able-bodied man to the war that had just broken out. The farmer's son was the only young man in the village who didn't have to go. He would live, while others would surely die.

The moral of this story provides a powerful lesson. The truth is, we *don't* know what's going to happen – we just think we do. Often we make a big deal out of something. We blow up scenarios in our minds about all the terrible things that are going to happen. Most of the time we are wrong. If we keep our cool and stay open to possibilities, we can be reasonably certain that, eventually, all will be well. Remember, maybe so, maybe not.

Source: Carlson, Richard (1998) *Don't Sweat the Small Stuff …
and It's All Small Stuff* London: Hodder Headline plc

We will apply this model to Text 8.4. The title forms the abstract though this is not always the case (compare with Text 8.7: how does the title *Coram Boy* relate to the following text?) and it is certainly true that some abstracts (e.g. those at the start of academic papers) can be more explicit about what is to come than others. One could argue that the title here does not provide many clues as to what is to come. The orientation occurs in the first paragraph (L1–L2) and then the action starts: the ox dies, the horse throws the son, and the troops arrive. The resolution to the narrative is that the son will not have to go to war. The evaluation (L30 *the moral* clearly responds to the 'so what?' question in Labov's model) and the coda (in this text the summary that appears in the final sentence *Remember, maybe so, maybe not*) both appear in the final paragraph. This kind of organization and sequencing of events in narrative is one way in which a text becomes a text.

One of the reasons why Text 8.3 is arguably not a text is that a reader has to work excessively hard to try to make any connection between one sentence and another. There is no obvious topic that links the three sentences nor is there any coherence between them (furniture + legal sentence + toys). There is no cohesion in the form or the structure of the three sentences: there is no link through ellipsis or the use of pronouns – which will be explained later in this chapter. There is no organizational structure to Text 8.3 such as that offered in Labov's model.

Activity 8.3 🔑

(a)   Identify the various stages of abstract, orientation, complicating action, evaluation, resolution and coda in Text 8.1.

(b)   Look at Texts 7.1, 7.2 and 7.6 and see whether any of the same analytical categories apply.

(c)   Texts 7.3, 7.4 and 7.5 are extracts taken from longer texts – which of the features identified by Labov are not evident in these Texts?

Texts are cohesive

Cohesion is part of the textual function of language (in Hallidayan terms) which is concerned with the way in which sentences within a text hold together and relate to each other. The lack of connection between the sentences in Text 8.3 is one reason why it is hard to call that text a text.

If sentences link to each other (this linking can appear in various ways) then they are said to be COHESIVE and this phenomenon is a characteristic of texts. The use of pronouns in the linguistic system of REFERENCE is a clear way of relating a later sentence to an earlier one. In Text 8.4, after he has been introduced, the farmer is later referred to using the pronoun *he* (L11). However, it should be noted that in direct speech the farmer refers to himself as *I* (L4) and *me* (L5). Other characters are referred to using the pronoun *he*: on L8 *he* is the wise man and on L18 *he* is the farmer's son. On L5 the pronoun *this* can only be understood if the reader looks back to a previous event in the narrative. Part of the skill of reading is working out the referent for each pronoun. Alternatively, part of the skill of writing is referring in an unambiguous way – unless ambiguity is needed within the text for some reason.

Activity 8.4 🔑

Identify all the pronouns in Text 8.4 and the referent for each pronoun. As you do this task, you will be exploring **deixis** which Trask (1997: 65) defines as 'linguistic pointing' (➜ 3.3).

Activity 8.5 🔑

Read Text 7.4 and identify the referent for each of the pronouns.

Activity 8.6

Some dictionaries (e.g. Encarta World English Dictionary) claim that *everybody, anybody, nobody* and *somebody* are examples of pronouns. Read Text 7.6 and decide whether you think this classification accords with the way the four words are used in this particular text.

Determiners in NPs can be part of the reference system. In Text 8.4 the existence of the village is asserted in L1 (*There was once a village*) and here the village is non-specified and the determiner used within the NP structure is the indefinite article *a*. The village does not have a name and the reader cannot refer to a map to identify it. In L3, the definite article *the* is used to specify that it is the same village that has been referred to earlier in the text. The reader can still not locate the village on a real-world map but can mentally locate it as the one that was mentioned earlier in the text. Now look at L3 and L6 to see how the farmer is referred to and at L1, L2 and L3 to see how the writer makes clear that in all three instances it is the same wise old man under discussion. The choice of determiners helps to create a coherent text.

The last part of the reference system involves comparison (of **adjectives** or of **adverbs**) and in Text 8.4 it is clearest in the use of superlative adjectives. As soon as the farmer says (L5, L15) to the wise man 'the worst thing' or 'the best thing that could have happened', there is an implicit comparison with everything that could possibly have happened in the village, if not in the world. Text 7.4 uses the comparative form in L1 with the idiom *the longer … the better*. Sometimes in a text the comparison is left implicit as, perhaps, the comparison between the readers of the various newspapers in Text 7.5.

ELLIPSIS and SUBSTITUTION can also be used to hold sentences of a text together. Ellipsis, the omission of linguistic elements within a clause, is evident in Text 8.4 when the subject element of the second clause in L3 appears to have been omitted (*a farmer […] went to the wise man and said […]*). A writer/speaker can omit the grammatical subject (and/or other elements) in a second or later coordinated clause, where that subject (or those other elements) is (are) the same as in the first clause. This process clearly links clauses together but there are important considerations of meaning. Consider the following two sentences:

The comparative form of the adjective *young* is *younger* and the superlative form *youngest*. For longer adjectives and adverbs, you use *more* and *most* e.g. *more interestingly, most interestingly*. Some have irregular forms e.g. *good, better, best* and *bad, worse, worst*.

(a) A man came into the pub and bought a pint of beer.
(b) A man came into the pub and a man bought a pint of beer.

How many men are involved in the actions in a) and in b)?

Rather than omitting words, a speaker/writer often substitutes one word for a previously used word or phrase. Substitution can be of three types, as demonstrated in these invented examples:

Clausal substitution:

A Can I help you?
B I think so.

where *so* (or *not* in a negative response such as 'I think not') substitutes for the clause *that you can help me*.

Verbal substitution:

A We need to feed the cat.
B I have done.

where *done* substitutes for the verb phrase *fed the cat*.

Nominal substitution:

A Which flowers would you like?
B I'd like those blue ones.

where *ones* substitutes for the noun *flowers*.

Activity 8.7 🔑

(a) In Text 8.4, the repeated verbless clauses *Maybe so, maybe not* are examples of substitution. Explain what kind of substitution is being used and demonstrate your understanding of the process by specifying for what they are substitutes.

(b) In Text 8.5 find and comment on three examples of elision.

One of the rules in older prescriptive grammars was that you should not begin a sentence with a coordinating conjunction: they were to join clauses not sentences. But such conjoining does happen very often – as here!

Conjunction is clearly a way by which clauses and sentences can be held together to create a text. Clauses and sentences can be coordinated with *and* (Text 8.1: L1, L2, L25) or *but* (Text 8.1: L3, L29) or *or*. They can also be bound together by subordinate conjunctions such as *while* (Text 8.4: L29) of *if* (Text 8.1: L32). Temporal conjunction occurs with phrases that indicate the sequence of events. The events of the narrative begin *One day* (Text 8.4: L3) and continue *The very next day* (Text 8.4: L9). *Once again* (Text 8.4: L20) the farmer cannot predict the future but *a few days later* (Text 8.4: L17) the next disaster hits him. You will find other examples throughout the text.

Text 8.5 Lily O'Brien's Italian Collection

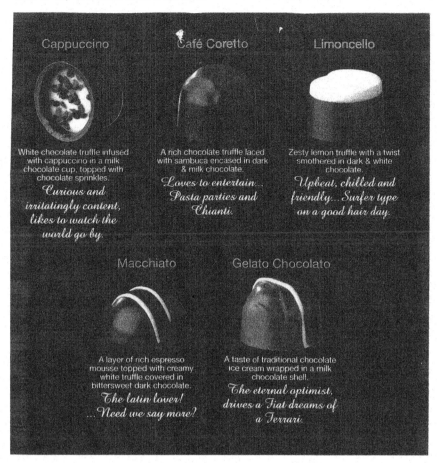

As we are now considering text, you are not being asked to analyse the detail of the clause construction. What is important in the next two activities is that you can understand and demonstrate (in whatever way you prefer but you are shown some ways of presenting this information) how the clauses and sentences hold together in the text.

Activity 8.8 🔑

(a) Identify all the examples of coordinate and subordinate conjunction in Text 8.1.

(b) Are all the examples you have found examples of clausal conjunction or are other elements within a clause also conjoined? If so, what elements are these?

Text 8.6 PM calls for a republic

PM calls for a republic – when the Queen dies

Australia should drop its ties to the British monarchy after the reign of Queen Elizabeth II ends, the nation's prime minister said yesterday. Julia Gillard, whose centre-left Labor party has long argued that the country should become a republic, said Australia had 'deep affection' for the Queen but that she should be its final monarch. 'The appropriate time for this nation to move to be a republic is when we see the monarch change.' said Gillard. 'Obviously I'm hoping for Queen Elizabeth that she lives a long and happy life, and having watched her mother I think that there's every chance that she will.' AP Canberra

Source: the *Guardian*, 18 August 2010, p. 11.

Activity 8.9 🔑

Use Text 8.6 PM *calls for a republic* to demonstrate your understanding of subordinate clauses and show how they indicate the chronology of the topics under discussion.

LEXICAL COHESION is a powerful way of holding a text together. Some of the lexical cohesive devices in Text 8.4 are:

- repetition: e.g. *the wise man, the farmer.*
- different ways of referring to the main protagonists: e.g. *the farmer, the man.*
- different ways of referring to the main place and its inhabitants: *the village, the villagers, his neighbors.*
- the terms relating to agricultural activities and animals such as *animal, plow, field, ox, horse* and *crop.*
- different verbs to indicate how the man went to see the wise man: *went, hurried back, stormed back, arrived, didn't have to go.* Whilst these last two examples refer to the actions of the troops, they are still part of the lexical field of verbs of movement (➜ 6.3).
- indicators of time: *once, one day, the very next day, once again, a few days later, this time.*

Such patterning through the text is one way of making sure the text coheres together and the lack of any such patterns in Text 8.3 is another reason why those sentences do not form a text.

Text 8.7 *Coram Boy* (Gavin 2000: 1)

A fine lady went to Stowe Fair. She was pregnant for the first time and, keen
2 to know what the future held for her, she consulted an old gypsy woman.
'Why, my dear, I do believe you will have seven babies,' said the gypsy woman
4 studying her hand. The fine lady went away and thought no more about it.
When the time came for her child to be born, a midwife was summoned to
6 attend the labour. 'What have we here?' she exclaimed, as she delivered first
one baby, then another and another.
8 'Oh no!' cried the young wife, remembering the gypsy's prophecy. 'That can't
be so!' She wept. But sure enough, one by one, seven little girls were born
10 and laid into a basket.
The fine lady was upset fit to die. 'I don't care what the gypsy prophesied;
12 I will only keep one baby. Take the other six away,' she begged the midwife.
'Drown them in the river, but whatever you do, don't tell my husband,' and
14 she pressed a purse of silver into her hand.
So the midwife took the basket of six babies down to the river. But on the
16 way she met the husband, a fine gentleman. He heard little squealings and
noises. 'Pray, what have you in that basket?' he asked.
18 'Oh it's nothing but six little kittens I am going to drown in the river,' quoth
she. 'I'm going that way myself,' said he. 'Give them to me. I shall deal with
20 them.' Whereupon he took the basket and rode down to the river.
When the husband got to the riverbank and opened the basket, what did he
22 see but six little newborn girls. He frowned a dark, dreadful frown then
closing the basket took it away to a secret place.
24 Seven years passed. The gentleman and his fine lady prepared to celebrate
their daughter's birthday and to give thanks to God for preserving her
26 through infancy. First they would go to church for a special service, then
afterwards throw a party to which the whole village was invited.
28 'And what shall our daughter wear for this special day?' the husband asked
his wife.
30 'Because she was born in October, I shall stitch her a dress of autumn
colours,' the fine lady told him.
32 The little girl's birthday dawned and she was all decked out in nut-brown
velvet trimmed in red. The gentleman and his fine lady set off for church
34 with their pretty little daughter between them.
They sat in the front pew and said their prayers. The organ played, the choir
36 sang. The minister raised his hand to give the blessing and make the sign of the
cross, but he was interrupted. The east door of the church swung open.
38 Everyone turned to see who had arrived so late. There standing on the threshold
were six little girls, all dressed in nut-brown velvet trimmed in red. All were
40 identical to the fine lady's daughter. At the sight of them, the fine lady gave one
dreadful scream and fell down dead.

Activity 8.10 🔑

Show how Text 8.7 *Coram Boy* is a coherent and cohesive text. You should consider:

(a)   the narrative structure of the text
(b)   the reference system
(c)   ellipsis and substitution
(d)   conjunction
(e)   lexical patterning.

8.4 WHO AND WHAT ARE TEXTS FOR?

When students produce a coherent text (oral or written) on a given topic, say an assignment for their tutor, it takes far more effort on their part than the effort needed when they are informally sitting with friends talking about the same topic. Why is that? Is it simply that this coherent version will be judged by tutors and that grades will be dependent on this specific text? If that is the case, then it is worth thinking about other written texts. It takes more effort to write a postcard or a letter (where grades are irrelevant – but perhaps we still care about what the reader thinks) than to make a phone call to transmit the same information. Many would say that it takes more effort to write a postcard or a letter than to send an email or to text a message. If that is true, then arguably the sheer physical effort of writing needs to be considered as well as the mental effort of organizing and creating the (oral or written) text. However, some will want to argue that texting somebody is easier than talking to the same person on the phone – why might that be?

Some will argue that modern technology might well make the physical process of writing easier for a writer, hence the suggestion that all student examinations should be word-processed and not handwritten as students lose the on-going experience of handwriting. Others will argue that the relative ease of writing with the assistance of modern technology (word processing, texting) means that there is less control over the writing process and that writers now use more words to make the same point than earlier writers did. It is certainly true that it is easier to edit a text with modern word processing facilities than it was in the past. However, there still remains the problem of deciding at what point the text is ready for public consideration – whether that text is commercially published or simply shared among friends or colleagues. There are many texts on the worldwide web and the author of each has decided that the text is in a state where it can be released to the world.

The texts considered so far in this chapter have been produced for a variety of purposes: as part of so-called self-help manuals, prefaces for longer texts, informative texts about a product or recent events. They have used language in more or less creative ways – and certainly with a great variety of syntactic structures to convey their content. They have been chosen for this chapter to demonstrate how smaller chunks of language combine to former larger chunks but none was originally written

with that intention: each of them appeared as language use in the real world at some time
or another.

Discourse analysts who adopt a *critical linguistic* approach to text argue that no text
(written or oral) is constructed in isolation. Fairclough (2001: 21) proposes a model
(Figure 8.2) which shows clearly how the text is central in the process of production
of the writer/speaker (or the *addresser*) and interpretation of the reader/hearer (or
addressee) and how that interaction is influenced by the social conditions of production
and interpretation. For example, there are social conventions as to how a formal letter
'should' (you might like to wonder where this moral compulsion comes from and
for what reason) be written or of how a marriage service should be conducted
(➜ 3.3). Of course, the addresser may well be the creator of the individual text as
s/he writes/speaks it. The addressee, however, interprets the text and therefore is
arguably creating his/her own understanding of the text which may be different
from another person's understanding of that same text and, indeed, from the meaning
intended by the addresser. Both addresser and addressee operate as individuals but
each works within more widely accepted constraints of what constitutes a particular
type of text.

Fairclough's view of 'language as discourse and as social practice' necessitates an
analysis of 'the relationship between texts, processes and their social conditions, both the
immediate conditions of the situational context and the more remote conditions of institutional and social structures' (2001: 21). This approach, which links the text with its
social **context** (➜ 1.2 Jakobson's model of communication) and an interest in power
relationships between the participants, becomes particularly relevant when looking at
news reports, whether oral or written.

> Critical linguistic analysis
> aims to address the social
> power relationships that
> operate between
> participants in an
> interaction – a dimension
> that critical discourse
> analysts saw as lacking in
> more formalist approaches
> to language.

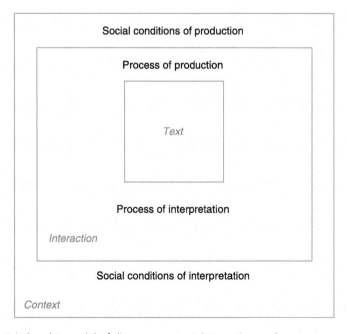

Figure 8.2 Fairclough's model of discourse as text, interaction and context

A classic example is to wonder whether to describe a participant as a *terrorist* or as a *freedom fighter* or a head of state by their full name (e.g. David Cameron) or by an abbreviated form (e.g. Dave) or simply by the role (e.g. the Prime Minister).

The reporter chooses which words and syntactic structures to use. But what are the implications of those choices? Despite all claims to unbiased and objective reporting, something as simple as the choice of words to refer to participants in the narrative (or the news article) can give an indication of the writer's own views. The way the writer refers to the individual in question provides the reader/listener with some sense of how the writer perceives that person even before any comment has been made.

Activity 8.11

Names are important.

(a) Think of people you know for whom you (and perhaps others) have nicknames.
(b) Are these nicknames affectionate or hostile, diminishing or empowering for the recipient of the nicknames? Do you use these nicknames to the individual's face or not?
(c) Does the individual know that you have these nicknames for them – and would you want them to know? Why (or why not)?

Activity 8.12 ⌐ for parts (a) and (b)

1   Look at Text 8.7 and Text 8.8.
(a) List the main characters in each article (narrative or story).
(b) If named, how is each participant named and is there any qualification to the name used?
(c) What is the effect of these naming conventions? Do they personalize the story or depersonalize it? Do the conventions indicate individuals or nameless authorities?
2   Look at Text 8.6 *PM calls for a republic*
(a) List all the naming conventions used in this article.
(b) If named, how is each participant named and is there any qualification to the name used?
(c) What is the implication of claiming that Australia has 'deep affection' for the Queen? Can a country feel affection?
3   Find reports from at least two different journalistic sources about a given event that is in the news at the time of your reading this. Do the same tasks as in (a) and (b) in this activity in relation to your chosen reports.

Text 8.8 Future tense

Future tense for third edition of dictionary

Publishers of the Oxford English Dictionary have confirmed that the third edition
2   may never appear in print. A team of 80 lexicographers began working on it
following the publication of the second edition in 1989. It is 28% finished. In
4   comments to a Sunday newspaper, Nigel Portwood, chief executive of Oxford
University Press which owns the dictionary, said 'The print dictionary market is
6   just disappearing. It is falling away by tens of percent a year'. Asked if he thought
the third edition would appear in printed format, he said: 'I don't think so'.
8   However, an OUP spokeswoman said no decision had been made. PA

Source: the *Guardian*, 30 August 2010, p. 11.

A news reporter has to choose whether to use **active** or **passive voice** (➔ 7.4.5): if the reporter states that X did Y (active voice) then responsibility for the action is stated but if the claim is that Y was done (passive voice), the reader might be left wondering who is responsible for the action and the writer cannot then be held responsible for the reader's interpretation of the report. An added bonus of using the passive is that the reporter cannot be sued for libel because they have not explicitly stated that a particular person is responsible for the action being reported. (See also the deniability of implicatures ➔ 3.6.5.)

The process of nominalization also protects the journalist from legal liability as the actors/agents are not named in the report. Examples can be found in Text 8.8: the date of *publication* of the second *edition* is given but the reader is left to assume that it was OUP (itself an institution some of whose individual employees will have done the actual work) who was the actor in both the act of publishing and editing the dictionary at that time. This all seems very mild and innocuous, but the use of nominalizations in news reporting can allow a journalist to appear to be reporting impartially when, in fact, they are leaving the reader to assume a lot of information. Activity 8.13 addresses linguistic choices such as these made by journalists.

Nominalizations allow only the process to be reported or narrated: talking about *murder* makes the assumption that A murdered B when in fact it might later prove to have been an accident; or talking about an *operation* or an *experiment* gives no information about who is doing what to whom.

Text 8.9 Claudy bombing

Priest rejects criticism of church over Claudy blast

A Catholic spokesman in Northern Ireland has described criticism of the
2   church's role in covering up a priest's involvement in the Claudy bombing as
'dancing on the head of a pin'. Fr Tim Bartlett said too much attention had
4   been paid to the church's part in moving James Chesney out of Northern
Ireland after the 1972 attack, which killed nine people. A report last week said
6   the church, British government and police had agreed to keep Chesney's role
secret, fearing a loyalist backlash against Catholic clergy. Bartlett urged those
8   who knew the truth of what happened to come forward

Source: the *Guardian*, 30 August 2010, p. 11.

We know that there is no grammatical future tense in English (despite the headline in Text 8.8) but what tense would you expect the news to be written in? Most people would expect the past tense, seeing news reports as an account of what has already happened. Look at or listen to news reports carefully and see what tenses are used. Are you surprised in any way? Why do you think the headline writer chose the particular headline for Text 8.8?

Activity 8.13 🔑

Consider the uses of the passive voice and nominalizations in Texts 8.8 and Text 8.9.

1　In Text 8.8
  (a)　If something is 28 per cent finished (passive voice), who do you think has been working on the task? Why has credit for this not been afforded explicitly and directly to them, do you think?
  (b)　Who do you think might make the decision referred to?
2　In Text 8.9
  (a)　Why use the noun *criticism* and not the verb *criticise*?
  (b)　Why use the noun *attack* – who attacked whom and why? All we are told is that the attack 'killed nine people'.
  (c)　Why use the noun *report* and not the verb *report*?
  (d)　Why use the noun *backlash* and not an appropriate verb (give suggestions as to which verbs might have been chosen)?
  (e)　Why use the nouns *blast* and *bombing* rather than their cognate verbs?

The poet John Donne wrote that 'No man is an Island, entire of it self [*sic*]'. We are all members of society or community as it is often now called (why the change, do you think?) and a society/community often has norms of behaviour to which members are supposed to adhere. Critical linguists argue that no text is created in isolation but always with reference to other texts and to social conditioning for the production of texts. So when someone starts to write a letter to their bank manager to ask for a loan or to their closest friend to share some good or bad news, there are wider influences on the writing than just the individual's own linguistic choices. Newer **communication** media such as email, social networking sites, or writing on the web are developing their own conventions. Texting is a particularly clear example of how the linguistic conventions are changing.

Activity 8.14

You might find it helpful to print out – or at the very least reread – the last dozen emails and texts you sent (not all to the same person as the range of addressees will be important for the last part of this activity) before you start this task. Never assume that you know what you do when you are using language – always check the evidence!

(a)　Consider how you write emails. Do you begin with 'Dear X', 'Hi!', just the name of the person you are writing to or do you go straight into the message?

How do you sign off at the end? How many signatures do you have (if any) and which do you use for whom? Does your email language represent spoken language more than written? In what ways? Does your email have only complete sentences in it? Do you use capital letters and other punctuation?

(b) Consider how you use language when you are texting. How do the conventions you follow when you are texting differ from those you follow when you are emailing?

(c) Whether texting or emailing, do you vary the conventions you adopt in relation to who is the recipient of your message? Why and how?

Activity 8.15

Are there any social events where, in your opinion, certain methods of communication might be inappropriate? If so which events and which forms of communication might be involved?

Some texts are written by the author and for only the author and are not intended at the time for a more public reading – diaries written to record the diarist's reflections on previous events are a very clear example. Whether the events were public or private, the reflections are often private and intended for the author's eyes only. Is a diary, therefore, no more than an aide-mémoire? Instructions are sometimes left in a writer's last will and testament that when s/he dies, their diaries, unread by anyone, are to be destroyed by their executors. Not all diaries are private documents, however. Politicians write diaries which are clearly intended to provide at a later date a public account of the private reasons behind the individual's political activities and such diaries often indicate the writer's private opinions of their colleagues.

A writer can be male or female – hence the use of a new form of the pronoun *s/he*. Note that the determiner *their* is now using a plural form to refer to a single referent (➔ 7.3). Language change is all about us all the time (➔ 17).

Activity 8.16

In 2010 when the UK had just changed government, there were several memoirs published by members of the previous government.

(a) Why do you think this should be the case?

(b) Do you think the memoirs would tell 'the truth, the whole truth and nothing but the truth'? Why (not)?

Figurative language use (e.g. simile, metaphor, idiom) can be contrasted with a literal use of language though the use of *literally* is changing markedly these days to mean not *literally* but used as an intensifier to mean *really* or *extremely*. Listen carefully to what is said around you. One of the authors remembers hearing somebody once say 'This is literally mind-blowing'.

Figurative language incorporates the use of metaphor (e.g. *ties to the British monarchy* in Text 8.6, *It is falling away* in Text 8.8, *covering up* and *backlash* in Text 8.9 or *clouded his triumph* in Text 7.2), and simile (e.g. *he works like a Trojan* or *her bedroom looks like a bombsite* – invented but often heard examples) and other non-literal uses of language (e.g. *pull your socks up!*), used every day in normal conversation as well as in literary works.

Even in so-claimed objective news reporting, figurative and metaphorical (➜ R2.6) language use abounds and the characteristics ascribed to participants are also important. In reports on currency and the financial markets, whether in good or bad financial times, journalists anthropomorphize the currencies by ascribing them human characteristics: the currencies sound like patients in that the pound/dollar/euro fails, recovers, rises, falls, weakens, strengthens, rallies, is strong/weak to give but some of the examples that can be found in the financial press. In political reports, you will find elections referred to in terms of war and battle. BBC reports of the 2012 UK presidential election seemed to be particular prone to this. You will find many more examples in news reports – just keep your eyes and ears open.

Instruction manuals are easily recognizable in a wide range of contexts. Texts instructing the reader how to set up a video, how to cook a favourite dish or meal (in this case called a recipe), how to construct a piece of furniture bought as flat-pack (sometimes called assembly instructions) or how to write an essay (often called study guides) all have basically the same structure. The reader is shown what tools and/or ingredients are needed to carry out the task (either by diagrams or in a list). The directions are provided in chronological order for the process that is to be carried out and are often numbered to make that quite explicit for the reader. The directions will, most probably, be in **imperative** mood – there are three examples (*press*, *press*, *keep* (*pressed*)) of imperative verbs in Text 8.10 to indicate the instructions. Other non-imperative verbs in the present tense give information that guides the programmer through the process. In an instruction text, literal language use will be adopted to ensure clarity as far as possible. There may be images (as in Text 8.10) to help the reader see what has to be done. There is unlikely to be any use of figurative language as the writer will want to ensure as far as possible that the reader has no scope for understanding the message in any other way than that intended by the writer.

Activity 8.17

Find two examples of instructive texts from different arenas of life. In the light of what you have just read and with these questions as a guide, identify some of the common features that are demonstrated in the texts you have chosen.

(a) Is there any visual support for the instructions? If so, are iconic or symbolic visuals used to represent various processes (➜ 1)?

(b) Identify the specialized lexis which relates to the area of instruction.

(c) Are the sentences in imperative mood? If not, how is it made clear to the reader what s/he must do?

(d) How is the order in which the instructions are to be carried out made clear? Are they numbered or is the sequence made clear in some other way?

Text 8.10 Programming the start function

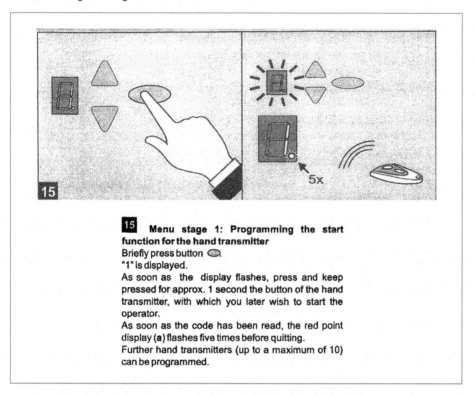

15 **Menu stage 1: Programming the start function for the hand transmitter**
Briefly press button ⬭.
"1" is displayed.
As soon as the display flashes, press and keep pressed for approx. 1 second the button of the hand transmitter, with which you later wish to start the operator.
As soon as the code has been read, the red point display (a) flashes five times before quitting.
Further hand transmitters (up to a maximum of 10) can be programmed.

Arguably self-help manuals are sets of instructions or suggestions to people as to how they might improve their lives but these are rarely written as a set of instructions. Why do you think that the author of Text 8.4 chose to write a piece of self-help advice in the form of a narrative?

Advertisements follow different conventions from instruction manuals and news reports. Whilst an advertiser is not allowed actually to lie about the product, there is scope for figurative and creative use of language to persuade the potential purchaser actually to buy the product. Quite simply, that is the purpose of the advertisement.

The text advertising Comfort Vaporesse (Text 8.11 *Heaven scent*) appeared in *Good Housekeeping* magazine in the UK in July 2002. The advertisement is for a fabric conditioner and the language works deliberately on two levels – talking about fabric and fabric care in the context of a newspaper article about the possible breakdown of a marriage.

The newspaper reader is clearly made out of fabric (her ring has a button where normally there would be a precious stone) as are the two main participants in the saved-marriage story. Lexical items which relate to the field of fabric and fabric care include the names of the main participants, Gary and Veronica <u>Paisley</u>, the reporters John <u>Tweedy</u> and Quentin <u>Quilter</u> and the county where the tanker spillage occurred (<u>Hemp</u>shire, a play on the name of a real UK county, Hampshire). The headline and one of the picture

Text 8.11 Heaven scent

captions revolve around a pun based on the **homophones**, *scent* and *sent* (both phonetically [sɛnt]) where the two meanings are clearly relevant to the tale being told. The other caption reports that Mr and Mrs Paisley can 'iron out' their problems – a caption that is clearly based on the literal meaning of ironing creased clothes (as in the picture) as well as the metaphorical use of the same **lexical item** in relation to abstract problem solving. The headline in the second article is also based on homophones, in this case *dye* and *die* (phonetically [daɪ]), and is reminiscent of the all too frequent newspaper headlines which proclaim that large numbers of people die in accidents daily (an example of intertextuality where one text is read with another text in mind). Figurative language use abounds in the text: 'spell the end of marriage guidance', 'heading straight for the divorce courts' and 'Our marriage has really lost its spark' are just some of the examples. Such language use entices the reader to read further. Modal verbs are widely used in advertisements and so the claims about the success of the product are acceptable (if unlikely in this case – will a fabric conditioner really spell the end of marriage guidance?) and within the UK guidelines that advertisements have to be legal, decent, honest and truthful. To claim that something is possible cannot be challenged in the same way as one can challenge a fact.

In this advertisement, there has been great play made on the newspaper industry. In the original, the name of the newspaper is printed on a red background, reminiscent of the UK tabloid newspapers which have a solid red band as masthead at the top of the front page but the check-pattern in the advertisement is reminiscent of gingham fabric, the name given to the "newspaper". The text is printed in columns. The language used to report the tanker spillage could almost read as a genuine accident: lorries do overturn, they do spill chemicals, experts do work overnight and emergency centres are set up for immediate victims. Such tabloid papers regularly have offers for the reader to 'win a luxury ...' – which in this text introduces the element of humour through bathos (or anti-climax) by the juxtaposition in the reader's mind (so another example of intertextuality) of the luxury night for two at a top hotel with the 'night for two at a dry-cleaners!'.

There is linguistic humour in the advertisement in:

- the pun on 'stained for life' which could be mentally compared with the oft-used 'scarred for life' in genuine reports
- the unlikely presence at an accident of 'stain removal experts' though experts are regularly present at genuine incidents
- the emergency centres here are for 'bleaching'.

This text is read with a typical accident report in mind – a form of intertextuality and linguistic humour reminiscent of that found in parody. Humour is often used within advertisements to encourage the consumer to purchase but it is important to note that advertisements, like literary texts, can borrow language from any and all registers for their particular purpose as can be seen in the advertisement for more! magazine (Text 8.12) which looks more like an invitation to a party than an advert for a magazine.

Advertisements also use sound patterning to make the slogan memorable and this is simply an extension of the way poetry uses sound patterning to particular effect. Think of the slogans for some of the products currently being advertised. Whether in print or on the broadcast media, there will be sound patterning to help the hearer/reader remember the advertisement, and therefore, hopefully, the product.

Text 8.12 *More!* Magazine advertisement

Activity 8.18

Find some advertisements and examine how they exploit the resources of the language. If you look at cosmetics advertisements, you might want to consider how often they exploit the **register** of science to support their claims about the product. Consider the language used to persuade the consumer to buy yet another computer, another phone or another car. How do banks advertise? Have banks changed their advertising since the financial crisis of 2008?

Activity 8.19

Find advertisements which focus on the sound patterning of the language. What phonological features in particular are being exploited?

Written text appears in all shapes, sizes and forms. Some texts are created simply for the pleasure of using language in an innovative, creative and entertaining way such as Text 8.13.

Text 8.13 *Hamlet* at Kennington

Hamlet at Kennington

Tube, or not Tube: that is the question:
2 Whether 'tis nobler in the mind to suffer
The stinks and elbows of obnoxious passengers,
4 Or to take refuge in your Walkman,
And by ignoring end them? To die: to nod off:
6 No more; and, by nodding off to say we end
The bone-ache, the delays, the thousand disturbances
8 The Underground is heir to, 'tis an escape
Devoutly to be wish'd. To die, to have a kip;
10 To sleep; perchance to miss our stop: ay, there's the rub.

Source: Tagholm 1996: 16.

The original text is well known and indeed is often quoted out of context in normal everyday conversation, if not in its entirety, then certainly the first few words. The source of a parody may well never have been seen before by the reader. Nevertheless, the reader recognizes that in some ways (but not in others) the text which they are reading is closely linked to some other text and they read the parody with the original text in mind.

Whether the speaker knows the source text is immaterial; texts find their way from the literary canons to which they originally belong and appear in many and much wider contexts. Not only literary texts are widely quoted: so too are religious texts such as the Bible (in surprising places, sometimes, even in linguistic textbooks (➔ 4, 16, 17) or catchphrases from current television programmes such as soap operas or quiz shows. Can you think of any?

Parody is 'a literary composition modeled on and imitating another work' (OED online), often created for humorous purposes by exaggerating features of the original.

Activity 8.20 🔑

(a) Reread Text 8.13. Find the original text.
(b) Analyse how close the parody is to the original in terms of lexis, syntax, rhythm and phonetic patterning, and meaning.

Parody is one very clear example of intertextuality in that one text is read in the context or with the knowledge of another text. The reader cannot fully appreciate the parody without recognizing the original text which is being parodied. Another example of intertextuality would be where an author quotes directly from another text. Some texts, such as novels and advertisements, borrow from all registers and styles of text. Other texts, such as legal texts or academic essays, are more constrained by their conventions.

8.5 HOW TO ANALYSE A TEXT

A text can be analysed in a variety of ways but a linguistic analysis will aim to show primarily how the finite resources of a language are used creatively to produce an individual text that serves the author's purposes. An analysis should be systematic so that results can be compared and thus contrasts between different types of text become more apparent. Consideration of the following questions will provide a clear and systematic approach to text analysis – the response to each question will vary in length and detail depending on the particular text under scrutiny. Whilst the following points can be addressed in any order, this sequence does provide a practical approach to the analysis of text but you should note that questions in each section are indicative rather than definitive.

(a)   What is the purpose of the text? Why has it been written? Is the reader, for example, simply to enjoy the text (as with a novel or a poem) or to carry out instructions, to consider taking the advice presented or to read the legal document very carefully before signing or just to do the shopping?

(b)   How is the text constructed? Is it a narrative, a descriptive or an instructive text? Or does it contain elements of all three? Is it simply a list or is it a carefully constructed argument putting thesis and antithesis before coming to a synthesis or conclusion?

(c)   Is there any deliberate manipulation of the **phonological** systems of the language? Are there aspects of rhyme (where the final vowel and consonant sequences of syllables are patterned as in *fared* which rhymes with *laird*, or *cough* which rhymes with *off* – remember it is the sound system you are considering here) or alliteration (where the initial consonants and vowels of syllables like *summer* and *sun*, *brother* and *brunch* are the same) which is often a feature of verse or poetic prose? Is the language metrically patterned (→ commentary on Activity 8.20) such that the rhythm of the language becomes marked or is the text written with the normal stress patterns that occur in every day language use?

(d)   What **lexical choices** have been made? Does the text have examples of formal or informal lexis? From what lexical sets are the lexical items taken? Is there a preponderance of homonymic words (with more than one unrelated meaning, e.g. *fair* (= 'just' or = 'village event'), *bank* (= 'riverine' or = 'financial institution'), or is the meaning of each word clear and unambiguous? Has modern lexis been used or, from the reader's perspective, are the lexical items ones that have fallen into disuse in the modern world? Is the language used figuratively (as, for example, where an untidy bedroom is described as looking like 'a bomb site'

or in sports reports where losing a match is described as a tragedy) or literally
(➜ R2.6)?

(e)   What syntactic choices have been made? Do **noun phrases** contain much modifica-
       tion or little? Are the sentences markedly long or short, or does one sentence stand
       out as being markedly different in length to those around it? Do they contain simple
       or complex **clause** structures? Does one syntactic **mood** predominate over others or
       is there a roughly equal mix? In which tense is the text written? Which syntactic
       voice has been chosen? What patterning or foregrounding of syntactic elements has
       been chosen?

8.6 SUMMARY

In this chapter, you have seen how a text can be constructed by choosing which words to
use in which grammatical pattern. Each individual text is constructed by its creator to suit
the intended audience (➜ 13) and to achieve the intended purpose. Texts can range from
the completely literal in order to prevent any possible misunderstanding to the highly
figurative where deliberate plays on language might allow for a multiplicity of meanings
to be expressed and retrieved. Despite the undeniable uniqueness of each text, there are
similarities across different individual texts where they are constructed for a similar
purpose and systematic analysis of the linguistic features of any text(s) allows for generic
comments to be made as well as specific.

8.7 FURTHER ACTIVITY

Text 8.14 English as a foreign language

Dnt u sumX rekn eng lang v lngwindd? 2mny wds & ltrs? ?nt we b usng lss time & papr? ?nt we b 4wd tnking + txt? 13yr grl frm w scot 2ndry schl sd ok. Sh rote GCSE eng sa (abt hr smmr hols in NY) in txt spk. (NO!) Sh sd sh 4t txt spk was "easr thn standrd eng". Sh 4t hr tcher wd b :) Hr tcher 4t it was nt so gr8! Sh was :(& talkd 2 newspprs (but askd 2 b anon). "I cdnt bleve wot I was cing! :o" -!-!-! OW2TE. Sh hd NI@A wot grl was on abt. Sh 4t her pupl was ritng in "hieroglyphics".

Edu xperts r c:-&. Thy r wrrd tht mobile fone spk has gn 2 far. SQA (Scot Qual Auth) has sd txt spk oftn apprs "inappropriately" in xms. Dr Cynthia McVey (Glasgw Cal Univ Psychol lect) sez "Yng pepl dnt rite ltrs so sitng dwn 2 rite is diff ... txting is more aTractve". (Sh is COl).   But Judith Gillespie spokeswmn 4 Scot parent/tcher assoc sez we mst stmp out use of txting 4 eng SAs (Y not hstry, geog, econ, etc? she dnt say). no1 can rite. no1 can spel. "u wd b :-o @ nos of 2ndry pupls wh cant distngsh btwEn 'ther' & ther'". R tchrs a prob? 2 mny tchrs (she sez) thnk pupls 3dom of xpreSn shd nt b inhibtd.

B frank. Do u care? Wot if all eng bcame txt spk? AAMOF eng lits gd in txt spk. "2BON2BTITQ." "2moro & 2moro & 2moro." C? Shakesprs gr8 in txt! 2dA he wd txt all hs wk. May b. Nethng is psble in txt spk.

2 tru. 13yr grl noes wots wot. I say 2 hr URA*! KUTGW! 1OTD yr tcher wll b tching txt. I say 2 edu xperts, 4COL! Gt rl! Eng lang must b COl 2 b xitng. Eat y <3 out! @TEOTD ths is 24/7 wrld! IIN! 01CnStpTxtng. Hax shd tke hEd. I no 1OTD Gdn wll b in ext.

Activity 8.21

Text 8.14 was published in *The Guardian*, one of the national broadsheet newspapers in the UK, after a public examination candidate had written their answers in text-language rather than in Standard British English. How does the language of this text vary from standard language as you know it? Consider the relationship between sound, spelling and punctuation. What is the journalist's view of the use of this **variety** of English in the context of examinations? How can you tell?

COMMENTARY ON ACTIVITIES

O—⊤ Remember that this symbol indicates that there is a commentary on the activity that you can find on the companion website at www.routledge.com/cw/merrison.

FURTHER READING and REFERENCES

Suggestions for further reading on the topics discussed in this chapter can be found on the companion website (www.routledge.com/cw/merrison).

Any piece of academic writing must always provide a list of publications to which reference has been made. Unusually and very unconventionally, this information is provided on the companion website (www.routledge.com/cw/merrison). Always ask your tutor about how you are to present references for any piece of work that you submit.

Chapter 9
Phonetics I: Voiceless Sounds

Key Ideas in this Chapter

- Phonetics is the study of how speech sounds are made and what their acoustic properties are.

- The speech sounds of any language can be represented graphically using the symbols of the International Phonetic Alphabet (IPA).

- Speech sounds are produced in the *vocal tract*: the air passages through which we breathe in and out, from the lungs to the lips and nostrils.

- Different speech sounds are made by (temporarily) closing or changing the shape of the vocal tract (especially the mouth) and by vibrating the vocal cords in the larynx at the top of the windpipe.

- Speech sounds can be described in terms of their place of articulation (e.g. lips vs. back of teeth) and manner of articulation (e.g. with vibrating vocal cords or not).

- Various consonant sounds can be made when the vocal folds are not vibrating (*voiceless* sounds). These include *fricatives* (like the 's'-sound), *plosives* (like the 'p'-sound), and *affricates* (like the 'ch'-sound).

9.1 INTRODUCTION

The vowel sound in English words like *fish*, *shin* and *tip* is pronounced in typically different ways by Australians and New Zealanders. A website about emigrating to New Zealand (➔ W9.1) offers this test of the difference:

If your companion likes eating 'feesh and cheeps,' he or she is Australian. If, on the other hand, they prefer 'fush and chups,' you are undoubtedly dealing with a New Zealander.

Actually, it's an exaggeration to claim that speakers of New Zealand English say 'fush', 'shun' and 'tup' for *fish*, *shin* and *tip*; and it would be a different exaggeration to write that Australian English speakers pronounce the same three words as 'feesh', 'sheen' and 'teep'. The exaggerations are capable of triggering recognition among speakers of other varieties of English who happen to have some acquaintance with Australian English and New Zealand English, but would be misleading for English speakers who had not heard English as spoken in the Antipodes. Adapted English spelling is simply an obstruction if you want to write to French or Japanese people about these pronunciations; an average user of French asked to read *fush* and *feesh* aloud would probably come up with different pronunciations from, for example, the pronunciations that an average speaker of British English would offer for these made-up spellings. And average users of Japanese who have learnt the basics of Western alphabetic writing would produce yet another pair of different pronunciations. Phoneticians can represent the words as: Australian [fiʃ], [ʃin], [tip] and New Zealand [fɪʃ], [ʃɪn], [tɪp].

One job that phonetics does is provide symbols to represent pronunciations. A phonetician can write down a phonetic representation of what a speaker of some language or other says and another phonetician, who hasn't heard the speaker and perhaps does not know the speaker's language, should be able to read out the phonetic symbols and sound pretty much like the original.

However, there is more to phonetics than just notation and performance. If the goal was merely the faithful reproduction of what speakers sounded like, we could do it with recordings and could email digitized files to anyone who was interested. Phonetics is concerned with understanding the nature of the sounds (PHONES) used in speech: how speakers produce sounds, what the acoustic characteristics are of speech sound waves and what the dimensions of similarity and difference are between speech sounds – in terms of producing them in our vocal tracts, their acoustic characteristics and how they are registered in human hearing. The origins of phonetic study lie in ancient India, where a sophisticated understanding of how speech sounds are produced was developed well over 2,000 years ago (Robins 1967: 141–143).

This subject involves an interesting blend of skills and theory. The skills that come with phonetic training include the following:

Actual speech-sound segments that can impinge on our eardrums are called PHONES

- hearing small differences in sound
- noticing how speakers move their lips, jaws, cheeks and other visible parts of their speech-making apparatus when they talk

- sensing the details of what is going on inside one's own vocal tract in the process of uttering
- imitating precisely how other people produce speech sounds.

The theories derive from:

- biology, for understanding the anatomy, muscles and controlled movements of speech (➜ R4.1)
- physics, for analysing speech sound waves, the sources of these and how they are modified by the resonances of the human throat, mouth and nose
- psychology, for trying to grasp how speech sounds are perceived (➜ 14; R4.8)
- linguistics, for knowing the roles of sounds in languages, which sounds are common and which are rare, and which sounds tend to replace which across time and language boundaries (➜ 11; R2.2).

For readers starting with little prior knowledge of phonetics, this chapter and the next aim to demystify the basics and show that phonetics can become familiar if you put effort into developing the necessary skills and learning some relevant concepts. Rather than have a large single chapter, after initial introductory material, we have split the remaining content according to how the vocal folds (➜ 9.2.1) behave to create what are called 'voiceless sounds' and 'voiced sounds'. The former are dealt with here in Chapter 9, the latter in Chapter 10.

If you already have a grasp of phonetics, then the hope is that you'll appreciate a different retelling of the material. This chapter begins with a glimpse into the use of phonetic symbols. From early in your reading of this chapter, you should be able to figure out the sounds that some of the symbols stand for, provided you do the activities (and read the margin notes and footnotes). By the end of the two chapters many of the symbols will have been introduced and what each of them stands for described. It will take plenty of subsequent practice to become a confident user of the symbols.

Together, Chapters 9 and 10 concentrate on ARTICULATORY PHONETICS, the ways that speech sounds are made, essentially through adaptations of our breathing, chewing and swallowing apparatus. In this chapter, an early section outlines the structure of the VOCAL TRACT, from the lungs, via the throat, to the lips and nostrils. The production of the simplest kind of vowel sound is explained. Then the class of **voiceless** consonant sounds is dealt with. Consonants are speech sounds in which articulators within the vocal tract typically come close together or form a complete closure. Voiceless sounds are so called because they are not accompanied by the buzz of vibrating vocal folds in the larynx, a buzz known as **voicing** (explained in Chapter 10).

Consonants (unlike vowels) are typically peripheral in a syllable (➜ 11.03.2, 11.04.1).

Advice: watch yourself

It really helps to keep a mirror with you when you are learning phonetics. You also need to abandon any inhibitions you might have about watching yourself make speech sounds, and indeed about making speech sounds again and again, in varied ways, to gain knowledgeable control over them.

9.1.1 Representing speech sounds: ði ɪntəˈnæʃənəl fəˈnɛtɪk əsəʊsiˈeɪʃn

The International Phonetic Association (➜ W9.2) was founded in 1886. It 'provides [...] a notational standard for the phonetic representation of all languages'. The phonetic transcription above is adapted from the heading to the Association's website.

Peter Gibbs is a weather forecaster often heard on the BBC, the UK's national broadcaster. When he utters the word *though*, the consonant sound at the beginning is like the one most native speakers of English use at the start of *think*, *thank* and *thistle*. (For a particularly clear example, ➜ W9.4, at 1 minute, 16 seconds). In the main, written *th* in English corresponds to two different speech sounds. For us, one of them occurs at the start of *thistle* and the other at the start of *this'll* (as in *This'll make you laugh*). Some native speakers of English use one of these sounds at the end of *with* and some native speakers of English use the other; and there are native speakers of English who sometimes use one and sometimes use the other (➜ 10). But how could we even parody such distinctions when English spelling gives us only *th* for representing both of the sounds? Well, some writers try to capture the distinction by referring to 'soft *th*' and 'hard *th*', or they employ a nonce distinction between *dh* and *th* (and they generally neglect to say that *th*, here, excludes the pronunciation that they are temporarily associating with *dh*). Some people who are interested in English pronunciations and spellings will intuit what is signified, in this sort of context, by 'hard' in contrast to 'soft', or by the written distinction *dh/th*, but there are quite likely to be some misunderstandings too. And if Russians or speakers of Hindi who are not steeped in English conventions are invited to say how they would pronounce *dhough* or '*this'll* with a hard *th*', their renditions are unlikely to sound like those of average speakers of English.

Phoneticians, around the world and regardless of their first languages, could be confident that other phoneticians would know which sounds were meant by: Peter Gibbs' pronunciation of *though* is [θəʊ]; some speakers of English use [θ] at the end of *with*, others have [ð]; and there are others who sometimes do *with* with [ð] and sometimes with [θ], in free variation; and an increasing number of speakers of British English have [f] and [v] instead of, respectively, [θ] and [ð]. (You will have noticed that square brackets are used for phonetic representations.)

> The website of the Linguistic Informatics centre at Tokyo University of Foreign Studies has a worthwhile tool for learning the International Phonetic Alphabet. Clicking on one of the phonetic symbols leads to a useful articulatory diagram and an audio file of someone making the associated speech sound ➜ W9.3.

Activity 9.1

Work out how the phonetic symbols in [ði ɪntəˈnæʃənəl fəˈnɛtɪk əsəʊsiˈeɪʃn] map to the English spelling of the name of the organization: *The International Phonetic Association*. Take time to work through all the pairings. Considering just this four-word title, see which phonetic symbols relate one-to-one with letters of the alphabet. Which mappings are consistent and which are inconsistent? Do this before reading further.

(For now, ignore the three short, raised verticals [ˈ]. They'll be asked about in the next activity box.)

The phonetic symbol [n] maps one-to-one onto the letter <n>, in this example. There is only one [l] and it maps to <l>. The single instance of [ð] corresponds to the DIGRAPH <Th>. Another digraph <Ph> corresponds to [f]. In the phonetic transcription there is a single [ɛ] and it maps to <e>, but there are two more occurrences of <e> and they map back onto different phonetic symbols. The two occurrences of [t] both correspond to the letter <t>, but the mapping is not one-to-one, because two other occurrences of <t> – in the digraph <ti> – correspond to the symbol [ʃ]. The mapping of [k] onto <c> isn't one-to-one, because <c> also maps onto [s]. And a different instance of [s] corresponds to <ss>.

<A> or <a> occurs four times. As the seventh letter of *Association* it relates to [eɪ]. This is how the name of the first letter of the alphabet <A> is recited in English. [eɪ] represents a two-part vowel sound of a kind known as a **diphthong** (and more will be said about them in the section on vowel sounds in Chapter 10). In the middle of the printed word *International*, the letter <a> corresponds to the sound [æ], which is the sound that teachers doing 'phonics' in initial English reading classes usually advise children to associate with <a>. The other two tokens of <a>/<A> go with the phonetic symbol [ə], which happens to be the segment of sound that occurs most often in spoken English. The name of [ə] is **schwa** (and schwa is the topic of a later section in this chapter ➜ 9.2.2). In the current example, [ə] is the phonetic counterpart of not only <a>, but also of <e> and <o>. The occurrences of <o> in *International* and *Phonetic* line up with phonetic schwas, but the first <o> in *Association* has a diphthong [əʊ] corresponding to it. The second <o> in *Association* has no counterpart in the phonetic transcription here. And – listen to yourself as you say *Association* aloud in a reasonably brisk and natural way – there is nothing particularly unusual about pronouncing this word without a vowel sound immediately before the [n]. The only occurrence of the letter <r> has nothing paired with it in the phonetic transcription, which signifies that it has no corresponding pronunciation here (and that is a clue to the variety of English that was transcribed: not Scottish English, not General American English).

Many speakers of Southern British English utter words such as *fish* and *chips* with the vowel sound that is phonetically represented by the symbol [ɪ], as at the start of *International* and in the final syllable of *Phonetic*. Australian speakers generally use a different vowel at these points: [i], the vowel sound in *The* in the example under discussion, as well as near the middle of [əsəʊsiˈeɪʃn]. (In British English, the word *the* is often pronounced with a schwa, [ðə], when the following word does not start with a vowel sound.) The correspondences are set out in Table 9.1, where thick bars mark those that, for the given example, are one-to-one mappings. If more data were included, these bars would have to be erased too. (For instance the phonetic symbol [f] relates not only to written <ph>, but also to <f> and to other English spellings.)

Activity 9.1 illustrates the widely recognized fact that English spelling is not a good guide to details of pronunciation. A system of phonetic notation is far more effective for

Angle brackets, for example <x>, are used to indicate a symbol as representing a unit in a writing (orthographic) system, a letter (or, a more technical term: a GRAPHEME). A DIGRAPH is a sequence of two letters working together.

A diphthong, such as [aʊ] in wow [waʊ], is a dynamic vowel that glides from one vowel quality to another within a single syllable.

Schwa is the name of a vowel sound, [ə].

Table 9.1 Correspondences, overlaps and gaps in the relation between phonetic symbols (top row) and English letters for the example given in Activity 9.1

f	ð	n	l	t		k	s	s	ʃ	ɪ	i	i	ɛ	ə	ə	æ	eɪ	əʊ	ə
Ph	Th	n	l	t	r	c	c	s(s)	ti	I/i	i	e	e	e	A/a	a	a	o	o	o

A useful online version of the IPA chart was prepared for Ladefoged (2005). Clicking on any of the phonetic symbols plays an audio example of it ➜ W9.5.

representing pronunciation, and the International Phonetic Alphabet (IPA) is the best-developed and most widely used one. A chart showing all the IPA symbols can be found at the back of this book. Notice that a phonetic alphabet aims to be a systematic way of representing all speech sounds. It is not a different way of spelling. In getting to know the IPA, you are not launched into learning that you should write [æ] when you would, in English, have written <a>, [k] when you would have written either <c> or <k> or <ck>, [ʃ] when you would have written <sh> or <ti>, [ə] for a range of different vowel symbols, [l] for <l> or <ll> and so on. No, the point is to use ['ækʃəl] only when what you hear is that *actual* sequence of sounds, regardless of which language is being spoken or how the word might be spelt in anyone's conventional writing system.

Activity 9.2 🔑

One of the following phonetic representations of the word *tomato* indicates the way it is pronounced in the Japanese language (and often by Japanese when they are speaking English), one indicates a mainstream American English pronunciation, and one a widespread southern variety of British English.

a) [tə.ˈmɑː.təʊ]
b) [tɔ.ma.tɔ]
c) [tə.ˈmeɪ.ɾoː]

Assuming that you have heard some of these ways of talking, which is which? It might help to look back at Activity 9.1 and identify the two diphthongs that figured there and also here.

The points [.] in a)–c) mark the divisions between syllables (see IPA chart, under SUPRASEGMENTALS). What do the short, raised verticals ['] represent; if you don't already know, can you guess? (Hint: they mark a feature of something that follows them. Again, comparison with the example in Activity 9.1 might be helpful.)

What is indicated by [ː]?

9.1.2 The scope of the subject

It is reasonable to wonder whether phonetic transcription has been rendered unnecessary by the existence of high-fidelity recording systems and analogue-to-digital converters. Collections of well-preserved examples are very useful in science, but they are not a substitute for analysis. Phonetics was stimulated by Alexander Graham Bell's invention of the phonograph in the nineteenth century and hugely helped by the availability of portable tape recorders in the twentieth century, but being able to replay interesting sounds does not constitute an understanding of them. Analysis requires generalization, the discernment of similarities embedded within differences of detail. Symbols are a way of keeping track of generalizations, without having to go through the full contextualized experience of rerunning reality every time.

There is more to the science of phonetics than collecting recordings and more even than transcribing those recordings with a consistent set of phonetic symbols. What if you were not just a user of sound files, but an engineer or other technical person who had to worry about the effects on the intelligibility of speech when acoustic information is degraded by compressing digital files for storage and transmission? You would need phonetic theories to do your analysis.

Language teachers, speech and language therapists, and voice coaches need more than ways of representing speech sounds. They need to understand the details of how speech sounds are made to help them devise exercises and explanations that succeed in teaching pronunciations.

Phonetic accounts of similarities in how sounds are made and in their acoustic characteristics enable us to explain why some varieties of English have [f] corresponding to [θ], and [v] corresponding to [ð]; and why it is reasonable that many speakers of French should, when they are speaking English, use [s] and [z] instead of [θ] and [ð], respectively; and why it is reasonable that many Fijians, when they are speaking English, use [ð] where English native speakers have either [θ] or [ð].

9.2 THE VOCAL TRACT: Y, Y, Y (AND Y)

Speech sounds are produced in the **vocal tract** – the airways through which we inhale and breathe out air. The lungs are at the lower end. Connection to the world outside our bodies is at our lips and nostrils. Part of the tract is also used for eating and drinking, and the safe containment of those activities depends on some valves and covers that have importance for speech production too. Schematically the vocal tract is a set of Y-shaped splitting (or joining) pipes, as shown in Figure 9.1.

The funny shape linking nose, mouth and chest in Figure 9.1(a) sketches a Y-shaped tube with the top part tilted over to the left. The lower part of the stem of the Y is the TRACHEA (the windpipe) connecting with the lungs. We can breathe in and out through either the nose or the mouth; and the upper two branches of the Y represent the space behind the nose (the NASAL CAVITY) and the inside of the mouth (the ORAL CAVITY). Still in 9.1(a), the upper part of the stem of the Y represents the PHARYNX. There is a little upside-down Y in 9.1(b) with a branch for each nostril. In 9.1(c) another upside-down

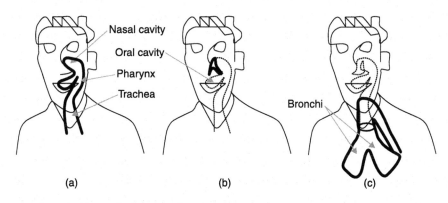

Figure 9.1 Tube map of Y-forkings in the vocal tract (not to scale)

Y represents the trachea splitting into two main BRONCHI (air pipes), one for each lung. At throat level in 9.1(c) there is another upside-down split (not all that Y-like in appearance, but it is a two-branch forking), where the OESOPHAGUS (food pipe) goes down behind the trachea to the stomach. The oesophagus is not part of the vocal tract, but it has been included here (its junction being the optionally bracketed *and* Y of this section's heading) as a reminder that our speech-producing vocal tracts are not only accommodated in our breathing equipment, but that the vocal tract also shares space with tubes that food and liquids pass through.

Muscles acting on the lungs allow us to inhale and exhale. Speech requires more effort from these muscles than quiet breathing does. Shouting demands even more effort. Most speech is produced by modifying exhaled breath. There are some phonetically interesting exceptions, such as click sounds. Also exceptional are speakers (who might want to give the appearance of having such important things to say that they are) so desperate not to leave gaps that could be butted into that they continue to speak even while gasping in more lungfuls of air to enable them to keep talking. Speech production requires more careful timing than unimpeded breathing does. One component of what we register as a STRESSED SYLLABLE may be achieved by a sharp, carefully calibrated contraction of the intercostal muscles; for example the fourth syllable in the English word *association* [ə.səʊ.si.ˈeɪ.ʃn] is uttered more loudly than the others. It is not as straightforward as this, however. Stress is also signalled by sudden variations in pitch, by a vowel sound being a bit longer than the norm, and/or by a combination of pitch change, loudness and length.

> A STRESSED SYLLABLE is more prominent than its neighbours.

9.2.1 Valves and lids: the lips, tongue, velum and vocal folds

Figure 9.2 shows the tubes and hollows of the vocal tract in a more nearly anatomically correct form than in Figure 9.1. It is also the sort of diagram that can be seen in many other phonetics books.

There are quite a number of ways of closing or changing the shapes of passages in this system. Among the benefits of this are: we are able to breathe while chewing; drink without drowning ourselves; chew food without having it fall out; send chewed food down through the pharynx to the oesophagus, without any of it heading up through the higher section of the pharynx into the nasal cavity; and so on. One of the 'and so ons' is significant here: these lids, valves and 'choke points' make speech possible. It is time to explore how some of them work in speech.

> The mark [:] indicates that the preceding sound is long, maybe lasting as long as twice the time duration typical for the sound indicated by the preceding symbol, but there is a great deal of relativity over length.

Activity 9.3

Say the English word *my* a few times: [maɪ maɪ maɪ]. Try to pay attention to what you do in producing the consonant sound [m], then make a very long version of it: [m:::::]. Do it again, but this time use a finger and thumb to hold your nostrils closed. What happens? What can you conclude from this?

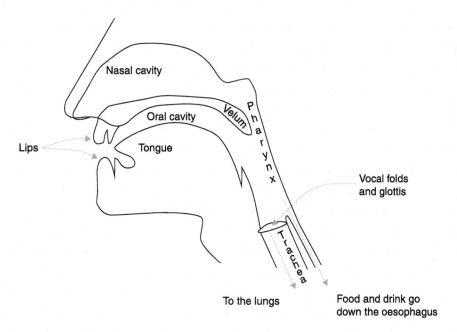

Figure 9.2 The vocal tract in a mid-line section through the head

Closing your nostrils very soon brings to a halt the [m] sound. Your finger and thumb are not part of the vocal tract, but using them to close the nostrils makes it obvious that the outflow of air for an [m] is through the nose, not through the mouth. When you make an [m], your lips being shut together stops air from flowing out through the mouth. Sounds that have complete shutting off of airflow through the oral cavity (see Figure 9.2, where the cavity is labelled) are called STOPS. Sounds that have their main or only airflow through the nose are called NASALS. Therefore [m] is a nasal, or a NASAL STOP. Because the stopping is done by putting the two lips together, a fuller label for [m] is BILABIAL NASAL STOP.

Labia is Latin for 'lips'; *bi-*, also Latin in origin, means 'two'.

The consonant sound [n] is also a nasal stop. It is an ALVEOLAR NASAL STOP. The stop in the oral cavity is made by pushing the tongue tip up against the alveolar ridge (see Figure 9.3). The sides of the tongue seal against the inner faces of the upper teeth, on each side. If you make an exaggeratedly long [n::::::] you can verify that, even though your lips will probably be parted, no air is coming out between them, because covering your mouth with your hand does not affect production of the [n]. But, as with [m], air can be shown to be flowing out via the nose because it is terminated by pinching your nostrils closed. The IPA has symbols for seven main kinds of nasal stop (see the second row of symbols in the CONSONANTS (PULMONIC) table at the top of the chart at the back of the book). These seven correspond to different positions where airflow can be stopped in the oral cavity, from the lips and teeth at the front, all the way back along the hard palate, then along the soft palate (called the VELUM) to the UVULA (the downward-dangling tip of the velum).

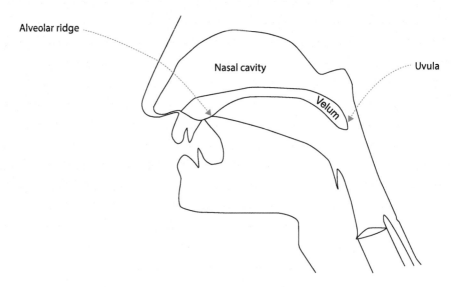

Figure 9.3 The vocal tract set for an alveolar nasal stop [n]

Advice: study the chart

You'll be lost in this introduction to phonetics if you neglect to look things up in the IPA chart, which is why one has been put in the back of this book. Try to become familiar with its layout.

In the IPA chart the symbol in the box to the right of [m] is [ɱ], a LABIODENTAL NASAL STOP. *Labiodental* signifies that the stopping of airflow through the oral cavity is done by shutting together the lower lip and upper teeth. You will probably make one of these labiodental nasal stops if you say *invariably* in a fluent and unmonitored way, not talking like an alphabetic automaton. If you allow yourself to relax, you will probably say something like [ɪɱˈveəɹiəbli], though there might be differences regarding the vowel sounds and kind of r-sound that you use (➔ 11.2.3). Watch yourself in a mirror as you speak the word in a natural way. What exactly happens when you produce the nasal stop? Is it both lips that you close together, as for [m], or do you make the closure between your bottom lip and top teeth? The nasal stop is likely to be labiodental [ɱ] because [v], the next consonant, though not a stop, involves a lip-and-teeth articulation, which makes it labiodental too (as you can see by looking three rows down from [ɱ] in the IPA table). If you see this happening in your mirror you will have witnessed what is called 'assimilation to place of articulation' (PLACE ASSIMILATION for short).

Oral stops, such as [p], show an additional valve in action. Oral stops necessitate blocking the passage of air into the nasal cavity at the back. This is done by raising the velum (the soft rear end of the palate; labelled in Figures 9.2 and 9.3). Try Activity 9.4.

Activity 9.4

Say the English word upper a few times: [ˈʌpəˈʌpəˈʌpə]. Looking at your face in a mirror, notice that your lips shut briefly for the consonant, because [p] is a bilabial stop. Now do it again, but for a couple of seconds hold the stoppage phase of the [p] – when your lips are shut together: [ʌp::::::ə]. Do it again, but this time pause when you are in the middle of the fully blocked stoppage and note that you can make your cheeks bulge by building up pressure from your lungs behind the lip closure, before letting the popping airburst happen at your lips. What do the bulging cheeks indicate about any role of the nasal cavity in the production of the oral stop [p]?

If you saw your cheeks bulge as they reacted to increased pressure behind the bilabial oral stop, then air was not able to escape up via the top of the pharynx, into the nasal cavity and out through your nostrils. There is no flow of air through the nasal cavity in (the stoppage stage of) an oral stop. You could double check that there is no airflow through the nose while you are pausing in the middle of a [p], by manually closing your nostrils as you did before. Whereas pinching the nostrils disrupts nasals, like [m] or [ɱ] or [n], it should have no effect on [p].

There is a technical term for raising the velum and pressing it against the back wall of the pharynx, thereby sealing off the top section of the pharynx and the nasal cavity from the rest of the pharynx and the oral cavity. It is called a VELIC CLOSURE. Figure 9.9 (later on in the chapter) depicts consonants made with velic closures (whereas there is a velic opening in Figures 9.2 and 9.3).

Vowel sounds characteristically involve velic closure. However, some languages have velic opening for some of their vowels. When there is a velic opening at the same time as a sound is being made in the oral cavity, the sound is said to be NASALIZED, and it is represented in phonetic notation by putting a TILDE [~] (a 'swung dash') above the symbol for the oral sound. French is a language that makes systematic use of nasalized vowels, for instance the word fin 'end' is pronounced [fɛ̃], with a nasalized vowel sound, but fait, the past participle of faire 'do', is pronounced with velic closure throughout: [fɛ].

Some speakers of English, some of the time, nasalize their vowels. The finger and thumb test of pinching your nose could show you whether you nasalize vowels when speaking English. Hold your nostrils shut while saying what the Giant said in Jack and the Beanstalk: [fiː faɪ fəʊ fʌm]. (Of course, shutting outflow through the nostrils will interfere with the production of that final bilabial nasal stop (making it into an unreleased 'b' sound [b̚]), but are you nasalizing the vowel sounds (and [f]) in these four syllables?)

The top of the trachea, coming up from the lungs into the pharynx, can be shut off by means of two muscled folds, the VOCAL FOLDS (for location see Figure 9.2). These lie from front to back in the cartilage framework of the LARYNX (the thyroid cartilage is usually externally visible on men, as what is called the 'Adam's apple', on the front of the throat, below the chin). The cartilages that anchor the rear ends of the vocal folds can be swivelled inwards and the muscles tightened to make a waterproof seal in the top of the trachea. Or the cartilage pivots at the rear ends can swing the vocal folds outwards to leave a clear passage between the trachea and the pharynx. The space between the vocal folds is called the GLOTTIS (see Figure 9.4).

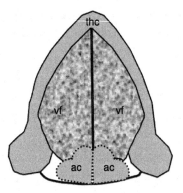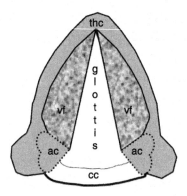

Figure 9.4 Vocal folds, cartilages and glottis in the larynx: glottis shut (left), and wide open (right) for breathing and fully voiceless sounds

Note: In these sketched cross-sections of the throat, the larynx is seen from above, oriented with its front towards the top of the page. The vocal folds are marked *vf*. The space between them is the glottis. At the front end the vocal folds are anchored in the angle of the thyroid cartilage (*thc*). At the rear the vocal folds are attached to the arytenoid cartilages (*ac*). Part of the back of the ring-shaped cricoid cartilage (*cc*) at the top of the trachea is also shown.

When you gargle for a sore throat, the glottis is held firmly enough closed for safety while you create just enough lung pressure from below to squeeze pulses of air between the vocal folds to bubble up through the gargle liquid. The glottis is where GLOTTAL STOPS are produced. The phonetic symbol for a glottal stop is [ʔ]. Non-linguistically, a glottal stop is used at the start of a throat-clearing cough. Do some mild pretend coughs and you may be able to sense the glottal stops. Have you heard adults utter a peremptory warning to animals and infants in the form of a vowel that starts sharply and ends sharply because it comes between glottal stops [ʔaʔ]? The glottal stop is a normal consonant in Arabic and it is a significant sound in Danish. Vibration of the vocal folds produces a component of speech sound called *voice*. It is of such importance that the whole of Chapter 10 is devoted to voiced sounds.

Advice: a phonetic font

Doulos SIL is a useful, usable and free phonetic font to install in either Mac or Windows systems. It can be downloaded from the SIL site (➜ W9.6).

9.2.2 Schwa [ə], a neutral vowel sound

SCHWA is common in English unstressed syllables, for example in *again* [əˈgem] and *famous* [ˈfeɪməs]. You can hear a schwa by clicking on the symbol [ə] in the online IPA chart from Ladefoged (2005) ➜ W9.7.

A tube can resonate. We can form a longish resonating tube through the throat and mouth, from the larynx to the lips, by raising the velum to shut off the nasal passage (called a velic closure, remember). For the internal size of the tube (its cross-sectional area) to be about the same all the way along its length, our lips and tongue need to be relaxed. Something like this pertains when you are breathing quietly through a partially open mouth and thinking of nothing in particular. If someone were then to give you a friendly slap on the back, you might utter a SCHWA vowel [ə].

In regard to sounds, saying that something RESONATES means that it selectively emphasizes sounds at certain pitches. We experience PITCH as varying between low (bass) and high (treble). Pitch can be measured in the FREQUENCY of vibrations, with units named HERTZ, abbreviated to Hz. At 2 Hz, two complete vibrations happen every second. If a vibration with a frequency as slow as 2 Hz was happening in liquid or cloth (think of pond surfaces and flapping banners) you could see and count each complete back-and-forth, sideways or up-and-down perturbation before it repeats itself in the next half-second period.

For tubes closed at one end and open at the other, and quite a lot longer than they are wide, the resonant frequencies depend on the length of the tube. A very long organ pipe of a particular length booms out a 16 Hz note, and standing close by you might feel parts of your clothing vibrating. A frequency of 16 Hz is somewhat faster than one can count. An organ pipe of half the length would have its main resonance one octave higher, at 32 Hz, which is about the frequency of the lowest C on a piano.

Figure 9.5 is a sketch of a spring drum called a 'Thunderer', made in Bali from recycled materials. To play this instrument, you hold the tube, open end up, and shake it to jangle the spring and vibrate the thin metal 'drumskin' that covers the base. The tube selectively enhances some components of the noise and it sounds a bit like rolling thunder. Thunder is different from speech; the tube is wider and it is made from hard cardboard; but the length is comparable with the human vocal tract set to produce the vowel schwa [ə].

The lowest resonance of this kind of tube is calculated by dividing four times the length of the tube into the speed of sound. The 'Thunderer' is 19 centimetres long (about 7½ inches). Nineteen cm = 0.19 metres. Multiplying, 4 × 0.19 m = 0.76 m. Dividing this number into the speed of sound, around 350 metres per second, gives a resonant frequency of (350/0.76 =) 460.5 Hz. This is close to the frequency of the note on a piano made by the fifth black key above Middle C (or, if you prefer, A sharp/B flat). Tubes like this have another resonance at three times the frequency of the lowest one, 3 × 460.5 = 1381.5 Hz. There are other resonances at five times (2302.5 Hz), seven times (3223.5 Hz), nine times (and so on with all the odd numbers as multipliers) the frequency of the lowest one.

In Figure 9.6 you can see how the vocal tract is configured for making a schwa vowel [ə]. Notice that it involves a velic closure. The spectrographic analysis shows the pitch components in a spoken syllable containing [ə].

The spectrum for a human-made [ə] vowel sound in Figure 9.6(b) reveals resonant frequencies at roughly 500 Hz, 1500 Hz, 2500 Hz and 3500 Hz. (A dark area on a spectrogram indicates the presence of sound energy at a pitch that can be read off on the vertical axis, continuing for a period of time indicated on the horizontal axis.) We can use the same formula as used for the Thunderer to estimate the length of the relaxed vocal

If you want to know why it is four times the tube's length and how the speed of sound comes into it, read Johnson (2003). This is acoustic science, dating back to August Kundt (1839–1894). Physics textbooks generally include acoustics.

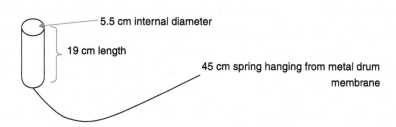

5.5 cm internal diameter

19 cm length

45 cm spring hanging from metal drum membrane

Figure 9.5 Thunderer spring drum

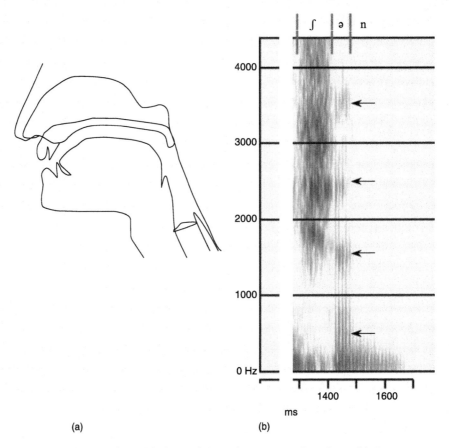

(a)   (b)

Figure 9.6 Producing schwa. (a) shows the vocal tract as set for schwa; (b) shows a portion of a spectrogram with the trace for schwa beginning at about 1430 ms and continuing to about 1480 ms

Source: (b) is adapted from Hagiwara (2009): < http://home.cc.umanitoba.ca/~robh/archives/arc0802.html>

Note: In the vertical slice corresponding to [ə] the arrowed smudgy marks represent bands of resonance (called FORMANTS) centred on, very approximately, 500 Hz, 1500 Hz, 2500 Hz and 3500 Hz. (The indications of energy in the lowest 200 Hz represent voicing and are not relevant to the discussion in this part of the chapter.)

tract of the speaker who uttered the schwa in Figure 9.6 (b), as follows. Like the Thunderer, the 'schwa tube' is open at the mouth end, and the vibrating vocal folds in the glottis amount to the lower end being shut (well, about 50 per cent of the time). (This has to be mentioned because the calculation uses a formula for parallel-sided tubes that are open at one end and closed at the other.)

lowest resonant frequency = speed of sound ÷ (4 × length of the tube)

or, rearranged

length of tube = speed of sound ÷ (4 × lowest resonant frequency)

For the human [ə] in Figure 9.6(b):

glottis-to-lips length of vocal tract in metres = 350 m/s ÷ (4 × 500) Hz

Doing the sums tells us that the speaker's neutral vocal tract was about 0.175 metres long, which is 17.5 cm (nearly 7 inches).

9.3 HISSES, POPS, POPPY HISSES: A SELECTION OF VOICELESS CONSONANT SOUNDS

The sounds to be described in Section 9.3 are collectively known as OBSTRUENTS. They are three classes of speech sound: PLOSIVES, FRICATIVES and AFFRICATES. It is easier to explain voiceless obstruents first – which is largely why their voiced counterparts will be dealt with in Chapter 10. The production of fricatives is the easiest to understand, so that is where we'll start.

9.3.1 Voiceless fricatives

When you lightly purse your lips and send out a directed draught of air to blow dust off the screen of a mobile phone, you make a sound [ɸ] that is used in some languages, for example as the first consonant in the name of Japan's iconic mountain: [ɸɯdzʲisaɴ], Fuji-san, i.e. Mt Fuji. Do a little puff of this kind at some imaginary dust on a mirror. You should be able to see in the mirror that the air is coming out of a narrow parting between your lips, maybe 15 mm from side to side and with a height in the centre, below the tip of your nose, of only about 2 mm. The noise of [ɸ] is created just in front of your mouth by the air rushing out of that narrow channel and tumbling into air molecules that were occupying the space between your lips and the mirror. The noise of air molecules turbulently brushing against other air molecules and squeezing through gaps between them is 'friction' noise, and speech sounds with friction noise are called FRICATIVES. The fricative [ɸ] is made at the exit from a channel created with both lips, so it is a BILABIAL FRICATIVE. Furthermore [ɸ] is a voiceless sound (and what that means will be explained in a later section of this chapter), so a full phonetic label for [ɸ] is VOICELESS BILABIAL FRICATIVE. All the sounds focused on in the rest of this chapter are voiceless ones.

Check two points: (1) that friction noise cannot be generated with a channel that is too wide and (2) that when you are making [ɸ] air is not simultaneously escaping through your nostrils. Perform the first check in front of a mirror by setting your lips at the opening they would have for the vowel schwa [ə], which you might have for the first syllable in the English word ahead or the vowel sound at the end of the word sofa. This involves lips spread to have a gap about 5 cm from left to right and a height of around 15 mm in the centre. (To estimate this you'll need to hold a ruler near your lips and be able to read mirror images of numbers!) Keeping the lips with that size of opening can you usefully blow dust off things a hand's length away from your lips? We can't and there's no audible friction noise from the vicinity of our lips. Conclusion, a narrow constriction is essential for making fricatives. The technical term in phonetics for an articulation that interferes with the flow through of air in the vocal tract is STRICTURE, and that term will be used from now on. The complete closure made for a stop, such as the bilabial closure for [p] or [m], obviously interferes with the flow of air, so complete CLOSURE is one kind of stricture. In the case of fricatives, two parts of our speech apparatus come close enough together to make noisy turbulence, but not close enough to shut off a passage entirely. In phonetics the full label for such a stricture is CLOSE APPROXIMATION.

Do the second check by making an audible voiceless bilabial fricative [ɸ] and simultaneously gently pinch your nostrils closed. For most people, closing the nostrils makes no difference to the [ɸ] sound, because no air was coming out via the nose. In general, fricatives are made with a velic closure blocking off escape of air up the pharynx behind the end of the soft palate into the nasal cavity. Fricatives require quite a reasonable amount of pressure to squirt air through a narrow channel and not enough pressure can be built up if air is leaking out via the nose. A speaker with a cleft palate that has not been surgically treated who aimed to make a bilabial voiceless fricative would produce a fainter sound [ɸ̃], where the tilde printed above the fricative symbol indicates that it is nasalized. These three generalizations hold for all fricatives: narrow channel, highish pressure and velic closure.

A point to understand about the transmission of sound is that it is not a matter of spraying other people's ears with molecules of air from your vocal tract. Sound travels by perturbations being passed on; sound transmission does not depend on wholesale transfer of air. As an analogy, think of people crowding towards a table where tea, coffee and biscuits are being served. Someone at the front drops a bunch of keys and bends down to pick them up. People in the immediate vicinity shift slightly to avoid being bumped into which leads to the next small arc of people outwards from the table having to shift position and so on. When the key dropper stands up, everyone can move back to where they were before. Without direct contact, the key dropper's sudden stoop can affect people some way off. In two other respects sound passing through air is similar to avoidance pulses in a crowd of people: it goes in all directions, even around corners, and it fades – people nearest the key dropper have to reposition themselves more than those further away, and ones still further away might not be impinged on at all.

EsH: the name of the sound [ʃ], heard in, for example, the English words *shoe* [ʃuː] and *fish* [fɪʃ].

Other fricatives have the narrow gap further back in the vocal tract than the bilabial position. And, in most cases, another factor adds to the noise: the blast of turbulent air hits a solid obstacle, not just stationary air. Let us consider [s] and [ʃ], depicted in Figure 9.7. The English words *see* and *sue* are pronounced with the consonant sound [s] at the beginning, by just about everyone. *She* and *shoe* are pronounced with an [ʃ] at the start, by almost all native speakers of English (though not by all second and foreign language speakers of English; Fijians and Finns, for instance, have to work to achieve an [ʃ] that is distinct from [s]).

The sound [s] is a VOICELESS ALVEOLAR FRICATIVE. The narrow channel is a front-to-back groove along the tip and part of the blade of the tongue with the roof of the channel being the alveolar ridge of the palate, just behind the top teeth. Air exiting from the front end of this groove makes friction noise. Tilting your head back a bit and studying your mouth in a mirror, in good light, while you make an [s] should show that the sides of your tongue are sealed against the side teeth of the upper jaw, to concentrate all of the outflow of air down a central channel formed by the tongue. The jet of air striking the backs and cutting edges of the upper incisors creates additional friction noise. Readers who chew gum might like to investigate how their [s] sound can be modified if they can make a bit of chewing gum stick on the rear of their upper incisors.

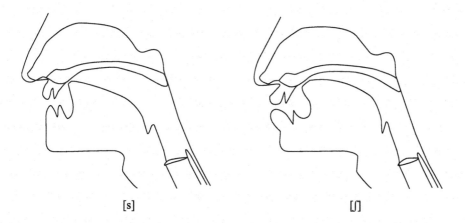

[s]   [ʃ]

Figure 9.7 Two fricatives: a stricture against the alveolar ridge for [s] *versus* a stricture just back from the alveolar ridge for [ʃ]

The VOICELESS POST-ALVEOLAR FRICATIVE [ʃ] has its stricture slightly further back and with a flatter surface on the tip and BLADE of the tongue, not so much of a groove. As in the case of [s], the sides of the tongue seal against the upper teeth. This time the blast of air gets additional noise from hitting the lower incisors. (Palatography tells us about contact between the tongue and roof of the mouth. It used to be done by spraying chocolate dust on to the palate, making a speech sound, then holding one's mouth open for the wipe-off to be photographed, using a mirror on a stalk. There are more sophisticated ways of making PALATOGRAMS now.)

> The BLADE of the tongue is the top surface of the tongue, near the front, just behind the tip.

Speech almost always uses EGRESSIVE breath (breathing out), but interesting observations are possible if you produce voiceless fricatives with INGRESSIVE breath (breathing in). Try saying [s] and then, holding the articulatory posture of the tongue constant, suck air in. You should feel a cold streak starting at your alveolar ridge, a bit behind the top front teeth and reaching back on to the forward part of your hard palate. Next, while continuing to hold the posture, check that you were indeed maintaining the position for [s] by sending an egressive airstream through the stricture. Then do an [ʃ] on ingressive air. The coldness now starts just behind the alveolar ridge, and it spreads a bit wider to the left and right too, doesn't it? If you know German or can persuade a competent speaker of German to train you to say ich 'I' [ɪç], where does the cold patch occur when you use ingressive breath for that voiceless PALATAL FRICATIVE [ç]? Answer: starting around where the hard palate ends and the soft palate begins, if you are doing it right.

> PALATOGRAMS are records of where the tongue touched the roof of the mouth. The corresponding record of contact on the tongue is a LINGUAGRAM.

> INGRESSIVE airflow is into the vocal tract such as can be heard when someone speaks while yawning.

Activity 9.5 0⚊

Study the cavities in front of the strictures in Figure 9.7. Even though they are strange shaped caves that do not have length as a salient dimension, which one is 'longer' from the opening of the lips to the narrowing at the alveolar ridge (or just behind it)? Thinking back to what was said earlier about organ pipes, which of these front cavities has the higher pitched resonant frequency?

The narrowness of the stricture channel in fricatives means that any sound generated in the cavity behind the stricture hardly gets heard at all. It is the resonance of the cavity in front of the stricture that gives a fricative its characteristics. If that front cavity is short, then higher pitched components of the noise will be emphasized and the longer the front cavity is, the lower will be the concentration of pitches in the noise. What we call NOISE is a whole mixture of pitches sounded together – many more notes than could be heard as a chord!

The voiceless bilabial fricative [ɸ] discussed at the start of this section is a rather faint sound because – blowing directly out into the world – it has no part of the vocal tract ahead of it to provide resonance. Furthermore there is no anatomical obstacle out there to be hit by the emerging jet of air and create additional turbulence noise. The stricture of a VOICELESS LABIODENTAL FRICATIVE [f], as in English *face*, *if* and *offer*, has the upper teeth coming close to the lower lip. There is not much of a front cavity ahead of it, but the outflowing jet of air can strike the upper lip to produce some additional turbulence. Explore the variations in sound that you can get making a long [f::::::] while using a finger to prod your top lip upwards. You could also try saying [f::::::] while using a finger and thumb, gently, to extend your top lip forwards.

Two more fricatives (diagrammed in Figure 9.8) are going to be used to illustrate two further points. The first is that there are places further back than the area behind the teeth where the tongue can be used to make fricative strictures. The second is that the details of how a fricative stricture is made at a given place can affect the resulting sound.

The sound [x] occurs in Spanish, in words such as *mujer* 'woman' [muxɛr], and in Scottish English, for example at the end of the word *loch* [lɔx]. Air rushes through a narrow slit made by raising the back of the tongue high towards the velum. Turbulence noise comes both from the air molecules emerging turbulently into the cavity in front of the stricture and – as you may be able to sense if you can make the sound – from this outflowing jet obliquely hitting the curved hard palate. A terminological point is that raising the tongue towards the velum forms a velar stricture. Recall that a *velic* closure is made by raising the velum itself to form a seal against the back wall of the pharynx. The diagram for [x] in Figure 9.8 illustrates both a VELAR STRICTURE (of close approximation) and a

In Scottish English, in words such as *loch* and *pot*, either of the vowels [ɔ] and [ɒ] can be heard (see tracks 22–25 in the online audio files of Hughes, Trudgill and Watt 2012).

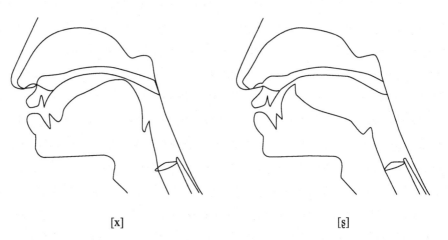

[x]   [ʂ]

Figure 9.8 Two fricatives: a stricture between the back of the tongue and the velum (i.e. the soft palate) for [x] and a retroflex post-alveolar stricture for [ʂ]

velic closure, allowing no air through between the main vocal tract and the nasal cavity. The vocal tract posture for [ʂ] has a velic closure, but no velar stricture of any kind.

Some languages, like Pǔtōnghuá (Mandarin Chinese) and Hindi, use a range of RETRO-FLEX sounds. Retroflection is the curling back of the tip of the tongue in the production of a sound. Because of the tongue being curled back, the close approximation is between the underside of the tongue and the post-alveolar area of the palate. This is the same place of articulation as for [ʃ], and English speakers learning Chinese often produce [ʃ] when [ʂ] is called for, and that sounds wrong to their teachers. It is not that retroflex sounds as such are difficult for native speakers of English: retroflection features in the r-sounds of many English native speakers. The sound [ɻ] is common in Scottish English, though less tightly curved back than in Belfast English, and the [ɹ] of Southern British English is often slightly retroflexed (Hughes, Trudgill and Watt 2012: 66). In many varieties of American English an 'r' sound that immediately follows a vowel is pronounced by lightly curling back the tip of the tongue towards the end of a vowel's duration (IPA diacritic [˞]); and perhaps using the root of the tongue to narrow the pharynx at the same time – the IPA offers a *retracted tongue root* diacritic for cases like this [̠]. Thus *fur* may be pronounced [fɚ̠ː].

DIACRITICS are subsidiary symbols added to vowel and consonant symbols. They mark details about the articulation of a sound.

Activity 9.6 ⌾━┳

What feature is common to all the symbols in the column headed *Retroflex* in the CONSONANTS (PULMONIC) part of the IPA chart, and not seen as a component of any of the other symbols in the consonants table?

9.3.2 Voiceless plosives

Plosives are an important species of stop. As the name suggests, these sounds typically involve small explosions, air pops. A PLOSIVE is a pulmonic, egressive stop. PULMONIC means that the lungs get the airstream moving and EGRESSIVE means that the sound is made with air flowing out from the lungs rather than on an inbreath. Thus, while it was correct, in Activity 9.4, to call the [p] in *upper* [ˈʌpə] a bilabial stop, it is a stop of the kind known as a plosive, specifically a VOICELESS BILABIAL PLOSIVE. The consonant sounds in the middle of the following two English words offer examples of two other plosives: *otter* [ˈɒtə] containing a VOICELESS ALVEOLAR PLOSIVE (though not for people who use a glottal stop in this position [ˈɒʔə]), and *ochre* '(pigment of) reddish soil' [ˈəʊkə] with a VOICELESS VELAR PLOSIVE. Figure 9.9 shows where the outflow of air is stopped in the oral cavity for these three plosives.

Plosives have velic closure: as can be seen in all three diagrams of Figure 9.9, the velum is raised against the back wall of the pharynx, preventing air that is pushed up from the lungs from going through into the nasal cavity. In one phase of the production of a plosive – the 'compression' phase shown in the diagrams of Figure 9.9 – airflow through the mouth is completely stopped: for [p] the lips are sealed; for [t] the tongue is on the alveolar ridge and the edges of the tongue complete the seal by pressing against the inside faces of the top teeth, on both sides; for [k] the back of the tongue is raised against the soft palate, touching around the sides too, fully blocking the passage into the mouth from

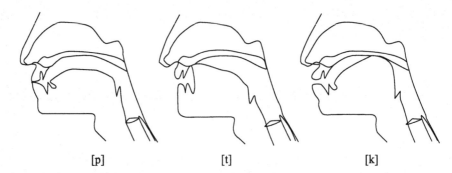

[p]   [t]   [k]

Figure 9.9 Diagrams showing the position of the stop for three plosives: bilabial [p], alveolar [t] and velar [k]

the pharynx. No outflow of air implies a period of silence; so the compression phases of [p], [t] and [k] 'sound' the same: simple silence.

Pressure builds behind the stop until it is forced open and the pent up air is suddenly released in a noisy burst. Noise, remember, is a disharmonic mixture of a lot of different pitches thrown together. The widest ranging mixture is heard for bilabial plosives, because there is no resonating 'tube' in front of the lips to selectively enhance some frequencies. The noise bursts of [t] and [k] are a bit more focused: the short cavity forward from the alveolar ridge to the lips, for [t], emphasizes higher pitched components than those picked out by the longer tube between [k]'s velar stop and the lips. Compare the three diagrams in Figure 9.9.

When edited excerpts of recordings containing just the bursts of plosives are listened to it is generally difficult to distinguish between [p], [t] and [k], perhaps because the burst is over so soon – too short to register properly. The spike of noise, lasting for only a couple of milliseconds, made by a stop being ruptured is a pop, impressionistically not even much like speech and rather similar-sounding regardless of which plosive it is. So how do we manage to hear the difference between [p], [t] and [k]? The most important part of the answer is the effect on neighbouring vowel sounds, and sound clips of plosives become a lot more easily recognizable provided at least a short section of an adjacent vowel is included. Another part of the answer is aspiration, which is dealt with briefly now.

The lungs build up pressure behind the stop. The plosive burst happens at the moment when the blockage is removed. Air may then continue to rush out of the lungs through the glottis (the gap between the vocal folds, in the larynx). Because even a wide-open glottis is a narrowing in the vocal tract (see Figure 9.4), this can create fricative noise where the glottis discharges into the pharynx: a glottal fricative. Following the burst of a voiceless plosive, it will be a VOICELESS GLOTTAL FRICATIVE [h]. A glottal fricative that has a subsidiary effect on the release of another sound is called ASPIRATION, and the symbol for it is a superscript [ʰ] added to the symbol for the main articulation. In most native varieties of English a voiceless plosive has aspiration when it stands alone at the beginning of a stressed syllable. For example, *pooh, too* and *coo* come out phonetically as [pʰuː], [tʰuː] and [kʰuː].

The aspiration lasts appreciably longer than the plosive burst and it can reveal what has just previously happened, as when a child stepping back from a shelf as you enter the kitchen enables you to infer what the snack target was. For quite a few milliseconds after the blowing open of the velar stop of an ASPIRATED VOICELESS VELAR PLOSIVE [kʰ] the back of the tongue is still going to be somewhat raised. (Have a look at the [k] diagram in Figure 9.9 and imagine the tongue dropping away from the soft palate.) Temporarily, the vocal tract amounts to two tubes coupled end-to-end, one from the glottis to the humped back of the tongue and the other between the hump and the lips. But for [tʰ], it is the tip and blade of the tongue that will be somewhat raised, separating a rather short front cavity between tongue tip and lips from a longer back cavity between the glottis and the ridge behind the top front teeth. Different combinations of tubes yield different resonances. If you say *ooh* in a quiet whisper [ɰ̥ː] it sounds similar to what aspiration reveals about a retreating [kʰ]; and it is different from the sound of aspiration on a [tʰ] that has opened quite a lot but has not yet vanished.

So far, this chapter has concentrated on three MANNERS OF ARTICULATION: nasals, fricatives and plosives. A plosive is different from the other two types because it involves a sequence of distinct phases: (1) making of the closure, then (2) compression behind the closure, then (3) the release of the pressure by the closure being blown open. With nasals and fricatives, on the other hand, once the posture of the articulators has been achieved they can be held steady while air is sent through the vocal tract, until the speaker chooses silence, or goes on to utter a different sound or runs out of air. Thus you could straightforwardly be asked, in Activity 9.3, to extend the duration of a nasal sound [m⋮⋮⋮], but, in Activity 9.4, it had to be specified for [ʌp⋮⋮⋮⋮ə] which phase of the plosive [p] was to be lengthened (and, in the case of a plosive, it is only the compression phase that can be lengthened to any great extent). A very rough indication of the durations of the components of a plosive are that Phase 2, compression, may last for about one tenth of a second (100 milliseconds) and Phases 1 and 3 are each about half as long.

When the plosives [p], [t] and [k] occur at the end of a syllable in Cantonese they are unreleased: [p̚], [t̚] and [k̚] (International Phonetic Association 1999: 60). When the syllable is also the last one before a pause it sounds weird to someone accustomed to English. Because the compression behind the closure is simply relaxed without exploding the closure – which is to say that the third phase does not occur – the speaker appears to have switched off suddenly, leaving one guessing rather helplessly what the last consonant sound was. However, it can happen in English too: Cruttenden (2008: 165) gives examples such as *captain*, *outpost* and *Blackpool*, where, in the accent he is describing, there is no audible release for the first of two plosives occurring in immediate succession – corresponding to the underlined letters in the words here. It depends on what you are used to hearing in which places. It takes practice to listen analytically, perhaps especially when the language is a familiar one.

Activity 9.7 🔑

Compare the diagram for [x] in Figure 9.8 with the [k] diagram in Figure 9.9. Using the correct phonetic label, where is the stricture in each case? Again using the appropriate label, what kind of stricture is it in each case?

Two more voiceless plosives will be briefly discussed now, using comparisons with the place of articulation of the voiceless velar plosive [k], as shown on the right in

Figure 9.9. The sound [k] represented in the figure is as used by English speakers in the word cock [kʰɒk].

1   The PALATAL PLOSIVE [c] is made with its stricture of complete closure forward from the closure for [k].
2   The UVULAR PLOSIVE [q] has its complete closure further back in the mouth than [k]. The Arabic word for 'heart' is pronounced [qalb] in many varieties of the language.

You should be able to gain a feeling for 'k' sounds at different places of articulation by saying cookie [ˈkʊci] a few times. The 'k' sounds are different because of anticipatory assimilation to the tongue positions required for the different vowels [ʊ] and [i]. Next, attempt to extract just the articulations for [k] and [c]. Now do [k] and [c] in front of a mirror with your mouth open wide enough for you to see the front of your tongue clearly. The front of the tongue is not directly involved in these articulations, but you should see that it comes forward for [c] and is withdrawn a bit for [k], because [c]'s stricture is made further forward than the velar stricture for [k], the one shown on the right in Figure 9.9. If you have made any headway with this, you should next be able to do a version with the first 'k' articulated against the uvula as [q]. (See Figure 9.3 if you need a reminder of where the uvula is located.)

> The difference between the written (orthographic) consonants in the two syllables of cookie, <c> and <k> is irrelevant (and, in this particular example, phonetically speaking, completely misleading – for the orthographic <c> is a phonetic [k] and the orthographic <k> is phonetically a [c].

Activity 9.8

Find [p], [t] and [k] in the CONSONANTS (PULMONIC) part of the IPA chart, bound into the back of this book, then say how the arrangement of the Plosive row of that table relates to the stricture positions shown in Figure 9.9. Do this before reading on.

The IPA's row of plosives is systematically arranged to put strictures in the forward parts of the vocal tract on the left of the table and strictures in the back and lower parts of the vocal tract on the right: bilabial [p] on the left, alveolar [t] near to the left, velar [k] well over towards the right and the glottal stop [ʔ] on the far right. The other pulmonic consonants, for example the nasals and fricatives, are similarly arranged, with strictures that are further forward in the vocal tract positioned further left in the table. That is why the saggital cross-sections of the head in this book (and in many other accounts of articulatory phonetics) have the head facing leftwards, to match how the IPA sets out the corresponding symbols.

> The layout of the vocal tract is rather directly portrayed in the IPA layout: lips at the left, with each column to the right representing a stricture further back towards the pharynx and, eventually, down to the glottis.

Each of the column headings on the IPA pulmonic consonants table (Bilabial, Labiodental, Dental, Alveolar and so on, through to Glottal) is traditionally termed a PLACE OF ARTICULATION. Each of the IPA table's row labels represents a MANNER OF ARTICULATION (Plosive, Nasal etc.). An important start on identifying a consonant sound is to state its place and manner of articulation, for example [m] is a bilabial nasal. Sounds discussed so far have shown one other descriptor in use, for instance [s] is a voiceless alveolar fricative, [k] is a voiceless velar plosive. Voicelessness is one pole of the dimension of voicing (the other is dealt with in Chapter 10).

The left–right arrangement of places of articulation is more than mere tidiness. The layout reflects an important dimension of similarity in sound. Strictures at the different places of articulation form vocal tract cavities of different lengths, which therefore have different resonance characteristics. Audible resonances are evidence towards the hearers' identification of where speakers are making the strictures. This was suggested in the commentary on Activity 9.7: a [k] sounds somewhat like an [x] because the cavity in front of the stricture is the same length. Another example is some French speakers' use of [s] as a replacement of [θ], in English words such as think; the resonance cavities ahead of the strictures of these two voiceless fricatives are fairly similar (compare the diagram second from left in Figure 9.10 and the right-hand diagram in Figure 9.11) and note that the symbols [θ] and [s] are in adjacent columns of the IPA layout.

9.3.3 Voiceless affricates

The manners of articulation described in the previous two subsections were fricative and plosive. An AFFRICATE is a coordinated sequence of a plosive followed immediately by a fricative at approximately the same place of articulation. It was noted above that there are three phases in the production of the plosive ((1) making the closure, (2) compression and (3) plosive release). An affricate has those three phases and then (4) a fricative, held for long enough to be clearly identifiable. Of course, as with other plosives and fricatives, there is normally a velic closure throughout, preventing escape of air into the nasal cavity.

The articulatory postures shown in Figure 9.10 for [s] and [ʃ] are the same as shown for the same two fricatives in Figure 9.7. However, Phase 2 (compression) is different between the two affricates in Figure 9.10. Phase 2 for the alveolar affricate [ts] is the same as shown for the plosive [t] in Figure 9.9, but the compression phase for [tʃ] is different, even though it has also been labelled [t]. Phoneticians can indicate the particular kind of [t] depicted in the third diagram from the left in Figure 9.10, the one that occurs before [ʃ] in the affricate [tʃ]. This is done with a minus sign added below the main phonetic symbol: [t̠]. The minus sign indicates that the tongue contact is further back than might be expected. It is listed in the IPA chart's diacritics table, but most of the add-ons in that table imply more precision than is appropriate for a first course in phonetics.

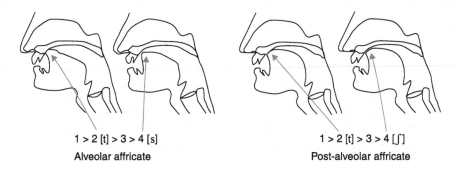

1 > 2 [t] > 3 > 4 [s]
Alveolar affricate

1 > 2 [t] > 3 > 4 [ʃ]
Post-alveolar affricate

Figure 9.10 Strictures for Phase 2 (compression) and Phase 4 (fricative) for two affricates: the pair on the left represents the VOICELESS ALVEOLAR AFFRICATE [ts], as in English eats [iːts]; the pair on the right represents the VOICELESS POST-ALVEOLAR AFFRICATE [tʃ] as in each [iːtʃ]. Phases 1 and 3 are not depicted in the diagrams

Comparing the diagrams in Figure 9.10, you should be able to make a plausible guess at what is going on: the tongue posture for the plosive component of an affricate antici-pates the tongue posture that will be needed for the fricative in the fourth and final phase in the production of an affricate. The [t̪] that is formed in anticipation of an upcoming [ʃ] has contact further back than for an alveolar [t]. Its contact on the roof of the mouth is at the boundary between the rear of the alveolar ridge and the front of the hard palate. This is a phonetic reason for regarding some affricates as not just a simple sequence of plosive + fricative. The affricate seems to be 'choreographed' as an item: the plosive closure is adapted to the fricative that immediately follows it.

Activity 9.9

There is an English word biff. Now say that word backwards. It would be reasonable to have uttered the word fib. If you tried to say a long 'f' at the beginning of 'ffib', then you are perhaps still too much in thrall to English spelling for this far into a chapter about phonetics.

What are your backwards versions of pots and patch? Say them aloud and remember what you said before reading on.

Arguably [ts] in English is just a sequence of plosive [t] followed by a fricative [s]. After all eat and the suffix -s are separately meaningful parts of the word eats (➔ 5). So we might expect many (possibly even most) readers of this book to have given [stɒp] as the reversed version of pots in Activity 9.9. A further reason for readers not to have said [tsɒp] is that [ts] does not occur at the start of English words, so English speakers find it difficult to say borrowed words with the affricate [ts] at the beginning, such as tsunami (from Japanese [tsɯnami]). After the December 2004 tsunami, some British broadcasters could be heard reporting on a disaster with a label that started with [s] or [z].

The diacritic [ˌ] represents voicelessness, manifested in some languages by some vowel sounds when adjacent to a voiceless sound.

On the other hand, the [tʃ] in each [iːtʃ] or church [tʃɜːtʃ] is widely thought of by English speakers as a 'single sound'. Readers of that persuasion should have produced chap [tʃæp] as the backwards version of patch. The spelling of patch could easily have led people to other answers, such as [tʃətæp] or even [həkətæp]. Notice that even the response [tʃətæp] treats [tʃ] as an item that does not have separate parts to reverse. (You have talent as an analytical phonetician if your answer was [ʃtæp].)

How speakers of a particular language think of sounds and what sequences of sounds are allowable in which languages are issues in phonology (➔ 11). Phonetics, our present concern, is about human speech-sound-making across all languages. Nonetheless, a nota-tion can be mentioned here: tie bars may be used to indicate that a sequence of two speech sounds is regarded as a single item, so pronunciations of each and church could be given as: [iːt͡ʃ] and [t͡ʃɜːt͡ʃ]. (See the list of OTHER SYMBOLS, some distance below mid page in the IPA chart.)

In German, a single letter <z> generally corresponds to an affricate [t͡s], in words such as Zeit 'time' [t͡saɪt], and this is one reason why a tie bar could be justified to link the [t] and the [s] when transcribing German. Phonetically the articulatory movements are virtually the same whether for [t͡s] in German *zehn* 'ten' [t͡seːn] or *Tanz* 'dance' [tant͡s] or for [ts] in English words such as *its* [ɪts], *itself* [ɪtˈsɛlf] or *eats* [iːts]. Elsewhere in this book, the tie bar is not usually going to be used for affricates.

Figure 9.11 depicts two phases in the production of a VOICELESS DENTAL AFFRICATE [tθ], which is used in English words like *eighth* [eɪtθ] and *width* [wɪtθ]. The right-hand diagram shows the fricative stricture of close approximation between the tongue tip and the backs and cutting edges of the top teeth. The tongue seals against the top teeth on both sides of the central channel. The diagram on the left shows the plosive [t]'s ANTICIPATORY ASSIMILATION to the fricative's place of articulation: the fricative [θ] has a dental stricture, and this is anticipated by closing the tongue against the top teeth for the plosive too: [t̪], where the little 'bridge' [̪] diacritic that marks a stricture against the top teeth can be used when that amount of detail is wanted.

Just as it is true that Frida Kahlo and Pablo Picasso were both painters, it is true that the plosive component of [tθ], [ts] and [tʃ] is [t], but there are differences between painters and there are different types of [t]. Specifics of how the plosive component of an affricate assimilates to the place of articulation of the fricative can be given if needed, for example [t̪] versus [t]. But, as noted by Ladefoged (2005: 13):

> **There is only a limited set of symbols in the International Phonetic Alphabet, and we often use a symbol to represent one sound in one language and a slightly different sound in another language.**

And this happens even in the transcription of a single language.

There is only one other widely-used voiceless affricate in English. It also starts with a [t], but the fricative component is [ɹ̝], as in *try* [tɹ̝aɪ] and *attract* [əˈtɹ̝ækt]. The 'up tack' diacritic [̝] below the [ɹ] indicates that the tip of the tongue is raised above the ordinary position for [ɹ], bringing it near enough to the alveolar ridge to create friction noise. And note that the [t] is retroflexed [ʈ] in anticipation of [ɹ̝]. Even if the details are hard

ANTICIPATORY ASSIMILATION (opposite of the PERSEVERATIVE kind) is seen when a sound's place or manner of articulation is modified towards a match with the articulation of an upcoming sound.

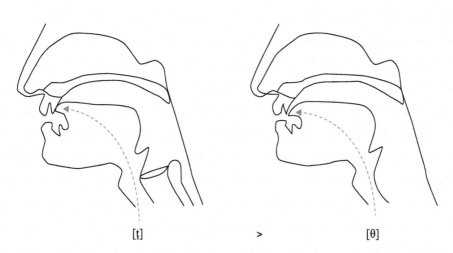

[t] > [θ]

Figure 9.11 The affricate [tθ], as at the end of English *eighth*. The diagrams are for the compression phase and the fricative phase

to follow here, compare how English speakers utter words that can be paired like *try* and *rye* [ɹaɪ], *attract* and *racked* [ɹækt]. It is likely, in words like this, that they will have a fricative sound after [t] – listen for the hissy noise – but not when [ɹ] is the first sound in a word.

Not all affricates start with a [t]. To give just one illustrative example, Standard German has a [pf] affricate in words such as *Pferd* 'horse' [pfɛɐt] and *Kopf* 'head' [kɔpf]. There is no space here to deal with the place assimilation involved in articulating this affricate but try watching a German speaker's mouth, if you can find someone willing to help by saying these words repeatedly for you.

9.4 SUMMARY

Phonetics is about the production, auditory characteristics and acoustics of speech sounds, across all languages. It is the foundation for phonology, the subject of Chapter 11. Phonetics combines science with performance. Imitation of speech sounds and reflection on what we are doing when we make them are essential.

Articulatory phonetics, the focus of this chapter, describes speech sounds in terms of postures and actions in the vocal tract. There is a concern with principles and generalizations as well as details. The International Phonetic Alphabet (IPA), displayed in the chart at the back of this book, provides symbols for a huge range of speech sounds. They are laid out according to the distinctions and dimensions of similarity that are relevant in languages. The phonetic alphabet is not an alternative writing system, but a way of recording speech, so that it can be systematically investigated. A goal of the chapter has been to encourage students to become familiar with the IPA symbols and the layout of the chart. Diacritics are marks added to basic phonetic symbols to denote subtle features of articulation.

Resonances in the vocal tract (the airways from the lungs to the lips and nostrils) selectively emphasize sounds at particular pitches. Different configurations of the tongue and the vocal tract's valves yield different patterns of resonance to modify the pitch composition of sound waves. Prominent frequency bands in the acoustic spectrum of a speech sound are called formants.

Consonant sounds are described in terms of their manner of articulation (nasal, fricative, plosive and so on) and the position of their stricture (from bilabial to glottal). Strictures are constrictions that interfere with the flow of air through the vocal tract. A stricture can be complete closure or a close approximation (causing friction noise). Assimilation is the modification of a sound's place or manner of articulation towards a match with the articulation of a neighbouring sound.

Sounds that have their main or only airflow through the nose are called nasals. Oral sounds are made with the soft palate raised to prevent airflow from the pharynx into the nasal cavity. Voiceless sounds originate in the hiss of air passing through a wide-open glottis. Other effects based on how the glottis is set are breathy voice and whisper.

Table 9.2 summarizes important points covered in the chapter.

Table 9.2 Articulatory properties of nasals, fricatives and plosives

| Manner of articulation | Does air flow out through | | Stricture tight enough for friction noise? |
	the mouth?	the nose?	
nasals	NO	YES	oral closure
fricatives	YES	usually NO	YES
plosives	NO, then YES	usually NO	closure

9.5 FURTHER ACTIVITY

Activity 9.10 ⊶

Write down in IPA symbols typical pronunciations of the words *church*, *table* and *fish* (you should have encountered all the necessary symbols somewhere in this chapter), then answer the following question. What are Hughes, Trudgill and Watt getting at with this statement: 'No native speaker of English would argue that the word *church* begins with the same sound as the word *table*, nor would he or she maintain that *church* ends with the same sound as does the word *fish*.' (2012: 45)?

COMMENTARY ON ACTIVITIES

⊶ Remember that this symbol indicates that there is a commentary on the activity that you can find on the companion website at www.routledge.com/cw/merrison.

FURTHER READING and REFERENCES

Suggestions for further reading on the topics discussed in this chapter can be found on the companion website (www.routledge.com/cw/merrison).

Any piece of academic writing must always provide a list of publications to which reference has been made. Unusually and very unconventionally, this information is provided on the companion website (www.routledge.com/cw/merrison). Always ask your tutor about how you are to present references for any piece of work that you submit.

Chapter 10
Phonetics II: Voiced Sounds

Key Ideas in this Chapter

- Voiced sounds are produced when air flowing through the glottis causes the vocal folds to vibrate and are the basis for vowels, many consonants, and tone/intonation.

- The distinctive sound of different vowels (*vowel quality*) depends on the shape of the oral cavity and the degree of lip rounding.

- Vowel quality can be specified with reference to 16 'landmark' vowel sounds, called the *cardinal vowels*.

- Voiced consonants, like unvoiced consonants, can be characterized in terms of their manner of articulation (e.g. whether there is airflow through the nose) and place of articulation (e.g. whether the lips are closed).

- *Approximants* are a class of vowel-like speech sounds which are produced when the flow of air through the vocal tract is only partially restricted.

- Assimilation occurs when a speech sound adapts its manner or place of articulation to that of a neighbouring speech sound.

10.1 INTRODUCTION

Note: unlike the other chapters in this book (which we believe can be read in any order), this chapter assumes that the reader will already sufficiently understand the material covered in Chapter 9 (Phonetics I).

Where Chapter 9 was concerned with voiceless sounds, the current chapter explains voicing and other ways of making sound in the larynx. We start by discussing VOICED **consonant** sounds. Thereafter, the characteristics of **vowel** sounds are discussed. Before we reach that discussion, however, it is hoped that you will have developed some acquaintance with the sounds represented by different vowel symbols, from attending to the various examples presented in this as well as the previous chapter. Near the end of the current chapter, there is a section on APPROXIMANTS, a category of vowel-like consonant sounds (such as those at the start of the English words *yet*, *wet* and *let*).

Most vowel sounds and a wide range of consonant sounds are produced by sending through the vocal tract a periodic sound wave that originates in vibration of the vocal folds. *Periodic* means that the sound is repetitive in a regular way: the vocal folds go open>shut>open>shut>open>shut … . Each opening lets a little puff of air through into the pharynx. This happens more than fifty times a second, and for a soprano several hundred times a second. Such an iterated series of air puffs coming from the glottis is called VOICE.

> For **vowel** sounds, air flows freely through the mouth. The sonorous, high energy part of a syllable is usually a vowel. Usually the syllable margins are **consonant** sounds. APPROXIMANTS are vowel-like consonants.

Activity 10.1 🔑

Say the English words *sip* [sɪp] and *zip* [zɪp] a few times. Next alternate between longer than usual versions of the consonants at the beginnings of the two words (because the pronunciation distinction between the words is in the initial consonants): [sːːzːːsːːzːːsːːzːː]. The consonant sound [s] is voiceless (air is flowing freely up through an open glottis), but for the voiced consonant sound [z] the vocal folds in the larynx are vibrating open and shut.

Try both of the following ways of increasing your awareness of vocal fold vibration:

a) Cup your hands over your ears while saying [sːːzːːsːːzːːsːːzːː]. Doing this reduces the amount you can hear of the sounds emerging from your mouth and you are, consequently, less likely to ignore the vibrations coming up (from the vocal folds) through the bone, cartilage and tissue of your neck and head.

b) Below your chin, lightly grasp your larynx between your thumb and first two fingers while saying [sːːzːːsːːzːːsːːzːː]. You may be able to feel the vocal fold vibrations that are present in [z], but absent in [s].

Here is a check on whether you have got it: is the bilabial nasal stop [m] voiced or voiceless? Find out by doing a) and b) while uttering long versions of this consonant sound: [mːːːːː].

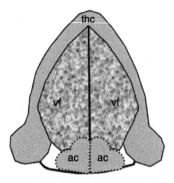

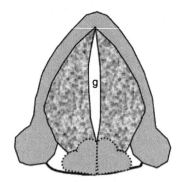

Figure 10.1 Two stages of vocal-fold vibration in modal voicing are depicted: glottis shut (left), and open (right) just before it snaps shut again

Note: In these sketched cross-sections of the throat, the larynx is seen from above, oriented with its front towards the top of the page. The vocal folds are marked *vf*. The space between them is the glottis (*g*). At the front end the vocal folds are anchored in the angle of the thyroid cartilage (*thc*). At the rear the vocal folds are attached to the arytenoid cartilages (*ac*).

A slow-motion animation of vocal fold vibration can be seen on the UCLA Phonetics Lab site (➔ W10.1). But it is the other way up compared to Figure 10.1.

In MODAL VOICING, the main kind in speech, the vocal folds open more gradually than the sharp snap shut that follows.

BREATHY VOICE is made by vibration of rather slack vocal folds overlaid with a hiss of voiceless air emerging from a chink between the arytenoids.

To describe voicing, let us start with the vocal folds in the position shown in the left-hand diagram of Figure 10.1. They are held firmly shut and lung pressure builds up below them until it rolls the folds apart into a long slit from front to back, as represented on the right in the figure. This has two immediate consequences: (1) the pressure that opened the glottis is temporarily relieved, so the vocal fold muscles begin to close the slit; (2) an effect named after (Daniel) Bernoulli (1700–1782) is that pressure falls when air speeds up (as it does through the now open glottis), and this drop in pressure sucks the vocal folds back together again. Then the cycle begins once more, with pressure building up until the glottal seal is pushed open. For MODAL VOICING, which is simply the kind that predominates in speech, the glottis is open about 50 per cent of the time. The characteristic time-profile of modal voicing is that air pushes the vocal folds open in a less sudden way than they subsequently close.

During the babbling phase in infancy (➔ 15.3.2) we learn how to balance muscular effort around the lungs against muscular adjustments in and around the larynx, to effortlessly achieve sustained voicing: rapid chains of equal puffs of air measured out with a high degree of regularity.

Figure 10.2 illustrates three other ways of using the larynx in speech. Shown on the left is the default setting: a wide-open glottis for breathing in and for voiceless sounds as well as the aspiration discussed in connection with English voiceless plosives, the [ʰ] in [tʰuː] *too*, for instance (see Chapter 9). An open glottis is also employed for quiet whispering that is not intended to be overheard. The middle picture shows the vocal folds held tightly shut, but with a gap between the arytenoids allowing through a noisy jet of air that is used in loud whispering. BREATHY VOICE, represented in the right-hand diagram, has air coming through that triangular aperture but at the same time the vocal folds are only loosely tensioned, allowing them to vibrate in a floppy way. This is used by some speakers of English on [ɦ] between vowels, as in *ahead* [əɦɛd]; and for some it is a component of a 'gushy' or 'sultry' style of talking.

The different settings of the glottis are in part made possible by the amazing mounting of the arytenoid cartilages, on the rear of the upper surface of the CRICOID CARTILAGE

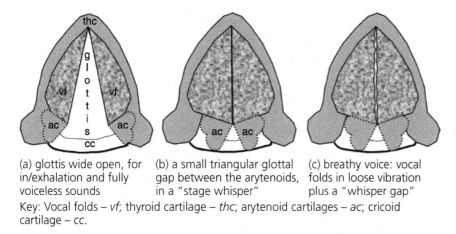

(a) glottis wide open, for in/exhalation and fully voiceless sounds

(b) a small triangular glottal gap between the arytenoids, in a "stage whisper"

(c) breathy voice: vocal folds in loose vibration plus a "whisper gap"

Key: Vocal folds – *vf*; thyroid cartilage – *thc*; arytenoid cartilages – *ac*; cricoid cartilage – *cc*.

Figure 10.2 Three settings of the vocal folds are shown in these sketches of the larynx viewed from above, looking down into the trachea when the glottis is open. Part of the back of the ring-shaped cricoid cartilage at the top of the trachea is shown

(which is a ring-shaped cartilage forming the upper end of the trachea). The arytenoids can be swivelled and also slid outwards or inwards. The elaborate musculature of the larynx allows the vocal folds to be adjusted in complicated ways, not only as shown in Figures 10.1 and 10.2. They can be stretched by independent movement of the cartilages they attach to at front and rear. Increasing tension in the vocal folds raises the pitch of the voice. The larynx as a whole can be moved up and down too.

Studied acoustically, voice is a complex periodic wave that can be analysed as comprising a fundamental frequency and harmonics. The FUNDAMENTAL FREQUENCY is the number of times per second that the vocal folds complete a cycle of opening and then returning to being shut again, measured in Hertz (Hz). Clark, Yallop and Fletcher (2007: 237) give the following as very approximate ranges for the fundamental frequencies of human voices:

children	200–500 Hz
women	150–300 Hz
men	80–200 Hz.

The HARMONICS are whole-number multiples of the fundamental frequency and they contribute to the overall effect of a complex periodic sound wave. Imagine an adult speaking with modal voice at a fundamental frequency of 150 Hz. This will be the strongest component of the sound of voice coming from their larynx, but contributory presences in that voice will be harmonics at 300 Hz, 450 Hz, 600 Hz, 750 Hz, and so on up in 150 Hz steps (or one octave higher each time, like overtones, if you understand musical theory). Each harmonic has slightly less amplitude than the previous lower one. (AMPLITUDE is energy, roughly the same as loudness in this context.) Voice is like a multi-pronged probe sent up through the vocal tract. Some of the harmonic 'prongs' will match resonances in the cavities of the vocal tract and they will be heard clearly in what emerges from the speaker's lips or nostrils (or both); others will be 'blunted' because they do not fit resonances in there. This is largely how listeners can infer, unconsciously, where the speaker's strictures are from moment to moment. In other words the emerging spectrum of that probe with some of its harmonic prongs strong and others blunted or missing (because they were wiped out by anti-resonances) is the main basis of speech perception. The 'strong prongs' that survive the passage are called *formants*, as will be briefly explained in the section on vowel sounds.

Changes in fundamental frequency along the length of an utterance are the foundation for **intonation**. An example is the way *You did it* said with a rise at the end counts as a query, whereas with a fall at the end it is more likely to be an assertion.

In languages with LEXICAL TONE, such as Pǔtōnghuá (Mandarin Chinese), a word is identified not only by its vowels and consonants but by its pitch pattern, which is essentially the contour of the fundamental frequency for that word. Some examples from Pǔtōnghuá are *cāi* 'figure out' with pitch level and near the top of the speaker's normal range, versus *cái* '(only) then' with the same consonant and vowels but spoken with a pitch rise from mid-range to high, versus *cài* 'vegetable' with a fall from high to low; and *mǎi* 'buy' with a fall from low in the speaker's normal range for fundamental frequency to the bottom of the range and then back up to highish, which contrasts with *mài* 'sell' with its fall from high to low.

Intonation is concerned with the pitch and loudness contour of an entire utterance, whether it is only one word long or several (➔ 2).

10.2 VOICED CONSONANT SOUNDS

With one exception, all the voiceless fricatives, plosives and affricates discussed in Chapter 9 have voiced counterparts. These will be introduced now and the presence of voice will also be seen as the default for other manners of articulating pulmonic consonants, the ones in the table at top left of the IPA chart.

Activity 10.2 ⚷

The voiceless alveolar fricative [s] has a counterpart in the voiced alveolar fricative [z], as should have become clear in Activity 10.1. Except for [z]'s addition of voice from a vibrating larynx, the articulation is the same as for [s]. The diagram of the stricture for [s] in Figure 9.7 could equally well have been presented as a diagram of the stricture for [z].

Fill in the blanks below to complete three-element descriptions for the three consonant sounds in square brackets down the left-hand side. Also complete the descriptions of their voiced counterparts, offer an English word that uses the voiced counterpart and, finally, try to find a symbol for each in the IPA chart. Three gaps have been done to get you started.

[f] voiceless _____ <u>fricative</u> as in [fɔːn] *fawn*
[ ] voiced _____ _____ as in [ ] _____

[θ] voiceless _____ _____ as in [θaɪ] *thigh*
[ ] voiced <u>dental</u> _____ as in [ ] _____

[ʃ] voiceless <u>post-alveolar</u> _____ as in [ʃɑːk] *shark*
[ ] voiced _____ _____ as in [ ] _____

What is systematic about the place in the IPA chart where you find the symbols for the voiced counterparts of the three sounds?

> **Advice: read the small print**
>
> There is important information in the sentences printed on the IPA chart at the foot of the CONSONANTS (PULMONIC) table and below the diagram for VOWELS.

For every voiceless fricative there is a matching voiced one. Eleven pairs are shown in the IPA's array of pulmonic consonants and you can find another pair, [ɕ] and [ʑ], under the heading OTHER SYMBOLS in the chart. The fricatives used in English are set out in Table 10.1 so as to match the IPA 'small print' convention that 'Where symbols appear in pairs, the one to the right represents a voiced consonant'. Table 10.1 gives an English example for each one. Not all speakers of English use all of these; for instance many British English speakers nowadays do not have dental fricatives [θ] and [ð]. And many non-Scottish speakers do not use the voiceless velar fricative [x].

Table 10.1 Fricatives that occur in English, according to place of articulation and whether voiceless (*vl.*) or voiced (*vd.*)

labiodental		dental		alveolar		post alveolar		velar		glottal	
vl.	**vd.**	**vl.**	**vd.**	**vl.**	**vd.**	**vl.**	**vd.**	**vl.**	**vd.**	**vl.**	**vd.**
f	v	θ	ð	s	z	ʃ	ʒ	x		h	ɦ
few	*view*	*oath*	*clothe*	*ass*	*as*	*ash*	*beige*	*loch*		*hi*	*ahoy*
fjuː	vjuː	əʊθ	kləʊð	æs	æz	æʃ	beɪʒ	lɒx		haɪ	əˈɦɔɪ

> **Activity 10.3** 🔑
>
> Here are two rather contrived sentences. Above the relevant parts of the spelling, write the phonetic symbols for the fricatives that might be used if the sentences were to be spoken. And put wavy underlining on the parts of each word that are likely to be voiced. Obviously you should interrupt the underlining for the voiceless parts. Note that vowel sounds are generally voiced.
>
> Och, she sees those vases ahead are safe.
> Earth has a few of these Asian shoes.

Voicing on fricatives is conceptually easy. Ignoring some details about voicing assimilation, it is reasonable to think of a fricative as being either voiceless throughout or voiced throughout. For instance, [f] is voiceless and [v] is voiced, and we could do wavy lines under just the voiced parts of the following English words to make this clear.

fail	[feɪl]
veil	[veɪl]
bluffer	[ˈblʌfə]
lover	[ˈlʌvə]
off	[ɒf]
of	[ɒv]

(The sound [l] is voiced, so are vowel sounds, and something will soon be said about [b]. Wavy underlining is not conventional for voice in phonetics, so it is put onto orthographic (spelt) forms of the words here.) If you were programming a machine to do artificial speech, then, as a start, a buzz from the larynx, i.e. voice, could be the default, with voicing switched off for the duration of [f], [θ], [s] and any other voiceless fricative.

Voice is less straightforward with plosives. Voicing requires airflow through the glottis, but where would the air go if there is a velic closure blocking the passage to the nasal cavity and there is a closure in the oral cavity too (and both of these closures are normal for plosives)? Figure 10.3 shows the compression phase for [b], the voiced counterpart of [p], to pose the problem of where the air could go if all outlets are blocked. (We have edited the oesophagus closed, because it is not really an escape route for air from the vocal tract.) The issue is the same for [d] and [g], the voiced counterparts of [t] and [k]. (See Figure 9.9 for diagrams of other plosives that could have been copied here.)

If nothing expands, then airflow through the glottis will stop in a few instants because the pressure will be the same above the glottis as below it. However, one's cheeks are flexible – as are some other parts of the vocal tract – so a bit of room can be made for inrushing air. Voicing can be kept going for a short time behind the closures of a plosive by letting the cheeks be puffed out and giving way at other places where there is flexibility. This is done more in some languages than in others. English voiced plosives at the beginning of an utterance are generally done without expansion of the kind just described, but Spanish initial voiced plosives have such expansion. The following explanation is adapted from Ladefoged (2005: 135–137), using his examples.

Any voicing during the compression phase of a stop sounds faint because it is transmitted through the walls of the throat, rather than emerging from between the speaker's lips.

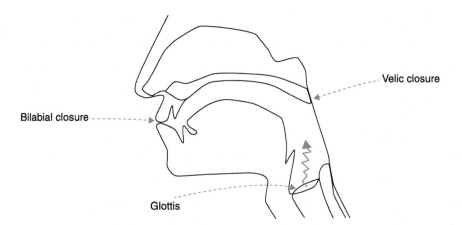

Figure 10.3 Closure for the compression phase of a voiced bilabial plosive, [b]. Where can the voice pulses (wavy arrow) go?

In Chapter 9 plosives were described as having three phases: (1) making the closure, (2) compression and (3) explosive release (➔ 9.3.2). These three phases are schematically represented in Figure 10.4, which compares, across three types of bilabial plosive, the onset of voicing in relation to the moment when the oral closure is popped open, the MOMENT OF PLOSION.

Vowels are normally voiced. A voiceless plosive, such as [p] is (by definition) not voiced. In Figure 10.4, English [pʰ] clearly fits this specification. None of the phases (1–3) of the plosive's production is voiced. The time interval between the moment of plosion and the onset of voicing (about 1/30 second, or 33 milliseconds in this case) is technically known as VOICE ONSET TIME (or VOT). If there is no voicing immediately after plosion, then up to the start of voicing there is likely to be voiceless outflow of air, which is aspiration, [ʰ]. The Spanish [b] represented in Figure 10.4 has to be regarded as voiced: voicing runs through phases 2 and 3 of the plosive. Voicing starts back in time before the moment of plosion, so it can be said to exhibit a negative VOT.

A paradox is seen when we compare the Spanish [p] and English [b] (as they are both typically articulated at the beginning of an utterance; the facts are different when they occur between vowels and elsewhere). With regard to VOT, this Spanish [p] and this English [b] are the same. Both of the symbols have some justification as labels for the voice pattern seen in the second and third lines of Figure 10.4: the symbol for a voiceless plosive [p] is appropriate for the Spanish sound because the whole of the compression phase is voiceless; the symbol for a voiced plosive [b] is justified for the English sound because a part of the production of the plosive, phase 3, is voiced. Maybe we should say

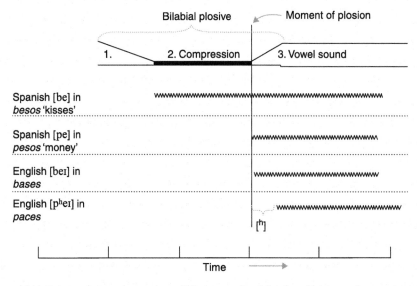

Figure 10.4 Schematic representation of the start of voicing in relation to the moment of plosion for four utterance-initial bilabial plosives: Spanish [b] and [p], English [b] and [pʰ]. The wavy lines represent voice. The successive phases of plosive production are numbered: (1) closure, (2) compression and (3) release after the moment of plosion. The delay between plosion and the onset of voicing for the vowel is a period of aspiration, marked by [ʰ]

Source: Adapted from Ladefoged 2005: 135–137.

that, while Spanish has [b] and [p] as bilabial stops, English has [p] and [pʰ]. But denying that [b] is widely heard in English would go against a long tradition of transcribing English as having [b] and [p].

The problem is complicated further by introducing the facts of Hindi, where four different types of plosive need to be recognized, for instance the bilabials [b], [p], [pʰ] and [b̤ʱ]. The first two of these are similar to the Spanish ones just discussed. Hindi [pʰ] tends to have a longer VOT (which is to say more aspiration) than English. Hindi [b̤ʱ] is similar to Spanish [b] and Hindi [b] in timing, but the voicing in phases 2 and 3 of the plosive is breathy (see Figure 10.2) (Ladefoged 2005: 140–143).

In practice there is no serious problem. Phoneticians engaged in general work on one of these languages will usually follow established conventions, for instance using the symbols [b] and [p] in transcribing English. If they are doing comparisons or focusing on plosives, then they can use diacritic marks to indicate detailed differences or analyse digital recordings of speech and report voice onset times.

Activity 10.4

Have another look at the IPA pulmonic consonants table. It shows symbols for six pairs of plosives. Remember that the one on the right in each pair is voiced: voiceless [p], voiced [b]; through to voiceless [q] and voiced [ɢ]. However, the glottal stop [ʔ] is not a member of a pair. Why not? From its position in the table, would you say it is a voiceless sound or a voiced sound?

Some people say [ʔaʔaː] to arrest action when they notice that an important step is about to be forgotten. The glottal stop is a plosive articulated by building up air pressure behind a tightly closed glottis until it is blown open by the pressure. It is a plosive made in the very place where voicing would have to be produced. That is why, as the wording on the IPA chart coyly puts it, a voiced glottal stop is 'judged impossible'. The symbol appears on the left in the *Glottal* column, so it is represented as a voiceless sound.

You may have inferred when doing Activity 10.1 that not just [m], but all the nasals are normally voiced. That is correct, and the IPA table has them over on the right in each column where they appear (even in the *Alveolar* column, although vertical lines have not been ruled there to guide your eyes). It is superfluous to add the qualifier *voiced* when describing a nasal, but if you hear a partially devoiced nasal, maybe because of perseverative assimilation from a preceding voiceless consonant, as in *snow* [sn̥əʊ], then the voicelessness should be mentioned by using the diacritic [̥] (Cruttenden 2008: 208).

Figure 9.3 showed the setting for an alveolar nasal [n]: a tube open from the glottis to the nostrils, with the oral cavity as a side tube going nowhere. It is a longer side tube for the bilabial nasal [m]; shorter for most of the other nasals. Johnson (2003: Chapter 9) explains how such side tubes selectively subtract their resonant frequencies from the voice spectrum (of fundamental plus harmonics) that we hear coming up through the nasal passage. The depletion of harmonics allows humans to hear where the oral strictures are, even when, as here, air is not coming out through the mouth. Different harmonics 'get swallowed up' down different lengths of mouth cavity 'dead ends'.

TRILLS and TAPS are the final consonant types to be described in this section. They all normally have velic closure, so the nasal cavity is shut off and all outflow of air is through the mouth. As can be seen in the IPA chart, they are listed in the right halves of their little boxes to indicate that they are usually voiced when used for speaking (as opposed to mere vocal play). Voicing itself – described in the previous section of this chapter – is a kind of trill. In a trill, a movable articulator (or a pair of them) is set into stable vibration, opening and shutting a narrow gap.

The (VOICED) BILABIAL TRILL [ʙ] is the sort of noise that you might make to indicate that you are feeling cold – commonly written as Brrr. Putting *voiced* in parentheses is an indication that it is not usually necessary to specify this; trills and taps are assumed to be voiced unless there is a specific indication of voicelessness. If you have not yet learnt how to make [ʙ], then you might like to try pouting your lips, closing them gently against each other and then blowing hard. Switch on voicing to get the voiced version. Italian has a (VOICED) ALVEOLAR TRILL [r], for instance in *terra* 'land' [ˈtɛrːa]. The tip of the tongue is set to trill against the alveolar ridge. For a (VOICED) UVULAR TRILL [ʀ] the back of the tongue is raised high and to the rear of the oral cavity. This allows the uvula (the dangling end of the velum) to vibrate against it. (The main body of the velum makes a velic closure while this is happening.) Uvular trills can be heard in some varieties of French, for example in the word *rue* 'street' [ʀy], and some varieties of German, for example *rot* 'red' [ʀoːt].

> Remember that you can hear examples of the sounds discussed in this chapter and the previous one by clicking on the associated IPA symbols on the Ladefoged (2005) and Tokyo University of Foreign Studies websites (→ W10.2, W10.3)

> Some varieties of French have a VOICED UVULAR FRICATIVE instead: [ʁ].

Taps (also known as FLAPS) are done by flicking the tongue tip up to give the roof of the mouth a single brief tap. Many speakers of American English have a (VOICED) ALVEOLAR TAP [ɾ] as the pronunciation of both "t" and "d" between vowels, when the second of the two syllables is unstressed (→ 9.2), as in *writer* [ˈɹăɪɾɚ] and *rider* [ˈɹaɪɾɚ]. (The little raised mark [˘], a 'breve' in the transcription of *writer* indicates that the vowel sound [a] is shorter than normal.) The length difference is the salient one between words in such pairs. Japanese has a (VOICED) RETROFLEX TAP [ɽ], for instance in *aru* 'a certain' [aɽu]. The underside of the tip of the tongue strikes the palate. If you are not a speaker of Japanese, ask a competent speaker of Japanese – who will probably need to be quite patient – to teach you how to say *arigatō* 'thanks' [aɽigatɔː] and focus your effort on trying to do the [ɽ] in this expression.

Activity 10.5 🔑

What is the common feature for all but one of the sounds represented by the phonetic symbols in each numbered set and which one does not belong in the set? A solution is given for the first set, as an example.

1   ɾ ɹ ɽ   Answer: [ɾ] and [ɽ] are taps. [ɹ] is out of place. (Saying that [ɽ] is retroflex and the others are not retroflex is a less diligent answer, because it makes the common feature a negative one.)

2   m ɱ ɾ ɳ
3   b m s z g
4   t d n ð s ɹ
5   ɸ ʙ θ t ʃ ʈ x
6   v θ ɬ ɻ ʒ ç h ʔ

10.3 VOWEL SOUNDS

Vowel sounds are normally voiced. They are mostly made with velic closure, so they are not nasalized (though two kinds of exception were mentioned when velic closure was described in Chapter 9). For vowel sounds there is rather free airflow through the oral cavity. If the tongue forms a stricture with any other part of the vocal tract and that stricture is narrow enough to create friction noise, then the sound is a fricative (➜ 9.3.1), not a vowel. The relatively unrestricted airflow of vowel sounds means that they are comparatively loud. As such, a vowel generally constitutes the energetic nucleus of a syllable, with consonant sounds as attachments at one end or the other, or both ends. Some vowels can, of course, also be syllables all on their own.

For consonant sounds, strictures are the foundation of a descriptive system that works in terms of places of articulation (labial, dental, alveolar and so on), as outlined up to now. This system does not really apply to vowel sounds because most of the narrowings involved in vowel production are wide ones. Activity 10.6 should enable you to begin to understand the articulations involved in what are known as front vowels.

Activity 10.6

In a mirror, study your lips and — to the extent that you can see them — your teeth, while uttering the following English words, in the order given here.

eat	[iːt]
eight	[eɪt]
ate	[ɛt] (If your version of the past tense form of *eat* sounds the same as the name of the number 8, then use the first syllable of *et cetera* instead.)
at	[æt]

and, if you are a speaker of Australian English or New Zealand English or can manage an imitation, add one more word to the list:

art	[aːt]

When you have done this a few times, say the vowel sounds by themselves, but in the given sequence [iː eɪ ɛ æ aː], while continuing to watch your lips and what you can see in the parting between them.

Not guaranteed, but perhaps when you were uttering just the vowel sounds you saw greater exposure of your teeth with each vowel as you went down the list. You will surely have noticed that your lips were SPREAD, i.e. the corners were drawn outwards, in the direction of the ear on each side. Maybe you noticed that your lips were most widely spread for [iː] and that they became a bit less spread as you went on through the list, with [æ] and [aː] having a neutral lip position (corners out, but not much).

Producing the front vowel sound [iː] involves raising the body of the tongue into a hump, with the top of the hump close to the forward part of the hard palate (but not close enough to produce friction noise). The top of the tongue is a bit further from the hard palate for each successive front vowel in Activity 10.6's list, until eventually there is a wide open space between the palate and the highest point on the tongue, for that Antipodean sound [aː]. One way of moving the tongue successively down from the palate is to lower your jaw in stages. If you did it that way, you would have seen your lips opening more to reveal your teeth as you went through the list of vowel sounds.

But the tongue has complex musculature, making it very versatile. There are people who seem to talk through clenched teeth. That's extreme, but try doing the whole of Activity 10.6 with your jaws held a fixed distance apart by biting very gently on the tip of your thumb. You'll find that it's possible to say the vowels from [iː] to [aː] by just changing tongue position within a framework of jaws that aren't being opened wider for each next one of the five vowels! That versatility is why you might not have seen your mouth opening while originally doing the list of front vowels, if you are a person whose jaw gap is habitually fairly steady when you are talking.

Vowel sounds are differentiated mainly by tongue postures shaping the vocal tract into 'tube resonators' of different lengths, coupled end-to-end. A hump of the tongue demarcates the vocal tract into cavities on either side of the hump (and sometimes a third one above the hump). In the earlier account of fricatives it was noted that the small aperture through which air is squeezed to make a fricative sound has the effect of suppressing any contribution that a cavity behind the stricture might have made to the overall sound. Because the gap is larger for vowels, resonances from the entire vocal tract above the glottis (though mostly not from the nasal cavity) contribute to what listeners hear.

Figure 10.5 shows tongue positions typical for five different vowel sounds. Two of them are the front vowels [i] and [a]. It also depicts LIP ROUNDING, on the back vowel [u]. The 'pout' of lip rounding lengthens the front end of the vocal tract.

The [i], [ɑ] and [u] corners of the quadrilateral in Figure 10.5 represent boundaries beyond which the tongue would move out of vowel production and into voiced fricative territory. Compare the tongue position for [u] in Figure 10.5 with that shown for [x] in Figure 9.8. Raising the tongue a bit higher from where it is for [u] yields [ɣ], the voiced velar fricative counterpart of [x]. Moving the tongue a bit up from [i] gives a voiced palatal fricative [j] and from [ɑ] you could back into a voiced pharyngeal fricative [ʕ] (which looks like the symbol for a glottal stop [ʔ] but faces the other way). The fourth corner [a] is also a boundary to the vowel-producing zone, in part because the tongue cannot be lowered below the bottom of the mouth!

Study the diagram for [i] in Figure 10.5 and think of how the vocal tract is separated into cavities by the posture of the tongue. There is a long back 'tube' from the glottis to the highest point of the hump of the tongue. Long tubes have low resonant frequencies, so, out of the array of fundamental voice pitch and harmonics coming from the glottis to energize the system, this tube will emphasize low notes. Forward of the hump there is a short cavity to the lips. This will emphasize much higher notes. There is also what amounts to a narrow tube between the hump and the roof of the mouth. It is not narrow enough for friction noise, but located between two cavities and being much smaller than them it resonates with (surprising as this may seem) rather low notes. Each of the resulting prominent pitch bands in the sound that emerges from the lips is called a FORMANT. Different vowels have different characteristic formants. Consider [ɑ]. It has a long front cavity and a shorter back one, but neither of them is the same length as the two main cavities for [i]; and [ɑ] does not have a narrow 'tube' connecting its front and back cavities, so it will not have a formant as low as the one that [i] gets from the narrowing against the roof of the mouth.

LIP ROUNDING: seen in a mirror, rounded lips have an approximately circular aperture; seen from the side it amounts to a "pout". Lip rounded vowel sounds contrast with UNROUNDED ones, the latter made with lips spread or in a neutral shape.

The sound [ɑ] is helpful for medical practitioners who need to inspect your pharynx.

FORMANTS: prominent frequency bands in the acoustic spectrum of a speech sound. The lowest formant of a given sound is labelled F_1, the next higher is F_2 and so on. The first three formants are important for recognizing speech sounds, especially vowels, or synthesizing speech by computer. Often the first two formants will suffice.

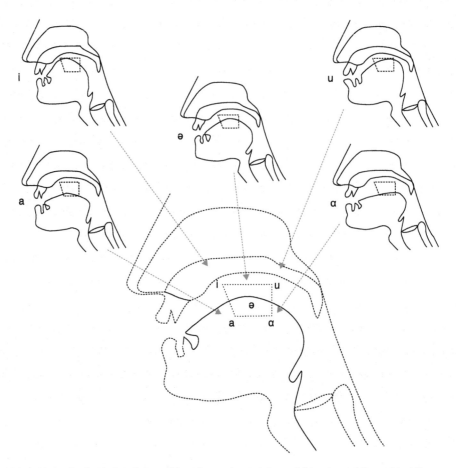

Figure 10.5 The basis for the traditional vowel quadrilateral (the dotted four-sided figure here). In the quadrilateral, the location of the highest point on the tongue's surface for each vowel sound's articulatory posture is represented on a front–back dimension and an open–close(-to-the-roof-of-the-mouth) dimension. The quadrilaterals are shown in a fixed position in the mouth in all six diagrams to highlight the different places where the top of the hump of the tongue is for different vowel sounds. The summary diagram is given with the tongue set for the vowel sound schwa [ə], a 'neutral' position (as also in the small diagram immediately above it)

The lowest three formants – and in some cases even just the lowest two – provide a basis for recognition by computers and humans of vowel sounds especially, but also nasals and the approximants discussed in the last headed section of this chapter. The identity of consonants adjacent to vowels is often carried by the transition into or out of the formant pattern of a vowel, by the way the formants bend before settling into the configuration that characterizes the particular vowel. This is probably the main source of information that hearers have for identifying plosives.

The labels that phoneticians use to talk about positions in the vowel producing area are shown in Figure 10.6, which also locates a few more vowel symbols and, where possible, offers English language examples, representing a Southern British accent.

In Figure 10.6, look out for the CLOSE CENTRAL UNROUNDED vowel [ɨ]. It is called BARRED I. Many New Zealanders use it in words such as fish [fɨʃ] and chips [tʃɨps]. There

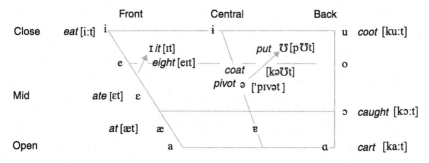

Figure 10.6 The vowel quadrilateral (set out here in the manner of the IPA *VOWELS* diagram), introducing a selection of important vowels. Note the *front–central–back* dimension and the *open–mid–close* dimension (the latter is often labelled *low–mid–high* instead). It should be clear why, for instance, schwa [ə] is termed a MID-CENTRAL vowel. The examples represent a Southern British English accent. The two arrows depict diphthongs, [eɪ] and [əʊ] (exemplified here by *eight* and *coat*, respectively)

are also speakers of New Zealand English who say these words as [fəʃ] and [tʃəps]. As further illustrations of how the grid works, consider [ʊ], located near the top right-hand corner of the quadrilateral, [æ], lower left side, and [ɐ], rightwards from there. The symbol [ʊ] represents a 'Near-close near-back rounded vowel'; [æ] a 'Near-open front unrounded vowel'; and [ɐ] a 'Near-open central vowel' (International Phonetic Association handbook 1999: 166 and 170). The reason for the slightly out-of-line position of [ɑ] in Figure 10.6 should become clear in the discussion of Figure 10.7.

Diphthongs are one-syllable complex vowel sounds. The start of a diphthong is a given vowel sound, but the oral cavity is then reset by degrees until the diphthong ends in the posture for a different vowel sound, as suggested by the arrow going from [ə] to [ʊ] for *coat* [kəʊt] in Figure 10.6. The identity of the vowel (which phoneticians label VOWEL QUALITY) changes dynamically in the production of a diphthong. A diphthong is not a sequence of two vowels each held steady (though the first component may be held for a while). However, a convenient notation for a diphthong uses the phonetic symbols for its initial and final vowel qualities. Another instance of an English diphthong is [ɔɪ], in *toy* [tɔɪ] and *oil* [ɔɪl] and so on. It could be represented by running an arrow across the vowel

VOWEL QUALITY is not a matter of how good a vowel is; it is simply the phoneticians' way of noting that there are different vowel sounds.

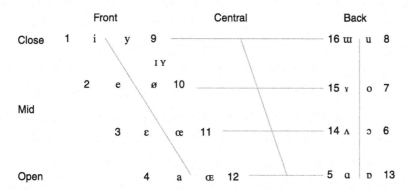

Figure 10.7 The vowel quadrilateral drawing attention to lip rounding (in each pair the left-hand vowel is unrounded and the right-hand one rounded). The numbers 1–8 identify the 'primary cardinal vowels', and 9–16 the 'secondary cardinal vowels'. The unnumbered vowels [ɪ] and [ʏ] are not cardinal vowels

quadrilateral from open-mid back rounded [ɔ] towards [ɪ] (though, to fit the phonetic facts, not quite reaching [ɪ]). Some varieties of English have as many as eight different diphthongs (➔ 11.2.3).

Small print below the IPA chart's diagram for VOWELS says that 'Where symbols appear in pairs, the one to the right represents a rounded vowel'. Figure 10.7 shows the pairs around the periphery. To limit complexity, eight central vowels and [ʊ] have been omitted. Numbers are given for the *cardinal vowels*, a system that will be outlined later.

The CLOSE FRONT UNROUNDED VOWEL [i] is used in many languages. In English it occurs most obviously in a long form [iː], as in *bee* [biː], *Eve* [iːv] and *siege* [siːdʒ]. If while uttering an [i] (or a long version of it [iː]) we keep everything constant but alter our lip posture from spread to rounded, the vowel sound becomes CLOSE FRONT ROUNDED [y] (or a long version of it [yː]). This is a sound used in French (for instance, in *duc* 'duke' [dyk] and *une* 'one' [yn]) and German (as in *Tür* 'door' [tyːɐ] and *über* 'over' [yːbɐ]). English speakers learning languages that use [y] often have trouble with the sound (➔ 15.6). They tend to mistake it for [u] because it is close and rounded and, because the English vowel with the quality [u] is a long vowel [uː], they tend to put that in its place, as when English beginners in French mispronounce *tu* 'you' [ty] as [tʰuː].

The other rounded front vowels [ʏ], [ø], [œ] and [ɶ], can likewise be produced by changing the posture of the lips to rounded while otherwise doing everything that would be necessary to make the spread or neutral partner vowel.

French has roundedness contrasts in three pairs of front vowels. French words given by Fougeron and Smith (1999: 78) to illustrate these contrasts are (and, unless, you are familiar with the IPA, it would be a good idea to locate the vowel symbols in Figure 10.7):

si 'if'	[si]	*su* 'known'	[sy]
ses 'his/hers_plural'	[se]	*ceux* 'these'	[sø]
serre 'greenhouse'	[sɛʁ]	*soeur* 'sister'	[sœʁ]

The symbol [ʁ] represents a uvular sound, but what is the manner of articulation? The answer can be found in the IPA chart.

Dutch also has three unround-*versus*-round distinctions among its front vowels, but with several of the vowels rather differently located from what is shown in Figure 10.7 (see Gussenhoven 1999: 76). Speakers of standard German distinguish between four unrounded front vowels [i], [ɪ], [e] and [ɛ] and four rounded counterparts of these vowels. German front-rounded vowels are generally somewhat more central than the ones depicted in Figure 10.7 (and there are diacritics that could be used to indicate where in the vowel space the summit of the tongue's hump is).

Turkish has roundedness distinctions for two pairs of front vowels, but also distinguishes a close back unrounded vowel [ɯ] from a close back rounded one [u]. A word pair given by Zimmer and Orgun (1999: 155) to illustrate the latter contrast is *kıl* 'hair' [kɯɫ] and *kul* 'slave' [kuɫ]. Japanese uses an unrounded [ɯ] (though with the lips generally not spread enough to justify use of the symbol [ɯ]) but not in contrast with [u]; no pairs of words are kept distinct in Japanese by an [ɯ]–[u] difference. A distinction made in most Southern accents of British English between members of a pair of back vowel sounds (those numbered 5 and 13 in Figure 10.7) is partly one of roundedness (but there is a length difference too); an example is *cart* [kɑːt] in contrast with *cot* [kɒt]. The sound [ɒ] is largely absent from American English. It is used in Australian and New Zealand English, but is not generally paired with a clearly back vowel there.

Two issues need to be tackled now: (1) the specification of vowels that fall within the boundaries of the vowel quadrilateral but do not have a recognized symbol; (2) how, in practical terms, one learns and applies the system introduced in Figures 10.5–7. These issues are interrelated.

An English pronunciation can be used to illustrate the first issue. Many speakers of Southern British English say the vowel in words like *come* and *blood* with a vowel that has the highest part of the tongue a bit lower than the [ɛœʌɔ] line shown in Figure 10.7 (which is to say that it is on the open side of the mid region) and the sound is also closer to the centre of the vowel quadrilateral than the rear boundary of the vowel producing area. The vowel is uttered with the lips in a neutral (that is, unrounded) position. Thus it is a centralized and lowered version of [ʌ]. The diacritic [ˌ] can be added to a phonetic symbol to denote a lowered (= more open) variant and [¨] indicates a centralized variant of a vowel. Adding both of the diacritics to the symbol [ʌ] gives the one needed for these particular pronunciations of *come* [kʰ̈ʌ̞m] and *blood* [bl̈ʌ̞d]. Of course there will be purposes that do not require such finesse, and then English *come* can satisfactorily be transcribed simply as [kʌm]. The vowel sounds [ɪ], [ʊ] and [ɐ] plotted in Figure 10.6 – and [ʏ] in Figure 10.7 – are so often transcribed that they have their own unitary symbols, avoiding the need to represent them with diacritics on cardinal vowel symbols.

Issue 2: how does a learner phonetician get to know what, for example, [ʌ] sounds like and what the average 'spacing' is between the vowel sounds around the edge of the quadrilateral, so as to be able to start working out how to utter and recognize a lowered and centralized variant of the sound? As in this chapter, you can be offered hints in the form of example words from languages that you might know or be able to hear spoken. But you could easily be misled because there are frequently competing ways of pronouncing words even within the same language. In Yorkshire English, for instance, *come* and *blood* are usually pronounced [kʰʊm] and [blʊd], respectively.

The system of numbered CARDINAL VOWELS displayed in Figure 10.7 was devised by Daniel Jones (1881–1967). Jones taught phonetics at University College London for more than 40 years and became the secretary to the International Phonetic Association in 1928, and eventually its president. With some reliance on X-ray pictures showing the position of the tongue in vowel articulations, he chose cardinal vowels 1 [i], 4 [a], 5 [ɑ] and 8 [u] as 'landmarks' because they delimit the extremities of the articulatory space in the mouth for vowels (see Figure 10.5). Then he relied on his own judgements of equal auditory intervals to establish further cardinal vowels between those. He trained his students to identify and produce the cardinal vowels. There are many sites on the Internet where you can listen to sound files of cardinal vowels (and indeed of other vowels).

Cardinal vowels 1–5 are made without lip rounding; 6–8 are rounded vowels. Jones termed these eight 'primary'. Anyone who wishes to make practical use of phonetics should become familiar with the eight primary cardinal vowels. Each of the secondary cardinal vowels, 9–16, is opposite in lip rounding to the primary one that it is paired with (as shown in Figure 10.7); so the secondaries are fairly easy to learn after the primaries have been mastered.

There is a tendency for the vowels that are most widespread across the languages of the world to be among the primary cardinal vowels, or similar to primary cardinal vowels. The secondary cardinal vowels tend to be less used. This matter will not be pursued here, but the following statement by Clark, Yallop and Fletcher (2007: 31) gives a flavour of the sorts of consideration that are relevant: 'Few languages distinguish unrounded back vowels from rounded back vowels, and where rounded front vowels occur, they are normally found in addition to front unrounded vowels and not instead of them.'

The CARDINAL VOWELS are a set of 16 'landmarks' along the front and back edges of the articulatory space for vowels. Other vowels are specified in relation to the cardinals.

There is a nicely annotated copy of a recording of Jones saying the cardinal vowels on YouTube (➔ W10.4).

10.4 APPROXIMANTS

APPROXIMANTS are vowel-like consonants. They are similar to vowel sounds in not having any stricture tight enough to create either full closure or fricative noise, though they do generally have a narrowing – termed an OPEN APPROXIMATION – that restricts the passage of air through the vocal tract more than for typical vowel sounds. In a syllable, the usual role of an approximant is similar to that of most consonants: not the main display of energy, but (part of) the syllable's onset or end. Normally, approximants are voiced sounds and there is usually a velic closure.

The last two rows of the IPA chart's CONSONANTS (PULMONIC) table classifies several approximants. Three more are listed in the OTHER SYMBOLS section of the chart. The saggital cross-sections in Figure 10.8 show the settings for three approximants.

English 'r' may manifest itself differently in different syllable positions, for example as a tap between vowels, as a fricative when it comes straight after a plosive (a voiceless fricative after voiceless plosives) and as retroflection towards the end of a vowel's articulation. Also, it may be systematically absent immediately after vowels in some varieties, when a written <r> suggests otherwise, e.g. in *car* or *rider* (➜ 11.2.1). However, the POST-ALVEOLAR APPROXIMANT [ɹ], on the left in Figure 10.8, occurs at the beginnings of words in many varieties of English: American, Australian, British, New Zealand and South African. Examples are: *right* [ɹaɪt], *rough* [ɹʌf], *room* [ɹuːm]. The edges of the back of the tongue make a seal against the upper molar teeth, but there is enough space between the tip of the tongue and post-alveolar region (the boundary between the alveolar ridge and the palate) to avoid audible friction. There would almost certainly be lip rounding on [ɹ] in a word like *room*, an anticipatory assimilation of the lip posture for the close back round vowel [uː]. But in English it is not uncommon for all instances of [ɹ] to be at least slightly lip rounded regardless of the quality of the vowel coming next.

LATERAL APPROXIMANTS are sounds where the air flows, without friction noise, around one side (or both sides) of the tongue because flow along the centre line of the tongue is blocked. In the case of the ALVEOLAR LATERAL APPROXIMANT [l] there is closure between the tip of the tongue and the centre of the alveolar ridge.

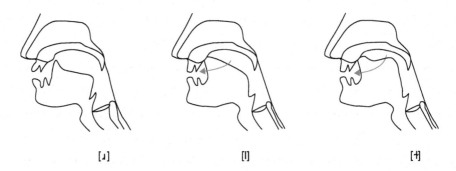

[ɹ]   [l]   [ɫ]

Figure 10.8 Articulatory postures for the post-alveolar approximant [ɹ] and two lateral approximants, 'clear' [l] and 'dark' [ɫ]. The arrows for the latter two indicate that airflow, blocked in the centre, is over the side(s) of the tongue

Activity 10.7

Use ingressive breath to explore the nature of the closure that you make for [l]. Say a word that starts with this sound, for example *lie* [laɪ]. After you have said it a few times, say just the [l], then do the [l] while sucking in air. It is hard (but not impossible) to do this with voicing. However, the observations can as easily be made with a voiceless ingressive airstream [l̥]. Is your [l] left-sided, right-sided, or do you feel a chill bilaterally on your palate? How far back on the palate do you feel the coldness? It is worth contrasting this with the chill produced by doing an ingressive [ɹ], as in a word like *rye* (and, again, it would be OK to do the ingressive one voicelessly).

Because the cross-sections in Figure 10.8 are on the centre line of the head, the diagram for [l] fails to show that there is some closure against the upper teeth to left and right of the tongue tip, and for a one-sided [l], where all the outflow of air goes over one side of the tongue, the closure also reaches a long way back, on the other side of the tongue, against the inside of the upper teeth preventing airflow over that side. This means that the closure for [l] is not just a barrier against airflow straight ahead, but also forms something of a pouch behind the tongue tip and under arch of the palate. This is important for the acoustic quality of laterals. It is a 'dead end' cavity and produces anti-resonances that subtract from the voicing spectrum of fundamental and harmonics coming up from the glottis (Johnson 2003: 160–163).

The IPA has a diacritic for velarization [~]. VELARIZATION is the raising of the body of the tongue towards the velum, which gives it a hump similar to that for the vowel-sound [ʊ]. A velarized [l] is symbolized [ɫ]. Impressionistically, it has an auditory overlay, which is recognizable as the quality of a close back vowel. Phoneticians generally refer to it as DARK L. Dark L is often produced with some lip rounding. In many varieties of English, 'l' is clear in front of a stressed vowel and dark elsewhere, so the word *lull* is pronounced [lʌɫ]. Liverpool English is noted for its velarization (Hughes, Trudgill and Watt 2012: 114), so its speakers generally have [ɫ] at both ends of their city's name.

In a lateral, if the side of the tongue (or both sides for utterers of bilateral laterals) that air is flowing over is (/are) slightly taughtened to narrow the sideways-facing slit, then fricative noise can be produced. This is because approximants involve open approximation, something not far from the close approximation strictures that yield audible friction. As soon as that boundary has been crossed, the sound will no longer be an approximant but a lateral fricative. Welsh has a VOICELESS LATERAL FRICATIVE [ɬ], for example in *llwyd* 'grey/brown' [ɬʊid]. Zulu has both the voiceless lateral fricative [ɬ] associated with the written digraph <hl>, as in *hlala* 'sit', and a voiced one [ɮ] corresponding to the written digraph <dl>, as in *indlovu* 'elephant'.

It is sometimes a shock for phonetics students whose main written language is English to discover that the phonetic symbol for the approximant at the start of *yacht* [jɒt], *you* [juː], *ewe* [juː] and *yodel* [ˈjəʊdɫ] is [j], where they might have expected something based on the orthographic symbol <Y>. For the PALATAL APPROXIMANT [j], the vocal tract posture starts in the vicinity of where everything would need to be for a close front unrounded vowel, as in the top left-hand diagram of Figure 10.5, then it quickly glides away from there to take up the posture of the vowel sound that follows it. Thus [j] is a rush away from [i] or [ɪ] to the start of another vowel sound.

The approximant [j] can come after another consonant and before a vowel in many varieties of British English (though not in Norfolk), in words like *beauty* [ˈbjuːti], *pure* [pjʊə], *tune* [tjuːn] and *cute* [cjuːt]. This happens in Australian, New Zealand and South African English too. However, the pronunciations just given for the last three words are implausible for anything outside of an old-fashioned elocution lesson. After a voiceless plosive ([p], [t] or [c]) in a stressed syllable, we would hear a voiceless palatal fricative [ç], not the approximant [j]; so *pure* [pᶜʊə], *tune* [tᶜuːn] and *cute* [cᶜuːt] (where the symbol [ç] is superscripted to indicate that it is held only briefly before the vowel starts).

The (VOICED) LABIAL—VELAR APPROXIMANT [w] in English words such as *wee* [wiː], *woo* [wuː], *what* [wɒt] and *away* [əˈweɪ] involves starting in the vicinity of [u] or [ʊ] with, as the term *velar* in the label indicates, the hump of the tongue near the velum (as in the top right-hand diagram of Figure 10.5), then gliding rapidly into the tongue posture for the following vowel. Additionally there is tight lip-rounding, the basis for the term *labial* in the label. If you look in a mirror while alternating between the words *Ooh* [uː] and *woo* [wuː], you should be able to see that the lips squeeze up to form a smaller opening for [w], than the lip-rounding of [uː] in *Ooh*, where there isn't an approximant at the start. The term GLIDE covers both [j] and [w].

The *OTHER SYMBOLS* section of the IPA chart that lists [w] also offers a VOICELESS LABIAL—VELAR FRICATIVE symbol [ʍ]. This is likely to be heard in stressed syllables with a preceding voiceless plosive, for example *twice* [tʍaɪs] and *queen* [kʍiːn]. And yet again this illustrates how near approximant articulation is to the borderline of fricativity.

A GLIDE, for example [j] or [w], is a vowel sound in a part of a syllable where consonant sounds are typically found.

10.5 SUMMARY

Voice is a sound source generated when air causes vibrations as it passes through the glottis (the space between the vocal folds in the larynx). Voice, the basis for much of speech, can be described as complex periodic sound waves with a fundamental frequency (variations in which are heard as tone and intonation in speech) and harmonics ('overtone' multiples of the fundamental pitch).

The quality of a vowel (its identity and formant patterns) depends largely on the sizes and shapes of cavities fore and aft of the highest point of the tongue. Lip rounding contributes too. Diphthongs are one-syllable sounds that begin with one vowel quality and end with another. The cardinal vowels are a set of 16 'landmark' vowel sounds that provide a practical basis for description. Other vowels are specified in relation to the cardinals. Diacritics are marks added to basic phonetic symbols to denote subtle features of articulation.

Consonant sounds are described in terms of their manner of articulation (nasal, fricative, plosive and so on) and the position of their stricture (from bilabial to glottal). Strictures are constrictions that interfere with the flow of air through the vocal tract. A stricture can be complete closure or a close approximation (causing friction noise) or an open approximation (for the vowel-like class of consonants called *approximants*, for example [ɹ], [w] and [l]). Assimilation is the modification of a sound's place or manner of articulation towards a match with the articulation of a neighbouring sound.

Sounds that have their main or only airflow through the nose are called nasals. Oral sounds are made with the soft palate raised to prevent airflow from the pharynx into the nasal cavity.

Table 10.2 is an addition to Table 9.2 and summarizes important points covered in both chapters on phonetics.

Table 10.2 Articulatory and voicing properties of the main classes of speech sound

Manner of articulation	Does air flow out through		Stricture tight enough for friction noise?	Voiced or voiceless?
	the mouth?	the nose?		
vowels	YES, easily	for some speakers and in some languages	NO	usually voiced
approximants	YES, fairly freely	usually NO	NO	usually voiced
nasals	NO	YES	oral closure	usually voiced
fricatives	YES	usually NO	YES	either
plosives	NO, then YES	usually NO	closure	either
trills and taps	YES, except at moment(s) of contact	usually NO	momentary closure(s)	usually voiced

10.6 FURTHER ACTIVITY

Activity 10.8

Find a phonetic transcription in the list (a)–(z) that is plausible for each English word given. Say the words and think about the pronunciations and transcriptions. Treat this as a more interesting task than just finding a letter to go with each number. One of the answers has to be used twice and the names of two, slightly unusual, salad ingredients have been thrown in as distractors! (The salady things are not the answers for any of 1–25, but you might try to identify them.)

1 picture	2 knight	3 live ('not dead')	4 tenth
5 night	6 live ('reside')	7 jet	8 fire
9 yes	10 Jess	11 yet	12 hand towel
13 shrivel	14 fearful	15 close ('nearby')	16 adjust
17 linger	18 close ('to shut')	19 colonel	20 listening
21 boyishly	22 unique	23 housing estate	24 unbearable
25 tourist spot			

a [naɪt]	b [lɪv]	c [laɪv]	d [ˈfɪəfʊl]
e [dʒɛs]	f [jɛt]	g [kləʊs]	h [jɛs]
i [kləʊz]	j [ˈpɪktʃə]	k [dʒɛt]	l [juːˈniːk]
m [ˈtʃɜːvl̩]	n [tɛŋθ]	o [ˈʃɹɪvl̩]	p [ˌʌmˈbɛəɹəbl̩]
q [ˈtʊəɹɪsʔspɒt]	r [əˈdʒʌst]	s [ˈlɪŋgə]	t [ˈlɪsnɪŋ]
u [ˈkɜːnəl]	v [ˈfaɪə]	w [ˈhænʔtaʊəl]	x [ˈbɔɪʃli]
y [ˈhaʊzɪŋɪˌsteɪt]	z [ˈwɔːtəˌkrɛs]		

COMMENTARY ON ACTIVITIES

O━┳ Remember that this symbol indicates that there is a commentary on the activity that you can find on the companion website at www.routledge.com/cw/merrison.

FURTHER READING and REFERENCES

Suggestions for further reading on the topics discussed in this chapter can be found on the companion website (www.routledge.com/cw/merrison).

Any piece of academic writing must always provide a list of publications to which reference has been made. Unusually and very unconventionally, this information is provided on the companion website (www.routledge.com/cw/merrison). Always ask your tutor about how you are to present references for any piece of work that you submit.

Chapter 11
Phonology

Key Ideas in this Chapter

- Phonology is concerned with the abstract contrastive units, such as phonemes, which underlie the actual spoken sounds that are studied in phonetics.

- The phonology of any given language is characterized by the set of phonemes it employs, how these phonemes are sequenced to make syllables, and how the sounds of the language are organized with respect to each other, as a system.

- Phonemes are abstract phonological units which allow speakers to distinguish words from other words.

- There can be several different pronunciations of a phoneme, but replacing one with another will not make a different word.

- The systematic nature of the phonological contrasts in a language can be captured by decomposing phonemes into a finite set of binary features.

- There are restrictions on how phonemes can be combined together within and across syllables (phonotactics).

- Word stress can be phonologically contrastive in English and other languages, distinguishing between different words which are composed of the same sequence of phonemes.

11.1 INTRODUCTION

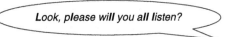

Look, please will you all listen?

Although you might think there is only one l-sound in English, in fact a range of distinct variants can be heard, not only between speakers of different **dialects** (➔ 12), but also in different positions and contexts in the utterances of a single individual. We will use this subclass of LATERALS (➔10.4) to illustrate here the basic idea of a **phoneme**, the central unit of **phonology**. The phonology of a language is its pronunciation system, with emphasis on *system*: speech sounds are stored and selected (normally unconsciously ➔ R3.2) in an organized way, rather than as a random miscellany which is dipped into as the need arises. Sounds like the l's in the speech bubble above have physical reality; they can make people's eardrums vibrate. But what unifies them is an abstract categorization: they count as different instances of 'the same thing': the English phoneme /l/.

The phoneme is a source of quiet satisfaction to many linguists: together with the descriptive tools of **phonetics** (➔ 9, 10), it provides a neat framework for understanding the nature of pronunciation systems. There are plenty of unresolved issues in phonology, but working out the phonemes of a language is a substantial and satisfying achievement; so the phoneme is an important topic in this chapter.

Phonetics is universalist: its notations and descriptions are intended to cover pronunciations in any language. Phonology has universalist interests too, but also has a central concern with understanding the pronunciation systems of separate languages and language varieties, investigating what is the pronunciation system of each variety (➔ 12; R2.2). Different languages and dialects can sound strikingly different, and adult language learners' pronunciations often disclose the phonological systems of earlier-learnt languages (➔ 15.6). Most of the examples discussed in this chapter come from the phonology of English, but occasionally from other languages. (Taking advantage of the knowledge of English that can be assumed for readers of this book makes it possible to keep an introduction to phonology within manageable proportions.)

The phonology of any given language or variety is characterized by three essential factors:

- Its PHONEME INVENTORY: the selection of sounds it employs from among all the phonetic resources available to humans. For instance at the beginning of *Viti*, the name of the country called Fiji in English, speakers of Fijian use a voiced bilabial fricative [β]. The sound [β] is not used in English. Another example is that while English has the sound [θ], in <u>th</u>ing, e<u>th</u>er, too<u>th</u> and so on, many other languages make no use of [θ].
- How sounds are sequenced to make SYLLABLES. For example, Greek words such as *psári* 'fish' and *psomí* 'bread', show that [ps] is an allowable sequence at the beginning of a syllable in that language, but in English [ps] is only possible at the end of a syllable. For instance in *lapse* [læps], or across the division between two syllables, as in *topsoil* [ˈtʰɒp.sɔɪɫ].
- How the inventory of sounds is organized. An illustration of this is that English has six plosives in three pairs, **voiceless** *versus* **voiced** [p] and [b], [t] and [d], [k] and [g],

The dot in the transcription of *topsoil* indicates the break between syllables.

whereas in Pǔtōnghuá (Mandarin Chinese), which has six similar plosives, they are all voiceless and paired as aspirated against unaspirated: [pʰ] and [p], [tʰ] and [t], [kʰ] and [k].

11.2 PHONEMES

11.2.1 Syllables, phonemes, and segments

A word form consists of one or more syllables. *Words* is a one-syllable word, whereas the word *syllables* has three syllables:

[wɜːdʒ]
[ˈsɪl.ə.bl̩z]

Syllables, in turn, are sequences of phonemes (as in the **hierarchy of rank** → Figure 7.1). A phoneme is an abstract unit, standing for only those aspects of pronunciation that enable users of the language or variety to distinguish words from other words. The phoneme omits details that do not have systematically contrastive signalling significance. Varieties of English usually have 40 or so phonemes. Some languages have more; a few have about three times as many; a few have less than half the total for English.

Some terminology is going to be needed for the parts of a syllable. Syllables consist of one or more SEGMENTS, discrete units of sound like consonants and vowels. The sonorous carrying-power of speech comes from its obligatory segment, the NUCLEUS. The nucleus is normally a vowel sound, though some languages allow other sounds as well. English, for instance, allows approximants and nasals to be nuclei (as when a syllabic-l forms the nucleus of the second syllable in *handle*, instead of a vowel being pronounced there: [ˈhændl̩]; or the syllabic-n in [ˈmɒdn̩], one way of saying *modern*). One or more consonants at the beginning of a syllable are its ONSET, and any consonants that the syllable ends with are its CODA. Syllables commonly have onsets, but there are languages that largely do without codas to their syllables (Japanese and the Nigerian language Igbo, for instance). Figure 11.1 shows the syllable structure of the two words used as examples above. It shows the middle syllable of *syllables* as having neither an onset nor a coda. The last syllable of *syllables* as represented here has an approximant [l̩] as its nucleus.

Figure 11.1 The syllables of two words. A Greek letter <σ> *sigma* heads each syllable's constituent segments. A vertical line drops from σ to its nucleus. Any consonants to the left of the nucleus within a given syllable constitute the onset; to the right the coda

Consider the words *label* and *level*, which many English speakers pronounce as, respectively, [ˈleɪbəl] and [ˈlɛvəl]. The phonetic difference between 'clear' [l] and 'dark' (or *velarized*) [l̩] was explained in the previous chapter (→ 10.4). The intuition that the segments [l] and [ɫ] in these words count as 'the same thing', that they are both l-sounds notwithstanding the difference between clear and dark, is captured by saying that both are manifestations of the same English phoneme, /l/, where the slashes signify that this is a phonological unit, not a phonetic unit. To be identifiable as the words *label* and *level*, what is spoken has to begin and end with phones that represent /l/ and not any other phoneme. The lower three rows in (1) show what happens when one or both of the /l/s goes unpronounced.

(1)   ['leɪbəɫ]   label   ['lɛvəɫ]   level
        ['eɪbəɫ]   able   ['ɛvəɫ]   not (yet) an English word
        ['leɪbə]   labour (for some) ['lɛvə]   leather (for many Brits)
        ['eɪbə]   not an English word ['ɛvə]   ever (for some)

If there is no phonetic segment representing an /l/, then we are not likely to be understood as saying *label* or *level*. *Label* with nothing in place of its initial /l/ is *able*, and when its final /l/ is missing it becomes *labour* in non-RHOTIC varieties of English (➜ Activity 12.4; R2.2), ones where there is no segment corresponding to the final written <r>. *Level* without anything for /l/ at the start yields something that happens not to be an English word, but sounds as if it could be one; without its final /l/ it is a now widespread British pronunciation of *leather*. If both /l/s are absent from *label*, the result could be an English word, but is not (yet). *Level* without /l/s is *ever* in accents where the <r> at the end is 'silent', i.e. non-rhotic ones.

If representatives of different English phonemes are put in place of one or both of the /l/ phonemes, then we get different words, as illustrated in (2a, 2b).

(2)   (a)   ['leɪbəɫ]   label
                ['beɪbəɫ]   Babel
                ['tʰeɪbəɫ]   table
                ['cʰeɪbəɫ]   cable
                ['geɪbəɫ]   gable
                ['meɪbəɫ]   Mabel
                ['feɪbəɫ]   fable
                ['seɪbəɫ]   sable
        (b)   ['lɛvəɫ]   level
                ['bɛvəɫ]   bevel
                ['dɛvəɫ]   devil
                ['nɛvəɫ]   Neville
                ['rɛvəɫ]   revel
                ['lɛvən]   leaven
                ['sɛvən]   seven
                ['hɛvən]   heaven

Comparisons within the sets of words in (2a, b) are evidence that the phonemes /b/, /t/, /d/, /k/, /g/, /m/, /n/, /f/, /s/, /r/ and /h/ contrast with /l/ and with each other, which is to say that they are responsible for distinguishing words from other words. Of course there are more phonemes in English, and we would need other sets of words to illustrate that.

11.2.2 Minimal pairs

A pair of words that differs only by the substitution of a single segment is a **minimal pair**. The relevance of the examples discussed above is that they are minimal pairs. For instance, in (2b) [ˈbɛvəɫ] and [ˈlɛvəɫ] differ only in whether the first segment is [b] or [l], and they are pronunciations of different words, bevel and level; so they are a minimal pair providing evidence for a phonemic distinction between /b/ and /l/. The difference between [ˈlɛvən] and [ˈlɛvəɫ] lies in just the last segment and they are different words, leaven and level, so they are a minimal pair testifying to /n/ and /l/ being separate phonemes. It may seem obvious to people who have grown up speaking a European language that [n] and [l] have to represent different phonemes, but in fact they do not have to; in some varieties of Chinese the difference between [n] and [l] is not phonemic; it does not signal differences between words.

> Similarly, [l] and [r] are allophones of the same phoneme in Chinese (hence the difficulty many Chinese-speaking learners of English have with distinguishing words like *rock* and *lock*).

Activity 11.1 🔑

Take the English words *local* [ˈləʊkəɫ] and *lawful* [ˈlɔːfʊɫ] and make some minimal pairs by substituting phonemes at their beginnings and/or ends to give different English words. Do your results offer any phonemes not listed in the examples in (2a, b)?

Now consider what the consequences are of exchanging a clear [l] for a dark [ɫ] in words such as *label* and *level*. What if, instead of [ˈleɪbəɫ] and [ˈlɛvəɫ], a speaker were to say [ˈleɪbəl] and [ˈlɛvəl]? The answer is that the speaker's words will be heard as *label* and *level*, but sounding as if spoken in a different accent of English, perhaps UK Tyneside, where all realizations of /l/ are characteristically clear (Hughes, Trudgill and Watt 2005: 124). While putting /n/ in place of the dark [ɫ] at the end of *level* changes it into a different word (*leaven*), putting [l] in place of the [ɫ] in *level* does not signal a different word. The phones [l] and [ɫ] do not contrast. They are exponents of the same phoneme, /l/. The pairs {[ˈleɪbəɫ], [ˈleɪbəl]} and {[ˈlɛvəɫ], [ˈlɛvəl]} are not minimal pairs. At the abstract level of phonology, the first two are /leɪbəl/ and the next two are /lɛvəl/, because phonemic representation ignores whatever is not contrastive.

Pronunciations with [ɫ] replacing the initial [l] in [ˈleɪbəɫ] and [ˈlɛvəɫ], likewise do not alter word identity: [ˈɫeɪbəɫ] will be heard as *label* and [ˈɫɛvəɫ] as *level*, but in a different accent again, perhaps as from a speaker of Liverpool English (Hughes, Trudgill and Watt 2005: 99). The conclusion is that English has a phoneme /l/, an abstract phonological unit in which clearness and darkness are irrelevant. What we have been considering are two of the phoneme's phonetic realizations, [l] and [ɫ], which therefore do not provide evidence for phonemic contrasts.

Activity 11.2 🔑

What contrasts do the minimal pair comparisons among the following set of four words provide evidence for?
    [lɪɫ] Lil' (short form of *Lillian*), [lɒɫ] loll, [lʌɫ] lull, [laɪɫ] Lyle

11.2.3 Allophones

A speech sound as a physical manifestation corresponding to a particular phoneme is called an ALLOPHONE of that phoneme. There will often be several allophones corresponding to a given phoneme. How the available sound space for speech is carved up into phonemes and allophones is part of the phonological system of each particular language. What are two phonemes in one language might be a pair of allophones of a single phoneme in another language, and this is something children must work out early in the acquisition process (➔ 15.3.1). So far, the phoneme /l/ in English has been shown to have two allophones [l] and [ɫ]. Clear allophones of /l/ occur when they are in the onset of a stressed syllable, either as the only consonant there (as in *low* or *loom*) or one of a cluster of consonants (as in *blue* or *gloomy*); [ɫ] is the manifestation for /l/ elsewhere in a syllable.

There is no obvious phonetic reason motivating the existence of a dark allophone of /l/ in English. There are varieties of English in which it does not occur; English as spoken on the Indian sub-continent (➔ 18) is a major example (Gargesh 2004, Mahboob and Ahmar 2004). The /l/ phonemes of French, German and Italian generally do not have dark allophones. Having [ɫ] as one of the allophones of /l/ seems simply to be one of the things that many native speakers of English acquire as part of learning their language (➔ 15) and becoming acculturated into their speech communities (➔ 13, 12). It will be seen later, however, that some other cases of allophony do have clear phonetic motivation.

Another two allophones of /l/, that is to say phones that, even though they are different, count as instances of /l/, are going to be introduced soon, but do Activity 11.3 first, to check your understanding of the phoneme concept and to get more practice in phonological analysis.

Activity 11.3 🔑

A speaker of Japanese is likely to respond [saɴ] to the question 'In Japanese, how do you say *three* when you are counting?' ([saɴ] is the usual pronunciation of the word in isolation. It is written 三 in Japanese, or *san* for Westerners.) The spoken word's last segment is a uvular nasal stop [ɴ], but different nasal sounds can be heard when the word occurs in longer expressions, for example:

[sambaɴ]	三番	*sanban* 'no. 3'
[san̪tɔ:]	三等	*santou* 'third class, third place, third prize'
[saŋkakɯ̥]	三角	*sankaku* 'triangle'
[san̪do]	三度	*sando* '3 degrees'
[saŋgatsɯ̥]	三月	*sangatsu* 'March'

a) Using the technical terms *phoneme* and *allophone*, make a statement of what the data above suggest about this/these nasal stop(s) in Japanese phonology. A one-sentence statement is all that is needed. It should be cautiously phrased because you have been given very little data here, and no minimal pairs.

b) Offer a guess as to why the Japanese word for '3' appears not always to end in [ɴ], but sometimes in [m], sometimes in [ɲ] and sometimes in [ŋ].

A phoneme is the unifying concept that groups together a set of phonetically similar allophones. The four allophones of Japanese /ɴ/ in Activity 11.3 are phonetically similar in all being nasal stops. The two allophones of English /l/ discussed above are phonetically similar too: [l] and [ɫ] are both lateral approximants.

At the start of a stressed syllable, the sequences /pl/ and /kl/ are manifested across many varieties of English with a voiceless allophone of /l/, which is written phonetically as [l̥]. This allophone of /l/ is clear as well as voiceless. Examples are given in (3a).

(3)	(a)	/pleɪz/	[pʰl̥eɪz̥]	plays
		/plæn/	[pʰl̥æn]	plan
		/kleɪz/	[kʰl̥eɪz̥]	clays
		/klæn/	[kʰl̥æn]	clan
	(b)	/leɪz/	[leɪz̥]	laze
		/læn/	[læn]	LAN (network)
	(c)	/bleɪz/	[bleɪz̥]	blaze
		/gleɪz/	[gleɪz̥]	glaze
		/blænd/	[blænd]	bland
		/glænd/	[glænd]	gland
	(d)	/ɛərəpleɪn/	[ˈɛərəpleɪn]	aeroplane
		/ɛərpleɪn/	[ˈɛə‑pleɪn]	airplane
		/prɒkləmeɪʃən/	[ˌpɹɒkləˈmeɪʃən]	proclamation

The [ˌ] at the start of [ˌpɹɒkləˈmeɪʃən] indicates SECONDARY STRESS on the first syllable. However, the focus of discussion here is the unstressed syllable [klə].

In minimally different words without the initial /p/ or /k/ (3b) we do not get the voiceless allophone; the first segment in *laze* and *LAN* is voiced. We also get the voiced allophone of /l/ when /p/ and /k/ are replaced by their voiced counterparts /b/ and /g/ (3c). Because of the final /d/, *bland* and *gland* do not form minimal pairs with *plan* and *clan*, but the words are comparable in relevant respects, and they form minimal pairs with *planned*. When the syllable with a /pl/ or /kl/ onset is not stressed (3d) it is the voiced allophone [l] that is generally used. So it is the presence of /p/ or /k/ before /l/ at the beginning of a stressed syllable that correlates with /l/'s voiceless allophone [l̥].

Across many varieties of English, /r/ has a voiceless allophone after a voiceless plosive in the onset of a stressed syllable, in words such as those listed in (4). The fact that this follows the same pattern as /l/ in (3a) demonstrates how languages have phonological systems, not just curious isolated phonetic facts.

(4)   pry, oppress, try, attract, cry, accrue

Hughes, Trudgill and Watt (2005: 45, 75) note an increasingly common feature of English in London and surrounding areas, and even further afield. To put it simply, a vowel sound [ʊ] is the allophone used in the places where [ɫ], the dark allophone of /l/, was described above as occurring, i.e. elsewhere than in the onsets of stressed syllables. Examples are given in (5).

(5)	/bɛl/	[bɛʊ]	bell
	/dɒl/	[dɒʊ]	doll
	/mɪlk/	[mɪʊˀk]	milk
	/lɪtəl/	[ˈlɪʔʊ]	little

According to Clark, Yallop and Fletcher (2007: 96) this allophone of /l/ is found in South Australian English too.

In the following couple of activities you can explore some of the many other allophone sets characteristic of English phonology.

Activity 11.4 ⊶

Study the pairs of words below. The plural form of English nouns is usually written with an <s>: *one cat, two or three cats*. Give phonetic transcriptions for the sound that the plural suffix would have if it were added to each of these six words.

/mɒp/ [mɒp] mop   /pæt/ [pæt] pat   /ræk/ [ɹæc] rack
/mɒb/ [mɒb] mob   /pæd/ [pæd] pad   /ræg/ [ɹæg] rag

Is there a systematic difference between the plural suffix on the words in the upper row and in the lower row? How do you characterize it?

Activity 11.5 ⊶

Study the list of English words below. They show two different allophones of /g/. In the accent represented here, when is the allophone [ɟ] used and when is [g] used?

/ˈgægɪŋ/   [ˈɟæɟiŋ]   gagging
/ˈgægəl/   [ˈɟægɫ]   gaggle
/ˈgɪgəl/   [ˈɟigɫ]   giggle
/ˈgɒgəl/   [ˈgɒgɫ]   goggle
/ˈguːgəl/   [ˈguːgɫ]   google
/ˈgɑːgəl/   [ˈgɑːgɫ]   gargle

Unless the answer is obvious to you, make a list of the sounds that follow each of the /g/ allophones in the data given, and then attempt to state concisely the kinds of sound in each set.

The phonetic symbol [ɟ] represents a VOICED PALATAL PLOSIVE. It is a g-like sound articulated towards the rear of the hard palate, which is to say the closure between the tongue and the roof of the mouth is a bit further forward than the area of the soft palate (the *velum*) where closure is made for [g]. In terms of how the tongue moves in the mouth when speaking, could there be a connection between the place of articulation of a given /g/ allophone and the nature of the sounds that follow it, i.e. is the allophony phonetically motivated?

11.2.4 English phoneme types and features

The main goal of this section is to illustrate that a language's selection of contrastive phonological units and dimensions tends to be systematic and that phonemes are organized into subsets with similarities that are relevant in the process of mapping mental phonological representations into sequences of phones, which amounts to an abstract account of the nature of speech production. The important concept of phonological DISTINCTIVE FEATURES will be introduced too. Some outline generalizations will be made, across different varieties of English.

→ 14 and 15 for more on the mental representation of language and on speech processes in the mind.

A book by Noam Chomsky and Morris Halle, *The Sound Pattern of English* (1968), gave modern phonology much of its impetus. An influential aspect of this work was the use of phonological distinctive features. They were extending ideas developed by the Prague School of linguistics in the 1920s and 1930s, particularly by Roman Jakobson (1896–1982). The contrastive properties of phonological units, such as phonemes, and the similarities between the units are distilled into specifications (usually binary, i.e. ±) on a limited number of distinctive features. For instance, phonemes that count as voiced are specified as [+voice]; voiceless ones as [-voice]. The English phoneme /p/ is:

- [-syllabic]
- [-SONORANT] (meaning that it is an OBSTRUENT)
- [+stop]
- [-nasal] (and [+stop, -nasal] segments are plosives)
- [+labial]
- [-voice]

The term OBSTRUENT covers plosives, fricatives and affricates. Types of sound that are not obstruents are SONORANTS.

The feature [-syllabic] indicates that, unlike vowels (which are +syllabic), /p/, as a consonant, cannot be the nucleus of a syllable.

A consonant inventory for English

The consonant phonemes underlying the pronunciation systems of many varieties of English are set out in Table 11.1. Though the layout is similar to that of the IPA chart, this table is different. The slashes are a reminder that these are phonological representations, not direct or specific indications of speech sound. And the aim here is an account of English, not an attempt to describe the sounds of all languages.

The top row of Table 11.1 has the phonemes that most clearly typify consonants (because the phones that manifest them in speech involve complete blockage of the airstream). That row and the one below it are [-sonorant], which is to say that they are obstruents (= plosives, affricates and fricatives, all of which relate to sounds having at least some increase in pressure behind an oral stricture). The phonemes in successively lower rows underlie speech sounds that allow increasingly free outflow of air, with the glides /j/ and /w/ in the last row, because the pronunciations associated with them have airflow as powerful as vowels (though generally for shorter durations). Glides are [-syllabic] because they cannot be syllable nuclei, but they also carry the feature specification [-consonantal] to indicate their borderline status.

Table 11.1 The 24-consonant phoneme array shared by many varieties of English

major class features				labial		labio-dental		alveolar		post-alveolar		velar		glottal
				-v	**+v**	**-v**	**+v**	**-v**	**+v**	**-v**	**+v**	**-v**	**+v**	**-v**
		−	−	/p/	/b/			/t/	/d/	/tʃ/	/dʒ/	/k/	/g/	
consonantal	− approximant	+ sonorant	+ continuant	/f/	/v/	/θ/	/ð/	/s/	/z/	/ʃ/	/ʒ/			/h/
+		−	−	/m/				/n/					/ŋ/	
	+ approximant	+ sonorant							/l/					
			+						/r/					
−	+		+		/w/								/j/	

Notes: All these consonants are negatively specified on the phonological distinctive feature *syllabic*, i.e. they are [-syllabic]; the sub-column headings -v abbreviate [-voice], i.e. voiceless; +v is for [+voice], i.e. voiced.

You might have observed that Table 11.1 fails to distinguish /l/ from /r/. Both are [+voice], alveolar in place of articulation and [+consonantal, +approximant, +sonorant, +continuant]. To avoid clutter in the table, readers are being relied upon to supply the differentiating feature [±lateral]: /l/ is [+lateral]; /r/ and all the other phonemes in the table are [-lateral].

Activity 11.6 🔑

In Table 11.1 'major class features' are represented in the columns to the left of the phonemes in the body of the table. According to the table, what are the major class features shared by:

- the glides /j/ and /w/ (besides their being [-syllabic, -consonantal])?
- the row of nasals (/m/, /n/ and /ŋ/)?
- the fricative row (/f/ through /h/)?

Table 11.1 shows a pattern of phonological contrasts. Across different varieties of English there can be quite different ways of realizing those contrasts in sound. Thus, while many kinds of English have fricatives [θ] and [ð] as the sounds that represent /θ/ and /ð/, Pakistani English (→ 18) has dental stops for these, as in [nɔːr̪t̪] *north* and [d̪en] *then* (Mahboob and Ahmar 2004: 1011).

Activity 11.7 🔑

Take the row of nine fricative phonemes in Table 11.1 and try to find sets of words – minimal pairs at least – that establish them as phonemes distinctive from each other in English. Do this task for syllable onset and for syllable coda position. Are any parts of this task impossible?

Examples:

- /fiː/ *fee*, /viː/ *V*, and /ðiː/ *thee* establish that /f/, /v/ and /ð/ are distinct phonemes in syllable onset position, but there are still six more fricatives to go.
- /liːf/ *leaf*, /liːv/ *leave*, and /liːθ/ *Leith* (Edinburgh's harbour) are distinct phonemes in coda position, but there are six more to go.

Consider using a different vowel. It need not be the same vowel in every pair. There could be other consonants in the words. Trying to do it with long words would make the task much harder.

A vowel inventory for English

English has simple vowel phonemes, both long (like /iː/) and short (like /æ/), and **diphthong** phonemes (two-part vowels, like /aʊ/; ➔ 9, 10). Table 11.2 sets out distinctive phonological features that can be used to state the contrastive characteristics of a set of simple vowels that suffice for describing quite a range of varieties of English.

Table 11.2 Phonological distinctive features for English simple vowel phonemes

	+front		-front, -back	+back		
	-round		-round	-round		+round
	+tense	-tense		+tense	-tense	+tense
+high	/iː/	/ɪ/			/ʊ/	/uː/
-high, -low	(/eɪ/)		/ə/			
	/ɛ/		/ɜː/		/ʌ/	/ɔː/
+low		/æ/		/ɑː/	/ɒ/	

Notes: All the vowels are positively specified on the phonological distinctive feature *syllabic*, i.e. they are [+syllabic]; the diphthong /eɪ/ is in this table because its first component would not otherwise be described in this chapter.

In terms of the binary features [±high] and [±low], the mid vowel phonemes, /ə/, /ɛ/, /ɜː/, /ʌ/ and /ɔː/, are [-high, -low]. In terms of [±front] and [±back], the central vowels, /ə/ and /ɜː/, are [-front, -back]. Thus /ə/ is [+syllabic, -high, -low, -front, -back, -round, -long] and /ɜː/ is [+syllabic, -high, -low, -front, -back, -round, +long].

In Chapter 9 the : symbol was introduced to mark length on vowels. It is a widely used notation in phonetics and phonology. In most major varieties of English there is a change in vowel quality between a 'long' vowel and its 'short' counterpart, as indicated by the choice of symbols in: /iː/ vs /ɪ/, /uː/ vs /ʊ/, /ɔː/ vs /ɒ/, and /ɑː/ vs /ɒ/ or /æ/. A better account of these phoneme distinctions is that the long vowels are [+tense] and the short ones are [-tense], the latter sometimes labelled *lax*. The phonetic manifestation of a tense vowel is that it is articulated closer to the boundaries of the vowel quadrilateral (➔ 10). Native speakers of English often wrongly think that a non-native speaker who says [hit] for /hɪt/ *hit* is saying *heat*, that is, the English native-speaker is guided more by the quality of the vowel than by its length (➔ 15.6). And native speakers of the sorts of English summarized in Table 11.2 are notoriously bad at producing the authentic quality of [i], [u], [ɔ] and [a], when these are required as short vowels in the pronunciation of other languages, tending to use allophones of the English [-tense] vowels instead: [ɪ], [ʊ], [ɒ] and [æ].

Quite a few languages have three-vowel systems as shown on the left in Figure 11.2. Many languages have five-vowel systems as shown on the right in the figure. Many of these languages have [±long] distinctions on all of their vowels, yielding either a six-vowel system or one with 10 vowels. There are often two diphthongs as well, usually /ai/ and /au/, taking the totals up to seven or 12 vowel phonemes.

The choice of the phoneme symbols here follows fairly well-established conventions in descriptions of English, where the most common allophone has generally guided selection of vowel symbol.

/i/	/u/	/i/	/u/
		/ɛ/	/ɔ/
/a/		/a/	

Figure 11.2 Three-vowel and five-vowel systems found in numerous languages around the world

Jamaican English (➔ 18) has a 15-vowel system, as set out by Devonish and Harry (2004: 459).

Different varieties of English generally have between 15 and 20 vowel phonemes. Table 11.3 lists the vowel phonemes of two varieties of English: General American English, which McMahon (2002: 5) characterizes as 'the most frequently encountered broadcasting variety in the United States' (henceforth GAE) and Educated Southern British English (ESBE). ESBE used to have an inventory of 20 vowel phonemes. Nowadays there are 19 vowel phonemes for the majority of ESBE speakers, because words such as *poor, sure* and *tour* that used to have a diphthong /ʊə/ are increasingly heard with /ɔː/, and this is marked by the greying out of a cell in the ESBE column. The body of the table has 20 rows to accommodate the older kind of ESBE.

The two main differences between these vowel systems are:

- The absence from GAE (see the crosshatched cell in the left-hand column) of a [+low, +back, +round, -tense] vowel /ɒ/. Some words with this vowel in ESBE are pronounced in GAE with /ɔː/, matching across the varieties in roundness but not in tongue height, and others with /ɑː/, matching in height but not in roundness.
- GAE is rhotic and preserves the historical possibility of pronouncing /r/ in syllable codas. In four cases ESBE has a systematically different vowel phoneme corresponding to an r-coda GAE vowel, differing either in length alone or in being a diphthong that ends in schwa.

Table 11.3 Comparisons of vowel nuclei (and vowel nuclei+/r/ sequences) in two varieties
of English with illustrative words

General American English (GAE)	Educated Southern British English (ESBE)
/iː/ beat	/iː/ beat
/ɪ/ bit	/ɪ/ bit
/ɛ/ bet	/ɛ/ bet
/æ/ bat	/æ/ bat
/uː/ boot	/uː/ boot
/ʊ/ put	/ʊ/ put
/ɔː/ dog, c<u>o</u>ffee, long, thought, sauce	/ɔː/ bought, thought, sauce, sure
/ʌ/ but	/ʌ/ but
////////////////////	/ɒ/ pot, dog, stop, c<u>o</u>ffee
/ɑː/ stop, sock, part, palm, father	/ɑː/ part, palm, father
/ə/ <u>a</u>bout	/ə/ <u>a</u>bout
/eɪ/ day	/eɪ/ day
/aɪ/ buy	/aɪ/ buy
/ɔɪ/ boy	/ɔɪ/ boy
/aʊ/ now	/aʊ/ now
/ɝ/ her	/ɜː/ her
/ir/ beer	/ɪə/ beer
/ɛr/ pair	/ɛə/ pair
/ʊr/ sure	(/ʊə/ sure) Words transferred to /ɔː/ by very many speakers now.
/əʊ/ so	/əʊ/ so

Activity 11.8 ⚿

Make a list of the diphthongs in the ESBE column of Table 11.3, including the
greyed-out one and, indicating the basis of your classification, sort them into three
kinds.

Phonologists are encouraged when they find that observations about pronunciation
systems can be economically stated in terms of distinctive features. Here is an example
based on features in Table 11.2: English [+syllabic, -tense] sounds do not occur at the
end of a word in syllables that lack a coda. A syllable with a nucleus but no coda is
called an OPEN SYLLABLE. All the other vowels can be used in open syllables at the ends
of words. The forms in (6a) could not be words in English with its current phonological
system. As seen in (6b), there are English words without final consonants that would
be close enough to make minimal pairs with the forms in (6a). This suggests that the

distinction [±tense] and the way English vowels have been specified in relation to it are capturing something real about the language (Hayes 2009: 81).

(6)   (a)   */spɪ/
                  */kɛ/
                  */mæ/
                  */pʊ/
                  */flʌ/
                  */hɒ/
         (b)   /spaɪ/   spy
                  /keɪ/   Kay
                  /mɑː/   Ma
                  /puː/   poo
                  /flɔː/   floor
                  /hɑː/   hah!

It is not contradictory to claim that English [-tense] vowels such as /ɪ/ cannot appear in an open syllable and also to acknowledge the existence of the first two words in (6b). In /spaɪ/ *spy* and /keɪ/ *Kay*, the vowels are the diphthongs /aɪ/ and /eɪ/. In the diphthongs, /ɪ/ is a [-syllabic] component, a glide, not an independent vowel.

An English dictionary that gives IPA representations for its entries (Seaton and Macaulay 2002) has /kəˈrɑːti/ as the pronunciation of *karate*. That is correct; it is the way that most speakers of English pronounce the name of this martial art. We have also heard English speakers say /kəˈrɑːˌteɪ/ for this word, among them people who have heard the Japanese pronunciation of the word: [karate]. The borrowed word has been squeezed into the phonological system of English (as is done in every language with borrowed words; → 17). Likewise English speakers usually pronounce two other borrowings from Japanese, [karaoke] *karaoke* and [sake] *sake* (a drink made from fermented rice), with an /i/ or an /eɪ/, even though the English vowel /ɛ/ would offer a good match to the [e] vowel sounds at the ends of the Japanese words. Because /ɛ/ is [-tense] it is not available in open syllables for English pronunciations of words like *karaoke*.

11.3 SEGMENT SEQUENCES

Cycling through Suva, the capital of Fiji, the attention of one of us was grabbed by a hand-painted sign on a roof, spaced as shown in Figure 11.3. Notice the unusual leftover after the hyphen.

Except in abbreviations, English orthography does not present us with examples of words beginning CT, so *CTURER* was eye-catching.

Figure 11.3 Surprising hyphenation in an advertisement seen in Fiji's capital city, Suva

Turning to pronunciation, there are sequences of phonological segments that occur in a language and others that do not. There is more to this, however, than merely a catalogue of those sequences that happen to be used by speakers and those that are not. The phonological system of a language systematically rules some patterns out, giving a three-way distinction between (using English as the language of illustration):

1   forms that are in use, for example /pæl/ *pal*, /kwɛl/ *quell*, /lɪŋ/ *ling*;
2   ones that could occur, being allowed by the phonology of English (but not yet put to use as words in the language), for example /pɛl/, /kwæl/, /næl/;
3   forms not accepted by the phonology of English, for example */pwɛl/, */lkwæ/, */ŋɪl/.

Such issues come under the heading of DISTRIBUTION and this technical notion is sketched in 11.3.1. Distribution determines the possibility of contrast and, because of that, is a foundation for the very concept of a phoneme. In 11.3.2 a brief survey is given of segment sequences in English. The section ends with a glance at other languages and a generalization about the distribution of segments in syllables that – if it could be formulated in the right way – might hold across all languages.

11.3.1 Distribution

Statements about the distribution of plant species indicate where we find the plants: high up or on coastal margins and so on. Plants found in a given habitat compete with each other, but alpine and maritime plants generally do not compete, because they are found in substantially separate zones.

The environments where we find phonemes distributed are mainly different kinds of syllables (stressed or unstressed) and places in syllables (the onset, nucleus and coda). Also relevant to specifying an environment are other phonemes present in the syllable, or present in components of the syllable, and sometimes in adjacent syllables too.

Two phonemes cannot contrast with each other unless at least some allophone representing each of them can appear in a given environment, allowing the substitution of one for another. This is because we then have the possibility of minimal pairs, in which substitution changes the word – or other expression – that is identified. For instance, each of the three nasal stop phonemes of English can appear as the only item in a syllable coda, so, for word identification, it can matter which one actually appears there. Take the syllable fragment /lɪ/, an onset and nucleus needing a coda (because English [-tense] vowels cannot appear in open syllables). This fragment is shown in (7) with each of the nasals as a coda.

(7)   /lɪm/   limb
        /lɪn/   Lynne
        /lɪŋ/   ling (a fish)

When two phones can occur in the same environment, then even if no minimal pairs happen to exist, the two phones could in principle contrast, for instance when a new word comes into the language; so they should not be allophones of the same phoneme.

Now consider putting the English nasals into the onset position of a syllable similar to the one used in (7), as in (8).

(8)   /mɪl/   mill
        /nɪl/   nil
      */ŋɪl/

The phonological system of English does not accept /ŋ/ in syllable onsets. If someone did try to use the pronunciation [ŋɪl] while ostensibly speaking English, it is likely that whoever was addressed would think it was a bizarre pronunciation of nil. An English speaker would need some skill as a phonetician even to say [ŋɪl]. (When speakers of English were first given the opportunity to say [ŋuː], the name for an African antelope, the gnu, the best most of them could manage was [nuː]. Some said it as [gəˈnuː].) In English, /ŋ/ has restricted distribution:

- It can be the sole coda consonant, as in /ræŋ/ rang. This is an environment where it contrasts with /m/ and /n/, in the words ram and ran, for instance.
- It can appear in the coda before one of a limited set of [-sonorant] phonemes: /d/, /z/ and /k/, as in /hæŋd/ hanged, /hæŋz/ hangs and /hæŋk/ hank. Contrast of /ŋ/ with /m/ and /n/ is possible before a /d/ or /z/ coda (cf. /hænd/ hand, /hænz/ Hans (in some English speakers' version of this name), /hæmd/ hammed, /hæmz/ hams). But before a /k/ coda English disallows [m] and [n]. *[hæmk] and *[hænk] are hard to say and don't sound English.
- In some varieties of English /ŋ/ can also appear in a coda before a /g/, in /lɒŋg/ long, for instance. Here, again, English speakers would struggle to say *[lɒmg] and *[lɒng]; and if they succeeded would be thought to be pronouncing long oddly, rather than saying some other word.

COMPLEMENTARY DISTRIBUTION of phones is a situation where putting any of those phones in place of the other(s) is not possible because there is no overlap at all in their distribution. In quite a number of varieties of English the phones [l], [ɭ] and [ɫ] are in complementary distribution. It was demonstrated in 11.2.1 that these allophones are confined to different syllable slots. This implies that they cannot contrast. A phonetic virtuoso who swaps clear and dark ls will just sound strange and won't succeed in changing the identity of words like level and label. Where there is complementary distribution it is possible that the phones distributed in this way are allophones of the same phoneme, as [l], [ɭ] and [ɫ] are allophones of /l/.

Complementary distribution makes it possible for two phones to be allophones of the same phoneme, but phonetic similarity is needed too, like that between the phones [l], [ɭ] and [ɫ].

Consider a case where phonetic similarity is absent and where two phones in complementary distribution, therefore, cannot reasonably be assigned as allophones to the same phoneme. It was seen that [ŋ] has rather restricted distribution in English: it occurs only in syllable codas – it is even more restricted than that, but restriction to syllable codas is enough to make the point. In the commentary on Activity 11.7 it was noted that [h] occurs only in syllable onsets (and your efforts in that activity to find minimal pairs should have persuaded you of the truth of this assertion). So, because [h] is restricted to onsets and [ŋ] to codas, they are in complementary distribution. This opens the possibility that they could be allophones of the same phoneme, but this is not a viable analysis. [h] and [ŋ] really are too dissimilar phonetically to be regarded as allophones of the same phoneme.

While speakers of English find it easy to accept that [l], [l̩] and [ɫ] are variants of the same thing (and some find it hard to hear differences between these three allophones), English speakers have no trouble distinguishing between the sounds [h] and [ŋ] and it would be counterintuitive to argue that they are variants of the same underlying unit. Complementary distribution is a precondition for allophony, but there has to be phonetic similarity to clinch it.

11.3.2 Phonotactics

The PHONOTACTICS of a language is an account of the permitted arrangements of its phonological units, usually focusing on sequences of phonemes. To keep the topic to manageable size, we'll deal here only with the phonotactics of consonants: where we find them in syllables and what sequences of consonants can occur. (The restriction that English [-tense] vowels do not appear in open syllables is about the phonotactics of vowels.)

Two or more consonants occurring in a sequence uninterrupted by vowels constitute what is called a CONSONANT CLUSTER. Usually consonant clusters are mainly of interest when they are in the same onset or coda, not spread across the coda of one syllable and the onset of another. In *They glimpsed streams from the helicopter*, the word *they* has a 'singleton' consonant onset /ð/ and no coda. The second word *glimpsed* is a single syllable /glɪmpst/ with a two-consonant onset cluster /gl/ and a coda cluster of four consonants /mpst/. The two words *glimpsed streams* include the unusual cross-word consonant cluster /mpst.str/.

English allows syllables lacking both onset and coda, for example /aɪ/ *I*, ones without onsets, like /aɪs/ *ice*, and (as all languages do) ones without codas, like /saɪ/ *sigh*. English is unusual in admitting rather long consonant clusters, up to three in a row for onsets and as many as four in codas (as in *glimpsed*). Many languages disallow them, or have very few types. For instance, clustering is rather limited in Japanese; so the German city *Frankfurt* is rendered as フランクフルト *Hurankufuruto*, with additional vowels having the effect of breaking up clusters that do not fit Japanese phonology.

Any of the consonants in Table 11.1, except for /ŋ/, can be a singleton onset in English; and any of the consonants in the table can be a singleton coda, except for /h/, /w/, /j/. In non-rhotic accents, /r/ is also ruled out of codas.

Onset clusters in English

We'll start with two-consonant onset clusters. The words *sphere, sphinx* and *svelte* testify to /sf/ and /sv/ being allowable onsets in English, though not many words can be cited for /sv/.

Activity 11.9 0—ᴛ

What else can appear after /s/ in an English syllable onset? Work systematically through the phonemes in Table 11.1 trying to find English words that begin with syllables having two-consonant onsets consisting of an /s/ followed by each of those consonants, with a vowel immediately afterwards. Which sequences are in use? Put asterisks in front /s/-onset sequences that are disallowed by the phonology of English.

When English three-segment onsets are examined there is a tighter set of constraints than what you saw in Activity 11.9. Here are the possibilities in the first, second and third onset slots:

1   The only consonant that can go into the first slot of an English three-consonant onset is /s/.
2   The only consonants that can go into the *second* slot are the voiceless plosives /p/, /t/ and /k/, which is to say the [-voice, -sonorant, -continuant] consonants (look back to Table 11.1 if this seems baffling).
3   And only [+approximant] consonants can go into the *third* slot (but there are some limits on combinations).

Examples illustrating this are given in (9) (with asterisks on the items that justify the parenthesized comment, above, regarding the third slot).

(9)   /spl/   splay
       */stl_/
       /skl/   sclerosis
       /spr/   spray
       /str/   stray
       /skr/   scrabble
       */spw_/
       */stw_/
       /skw/   square
       /spj/   spew
       /stj/   stew (though not for GAE and some other varieties)
       /skj/   skew

Looking at English two-consonant onsets other than the /s/-initial ones considered in Activity 11.9, it is interesting that the segment just before the vowel is always a [+approximant] consonant. Examples – not a full listing of possibilities – are given in (10) (though the ones with /j/ do not occur in some accents that accept other patterns exemplified here).

(10)   /pl/   ply
        /pr/   pray
        /pj/   puma
        /bl/   blue
        /br/   bran
        /tr/   true
        /dw/   dwell
        /kj/   cute
        /gr/   gran
        /fl/   flea
        /fr/   free
        /fj/   few
        /θr/   three
        /ʃr/   shrew

/hj/   huge
/mj/   music
/nj/   newt

Some English coda clusters

Examples are given in (11) of English three- and four-consonant codas.

(11)   /lɪŋks/   lynx
         /hændz/   hands
         /twɛlfθ/   twelfth
         /twɛlfθs/   twelfths
         /tɛksts/   texts

It is not practicable to cover the full range of patterns here. See Roach (2000: 70–76) for a compact and very orderly account of the phonotactics of English consonant clusters. Some highlights are going to be noted about two-consonant codas and then we'll move on.

Activity 11.10 🔑

Restricting attention to two-consonant codas that have a [-sonorant] consonant (a plosive or a fricative, as shown in Table 11.1) coming straight after the vowel, it turns out that the only type of consonant possible in the second coda slot is also [-sonorant], but limited to the subset {[p], [t], [d], [k], [θ], [s], [z]}. There are two distinct patterns, exemplified in a) and b), which are meant to illustrate the full range of two-obstruent codas in English.

a)   /skrɪpt/   script
        /dɛpθ/   depth
        /kɒps/   copse
        /əʊts/   oats
        /eɪtθ/   eighth
        /iːdɪkt/   edict
        /æks/   axe
        /fɛtʃt/   fetched
        /drɪft/   drift
        /fɪfθ/   fifth
        /kʌfs/   cuffs
        /ʃiːθt/   sheathed
        /grəʊθs/   growths
        /rɑːsp/   rasp
        /lɪst/   list
        /bʌsk/   busk
        /liːʃt/   leashed
b)   /rɒbd/   robbed
        /rɒbz/   robs

/ædz/	adze
/bægd/	bagged
/gʊdz/	goods
/ɛŋgeɪdʒd/	engaged
/lʌvd/	loved
/lʌvz/	loves
/ləʊðd/	loathed
/ləʊðz/	loathes
/sɪvɪlaɪzd/	civilized
/ruːʒd/	rouged

What is the important phonological difference between the codas in a) and b)? Try to formulate an interesting phonological generalization about English two-consonant [-sonorant] coda clusters.

English has other two-consonant codas, besides the ones in Activity 11.10. These have a nasal or /l/ or, in rhotic accents, /r/ in the first coda slot, and then it is possible to mix voiceless and voiced consonants in a two-consonant coda. A small sample is given in (12).

(12)
/dʌmp/	dump
/dʒæmd/	jammed
/lʌntʃ/	lunch
/lʌndʒ/	lunge
/rɪŋk/	rink
/rɪŋz/	rings
/bɛlt/	belt
/bəʊld/	bold
/kɑːrt/	cart
/kɑːrt/	card

Activity 11.11 🔑

It requires careful study of a language to analyse its phonotactics, but it is possible to gain an impression of the system from quite a small sample. The sentences given below are from Fijian, a language that is phonotactically very different from English. Make some tentative generalizations about syllable structure in Fijian. You will be giving enough detail if you talk about vowels and consonants, in onsets, nuclei and codas. The Fijian adaptations of four words borrowed from English are informative (so you should attempt to guess which words they are). The data are presented in the Fijian writing system but, as Geraghty (1994: 12) notes, this is almost a phonemic representation, because the alphabet 'was devised relatively recently (in the 1830s) by a missionary who was also a very competent linguist ...'.

> 1   *Au via lako i na ikelekele ni basi ni Suva.* 'I want to go to the Suva bus stop.'
> 2   *O iko mai vei?* 'Where are you from?'
> 3   *Au kilā na vosa vakafaranisē.* 'I speak French.'
> 4   *Au kilā na vosa vakasipeni.* 'I speak Spanish.'
> 5   *E mosi i kē.* 'It hurts here.'
> 6   *Au vinakata na rumu taurua.* 'I would like a double room.'
>   (Fijian sentences and their English translations from Geraghty 1994.)

11.4 SYLLABLE STRUCTURE AND STRESS

11.4.1 Splitting segment sequences into syllables

In English the three-syllable sequences in (13) form a minimal pair, hinging on the /s/ versus /z/ difference. Where are the divisions between syllables?

(13)   /draɪvɪŋskuːl/   /draɪvɪŋzkuːl/

First consider the syllable break in the consonant sequences /ŋsk/ and /ŋzk/. Neither of these sequences is an allowable onset or coda in English; so they have to be divided between the second and third syllables of the sequences in (13). What is allowed and what is prohibited in English onsets and codas determines where the divisions are made. Here are some relevant points that were noted earlier and their consequences for (13).

- English /ŋ/ is restricted to codas, so these onsets are disallowed: */ŋz_/ and */ŋs_/. And anything that goes with /ŋ/ in the coda has to follow and must be one of /d/, /z/ or /k/ (➔ 11.3.1); so /_ŋz/ is a possible coda, but */–ŋs/ (i.e. this is not an allowable coda).
- The onset cluster /sk_/ is found in English (➔ 11.3.2, Activity 11.9); so /_ŋ.sk_/ would be an allowable coda-followed-by-onset, with the split where the point has been put.
- No English onset clusters with /z/ in them were given in the list presented in (10) (➔ 11.3.2) because, in an onset, /z/ can occur only on its own; so */zk_/.

This forces the splits shown by the dots in (14), which accord with the intuitions of people who know English and probably contribute to listeners hearing the words as indicated.

(14)   /draɪvɪŋ.skuːl/   *driving school*
           /draɪvɪŋz.kuːl/   *driving's cool*

A basic schema for splitting segment sequences into syllables (BSSS) in any language is the following (adapted from Hayes 2009: Chapter 13):

(a)   Every [+syllabic] segment is the nucleus of a syllable (σ).

(b)   Onset maximization: to the maximum extent possible, join consonants to syllables that follow them, as long as the onsets formed in this way are allowable in the language.

(c)   Create codas, if any, by joining any leftover consonants to the syllables that precede them.

Figure 11.4 shows the effects of (a–c) on the English phoneme sequence /ɛkstrə/ *extra*. (Recall from 11.3.2 that the longest possible onset clusters in English are /s/ followed by /p/, /t/ or /k/, followed by an approximant consonant.)

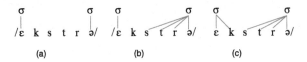

Figure 11.4 Schema for allocating segments to syllables (BSSS), as applied to the English word *extra*, showing: (a) every [+syllabic] segment is a syllable nucleus, (b) onset maximization and (c) coda formed from what is left over

In the commentary on Activity 11.11 it was pointed out that Fijian words such as *lako* could, in principle, be /la.ko/ or /lak.o/. The BSSS settles this: it has to be /la.ko/, as shown in Figure 11.5 (and this concurs with what wider study of Fijian shows: any Fijian consonant can be an onset; but codas do not occur).

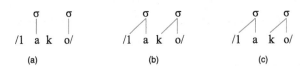

Figure 11.5 Schema for allocating segments to syllables, as applied to the Fijian word *lako* 'go', showing: (a) every [+syllabic] segment is a syllable nucleus, (b) onset maximization and (c) no leftovers, so no codas are formed

11.4.2 Word stress in English

Some languages have fixed stress for words with more than one syllable. In French for instance the final syllable of a word is stressed. This almost certainly helps the addressee hear where the word boundaries are when listening to French, but it means that stress cannot differentiate between words in French. In some other languages the position of stress can be phonologically contrastive, for example in Russian, **bronj**a means 'reservation, booking' but **bronj**a is 'armour-plating'.

McMahon (2002: 120) explains why English has features of both of these types:

For an account of the origins and history of English → 17.

English inherited from Germanic a system with fixed stress falling on the first syllable of the stem; but it has subsequently been strongly influenced by Latin, French and other Romance languages, because of the sheer number of

words it has borrowed. It has therefore ended up with a mixture of the Germanic and Romance stress systems.

Stress belongs in an introduction to phonology, particularly when there is a focus on the phonology of English, because it is often part of the specification of the environment in which allophones occur (for instance for clear and dark /l/, discussed in 11.2.1). Word stress is also central to any account of speech rhythm in English, because the beats that are spaced at roughly equal intervals of time in connected speech fall on the main-stressed syllables of words, with intervening unstressed syllables being 'squashed up' if necessary to keep the rhythm even.

In English the position of the main stress in a word is phonologically contrastive in a special way. It sometimes signals the syntactic class of words, particularly the difference between, on the one hand, nouns and adjectives; and, on the other, verbs (➔ 7). Examples are seen in the words of (15) that have a stress mark in front of their strongly stressed syllable. Context is provided to cue readings as nouns (and one adjective, *abstract*) in the left-hand column, and as verbs on the right.

Word stress is also important in poetry, where rhythm is called *metre*; ➔ Commentary on Activity 8.20.

(15)	/ˈɪnsʌlt/	That's an **in**sult	/ɪnˈsʌlt/	Don't in**sult** us
	/ˈæbstrækt/	It's **ab**stract art	/æbˈstrækt/	Can you ab**stract** it?
	/ˈɪmpɔːts/	**Im**ports come in	/ɪmˈpɔːts/	She im**ports** them
	/ˈaʊtɹeɪdʒ/	It's an **out**rage	/aʊtˈɹeɪdʒ/	They out**rage** me
	/ˈɛkspɔːt/	It's a key **ex**port	/ɪkˈspɔːt/	We ex**port** things
	/ˈprɒdjuːs/	Organic **pro**duce	/prəˈdjuːs/	They pro**duce** it
	/ˈsʌspɛkt/	Who's the **sus**pect?	/səˈspɛkt/	I don't su**spect** him

The position of main stress in compounds is subject to variation in English: ➔ 12.2.5.

The first four contrasts in (15) are minimal pairs for stress. In the final three pairs there is a vowel difference as well as a stress difference, and this latter is the more usual situation.

As long as we know whether we are dealing with a noun (or adjective) or a verb, the position of the main stress in English words is to an extent predictable from the nature of the nuclei and codas of syllables and their position in the word. The onsets are not relevant to this. The sketch of syllable division in 11.4.1 (BSSS) is the basis for a brief account that will be given here of the assignment of stress in English nouns, in a non-rhotic accent. The principles apply to rhotic varieties of English too. Only the main stress in words is considered here. Compound nouns and ones with prefixes or suffixes (➔ 5, 7) are also largely ignored, to avoid going into the additional details needed to cover them.

Stress assignment in English is fairly complicated, but it is part of the tacit phonological knowledge of speakers of English. One thing that suggests this is the way speakers generally agree on where to misplace the stress in foreign words! For instance, English speakers usually call Greece's big northern city /θɛsaˈlɒnɪkə/ or /θɛsaˈlɒnɪkɪ/, stressing the antepenultimate syllable (i.e. the third one in from the right), though its Greek name, Θεσσαλονίκη, *Thessaloniki*, is stressed on the penultimate (the next to last) syllable. It will be seen below that the English stressing of this place name follows a regular pattern.

A distinction is needed between what are called *heavy* and *light* syllables. The essentials of stress assignment can then be systematically explained in terms of this 'weight' distinction. (The presence or absence of an onset has no bearing on syllable weight.) A LIGHT SYLLABLE (L) either:

- has **schwa** /ə/ as its only vowel (→ 9.2.2), for example /ə/ in /ə.ˈbaʊt/ *about*, /ləs/ in /ˈkɛə.ləs/ *careless*, or /ʃə/ in /ʃə.ˈlɒt/ *shallot*
- or is an OPEN syllable (= one lacking a coda) having as its nucleus any short vowel, for example /rɪ/ in /rɪ.ˈgɑːd/ *regard*, /tæ/ in /tæ.ˈbuː/ *taboo*, or /ɛ/ and /ʃə/ in /ˈɛ.ʃə.lɒn/ *echelon*.

The first kind of light syllable – those with /ə/ as the only vowel – does not carry stress in English. The second kind – open syllables with short vowels – tend not to carry main stress; the main stress goes instead on to a nearby heavy syllable, if there is an appropriately positioned one. (We'll soon see why the light syllable in *echelon* nevertheless bears that word's main stress.)

HEAVY SYLLABLES (H) are the kinds that tend to bear stress – not always, but they are the prime locus for it. It is easy to define them: they are not light, which is to say they are:

- CLOSED syllables (= ones with a coda), like /siːd/ *seed* or /tʌsk/ *tusk*, or /kɒn/ in /ˌkɒntrɪˈbjuːʃən/ *contribution* (but remember that ones with schwa as the only vowel, such as /ʃən/ in this word, have already been claimed for the light syllables);

→ Figure 10.6 for examples of English long vowels and diphthongs.

- or syllables that have a long vowel or a diphthong, regardless of whether or not there is a coda, for example /bjuː/ in /ˌkɒntrɪˈbjuːʃən/ *contribution*, or /laɪ/ in /laɪ/ *lie* or /laɪk/ *like*.

Hayes (2009: 282–286) delineates 'a surprisingly common stress rule among the languages of the world'. His rule is informally paraphrased below and examples will be given to show how it accounts quite well for the placement of main stress on English nouns, no matter how long or short the words are.

> GENERAL STRESS RULE **(GSR), which also works for many English nouns: Start at the end of the word, ready to assign stress to the first heavy syllable found, but, if the word has at least two syllables, skip the final syllable and assign main stress to the penultimate syllable; however, if that penultimate syllable is light and the word has at least three syllables, assign stress to the antepenultimate syllable.**

The operation of the GSR is shown in (16) for four words of different lengths (pronounced as in ESBE). The words are identified in (16a); how they split into syllables is shown in (16b); the syllables are classified as light (L) or heavy (H) in (16c); and the position of main stress is shown in (16d).

(16)	(a)	analysis	echelon	salon	long
	(b)	/ə.næ.lɪ.sɪs/	/ɛ.ʃə.lɒn/	/sæ.lɒn/	/lɒŋ/
	(c)	L L L H	L L H	L H	H
	(d)	/əˈnælɪsɪs/	/ˈɛʃəlɒn/	/ˈsælɒn/	/ˈlɒŋ/

Note in (16c) that the pattern of light and heavy syllables for each of the shorter words is a sub-sequence of the pattern to its left. The GSR, as given earlier, works for words of different lengths. Starting at the right-hand end of the word, it deals with words of one, two or three syllables, or more. The goal of the GSR is to assign main stress to a heavy syllable that lies penultimate in the word. A one-syllable word that, like *long*, is heavy (i.e. H) does not have a penultimate syllable leftwards, so the main stress goes on the only syllable. The penultimate position is the basic location for stress and that is where it goes in *salon*, even though the syllable /sæ/ is L and /lɒn/ is H. But when there is another syllable to the left of a penultimate L, that antepenultimate syllable gets the stress, as in *echelon*, regardless of its weight (L in the case of *echelon*'s /ɛ/). Movement back towards the beginning of the word stops there; so *analysis*, with four syllables, has the same GSR stress pattern as *echelon* (counting in from the right-hand side), because the final three syllables of both words are LLH.

In (16c) the penultimate syllable is light: L<u>L</u>H. We need to see what happens when the penultimate is heavy, as in H<u>H</u>H, L<u>H</u>H and L<u>H</u>L. Words fitting these three specifications are given in (17), and it can be seen that the GSR yields the right results for them.

(17)	(a)	intensive	electron	horizon
	(b)	/ɪn.tɛn.sɪv/	/ɪ.lɛk.trɒn/	/hə.raɪ.zən/
	(c)	H H H	L H H	L H L
	(d)	/ɪnˈtɛnsɪv/	/ɪˈlɛktrɒn/	/həˈraɪzən/

There are eight possible three-syllable combinations of L and H. Four of these have been exemplified in (16) and (17): LLH, HHH, LHH and LHL. Examples of the GSR applying correctly to the other four combinations are given in (18).

(18)	(a)	suicide	adventure	oxygen	miracle
	(b)	/suː.ɪ.saɪd/	/æd.vɛn.tʃə/	/ɒk.sɪ.dʒən/	/mɪ.rə.kəl/
	(c)	H L H	H H L	H L L	L L L
	(d)	/ˈsuːɪsaɪd/	/ædˈvɛntʃə/	/ˈɒksɪdʒən/	/ˈmɪrəkəl/

Where the penultimate syllable is heavy, it takes the main stress, as in *adventure*, as well as all three words in (17); where the penultimate is light and there is an antepenultimate syllable, then that is where the main stress goes, as in *suicide*, *oxygen* and *miracle*.

Words with more than three syllables generally fit these patterns too, for example the five-syllabled *xenophobia* /zɛ.nə.ˈfəʊ.bɪ.ə/ is LLHLL. Its last three syllables have the same weight distribution as *oxygen*, HLL, in (18) and indeed, like *oxygen*, its main stress is on the antepenultimate syllable. *Ecology* has four syllables and the scheme explained so far divides and stresses them correctly, as /ɪ.ˈkɒ.lə.dʒɪ/ LLLL, comparable in the weights of the final three syllables to *miracle* in (18).

Activity 11.12 🔑

Divide the following phonemic sequences into syllables, in accordance with the BSSS given in 11.4.1. Then, using the definitions of H and L syllables and the GSR, from earlier in 11.4.2, determine the pattern of syllable weights and predict where the main stress will go in each of these sequences, which represent English words:

/ɪksaɪtɪŋ/
/stælǝktaɪt/
/zaɪlǝphǝʊn/
/kɒmpjuːtǝ/
/hɛmɪsfɪǝ/
/pɛdɪɡriː/
/bɪheɪvjǝ/
/kʌmpǝnɪ/
/kɒmǝdɪ/

The point is not so much to say where the main stress is, but to see how it can be derived from syllable division, syllable weight and the GSR.

In (19) all possible two-syllable pairings of the weights L and H are shown with examples.

(19)	(a)	programme	thousand	office	comma
	(b)	/prǝʊ.ɡræm/	/θaʊ.zǝnd/	/ɒ.fɪs/	/kɒ.mǝ/
	(c)	H H	H L	L H	L L
	(d)	/ˈprǝʊɡræm/	/ˈθaʊzǝnd/	/ˈɒfɪs/	/ˈkɒmǝ/

The words in (19) all have penultimate stress, but that is what the GSR predicts for *bisyllabic* (two-syllable) nouns.

This section has not told the whole story of English stress patterns. Verbs, which generally have their main stress one syllable closer to the end of the word, have been neglected. Even for nouns, there are exceptions that the GSR does not predict. For instance, some prefixes and suffixes affect stress; some do not. There is no room to consider the matter here, but Activity 11.15, at the end of the chapter, invites you to explore the effect of three suffixes on stress placement.

11.5 SUMMARY

Phonology, the study of how speech sound is systematically organized, is built on phonetics, the subject of Chapters 9 and 10. Phonology is concerned with abstract contrastive units, such as the phoneme, underlying the actual spoken (allo)phones that are studied in phonetics. Extended examples, drawn principally from English, were used in the chapter to explain phoneme principles, the sequential arrangement of phonemes and the orderliness of consonant and vowel inventories. A basic schema for dividing words into syllables was recounted and then utilized in an elementary description of stress placement in English.

11.6 FURTHER ACTIVITIES

Activity 11.13

Numerous English expressions have been adopted into Japanese, filtered through the phonological system of Japanese. Here is how some words with /s/ in English are pronounced in Japanese:

- CD [ɕiːdʑiː]
- chess [tʃɛsɯ]
- DC (power supply) [diːɕiː]
- disco [dʑisɯkɔ]
- set (in tennis) [sɛt̚tɔ]
- singles (in tennis) [ɕiŋɡɯrɯsɯ]

Japanese has a phoneme /s/. What are its allophones insofar as they appear in the data above? Also state the distribution of these allophones. CD is /siːdiː/ in English. It might help to write out at least the English phonological form of each of the other words too.

Activity 11.14

Compare (a) which might have been spoken in an American variety of English with (b) a possible first response from a speaker of a British variety of English.

(a) [aɪkæ̃nbɛɹjɚˈbiɹ]   I can't bear your beer.
(b) [juːkɑˑmbɛəɹɑʊˈbɪə]   You can't bear our beer?

What are the phonemic representations for the two utterances? Comment on phonemic forms that do not map to heard allophones. Of course you can consult reference descriptions of American and British English.

Activity 11.15

Mark the position of the main stress on each of the English words in the list below, then add the suffix -ic and see what happens to the position of stress. What generalization can be made about the effect of this suffix on stress?

- *acrobat, electron, metal, drama, autocrat, microscope, catastrophe, geometry*

Do the same with the following and the suffix -ity.

- *adaptable, flexible, monstrous, hostile, morbid*

And the following with -*able*.

- *measure, disagree, recognize, demolish, prohibit*

COMMENTARY ON ACTIVITIES

⊙━┳ Remember that this symbol indicates that there is a commentary on the activity that you can find on the companion website at www.routledge.com/cw/merrison.

FURTHER READING and REFERENCES

Suggestions for further reading on the topics discussed in this chapter can be found on the companion website (www.routledge.com/cw/merrison).

Any piece of academic writing must always provide a list of publications to which reference has been made. Unusually and very unconventionally, this information is provided on the companion website (www.routledge.com/cw/merrison). Always ask your tutor about how you are to present references for any piece of work that you submit.

Chapter 12
Variety in Language

Key Ideas in this Chapter

- Different ways of using language are to be found everywhere language is used.

- The terms *dialect*, *accent* and *language* are distinguished from each other.

- Why are some forms of language deemed to be more prestigious than others – who might make such decisions and why?

- Many branches of linguistics help to describe and even explain different varieties.

- What factors cause language to vary?

- Is variety in language to be welcomed or shunned?

- Prescriptive approaches (how some people think language *should* be used) and descriptive approaches (how language actually *is* used) are considered.

12.1 INTRODUCTION

Do you speak the same way that you write? Would you write a love letter the same way as a shopping list? Do you use language the same way as your grandparents, or even as your parents? Do you address your teachers the same way as you do your friends? Do you use language now the same way that you did when you were three years old? We could keep asking this sort of question for pages. We might wager that you answered 'No' to them all and we would also hope that some of you may even have thought 'Of course not – don't be so stupid!!'. Why? Because appropriately different ways of using language are absolutely everywhere – and that is what this chapter is about: *variety in language*.

Material from all of the other chapters has the potential of being reasonably incorporated into a discussion of the concept of VARIETY in language. In the next few pages it will not be possible to cover anything like all that material and so our ultimate aim is much more modest. The purpose of this chapter is to show that language in use is incredibly diverse. This involves two aspects: (a) we will uncover just the very tip of the language variety iceberg to give some idea of how incredibly vast the possibilities are and (b) at the same time, we will address how and why there is such diversity with the intention of making the incredible credible.

Activity 12.1

It is probably unlikely that you would talk to an eight-year-old, eighteen-year-old or eighty-year-old in exactly the same way. This is but one example of how language is used in different ways. For this activity, list as many different ways as you can in one minute. If possible, compare your list with someone else.

There is no commentary as the whole of this chapter is effectively the commentary to this activity.

While Activity 12.1 should have been relatively simple enough to do, it could actually have taken you rather longer than a minute because (as you may have realized) almost anything can affect how language is used.

12.1.1 What the chapter can do for you and what it can't

To get another perspective on this, try thinking about how language has changed in your lifetime (➜ 17).

Having attempted Activity 12.1, you should have begun to realize that language in use is certainly dynamic and that in any living language, variety (difference) is everywhere – both linguistically as well as socially. The role of this chapter is primarily to provide an introduction to some of the terms and concepts relevant to the study of regional and social varieties of language. While it includes examples from selected language varieties, this chapter isn't designed to be a **descriptive** guide to any specific language variety in particular. Nor is it an introduction to any particular sociolinguistic theory – that we do in the following chapter (➜ 13).

12.1.2 An initial illustration

We can't encounter language without instantly being confronted with variety of some sort. A walk down the high street in Sheffield, UK (the setting for the film *The Full Monty*) revealed the wealth of greeting types between people from the same community, in theory sharing the same native language shown in Extract 12.1.

Extract 12.1

Nah den
Ah reet
Hi
Hiya
Morning
Mornin'
'ello luv
Geoff! (accompanied by a hand wave)

So why is there so much variety in the ways these few people chose to express themselves? Well, at the most microscopic level, every speaker's language use is unique in often subtle but complex ways. In other words, every person has their own IDIOLECT. Yet every speaker shares some characteristics of the way they use language with other speakers – at a personal, local, regional, national and even global level. The variation we see in the way people use language generally falls into some more or less ordered and sophisticated pattern – how else would we be able to understand speakers of the same language but from different regions, walks of life, age groups, and so on? And how would we be able to tell that they belong to these various categories? Activity 12.2 illustrates that we do indeed have (though admittedly to varying extents) an ability to make judgements about people based on the type of language that they use.

An idiolect is an individual's way of using language.

> **Activity 12.2** 🔑
>
> Try making some predictions about each of the speakers in the data from Extract 12.1. For example, what might you guess to be their age, gender, geographical origin and social status?

How accurately you feel you can make these types of social judgements will clearly depend upon your knowledge of the communities that the speakers belong to. For example non-UK residents might have found Activity 12.2 harder than speakers from London, who in turn might have found it harder than speakers from the north of England, who in turn might have found it harder than speakers from Sheffield. In short, the more familiar we are with a particular variety of language use, the more likely we are to be able to recognize and identify it accurately. Just in case you think Activity 12.2 was simply a contrived exercise and you really don't believe that people pay that much attention to such matters, consider Internet chatrooms where quite often one of the very first questions asked is 'age/sex/location?'. If social attributes didn't matter to people, surely they wouldn't bother asking such questions.

But why is it useful to be able to categorize people in this way? Using Extract 12.1 as an example, considering who produced which greeting (old or young, male or female, approximate social status, geographical origin, etc.) could give linguists information (very impressionistic in this case) to feed into data banks about which people are likely to speak in which ways. This information could then, in future, help linguists suggest likely attributes of other speakers from samples of their language. Knowledge like this can also have applications beyond the purely academic; for example, it is the kind of information that forensic linguists focus on in helping the police to solve crimes, it affects how well novelists manage to write convincing regional dialogue and it is also how advertisers can attempt to target their advertisements to particular markets.

Some people argue that 'snap judgements' like this are potentially dangerous. What dangers can you think of?

12.1.3 Initial impressions

Before we start on some key definitions, stop to consider your views on the questions in Activity 12.3.

Activity 12.3 0—🔑

Note down your responses to the following questions:

1   Why are there so many varieties of language?
2   How do varieties come about?
3   Why do they persist?
4   Is variety in language declining in an age of mass media and social mobility?
5   Why are varieties unequally valued?
6   Are new varieties coming into existence now and if so can you identify any?
7   How can knowledge of varieties be useful in 'real life'?

To help you to develop your answers to these questions, this chapter will now provide an insight into the concepts, scope and importance of social and regional language variation. Even at an introductory level, there are many facets to this very broad field so the approach here is to focus on some of the key terms and ideas with brief examples which it is hoped will spark ideas for work on your own varieties data.

12.2 KEY TERMS

12.2.1 Variety

In linguistics, the term *variety* is commonly used simply to refer to any way of using language which is somehow systematically different from other ways. That, however, just shifts the issue to the problem of defining language.

12.2.2 Language

It might feel like 'language' is a completely unproblematical concept. That is not actually the case (➔ 1). Nevertheless, although it is something of a simplification, for current purposes we will assume that **language** refers to 'the [abstract] systems assumed to be inherent in the linguistic behaviour of a community and in their literature' (Le Page and Tabouret-Keller 1985: 190f.). Of course, by this definition, Language X becomes the system underlying the linguistic behaviour of Community X and that just shifts the problem from defining language to the equally problematic task of defining community and although many people speak 'English' in England, the Channel Islands, Australia, the USA, the Caribbean, South Africa and so on (➔ 18), it often makes little sense to say that inhabitants of these countries belong to the same community (➔ 13.3.2, 13.3.3 and 13.3.4). For example, while English is spoken in both York (in the north of England) and Jersey (in the Channel Islands) and while both locations are governed by the British monarch, people from Jersey probably have much more in common with their Norman French heritage (and it certainly makes much less sense to say that the inhabitants of York and Jersey belong to the same community as folks from New York and New Jersey in the USA).

12.2.3 Standard language

As we have seen (and shall continue to see), even speakers of the same language persist in using both spoken and written language in systematically different ways. However, some people argue that all speakers of a language should strive to use just one form of that language in a set way. That form of the language will often be held to be the **standard** – a subset of whatever it is that is covered by the term 'language'. It tends to be the type of language which is used in academic, government and religious settings, and which is often associated with written and published material (➔ 13.3.5). Because of its use in these rather important-seeming contexts, and in written material, a standard often carries prestige. It is easy to see how this can give rise to situations where the standard starts to be seen as 'the' language, and differing ways of speaking or writing – often ones linked to particular locales or less powerful social groups – are somehow deemed 'deviant' or 'substandard' and these negative associations can quickly carry over into judgements on non-linguistic characteristics of speakers. A slightly more neutral alternative to the loaded term substandard (below standard) is 'non-standard'.

12.2.4 Code

To get around some of the difficulties associated with the term 'language', linguists often prefer to use the term **code** (➔ 1, 3) to mean a set of arbitrary conventions for converting one system of signals into another – just as in Morse code where ··· − − − ··· represents <SOS>, or when at the end of a date 'Would you like to come in for coffee?' often signals an invitation to pleasures beyond those offered by a caffeinated beverage!

12.2.5 Accent

One way in which speakers can differ in the way they use language is in their pronunciation or **accent**. This includes the choice of sounds used as segments (**phonemes ➔** 11), in particular words as well as prosodic **suprasegmentals** such as **stress** and **intonation**. Often a spoken standard will be associated with a particular accent. In England it is often referred to as **Received Pronunciation** (abbreviated as **RP** and sometimes also referred to as the Queen's English or BBC English – though it should be noted that these two types of pronunciation have changed over the decades: BBC presenters no longer talk in the clipped tones of the early television broadcasts from Alexandra Palace in the 1930s and even the Queen has shifted her accent over the years of her reign). In the USA, the standard accent used in much media broadcasting is called *General American*.

Orthographic representations of different pronunciations appeared in Activity 12.2. The back rounded vowel [ʊ] is used in many northern accents in Britain where RP would use the vowel [ʌ] (➔ 10). So, for example, in such accents there is no **phonetic** distinction between the words *put* and *putt*, both being pronounced [pʊt], whereas in RP the pronunciations would be [pʊt] and [pʌt] respectively. Other very common pronunciations across various varieties of English would include the following:

- [ɑ]/[a] for the vowel in words such as *grass, glass, bath*
- [ɪŋ]/[ɪn]/[ɪŋg] in the final consonants of words ending in the morpheme {-ing}
- [h]/ø – i.e. [h] or nothing at all – in syllable-initial positions in words such as h̲ungry h̲orses h̲ate h̲orrible h̲ay
- [ɹ]/ø in English words with an <r> after a vowel (known as post-vocalic r) as in fou̲r̲th and floo̲r̲ (see Labov 1972b)
- [ð]/[v]/[d] in words such as t̲h̲is, t̲h̲at, t̲h̲ese, mo̲t̲h̲er, fa̲t̲h̲er and bro̲t̲h̲er
- [θ]/[f]/[t] in words such as t̲h̲ink, t̲h̲ing and t̲h̲ree
- [ju:]/[u:] in words such as n̲e̲w̲ and tu̲ne

and many more.

> The mathematical symbol <ø>, for ZERO, is used to indicate that a feature is not present.

While the above are examples of variety in segments (**vowels** or **consonants**), accent can also include suprasegmental variation (though this is less diverse). Perhaps the most recognizable intonational feature in an accent is the occurrence of high-rising terminals (HRTs) associated with Australian English. Put simply, a high-rising terminal means that there is a noticeably high rise in pitch at the end (terminal) of an utterance. Such an intonation is typical of **interrogative** syntax (questions) in many English accents (➔ 7), but in Australian, these HRTs also occur on **declarative** sentences (statements). This is why Australians (and others who have taken up this way of talking) can sound (at least to non-HRT speakers) like they are either always asking questions or are in constant need of confirmation from their **interlocutors**. This phenomenon is sometimes also known as *Australian Question Intonation* (or AQI).

Another form of suprasegmental variation involves the placement of the main (or primary) stress (➔ 9.2, 11.4). In English, the placement of primary stress (marked in phonetics by a < ' > before the stressed syllable) habitually moves when differentiating between nouns and verbs:

Verb	Noun
irrigate	irri**ga**tion
promulgate	promul**ga**tion
e**lu**cidate	eluci**da**tion

The diacritic < ' > is used in phonetic script. In orthographic script as here, the stressed syllable is often shown in **bold** font, as we do in this book.

Of course, here, there is additional morphological (and hence phonetic) material to distinguish the two forms over and above the stress placement. However, in a few cases, stress bears the majority of the responsibility for marking the distinction:

Verb	Noun
con**tract**	**con**tract
dis**pute**	**dis**pute
ex**port**	**ex**port
ex**tract**	**ex**tract
im**port**	**im**port

Now these examples of variable stress location affect the meaning of the words so in terms of just accent, they are not very interesting (yet interesting enough to note in passing). However some accents seem to employ different stress patterns on words with the *same* semantic meanings. The following lists show how stress is employed differently by two speakers – one from Cambridgeshire, in the south of England, the other from West Yorkshire, in the north of England:

Southerner	Northerner
ad**ver**tisement	adver**tise**ment
dis**tri**buted	**dis**tributed
caravan	cara**van**
tinfoil	tin**foil**
chocolate cake	**choc**olate **cake**
pork **pie**	**pork pie**

In *tinfoil*, *chocolate cake* and *pork pie*, the variant stress locations are arguably to make a very subtle semantic distinction between whether or not the lexical items in question are **compound words** (➔ 5), and therefore perhaps even these examples are not truly indicative of geographical accent alone.

Another particularly fine source of alternative stress patterns from those used in RP can be found in speakers from the West Indies – for example West Indian: Ca**ri**bbean *versus* RP: Carib**bean**.

Activity 12.4 🔑

1   Think about the sorts of accent variations we have just encountered. Can you ascribe any of the variants listed to any particular groups (geographical or social)?
2   If you are familiar with, or even speak any other notable accent, think about the ways it differs phonetically from whatever you consider to be the standard form of your language. (Hint: you are likely to find most variation in the use of vowels.)

As a final point in this section, it should be noted that 'accent' is concerned with the phonetics of an utterance – the way it sounds. It is therefore impossible not to speak with an accent of some kind – even when speaking a standard variety: when a spoken standard is associated with a particular accent it is still an accent – RP and General American are both accents of English. Once differences extend beyond phonetics, however, we have to use a different term: *dialect*.

12.2.6 Dialect

Dialect is the term used when a variety of language is distinct in matters of **morphology** (➔ 5), **lexis** (➔ 5), **semantics** (➔ 6) or **syntax** (➔ 7). It is often assumed that a dialect must be different from the standard. Technically, this is not so: any standard is but a particular (admittedly privileged) dialect of the language concerned. The most common dialectal differences involve the existence of entirely different words. Because dialects are usually associated with *regional* types of language they also tend to involve a non-standard accent. Activity 12.5 deals with some examples of English dialect words.

Activity 12.5 ⚷

1 Do you recognize any of the following dialect words?
2 Do you use any of them? If so, when?
3 What do they mean?
4 Where (for example, geographically) might they be used?

Note

- In this activity we are assuming British English to be the standard.
- Some words might have other meanings in Standard English.
- For some of these words (such as *agait*) the spelling is indicative only.

01 agait	14 dunny	27 lark	40 spogs
02 baguette	15 eagle	28 like	41 strides
03 banner	16 feast	29 manchester	42 titfer
04 bar	17 gannin	30 muggle	43 togs
05 bizzies	18 gate	31 netty	44 trews
06 bog	19 goodies	32 pants	45 trunks
07 charlie	20 greeting	33 pigs	46 tucker
08 chow	21 grub	34 pukka	47 twat
09 crack	22 huggy	35 rozzers	48 ute
10 docky	23 illocution	36 scran	49 while
11 dods	24 john	37 snap	50 yankee
12 driv	25 kecks	38 sneeped	
13 dumpy	26 lake	39 spice	

A commentary is provided for questions 3 and 4.

Activity 12.5 reveals several issues that, sadly, are far too complex to do any real justice to here, but yet important enough to at least raise. For example, was that list really a list of non-standard dialect terms or simply a list of more or less universally recognized colloquial words? Might some words, in fact, be standard English words but just so unusual or obscure that they *seem* to be dialect terms? Are some words, in fact, simply pronunciation variants on other words, in which case it is a matter not of dialect but rather of accent? And at what stage does one word change so much that speakers say that it has mutated into a different word, in which case it is a question of dialect? Extract 12.2 provides an example which illustrates this problem:

Extract 12.2

01 Andrew: Do you want a coffee Sally?

02 Sally: What sort are you making?

03 Andrew: I'm making real coffee.

04 Sally: Oh: (.) no thanks. (2.0)

05   Oh alright then I'll have a rail coffee

06 Andrew: No you won't (.) that's what you get on trains!

07 Sally: Huh?

08 Andrew: Rail coffee.

09 Sally: Ha ha!

10 Andrew: I'm going to use that in my chapter on language varieties.

11 Sally: Piss off!

Admittedly, Andrew was making a linguistic joke on Sally's West Yorkshire pronunciation of *real* in L05, which sounds like (and hence is transcribed as) *rail*. Nevertheless, the fact that she didn't understand the (albeit poor) pun (see L07) and her condescension in L09 indicate that for her the issue was a matter of accent while for him it was a matter of dialect. Sally's angered retort in L11 is also worth mentioning in that it illustrates how use of language can be a personal and therefore potentially sensitive issue.

12.2.7 Jargon

Another point to be drawn from Activity 12.5 is the fact that dialect words do not necessarily have to be regional in origin. The (alternative) meanings for *baguette, eagle, illocution, muggle* and *yankee* are examples. They all 'belong' to Standard English (*muggle* will surely eventually make it into the dictionary ➜ 7) but the meanings used here all have a very restricted sense. They are words which clearly pertain to particular groups (architects, golfers, linguists, Harry Potter fans and gamblers) – in other words they count as jargon or **technical words** (➜ 7).

12.2.8 Register

It can also be possible to recognize certain *social* (i.e. non-regional) varieties of language use even in cases where specialized terminology is not employed. The technical term used for such a variety is **register**. Register is sometimes further subdivided into **field of discourse** (subject matter, e.g. chemistry/linguistics/music), **tenor of discourse** (sometimes referred to as *style*, e.g. formal/informal) and **mode of discourse** (medium of the language activity, e.g. written/spoken) (➔ 7). Most speakers have a range of registers available to them independently of the dialect(s) they speak. They know, for example, that the lexical choice *kid* is used in informal styles of speaking, that *infant* might be more appropriate for a written medical report, and that *child* is a neutral choice. This is part of what is called a speaker's linguistic repertoire (➔ 16.3.2).

So far this chapter has mainly been concerned with variation in phonetics and lexis (both in terms of morphology and semantics), but regular variation in the syntax and the structure (including layout) of the discourse can also be found in registers. Activity 12.8 at the end of the chapter provides several examples of various registers.

12.3 LINKS WITH BRANCHES OF LINGUISTICS

Any consideration of regional varieties (based on geographical locality) and social varieties (based on other criteria such as age, gender, class, profession, mode of discourse and so on) requires some reflection on ideas and approaches from several linked disciplines within linguistics. The study of dialects became popular in the nineteenth century, though many involved were self-trained enthusiasts rather than academics. The study of dialect gained academic respectability in the twentieth century and major surveys of regional variation were undertaken in England (for example, the Survey of English Dialects – see Orton 1962), the United States and Canada, and elsewhere. In this traditional dialectology, the focus was largely on very specific types of informant who were anticipated to speak strong and old fashioned forms of local varieties (the so-called NORMs: non-mobile, older, rural males), and the approach was geared at producing dialect maps (not dissimilar in type to (but very different in detail from) those to be found in Figures 17.3 and 17.4) and showing links with older forms of language (hence its alternative name of *dialect geography*).

In the 1960s, several new approaches gained huge popularity. Largely following the lead of William Labov (1963 in Martha's Vineyard, USA; 1966 and 1972 in New York City, USA – see Labov 1972b for a summary) and later Peter Trudgill (1972; 1974 in Norwich, UK), the field of urban dialectology broadened the focus and aims of dialect work. Urban dialectologists are interested in the varieties of language spoken in particular locales (specifically towns, thought by traditional dialectologists to be unsuitable for their purposes). They are also interested in why there is variation even within those locales in terms of 'who speaks what way'. Furthermore, why do some people change the way they speak from one situation to the next? How and why do new varieties develop and change over time and what is their relationship to the standard language of that area? In order to answer these questions, and more, urban dialectologists developed new methodologies including new indirect oral interview techniques and ways of classifying informants according to social background. Their approaches also require a more inclusive cross-section of informants, incorporating women, who had tended to be very poorly represented in traditional dialectology work. (For a fuller background on the development of traditional and urban dialectology, see Chambers and Trudgill 1980; for a selection of recent detailed studies of urban dialects, see Foulkes and Docherty 1999; for a critique on gender representation, see Coates 1993: Chapter 3.)

From this base, the broader field of **sociolinguistics** has developed (➔ 13). Though originally more or less synonymous with urban dialectology, sociolinguistics has grown into a multi-faceted beast, linking many now virtually autonomous branches of linguistics, including (in addition to dialectologists) those studying language and gender, language and power (➔ 4) and discourse and conversation (➔ 2). While sociolinguistics studies the relationship between language and society, the balance between these two foci in researchers' approaches can vary. Some are most interested in what language can tell them about society and this approach is usually heavily linked to the social sciences. Others focus on what society can tell them about language, and this is more allied to a firmly linguistic approach. Some of the main approaches to sociolinguistics are outlined in Chapter 13.

12.4 WHAT FACTORS CAUSE LANGUAGE TO VARY?

There are many factors which can cause language to vary. One way of classifying factors which can cause language variation is to divide them into two broad groupings: the first comprises characteristics of the language users themselves (which can be called USER FACTORS); the second is made up of features of the situation in which language is used and what it is being used for (SITUATIONAL FACTORS).

12.4.1 User factors: WHO?

The WHO factors focus on the characteristics of the individuals involved – they include aspects such as the users' age, gender, profession, class, level of education, nation/region of origin, ethnicity, religion, disability, personality. These things matter for *all* the individuals involved – we cannot simplify it to just speaker (or writer) issues. For example, consider a white, Anglo-Saxon, protestant, middle-class, university-educated male, in his late forties. Let's say he's an enthusiastic, friendly linguistics lecturer from the county of Cambridgeshire in England. Now here's the point: although we have accounted for many of his personal attributes (and so we can probably predict some of the ways in which he might use language differently from, say, a twenty-something, lower-class, uneducated, violent gangster rapper from New Jersey), unless we take into account who else is involved in the interaction, we will have only part of the story. For example, it is almost certain that he would use language differently when addressing one of his PhD students compared to how he would interact with his eight-year-old son. Indeed, the age difference needn't be so extreme – he would probably even speak differently, in some respects, to first year students compared to second years! So hearer (or reader) characteristics can matter just as much as those of speaker (or writer). Indeed it is also possible that language can be affected by a non-addressed (and even non-present) third party (see Bell 1997; Clark and Schaefer 1987; Schober and Clark 1989).

Over 50 years of sociolinguistic research has suggested that various user factors can help generate distinctive patterns in the way language is used. For example, in many cultures women have been found to be more cooperative and mutually supportive language users than their male counterparts. Nonetheless, there are differences in the way, and the extent to which, this is realized cross-culturally – comparing Japanese women and North American women, for example. And of course, there is variety amongst American women and amongst Japanese women!

What is important to stress is that simply being a woman, a child, someone from Singapore, someone from a lower socio-economic background and so on does not guarantee that a person will use language in a particular way. Each person represents a unique cocktail of influences and this is reflected in their personally-distinctive language use, or idiolect, as outlined above.

Some of the longer-established potential causes of language variation are not without controversy or difficulty. For example, how should social background be determined? The early work of Labov and Trudgill (mentioned above) established classifications largely based on status, occupation and income and they were quite closely tied to the social situations at the time of study in their respective nations (the USA and UK respectively). Even at the time, their 'class'-based categories and methods were questioned – for example, they excluded consideration of important social background influences such as education – and they have been revised or abandoned by later researchers in favour of other approaches, including social networks, described below (➔ 13.3.3 and 13.3.4).

So, the use of particular language patterns can identify us not just as individuals through our idiolects but as members of groups or communities. For each of us, there is a conscious or unconscious choice of how far we conform to the norms of language use in our speech community regarding issues like gender, age, social background, etc. It's worth noting that as individuals we may belong to several speech communities, each exerting different types of influence upon us and which may intersect with each other. For example, a teenage boy of Chinese ethnic origin, born and raised in Sydney, Australia, may mark membership of several groups in his use of language:

- local Sydney teenage culture and specific male peer groups to which he belongs and in which he uses particular rather non-standard forms of Australian English
- the broader standard English-speaking community in Australia
- the Chinese-speaking community in his area, including his family and family friends.

These considerations have suggested that there is an alternative way of reflecting an individual's language use and the influences on him or her to that offered by the potentially crude pigeonholing of *social class* and that is one based on social networks. This approach can also explain how the shared norms of group language behaviour are developed and perpetuated, as well as explaining individual behaviour.

A social network approach looks at the frequency and the types of contact between individuals in groups. These groups might be based around friendship, family or neighbourhood ties or on a place of work or education; they might even be very large-scale groups such as ones based on a particular religion. The basic principle is that the more we interact with other people in our various groups or networks (including virtual cyber communities), the more likely we are to identify with them and show this by adopting the language patterns of those groups. If we feel peripheral to a group, we are likely to show weaker linguistic ties with it. Labov (1972a) was one of the first sociolinguists to demonstrate this in his study of teenage gangs in Harlem, New York City (USA): central gang members showed the most distinctive language traits of the group and those on the fringes, dubbed *lames*, showed the weakest links linguistically.

Work that was carried out many years ago needs to be judged within the context of the time of production – and not with the advantage of critical hindsight.

12.4.2 Situational factors: WHEN? and WHY?

The WHEN and WHY factors are potentially infinite. They relate to the situation that the language is used in and what it is used for. For example, irrespective of who is using it, language is likely to be used differently when:

- in a courtroom, a classroom, a bedroom, a market, a therapy session, a playground, a job interview, a political speech, a poem, a horoscope, an obituary, a love letter, a suicide note, a football commentary, a horse racing commentary, an advice (agony aunt) column in a women's magazine, an advice (agony aunt/uncle?) column in a men's magazine, a personal ad., a movie trailer, a plane, a sitcom, an opera, a soap opera, a will, a delicatessen, a lecture, a tutorial, a textbook, a diary, a dairy, a children's story, a child's story, an undergraduate essay, a PhD thesis, a proposal (business or marriage), a synagogue, a mosque, a chapel, a church, a temple, a chatroom, a pool hall, a different country
- on a basketball court, a deathbed, a bus, a train, a driving lesson, a shopping list, a breakfast cereal packet, a wedding invitation
- at a bank robbery, a marriage ceremony, a grocery checkout, a shrine, a bowling alley, a nursery (plant or child) or at a funeral.

It is also likely to be used differently depending on what we use it for, for example when it is used to:

- accuse, amuse, apologize, assert, boast, congratulate, console, demand, excuse, free, gloat, greet, hail, insult, jibe, kid, leer, mock, name, offer, persuade, please, promise, query, recommend, recriminate, scare, suggest, thank, urge, value, warn or to yearn (if you've already read Chapter 3, this list should look familiar).

All these issues (WHO/WHEN/WHY) show that how language is used is intimately dependent on a variety of social contexts and as such, they could reasonably be investigated by a sociologist. This book, however, has been written by and for linguists, and what makes us different from sociologists is that any linguist interested in different ways of using language (for that is essentially what variety is about) must also be interested in linguistic matters – which might be called the WHAT factors. In other words, when linguists are interested in variety they are also concerned with what it is in the language that varies. Again, the answer to the WHAT question can be anything – *accent*: phonetics, **phonology**, prosody (intonation and stress); *dialect*: morphology, lexis, syntax, choice of language; and *style* including issues such as the formality and overall structure of the discourse. Activity 12.8 at the end of the chapter provides opportunities to analyse several varieties. But if you just can't wait, try Activity 12.6.

Activity 12.6

Choose three user factors (WHO) and three situational factors (WHEN/WHY) and think about exactly how they might make a difference to language in use (WHAT). If possible, discuss your ideas with other students (who may well have chosen other factors).

12.5 VARIETY – VIVE LA DIFFERENCE!

Whichever way you look at it, the kinds of variation (or *différence*) in language that have so far only been hinted at here (though rest assured that Activity 12.8 will come) are vital for any language which is alive and kicking (hence *vive*) and want to remain so! The existence of systematic variation within a language means that speakers are really using that language on a regular basis as part of a range of aspects of their lives and that they have made it their own by favouring particular forms of it. In other words, the language varieties people use will express a key part of their personal, regional and social identity. Since all sorts of people make up communities, there will be variation in the language they use, even if they are all technically speaking 'the same language'.

Each author led on different chapters (though all the authors offered comments on all the chapters). Can you work out which chapters were mainly written by each author? If you think you can, then you must be working on individual writer characteristics.

Unless communities are using language this way, languages will tend to fossilize and then die out when they are no longer able to express the concepts, needs and feelings of a range of different types of user, or when they start to seem remote or alien to their users. In a sense, this is the position with the so-called 'dead' languages like Latin. Welsh (spoken in Wales in the UK) was on the road to that fate (so-called *language loss* or *language death*) before a resurgence of linguistic and national interest, plus some language planning on behalf of government bodies, began to restore the dwindling numbers of speakers (➔ 16).

12.6 PRESCRIPTIVE/DESCRIPTIVE APPROACHES

This section returns to the notion of standard for it may be thought that if variety is equivalent to difference, then it must inherently be not standard. Not so; variety and standard are not **complementary** (mutually exclusive) terms because any standard language is but a particular variety of that language – admittedly a powerful and prestigious variety, but nonetheless a variety and often an accidental variety at that (➔ 17). This is a very important point which should not be forgotten. If it *is* forgotten, then differing ways of speaking or writing (non-standard ones often linked to particular locales or less powerful social groups) might be deemed somehow 'deviant' or 'substandard' and these prejudiced, negative associations could quickly carry over into prejudiced, negative judgements on non-linguistic characteristics of speakers.

Within linguistics, a descriptive approach to the study of language is usually favoured. This is the approach set out in this book. Linguists strive to describe and study languages and the systematic ways in which any particular language is used, including the range of varieties of that language, standard or non-standard. This approach is based on the view that all varieties of a language which are systematically and successfully used by communities of speakers are linguistically valid and worthy of study. The term 'variety' is therefore adopted as a non-loaded term; it supposedly carries no judgements. Descriptive linguists will, of course, acknowledge that *socially*, the standard form may have more prestige but most would point out that it is wrong to assume it will be any 'better' as a *linguistic system*. In many cases, prestige or standard forms of languages are raised to their elevated positions purely by chance – by being 'in the right place at the right time' and spoken by the right people, as it were, and the rise of standard English in Britain is a wonderful case in point here (➔ 17.2.2).

There is another, alternative stance on standard language which we are all probably quite familiar with. A **prescriptive** approach to the study of language literally 'prescribes' how language *should* be used, rather than trying to chart objectively how it is used, as a descriptive linguist would. This usually boils down to prescribing that all speakers of a language should use the standard form. Prescriptive arguments are usually tied to a rather nostalgic (often personal) view whereby whatever language is under discussion is seen to be in peril from current trends in usage, and effectively the so-called standard of yesteryear is held up as the 'true', 'pure', 'correct', 'beautiful' and 'complex' language. So a prescriptive approach would condemn the first sentence in this paragraph because it ends with a **preposition** – a use of language up with which prescriptivists just will not put (➜ 7)! Prescriptivists tend to consider regional and social varieties of a language as inferior to the standard – both socially and linguistically. Extreme prescriptivists have difficulty seeing that anything other than the standard form of a language has any linguistic system, complexity, logic or ability to express a range of concepts and emotions. This view can apply not only to non-standard social and regional varieties but also to any new trends in language use adopted by otherwise standard language users (see, for example, Activity 8.21). Hopefully it is clear, from earlier discussion, that we feel there are some fundamental problems with a prescriptivist approach: variety and variation simply show that a language is alive – and they also keep it alive. Whatever the prescriptivists claim, languages do continue to change and change is now viewed by most linguists as both natural and inevitable.

However, there are thorny issues linked to the descriptive–prescriptive debate, not least of which are ones like those in Activity 12.7.

Activity 12.7 ⚬╍

Using the terminology introduced so far as much as possible, and identifying descriptive and prescriptive viewpoints in relation to each question, consider your responses to the following:

1   If all varieties of a language are linguistically valid, should we (and who would be meant by *we*?) still choose a single variety (for example, the existing standard) as a medium of education, government, religion, etc.?
2   Is there consensus on what the standard variety of any language actually is?
3   How do we (and who might that be?) decide where standard language ends and non-standard language begins?

To round off this section, it is worth returning to what was said earlier in this chapter: even speakers of the same language persist in using both spoken and written language in systematically different ways. Descriptive linguists argue that variation in language use is a key way of keeping the language alive. Variation in language is inevitable: it is part of human nature to mark our identity by the way we speak (or write) and that means showing how we are like those around us whom we admire as well as showing how we are different from those outwith those groups.

12.7 PUTTING ALL THIS INTO PRACTICE

> ## Activity 12.8 ⚬━┳
>
> This is the final activity of this chapter and it is designed to offer you more detailed practice in using the terms and concepts introduced thus far.
>
> Consider the following **texts** and analyse each in terms of field, tenor and mode and hence overall register of the discourse. Pay attention to as many WHO/WHEN/WHY/WHAT aspects as possible. This type of analysis that you are about to do is sometimes known as 'genre analysis' or 'stylistics'.

Text is a cover term for representations of both written and spoken language data (➜ 7, 8).

Text 12.1 Snowee and Multee (Teah Bennett)

Text 12.2 Loan agreement (AJM/SAF/SEH)

> We the undersigned, <FULL NAME> and <FULL NAME>, hereinafter referred to as 'the borrowers', both residing at <FULL ADDRESS> ... Edinburgh in the region of Lothian Scotland hereby acknowledge that we have received a loan of twelve thousand pounds sterling from Sheila Ena <SURNAME> of <FULL ADDRESS> ... Peterborough in the county of Cambridge England, hereinafter referred to as 'the lender'.
>
> (DOCUMENT CONTINUES)

Text 12.3 Signature and Stamp (AJM/SPECS)

Hi

SORRY, SORRY, SORRY, SORRY
I'M SO EMBARREST AND SORRY THAT
I'VE BEEN SO SLOPPY (MAYBE NOT THE RIGHT WORD?)
I HOPE THIS CARD AND MY SIGNATURE
+ THE STAMP WILL HELP TO GET SOME
MONEY BACK.
I'VE BEEN SO BUSY —
GOING ON HOLIDAYS ! FIRST A WEEK
AT MALLORCA TO PLAY GOLF AND NEXT
THE YEARLY HOLIDAY IN SKAGEN WITH
PER, KARSTEN AND MY FATHER. AND
NOW i'M WAITING FOR THE GOLFSEASON
TO BEGIN HERE IN DENMARK

ALL THE BEST
LOVE TO YOU ALL

Text 12.4 Barrier Reef (AJM/MUM)

Mon 3 Nov.
Had a wonderful day on the Barrier Reef.
Huge Catamaran, 4 Decks, travelled 70 miles
out to a huge pontoon moored at the reef. We
could step back & forth ship/pontoon. Top left
picture shows the inside of semi submersible,
passengers were under the water, but deck of sub
was still above water. It was so enjoyable
we went down twice, each trip lasting 30 min
Weather was very hot, calm seas, blue sky.
Perfect. Lunch provided.
It was a whole day — 8.30 am
& returned at 4.

is the Great Barrier Reef

Marina Mirage, Port Douglas, Qld. 4871 Australia.

Love
Mum.
x
x

Text 12.5 Good boy (M&M/M1/SA)

```
01  A:   Right can you see the church?=
    C:   =Yes.= ((simultaneously nods))
    A:   =Near it.=Yes. ((simultaneously nods)) OK go down to that church.
         ((pause)) From the traffic lights to the church.
05       ((pause))
    C:   °Done it°
    A:   Done it good boy, OK.=Turn off and go over the bridge.
         ((pause))
    C:   °Bridge°
10       ((pause))
    C:   Found it! ((simultaneously points to map))
    A:   Good boy.
         ((pause))
    C:   .hh There.
15  A:   Good boy. .hh Keep going until you get to the roundabout.
         ((pause))
         ((C points to the roundabout))
    C:   Found it.
    A:   Good boy then
20  C:   (°X round°)
         ((pause while C completes drawing then sits))
    A:   [[(°°X°°) ]
    C:   [[°Done it.°]
    A:   You've done it so you're ready. Good boy.
```

Text 12.6 Extract from Jaworski et al. (2004) (AJ/MK/SL/VYM/SS15/EX2 (modified))

```
01  V      you need the bowl? (.) I give for cheap price (.) you can go in (.) I have
02         (unclear) go inside don't mind no problem (.) ooh (.) you see I'm
03         mister cheap (.) I work with myself (.) anything you like I give
04         something for secret price anything (.) you have three wise monkeys (.)
05         thinking man and the (mother? unclear) (.) half faces (.) man who play
06         the kora (.) Africa kora
07  T1     is that an instrument (.)
08  T2     [yeah
09  Tchr   [yeah
10  T1     what's the instrument called
11  V      kora (.) kora kora (.) the man who play the kora
12  T      hmm mm
13  V      just feel it
14         ((feeling))
```

15	V	this this Black and white
16	T1	hmm hmm
17	V	you know no problem I just offer [( ) you something for
18	T2	[( ) OK just looking
19	V	listen <u>listen</u> I just offer you something for hundred seventy-five (.) its secret (.)
21	T1	hmm mm
22	V	anything you like you just tell you just tell and we can discu [ss
23	T1	[OK
24	V	because you are my first customer (.) anything you like hundred
25		and seventy-five (.) fifty (.) I give to you lower (.) you don't like this small
26		(mother) [yes?
27	T	[hmm
28		((laugh[ter))
29	V	[yes feel it (.) just feel it (.) don't mind (.)
30		yes no problem (.) ((sound of clackers)) it's my role

Text 12.7 Extract from Harris (1995: 127) (modified)

01	P:	how do you think he went down those stairs then
02	S:	well I don't know − (I just) I I I think he must have fell down them
03	P:	were you there when he fell down
04	S:	no I was not − I was in bed − all right − I must have been in bed
05	P:	you're sure of that
06	S:	I'm sure of it − I must have been in bed − yeh I was in bed anyhow (2) (yeh)
07	P:	you weren't at the top of the stairs
08	S:	no (2) I was not
09	P:	you had an argument in the morning didn't you
10	S:	in the morning [aye − but that wouldn't be nothin [g ( )
11	P:	[hmmm [what d'you
12		mean it'd be nothing
13	S:	that would be nothin' − an anyway that would only be a bit of − crack − that's
14		what I'd (think) − that it was the crack you know
15	P:	when you've had a few to drink and you had a few that morning
16	S:	yeh
17		(2)
18	P:	you're a bit argumentative aren't you
19	S:	(be Jesus) I wouldn't think so
20	P:	you don't think so

Text 12.8 'Shitwork' (AJM/LC/3LS050 (modified))

01	F1	Right, can I get on with this now?
	L	She does as well, oh I see
	F	She's put it on …
	F1	It's quarter to eleven, come on, pay attention. I can do that now can't I
05		((louder)) It's a quarter to eleven
	L	And I'm gonna do Sacks' bit first
	F1	Eh? No you're not. Three before break, three after break come on, don't be rotten
		((general hubbub))
	F1	Right. So, basically, er the definition of appropriate versus inappropriate
10		conversation she says, is the male's choice therefore he decides what their reality is
		but the women work harder at the interactions therefore they erm … basically, they do
		all the routine work but they don't reap the benefits. And on page four-two-six
		we have just the biggest giveaway that she went in there with an agenda, it's 'women
		are the "shit" workers of routine interactions'.
15	F4	Yes
	F1	Now the lexical choice of 'shit' oh how emotively written is that! You know, I
		erm, I do think … anyway

12.8 SUMMARY

This chapter has shown that language in use is incredibly diverse and yet that this diversity – this difference – is not random, but systematic. This chapter also provided an introduction to terms and concepts relevant to the study of regional and social varieties of language. In other words, it has provided an initial introduction to sociolinguistics – an introduction which we continue in Chapter 13.

12.8.1 What has not been covered

Sociolinguistics is a vast field and a truly comprehensive coverage would have to be encyclopaedic in magnitude. There is therefore so very much that has had to be left out. However, you may like to extend your studies in areas such as: accommodation; acts of identity; advertising; attitudes to language; audience design; code-mixing and **code-switching**; communicative competence; communities of practice; **diglossia**; forensic linguistics; guise experiments (matched or otherwise); institutional language; interactional linguistics; language and culture; language and gender; language and the Internet; language change; language disorder; motherese; pidgins and creoles; politeness; power; stereotypes; taboo language and many more.

Some of these sociolinguistic issues are addressed in the other chapters (especially Chapter 13). Others are not. Clearly it is not possible to go into details about what these concepts are about (this is a 'what has not been covered' section after all), but suffice to say that all these many different varieties of sociolinguistics are fascinating. And the variety in sociolinguistics exists because there is variety in language use.

Throughout this chapter, quoting from many sources has been resisted, however it seems appropriate to close with the thoughts of some very eminent sociolinguists, starting with Hudson (1996: 18) who comments: 'as soon as we start to consider language as an object of research, social considerations are hard to ignore'. Next, Labov (1997: 23, original italics) has admitted that he has 'resisted the term *sociolinguistics* for many years, since it implies that there can be a successful linguistic theory or practice which is not social'. Finally, Le Page and Tabouret-Keller (1985: 188) note: 'We should constantly remind ourselves that languages do not do things; people do things, languages are abstractions from what people do'.

So as long as human beings gather together in a variety of identifiable social and regional communities for a variety of different social and regional purposes – in short, to do a variety of different things – then there will always be differences in the way they use their linguistic resources. Even if you have learnt nothing else from this chapter, we hope you now realize that *variety in language is everywhere* because *everything in language is some variety*. Consequently, *any* linguistic data can be analysed in terms of regional and/or social variation. There are therefore many examples in all the chapters throughout this book.

If variety really is the spice of life, let's keep it spicy and *vive la différence* – or should that be *vivent les différences*?!

12.9 FURTHER ACTIVITY

Activity 12.9

As per Activity 12.5:

1   Do you recognize any of the following dialect words?
2   Do you use any of them? If so, when?
3   What do they mean?
4   Where (for example, geographically) might they be used?

As before, there are some small clusters of terms (including ones relating to alleyways, being pleased, drinking receptacles, stickiness, talking and truancy).

01 aye	14 claggy	27 made up	40 snog
02 bairn	15 clarty	28 minging	41 stubby
03 barnet	16 crook	29 nick off	42 suited
04 blethering	17 divn't	30 nowt	43 summat
05 blower	18 dram	31 oldies	44 this avo
06 bonce	19 fag	32 owt	45 tinny
07 bonny	20 gigs	33 pinkie	46 tubular
08 booger	21 ginnel	34 play hooky	47 twag
09 brae	22 gobsmacked	35 ranchslider	48 wag
10 brass	23 happen	36 rellies	49 wee
11 bunk off	24 heffalump	37 skive	50 yammering
12 char	25 hood	38 snicket	
13 chuntering	26 low-set	39 snickleway	

COMMENTARY ON ACTIVITIES

⚷ Remember that this symbol indicates that there is a commentary on the activity that you can find on the companion website at www.routledge.com/cw/merrison.

FURTHER READING and REFERENCES

Suggestions for further reading on the topics discussed in this chapter can be found on the companion website (www.routledge.com/cw/merrison).

Any piece of academic writing must always provide a list of publications to which reference has been made. Unusually and very unconventionally, this information is provided on the companion website (www.routledge.com/cw/merrison). Always ask your tutor about how you are to present references for any piece of work that you submit.

Chapter 13
Sociolinguistics

Key Ideas in this Chapter

- Several key concepts in sociolinguistics are presented: communicative competence, speech community, social networks, communities of practice, diglossia and language choice.

- There are many approaches to sociolinguistics: in this chapter we address ethnography; variationist approaches to sociolinguistics; interactional sociolinguistics; and some approaches that might be labelled as post-Labovian, in particular Accommodation Theory, Audience Design and Acts of Identity.

- For each of these paradigms, we discuss the questions, data, methods and theories with which they are concerned.

13.1 INTRODUCTION

Like many areas of linguistic study, sociolinguistics is simultaneously blessed and cursed with its transparent **morphological** formation: {socio} + {linguistics}. The blessing is that it is clear that socio-linguistics must, therefore, simply be the study of the relationship between *society* and *language*. The curse, of course, is that that requires us to answer two further questions – viz. *'what is 'society'?'* and *'what is 'language'?'*. And while both those questions are simple, the answers to them are not. The way that we will deal with these problematic issues in this chapter is necessarily practical. Here, in addition to assuming that 'language' is 'the abstract system underlying the linguistic behaviour of a community based on conventions for the use of sounds or signs' (➜ glossary), sociolinguists also use it to refer to the linguistic behaviour (the language in *use*) itself (and in whatever form).

Defining the term 'society' properly is harder. We therefore take the easy way out (because it is sufficient for our current purposes) and quote the OED (online): 'society [is] the aggregate of people living together in a more or less ordered community' which thus requires a definition of community (also taken from the OED online) 'a group of people [...] having a particular characteristic in common'. (We will return to the idea of community in 13.3.2 below.)

So, for our current purposes, a society is any set of individuals (with more than one member) with some characteristic in common and language is the linguistic behaviour used by those individuals.

In this book, we take the same approach as Fishman (1972 [1965]) – and therefore, indirectly, Wardhaugh (2010: 16) – who suggests that sociolinguistics (though in 1972, Fishman called it 'the descriptive sociology of language') should seek 'to provide an answer to the question "who speaks (or writes) what language (or what language variety) to whom and when and to what end?"' (Fishman, 1972 [1965]: 46).

For that reason, Chapter 12 covers some introductory issues relating to the vast potential for there to be *variety* in language use depending on (a) user factors (i.e. *who* is using the language) and (b) situational factors (i.e. *when* and *why* the language is being used). It also introduces the following technical terms: **variety**, **language**, **standard language**, **code**, **accent**, **dialect**, **jargon**, **register** and describes many ways in which various bits of language stuff varies.

Similarly – and, we would hope from the title of this book, evidently – we also believe that sociolinguistic research should be firmly based on actual observations of actual occurrences of actual language behaviour (hence *language in use*). In other words, sociolinguistics should be *data-driven*. But collecting data is not usually where sociolinguists start. Data collection should be purposive. As Wardhaugh (2010: 16) comments, 'We must collect data for a purpose and that purpose should be to find an answer, or answers, to an interesting question'. Consequently, as he goes on to add, 'Those who seek to investigate the possible relationships between language and society must have a twofold concern: they must ask good questions, and they must find the right kinds of data that bear on those questions'. And these two things are, of course, inter-connected: it is not until we know the questions we wish to investigate that we will know what data are appropriate to answer those questions or, if you prefer, it is not until we know what data we have available that we will know what interesting questions can be reasonably asked.

QUESTIONS  DATA

However, merely having interesting questions and gathering an array of appropriately interesting exemplars of linguistic variation is insufficient for proper, methodical, scientific study. What is needed for proper methodical, scientific study is proper scientific *method* (defined by the OED online as 'a method of procedure [...] consisting in systematic observation, measurement, and experiment, and the formulation, testing, and modification of hypotheses').

However, merely employing scientific method is insufficient for the ultimate purposes of scientific research. The reason that data are methodically collected, observed, measured, experimented on and tested is to provide some answer(s) to the interesting question(s) (often expressed in the form of hypotheses). In short, the goal of scientific method is to provide some explanation(s) of – and in the long run, prediction(s) about – the phenomena under investigation. It is such a collection of interrelated explanations and predictions that scientists call *theories* and, like questions and data, methods and theories are similarly inter-connected.

METHODS

THEORIES

And, of course, questions and data are also inter-connected with both methods and theories: certain methods are required to answer certain questions; certain data are usable only with certain methods; certain data are particularly relevant for certain theories; and certain theories definitely prioritize certain questions. What this results in is an inter-connectedness of inter-connected issues with research being affected by all four aspects of questions, data, methods and theories (see McNeill 1990: 125):

METHODS

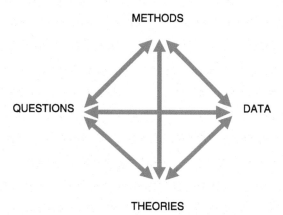

QUESTIONS   DATA

THEORIES

The purpose of this chapter, then, is to use some of the ideas discussed in Chapter 12 in order to explore just some of the interrelated questions, data, methods and theories that that chapter did not cover.

13.2 THE SCOPE OF SOCIOLINGUISTICS

Prior to the emergence of sociolinguistics as a distinct discipline in the early 1960s, the study of language had largely been the study of linguistic forms – concerned essentially with issues of grammar (in the broader sense of phonology (➔ 11), morphology (➔ 5), syntax (➔ 7) and semantics (➔ 6)) as well as with the traditions of philology and historical linguistics (➔ 17).

In 1974, Dell Hymes (who, with William Labov, was one of the founding fathers of modern sociolinguistic study) made one of those 'oh-so-obvious-when-you-say-it-out-loud' remarks:

> **It is not obvious, is it, after all, that the energies of linguistics should be devoted entirely to the signals that tell where things can be bought in department stores, and not at all to the signals that tell where the people in department stores have come from, are now, and aspire to be?**
>
> (Hymes 1974: 200)

Along with this refocusing of attention onto the human aspect of human communication (not surprising given that Hymes' academic heritage had its roots in anthropology), he also set out a clear programmatic statement for those who would study the subject. He urged that sociolinguistics should be:

1   SOCIAL and LINGUISTIC
     i.e. sociolinguistics is not sociology and nor is it a theory of grammar, but rather it is a discipline at the interface of both

2   socially REALISTIC
     i.e. instead of treating idealized (and often researcher-generated) language forms as acceptable data, it should concern itself only with data that is *real* (what we are calling *language in use*)

3   socially CONSTITUTED
     i.e. it should recognize that it is social action/function which gives rise to the particular linguistic structures that are put to use.

In addition to these exhortations, Hymes also suggested that 'the final goal of sociolinguistics […] must be to preside over its own liquidation' (Hymes 1974: 206). For a founding father of a discipline to advocate the annihilation of that discipline seems counterintuitive to say the least – even more so given that it is a position that Labov also evidently ascribed to. The confusion disappears, however, when, rather than consider what Hymes *said*, we work out what he *meant*. Labov's (1972: xix) version of the sentiment makes it perfectly clear: 'I have resisted the term sociolinguistics for many years, since it implies that there can be a successful theory or practice which is not social'. In other words, according to these two 'socio'-linguists, doing 'linguistics' properly cannot be achieved without taking into account social aspects of language in use. The corollary, then, is that when the discipline of linguistics ultimately becomes inherently social, we will no longer need the morphological marking of 'socio' to be attached to the term 'linguistics'. What Hymes meant, then, was not that the *discipline* should be wound up but only the use of the sub-ordinate 'socio' *nomenclature*.

Half a century later, although the field of sociolinguistics has grown massively, it is nowhere close to the 'socio'-liquidation that Hymes and Labov had hoped for. We are thus – for the foreseeable (if not permanent) future at least – stuck with the term.

13.3 KEY CONCEPTS IN SOCIOLINGUISTICS

Although sociolinguistics is a very broad church (as we shall soon see in 13.4), there are some concepts and terms that most practitioners would recognize. Several of these are covered in Chapter 12 because they concern the actual *stuff* of sociolinguistic study – the multiple types of linguistic behaviour: *variety, language, code, accent, dialect, jargon, register*. In the next sections, then, we introduce terms relating not to the stuff itself, but rather to some theoretical concepts *about the stuff: communicative competence, speech community, community of practice* and *diglossia*. Unfortunately, these introductions will necessarily be brief.

13.3.1 Communicative competence

In response to Chomsky's earlier (1965) notion of 'competence', Hymes introduced the term COMMUNICATIVE COMPETENCE. In defining competence only in terms of the *grammatical* knowledge speakers have, Chomsky essentially redefined the nature of linguistic theory. Hymes, on the other hand, suggested that while a theory of grammar is necessary for a theory of language, it is by no means sufficient. For Hymes (1972b [1971]: 281), an adequate approach to linguistic study should be concerned with four distinct issues:

1   *possibility* – whether and to what extent something is formally (theoretically) possible within the system even if it has never actually been uttered (in essence, this is the limit of Chomskyan competence)
2   *feasibility* – whether and to what extent something is reasonably possible given the affordances and constraints within the given system
3   *appropriacy* – whether and to what extent something is (in a given context) suitable, effective, felicitous and so on
4   *occurrence* – whether and to what extent something actually happens.

This he illustrates by saying 'a sentence may be grammatical, awkward, tactful and rare' (1972b [1971]: 281f.). Of all these, it is *appropriacy* which is arguably of the most consequential importance to sociolinguistics. Elsewhere in the same publication, Hymes (1972b [1971]: 277) puts it like this:

> We have to account for the fact that a normal child acquires knowledge of sentences, not only as grammatical, but also as appropriate. He or she acquires competence as to when to speak, when not, and as to what to talk about with whom, when, where, in what manner.

Chomsky's concept of **competence** relates to a person's (mostly implicit) knowledge of whether or not a particular string of words in their language would be considered to be grammatical. In this way, even though Chomsky's famous string of English words – *colourless green ideas sleep furiously* – is undoubtedly semantically and pragmatically odd, all competent English users will know that, as a sentence of English, it is syntactically perfectly well-formed (➜ 1, 7, 16).

In short, then, in order to be a competent user of a language, one needs to know much more than whether or not a given structure is syntactically acceptable.

13.3.2 Speech community

We cite a first year undergraduate essay here for the same reason that we published an undergraduate essay in the sister Reader to this volume – to remind academically young readers that 'simply being a *new* student in the field does not necessarily mean being unable to contribute to it' (Griffiths, Merrison and Bloomer 2010: 6).

The word 'communication' comes from the Latin verb *communicare*, meaning to make common, or to share.

Man is by nature a sociable being; he organises himself into various groups of people with whom he shares a way of life: a sharing of a culture, of a name with which the members of the group relate, of a common folklore, of a common history and of a network for contact are 'all largely dependent on having a common mode of communication' (Saville-Troike 1982: 22).

(Merrison 1988: 1)

Merrison's point is a simple but important one: the population of communities is more than a matter of mere side-by-side living (cohabitation) – it is also a matter of sharing (communication) and the way that we do this is invariably through some common linguistic variety (or *language, code, accent, dialect, jargon, register* ...). It is this notion of some shared linguistic form that is at the basis of the concept of *speech community*. The use of the word 'speech' in this terminology is slightly problematic for it is certainly not meant to imply an exclusion of sign languages – rather, it is meant to recognize that while an alternative term might have perhaps been *language community*, the common factor that binds a community together may often be much more subtle than a full-blown language. The next 'problem' is that there are almost as many definitions of the 'speech community' as there are definers! We offer a range below:

1   Lyons (1970: 326)
     Speech community: all the people who use a given language (or dialect).

2   Bloomfield (1933: 42)
     A speech community is a group of people who interact by means of speech.

3   Gumperz (1972 [1968]: 219)
     The speech community: any human aggregate characterized by regular and frequent interaction by means of a shared body of verbal signs and set off from similar aggregates by significant differences in language usage.

4   Labov (1972: 120f.)
     The speech community is not defined by any marked agreement in the use of language elements, so much as by participation in a set of shared norms.

Lyons' definition (1) is perhaps the simplest in that it does not require any social or cultural unity. Because of this, such a loose definition would, for example enable (*inter alia*) Americans, Australians, Brits, Canadians, New Zealanders, South Africans, as well as all the people in the world who have English as a second or additional language to be considered as 'a' community – even though its 'members' would be geographically disparate, at different levels of competence and (for the vast majority) unknown to each other (➜ 18). Bloomfield's definition (2) shifts the *sine qua non* to interaction – people who do not interact with each other cannot be considered to be members of the same community. The refinement offered by Gumperz (3) is to specify a difference in the language use of the members within the speech community and that of those who are outwith it (a sense of 'us versus them'); this (importantly) distinguishes for example, English-speaking Australians from English-speaking New Zealanders, Americans from Canadians, and Geordies (from Newcastle upon Tyne, UK) from Mackems (from Sunderland on Wearside, UK (just over a dozen or so miles south-east of Newcastle)). Finally, Labov's definition (4) emphasizes the importance of attitudes to language focusing on an 'us'-group behaving differently from a 'them'-group according to a set of normative practices.

We can see, then, that the precise definition of 'speech community' is not at all a simple task – indeed, as Hudson (1980: 30) has commented 'it is possible that speech communities do not really exist in society except in the minds of people, in which case the search for the "true" definition of "speech community" is just a wild goose chase'. Whether we are in fact chasing wild geese is not of crucial importance to this chapter. What is required though, is an acceptance that people do exist in communities where the various ways in which they use language is indeed a unifying thread.

It is for this reason that we adopt Wardhaugh's (2010: 118) more general working definition:

> [A] speech community is no more than some kind of social group whose speech characteristics are of interest and can be described in a coherent manner.

Activity 13.1

In just one minute, make a list of as many groups as you can think of where the members of one group might use language somehow differently to the members in the others.

13.3.3 Social networks

Often, sociolinguists who invoke the notion of speech communities may be found drawing on the idea of social networks – a concept most associated with the work of Lesley and James Milroy (L. Milroy, 1980, 1987; J. Milroy and L. Milroy 1985). In brief, it is a method of describing how the various members of speech communities are inter-connected. There are two main dimensions of connectivity: one which relates to how many people know how many people (few = *loose*; many = *dense*); and one which relates to the ways in/through which people know each other (mostly one = *uniplex*; mostly many = *multiplex*).

So in this way, a community in which (mostly) everyone knows everyone else is said to be a *dense* network. Conversely, a *loose* network is one in which (mostly) everyone knows only some of the other members. We can visualize this (indeed there used to be a Facebook application called Friend Wheel that did this very thing) as a diagram where everyone who knows person A is connected to them by a line. The same for person B, C, D and so on. The most dense network is one where absolutely everyone in the community knows (and so would be connected to) everyone else in the community. A simple example might be the people who were in your form group/home room at school.

Multiplex networks are those where the people who are connected to each other are connected for multiple reasons. Members of a multiplex network might work together, socialize together (go to the same sports events, parties, weddings and so on), worship at the same religious institution and inter-marry. (In diagram form, person A might be connected to B by a red line because they work in the same factory, by a blue line because they support the same sports team, by a yellow line because they are members of the same church and by a green line because they are in-laws.) In the UK, dense multiplex networks are often found at the far extremes of the social-class structure where strong bonds of social identity keep these birds of a feather flocking together. It is people from the middle classes who generally have less intricately inter-connected social lives, living instead in communities where the ties within their networks are at the more loose and simplex ends of the respective spectra. It is these various representations of the degree(s) of solidarity and interconnected group identity which the Milroys (*inter alia*) have used to explain how innovations in language use can be introduced and spread throughout a social network.

Activity 13.2

Make a list of the first ten people whom you interacted with today (or, if you haven't yet hit ten, any day before today). Put these names (including your own) in a circle. Draw a line to connect each pair of people who you know interact with each other (you will necessarily be connected to all ten others, though not all ten others will necessarily be connected to anyone else). In a different colour (or a different line style – dotted, dashed, wiggly …) connect each pair of people who are members of the same household. In a different colour (or line style) connect each pair of people work (or study) together. In a final different colour connect each pair of people who socialize (or play) together.

What you will have created is a very simple social network diagram for these people. You can make it more complex in several ways: (a) add more people; (b) add more types of association; (c) rearrange the people not in a circle, but into more or less highly discrete clusters of people according to the cohesiveness of their inter-connectivity (so for example you might have a housemates cluster, a linguists cluster and another bunch of peripheral members with whom you have only minimal (and mono-functional) contact (such as bus drivers, cleaners, coffee shop staff and, for many of you, lecturers).

13.3.4 Communities of practice

In recent years, a concept related to speech communities and social networks has begun to take hold within the field of sociolinguistics. The idea of COMMUNITY OF PRACTICE was initially coined in 1991 by Lave and Wenger who used it in their discussions of situated learning. Wenger's (1998: 73) definition requires a community of practice to exhibit the following three features:

1   mutual engagement
2   a joint enterprise
3   a shared repertoire.

The term subsequently entered the linguistic literature when Eckert and McConnell-Ginet used it in relation to gendered language:

> A community of practice is an aggregate of people who come together around mutual engagement in an endeavor. Ways of doing things, ways of talking, beliefs, values, power relations – in short practices – emerge in the course of this mutual endeavor.
>
> (Eckert and McConnell-Ginet 1992: 464)

A very useful discussion is offered by Davies (2005) who, among other things, has noted that an important aspect of communities of practice is that they are self-regulating. In her words:

> Individuals do not have open access to the communities based solely on their desire to be part of that community and to take part in its practices. While practices may define the community, the community determines who has access to that practice.
>
> (Davies 2005: 558)

13.3.5 Diglossia

Diglossia is a term first introduced by Ferguson in 1959 (➜ 16). It refers to a speech community where there are two distinct varieties, each with its own specialized functions. These two varieties Ferguson called high (H) and low (L) where 'In one set of situations only H is appropriate and in another only L, with the two sets overlapping only very slightly' (Ferguson 1972 [1959]: 235f.). Some examples of such functions (based on Ferguson 1972 [1959]: 236) are given in Table 13.1.

The common differences between H and L are that L is a vernacular (i.e. it is learned as a mother tongue) whereas H is generally a prestigious standardized variety often with an established historic and literary heritage which is learned via formal education as an additional language (see Table 13.1).

Although Ferguson's original definition rigidly adheres to the existence of only two varieties, Fasold (1984: 40) notes that a refinement was later made by Fishman who, following Gumperz, allowed for the presence of 'several separate codes' whilst still acknowledging the fact that the separation is indeed most often into high and low. In Fishman's words (cited by Fasold 1984: 40, original emphasis), diglossia also exists 'in societies which employ separate dialects, registers, or *functionally differentiated language varieties of whatever kind*'. This description therefore includes everything from the subtlest of stylistic distinctions within

The four diglossic cases cited by Ferguson were: Standard German (H) vs. Swiss German (L); classical Arabic (H) vs. local (colloquial) Arabic (L); Modern Greek katharévusa (H) vs. dhimotiki (L) and French (H) vs. Haitian Creole (L).

Table 13.1 Diglossic functions of high and low varieties

	High	Low
Religious sermons	X	
Political speech	X	
University lecture	X	
News broadcast	X	
Newspaper editorial, news story, caption on a picture	X	
Poetry	X	
Instructions to servants, waiters, workmen, clerks		X
Personal letter		X
Conversation with family/friends		X
Soap opera		X
Caption on a political cartoon		X
Folk literature		X

one particular language, to the use of two completely different languages and, as such, therefore subsumes Ferguson's original definition.

Diglossia is evidently a phenomenon which is closely linked with intimacy of the situation and while people tend to reflect the degree of this intimacy by 'subtle stylistic shifts within the same language, by switching between two moderately distinct "dialects", or by selecting entirely different languages [... the] social phenomenon is the same, regardless of the nature of the linguistic means used to accomplish it' (Fasold 1984: 51f.). It is this broader social phenomenon (as opposed to the precise linguistic methods by which it is implemented) that is the most important factor and thus, as Fasold suggests (1984: 53), the term 'diglossia' may be kept as long as it is remembered that {di-} only refers loosely to the 'two ends of the formality–intimacy continuum of language use, rather than to two linguistic varieties'.

What diglossic situations show us is an extreme example of the way that users of language adapt their speech to suit their surroundings (indeed it is tempting to refer to such users as 'linguistic chameleons'): humans can be creative in their use of language, and, as Hymes (1974: 123) has said, part of that creativity 'lies in the freedom to determine what and how much linguistic difference matters'. This notion of motivated choice is at the very heart of sociolinguistics.

13.3.6 Language choice

Above, we offered one definition of 'language' as 'the abstract system underlying the linguistic behaviour of a community based on conventions for the use of sounds or signs'. The key term here is *system*. Languages are, to be sure, collections of a vast range of possibilities at all linguistic levels (phonology (➔ 11), morphology (➔ 5), syntax (➔ 7), semantics (➔ 6), discourse (➔ 8)) and the reason that languages work the way that they do is because although the choices we actually make are always from an array of possibilities, those choices are not random – they are *systematic*. At every point, language users are faced both with syntagmatic choices (what class of words can and cannot come next in an on-going structure) as well as paradigmatic options (what words are interchangeably 'choosable' at any given point) and thus, as Halliday (1973: 55) remarked, 'Each choice takes place in the environment of other choices'. For example, if you were hungry and wanted to convey that proposition to someone else, you might reasonably say something like 'I am hungry' (and not 'I am thirsty' or 'I am cold' or 'I am tired' or 'I am bored with reading so many linguistic examples'). Similarly, if you were very hungry, you might say 'I am very hungry', though other alternatives are, of course, also available, including 'I could eat a horse', 'I am starving', 'I am ravenous', 'I am famished' and even (though undoubtedly much less likely) 'I am esurient'. What it is important for sociolinguists to remember, then, is that 'in the study of language in a social perspective we need both to pay attention to what is said and at the same time to relate it systematically to *what might* [reasonably] *have been said but was not*' (Halliday 1973: 67, emphasis added). This notion of negative definition is at the very heart of sociolinguistics: we are who we are not only because of the characteristics we exhibit, but also because of those we do not. (Or, if you prefer, a duck is a duck because it's a duck, but also because it's not a rabbit!)

How we perceive ourselves, how we perceive others, how we perceive ourselves in relation to others, how others perceive us perceiving ourselves in relation to them and how all that is finely mediated and represented through our myriad choices of linguistic behaviour is, in essence, what socio-linguistics is all about – and exactly how sociolinguists go about answering those questions depends largely on how they stand in relation to the four inter-connected aspects of questions, data, methods and theories. In the next section, we will discuss each of these four issues for some of the major approaches to doing sociolinguistics.

13.4 APPROACHES TO SOCIOLINGUISTICS

Because it is concerned with the interpretation of variable human behaviour, studying the social sciences (such as anthropology, archaeology, criminology, history, law, linguistics, philosophy, psychology, and sociology) is often thought to not be the same as studying other sciences (such as mathematics, physics, chemistry and biology) with approaches to social science generally being considered more eclectic. If this is true of social science, then it is true of linguistics and it is also true of sociolinguistics. In short, what can be found in the field of sociolinguistics is truly vast. In addition, the boundaries are not always clearly defined. That said, it is possible to distinguish several relatively internally coherent approaches to studying the interface between language and society, and this we do here. We will cover: ethnography; variationist sociolinguistics; interactional sociolinguistics; and post-Labovian sociolinguistics (encompassing Accommodation Theory, Audience Design and Acts of Identity).

13.4.1 Ethnography of Communication (EC)

Questions

Ethnography is another relatively transparent term morphologically speaking. The {ethno} part refers to people (Greek ἔθνος [ethnos] as in 'ethnic') and the {graph} relates to writing (Greek γράφω [grapho]). In essence it is an approach which asks questions about the organization of phenomena (linguistic knowledge, interaction skills, cultural knowledge) within a given group by carrying out detailed observations and ultimately leading to rich (written) descriptions. Ethnography is a predominantly qualitative methodology. It has clear links with anthropology (which largely ignores language) and while it is (almost necessarily) ethnocentric, it is also an open-minded paradigm in that it takes a(n) holistic approach in considering the inter-action [sic] of a wide range of cultural forms/activities (and not just a couple of variables – cf. *variationist sociolinguistics*, below). Because the currency of ethnography is culture, new students often believe that only remote exotic communities count as interesting. This is not so. It must be remembered that *any* cultural organization, no matter how apparently quotidian, mundane or just plain 'ordinary', can, if studied closely, yield interesting insights into what actually goes into making our social world(s).

> Ethnography shouldn't be restricted only to 'exotic' cultures. The organization of all social groups can tell us about the structure of human civilization.

Data

Ethnographers will use absolutely any data that can help them better understand the workings of a cultural group. This can include the following (see Saville-Troike 1989: 114–137):

1   *Background information*
    All sorts of background information can be useful: history, geography, population, religions, education, sources of employment.

2   *Material artefacts*
    Physical objects which are present and used in the community may be relevant in understanding the organization of that community.

3   *Social organization*
    This can include the (potentially hierarchical) structures within recognized institutions (such as education, religion, family, professions) and who has what sorts of power/influence.

4   *Legal information*
    Aspects of language use which are given special legal status can be illuminating (for example 'slander', 'libel', 'obscenity', 'offence', 'hate speech', 'contract', 'offer', 'freedom of speech' etc.).

5   *Artistic data*
     Value systems and other aspects of cultural identity can often be found in literature, poetry, drama, song lyrics, and nursery rhymes.

6   *Common knowledge*
     Statements such as 'everyone knows that …' and 'as they say …' as well as aphorisms, mantras, maxims and proverbs can all shed light on what a culture takes for granted. Ethnosemantics and ethnomethodology (see *Methods*, below) use this type of data.

7   *Beliefs about language use*
     This is interrelated with issues of im/politeness (➔ 4) and taboo. It involves beliefs about what can and can't, should and shouldn't, must and mustn't be uttered – in essence it concerns the nature of (in)appropriate language use and its consequences.

8   *Data on linguistic code*
     Given 'code' is a broader term than 'language' (➔ 12), this aspect of data collection includes accessing not just any pre-existing dictionaries and grammars but also wider aspects of paralinguistic features (such as the intonation, pitch, stress and volume associated with prosody) and other nonverbal (gestural) behaviour.

One of the authors owns several polo shirts with linguistic slogans on the back. One of his favourites is: *Of course, if it really goes without saying …*

Methods

Ethnographic data can be collected using a wide variety of methods. These include at least the following (for more detail see Saville-Troike 1989: 118–135):

1   *Introspection*
     Ethnographers who are also members of the culture they are researching can call on their own sense of how to communicate in that culture.

2   *Participant-observation*
     The most common method of collecting ethnographic data is as a fully-functioning ratified member (participant) of the given community, but one who, as far as is possible, makes objective (detached) observations in order to test hypotheses about organizational rules and principles. While it is not necessary to be a 'native' of the culture under research, it is generally thought that the longer non-native ethnographers can immerse themselves in the community, the better.

3   *Observation*
     Sometimes – for whatever reason(s) – it is just not possible to become a legitimate member of a community (Davies 2005). A simple case in point would be Eckert's study of American high school children: no matter how she might have tried, Eckert had no way of becoming a teenager (see Eckert 1989, 1997 [1989]). In such cases, peripheral observation is necessary.

4   *Interviewing*
     Semi-structured interviewing procedures (usually employing mainly open-ended questioning) can be vital for gathering a sufficiently comprehensive range of cultural information (some of which might be so rarely occurring that even a long-term participant-observer may never get to witness it).

5   *Ethnosemantics*

Ethnosemantics is concerned with the meanings (semantics) that people (ethnos) attribute to various collections of related parts of reality. This often involves the construction of a taxonomic system. Examples would include categorization systems for such things as colours, kinship terms, reading material, religious celebrations, insults, footwear, musical genres, compliments, professions, and so on and so on.

6   *Ethnomethodology*

Ethnomethodology is the study of the methods by which people produce and interpret their communicative interactions. It is, in large part, concerned with the sort of situated meaning-making and meaning-understanding that is covered in Chapter 2 on Conversation Analysis (though aspects that are covered in Chapter 3 on **deixis**, speech act theory and implicitness, and in Chapter 4 on Power and Politeness are also at play here).

7   *Philology*

Philology concerns the interpretation of the language in written sources (texts). This may include such coverage as governmental publications, newspapers, writings on etiquette, obituaries, personal ads, and so on.

Hymes (1972a [1964]: 22) proposed a framework for ensuring that communicative events are methodically and comprehensively analysed. It comprises a list of the necessary components of communicative events that should be considered. While other variations of the list exist (see, for example, Hymes 1972c: 59ff or Saville-Troike 1989: 138ff), the version which is most well known is organized by the eight-letter acronym SPEAKING (Figure 13.1).

S etting [physical circumstances]
  & Scene [event type]
P articipants
  [speaker, addressee, addressor, audience and the roles that these
  people play]
E nds
  [cultural and individual goals (anticipated outcomes) of a communicative
  exchange]
A cts and sequence of acts
  [message content (the topics) and the message form (how it is done,
  including the sequential ordering)]
K ey
  [the tone or manner (sometimes known as *tenor*) of the communication
  (formal, casual, serious, jocular, sarcastic, etc.)]
I nstrumentalities
  [the method (*mode*) by which communication takes place: speech, sign,
  writing, whistling, text messaging, gesture, drumming, etc.]
N orms of interaction and interpretation
  [in general what is considered and accepted as constituting
  (in)appropriate behaviour]
G enres
  [the (often nameable) type of the communication (such as chat, lecture,
  poem, wedding speech, interrogation etc.)]

Figure 13.1 SPEAKING

Theories

In a section entitled 'Towards a Descriptive Theory', Hymes (1972c) offers an overarching hierarchy of units relevant for ethnography of communication: *situation, event,* and *act.* These units are interrelated in that acts are parts of events and events are parts of situations. This embeddedness is represented as in Figure 13.2:

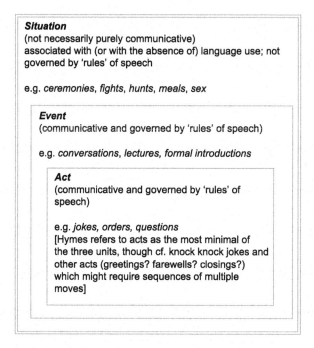

Situation
(not necessarily purely communicative)
associated with (or with the absence of) language use; not
governed by 'rules' of speech

e.g. *ceremonies, fights, hunts, meals, sex*

> **Event**
> (communicative and governed by 'rules' of speech)
>
> e.g. *conversations, lectures, formal introductions*
>
> > **Act**
> > (communicative and governed by 'rules' of
> > speech)
> >
> > e.g. *jokes, orders, questions*
> > [Hymes refers to acts as the most minimal of
> > the three units, though cf. knock knock jokes and
> > other acts (greetings? farewells? closings?)
> > which might require sequences of multiple
> > moves]

Figure 13.2 The embeddedness of situations, events and acts

The Sapir–Whorf Hypothesis (linguistic determinism)

Within the study of cultural organization, one very long-established theory that all socio-linguists should be aware of is known as the Sapir–Whorf Hypothesis (also known as LINGUISTIC DETERMINISM). In essence, it suggests that language and thought are inter-connected and because all languages are different, each of us has our own personal idea of 'reality'.

There are two main versions of this: one weaker, one stronger.

Weaker version

Language and culture are interrelated and people's behaviour will tend to be *guided* by the linguistic categories of their languages.

This can be found in the writings of Sapir (1961 [1929]: 69):

Human beings do not live in the objective world alone, nor alone in the world of social activity as ordinarily understood, but are very much at the mercy of the particular language which has become the medium of expression of their society. It is quite an illusion to imagine that one adjusts to reality essentially without the use of language and that language is merely an incidental means of solving specific problems of communication or reflection. The fact of the matter is that the 'real world' is to a large extent unconsciously built up on the language habits of the group. No two languages are ever sufficiently similar to be considered as representing the same social reality. The worlds in which different societies live are distinct worlds, not merely the same world with different labels attached. [...] We see and hear and otherwise experience very largely as we do because the language habits of our community predispose certain choices of interpretation.

Stronger version

People's concepts are *determined* by their language.

This can be found in the subsequent writings of Whorf (1956 [1940]: 213f., original emphasis):

> We dissect nature along lines laid down by our native languages. The categories and types that we isolate from the world of phenomena we do not find there because they stare every observer in the face [... but rather] because we are parties to an agreement to organize it in this way – an agreement that holds throughout our speech community and is codified in the patterns of our language. The agreement is, of course, an implicit and unstated one, BUT ITS TERMS ARE ABSOLUTELY OBLIGATORY; we cannot talk at all except by subscribing to the organization and classification of data which the agreement decrees. [...] all observers are not led by the same physical evidence to the same picture of the universe, unless their linguistic backgrounds are similar or can in some way be calibrated.

Clark and Clark (1977: 556) cite a study by Glucksberg and Weisberg which demonstrates this principle. Its results are so robust that we have used it (with some minor changes) every year in sociolinguistics classes for the past 15 years. People are given a candle (we use a tea light devoid of its foil casing), some drawing pins (thumb tacks) and a box of matches. People in condition A get the objects and a separately labelled inventory: box, drawing pins, candle, matches. People in condition B get the objects but without any labels.

In both conditions the participants are told to fix the candle to a wall in an upright position so that, when lit, it won't drip. To solve the problem, it is necessary to see that the box that the matches are kept in can be used, when pinned to the wall, as a support for the candle.

The result of Glucksberg and Weisberg's experiment was that on average, people performing under condition A completed the task successfully in about 37 seconds, whereas those in condition B took almost 9 minutes (nearly 15 times as long). The explanation that Clark and Clark (1977: 556) offer is that the explicit labels 'encourage people to pay attention to each object separately' which, in turn, 'enables them to see the box not merely as a holder but as an object that may figure in the solution to the problem'. In short, the words we use to describe the world constrain (or enable) us to view it in a certain way.

Activity 13.3

Repeat the candle experiment. See whether you get similar results.

13.4.2 Variationist Sociolinguistics (VS)

Where ethnography is essentially a qualitative paradigm, variationist sociolinguistics (VS) is a quantitative one. What this means is that it often deals with numbers rather than descriptions. Its founding father is William Labov.

Qualitative approaches are essentially descriptive (and from there explanatory) of naturally occurring language in use. Quantitative approaches are essentially statistical and analyse distribution and frequency of occurrence of specific linguistic items.

Questions

Once again, transparent morphological nomenclature is sufficient to indicate that variationist sociolinguists are interested in variation. What many VS studies are interested in finding out about is not just the social variation in language varieties in and of itself, but rather the nature of language *change* – a topic on which, over the past couple of decades, Labov has published three sizeable volumes totalling over 1,700 pages (Labov 1994, 2001, 2010). Clearly our discussions will have to be somewhat more brief.

Data

The sorts of variation that variationists are generally interested in are of relatively well-defined things. They call these things *variables*. They come in two major subtypes: (i) *independent variables* (such as geography, age, gender (though often reduced simply to biological sex) and socioeconomic class, and (ii) *dependent variables* (such as phonology (➔ 11), morphology (➔ 5), syntax (➔ 7) and discourse structure (➔ 8)). Of these, many studies have seemed to be interested in phonological variables, with perhaps the most well known being Labov's (1972) New York department store study on rhoticity (post-vocalic /r/) and Trudgill's (1997a) [1974] Norwich study on the word-final realization of the /ŋ/ phoneme in the {-ing} suffix in words such as *walking, talking, dancing* and the like. Generally, dependent variables have no more than two main possible realizations. In Labov's New York study, the variable for rhoticity was called (r) and the realizations were either /r/ being present or absent. In Norwich, the {-ing} suffix variable was known as (ng) and the phonetic realizations were either [ɪŋ] or [ɪn].

Variables can be themselves controversial. Establishing objective criteria for socio-economic class, for example, is not without its problems. In the UK, the Office for National Statistics offers a comprehensive categorization system which is based on employment (see Office for National Statistics 2010).

The general assumption underlying VS studies is that the dependent variables exhibit the distributions that they do because of their relationship to the various independent variables – in short, it is the *dependent* variables which vary in accordance with (depend on) the fixed independent variables. Think of it like this: at any given point in time, no matter how you might try, you cannot change your age, your biological sex or your social class – these things, while variable in the total population, are fixed for any given individual. What is less fixed is the way in which an individual might pronounce certain sounds in certain contexts.

Methods

Variationists tend to employ similar methods of data collection and analysis. First they identify the particular dependent linguistic variables that they are interested in. Next they organize a sample of the right sorts of people according to the required independent social variables that they wish to investigate as being responsible for the linguistic variation under scrutiny (such as old people, young people; men, women; lower working class, upper working class, lower middle class, upper middle class; and so on).

Once an appropriate sample of informants has been established, the next task for the variationist is to elicit specimens of language from them. This they generally do in a range of styles. The most common styles are, in order from most to least formal:

Elsewhere in the literature, you might find formal style (FS) called Interview Style and abbreviated to IS. We prefer to use IS for Interactional Sociolinguistics (13.4.3).

- casual style (CS) – generated via free conversational speech
- formal style (FS) – generated via semi-structured interview
- reading passage style (RPS) – generated via reading a passage
- word list style (WLS) – generated via reading out a word list
- minimal pair style (MPS) – generated via reading a list of **minimal pairs**.

The last three styles can be manipulated by the researcher so that they contain the relevant linguistic variables in all relevant environments (such as word-initially, word-medially, word-finally, and before/after certain vowels/consonants and so on). Interview data can sometimes be steered towards certain topics which might generate particularly useful words, but on the whole, FS and CS styles cannot readily be controlled.

Once speech samples have been garnered for all relevant styles from all relevant participant types, the quantification can begin. What this amounts to is counting how many times each realization actually occurs out of all the possible times it might have occurred. What tends to be counted is the presence of just one of the options – usually the one considered to be the most prestigious. This then yields a percentage score (by dividing actual occurrences by possible occurrences). This process is repeated for each social variable in each style and results are then tabulated and graphed. Some of the results from Trudgill's (1997a) [1974] study of (ng) in Norwich are re-presented in Table 13.2 and Figure 13.3:

Table 13.2 Trudgill's (ng) index for 1970s Norwich by class and style (% of [ŋ])

Class	Style			
	CS	FS	RPS	WLS
MMC	072	097	100	100
LMC	058	085	090	100
UWC	013	026	085	095
MWC	005	012	056	077
LWC	000	002	034	071

Key: L = Lower; M = Middle; U = Upper; W = Working; C = Class

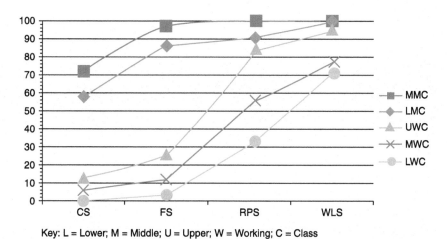

Key: L = Lower; M = Middle; U = Upper; W = Working; C = Class

Figure 13.3 Trudgill's (ng) variable for 1970s Norwich by class and style (% of [ŋ])

Theories

The data above provide empirical evidence for several basic theoretical assumptions of VS (see Labov 1972: 239f.), namely:

1   Different sections of society (as defined by various independent social variables –
     here, social class) will display discrete patterns of linguistic behaviour that separate
     each from the other; this is known as SOCIAL STRATIFICATION.
2   The more attention people pay to their speech (in essence, the more formal the situ-
     ation), the more they are likely to produce prestigious realizations of the linguistic
     variables; in such cases, the resultant graphs show sloping lines and the relevant
     variables are known as sociolinguistic *markers*. If the lines are horizontally flat, this
     shows that the variable carries no prestigious value judgements within the given
     speech community and the variable is known as a sociolinguistic *indicator*.
3   The greatest level of stylistic variation is often associated with classes on the border-
     line between social groups (in this study, the upper working class) – this extreme
     variation is often referred to as displaying 'linguistic insecurity'.
4   'Although it is impossible to [fully] predict for any one utterance which variant a
     speaker will use, the striking regularity of [Figure 13.3] emerges from samples with
     as few as five individuals in one subgroup, and no more than five or ten utterances
     in a given speech style for each individual' (Labov 1972: 240). Because of this fairly
     robust sociolinguistic patterning, it is, therefore, possible to at least partially predict
     either what linguistic behaviour a certain individual might produce in a given
     context, or, from the alternate point of view, from a certain utterance of a variable in
     a given context, it may be possible to partially predict what type of person uttered it.
5   The predictive utility of variationist findings does come with a caveat, however.
     What the MMC-CS score of 72 and the LWC-WLS score of 71 demonstrate is that, as
     Labov (1972: 240) himself noted, 'The same sociolinguistic variable is used to signal
     social and stylistic stratification. It may therefore be difficult to interpret any signal by
     itself – to distinguish, for example, a casual salesman from a careful pipefitter'.

13.4.3 Interactional Sociolinguistics (IS)

While interactional sociolinguists can be interested in the cultural differences across various cultural communities and might indeed also be interested in variations across particular variables, what they are always interested in is the way in which people conduct themselves in social interactions.

Questions

Although there is a vast multitude of studies in interactional sociolinguistics, each tries to answer the same simple question: HOW DO WE INTERACT WITH ONE ANOTHER? More fundamentally, we would argue that the single question that they are addressing is, in essence, the biggest question in linguistics, namely: HOW DO WE UNDERSTAND ONE ANOTHER?

Data

The data that interactional sociolinguists use are interactions – in whatever format: conversations, letters of complaint, personal ads, political interviews, wedding speeches, gossip, service encounters, classroom interactions, SMS (text) messages, banter, religious sermons, comedy hecklers … the list really is endless. Just some of the types of data that we have studied include emails between students and university staff (Davies, Merrison and Goddard 2005; Merrison, Wilson, Davies and Haugh 2012), speech and language therapy interactions (Merrison and Merrison 2005), chat-up routines (Hambling-Jones and Merrison 2012), online Christian advice forums (Wilson, Merrison and Graham in prep.), virtual learning environments (Gilroy and Merrison in prep.), task-oriented interactions (Merrison 1992, 1998, Merrison 2011), and professionally interpreted (mediated) interactions (Merrison and Turner in prep.).

Methods

There are simply too many methods to cover in this short section. Luckily, some of those that are particularly relevant are discussed in other chapters: conversation analysis (➜ 2), pragmatics (➜ 3) and politeness (➜ 4), though others would include critical discourse analysis (➜ 8) and corpus linguistics (➜ 5).

But whatever the precise details of the methods employed, all interactional sociolinguists will gather examples of (generally extended) interactions. This will often involve audio (and/or) video recordings of people talking to one another which must then be transcribed to an appropriately detailed degree in order to interrogate the particular issue(s) in question. In cases involving computer-mediated communication (such as instant messenger (online chat) conversations, posts on online forums, emails, text messages etc.) it will involve copying and pasting relevant extracts into some form of unified corpus database. The benefits of such text-based studies include the relative ease of data collection. It also often has the bonus of data being publically available and thus collectable without the knowledge of the producers of the data – and in such cases, the problems of the observer's paradox are thus avoided.

The essence of the observer's paradox is that we really want to observe naturally-ocurring linguistic behaviour. However, as soon as participants know that they are being observed, we have 'messed' with the naturalness of the situation and this can, in turn, affect the sort of linguistic behaviour that is (or is not) produced.

Theories

In some approaches to the study of interaction (such as conversation analysis ➜ 2), theorizing – in its sense of hypothesis testing – does not play much of a part. Rather, detailed descriptions and explications of collections of exemplars of particular types of data enable analysts to build an overarching account of some phenomena (e.g. turn-taking, conversational repair, preference structure). In other approaches, particular theoretical frameworks can be invoked in order to help in those analytical descriptions. Some of the frameworks that have been adopted in the list of Merrison's research mentioned above include Speech Act Theory, Face and Politeness Theory, and Equity Theory. The first two are partially and, for current purposes, sufficiently addressed in Chapters 3 and 4. Here, then, we devote some space to a summary of what is meant by equity.

The conceptualization of equity that we subscribe to is closely aligned with Clark's Equity Principle (1996: 295). This simply claims that individuals enter into joint projects *presupposing* a method for maintaining equity. In essence, it is concerned with balancing costs *versus* benefits. It is important to note that like 'benefits', 'costs' are not necessarily financial. More specifically, it involves an individual's attempts to maximize the resultant outcomes of their benefits minus their costs. Hambling-Jones and Merrison (2012: 1120) discuss equity and, invoking a quote from Goffman, its connection to the notion of 'face':

> The similarity with Goffman's description of face maintenance as 'a condition of interaction, not its objective' (1967 [1955]: 12) is obvious: we maintain that the reason for this is that both concepts are fundamentally interconnected. Where Clark is concerned with balancing costs vs. benefits, Goffman was concerned with the balancing of the ritual order achieved via facework. The latter conceptualisation can be seen in Goffman's references to ritual equilibrium. For example, when participants attempt to correct for the effects of a ratified threat then:
>
> > At this point one or more participants find themselves in an established state of ritual disequilibrium or disgrace, and an attempt must be made to re-establish a satisfactory ritual state for them [...] the imagery of equilibrium is apt here because the length and intensity of the corrective effort is nicely adapted to the persistence and intensity of the threat [...] the sequence of acts set in motion by an acknowledged threat to face, and terminating in the re-establishment of ritual equilibrium, I shall call an *interchange*.
> >
> > (Goffman 1967 [1955]: 19, original emphasis)

As an illustration of the cost–benefit aspect of equity, Hambling-Jones and Merrison (2012: 1119, original emphasis) consider two main methods for the dilemma of dividing a restaurant bill between a group of diners:

> One way is for each diner to contribute *exactly* their portion of the overall cost (the 'calculating payer' method). The other is to divide the whole cost equally by the number of diners (the 'equal payer' method). Taking the first method absolutely guarantees *financial* equity. Taking the second method means that some will pay slightly more and some slightly less than the actual

cost of their meal, and thus, financial *inequity* is virtually guaranteed. However, method-2 can also be seen to have associated *social* 'benefits' which, by virtue of their absence in method-1, can be considered as method-1's losses (or 'costs'). Over and above making for an easier calculation, dividing the bill equally also has at least the following face gains: it engenders a sense of group solidarity, and it may demonstrate commitment to the future(s) of the ongoing relationship(s) between the participants, since, over time, the financial loss on this particular occasion will potentially be recouped in some future exchange. However, we would argue that there is also a potential social loss for the 'calculating payer' since this behaviour carries a negative other-assessment by those who value ritual, *social* equilibrium over the financial. For the 'equal payer', the absence of this cost is effectively a further benefit. And yet, despite the apparent benefits of dividing the costs equally, there are 'calculating payers' who choose to forego them.

In a comprehensive account of social action, we must remember that people are driven by things other than face alone. For example, people can cheat, abuse and lie, but the explanation for this cannot always be that they actually *have no concerns* for face – it just so happens that agents may reckon that, in maximising their outcomes, there is more to be gained (or less to be lost) than by orienting to those concerns. Indeed, as Brown and Levinson (1987: 62) note: 'Face can be, and routinely is, ignored, not just in cases of social breakdown (affrontery) but also in cases of urgent cooperation, or in the interests of efficiency'. However, whilst we take it that face is foremost an interpersonally achieved construct, we are talking not just about (not) 'paying' face due to *others*, but also (not) choosing to display concern for the treatment of our *own* face, contingent upon rationalising our wants vs. needs for dues from others. We would argue then, that while face and ritual social equilibrium are invariably (and ordinarily) at play, equity *always is*.

13.4.4 Post-Labovian Sociolinguistics (PLS)

The variationist (Labovian) paradigm studies the inter-connectedness of both various social groups and various formalities of speech style. It is, however, fundamentally concerned more with the former rather than the latter. Labovian sociolinguistics investigates the variation according to the stratification of society into various social groups – *social variation*. Post-Labovian sociolinguistics, on the other hand, is a term sometimes used to cover the other side of the variationist divide. It is concerned predominantly with variation within individuals – *stylistic variation*. To end this chapter, we will sketch three main approaches to Post-Labovian sociolinguistics (PLS): Accommodation Theory, Audience Design, and Acts of Identity.

Questions

The common question that PLS asks is this: HOW DO PEOPLE ADAPT THE STYLE OF THEIR LANGUAGE ACCORDING TO THE ENVIRONMENT IN WHICH THEY FIND THEMSELVES? (In essence, we are back to the chameleonesque behaviour that we alluded to in the discussion of diglossia in 12.3.5.) In Bell's (1997: 240) words, 'style involves the ways in which speakers talk differently on different occasions rather than the way in which different speakers talk differently from each other' and thus the focus of PLS moves away from the behaviour of social groups to the linguistic behaviour and, with that, the linguistic identity of the individual.

Data

The data used in PLS is wide ranging and concerned with any linguistic level: phonology (➔ 11), morphology (➔ 5), semantics (➔ 6), syntax (➔ 7), discourse (➔ 8). In short, because anything can be different, anything can make a difference.

Methods

The methods used in PLS are also necessarily similarly eclectic. It is equally as possible to gather rich ethnographic descriptions as it is to collect data samples and carry out variationist quantifications of specific variables. What 'separates' these approaches is the theoretical frameworks that they espouse (and even then, the fundamental similarities are really quite evident).

Theories

Accommodation Theory

Accommodation Theory (always referred to as Accommodation Theory, never *the* Accommodation Theory) has its roots in the social psychological research on similarity-attraction. It is perhaps most associated with the work of Howard Giles and colleagues and has one major premise: 'an individual can induce another to evaluate him more favourably by reducing dissimilarities between them' (Giles and Powesland 1997 [1975]: 233). This positive evaluation is not necessarily affective – it can also relate to increased intelligibility.

Giles and Powesland (1997 [1975]: 236) provide the following schema representing the rationale behind accommodative behaviour:

> There is a dyad consisting of speakers A and B
> Assume that A wishes to gain B's approval
> A then
>
> 1. Samples B's speech and
>   (i)   draws inferences as to the personality characteristics of B (or at least the characteristics which [A assumes] B wishes to project as being his)
>   (ii) assumes that B values and approves of such characteristics
>   (iii) assumes that B will approve of him (A) to the extent that he (A) displays similar characteristics
> 2. Chooses from his speech-repertoire patterns of speech which project characteristics of which B is assumed to approve.

(NB: at each stage in this schema, accommodation is based on assumption (and, as the joke goes, sometimes, if we assume incorrectly we might find that the result makes an *ass* out of u and *me*).)

In certain circumstances, convergence may also be costly (even dangerous) if it is interpreted as patronizing, condescending or threatening, or ingratiating.

If A does this, the result is called CONVERGENCE (if it is in the direction of a prestige variety it is called upward convergence, if in the direction of a non-prestige it is called downward convergence). If B does likewise, the result is mutual convergence. If, on the other hand, A attempts to sound *less* like B, this is called DIVERGENCE.

Giles and Smith (1979: 47) discuss factors which can affect the extent to which convergence might occur (cf. Le Page, below) including:

1   range of the speaker's repertoire
2   the probability of future interactions with the listener
3   status relationships
4   recollections of previous shifts made by the listener.

Although Accommodation Theory is generally considered in relation to the benefits of convergent (or divergent) behaviour, there are, of course, also costs to be taken into account. The following words of Giles and Smith (1979: 48) should (if you have read the section on Equity Theory) sound somewhat familiar:

> The similarity-attraction model tends to emphasize only the rewards attending a convergent act, that is, an increase in attraction and or approval. However it is likely that certain *costs* would be involved too, such as the increased effort made to converge, a loss of perceived integrity and [a loss of] personal (and sometimes group) identity. Social exchange theory, again in its simplest form, states that prior to acting, we attempt to assess the rewards and costs of alternate courses of action (Homas, 1961). Thus, if we have a choice of doing (or saying) A or B, we tend to choose the alternative which maximizes the chances of a positive outcome, and minimizes the chances of an unpleasant one. Engaging in convergent speech acts should then incur more potential rewards for the speaker than costs.

Before we move on to audience design, it is worth mentioning three final points that Giles and Smith (1979) make about Accommodation Theory. We will not comment on them, however, but just let the quotes speak for themselves:

> A corollary of the notion of that convergence might result in increased approval is the idea that the greater one's need for approval, the greater will be one's tendency to converge.
>
> (1979: 47)

> Research on causal attribution theory [...] suggests that we interpret other people's behaviour and evaluate the persons themselves in terms of the motives and intentions that we attribute as the cause of their behaviour. For example, we do not just observe a man donating money to a charity and automatically evaluate him as kind and generous. We often consider, as best we can, his motives first. In this case, an attribution of a motive of personal gain from this act might temper our evaluative enthusiasm, or even to assess him somewhat negatively as [M]achiavellian and untrustworthy. We might expect that such processes operate in the perception of speech convergence as well [...].
>
> (1979: 50)

we like more those people whose respect we are *acquiring* rather than those whose admiration we already possess [… and] we *dislike* most those whose respect we appear to be losing, rather than those who have never held us in high esteem.

(1979: 62, original emphasis)

Audience Design

Audience Design is associated with Allan Bell. In his (1997: 243–248) paper, he summarizes the main points of this framework. Below, each initial italicization represents a direct quotation from Bell while the subsequent plain font is our explanatory commentary.

1   *Style is what an individual speaker does with a language in relation to other people.* Style is about how we consider other people, and not (*contra* the Labovians) about the amount of attention we pay to our speech.

2   *Style derives its meaning from the association of linguistic features with particular social groups.* In other words, the social values that we assign to linguistic features used by certain groups are related to the social values assigned to the groups themselves – so vowels used by 'posh' people are considered posh because the people who use them are considered posh and, *mutatis mutandis*, the same for common sounds and common people.

3   *Speakers design their style primarily for and in response to their audience.* This makes style shifting a responsive behaviour (our style choice depends on whom we are talking to).

4   *Audience design applies to all codes and levels of a language repertoire, monolingual and multilingual.* Anything can be different. Anything can make a difference.

5   *Variation on the style dimension within the speech of a single speaker derives from and echoes the variation which exists between speakers on the 'social' dimension.* The different styles individuals employ are not created out of nowhere, but rather originate in the linguistics differences of different groups.

6   *Speakers show a fine-grained ability to design their style for a range of different addressees, and to a lesser degree for other audience members.* According to Goffman (1981 [1979]), people who can hear what we are saying come in different types. There are the people who, at that moment, we are speaking directly to (our addressees); people who are part of the wider group of ratified (though not currently active) side participants (auditors); bystanders who are people known to be present and in earshot but not ratified as official participants in the ongoing exchange (overhearers); and people who we don't even know are able to hear us (eavesdroppers). And Bell's point is that we can (if we so choose) style shift in response to any of them.

7   *Style shifts according to topic or setting derive their meaning and direction of shift from the underlying association of topics or settings with typical audience members.* In essence, this claim hypothesizes that for example when we talk about school our style echoes the way we would talk to our teachers and when we talk about work it sounds like the way we would talk to our employer. This is the one that often causes students serious problems. Fortunately, Bell has an escape clause, in that he suggests that this hypothesis is only a tentative one. We would, however, suggest that even 'tentative' is perhaps something of an overstatement.

8   *As well as the 'responsive' dimension of style, there is the 'initiative' dimension.* While our style can be a
    response to a certain situation (we may talk quieter when we enter a place of worship,
    we may swear more when we are talking to our closest friends, we may use Latinate
    vocabulary as a *sine qua non* of academic writing), by employing certain styles we can
    actually shape the situation (so by speaking in hushed tones, we can invoke a sense of
    reverence and gravitas; by swearing more we might indicate that we are treating the
    addressees as intimates; and by using foreign phrases we may lay claim to being
    members of the intelligentsia).

9   *Initiative style shifts are in essence 'referee design', by which the linguistic features associated with a group can
    be used to express identification with that group.* This criterion is what particularly differentiates
    Audience Design from Accommodation Theory. While the latter suggests that our
    style shifts according to who we are talking *to*, 'referee design' accounts for the
    possibility that there may be occasions where we shift style in order to affiliate with a
    non-present reference group. In the sociolinguistic literature, examples of 'referee
    design' are also known by another name — they are what Bob Le Page called *Acts
    of Identity*.

Acts of Identity

Although Bob Le Page was already publishing his ideas about projection, focusing and
diffusion in 1968, the major work in which he develops them was co-authored with
Andrée Tabouret-Keller (and published in 1985). Extracts from this book were included
in the sister reader to this volume (➜ R3.1) and it is parts of the same sections (1985:
181–182) that we reproduce here:

> a major bastion in our general theory [...] is that *all* utterances are affected by
> the audience, the topic and the setting, and that in general terms [...] the indi-
> vidual creates for himself the patterns of his linguistic behaviour so as
> to resemble those of the group or groups with which from time to time he
> wishes to be identified, or so as to be unlike those from whom he wishes to be
> distinguished.

> *Projection, focussing, diffusion.* There are constraints upon the individual's
> ability to create these patterns, which we shall deal with in a moment. Within
> this general theory we see speech acts as acts of projection: the speaker is
> projecting his inner universe, implicitly with the invitation to others to share
> it, at least insofar as they recognize his language as an accurate symboliza-
> tion of the world, and to share his attitude towards it. By verbalizing as he
> does, he is seeking to reinforce his models of the world, and hopes for acts of
> solidarity from those with whom he wishes to identify. The feedback he
> receives from those with whom he talks may reinforce him, or may cause him
> to modify his projections, both in their form and in their content. To the
> extent that he is reinforced, his behaviour in that particular context may
> become more regular, more focussed; to the extent that he modifies his
> behaviour to accommodate to others it may for a time become more vari-
> able, more diffuse, but in time the behaviour of the group – that is, he and
> those with whom he is trying to identify – will become more focussed. Thus
> we may speak of focussed and of diffuse, or non-focussed, linguistic systems,

both in individuals and in groups, with each individual's knowledge of the systems of his groups the lynch-pin upon which the shared concept of communal languages or varieties turns.

The constraints upon our acts of identity. Our ability to get into focus with those with whom we wish to identify, however, is constrained, as we have already said, and the constraints can in general terms be categorized under four heads [...]. We can only behave according to the behavioural patterns of groups we find it desirable to identify with to the extent that:

(i)   we can identify the groups
(ii)   we have both adequate access to the groups and ability to analyse their behavioural patterns
(iii)   the motivation to join the groups is sufficiently powerful, and is either reinforced or reversed by feedback from the groups
(iv)   we have the ability to modify our behaviour.

Activity 13.4 🔑

1   In just one minute, list as many groups as you can think of with which (from time to time) you either do, or would like to identify.
2   Then think about *when* you actively identify with which groups.
3   Then think about *why* you do so.
4   Finally think about *how* you do so.

The social groups we identify with do, of course, overlap – massively. For example, it is entirely possible to simultaneously be a 44-year-old vegetarian bridge-playing dyslexic catholic lesbian accountant called Ernestine from Berlin who is a first-time mother ecstatically happy at the birth of her baby despite some serious fears about her own health. While this example is of course contrived, the point is that humans are generally not defined by any one characteristic – our individuality comes from the delicate interconnection of the myriad characteristics which we possess and the multifarious groups with whom we identify. The related linguistic point is that while we are always members of many categories, the way that we use language will, at any time, depend on which category(ies) is (are) currently most actively relevant. So for example, at work, Ernestine's way of speaking may mostly resemble that of other accountants; at church it may mostly be like that of other practicing Catholics; and in her post-natal classes she is likely to talk like many other first-time mothers.

This is what a simple audience design would predict: our style shifts according to our audience. What an acts of identity model offers in addition to this is why, when she is on holiday in Vienna, she is likely to be perceived as being German rather than Austrian (unless, of course, she has sufficient motivation and ability to do otherwise).

Activity 13.5

Most people have heard of the Beatles (if you haven't, they were once quite a popular beat combo from Liverpool). Find some of their earlier and later recordings – *She loves you* (1963) and *Across the universe* (1970) will work particularly well for starters – and listen to the pronunciation of their singing. (For comparison purposes, if you can, also try to find the very non-American version of *She loves you* by Ted Chippington – at the time of writing, it's available on YouTube.) You should be able to tell that the Beatles' early songs sound much more American than the later ones. Why do you think this might be so?

There is no commentary to this activity but an interesting account of how the Beatles changed their singing pronunciation over the years can be found in Trudgill's (1997b) [1983] paper, *Acts of Conflicting Identity: The Sociolinguistics of British Pop-song Pronunciation.*

13.5 SUMMARY

In 1964 there was a conference held at the University of California, Los Angeles (UCLA). In the published proceedings, Bright (1966) suggests that it was perhaps the first ever conference to focus on the then developing field of sociolinguistics. There were just 25 participants. A few years later in the early 1970s, the Sociolinguistics Symposia were founded 'by a group of sociolinguists who saw the need for a forum to discuss research findings and to debate theoretical and methodological issues concerning language in society' and according to the same Sociolinguistics Symposium website, 'The symposium has since grown into a large, international conference, now attracting more than 600 participants'.

We know that for many readers of this chapter, 50 years ago is like 'so last century', but for those of us who were there, the time since the mid-1960s is really but a blink of an eye. While we may never witness the liquidation of the term that Hymes and Labov wished for, the fact that sociolinguistics has come so very far in such a relatively short time is testament to the fact that many people – including us – are at least thinking about the very many sociolinguistic patterns which shape (some would argue, which *create*) our social reality. Quotations from many of the sociolinguists we have met in this chapter support this view:

> The fact of the matter is that the 'real world' is to a large extent unconsciously built up on the language habits of the group.
>
> Sapir (1961 [1929]: 69)

> In all these cases, people may be converging their speech to how they believe others in the situation would best receive it.
>
> (Giles and Smith 1979: 47)

> [W]e do not necessarily adapt to the style of the interlocutor, but rather the image we have of ourselves in relation to our interlocutor …
>
> (Le Page 1997: 28, original italics)

As we said above, how we perceive ourselves, how we perceive others, how we perceive ourselves in relation to others, how others perceive us perceiving ourselves in relation to them and how all that is finely mediated and represented through our myriad choices of linguistic behaviour is, in essence, what sociolinguistics is all about – and exactly how sociolinguists go about answering those questions depends largely on how they stand in relation to the four inter-connected aspects of questions, data, methods and theories.

But if sociolinguists differentiate themselves according to their stance on questions, data, methods and theories, they are all united in the fact that they are linguists who believe in the primary importance of the fundamental 'socialness' of language. After all is said and done, as Le Page and Tabouret-Keller (1985: 188) have long since noted:

> **We should constantly remind ourselves that languages do not do things; people do things, languages are abstractions from what people do.**

COMMENTARY ON ACTIVITIES

O— Remember that this symbol indicates that there is a commentary on the activity that you can find on the companion website at www.routledge.com/cw/merrison.

FURTHER READING and REFERENCES

Suggestions for further reading on the topics discussed in this chapter can be found on the companion website (www.routledge.com/cw/merrison).

Any piece of academic writing must always provide a list of publications to which reference has been made. Unusually and very unconventionally, this information is provided on the companion website (www.routledge.com/cw/merrison). Always ask your tutor about how you are to present references for any piece of work that you submit.

Chapter 14
Psycholinguistics

Key Ideas in this Chapter

- Language is a biological and psychological phenomenon as well as a social and cultural one.

- Psycholinguists study how language is stored in the mind (MENTAL REPRESENTATION) and how it is used during speaking, listening, reading, writing, and signing (PROCESSING).

- Neurolinguists study the brain structures and neurological processes underlying the mental representation and processing of language.

- These brain structures and processes are concentrated in the left cerebral hemisphere for most people, with a special role played by neural circuits in Broca's area and Wernicke's area.

- Broadly speaking, theories of mental representation and processing fall into two classes: CONNECTIONIST accounts, which are closer to the complex biological reality of neural circuits; and MODULAR accounts, which are closer to the kinds of symbolic descriptions of language used throughout this book.

- Language production involves the rapid selection of linguistic structures on different levels. In speaking, it starts with the activation of meaning and finishes with the articulation of speech.

- Language comprehension is more of a 'guessing-game', in which cues from accumulating speech (or text or signing), context and background knowledge, are all exploited in parallel to make understanding happen at lightning speeds.

14.1 INTRODUCTION

In books and films from the genres of science fiction and fantasy, one encounters characters who can read the thoughts of others and/or communicate their own thoughts without using a physical channel. Sometimes it is a specialized skill that only some individuals possess, like several wizards in the *Harry Potter* books, or the Jedi knights in the *Star Wars* movies. And sometimes it is a property of a whole species, like the Vulcans on TV's *Star Trek*, or the elves in Tolkien's *Lord of the Rings*. There are also many entertainers from our own real-life species who have claimed such powers – perhaps most famously Uri Geller, who could also bend spoons by 'mind power' alone.

But telepathy is a physical impossibility, and if it *were* something that human beings were capable of, then we wouldn't need language. In a sense, language is the next best thing to telepathy, and indeed we could argue that it has distinct advantages over it. Spoken and signed language works to communicate and construct meanings with others at lightning speeds and, because we can 'switch it on and off' in production, we can keep our thoughts to ourselves most of the time (useful for privacy, modesty, good taste, subterfuge, *etc.*).

From this perspective, language is a property of the human mind, a psychological system housed in the brain. It is this system that allows human minds to interact through the physical channels of speech, text and sign (the medium of sign languages for deaf people and those whose hearing is impaired). So although in most of this book we concentrate on its social nature, we must always bear in mind that language is also simultaneously psychological. It is constructed in infancy inside our brains, develops there throughout our lives, is activated there whenever we read, write, listen, speak or sign (even to ourselves), and can be lost or compromised if our brains are impaired through injury, illness or old age.

The area of study which explores these issues, psycholinguistics, is our principal concern here. In this chapter, we examine language from the perspectives of brain and mind, and introduce two major kinds of psycholinguistic theory, before sketching some of the processes involved in speaking and listening. There is a separate chapter for one central topic in psycholinguistics, LANGUAGE ACQUISITION, which studies the way in which human beings construct language systems in their minds, in infancy and adulthood (➜ 15).

14.2 LANGUAGE, COGNITION AND THE BRAIN

Before we address some of the core issues in the psychology of language, we should try to clarify the difference between mind (an abstract concept) and the brain (a physical entity). As part of human COGNITION, linguistic communication involves mental processes and happens almost instantaneously, so to that extent resembles telepathy. But it is not a supernatural phenomenon: language is very physically grounded, a function of the organic brain. It necessarily involves MOTOR CONTROL on the part of the speaker, writer or signer to generate and direct the physical energy required to span the physical gap between producer and receiver,

Human COGNITION refers to the mental processes, both conscious and unconscious, involved in the ways we perceive, learn, remember, know, categorize, and connect information – and thus how we reason. It is studied by psychologists, linguists, philosophers, neuroscientists, anthropologists, computer scientists and others.

and it relies on SENSORY PERCEPTION on the part of the receiver to *hear* speech and *see* text or sign.

From this perspective, language is a system, located in the brain, which outputs motor activity through the **vocal tract** in speech (➔ 9, 10) and the upper limbs in writing and signing, and receives sensory input through the ears in listening, the eyes in reading text or understanding sign, and the finger tips for reading braille. But how can abstract phenomena like morphemes, word meanings, verb groups, and discourse principles be stored and operate in the organic material of the brain? Where exactly in the brain is language located, and what actually happens when we use it? This is part of a larger question about the relationship between physical and mental structures and processes, or in other words about how the functional architecture of the brain relates to its physical workings.

> The terms *input* and *output*, like many used in psycholinguistics, are borrowed from computer science, a rich source of metaphors for trying to understand how the mind works (but not always helpful if the analogy is pushed too far).

Activity 14.1

If you are or were a reader of British children's comics, you might be familiar with 'The Numskulls' from the *Beezer* (and later the *Beano*), relating episodes in the mental life of an unnamed man. Take a look at Figure 14.1, and make a list of the problems it presents as the basis for an explanation of how the mind, the brain, the senses and language work.

The main problem with a Numskull-style representation of cognitive systems like language is that it explains away thinking, seeing, hearing etc. by populating our heads with 'mini-me's' that do the thinking, seeing, hearing etc. for us. But of course this is circular: it cannot be the case that the way we see things is by the images passing through our eyes and then themselves being 'seen' inside our heads. Or that we remember things because someone or something inside us writes them down, or stores an image of them, that 'we' can 'look at' at a later date. Explanations like these are called *homunculus* arguments, from the medieval idea of the 'little human' (the soul) within each of us. They are arguments of infinite regress: presumably the Numskulls (the 'homunculi' of the comic) can talk to each other and read and write because they themselves have mini-Numskulls in their own heads, who have mini-mini-Numskulls inside their heads, and so on, *ad infinitum*.

There are essentially two different strategies we can adopt to study cognition (as well as sensory perception and motor activity), and neither of them require the postulation of 'homunculi'. We can take the closest possible view, that of COGNITIVE NEUROSCIENCE, and examine the physical structures that underpin cognitive processes. Or we can step back and take a more general view, that of COGNITIVE PSYCHOLOGY, in which we abstract away from physical structures and processes to highlight more general informational ones (the mind's 'functional architecture'). In practice, psycholinguists draw on methods and insights associated with both strategies. For example, to investigate how morphologically complex words are processed, they might conduct experiments in which people are asked to read prefixed words, suffixed words, and bare stems, using NEUROIMAGING techniques from a neuroscience perspective, and CHRONOMETRIC techniques from a psychology perspective.

If the difference between the two perspectives is not clear, maybe an analogy will help. Think of an image file on a computer, like the one in the lower panel of Figure 14.2. If you

> Functional NEUROIMAGING (➔ R4.1) measures activity in the brain during different kinds of mental activities to see which areas are activated. CHRONOMETRIC TECHNIQUES measure reaction times to different kinds of stimuli (here linguistic structures), and the times are taken to reflect processing complexity.

Figure 14.1 An episode of 'The Numskulls' from *The Beezer*, published by DC Thomson and Co. Ltd 1988

are interested in the mechanics of how the photo is formed and how the whole is composed of its constituent parts, you can zoom in to examine how the different parts of the image are represented via shades of greyscale in a particular pattern of pixels (as in the detail of the central section of the main window presented in the upper panel). Or, if you are interested in what the photo *represents*, you can look at the whole image and contemplate a church, with all the encyclopaedic knowledge (➜ 6.1.2) that recognition of the image as a church might trigger. It is at this level also that you might recognize it as a particular *instance* of a church (York Minster) that you have encountered before in a photo or on a visit.

This is the essential difference between looking at language in the brain and looking at language in the mind. **Neurolinguistics** concentrates on language in the brain (≈ how

Figure 14.2 Partial image of York Minster from the south, with zoomed-in detail of the centre of the Rose Window (photo: James Bozadjian)

the pixels form the image), while psycholinguistics studies language in the mind (≈ what the image represents). Brain and mind are essentially the same thing, approached from two different perspectives.

As mentioned, the two perspectives are increasingly being combined by scholars to give us greater understanding of the mystery of how we develop and share thought through language. But it is *psycho*linguistic research that has more direct connection with the kinds of language issues covered in the rest of this book. If we look inside a random adult human brain using neuroimaging techniques or dissection, we can't tell which language(s) the individual knows (➔ 16), nor whether they are speakers or signers, literate or illiterate (➔ 1). We can't estimate the size of their vocabulary (➔ 5) or know which dialect they speak (➔ 12). But we *can* locate and measure different kinds of language activity, and this can inform psycholinguistic theory in important ways, as we demonstrate in the rest of this section.

14.2.1 How the brain works

The human brain is a physical organ of immense structural complexity which operates on the basis of, as yet, only poorly understood principles. The workings of the brain can perhaps best be understood in terms of an immense network or system of circuits, through which information flows in parallel, in a constant frenzy of electrochemical currents. The circuits are composed of billions of cells (NEURONS), connected through SYNAPSES. Neuronal networks together constitute a set of anatomical structures which stretch all the way from the nerves in your toes, up to the spinal cord, through the brain stem and thence to the two CEREBRAL HEMISPHERES, the bulging top of the brain made up of a left and a right half. Nerve endings all the way around the body allow us to experience localized sensations (like being tickled on the soles of the feet) and to move the different parts of our bodies independently of each other (e.g. using a foot to depress the accelerator pedal on a car).

Up in the head, the 'higher order' mental functions associated with cognition are mostly under the control of dense neural networks in the CORTEX, a layer of tissue only 2–4 mm deep covering the cerebral hemispheres. The left and right hemispheres, connected together by a bundle of nerve fibres called the CORPUS CALLOSUM, mirror each other in their 'formal architecture', but differ in significant aspects of function. For example, circuits in the left cerebral hemisphere control motor activity and sensory input associated with the right side of the body, and vice-versa (➔ R4.8). Thus, the operation of a car's accelerator starts with activity in your left cerebral hemisphere, even though the pedal is depressed with the right foot.

Also, the left cerebral hemisphere is more involved in analytic processes involving temporal sequencing (like adding numbers together or playing chess), whereas the right has greater responsibility for holistic processes involving spatial dimensions (like steering your car round a corner or admiring a large painting in a gallery). The memory systems underlying your ability to perform these activities are physically grounded in the interconnected neural circuitry of the hemispheres (and in other brain structures we will not discuss here). During actual performance, energy passes through the circuits in patterned ways, activating different portions of the neuronal network, and this results in sensory experience, logical or intuitive reasoning, voluntary and involuntary movement, etc.

Distinct areas of the cortex in both hemispheres are specialized for different sensory and motor control functions. In Figure 14.3, we have indicated the approximate

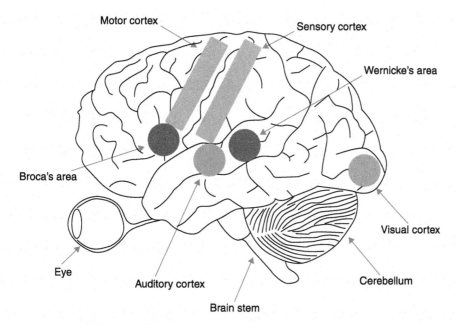

Figure 14.3 The left cerebral hemisphere of the brain (with eye to indicate orientation), showing the approximate location of significant regions

location of the MOTOR CORTEX and the SENSORY CORTEX, on either side of a central fissure that runs down from the top of the head to above the ear. Neural circuits in the former control movement in different parts of the body, depending on the circuits' location in the cortex, while those in the latter are responsible for sensory experience in corresponding regions. For example, wriggling the toes (movement) and stubbing them (sensation), are both associated with the lowest regions of the motor cortex and sensory cortex. Two other regions, the AUDITORY CORTEX and VISUAL CORTEX, are concerned with detailed handling of input from the ears and eyes, respectively. The specialization of distinct neurological structures and areas like this is known as MODULARITY.

14.2.2 Language in the brain

A person's knowledge of the nuts and bolts of language is encoded in constellations of neurons that for most people are concentrated in the left cerebral hemisphere. Over 95 per cent of right-handed individuals are left-dominant for language, as are around 70 per cent of left-handed individuals; of the remainder, half are right-dominant, and half appear to have language spread across both hemispheres (see Fernández and Smith Cairns 2011: 84–89). It should come as no surprise that language shares the same hemisphere as analytic processes such as arithmetic and chess-playing. As described at length in the central chapters of this book (➜ 7–11), language use involves the coordinated sequencing and patterning of separate units on various different levels, from phonemes to sentences. Just like maths and chess.

Within the dominant hemisphere, there is evidence that different units of language structure, and different stages and processes of language use, are associated with different anatomical regions. This also should not be surprising, given the cortical modularity for sensory processing and motor control that we have already noted. Comparisons of the language of people with brain damage, post-mortem examination of brains, and neuroimaging from impaired and unimpaired brains, suggest that there are two particular areas associated with language, on either side of another major fissure, the SYLVIAN FISSURE, which runs roughly back from behind the eye to above the ear. These two areas are named after the nineteenth-century physicians who first associated them with language functions: Paul Broca (BROCA'S AREA) and Carl Wernicke (WERNICKE'S AREA).

Exactly which aspects of language structure and use are associated with which area is a matter of considerable debate. Originally it was thought that Broca's area controlled the processes involved in speaking and that Wernicke's area controlled those for listening. The proximity of Broca's area to the motor cortex, and of Wernicke's area to the auditory cortex, seems consistent with this: speaking involves fine muscular control and listening, of course, requires the processing of sound. Broca's area has also been claimed to be where grammar is 'located', whereas Wernicke's area has been argued to be the seat of word meaning. The main evidence for these claims comes from studies of people with language disability or loss, especially **aphasia**, a condition in which language is disrupted independently of other cognitive functions (➜ R4.2).

Activity 14.2 🔑

Look at the following two-minute stretches of discourse, from aphasic speakers telling the Cinderella story (Berndt 2007: 566):

A. long ago uh (2 sec) one time uh many years ago (2 sec) uh step (2 sec) two sisters and one (2 sec) god mothers yeah uh (6 sec) Cinderella is uh washing uh clothes and uh (2 sec) mop floor (4 sec) one day Cinderella big party in the castle (5 sec) two uh girls (13 sec) dresses is beautiful (2 sec) Cinderella is poor.

B. this is uh something for that and it starts out as and um there is /**praetihds**/ and he has things to do and ... but anyway ... uh stuff is going along and then they think something and they think okay so he goes now he goes ... This goes on and takes all that and we see that we have things for that ... it's a thing and other things ... and then we /**djuz**/ all that and he sees that /**erawl**/ that well he happens to get up and goes things and he's that's good and see so good ...

How would you characterize the language of each? On the basis of what you have read of this chapter so far, which do you think has experienced damage to Broca's area, and which to Wernicke's? What evidence can you offer for your conclusions?

Many people with language disabilities who have trouble combining words and morphemes together fluently have damage to Broca's area, while those with damage to Wernicke's area often speak fluently but with semantically inappropriate word combinations. In Activity 14.2, sample A is from a person with what is called BROCA'S APHASIA and sample B is from a person with what is called WERNICKE'S APHASIA.

Recent advances in neurolinguistics have, however, revealed many cases of people with aphasia in which: (a) damage to Broca's area results in Wernicke-style symptoms and vice-versa; and (b) damage to other parts of the brain results in language behaviours such as those illustrated in Activity 14.2. Additionally, sophisticated neuroimaging techniques have demonstrated that normal linguistic activity involves numerous parts of the brain, including the right cerebral hemisphere and even other parts of the brain, suggesting that language is distributed, rather than located only in the main 'language centres' around the sylvian fissure in the left-hand side of the brain.

14.3 LANGUAGE IN THE MIND

Although the development of neuroimaging techniques means that language can now be studied in the brains of living people without language disabilities, there are still considerable shortcomings associated with neurolinguistic methods. In any case, psycholinguists need to use abstract, psychological concepts in order to characterize the linguistic phenomena they explore in the brain and link them to the categories used in descriptive linguistics. (That is to say, they need to be able to talk about language in the mind, as well as language in the brain.)

See Byrd and Mintz (2010: 255–262) for a brief discussion of the challenges and opportunities of neuroimaging.

> ### Activity 14.3 🔑
>
> Cast your eyes briefly over Figures 14.4 and 14.6 on the next few pages, without reading the captions beneath, but paying attention to the overall design and composition of the diagrams. What are the major differences between them? From what you have read about language in the mind so far, which one looks closer to how language is represented physically in the brain, as opposed to functionally, in the mind?

Psycholinguists view language in the mind in essentially two ways, one of which is closer to the neurolinguistic perspective, and is called *connectionist*, and the other which is closer to the linguistic perspective, and is called *modular*.

- Modular theories view language as a symbol- and rule-based computational system, 'hard-wired' into our brains by our genetic code (➔ R4.3), containing specialized knowledge sources (one for phonology, one for syntax, etc.) which are used to run specialized programmes for different aspects of language use, like assembling the sequence of phonemes required by the motor system for an utterance to be produced (PHONOLOGY ➔ 11), or working out who did what to whom when we hear a passive sentence (SYNTAX ➔ 7);
- Connectionist theories view language as a more organic brain-style system, emerging from our experience rather than determined by genetic endowment (➔R4.5), composed of vast interactive networks of neuron-like units which can be activated or deactivated to different degrees via interconnections of different strengths, with no separate sub-systems for syntax, phonology, etc.

In both views, the job of language in the mind is fundamentally the same: to encode aspects of thought into speech, text or sign (in the processes of speaking, writing and signing ➔ 14.4), and to derive thoughts from speech, text or sign (in the processes of listening, reading and comprehending sign ➔ 14.5). Although the modular and connectionist views are pitted against each other as alternatives in the research literature, and some scholars reject one or the other view completely, it is perhaps more helpful to try to understand the advantages and disadvantages of each, as well as their ultimate complementarity.

14.3.1 Modules and symbols

Although the brain might not be as compartmentalized as the rooms of the Numskulls in their oblivious host's head (Figure 14.1), it can be helpful to think of the mind in terms of separate modules, in order to see the wood for the trees – or the cathedral for the pixels in the example of Figure 14.2. We want to be able to look at the image of York Minster and talk about what we see in terms of walls, windows, turrets and towers, rather than the intrinsically meaningless greyscale pixels which actually form the image. In the same way, we want to be able to discuss the psychology of language in terms of phonemes, syllables, morphemes and phrases, and the ways we combine them, rather than the dense and complex networks of connected neurons which constitute them at the physical level.

The modular view thus parallels the view of many descriptive and theoretical linguists, who recognize separate classes of language structures and rules at different levels, as we have done in some of the central chapters of this book (➔ 5, 7, 8, 11). One formulation of the modular view is illustrated in Figure 14.4 (inspired by Jackendoff 1997). You will see that the upper three modules encapsulate rules (in the sense of regularities) in the three domains of phonology, syntax and concepts, and the arrows in each module indicate that these rules govern sets of possible structures of the corresponding kind.

This is parallel to the notion of the **hierarchy of rank** (➔ Figure 7.1), through which smaller units combine to make successively larger units, all the way from phonemes to texts. The difference is that the hierarchy of rank is a generalization about abstract systems (independent of individual minds) which can characterize the knowledge of a group of speakers of a particular language or variety (Canadian English, Mexican Spanish, Cantonese, etc.), whereas modularity is a theory about how individual speakers *store* and *access* the language system in their own minds: it attempts to explain the MENTAL REPRESEN-TATION and PROCESSING of language as a property of the species, rather than of individual languages.

Mental representation is the (temporary or long-term) storage in memory of what we have learned, what we have experienced, what we think, feel, understand, believe, assume, etc. Language rules and structures are assumed to be part of what is represented. Proponents of modularity argue that mental representation can be conceived of in terms of symbolic systems, and that when we access this information, we *process* these symbols

Speakers of languages which use a lot of grammatical **morphemes** (➔ 5, 7) are assumed to have corresponding modules in their minds for **inflectional** rules and structures too. Unfortunately, we cannot discuss the psycholinguistics of **morphology** here, for reasons of space, but you will find an accessible introduction in Chapter 11 of Aitchison (2003).

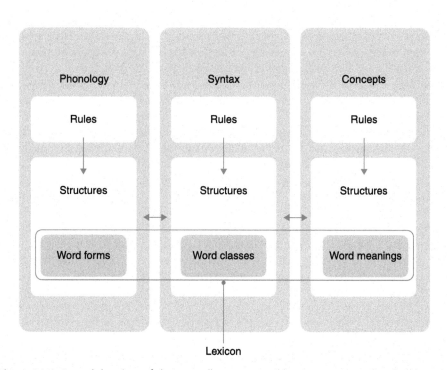

Figure 14.4 A modular view of the mentally represented language system (inspired by Jackendoff 1997)

in the same way a word processing program on a computer takes as input keystrokes and yields as output letters on a monitor.

The rules 'contained' in the first module in Figure 14.4 will constitute the regular patterns by which a speaker combines phonemes in phonological structures like syllables and words (➔ 11). Similarly, the rules in the second module will be those that represent the patterns by which the speaker combines words as phrases, and phrases as clauses and sentences (➔ 7). The third module is, in effect, the stuff of thought itself: where we mentally create, store and connect together conceptualizations of entities such as 'physical objects, events, properties, times, quantities and intentions' (Jackendoff 1997: 31). Many of these conceptualized entities can be expressed through linguistic structures, from individual morphemes to whole texts, and so constitute the *meanings* of these structures (➔ 6, 7).

In Figure 14.4, the place we store the words we know, the MENTAL LEXICON, is represented as embracing a triad of structures from each of the modules, and this corresponds to three different aspects of what it means to know a word (together 'a knot joining some threads', as we put it in Chapter 5). The three threads are: how the word is pronounced/ written/signed (*word form*); how it is used in phrases (most importantly *word class*, like noun, verb and adjective ➔ 7); and the concept(s) it is used to express (*word meaning*). For example, the word *apple* will be represented in the mind as three related mental representations (the word's LEXICAL ENTRY) which include the following information:

- the phonological structure: /æpl/
- the word class: noun
- the meaning: 'a spherical red, green or yellow fruit that grows on a tree'.

Of course our word knowledge is much richer than this and the use of a dictionary-style definition to represent the core meaning of the word is an especially flagrant oversimplification (one which we will attempt to unpack a little in the next section).

We have spent some time here on modularity, not because we believe it necessarily provides a superior account of the psychology of language, but because it is (relatively) more accessible to students (and descriptive linguists). Essentially, it is a way of viewing language in the mind which simplifies away from the underlying neural complexity by relying on metaphor: SYMBOLS (➔ 1), which 'stand for' more complex internal states, RULES operating on these symbols, which characterize how the symbols are combined, and MODULES, which are compartments of the mind inhabited by particular kinds of symbols, rules and procedures.

We can easily represent this view of language in the mind visually, using boxes connected by lines and arrows, labelled with English words. The next section points out, however, that if we look closer at the boxes, their borders may start to look less rigid; and if we think about it for a moment, the labels themselves are just words that themselves need unpacking. If this thorny issue is not tackled, the homunculus problem arises once again (➔ 14.2).

A non-modular approach to language in the mind is adopted by the proponents of COGNITIVE LINGUISTICS (e.g. Evans and Green 2006), according to which linguistic systems are constrained by usage in social contexts, rather than by brain structures, and are not separate from other aspects of cognition.

14.3.2 Networks and connections

Modules are ways of conceiving language in the mind as a series of functionally defined boxes and arrows containing symbols and rules. This is not the most insightful metaphorical stance for all aspects of language structure and use. We passed quite quickly over the tricky notion of concepts and word meaning in the previous section, and yet they are critical notions in psycholinguistics. They are also more accurately understood in terms of interconnected networks of shared features, rather than as separate, modular entities (like dictionary entries in lists), so we discuss them in a little more depth here.

Most linguists and psycholinguists, including proponents of modularity, assume that concepts, many of which are associated with individual words, can be broken down into smaller elements, represented by clusters of 'semantic features'. Our mentally represented knowledge of word meanings includes the ways they relate to each other (➜ 6.1). For example, we know that the words *jog* and *sprint* are related semantically because they both include the meaning of *run* (they are **co-hyponyms** of the superordinate word, to use the technical terms introduced in Chapter 6).

From a psycholinguistic perspective, it makes sense to think of this in terms of combinations of **semantic** features, which we indicate here in bracketed small capitals. For example, we can say that the meaning associated with the phonological structure /wʊmən/ (*woman*) is the concept in the mind corresponding to the combination of the features [FEMALE], [HUMAN], and [ADULT]. In similar fashion, the concept expressed by the word form *jog* shares a common set of features with that expressed by the word form *sprint*: namely those which in combination make the meaning of the verb *run*. In addition, the *run* features have also been combined with a modifying feature [SLOWLY] for *jog* and [FAST] for *sprint*.

Activity 14.4

Our mental lexicons contain instances where a single set of semantic features (word meaning) is associated with more than one phonological structure (word form). In other cases, the opposite holds: two different sets of semantic features are associated with a single phonological structure. Try to think of three examples of each.

If you are drawing a blank, look at Section 6.3. See if you can find the technical terms there which linguists use to label these phenomena.

The configuration in which two word forms are connected with the same meaning is called SYNONYMY in semantics (➜ 6.3.2). Examples include *sofa* and *couch, amble* and *stroll, post* and *mail*. The opposite is HOMONYMY, in which one word form serves to express different meanings (➜ 6.4.2). Examples include *case* ('item of luggage', 'instance', 'argument', etc.), *post* ('upright pole', 'mail', 'position in organization' etc.) and *pen* ('writing instrument', 'animal enclosure', etc.). Cases in which a single word form is associated with different but closely overlapping constellations of semantic features in conceptual structure, e.g. the verb *get* in 'get arrested' and 'get a new car', are called POLYSEMY (➜ 6.4.2).

Activity 14.5 🔑

Now consider word class. The sentences *It's about to rain again* and *Here comes the rain again* are associated with the same conceptual structure (i.e., they mean the same thing independent of contextual factors). One of the main differences between them is that in the first, *rain* is used as a verb, and in the second, as a noun. Can you think of five more words like this (not weather-related), which have the same phonological structure, are associated with almost identical semantic features, but differ in word class?

These examples show that our mental lexicon is more like a 'word-web' (Aitchison 2003) than the ordered columns of a dictionary (i.e. more connectionist than modular). Words are not just lists of word forms paired with word meanings. Apart from the complexity of hyponymy, synonymy, homonymy and polysemy, there are also multiple connections between grammatically similar words, such as all the nouns, all the non-count nouns (➔ 7, 17), and—for speakers of languages like German and Spanish with grammatical gender—all the words which are masculine, feminine, or neuter. Grammatical information of this kind constitutes a level of representation in each word's lexical entry which is called the *lemma* in some theories (e.g. Levelt 1989).

In the next section we will see that the mind also makes connections between word forms, e.g. all the words beginning with /str/ (*straddle, straggle, straight, strain, straw*, etc.) and all the words that rhyme with *post* (*boast, coast, ghost, host*, etc.). So the fact that word forms, classes and meanings are related in so many different ways suggests that a modular account might not be the most illuminating perspective on all aspects of the mental representation and processing of language. The metaphor of networks seems more appropriate, as illustrated in Figure 14.5.

In a connectionist approach to the mind, and therefore to language as part of cognition, our mental representations cannot be symbols (like 'V' for verb), because that ultimately requires a homunculus-type commitment (there would have to be a Numskull inside us who understands what 'V' stands for, so he/she would have to have a mind, and how does it work?). Rather, what we as linguists understand as 'V' (*verb-ness*), is actually a state of the neuronal networks in the brain. Neurolinguists have not yet been able to describe that state, although there is aphasic evidence that verbs can be selectively damaged, leaving other word classes unaffected (e.g. Caramazza and Hillis 1991).

Connectionist descriptions of language in the mind cannot, therefore, be typed onto a page, like the descriptions we use in the rest of this book, because their purpose is to delve beneath the short-hand of symbols, and get closer to the 'sub-symbolic' biological reality of language in the brain. They have, therefore, been modelled in computer programs which simulate brain-style representation and processing (as such, they form part of ARTIFICIAL INTELLIGENCE).

ARTIFICIAL INTELLIGENCE (AI) is the branch of computer science dedicated to the simulation and development of intelligent behaviour in machines, including understanding and producing speech.

Many connectionist networks on computers have modelled acquisition (➔ 15), rather than processing, although it is important to recognize that processing is a major part of acquisition: the first thing to happen in children's attempts to work out the rules and structures behind the language in their environment is that they receive acoustic input (manual input for sign languages) and process it. Acquisition simulations start with massively interconnected networks of simple neuron-like units, as yet unassociated with

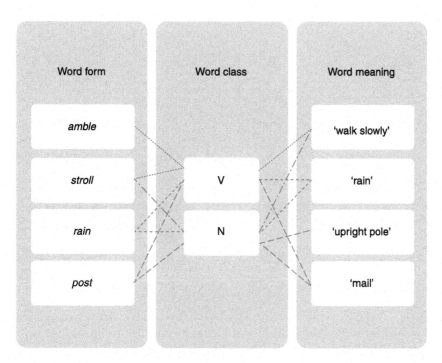

Figure 14.5 Fragments of the network of word forms, classes and meanings that together constitute some of the information in the mental lexicon

any content. Input is repeatedly fed into the model from the environment, and patterns begin to emerge in the strengths of connections activated and the ways some patterns inhibit others (i.e. deactivate them). Intelligent, rule-like behaviour emerges from the patterning of many simple units which, on their own, are meaningless. A well-known early attempt to model the English-speaking child's acquisition of regular and irregular past tense forms (Rumelhart and McClelland 1986) can provide us with an illustration of connectionist formulations of the mental representation of language.

In Figure 14.6 you can see two different states of one part of a (considerably oversimplified) network representing the end state of the learning of the past tense of two English verbs, one regular and one irregular (i.e. part of the mind of a child who has learnt some verb morphology ➔ 5). The first is for the irregular verb ring and the second for the regular verb link. The activated nodes in the left-hand column represent the child's knowledge of the verb root, and the activated nodes in the right-hand column represent the past-tense form that the child comes to associate with it (there are other, hidden columns of connections in between which we are glossing over here). Each node is short-hand for more dense networks which represent phonological structures (in this case ordered pairs of phonemes) that in combination are associated with word forms.

So in the first network state, /rɪ/ and /ɪŋ/ are together activated by the input [rɪŋ] (ring). The word form /rɪŋ/ is associated with /ræŋ/ in the past tense, and this is indicated in the model by the solid lines connecting the /rɪ/ and /ɪŋ/ nodes on the left with the /ræ/ and /æŋ/ nodes on the right. The knowledge that this is an irregular verb is reflected in the inhibitory links between /rɪŋ/ and /rɪŋd/ (ringed), represented by the

The phonemes in the network fragments are represented in ordered pairs to capture the child's knowledge of their sequence in the word: /rɪ/ and /ɪŋ/ fit together to make /rɪŋ/ (ring) via the shared phoneme /ɪ/.

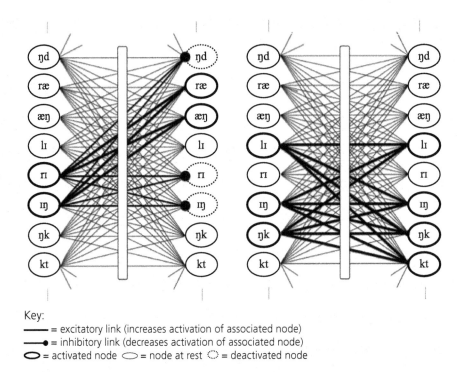

Key:
——— = excitatory link (increases activation of associated node)
——● = inhibitory link (decreases activation of associated node)
⬭ = activated node ⬭ = node at rest ⬭ = deactivated node

Figure 14.6 A fragment of a connectionist network in two states, showing the association between irregular *ring* and *rang* in the first, and between regular *link* and *linked* in the second

nodes /rɪ/, /ɪŋ/ and /ŋd/. The second network state shows the connections for the regular verb link /lɪŋk/ and its past tense linked /lɪŋkt/.

In a connectionist model of the past tense, the mind does not explicitly represent a rule about adding -*ed* at the end of verb roots (and therefore encodes no essential distinction between regular and irregular inflection): the patterns emerge from the distribution of activation and association in the network, on the basis of how often, and in what company, the different structures are heard in the input (for an alternative, modular account, see Pinker 1999).

Now that you have an idea of the ways in which psycholinguists describe the mental representation of language, we can proceed to discuss how these representations are accessed in production and comprehension. To keep things (relatively!) simple, we restrict the discussion to spoken language, the 'default' modality.

14.4 LANGUAGE PRODUCTION

For a sociocultural perspective on speakers' potential for making meaning with others, see M.A.K. Halliday's *Language in a Social Perspective* (➜ R2.3).

When we speak, the linguistic structures we need in order to make meaning with others are normally activated without effort, below the level of consciousness. If the structures have been used frequently enough on previous occasions they will be *selected* for articulation from memory, as pre-assembled combinations of phonemes and morphemes (for words) and combinations of words (for phrases and sentences). Most of the words we use on a daily basis, for example, are stored and retrieved as wholes. But so are many phrases, including idioms (*over the hill*, meaning 'old', *at the end of the day*, meaning 'ultimately', etc.) and also many thousands of familiar LEXICAL BUNDLES, including 'templates' with slots, like *Can-I-have-some-X; Y- {be} -looking-forward-to-Z*; etc.). In a sense, then, words and many phrases are 'off-the-peg' structures: they are not new structures, built by 'productive' rule use (➜ 1.4).

Regularly, however, we also say entirely new things by combining previously known units to produce previously unheard or unspoken structures needed for novel meanings and purposes (➜ 1.4, 5.3.2). This happens via the use of rules in modular theories, or analogy with other structures in connectionist theories. For example, the writer who first coined the prefixed noun *post-hacking* (see the blog at Katwala 2011, for a contender) unconsciously invoked either a mental rule (the prefix {post-} is added to nouns to mean 'after [noun]') or a mental analogy (*post-hacking* follows from *post-war, post-punk*, etc.). This kind of morphological innovation (➜ R2.1) is much less frequent than creativity at the sentence level, as the many thousands of brand-new sentences in this book (or in any corpus) attest to.

14.4.1 Speech errors

The activation of the structures we need when speaking is *normally* effortless and unconscious. But on occasions something goes wrong in language production, and what are called *speech errors* result. These errors reveal something about the mental events that are involved in successful language production, and constitute evidence for theoretical models that have been proposed to shed light on the processes involved. The next activity should be attempted before you read on.

Activity 14.6

Consider the following authentic speech errors, collected by the eminent psycholinguist Victoria Fromkin (1923–2000), available in a browsable online corpus ➜ W14.1.

1   a fifty pound dog of bag food
2   a first fine half
3   Amos Mansdorf from Tel Aviv, Italy
4   and what makes you competent — confident in the figures?
5   and you've prevented — presented us with a problem.

Describe, as fully and explicitly as you can, what you think has happened in each case. On the basis of this very limited set of data, see if you can draw any initial conclusions about: (a) the order in which a speaker selects the words from their mental lexicon and places them in the appropriate syntactic sequence; and (b) the ways that lexical entries are organized together in the mental lexicon.

The first couple of errors in Activity 14.6 indicate that speakers don't just look up the words they need in the order in which the grammatical rules require them to be sequenced. In the first example, the words *dog* and *bag* have been placed in each other's positions, and in the second, *fine* and *first* come out in the wrong order. This suggests that the words are activated *before* they are put into a sequence for delivery in speech.

Of course when we speak, it happens at lightning speed, so we're not aware of the order in which these 'micro events' happen in our minds. McMahon (2002: 2) states: 'we decide to speak, and what about, but the nuts and bolts of speech production are beyond our conscious reach …'. The evidence from speech errors, together with data from neuroimaging and experimental techniques (to be discussed in the next section), reveal a definite time course to language processing, measured in thousandths of a second (milliseconds or ms for short). For example, it has been calculated (Yuan *et al.* 2006) that the average speech rate for English is between 150 and 170 words a minute (that is, one every 350–400 ms).

The multiple connections between words in the mental lexicon facilitate the speed with which we can express ourselves in speech. The third and fourth speech errors in Activity 14.6 involve the activation of the wrong word: *Italy* for *Israel* and *competent* for *confident*. You will no doubt have noticed that in each case the word produced resembles the word intended, both in form and meaning. This is evidence for the kind of connectivity we discussed in 14.3.2: the massive parallel activity in the lexical network ends up activating entries which are closely related to the target entry, because they share semantic features (e.g. [NATION] for *Italy/Israel*, [PERSONAL QUALITY] for *competent/confident*) and form features (initial phoneme, number of syllables, and stress pattern, for both pairs).

You may have noticed too that the pairs of words exchanged and words substituted share another feature: word class (➜ 7.3). Nouns exchange places with other nouns, adjectives with other adjectives. Similarly, nouns are produced instead of other nouns, adjectives instead of other adjectives. In the fifth error, a verb in the past tense (*prevented*) is substituted for another verb in the past tense (*presented*). This is not a coincidence: it follows from a model of production in which: (a) words are activated to match the meanings required; and then (b), in a subsequent stage of grammatical encoding, are placed in the positions dictated by the grammatical rules that the speaker knows.

If syntactic encoding (the construction of sentences) follows word activation in the time course of spoken language production, we should expect grammatical morphemes (closed class words (➜ 7.3.2) and **inflections**) to be added at this stage too, since their activation is often dependent on (follows from) the syntactic structure selected. For example, the selection of the present participle instead of simple present in English requires the activation of the {-ing} morpheme to be added to the activated verb, as well as the auxiliary verb *be* to precede the verb.

Similarly, in passive sentences an NP which is not the actor appears in subject position, and the auxiliary *be* and the past participle {-en} are required instead of simple past {-ed} (➜ 7.4.5). A single communicative situation, involving (almost) identical lexical-semantic content, can lead to the selection of different grammatical structures. Take, for example, the following situations:

A   *A nappy-changing situation:*
    a   Michael was changing Ben's nappy (when I left the house).
    b   Michael changed Ben's nappy (as I left the house).

B   *A garden-showing situation:*
    a   Mary showed the visitors the garden.
    b   The visitors were shown the garden (by Mary).

The first thing that happens in production is that concepts are activated, and this in turn leads to the activation of content words to express these concepts. In the case of the nappy-changing and garden-showing situations in A and B above, these are as follows (where word classes are indicated with subscript N for noun and V for verb):

A $\{Michael\}_{N1}$, $\{Ben\}_{N2}$, $\{nappy\}_{N3}$, $\{change\}_V$
B $\{Mary\}_{N1}$, $\{visitor + s\}_{N2}$, $\{garden\}_{N3}$, $\{show\}_V$

Next a grammatical template is constructed (through rule use or analogy), including word order and grammatical morphemes:

A   *Nappy-changing:*
       a $\{\_\_\}_{N1}$ $\{was\}$ $\{\_\_\}_V\{-ing\}$ $\{\_\_\}_{N2}\{'s\}$ $\{\_\_\}_{N3}$
       b $\{\_\_\}_{N1}$ $\{\_\_\}_V\{-ed\}$ $\{\_\_\}_{N2}\{'s\}$ $\{\_\_\}_{N3}$

B   *Garden-showing:*
       a $\{\_\_\}_{N1}$ $\{\_\_\}_V\{-ed\}$ $\{the\}$ $\{\_\_\}_{N2}$ $\{the\}$ $\{\_\_\}_{N3}$
       b $\{the\}$ $\{\_\_\}_{N2}$ $\{were\}$ $\{\_\_\}_V\{-en\}$ $\{the\}$ $\{\_\_\}_{N3}\{by\}$ $\{\_\_\}_{N1}$

If grammatical morphemes are added after word selection, we might predict that sometimes when the wrong word is selected for the wrong slot in the grammatical template, then they will show up with the wrong morpheme. This happens in the following speech error from Fromkin's database, where the plural inflection is in the right place, but the wrong noun has been inserted:

(1)   I would rather gamble $125 than have a hole full of floors.

In the example, the $\{-s\}$ of the intended *holes* is in its syntactically appropriate place, but is attached to *floor*, which should have been inserted in the slot where *hole* actually appears. This preservation of the grammatical template with content words 'dropping into the wrong slots' is commonplace in speech error corpora.

A simple model which encapsulates these insights, and is consistent with speech error data and evidence from aphasia research, is sketched in Figure 14.7 (see also Garrett 1980; Levelt 1989).

The model is clearly a modular one (with boxes and arrows), and helps us to capture the overall sequencing in the process of linguistic encoding. If we want to understand the micro-level mental processes that govern specific lexical choices and outcomes, however, a connectionist account can be more helpful. For example, at the level of phonological structure, we need to be able to explain how speakers select the correct past tense form for the homophonous verbs *ring* ('cause to sound') and *ring* ('encircle') in sentences (2) and (3) below:

(2)   Riot police rang the bell before entering.
(3)   Riot police ringed the building before entering.

There must be quite complex connections between conceptual structure, the grammatical template level and particular lexical entries to ensure that the $\{past\}$ morpheme at the grammatical level picks out the irregular morphemes in the lexicon for the 'sounding' concept and the regular morpheme for the 'encircling' concept. Computer simulations of the kind illustrated in Figure 14.6 are well suited to handle this.

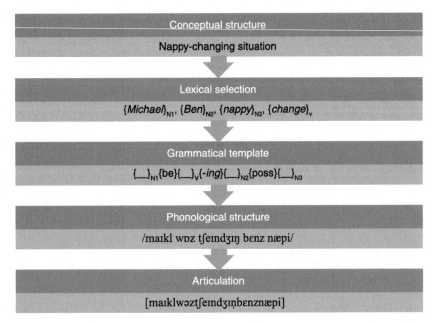

Figure 14.7 A model of language production, showing stages in the production of the sentence *Michael was changing Ben's nappy*

14.4.2 Tip-of-the-tongue states

Consider now another kind of speech error, where the intended word is neither moved nor substituted, but is temporarily unavailable: the so-called tip-of-the-tongue (or TOT) phenomenon. This is a familiar experience for most people: estimates suggest that young adults find themselves in a TOT state on average once a week, and this increases significantly with age. In a TOT state, speakers have passed through the first three stages of linguistic encoding in Figure 14.7, but cannot access the phonological structure of one of the words they want to produce.

One example (from the same online corpus site we used for previous errors) concerns a speaker's mental search for a proper name, Charles Hartshorn. Especially interesting for psycholinguists is the nature of related words that the speaker *does* manage to activate. In this case, they included *reindeer* and *antler*.

> ### Activity 14.7
>
> Why do you think the words *reindeer* and *antler* came to the speaker's mind when they were trying to recall the name Charles Hartshorn? How can we explain this in terms of the mind's connectionist architecture?

The speaker has activated words that are related in meaning to elements of the target word *Hartshorn*: *hart* and *reindeer* are both deer, and these have prominent *antlers*, which are like *horns* on other animals. The mind stores word meanings in word-sized bundles of semantic features, connected to phonological structures (word forms) in the mental lexicon. In cases where (some of) the features for one word are shared with *other* word meanings (e.g. [DEER] in the concepts 'reindeer', 'hart', 'stag' etc.), they must be connected to *several* phonological structures (/ˈreɪndɪə/, /hɑːt/, /stæg/ etc.).

In speaking, it appears that activation flows along *all* the conceptual-lexical connections, independently of whether the word forms at the other end are the intended ones or not. Normally, the word form which best matches all the features will be the one which is most highly activated and actually gets spoken. But in TOT states, the connection is temporarily out of action, and so unintended but related words rise to the level of consciousness.

Over a period of ten years, Peter Ecke, a multilingual TOT researcher, recorded details of over 100 of his own TOT states, including any partial information and related words that occurred to him during his attempts at lexical selection (Ecke and Hall 2012). Here are some examples:

- Speaking in English (his third language), Peter intended to say the word *fertility* in the sentence *The egg is a symbol of __*. He immediately came up with the translation equivalent *Fruchtbarkeit* in German, his first language, and within seconds produced the English word *fruitfulness*, followed by *maturity*. It wasn't until two minutes later that he was able to access the target word *fertility*.
- Speaking in German (his first language), Peter wanted to say *Inventur* ('stocktaking'), in the sentence *Der Laden macht heute __* ('The shop is doing ___ today'). Within seconds, he knew that the target word began with *In-*, and after a minute came up with the German word *Inversion* ('inversion'), again needing another minute before he succeeded in finding the target word *Inventur*.
- Speaking in Spanish (his fourth language), Peter was looking for the word *esposas* ('handcuffs'), in the sentence *Usaron __* ('They used ___'). He initially thought the word he wanted started with /p/, had four syllables, and was feminine in gender. Over the next 40 seconds, he came up with *pinzas* ('pincers'), *parejas* ('couples'), and *gemelos* ('twins'). After a minute he had the target word *esposas*.

Do the following activity before reading further.

Activity 14.8

In the Hartshorn example, the related words that came to the speaker's mind during the TOT state were activated through connections between semantic features and entries in the mental lexicon.

Now see if you can answer the following questions about Peter's multilingual TOT data, using ideas from the connectionist perspective on language in the mind. Look again at Figures 14.5 and 14.7 before attempting this activity.

1   In the English example, can you explain how and why the speaker might have activated the series of words *Fruchtbarkeit*, *fruitfulness* and *maturity*, in that order?

2   In the German example, how come the speaker very quickly felt that the word
started with In-, and then produced *Inversion* on the way to the correct word
Inventur?

3   In the Spanish example, why do you think he was able to correctly guess the
gender (feminine) of the intended word? (Hint: gender is one of the word
properties represented in the lemma, since it is a grammatical, not a phonological or semantic property.) Also, can you speculate as to why he might have
thought the word began with /p/? (Hint: *esposas* has main stress (➔ 11) on
the second syllable.)

The first example shows that in multilinguals, words from other languages can be activated, even if those languages are not currently being used by the speaker (➔ Activity
15.4). In his search for *fertility*, the German word *Fruchtbarkeit* first comes to Peter's mind,
possibly because it is better known to him: in connectionist terms, the activation route
between the concept and the L1 lexical entry is stronger (has been used more) than the
route to the L3 word. This interconnectedness between the mental representations of his
different languages is also demonstrated in the third guess. It appears that the activation
of *Fruchtbarkeit* sends secondary activation to an L3 word, *fruitfulness*, which is similar in
both sound and meaning to it and to the target word (it is also of three syllables, and the
first one is a COGNATE: *Frucht* in German is *fruit* in English). The third guess, *maturity*, is now
in the right language, and is similar in meaning to the target, sharing also its suffix. Some
research has suggested that the separate activation of prefixes and suffixes is another quite
common occurrence in TOT states.

The second TOT example also suggests a heightened role for affixes, this time a prefix,
{in-}. This is a very common prefix in many Romance languages and those (like German
and English) which have borrowed heavily from Latin. This might explain why Peter
comes up with the prefix so fast, and his first guess is a word starting with that prefix.

Finally, the third example shows that TOTs involve access to the lemma of the word,
where word class and other grammatical properties like gender are represented. Vigliocco,
Antonini, and Garrett (1997) have shown that Italian speakers regularly have access to the
gender of nouns they are searching for in a TOT state; Vigliocco, Vinson, Martin, and
Garrett (1999) further demonstrated that English speakers know whether a TOT noun is
count or non-count.

So having a word on the tip of the tongue means that you have got as far as the lexical
entry, but that access to the phonological structure is blocked, or only partially available.
Some parts of the phonological structure seem to be more accessible than others: most
salient are initial phonemes, number of syllables, and possibly also stress pattern (this
might explain Peter's activation of /p/, the initial phoneme of the stressed syllable in
esposas).

A final word about TOT states and language production, before we move on to the
flip-side of the process, language comprehension. The kind of words that sometimes get
as far as the tip of your tongue but no further are relatively uncommon: *Hartshorn*, *fertility*,
handcuffs, *stocktaking*, rather than *heart-attack*, *furniture*, *happiness*, *statement*. This is because word
frequency is psychologically real. Frequency estimates using language **corpora** measure
the number of times a word appears in a large number of texts (➔ 5.3.2), by different

speakers and writers in different contexts. But in individual minds, frequency manifests itself in terms of the relative 'state of rest' of the mentally represented lexical entry. Less frequently accessed words take more activating, and sometimes the amount of activation is not enough for the (full) phonological structure to become available for articulation: this is the case of TOTs.

14.5 LANGUAGE COMPREHENSION

When someone produces language, it is usually because there is someone around to hear it, and they are participating in talk-in-interaction (➔ 2). So what is happening in the minds of listeners as speakers speak? Both speaking and listening draw upon language structure and contextual knowledge in the social act of talk, but they involve fundamentally different mental events. Speakers devise and execute a plan, selecting and constructing linguistic structure to represent the meaning or message they wish to share; listeners, on the other hand, are essentially involved in a guessing-game, identifying clues to meaning from the accumulating speech stream, in a time frame over which they have little control. But like production, the comprehension process can be usefully modelled and explained using elements of both connectionist and modular theories of language and mind.

Although human beings cannot read the thoughts of others telepathically, they can recover meaning from sound at lightning speeds. In moments so brief that they seem to us instantaneous, we decode phonological, morphological, lexical, syntactic, and semantic structure, using data from the acoustic energy of the speech signal, represented temporarily in WORKING MEMORY, and from our own knowledge of language, stored in LONG-TERM MEMORY.

At the heart of the process is word recognition: the activation of entries in our mental lexicons that best match the sounds we are hearing, so that their meanings can in turn be activated and the basic elements of the speaker's message can be assembled.

Prior context plays a central role in making the word recognition process so fast. If context is informative enough, hearers don't actually have to hear every word being spoken to them, and the next best thing to telepathy occurs. For example, the odds are good that with the prior context *Sally burst out*, the most highly activated candidate to follow will be *laughing*, even though other words are possible. If you had richer prior context and knew Sally was sad, she is more likely to have burst out *crying*. But *laughing* is much more frequent in this position, as well as being more frequent overall. We saw in our discussion of TOTs that less frequent words are harder to select for production. They are also slower to be recognized in comprehension.

In the British National Corpus (BNC; ➔ W14.2), *laughing* occurs 2448 times, compared with 1873 times for *crying*. It occurs 123 times after *burst out*, compared with only six times for *crying*.

Activity 14.9 🔑

Can you guess what the next word might be in the following contexts (not necessarily one that ends the utterance)? If you can't, is there any other attribute of the word that you can be reasonably sure of?

> 1   They met at a jazz club in New ____
> 2   The organizers give a prize ____
> 3   Mary reached for ____
> 4   She pursed her ____
> 5   Bob read an ____
>
> Now try to identify what kinds of knowledge were activated in your mind to guess the word or its attribute. Be as precise as possible.

During comprehension, hearers can exploit many different kinds of information in order to make upcoming input more quickly and easily decodable: cues in the speech signal itself, properties of their mentally-represented lexicon and grammar, and stored knowledge of the world as they have experienced it. The use of mentally-represented information not present in the acoustic input is called *top-down* processing, and the use of cues in the speech signal itself is called *bottom-up* processing. In top-down processing, the non-linguistic information can come either from the immediate physical or social environment, or from knowledge accumulated through previous experience. Linguistic information can be from any level in the hierarchy of rank (➔ Figure 7.1), from the text level to the phonological.

Working together and in parallel, the top-down and bottom-up processes will generate a variety of possible analyses of the input at any given moment, but some will be more highly activated in working memory than others. For example, imagine you are hearing the utterance in (4) during a conversation in the London office where you work. Let us focus on what is happening in your mind at the point where you have heard the acoustic input corresponding to the first two phonemes of the word *Paris* (indicated by the vertical bar)—about a second into the utterance.

(4)   Jacques worked in Pa|ris before he joined us here.

Encyclopaedic knowledge (➔ 6.1.2) activated by knowledge of who *Jacques* is (or of the French name *Jacques*, if you don't know the person) might send some activation to the lexical entry *Paris* early on in the utterance (it might even be triggered by the francophone word-initial phoneme /ʒ/). Once recognized, the meaning of the word *worked*, in combination with *in*, will lead you to expect a location or area of business. Once you have recognized the word form *in*, you can activate its word class (preposition), and this will in turn activate syntactic knowledge that the prepositional phrase it heads will contain a following noun phrase, headed by a noun (➔ 7.4.2). So you will (subconsciously) be expecting a noun.

From the speech stream itself, the pronunciation of *in* as [ɪm] will already have given you a head-start with the phonological structure of the noun, by setting you up to expect a bilabial initial consonant (*in* takes the form [ɪm] due to what is called *anticipatory assimilation* (➔ 9) with the following consonant). All this evidence will converge on the likelihood that the word you have begun to hear is *Paris* (as opposed to *Pakistan, pantomime*, etc.) and to inhibit other possible analyses (such as *impassively*). So maybe you do not need to hear what is left of the word (i.e. the [rɪs] of *Paris*) before you recognize it?

This is indeed what the evidence from psycholinguistic experiments suggests. Let us take a look at one such experiment, conducted by William Marslen-Wilson and Lorraine

Tyler over 30 years ago (Marslen-Wilson and Tyler 1980), a classic demonstration of how context is used to speed processing. The experiment used PRIMING, one of the most common techniques used in psycholinguistics. In SEMANTIC PRIMING, a word related in meaning to the target is provided to participants in advance. This reliably decreases the amount of time needed to recognize the target word, compared with unrelated primes. For example, priming *table* with *chair* will make it faster to recognize than priming it with *hair*. Similar effects occur with PHONOLOGICAL PRIMING (e.g. *table* primed by *taper*). Such effects provide compelling evidence for the interactive flow of information in the networks which constitute the mental lexicon.

The goal of Marslen-Wilson and Tyler's (1980) study was to shed light on the role of syntactic and semantic knowledge in the time course of spoken word recognition. Specifically, they wanted to test whether all sources of knowledge used in processing interact and operate in parallel, or whether they are serially ordered, as reflected in the hierarchy of rank. The task required participants in the experiment to listen to pairs of sentences through earphones, and press a response button as fast as possible when they heard a word which had been primed in advance. For example, in the following pair of sentences, they would be asked to press the button as soon as they heard the word *lead*.

(5)   The church was broken into last night. Some thieves stole most of the *lead* off the roof.

The average time taken to respond to the target word (for 45 participants listening to nine pairs of sentences each) was 273 ms. This is 94 ms shorter than the average duration of the target words. The researchers estimate that between 50 and 75 ms is needed to decide to respond and then do so. This gives us an estimate of around 200 ms for word recognition, a figure that has been confirmed by many other experiments as an average for word recognition in English. This result shows the extreme speed with which hearers are able to match the input with words in their mental lexicons. (To put these times into perspective, it took one of us 15,430 ms to look up the word *lead* as fast as we could in the print version of *The Concise Oxford Dictionary*, according to a digital stopwatch.)

To measure the effect of syntactic and semantic context, the researchers also played participants pairs of sentences like the following:

(6)   The power was located into great water. No buns puzzle some in the *lead* off the text.
(7)   Into was power water the great located. Some the no puzzle buns in *lead* text the off.

The pair of sentences in (6) has exactly the same syntactic structure as (5), but the words do not make sense together. The word *lead* appears at exactly the same point in the input as it did in (5), but this time there is no prior semantic context. In (7), the syntactic context is also removed, leaving no useful prior context at all. The average reaction time for targets in pairs of sentences of type (6) was 331 ms. For target words in sentence pairs like (7), the average reaction time increased to 358 ms. Statistical tests show that these differences are very unlikely to be the result of chance.

So Marslen-Wilson and Tyler's study found that when hearing a word with both syntactic and semantic prior context (i.e. the way we normally hear words), its recognition is around 85 ms faster than when hearing it with no prior context (e.g. in sentence pairs of type (7)). But when there is syntactic context (e.g. in sentence pairs of type (6)), the difference is reduced to 58 ms. This suggests that hearers are using prior context to recognize words faster, and that meaning contributes more than grammar to the task. But the fact that syntactic structure provides a 27 ms advantage over random words suggests that even when meaning is absent, syntactic processing is going on and interacts with lexical processing. This is consistent with elements of both modularity and connectionism.

First, from a modular perspective, the experiment shows that the syntactic processor functions independently of the presence of a communicative act. We cannot help but work out the grammatical relationship between words, even when there is no meaning to decode. In this sense, processing is modular, using separate sources of knowledge which function independently of each other. But these independent processing modules exchange information in order for the whole system to operate more effectively.

In other words, the modules interact. And this makes sense from a connectionist perspective, according to which processing happens in parallel, with all sources of information being tapped simultaneously and spreading activation throughout the whole network of processing units. In the case of word recognition that we have been discussing here, candidate mental representations of word forms can be activated during comprehension on the basis of activation from syntactic and semantic representations being built for previously processed structures. So once more, the connectionist brain seems to sit at ease in a modular mind: only the perspective changes.

Activity 14.10 ⚿

One of us overheard the following exchange between a native-speaker of English, about to make a big pot of tea, and a native-speaker of Turkish with advanced-level competence in English:

'Will four teabags be enough?'
'Forty bags?!'

Can you provide a psycholinguistic account for what is happening here, and suggest why this particular misunderstanding is unlikely to occur between two native speakers of English? (Hint: You may want to look at the commentary on Activity 9.2.)

14.6 OTHER TOPICS IN PSYCHOLINGUISTICS

There are many other issues of interest to psycholinguists beyond those discussed here. We end this chapter by acknowledging some of them and giving some pointers to further information for readers interested in following them up. The issues selected for mention here fall into five broad areas:

- the relationship between language and thought
- levels of processing
- different modalities for language use
- language disability
- bilingual/multilingual representation and processing.

First, in the most general area of language and mind, we have not touched upon the extent to which the evolution of language in the species has driven or been driven by developments in other areas of our capacity for, and exercise of, cognition (see Aitchison 2000). For example, was the evolution of language possible because we developed complex patterns of thought, or was it the other way round? Related to this, and of long-running popular interest, is the extent to which the particular languages we speak can mould the ways we perceive and interact with the world (➔ 1, 13; Steinberg and Sciarini 2006 Chapter 9). For example, do we think more or more precisely about certain concepts because we have words for them?

Next, there are many issues in processing that are the object of rigorous ongoing research, but have not been discussed here. At the speech end of processing, we have not addressed the question of how speakers' activation of word forms leads to actual articulation (see Levelt 1989, Chapters 8–11; ➔ 9 and 10). Neither have we addressed how the vibration of air molecules caused by articulation impinges on hearers' eardrums, nor how linguistic information is extracted from it (see Byrd and Mintz 2010, Chapter 5). At the conceptual end of processing, we have not discussed how speakers package their messages into text-level or discourse units, nor how hearers use pragmatic and other knowledge to interpret such units (see Fernández and Smith Cairns 2011, Chapter 8; ➔ 3). The morphological level of processing is another intriguing area of study, for those languages that make any significant use of derivation and inflection (see Marslen-Wilson 2007).

Thirdly, we have restricted our discussion to speaking, listening and phonological representation, although for many people, especially those involved in teaching, it is reading, writing and signing that are of particular interest (the use of phonics in literacy teaching is an especially controversial question rooted in psycholinguistic research: see Harley 2008, Chapter 8). The question of how we process written text is a fascinating one, especially with respect to the role of phonological representations in reading and writing, and the type of writing systems associated with particular languages (see Harley 2008, Chapter 7; ➔ R3.2). Similarly, the processing of sign language (and the extent to which it resembles or differs from the processing of speech) continues to intrigue psycholinguists (see Emmorey 2002, Chapter 4; ➔ R3.5).

Fourthly, psycholinguists are very interested in cases where language representation and processing are impaired in some way (see Ingram 2007). For one thing, such cases reveal how the 'normal' system works (as discussed in 14.2.2); but, more importantly, we can use psycholinguistic theory in the assessment and treatment of people with brain-related language disabilities (Hall *et al.* 2011, Chapter 14). Apart from aphasia, there is also particular public interest in psycholinguistic models of DYSLEXIA, a common disability affecting the processing of alphabetic text (see Byrd and Mintz 2010, Chapter 12).

Finally, there is the issue of storing and using more than one language. Do multilingual speakers store their languages in separate language modules, or do they interact in one multilingual network? (The evidence suggests the latter: see Schwartz and Kroll 2006; ➔ Activity 15.4). There is also a lot of interesting work on the relationship between multilingualism (➔ 16) and cognition in general, especially with regard to whether knowing more than one language confers advantages in cognitive abilities beyond language, such as in creativity and 'metacognitive' processes (see Baker 2011, Chapter 7).

14.7 SUMMARY

The study of language in use considers not only the organization of talk, text and signing as they figure in social and cultural domains, but also how they are implemented at the biological and psychological levels. Neurolinguistic and psycholinguistic theories attempt to explain the representation and processing of language in the brain and the mind from different vantage points.

- Neurolinguistic research has pinpointed some of the areas of the brain which are responsible for speaking, listening, reading, writing and signing. Although many parts of the brain are involved, a central role appears to be played by neural circuits around the Sylvian Fissure in the left cerebral hemisphere. The evidence comes principally from the study of language impairments and from neuroimaging techniques.
- Psycholinguistic research investigates language in the mind, at a level which abstracts away from the biological reality of brain structures and processes. There are two main ways in which psycholinguists approach the phenomenon of human language:
  - Connectionist approaches, which emphasize the sub-symbolic 'brain-style' nature of representation and processing, which emerges during development in vast distributed networks of simple units, through which activation flows in parallel.
  - Modular approaches, which emphasize the different kinds of knowledge encapsulated in symbolic representations of language, and how they are accessed in processing at separate stages from separate (possibly innate) components of mind.

COMMENTARY ON ACTIVITIES

O— Remember that this symbol indicates that there is a commentary on the activity that you can find on the companion website at www.routledge.com/cw/merrison.

FURTHER READING and REFERENCES

Suggestions for further reading on the topics discussed in this chapter can be found on the companion website (www.routledge.com/cw/merrison).

Any piece of academic writing must always provide a list of publications to which reference has been made. Unusually and very unconventionally, this information is provided on the companion website (www.routledge.com/cw/merrison). Always ask your tutor about how you are to present references for any piece of work that you submit.

Chapter 15
Language Acquisition

Key Ideas in this Chapter

- Children build their own language systems by participating in linguistic interactions, and as young as six months old they begin to understand some expressions.

- Children simultaneously have to learn vocabulary, patterns for making sentences, a system of pronunciation, conventions of appropriate use, while also developing skills for fluent production and comprehension.

- Pronunciation starts with unsystematic 'chunks', but becomes increasingly patterned.

- Within their first year, children become less sensitive to phonological distinctions not relevant in the language they are acquiring.

- Word learning starts slowly, but sustained acceleration begins around the middle of the second year, when the first sentences are also constructed.

- Hierarchical constituent structure, recursion and coordination appear in child syntax around the age of two years.

- Over the past century second language acquisition theories have successively concentrated on structural linguistic aspects of the process, on its psycholinguistic requirements, and on the socio-cultural dimension of communication with other people.

15.1 INTRODUCTION

Closed doors can be frustrating for toddlers. An adult might offer help by saying 'Shall I open the door?' or '(Do you) want me to open the door?'. A young child, attending mainly to the final word *door*, could think that it means something like 'do it'. Perhaps this is how a girl aged 22½ months came to use the word *door* to ask an adult to unscrew the nuts on a construction toy, as in (1), where R identifies the child, *Ad* the adult.

(1)   Ad: Those go on there. (Ad is screwing on two big nuts.)
        R: Please. (R's gestures indicate that she wants the nuts off.)
        R: Door, door.
        Ad: Now just wait and see a minute and I think you'll like it.
                (Ad persists in screwing the nuts on.)
        R: Door, door.
        R: Door, door please.

                                            (Griffiths and Atkinson 1978: 313)

The other four children studied on the same project used different words (*out*, *open* and *shut*, also adopted from people they had heard talking) to make a similar range of requests for action.

The child was one of seven being recorded by researchers in weekly visits to their separate homes. She and another two of the children fairly often used *door* in comparable ways: to ask for the removal of lids, for help with extricating a pencil from a shirt sleeve, trying to persuade the research team to disconnect the cable from a microphone, requesting that a doll's shoe and its dress be taken off, to get assistance in pressing a bung into a hole in the base of a toy telephone, etc.

Children acquire their first language by intuitive analysis of instances of the language that they have heard being used in context. Their analysis is intuitive in the sense that it happens instinctively, below the level of consciousness, as the automatic realization of their innate capacity to develop a language. Chomsky (1986) calls this capacity the *Language Acquisition Device*, and argues that it is a cognitive mechanism (➜ 14) which derives actual adult languages (like English, Japanese, Arabic, etc.) from a genetically specified UNIVERSAL GRAMMAR (➜ 1.4). Other scholars believe that children's ability to acquire language derives from more general cognitive capacities, not specific to language (e.g. MacWhinney 1999). But however specific it is to human language, the key to unlocking this innate potential is without doubt the child's encounters with language *in use*, the central theme of this book. Although theorists differ on the question of what is innate and how specific it is to language (e.g. Pinker 1994; Tomasello 2003), all agree that without socially contextualized input, language acquisition would be impossible.

In (1), child R's use of *door* must have come from hearing people say it. The parents of each of the three children had earlier reported that their child was saying the word *door* in connection with doors. When their child said *door* to ask for help with opening a door, the parents perhaps thought that the child was referring to the door that should be opened. But it seems probable that, around the age of two years, these children treated *door* as a general-purpose request for action.

15.1.1 Holophrases

We could say that *door* was being used as a verb, instead of the noun that it is in adult English. However, the concept VERB belongs to syntax (➜ 7) and, at this phase in the children's development, *door* was a freestanding item, not a part of a sentence (and the same is true of the other items mentioned in the margin note above). The conveyed meaning '(You) do it' is more like the meaning of a simple sentence than of a word. HOLOPHRASE is the technical term for an utterance that packs in the meaning of a whole sentence, but in its spoken form is only the length of a single word.

That the children had actively used their brains to arrive at holophrase uses of *door* (and of *out, open* and *shut*) is indicated by the words not simply having been taken over with the meanings that they have in the adult language. Language acquisition involves more than mimicry.

Making sense of the organization of their first language is challenging for children and complicated skills have to be learnt to achieve fluency. First language acquisition is not a matter, however, of assembling all the separate items and skills and only then utilizing them. Instead, children launch themselves into communication very early and construct the vehicle as they go.

Infants show signs of understanding language in rudimentary ways from as young as six months old. Leopold (1939: 20) noted in a very detailed diary report that his daughter, shortly before the age of seven months, would usually turn expectantly towards anyone speaking her name, *Hildegard*. Starting at age nine months, another expression, *peek-a-boo*, was a cue for Hildegard to hide behind a blanket (1939: 118). In descriptions of child language there are many other accounts of children reacting similarly: showing basic recognition of particular words and phrases during the second half of the first year.

At around one year old, when children produce the first 'words' recognizable to their regular adult conversation partners, these holophrases are employed communicatively. For example, a precocious nine-month-old boy was reported as using [bø] to convey 'I want my ball' (Halliday 1975). The pronunciation is only approximately like *ball*, and it is a holophrase rather than a sentence. (For help with the phonetic symbols given in square brackets ➜ 9, 10 and see the International Phonetic Alphabet chart at the end of the book.)

15.1.2 Building capacity for communication

Communication is possible from early on, with infants starting to use utterances to convey their wants and emotions and beginning to understand what other people say. One circumstance making this possible is that first language learning takes place in social interaction, with child and adult generally sharing the same focus of attention at the time of utterance, thanks to being sensitive to each other's gaze and pointing (Clark 2003: 138–139). Also, children use gestures communicatively before they communicate verbally (➜ 1), for instance requesting things with an open-handed reach, or indicating refusal by a turning away of the head (Zinober and Martlew 1985). Some early language learning thus involves discovering how to translate into speech what can already be signalled with gesture.

Written language is generally learnt during the school years and vocabulary learning goes on throughout life, but children's preschool years are ones where a great deal of knowledge of language is acquired, as they develop their own language comprehension and production systems (➜ 14.5, 14.4), then extend and refine them in use. What children have to acquire to become language users includes the following:

- lots of words, with their meanings (➔ 5, 6)
- patterns for putting morphemes together to make complex words (➔ 5)
- the pronunciation system (➔ 11)
- syntax, for linking words into phrases, clauses, sentences and texts (➔ 7, 8)
- knowledge of how syntax contributes to meaning (➔ 6, 7)
- strategies and conventions on how to use language, e.g. how to be polite, how to be rude, how to get your own way, how to speak indirectly (and understand other people's indirectness), what it is appropriate to talk about in a range of different settings (➔ 3, 4)
- the skills needed for rapid decoding and fluency in the assembly of utterances (➔ 14).

Young children do not develop these separately. The different kinds of knowledge and skill have to be used together in conversations that they participate in from some point in their first year onwards. But, for clarity of presentation, the overview in this chapter deals successively with SEMANTICS, PHONOLOGY, SYNTAX and PRAGMATICS.

Arguably it is in the period from birth to two and a half years that children become users of language in the characteristically human sense discussed in Chapter 1, with much of later development consisting of adding more items and structures to the framework rather than altering the overall scheme. We therefore concentrate on the first thirty months of a child's life here.

The sheer size and complexity of any language makes it interesting to investigate how children gain control of one (or more than one ➔ 16). Because language is a human speciality, studying its acquisition also offers clues to human nature. Child language research is relevant to the work of speech and language therapists too, and has been a major source of ideas for teaching literacy (➔ R3.2) and second languages (➔ 15.6).

A broad sample of the ideas and findings that make the investigation of young children's language acquisition a fascinating subject is set out in sections 15.2–5. (See our companion website ➔ W15.1 for an overview of theoretical issues.) For second language acquisition, we adopt the opposite strategy, presenting an overview of different theoretical approaches. The incredible diversity of experiences and outcomes that language learning entails after infants have acquired their first language(s) means that there is little in the process that is typical for all learners, and there is much disagreement about how best to study the phenomenon.

15.2 WORDS AND THEIR MEANINGS

Children's ages are given in the format *[YEARS]; [MONTHS].[DAYS]* (so '2;1.18' stands for 2 years 1 month and 18 days), or just *[YEARS];[MONTHS]* (for example 1;6 for age 1 year 6 months).

Activity 15.1 0──

Recordings of children talking can be informative about their developing competence. A turn in conversation from Child J, aged 2;1.18 (Griffiths 1986), is presented here, together with a note about one aspect of his vocabulary. He was looking at and handling a toy plastic elephant as he spoke.

Child J: A cow, sheep, another cow.

In weekly recordings over the preceding three months and according to weekly vocabulary questionnaire entries from his mother J had produced some 19 different animal terms by the time he was 2;1.18 (*cow* and *sheep* were two of them), but it would be a few more weeks before he spontaneously said *elephant*.

1   How would you describe J's utterance, above? What does he seem to be trying to do?
2   Does his utterance suggest anything about his mental filing system (➜ 14.3.2) for English word meanings?
3   Any guesses about the features of the toy that influenced his choice of label for it?
4   Consider the **function words**, *a* and *another* (➜ 5.3.2). J didn't just say 'Cow, sheep, cow'. Comment briefly on what the utterance might indicate about his knowledge of syntax and pragmatics.

15.2.1 How many words?

Figure 15.1 summarizes the start that young children make on the task of learning the thousands of words they will have by adulthood. It is based on vocabulary research done for the MacArthur-Bates Communicative Development Inventory (or CDI ➜ W15.2; see Fenson *et al.* 1993; Dale and Fenson 1996). This large North American sample comprised substantial numbers of children representing each month over the age range 8–30 months. Their carers were asked to study lists of words that young children might know

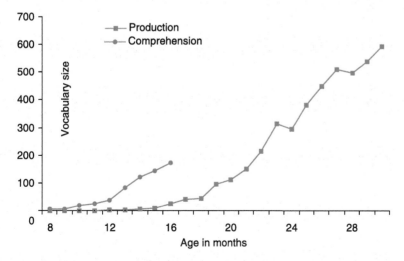

Figure 15.1 Words reported in the production and comprehension vocabularies of children aged 8–30 months, a different group of children for each month (based on CDI data from Dale and Fenson 1996)

and to mark each word that their child had been heard to say. On the 'Infant' form of the CDI, used for the age range 8–16 months, carers were also asked to indicate the words their child understood. This version of the CDI did not tap information about comprehension in children older than 16 months.

Figure 15.1 reflects the numbers of words that at least half of the children at each age were reported as knowing. The graph lines for production and comprehension over the age range 8–16 months derive from the Infant form of the CDI. The part of the graph covering production from 16–30 months is based on the Toddler CDI, a separate questionnaire for the older age range. An average value for age 16 months has been used to join the two sets of production results into a single line here. (It looks as if vocabulary declines at 24 months and 28 months, but these falls in the graph line are probably just accidents of sampling, not developmental trends. Remember that results for each month are based on data from different groups of children.)

An adult who is there for most of a young child's waking hours is a good source of information about which words the child knows, so the fact that carers are the source of the data is a real strength of the CDI vocabulary figures. Another is that they are based on hundreds of children. Large samples are feasible because the CDI is an indirect method of estimating children's vocabulary: the information is collected simply by adults working through checklists of words. There are versions in other languages too, including Chinese (Mandarin and Cantonese), Dutch, Canadian French, European French, three varieties of Spanish, and several other languages (➔ W15.3).

It takes much longer to make hours of recordings of individual children and then extract vocabulary lists from transcripts of the recordings; so direct methods are generally applied to only small samples of children. Comprehension testing takes even longer, though it can be done. For instance, Harris et al. (1995) systematically tested comprehension of words by six children up to the age of two years, as well as cataloguing the words that they produced. Getting vocabulary information from working directly with children provides details that checklists might not (for example, the surprising uses of *door* mentioned earlier). But of course, recordings at intervals can miss words that the child happens not to say while the microphone is on.

Two potential problems with checklist data should be noted:

1   Words that happen not to be included in the checklist stand a strong chance of not being reported, leading to underestimates of children's vocabularies. This is a problem even when the checklist offers write-in spaces for adding words to the list.
2   Some parents might have a tendency – an unconscious one, perhaps – to over-report what their child can do.

Recognizing that the numbers could be over- or under-estimates, Figure 15.1 nonetheless illustrates some important general points about vocabulary growth:

- comprehension begins earlier than production
- comprehension vocabulary increases faster than production vocabulary, up to age 16 months at least
- the age for speaking the first one or two recognizable 'words' is about 12 months
- children generally know between 100 and 200 words at around 1;6
- there is an acceleration, somewhere between 15 and 20 months, in the rate at which new words are acquired in production: an almost flat slope to 15 months turns into one that rises more steeply.

The last-mentioned of these features is called the 'word spurt': within a few months of age 1;6, a noticeable increase occurs in the rate of acquisition of new words. It is also around age 1;6 that many children produce their first sentences, initially only two words in length.

For more on the 'word spurt' ➜ W15.4.

15.2.2 Working out word meanings

Activity 15.2 🔑

Child R's parents reported that she had learnt the word *shoe* for her own shoes. In a one-hour recording session when she was 1;7.4, R spontaneously said 'shoe' in each of the following circumstances:

1. as she pointed at the shoes being worn by a doll
2. as she picked up one of the doll's shoes
3. as she handed one of the doll's shoes to an adult
4. when an adult was putting a shoe on the doll (three different times)
5. as she put a sock on the doll
6. as she passed the doll's second arm to an adult who had just refitted the first (the arms having become detached)
7. as she handled her teddy bear's shoeless feet.

(Griffiths 1986)

In what ways did R's word *shoe* have a similar meaning to the adult English word *shoe* and in what ways did it apparently differ in meaning? In (7) was R using the word *shoe* to label the bear's feet, or can you suggest anything different that she might have been trying to communicate?

Syntax is going to be discussed later, but note that part of the difficulty over deciding what R meant when she felt her teddy bear's feet and said *shoe* is that a holophrase lacks the syntactic pointers needed to signal reference.

Shape might have been a relevant link across some items in R's *shoe* category. Similarity in shape perhaps led Child J (Activity 15.1) to consider classifying an elephant either with the animals that he called *cow* or into his *sheep* category. Landau *et al.* (1988) drew attention to a bias that young children seem to have for using shape as the link holding together items in the categories denoted by their words. Bloom (2001: 172–173) points out that the shape of an object is often a good clue to the object's function, i.e. what it can do.

Various other biases have been proposed as explanations for the rapid success of young children's word learning. For instance, from the beginning of vocabulary learning, infants seem to have a "whole-object" bias: a strong inclination, when adults use a new word in connection with a physical object, to understand the word as denoting the whole object rather than one of its parts or its size, colour, etc. (Bloom 2002: 97–105).

Markman and Wachtel (1988) suggested that young children operate with a 'mutual exclusivity' bias: a tendency to avoid having more than one label for anything. If word meanings were rigorously constrained by mutual exclusivity, then *puppies* could not also be *dogs*. Of course they are: puppies are a subset of dogs. There is also obviously overlap between the categories denoted by the words *pet*, *dogs* and *puppies*. Nonetheless, it could be a helpful simplification for children in their earliest years if all pairs of words were treated like *cat* and *dog*, with no shared members. An experiment by Merriman and Stevenson (1997) showed that two-year-olds, at least some of the time, appear to have a mutual exclusivity bias. However, as they grow older, children have to relax the constraint and allow overlap in some cases. Au and Glusman (1990) found that four-year-olds were prepared to accept more than one label for a given thing.

There are three possibilities about the source of such biases, if they indeed exist to steer children towards humanly reasonable meanings for their words. They might be:

See the companion website for a summary of some evidence that the language being learnt is itself a guide to the learning of word meanings (→ W15.5)

- part of the general intelligence of infants (Bloom 2001)
- built up during the laborious learning of the child's first batch of words, i.e. a matter of learning how to learn (probably the position of Goldfield and Reznick 1996)
- part of the potential for language that humans are born with (our innate capacity for language → 1.4).

At present there is no conclusive evidence for choosing between the three positions, and it may be that two or all three of them operate together to produce the biases.

15.3 PHONOLOGY

Young children's pronunciations can be unintelligible, as when a child aged 1;0 pronounced *pen* as [ᵐbõ] (an example to be discussed later). Are such 'unadultlike' pronunciations attributable to lack of experience articulating speech or to lack of familiarity with hearing important features of the target sounds?

15.3.1 Hearing the important contrasts

Languages differ over which pronunciation differences matter for distinguishing words and which can be ignored (→ 11.2.3). For instance, Japanese, Fijian and English all require listeners to distinguish between short and long vowels; so a *ship* is something different from a *sheep*, and *pull* must be distinguished from *pool*. But, among these three languages, only in Japanese is there a significant distinction between short and long consonants, in many pairs such as /saka/ 'slope' and /sak:a/ 'writer', /ɔtɔ/ 'noise' and /ɔt:ɔ/ 'husband'. Consonant length is distinctive in Italian too. Another example is that English, but not Fijian, contrasts voiceless /θ/ with voiced /ð/, e.g. in the words *thigh* and *thy*.

The symbol /ː/ after /k/ and /t/ marks them as long (→ 9)

There are two possibilities regarding how children home in on the phonological contrasts relevant in their language:

- They might start out generally incapable of hearing differences between speech sounds, then learn the ones that their speech community requires.
- They might be able to hear all the differences used in any language, then learn to be less sensitive to ones not needed for their language.

A survey of research reports by Bohn (2000: 7) indicates that the second possibility is very likely correct:

> These studies showed that up to the age of 8 months, infants can discriminate any consonant contrast including those which have no phonological status [that is including ones that have no distinctive signalling value] in their L1 [= first language]. Between the ages of 10–12 months, however, infants attune to the contrasts of their ambient language so that only those contrasts which are phonologically relevant in their L1 remain highly discriminable.

According to Bohn's survey, infant perception of vowel distinctions (➔ 10) narrows down to those relevant in their own language even earlier than this age.

15.3.2 Pronouncing words

Infant pronunciations show that learning to articulate words is a substantial task. The BABBLING stage, starting after around five months and lasting around seven months or so, is when infants appear to be 'trying out' speech sounds. They start with a wide variety of sounds, including those that they won't be needing in the language they are acquiring, but gradually home in on those speech sounds they hear around them (in line with the research findings discussed in the previous section). By around the age of one, infants have an emerging **phoneme inventory** (➔ 11) for their language and start to produce their first words, although the process of fixing their pronunciations is far from over.

In a half-hour recording, one one-year-old girl said the word *pen* in ten different ways (Ferguson and Farwell 1975), including those shown in (2).

(2)   (a)   [pʰɪn]
       (b)   [tʰn̩tʰn̩tʰn̩]
       (c)   [ᵐbõ]

The target is an adult pronunciation like [pʰɛ̃n] and in (2a) the child obviously comes close. Versions (2b) and especially (2c) seem unrecognizable for *pen*, but they both contain a fair number of the necessary ingredients, just somewhat out of sequence (see Table 15.1). That there should be sequencing problems is not surprising, given the speed at which human speech is produced (at rates of between between 150 and 170 words a minute ➔ 14.4.1).

To understand Table 15.1, first read the whole of the Target column for a description of the sounds that make up the target word *pen*. Then start again at the top and, following rows across, see in the columns to the right how each target sound was changed in the child's attempts to say the word. The point to notice is that quite a number of phonetic features of the target pronunciations are carried across into (b) and (c). In both (b) and (c), the child has apparently compressed the vowel and final consonant into the same slot, making it a consonant with vowel-like syllabic force (➔ 11.2.1) in (b), but a vowel with an overlay of the consonant's nasality in (c). All speech shows anticipations of following sounds (➔ 9), as when a vowel is nasalized (to varying degrees) ahead of an upcoming nasal consonant. This child's anticipations are just a little different from some that adults would make, for example

Table 15.1 The phonetics of *pen* and a one-year-old's attempts to say it (data from Ferguson and Farwell 1975; ➜ 9, 10 for phonetic symbols and terms)

	Target [pʰɛ̃n]	Child's version (b) [tʰn̩]	Child's version (c) [ᵐbõ]
1st consonant	voiceless bilabial [pʰ] (raised [ʰ] marks aspiration)	[tʰ] voiceless and aspirated, but anticipates alveolar position of the [n̩]	not voiceless, but [ᵐb] is bilabial; pre-nasalization [ᵐ] anticipates nasalized vowel
Vowel	front, mid, unrounded vowel ([˜] on [ɛ] marks nasality, anticipating [n])	no vowel, but [ˌ] below [n] indicates that [n̩] has syllabic force, like a vowel	mid, but back rounded; has the expected nasality
End consonant	alveolar nasal [n]	present, but in the vowel slot	missing, but consonant and vowel preserve traces of nasal

when, at the beginning of the word in (b), she uses the alveolar place of articulation required for the [n] at the end, and when nasality (and voicing) are there from the start of the syllable in (c).

Adults employ relatively small sets of vowels and consonants to produce all of their speech – around 40 distinctive sounds in the phoneme inventory of most varieties of English (➜ 11). But infants' first 'words' are produced as wholes, instead of being assembled from a limited number of vowels and consonants. Near the beginning of this chapter a nine-month-old's holophrase [bø] 'I want my ball' was cited. Two other holophrases in the repertoire of this child at the same age were [nã] 'Give me that!' and [gʷɤi] 'I'm sleepy' (Halliday 1975). The child's expression meaning 'Give me that!' consists of the consonant [n] followed by a nasalized vowel, but neither of these sounds occurs in his ways of communicating 'I want my ball' or 'I'm sleepy'. None of the expressions shares sounds with the others. The pronunciation system of a child a few months older will be outlined next to illustrate a different phase in development.

Around the age of 1;3 the words of a child described by Cruttenden (1981) were each formed with only one out of just five consonants /b/, /d/, /g/, /m/ or /n/ and a vowel chosen from a small set. The words consisted either of a consonant followed by a vowel, for example /da/, /ga/, /dɛ/, or of such a consonant-vowel sequence repeated (in technical terms *reduplicated*), e.g. /baba/, /dada/, /gaga/, /mama/ and /nunu/. By contrast with this neat patterning, [bø], [nã] and [gʷɤi] – see previous paragraph – do not appear to be *constructed* according to a pattern. It seems that soon after the age of one year a child has a phonological system (➜ 11) for *assembling* pronunciations, rather than just a collection of unanalysed whole pronunciations. This is an early sign of the child's development of the feature of PRODUCTIVITY (➜ 1), their implicit knowledge that linguistic structures at one level are the product of units combined in a principled, systematic way from units at a lower level (as characterized in the **hierarchy of rank** ➜ Figure 7.1).

A small number of words that do not quite fit the described pattern are being ignored here.

Figure 15.2 Stripes

Possible explanations were discussed earlier in this chapter for a word spurt around 15–18 months. Another candidate explanation is that the spurt perhaps occurs because it is much easier to store and produce words once a child has an elementary phonological system.

From 15 months, children's phonological systems take at least another two and a half years to develop. It is interesting to see how they modify adult words to fit their developing systems. Three kinds of adaptation have been observed:

- *Consonant harmony* makes it possible to squeeze some kinds of words into patterns that are closer to reduplication. The different consonants are produced with the same place of articulation, e.g. *doggy* might be pronounced [gɒgɪ]. Anticipation of velar articulation, as in this case, is very common.
- *Cluster reduction* simply drops some consonants to fit words such as *stripes* /straɪps/ into child patterns that do not allow consonants to occur next to each other, e.g. *stripes* is pronounced as [daɪp]. Or a vowel can be inserted between two consonants to break up a cluster, turning *stripes* into [daɪpɪs]. In such ways, they are adapting the *phonotactics* of words to their current articulatory capacity (➔ 11.3.2). Applying both consonant harmony and cluster reduction, some children pronounce *stripes* as [baɪp], where the bilabial articulation of [p] is anticipated in the first consonant of the word (Figure 15.2).
- *Substitutions* by sounds already in the child's system for ones not yet included are common, e.g. [d] in place of [ð], to give [dat] for *that*.

15.4 SYNTAX

Syntax (➔ 7) enables language users to express meanings with greater precision than can be done with holophrases. Chapter 3 explains the distinction between sentence types (differentiated from each other syntactically: declaratives, interrogatives and imperatives) and **speech acts** (the conventional uses of utterances: as assertions, questions, requests, orders, promises, etc.). Holophrases are used to perform speech acts (such as requesting and rejecting) but they lack syntax. As well as acquiring syntax, children have to learn the partial correspondences that there are between sentence type and different kinds of speech act.

What do people generally use interrogative sentences (like the one you are reading now) for? Answer: interrogative sentences are normally used for asking questions (but ➔ 3.4.5). However, Halliday (1975: 31–32) reports that around age 1;10 his son used interrogative sentences not as questions (to ask for information), but to *give* information that would be news to the listener (i.e. he was using interrogatives for telling rather than asking):

> for example, if he was building a tower and the tower fell down, he would say to someone who was present and who was taking part with him *The tower fell down*. But to someone who had not been in the room at the time, and for whom the information was new, he would say *Did the tower fall down?*

Halliday's child had learnt a syntactic pattern: how to construct interrogatives as a sentence type, but his speech act use of them as assertions was creatively different from what is conventional in adult English. The point having been made that appropriate uses of sentence types have to be learnt, the rest of what is said about syntax here will focus more narrowly on how children begin to assemble sentences from parts.

A two-and-a-half-year-old assembling the sentence *Where's my mummy gone?* demonstrates syntactic knowledge of the following different kinds:

- The 'building blocks' of sentences are syntactic classes of words, such as nouns (e.g. *mummy*) and verbs (e.g. *gone*).
- Sequences of words are grouped into phrases (such as the noun phrase *my mummy*).
- Phrases act as units and fulfil various roles in sentences (*my mummy* is the subject of the example sentence).
- Some words are grammatically marked, e.g. *my* (not *I* or *me*) is used when the word is a determiner, as in *my mummy*; and the main (lexical) verb must be *gone* (not *go* or *went*), because that is the form needed with *has*.

In the example discussed here, *'s* on *Where's* is short for the auxiliary verb *has*.

The following is a selection of theoretically interesting milestones in the early acquisition of syntax. In practice it can be hard to be sure when an individual child reaches a particular milestone, so the list is an idealization and the ages given in round brackets are approximate. Milestones 1, 2 and 3 establish the hierarchy of rank (words make phrases, or groups, which make clauses, and clauses make sentences ➔ Figure 7.1).

1   (1;6) INITIAL SYNTAX: The first sentences are produced, just two words long.

2   (1;10) HIERARCHICAL STRUCTURE: Three-word sentences appear and, from now on, grouping of words into phrases can be significant, e.g. *Want my ball* or *My tower fall*, where the underlined words constitute phrases.

3   (2;0) RECURSION: One clause is now sometimes put into another clause, e.g. *I don't know where's a boat* (from J, the child in Activities 15.1 and 15.3, at age 2;6.20). The subordinate clause *where's a boat* is a complement of the verb *know* (➔ 7.5.3).

4   (2;3) COORDINATION: Two clauses can now be coordinated with *and*, e.g. (from a child aged 3;0.4): *One is big and one is small* (Fletcher 1985: 96). As much as six months

earlier two related clauses may be spoken as a single utterance without a linking conjunction *and*.

Language gains its tremendous communicative power – the possibility of making a sentence to suit any occasion – from features picked out for this list (milestones 2–4): hierarchical structure, recursion (also called *rankshifting*) and coordination (➔ 7.6.1).

Here are two quotations about early instances of two-word sentences (milestone 1). They are from a chapter on children's language development in a book by a professor of education. (In the first the child is his son B. The second was spoken by EW, daughter of one of his students.)

> We find B's first two-word sentences, 'Dada gone,' at 1;8½ preceded by the use of 'go' (gone) alone at 1;5¾, spoken when something had disappeared.
>
> (Valentine 1942: 422)

> EW at 1;9 (who had often heard herself called a 'good girl'), apparently wishing to express her approbation of something that her father had done, said 'Daddy good girl.' But here 'good girl' is evidently not the expression of two ideas ...
>
> (Valentine 1942: 421)

The evidence for treating B's sentence as the putting together of two items is that *Dada* had already been used for a year as a holophrase (described by Valentine as a 'father-joy-play cry', 1942: 406) and *gone* for nearly three months. On the other hand EW's *good girl* seems, at 1;9, to have been a single item meaning 'good', making it reasonable to regard her 'Daddy good girl' as also a 'two-word' sentence.

These are typical of children's first sentences. **Content words** are given priority, while function words tend to be absent (➔ 5, 7): B did not use an auxiliary verb *has* (or *is*) ahead of *gone*; EW's sentence omitted *is*. (If EW's *good girl* is thought of as a noun, like *goody-goody* or *saint* – a single noun meaning 'good person' – then a fully grammatical adult version would need the indefinite article *a* as well as *is*.)

Instead of the first of the two-word sentences quoted above, a rather older child might have said *Daddy has gone* or *My father has gone*. If Valentine's son aged 1;8½ had said 'My father has gone', then (without more evidence) we would not be able to tell whether it was an imitation of what he had heard someone else say or a rather precocious construction of his own. Omission from 'Dada gone' of words that a proficient speaker would have included, *has* (and perhaps also *my*), strongly suggests that this utterance was constructed out of parts, not *memorized* as a whole. Young children often do pick up unanalysed wholes from other people, and sometimes things that adults would rather they didn't repeat! Some of their utterances are constructed and some are imitated. Fully grammatical utterances might have been constructed or might have been imitated; ungrammatical utterances are most probably constructed by the child.

A tendency to keep the content words while omitting function words and inflections does not necessarily indicate ignorance of syntax. Infants might learn much about syntax through comprehension before they first produce sentences. Perhaps the sheer difficulty of organizing speech output causes them to leave out the grammatical markers (compare this with Broca's aphasia ➔ 14.2.2).

A belief that first language acquisition is essentially imitation is effectively challenged by the pervasiveness of OVERGENERALIZATION, whereby children produce forms which follow a general rule (e.g. *drinked*, *foots*) but do not occur in the speech used around them. This illustrates that in addition to IMITATING forms that they hear, they can also CONSTRUCT new expressions by subconsciously analysing how the forms pattern.

Hyams (1998) argues that it cannot be lack of syntactic knowledge that accounts for the dearth of verb inflections, subject pronouns and determiners in children's early utterances. She notes that, as well as omitting such items, children also often do produce these in their utterances from the earliest ages. She has evidence too that important syntactic distinctions are observed in the utterances of young children. For instance, she reports studies showing young French children matching adult French syntax by placing the negation *pas* after finite verbs (as in *Veux pas lolo* 'I don't want water'), but before infinitive verb forms (as in *Pas manger la poupée* 'The doll doesn't eat').

Against this, however, are results that point to lack of syntactic sophistication in young children. For instance Theakston *et al.* (2002) investigated the learning of *go, going, goes, gone* and *went* by 11 children, over the whole of their third year. In adult English these are five different inflectional forms (➔ 7) of one verb GO (members of a single lemma ➔ 5), but Theakston *et al.* found that they were initially unconnected in the children's systems, tending to be restricted to different meanings, e.g. *goes* was predominantly used to say where something belonged, but the main meaning of *gone* was 'disappeared' and *went* was most often used to talk about movement; *going* was used about equally for movement and future intent. Tomasello (1992) introduced the term *islands* for potentially relatable verb forms that have not yet been linked by the child. (See McClure *et al.* 2006, for an extension of Tomasello's findings and refinement of his proposals.) The issue of children's early knowledge of syntax is still open.

15.5 COMMUNICATIVE STYLES

Ervin-Tripp *et al.* (1984) recorded children in family interactions. The researchers themselves often participated in the conversations. One of their findings was that two- and three-year-olds used polite expressions much more often to the researchers than to their parents or to other children.

Platt (1986) reports data from four children between 2;1 and 3;9 growing up as speakers of Samoan. These children generally used the request form *sau* 'come' only to children younger than themselves. This is in accord with a Samoan view that a summons to come should be issued only to persons lower in status than the speaker.

The two observations above are about conventions for using language (➔ 4) – something beyond vocabulary, pronunciation and syntax. Such conventions differ between speech communities. In Fiji one is expected to use a specific apology, *Tilou*, when encroaching into other people's space, including passing behind them when they are seated. In Japan, no one at a meal should start eating until the Japanese expression *Itadakimasu* has been said. See Berko Gleason *et al.* (1984) for an interesting account of the acquisition of *please* and *thank you* by English-speaking children.

Speech communities are not uniform and children are not exact replicas of one another. One difference that has been noted, between the ages of one year and about 2;6, is probably the product of both the child's individuality and the style of interaction favoured by the people from whom the child most immediately learns language. The two poles of the distinction have been labelled *expressive* and *referential* (Nelson 1973).

Children with an expressive style operate as if their motto was 'Conversation first!' (Boysson-Bardies 1999: 167). They seem to enjoy interacting with others. Their holophrases can be several syllables long and the intonation pattern is more likely to be reliably reproduced than the vowels and consonants. Conversationally versatile expressions seem to be the ones they use most, for example a French child at 16 months had in her repertoire *C'est beau ça* ('That's nice'). This was a holophrase for her, not a sentence constructed out of parts and it was pronounced as [ebotsa] (Boysson-Bardies 1999: 163). Children with an expressive predilection also acquire greetings and the names of quite a range of people from early on.

Children exhibiting a referential preference concentrate first on noun learning. They interact less readily than expressive children and build up a vocabulary of labels for things in the environment. Their utterances tend to be shorter and less varied than those of expressive children. They apparently pattern their utterances according to a phonological system from a younger age.

No child uses either of these styles exclusively, and by the age of two and a half or three years obvious differences, such as the proportion of nouns in the child's vocabulary, have usually disappeared. Nonetheless, they may represent nursery forerunners of later style differences (➜ 12), such as those found between conversation and academic discourse, or between speech and writing.

Social and pragmatic development continues well into the school years. Two other topics deserve at least a mention, but cannot be surveyed fully here. One is gender differences in children's ways of talking. Coates (1993) gives a good overview. The other is children's learning of the many speech acts needed for practical communication. See Griffiths (1985) for a start on the description of speech act development.

15.6 SECOND LANGUAGE ACQUISITION

So far in this chapter we have made the simplifying assumption that the infant's task is to acquire a single language: the only one that is used around them. This is indeed the case for many children in countries where one language dominates. Monolingual societies often arise because the dominant language was associated with a powerful group of speakers which has displaced speakers of other local languages (e.g. English in the British Isles ➜ 17) and/or because cultural isolation has constrained linguistic diversity (e.g. in Japan or Iceland). But in the majority of societies around the planet, the default situation is multilingualism, and many infants acquire more than one native language, simultaneously (➜ 16).

But even in predominantly monolingual countries, there are many people who are learning or have learnt a second language after their first. For example, almost 90 per cent of Swedes claim to be able to sustain a conversation in English as a second language, even though Swedish is the first language acquired by the majority (European Commission 2006 ➜ W15.6). And the British Council have estimated that 1.88 million people are *teaching* English in primary and secondary schools in India (British Council 2009 ➜ W15.7). So language acquisition doesn't only involve the natural development of a first language by children, but also the more or less deliberate learning of a second language, often with the aid of a teacher and textbook.

The defining feature of **second language acquisition** (SLA) is, of course, that it happens after a first language has been acquired. As we have seen in the preceding sections, an infant has to work out what kind of things words, phonology and syntax *are*, what range of meanings they can *express* (semantics), and the ways they are *used* in different social acts (pragmatics). A child or adult learning a second language, on the other hand, has already acquired the phonology, syntax, semantics, pragmatics and at least several thousand words from a previous language (or more than one: ➔ 16). To what extent is learning and knowing a second language (an L2) similar to learning and knowing a first language (the L1)? Can we make the same kinds of generalizations for L2 that we have for L1?

Undoubtedly, first and second language acquisition have many features in common; but the fact that SLA is now a subfield of linguistics in its own right reflects scholars' recognition that many elements of the process are unique to it. For an initial appreciation of this, let us examine Pinker's (1994) contention that language is more a natural instinct than a learned skill. Here is the quotation from his book *The Language Instinct* that we also discuss in Chapter 1 (➔ 1.4), this time with numbers added to highlight the INSTINCTUAL features he ascribes to human language:

> [language] develops in the child [1] spontaneously, [2] without conscious effort or [3] formal instruction, [4] is deployed without awareness of its underlying logic, [5] is qualitatively the same in every individual, and [6] is distinct from more general abilities to process information or behave intelligently.
>
> (Pinker 1994: 18; numerals added)

Activity 15.3

Reflect on the degree to which Pinker's six features, quoted above, also characterize the acquisition and use of a second language. If you have learned (or started to learn) a second language yourself, note down any experiences you have had with it which would appear to question the applicability of Pinker's features. If you haven't learned a second language, present the features to someone who has, and ask them what they think.

The result of your reflection is probably that Pinker's features either do not hold for SLA, or only hold under exceptional or infrequent circumstances. Most scholarship in SLA over the past century has stressed the 'fundamental difference' between child language acquisition and SLA (Bley-Vroman 1989). As a start, let us look at each of Pinker's features in turn from an SLA perspective:

1   *Spontaneity of development*: Although first languages emerge spontaneously in all normal children as they participate in the communicative activities that unfold around them, second languages will only do so exceptionally, where learners are involved in large amounts of communicative activity and enjoy strong motivation, e.g. when an immigrant tries to integrate into local L1 speech communities.
2   *Lack of conscious effort*: Even in migrant contexts, success can be limited unless the learner deliberately attempts to remember and use new words, pays special attention to the pronunciation of native speakers, and consciously practises new aspects of syntax and new pragmatic routines.

3   *Lack of formal instruction:* Most learners of a second language do not have any sustained
     opportunity to participate in a community of target language speakers, so they
     learn the language with the help of a teacher (at school or in private classes) or on their
     own (from books or through electronic media). Children, of course, do not need
     to rely on explicit teaching or study materials to acquire the essential elements of their
     L1, with the exception of its writing system (➔ R3.2) and specialized vocabulary
     (➔ 5).

4   *Lack of awareness of structure:* Through deliberate study, many learners become very
     familiar with (at least superficial aspects of) the syntax and morphology of the L2,
     sometimes in group drills, repetition, and the memorization of inflectional tables
     (and especially CONJUGATIONS and DECLENSIONS). Many researchers (e.g. Schmidt
     2001) claim that awareness, in the form of deliberate focusing of attention, is a
     necessary component of L2 grammar learning.

CONJUGATIONS and DECLENSIONS list the different inflectional forms taken by (classes of) verbs and nouns, respectively, for a given language (➔ 5.5.1, 7.3.1).

5   *Homogeneity:* L2 learners are an extremely heterogenous population who end up with
     many different kinds and degrees of L2 knowledge. Unlike L1 acquisition, which is
     substantially complete (except for vocabulary, writing and pragmatics) by the time
     the child goes to school, SLA is an optional activity that can be engaged in at any age
     after infancy, all the way from primary school to retirement. Learners differ in many
     other ways too, including:
     - the styles and strategies they use to learn
     - the motivations and objectives they bring to the learning task
     - the amount of (a) exposure they get to L2 input and (b) interaction with other
       L2 users
     - the type and quality of teaching they receive
     - the L1 they speak.

     These factors and others lead to vastly different learning outcomes. Some learners
     might become very successful communicators in the L2; others may get stuck at
     only very rudimentary levels of knowledge; and few will use the language in a way
     that is indistinguishable from native speaker usage.

6   *Cognitive distinctiveness:* Many adult learners approach L2 syntax and morphology as
     they would other logical puzzles, like sudoku or chess. Bley-Vroman (1989) and
     others claim that second languages are learnt not by the human universal capacity
     for first language acquisition posited by Chomsky (e.g. 1986; ➔ 1.4), but by general
     problem-solving skills.

There are other big differences too, most significant among them perhaps being that
second language acquirers have not only an established first language, but also an established set of meanings to express (➔ 15.2) and an established set of cultural beliefs and
practices to enact (➔ 15.5). Because of these and other fundamental differences, it would
make little sense to retrace below the same sequence we used for first language acquisition. Instead, we follow the development of scholars' understanding of the subject, as it
has built upon, and subsequently emancipated itself from, research on L1 acquisition.

15.6.1 Linguistic approaches

In the first half of the last century, SLA wasn't yet established as a separate field of enquiry.
Scholars interested in the process were very language-focused, inspired in the structuralist

tradition of the Swiss linguist Ferdinand de Saussure (➔ 1.4), who highlighted the abstract formal systematicity of languages. In line with contemporary theory that L1 habits could 'interfere' with the L2, leading to errors, CONTRASTIVE ANALYSIS was used to attempt to identify areas of divergence between the two adult systems, in order to predict elements of the L2 which would be harder for the learner to learn, and so should be focused on in teaching.

For example, with respect to word order, Japanese should present more problems for English-speaking learners than Mandarin Chinese, since Japanese is predominantly subject-object-verb, but Mandarin is subject-verb-object, like English. With respect to phonology, we might predict that Fijian-speaking learners of English might have a hard time distinguishing the consonants in the words *either* and *ether*, because the voicing contrast between [ð] and [θ] (➔ 9, 10, 18) does not exist in their L1.

The effects of the known L1 on the unknown L2 are still much studied in contemporary SLA research, especially at the level of words and pronunciation. But the emphasis now is on understanding how SLA happens rather than revealing the source of 'bad habits'. Instead of *interference* the more positive terms *transfer* and **cross-linguistic influence** are preferred. Research goals include understanding how the **mental lexicon** is organized and added to (➔ 14, Activity 15.4 below) and why many non-native users of English have distinctive accents (➔ 18).

In the 1970s, the academic study of SLA came into its own and was highly influenced by Noam Chomsky's developing theory of GRAMMATICAL COMPETENCE, speakers' unconscious mental knowledge of the syntax and phonology of their first language. Chomsky (e.g. 1986) conceived the central task of linguistics to be the resolution of the 'logical problem' of child language acquisition, namely how children come to acquire such a complex system so quickly and on the basis of hearing utterances which 'violate' underlying rules, because interlocutors overlap and interrupt each other in talk-in-interaction (➔ 2), and accidentally produce utterances which are not what they intended (so-called SPEECH ERRORS ➔ 14.4.1).

The conclusion Chomsky reached was that human beings have innate (genetically inherited) mental knowledge of the possible syntactic and phonological resources available to all human languages and the ways in which these resources can be configured in particular languages like English, Japanese, or Turkish (➔ R4.3, R4.5). For example, all human languages use recursion for nesting phrases and clauses within other phrases and clauses (milestone 3 in Section 15.4, above). Chomsky's theory of human language was centred around his concept of UNIVERSAL GRAMMAR (UG), an abstract formulation of the innate system that he believes constrains the shape of human languages and allows children to acquire them (➔ 1.4).

Chomsky's argument that children build their own complex mental grammars, rather than just imitating adult speech, had a profound impact on the study of SLA. Corder (1967), for example, pioneered ERROR ANALYSIS, the systematic study of learners' spoken and written output. The objective was to explore how learners were actually building the 'target' grammar in their minds, rather than to predict in advance the 'bad habits' that learners would need to overcome, as the earlier contrastive analysis of native speakers' grammars had sought to do.

Later, Selinker (1972) elaborated the notion of INTERLANGUAGE, the dynamic linguistic systems developing in learners' minds, which, he claimed, could be characterized independently of both the learner's L1 system and that of native speakers of the L2. Subsequent

The International Corpus of Learner English (Granger et al. 2009) provides 3.75 million words of analysable interlanguage data from essays written by learners in 16 countries. Florence Myles and Rosamund Mitchell have made available spoken data for L2 French at their French Learner Language Oral Corpora website (➔ W15.8).

work has investigated the extent to which UG might be active in SLA, an issue that continues to be hotly debated today (see Mitchell and Myles 2004: Chapter 3). Apart from disagreement over the innateness of grammatical knowledge, one of the main issues in this debate has been about the so-called CRITICAL PERIOD during which languages can be acquired naturally. It has been argued that if there is an innate part of the mind dedicated to language acquisition, it will function like other maturational characteristics of the species, and become inactive after puberty.

15.6.2 Cognitive approaches

The 1980s saw SLA theory develop rapidly, as scholars increasingly recognized that the process was unlikely to be just a re-run of first language acquisition, but was governed by a more complex array of factors, both social and psychological. Stephen Krashen (e.g. Krashen 1981 ➜ W15.9) distinguished between unconscious processes of *acquisition*, such as those governing children's linguistic development, from more deliberate acts of *learning*, which play a major role in adult second language development, especially when the additional language is *taught*.

Krashen's (1981) MONITOR THEORY revolves around the idea that *learning* is not the process by which most L2 knowledge develops (it serves only to allow learners to monitor their output for accuracy). Instead, he argued, the key process was acquisition, through which the mind unconsciously and automatically extracts grammatical regularities from COMPREHENSIBLE INPUT. Comprehensible input is language that learners are exposed to which they are able to understand because it is used in contexts which are meaningful to them. It is the main ingredient in Krashen's (much challenged) recipe for successful SLA, the 'Natural Approach', which calls for input only slightly ahead of the learner's current levels of competence ('i+1', where i = interlanguage).

The notion that SLA can be more effective if the conditions approximate those leading to natural acquisition by children has a long history: François Gouin (1892: 4–5 ➜ W15.10) proposed a teaching method which was inspired by the contrast he observed between his own failure to learn German through deliberate study of grammar and vocabulary, and his two-and-a-half-year-old nephew's spectacular success in acquiring his own first language, French, during the same ten-month period. He proposed (1892: 5) that '[n]ature has already solved the problem that we are investigating', arguing with unbridled enthusiasm (and cheerful disregard for the evidence) that:

> the child learns in six months, in a year at the outside, to talk and also to think. The youth or the adult having to do but a portion of the work, since he already knows how to think, should therefore be able without trouble to learn in six months, or in a year at the outside, to speak any given language, be it Chinese, Japanese, Arabic, Sanscrit [*sic*], German, English, or French. And he certainly can do this on condition that he follow the special process known and so well applied by our own mothers.
>
> (Gouin 1892: 6–7)

Gouin's 'Natural Method' of second language teaching involved contextualized language use in sequenced activities, rather than the inflectional tables and invented example sentences that dominated most second language teaching at the time.

Krashen's concern with natural input in the 1980s was followed by a stream of research exploring how learners process the speech and text they encounter and produce, and how this performance feeds into developing competence. Pienemann's PROCESS-ABILITY THEORY (1998), for example, held that learners operate according to an inbuilt mental curriculum which constrains the acquisition of certain grammatical structures to the appropriate developmental stage, as illustrated for English in Table 15.2. L2 structures are processable (and so acquirable for subsequent use) when the learner has the necessary knowledge and cognitive resources to unpack their structure and extract the intended meaning from them. At the beginning, little is processable. For example, learners of French might not be able to isolate the definite article in a phrase like *Ouvrez la fenêtre* ('Open the window'). (Indeed, for much of his first few months of French classes one of us thought that the word for window was *lafenêtre*!)

Another avenue of cognitively-oriented (or psycholinguistic) research in SLA concerns the development and organization of the bilingual mind, especially at the lexical level. For example, do learners build a separate vocabulary store for L2 words, or is each L2 word tagged on to an L1 word as a translation, as in a bilingual dictionary? If L1 and L2 words are kept together in a combined memory store, does that mean that when using L2 vocabulary speakers first 'look up' the L1 word and unconsciously translate it into the L2 (➔ 14)?

Table 15.2 SLA stages according to Processability Theory (Pienemann 1998)

Stage	Processing strategy	Example structures
1	Memorizing individual words or unanalysed sequences of words.	[maɪneɪmɪz]* Felix
2	Using basic word order (for English: subject-verb-object)	Cat like milk
3	Recognising the relations between elements *within* phrases	(These$_{pl}$ cats$_{pl}$) like milk
4	Placing elements at the beginning of sentences	Do (cats like milk)?
5	Recognising the relations between elements *between* phrases	(The cat$_{sing}$) (likes$_{sing}$ milk)
6	Embedding subordinate clauses within sentences (one kind of recursion)	She saw (the cat who likes milk)

* = "My name is"

Activity 15.4 ⊙━┳

Look at the following list of Spanish nouns. If you don't know any Spanish, can you guess at the meaning of any of them? Which do you think might present fewer problems for English-speaking learners? Why? What do you think this might reveal about the way learners store L2 words in their minds?

Resist the temptation to look up the English translations on your first attempt to answer these questions, then do so and revise your initial answers if necessary. (A good online Spanish-English dictionary is *SpanishDict* ➜ W15.11.)

- almohada
- botella
- mesa
- librería
- manzana
- organización
- palabra
- persona
- tuna
- verbo

If this activity was too easy for you because you already know Spanish, have a look at the following list of English words, some of which were used in a study which investigates learners' implicit assumptions about L2 word meanings (Hall 2002). Which of these words do you think Spanish-speaking learners in their second year of EFL (English as a Foreign Language) might report being familiar with? Why? What might this tell us about how learners' minds process and store new L2 words?

- atraverse
- marcescent
- menesterous
- mirl
- moil
- tarm
- thrawn
- thrimble
- trundle
- smatter

So far, we've been concentrating on universal cognitive processes in SLA, in line with Pinker's (1994) homogeneity feature: that the human brain (where mental grammars are stored; ➜ 14) has the same basic structure in all members of our species and that this constrains the forms of language learning and language processing for all human beings. But the research on what happens in learners' minds has also highlighted INDIVIDUAL DIFFERENCES, for example in aptitude, motivation, unconscious learning styles, and conscious learning strategies, which potentially account for the wide variety of paths followed and ultimate outcomes achieved in SLA (see Erhman, Leaver and Oxford 2003 for an overview and references). The recognition that motivation is one of the biggest differences between successful and unsuccessful learners is embodied in a European Union project called *Don't Give Up* (➔ W15.12), which provides examples of best practice for helping adult language learners build motivation.

15.6.3 Sociocultural approaches

The explosion of work on individual differences in the 1980s reflected wider dissatisfaction with narrowly linguistic and psycholinguistic approaches to SLA. As most learners know, success in the language depends on so much more than the development of grammatical competence and accuracy in use. The anthropologist Dell Hymes had proposed in the 1970s the notion of **communicative competence**, which extended Chomsky's notion of grammatical competence to include knowledge of how to use language appropriately and strategically in actual situations of use (Hymes 1974). So English native speakers know that to ask a question in English they can put the auxiliary verb before the subject (e.g. *Can you help me?*); but they also know that they have to add *please* when addressing a stranger and that an unadorned yes/no answer is not expected (➔ 4).

The distinction between grammatical and communicative competence struck a chord with second language researchers and teachers, and the focus began to shift from what language *is* and how it *works* to what it *does*: mediate socially and culturally situated action. It was hypothesized that L2 learners respond better to the challenge when their objective is not simply accurate deployment of syntax and vocabulary, but rather the fluent and effective negotiation of meanings in sociocultural contexts. Discourse analysis is now as common a tool in SLA research as interlanguage analysis and psycholinguistic experiments. Foster and Ohta (2005), for example, demonstrate how learners assist each other in classroom communicative activities, and suggest that cooperative discourse is more important to the learners than comprehensible input. They report data such as the following, from three English-speaking learners of Japanese discussing the homestay experience (422–423):

1	E:	Hehehe. Ii kazoku dattara ii desu. Moshi kazoku ga dame dattara
		Hehehe. If you have a good family then it's a good thing. But if you have a bad family
2	I:	dame desu.
		then it's no good
3	J:	Un.
		yeah.
4	E:	Exactly desu.
		Exactly
5	I:	Oh. ee aa kazoku no yoo na (.) Does that work? Depending on family?
		Oh. uh uh like a family (.) Does that work? Depending on family?
6	J:	ah ah ah
7	E:	Yes.
8	J:	Yotei? yote? Kazoku kazoku ni yoote:.
		(J attempts to say 'Kazoku ni yotte' 'depending on the family' but mispronounces the verb)
9	E:	Kazoku ni yotte.
		Depending on the family (correct)
10	I:	Kazoku ni yotte
		Depending on the family

Notice how I completes E's utterance on line 2, and then seeks assistance from E and J in line 5 for an expression in Japanese that he is unsure of. E initially responds to the content, rather than the form of what I wants to say (*yes* in line 7), then both supply corrected forms of the utterance, with I repeating E's correct version in the last line of the excerpt. This shift of emphasis towards sociocultural processes in SLA research once more mirrors what we know about first language acquisition, which, as we saw at the beginning of the chapter, happens through social interaction (Clark 2003: 138–139).

The work of Vygotsky, Luria and Leontiev (published in Russia in the 1920s and 30s and first translated into English in the 1970s) provide the main principles of SOCIOCUL-TURAL THEORY (SCT), which began to inform SLA research in the mid-1980s (e.g. Frawley and Lantolf 1985) and has become increasingly influential in the field. SCT is an approach to human development which claims that our higher order functions (like general problem-solving or language) are the product of exposure to, and participation in, social interaction.

While other approaches to SLA assume a separation between the individual (within whom the psychological processes of language acquisition operate) and the social (where language use happens and shared meaning is created), SCT reconfigures the relationship. For Vygotsky and other socio-cultural theorists, language emerges from social and cultural activity and only later becomes reconstructed as an individual, psychological phenom-enon. In this way of thinking, SLA theory should explain not only the cognitive process of acquiring new sounds and structures and then using them to communicate, but also the social process of participating in interactions with other learners and users of the language (e.g. developing skills in using English as a **lingua franca** ➔ 18.7).

15.7 SUMMARY

Child language acquisition is one of the most impressive achievements of humans, made possible through a combination of the human capacity for language, our general intel-lectual abilities and interactive practice. Children usually show understanding of language before age one year, which is roughly when they produce their first word. Initial vocabu-lary growth is slow, but it accelerates and they soon have hundreds of words. Infants under one year old can hear more sound distinctions than they need, but producing speech is a complicated skill. The earliest sentences are made around the age of one and a half years. By age two and a half years many children are producing sentences that exhibit hierar-chical structure, recursion (of clauses within clauses) and coordination. Conventions for the use of language are another substantial learning task.

Second language acquisition appears to be fundamentally different from first language acquisition. Over the past century, scholars have attempted to tame the diversity inherent in the subject in a succession of approaches highlighting different aspects of SLA. First the emphasis was placed squarely on the linguistic systems themselves: the grammars, vocab-ularies and pronunciation systems of the learner's L1 and the target L2. The learner was not directly an object of study. This changed after Chomsky painted grammatical compe-tence as a cognitive faculty, and this concept was applied to SLA. But still linguistic organ-izational principles were the focus. The cognitive dimension subsequently came to the forefront, with researchers examining second language input, output, and processing, essentially psycholinguistic constructs. But input and output are embedded in social inter-action, and more recently the focus of SLA studies has shifted to the sociocultural domain, where communication with other users in context is as fundamental as command of native-like linguistic structure during language processing.

15.8 FURTHER ACTIVITIES

Activity 15.5

If possible, find a video- or audiotape or written diary account of some part of your own preschool language development. Talk to people who knew you before you turned five. Look through the data carefully, trying to see the ways in which it fits with or contradicts what has been said in this chapter and other sources. If you cannot locate records about yourself, ask people currently bringing up a preschooler for permission to use some of their recordings or diary material. Of course, if you are yourself caring for an infant or toddler you should be able to make observations directly. If two or more students can get together to discuss each other's data, so much the better.

Activity 15.6

If you studied or are studying another language apart from the one(s) you acquired in infancy, examine evidence of how your learning developed, in the form of schoolwork, audio- or video recordings if you have them, letters or emails to exchange partners, etc. As with the previous activity, look through the data carefully, trying to see the ways in which it fits with or contradicts the findings and approaches of scholars reviewed in this chapter and other sources.

COMMENTARY ON ACTIVITIES

O—╥ Remember that this symbol indicates that there is a commentary on the activity that you can find on the companion website at www.routledge.com/cw/merrison.

FURTHER READING and REFERENCES

Suggestions for further reading on the topics discussed in this chapter can be found on the companion website (www.routledge.com/cw/merrison).

Any piece of academic writing must always provide a list of publications to which reference has been made. Unusually and very unconventionally, this information is provided on the companion website (www.routledge.com/cw/merrison). Always ask your tutor about how you are to present references for any piece of work that you submit.

Chapter 16
Multilingualism

Key Ideas in this Chapter

- It is common for both individual speakers and whole societies to use more than one language on a regular basis, although few multilinguals are completely balanced in their language competences.

- For many multilinguals, the complementary resources they have from each language often form a single communicative competence.

- In *subtractive* educational processes, the intention is to replace an individual's L1 with an L2 (normally the principal language of a state). *Additive* bilingual education complements L1 knowledge with L2 knowledge.

- It is common for individuals to switch languages in everyday speech. This process, known as multilingual *code-switching*, is regular, not random, and responds to various social and communicative needs.

- In the phenomenon known as *diglossia*, societies assign their languages or varieties to distinct domains and purposes of use.

- Although most states are multilingual, many have elevated one language to a privileged position and the idea of 'one language, one nation' is often assumed to be the natural state, especially in more industrialized, powerful nations.

- Through language policy and planning, governments take steps to promote or suppress multilingualism.

16.1 INTRODUCTION

Most religions have stories to explain why we speak different languages, instead of the one 'sacred tongue' originally given us by a deity or deities. A common element of many of the stories is that our speech was 'sundered' as punishment for challenging divine power. The Tower of Babel (Figure 16.1), in which humanity is punished for trying to build a tower to heaven, is one such myth, and is paralleled by others from India to Mexico. But as Barthes observed:

> Language diversity has been historically under the influence of two contrasting myths: in the name of Babel, humankind has been punished with the confusion of the languages. In the name of Pentecost, the plurality of languages is on the contrary understood as a gift to humankind.
>
> (Barthes 1977, cited in Jacquemet 2005: 273)

In the Christian story of Pentecost, the apostles are given the ability to speak different languages by the Holy Spirit, which allowed them to overcome the confusion of Babel (and so spread the church beyond Palestine). So language diversity is conceived of as both curse and gift: curse for communities in general who cannot communicate with each other, but gift for those individuals who can speak to, and understand, members of more than one community. In this chapter we discuss both multilingual societies and multilingual individuals, emphasizing 'the gift' of Pentecost over 'the curse' of Babel.

Given today's globalized individuals and nations, one would think that multilingualism would always be considered a 'gift'. And yet as we illustrate in this chapter, it is often stigmatized or mismanaged. Understanding the nature of multilingualism and its role in the world is a crucial challenge for societies as they deal with complicated and emotive issues such as migration, bilingual education, and minority rights. The topic of this

Figure 16.1 The Tower of Babel, by Pieter Bruegel the Elder (1563)

chapter is therefore not only intrinsically interesting, but also of critical importance for individuals and nations.

16.2 MONOLINGUALISM, BILINGUALISM, MULTILINGUALISM

The study of multilingualism is plagued by considerable imprecision in terminology and by quite a few erroneous assumptions. This is especially evident among speakers of major languages (including linguists) in the West, as well as in other powerful states where a single language dominates, such as China and Japan. For example, most major languages use a term equivalent to the English 'mother tongue', which implies only one language for each individual (that of your mother), thus assuming *monolingualism* as the default or norm. *Bilingualism* is often taken to refer to (a) those speakers who have acquired the knowledge corresponding to that of two monolingual speakers of different languages; and (b) those societies in which two languages may be used for official purposes (e.g. Canada's use of French and English). By extension, *multilingualism* is assumed by many to refer to 'three or more' languages in the same definitions. In the sections to come we will see that we need to talk about Babel and Pentecost in more nuanced ways.

> The term *mother tongue education* is regularly used in the context of indigenous and immigrant children's rights to be taught in their own language, at least at primary level. We discuss this further in our case studies in 16.5, and more information can be found on UNESCO's website (➔ W16.1)

For a start, many individuals acquire more than one language from birth or early infancy, and so it makes sense to refer to *first language*(s), instead of mother tongue(s) (this is the convention we follow in Chapter 15, Language Acquisition). However, many people use languages regularly which they have acquired *after* their first language(s), in the process of **second language acquisition** (➔ 15.6). These language users are often thought of as bilingual when their proficiency in the second language is advanced.

In this chapter we use *bilingualism* to refer only to people's and societies' knowledge and use of two languages (reflecting the word's Latin etymology: *bi* = 'two' + *lingua* = 'language'), even though other linguists use the term to cover two or more languages. Despite theoretical discussions about the differences (Wei 2000a), we use *multilingualism* to refer to the general concept of knowing/using more than one language (i.e. including *bilingualism*), unless otherwise stated.

Multilingualism holds for individual people and communities or societies, and involves various levels of proficiency, efficiency, and frequency of use. It also correlates and co-varies with context, identity, and purpose. In this chapter we address both INDIVIDUAL and SOCIETAL MULTILINGUALISM, and discuss issues of balance and imbalance between the languages.

16.3 INDIVIDUAL MULTILINGUALISM

In this section we explore individual multilingualism, a more common phenomenon than generally assumed by people from largely monolingual societies. The number of people who use more than one language to negotiate their lives with others is certainly bigger than the number who get by with just one language. But estimates cited by linguists (e.g. Tucker 1999) rarely get more precise than 'more than 50 per cent of the world's population', mostly due to lack of census data (and problems with data that *are* available: see Baker 2011: 37–38). The other problem with counting multilinguals is, of course, that it presupposes a category that you are either in or out of, and this is the major issue we need to tackle here. We start by discussing different kinds of individuals who might be called multilingual and introduce the idea that the phenomenon is perhaps better conceptualized as a continuum than as a monolithic category. We then address the issue of the costs and benefits that different kinds of multilingualism might bring to the individuals concerned.

16.3.1 Kinds of multilingual individuals

Activity 16.1 🔑

Read the following linguistic autobiography, excerpted from a blog posting in English of over 1000 words written by 'Purity Purple', a student in Malaysia, whose other blogs are all in the Malay language. Would you describe the blogger as multilingual or not? If so, why and in how many languages? If not, why not? Ask other people what they think.

> I am the daughter of Malay speakers. I grew up in a home in which my parents and grandparents spoke in Terengganu dialect, which is apart of Malay language, to each other. [...] My mother tongue is of course, Malay. When I grew up, I think informally, I've been influenced with many languages which are English, Chinese, Hindi and Tamil from the television. As I remember, when I was about five years old, I enjoy watching Hindi movies very much, and sometimes I would follow when the actor or actress sing. But I don't know what they said. [...] I live in a small village in Kuala Terengganu and all of the villagers were Malays and their mother tongue were Malay, so that, I've grew up in a largely monolingual environment. [...] I started to learn English when I enter kindergarten [...] As English is our second language, I've learn English when I went to primary school [...] I've tried to learn English as good as possible and always discuss in groups regarding to English. Luckily, during [primary school], I could score A for my English subject. [...] After [primary school], I furthered my study in religious boarding-school [...]. In the school, we are compulsory to learn Arabic. I know nothing about the language and I've to learn from the basic part. [...] When I was in form two, my interest towards Arabic is decrease because we started to learn the language in depth and I found difficult to follow and understand. [...] When I was in form four and five, I'm one of the students that got high mark in English subject in my class. That's the reasons why I felt motivated to further study in English. [...] [A]fter finished studying law [at university], I applied for English Language Studies in [University X], and I feel very lucky to be in [University X] and learn English.
>
> (Purity Purple 2009)

Responses to this autobiography will probably yield many opinions about actually who 'should count' as multilingual. Any definition is likely to be controversial. Bloomfield's (1933: 56) classic definition of bilinguals as having 'native-like control of two languages' has always been problematic in that it begged the question of what 'native-like control' means. Do all native speakers of any given language have the same abilities with and in that language? Some research (Harley and Wang, cited in Harley 2008: 155) suggests that 'monolingual-like attainment in each of a bilingual's two languages is probably a myth (at any age)'. Baker (2011: 8) cites Diebold's concept of 'incipient bilingualism', which he defines as the state of 'hav[ing] one well-developed language, and the other [...] in the early stages of development'. This is almost at the other extreme from Bloomfield's definition and begins to conflict with the more widespread understanding and use of the term (although it is regularly used in psycholinguistic research ➜ 14).

There are many labels that can be used to describe the different levels and kinds of individual multilingualism (see Wei 2000a). One particularly useful distinction regards the relative timing of language learning in bilingualism:

- SIMULTANEOUS BILINGUALISM is when both languages are learned more or less at the same time, in early infancy, as L1s
- SEQUENTIAL BILINGUALISM is when one language is learnt after another (through second language acquisition ➜ 15.6), within which are distinguished
  - EARLY SEQUENTIAL BILINGUALISM, in which the L2 is learnt before puberty, more or less independently of schooling
  - LATE SEQUENTIAL BILINGUALISM, where the L2 is learnt during adolescence or adulthood, usually through deliberate study.

In discussions of language learning, language teaching and multilingualism, first language is often abbreviated as *L1* and second language as *L2*. Some researchers use L2 to refer to any languages learnt after the first, whereas others prefer to distinguish L3, L4, etc.

Harley (2008: 154) notes that '[e]arly sequential bilinguals form the largest group worldwide and the number is increasing, particularly in countries with large immigration rates'.

Of the languages that an individual uses, there may be one that can be classified as that individual's DOMINANT LANGUAGE, even for those who may describe themselves as BALANCED BILINGUALS, with roughly equal competence in both. This may be the language that is used most frequently, and/or the one that the individual feels most comfortable using. It is not necessarily L1: there are situations, such as living in another country for an extended period of time, in which L2 (or L3, L4, etc.) becomes dominant. Jacinto from Chile (featured in Activity 16.3 below), on returning to his home country after an absence of about 20 years living in England, commented that he sometimes found it more of an effort to speak Spanish (his L1) than English in some situations.

The CHILDES corpus includes interactional data involving children acquiring more than one language, either as L1 or L2, including Arabic and Chinese (Mandarin and Cantonese), as well as several European languages (➜ W16.3; click on *Database Manuals* for details, and *Databases* for the data itself).

Activity 16.2 ○━┳

Denise is American and has lived in Switzerland for 35 years. She says of her family:

> I am not bilingual – that would be stretching it a good deal … because I am not fluent. I can get by very well on the everyday things but if it comes to a complicated conversation I'm not that good and I don't feel that good expressing myself in German. [My husband] is Swedish and his English is perfect. He speaks German and Danish and Norwegian all fluently and he would probably have to say that his English and German are probably the best. [My daughters] were born here [Switzerland] and they heard English for their first year. Then they started playing with other children, they picked up Swiss German very rapidly and then all their schooling was in Swiss German. I must say their best language is Swiss German. We all speak English together but when just the two girls are together, they speak Swiss German because for them it is their most natural language, it is their stronger language.

From what she says, how is Denise defining 'being bilingual'? What are the implications of what she says about her daughters in relation to the concepts of 'mother tongue' and 'dominant language'?

16.3.2 Individual multilingualism as a continuum

The idea of a LINGUISTIC REPERTOIRE is a common way of conceptualizing all the different grammatical, lexical, pragmatic and stylistic resources a single individual can use from all the languages that they know.

Multilingualism is not a static concept. Any (monolingual or multilingual) individual's language or languages is continually developing and that development is very individual. No two individuals are equal in multilingualism, and there is no single threshold that must be crossed to 'enter the club'. One way to characterize multilingualism is as a continuum, rather than as simply 'the opposite of monolingualism'. Towards one pole would cluster cases in which an individual's LINGUISTIC REPERTOIRE (➔ 12.2.8) is pretty much restricted to resources from only one language (i.e. complete monolingualism), and towards the other would be cases of people with the richest possible linguistic repertoires, from (two or more) different languages.

Activity 16.3 🗝

Consider each of the following individual cases and decide roughly where each might fall on a multilingual continuum with *less multilingual* at one end and *more multilingual* at the other. Who in the list seems to fit which of the different kinds of bilingual mentioned in 16.2? Do you need any other information to help you form a judgement?

1   Anne is a British citizen from a monolingual English-speaking family, with a degree in French Studies from an English university.
2   Bien is a Vietnamese refugee who arrived in the UK 25 years ago and claims he can use Vietnamese, Mandarin Chinese and English fluently in any situation.
3   Carla is a child just learning to talk and is spoken to in English by her Australian mother and Spanish by her Chilean father.
4   Dunja is a refugee who speaks Croatian as his first language and who can greet an official in English and in French but achieve nothing more through the medium of either language.
5   Elise is a Belgian citizen who has an English language degree from an Irish University.
6   Fakir is a nine-year-old child living in San Francisco who regularly uses Gujarati at home with the family and as the language of play with some friends, Hindi as the language of play with other friends, and occasionally English as the language of play at school where English is the medium of instruction.
7   Geraldine is an elderly French lady who lived in Britain throughout her adult life, who was in hospital in Aylesbury (England) after suffering a stroke, after which she could apparently only use French despite having used English fluently for many years.
8   Hu is a Shanghai-based translator of technical manuals from English to Chinese, her L1.
9   Ingmar is a Swedish employee of a multinational firm, who uses English to socialize with Japanese employees of the same firm when he attends meetings held at the company headquarters in Brazil. All work-related communication is conducted through interpreters.
10   Jacinto is a Chilean who chose to come to the UK to study for a Master's Degree, met and married an English person and stayed in the UK for the next 20 years before returning to Chile on the English spouse's retirement.
11   Melissa is a deaf user of American Sign Language (ASL) who reads and writes in English.
12   You and your own knowledge of language(s).

Another kind of multilingual continuum relates not to differences between individuals' language resources, but rather to how much those resources are activated across situations in which a single individual participates. This is what Grosjean (e.g. 2001) refers to as a bilingual's MODE: the degree to which their different languages are currently activated in memory (➔ 14). For example, a reasonably balanced French-English bilingual might be:

- in MONOLINGUAL FRENCH MODE when reading a French novel
- in MONOLINGUAL ENGLISH MODE when chatting in English with a monolingual English speaker
- in BILINGUAL FRENCH MODE when discussing a recipe for *boeuf bourguignon* in French during a relaxed mixed-language conversation with another balanced bilingual (➔ 16.4.1)
- TOWARDS THE FRENCH MONOLINGUAL END OF THE CONTINUUM when using an English phrase in a generally French-medium conversation with a French speaker with limited English proficiency
- MIDWAY ALONG THE CONTINUUM when explaining an English TV programme she has seen, in French, to a bilingual French/English speaker.

Shifting between modes along the continuum is thus similar to the way that a monolingual individual might juggle different **registers** in some situations (➔ 12.2.8).

16.3.3 The (costs and) benefits of multilingualism

It is regularly assumed by non-experts that the natural development or adoption of more than one language (CIRCUMSTANTIAL BILINGUALISM) represents a deficit situation: that no single language in an individual's linguistic repertoire will be known fully or 'properly' and that this will lead to lower intelligence and lack of personal equilibrium. Baker (2011: 139) quotes a nineteenth-century professor from Cambridge University who wrote:

> If it were possible for a child to live in two languages at once and equally well, so much the worse. His intellectual and spiritual growth would not thereby be doubled, but halved. Unity of mind and character would have great difficulty in asserting itself in such circumstances.

This view, however, is not usually extended to those monolinguals (normally from wealthier families in industrialized Western countries) who, out of choice rather than circumstance or necessity, study a prestigious foreign language at school and/or university and become proficient in it (a phenomenon known as ELECTIVE or ELITE BILINGUALISM: see Romaine 1999). Examples of circumstantial bilingualism would be the children of Polish economic migrants in the UK acquiring English through local state schooling, and examples of elective bilingualism would be children of wealthier Poles who studied in a private English-medium school in Poland.

In the 1960s the term *semilingual* was first used in Scandinavia to label circumstantial bilinguals who displayed a proficiency in their languages that was not perceived to be equal to that of monolinguals. Hansegård (1975, cited in Skutnabb-Kangas 1981: 253) characterized the semilingual as someone who 'shows quantitative deficiencies (smaller vocabulary, etc.) compared with [monolinguals] [...] and [...] in addition to this deviates more from the normal for the two languages [...].' He goes on to claim (p. 254) that semilinguals are 'not fully affected emotionally by a language [...] [due to] a poverty of individual semantic experiences.'

The concept and the term *semilingual* were used by some in educational circles to explain poor examination results by pupils attending schools conducted in a language that is not much used in their homes, for example, children from ethnic minorities in Europe and North America, without regard to the wider context of the individual student's learning. The term is now avoided due to its overriding negativity and its association with bilingual education which is SUBTRACTIVE, i.e. the replacement of the pupil's L1 with an L2 which is the one used in mainstream schooling and society at large. Subtractive bilingualism often damages speakers' self-image and sense of cultural or ethnic identity, as well as undermining their potential to benefit from education as much as native speakers of the language. The alternative is ADDITIVE bilingualism, in which the second language complements, rather than displaces, the first language, and is introduced gradually in the individual's progress through school.

François Grosjean (2008: 14) uses a compelling analogy from athletics to provide a less deficit-oriented alternative to Bloomfield's (1933: 56) view of bilingualism as double monolingualism:

> The high hurdler blends two types of competencies, that of high jumping and that of sprinting. When compared individually with the sprinter or the high jumper, the hurdler meets neither level of competence, and yet when taken as a whole the hurdler is an athlete in his or her own right. [...] A high hurdler is an integrated whole, a unique and specific athlete, who can attain the highest levels of world competition in the same way that the sprinter and the high jumper can. In many ways, the bilingual is like the high hurdler: an integrated whole, a unique and specific speakerhearer, and not the sum of two complete or incomplete monolinguals.

Noam Chomsky (➔ 1.4) used the term *grammatical competence* to refer to the language units that speakers acquire and the rules they construct to combine these units. Dell Hymes later proposed an expanded notion, **communicative competence** (➔ 13.3.1), which embraced speakers' implicit knowledge of how their grammatical competence is used effectively and appropriately by members of their speech community in actual usage contexts.

According to this view (Figure 16.2), what we have called circumstantial bilinguals have a single **communicative competence**, just like monolinguals. The difference is that for a bilingual the competence draws from the resources of two language systems. We take up this idea again in Section 16.5.1.

Hoffmann (1991: 126) represents the majority of scholars who recognize the benefits of bilingualism when he states that:

> bilinguals have a wider and more varied range of experience than monolinguals, as they have access to two cultures and operate in two different systems ... Their need to switch from one code to another has also been seen as beneficial to flexible thinking, as each language may provide the speaker with distinct perspectives.

Some of the major research on cognitive costs and benefits is summarized by Baker (2011: Chapter 7). He recognizes that there are benefits associated with being bilingual, for example in terms of the ability to think *about* language (metalinguistic ability ➔ 7.1, linked to literacy development ➔ R3.2) and sensitivity to the communicative needs of a

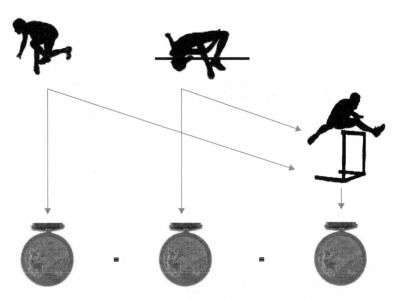

Figure 16.2 An athletic analogy for bilingualism, in which the hurdler resembles a bilingual, the sprinter and high jumper are like monolinguals, and the gold medals correspond to overall communicative competence (see Grosjean 2008: 14)

situation. But he also sounds cautionary notes about methodological limitations of the currently available empirical research, and points out that there are also superficial costs of bilingualism associated with certain processes and situations (e.g. in word-finding ➔ 14). He concludes, however, that in assessing the link between intelligence and bilingualism, 'a simple negative relationship is a misconception' (p. 161).

16.4 MANAGING MORE THAN ONE LANGUAGE

A multilingual's linguistic experience involves constant *choices* (some deliberate, most below the level of consciousness) and constant *change* (from one language to another, from monolingual to multilingual mode). How are these choices and changes played out? Part of the answer lies in the organization and operation of the multilingual mind, and psycholinguists are engaged in studying whether a bilingual's languages are stored and accessed separately or together (➔14.4.2, 14.6). In this section, however, we take more descriptive and sociolinguistic approaches to the issue.

16.4.1 Code-switching

Whether or not an individual's languages are stored separately in memory, multilinguals regularly use different languages within the same interaction and this process shows a variety of patterns. Table 16.1 presents some data featuring five different languages:

Table 16.1 Three examples of code-switching

1	**Come to the table. Bwyd yn barod** 'Come to the table. Food is ready'	
Eng	*Come to the table*	
Wel		*Bwyd yn barod*

2	**Tell them you'll buy xune-ye jaedid when you sell your own house.** 'Tell them you'll buy a new house when you sell your own house.'		
Eng	*Tell them you'll buy*		*when you sell your own house*
Far		*xune-ye jaedid*	

3	**I-chiefs isidle nge-referee's optional time, otherwise ngabe ihambe sleg.** **Maar why benga stopi this system ye-injury time?**								
	'Chiefs [a football team] have won owing to the referee's optional time, otherwise they could have lost.								
	But why is this system of injury time not phased out?'								
Eng	*chiefs*		*referee's optional time, otherwise*			*why*		*this system*	*injury time?*
Zul	*I-*		*isidle nge-*		*ngabe*		*benga*		*ye-*
Afr					*ihambe sleg. Maar*		*stopi*		

Key: Eng = English; Wel = Welsh; Far = Farsi; Zul = Zulu; Afr = Afrikaans

Sources: (1) Baker 2011: 107; (2) Mahootian 1993: 152; cited in MacSwan 2004: 306; (3) Mfusi, 1989; cited in de Klerk and Gough 2002: 370.

In the first example, one sentence is in English, and the next is in Welsh (a case of INTERSENTENTIAL SWITCHING). In the second, a Farsi noun group is embedded within an English sentence (a case of INTRASENTENTIAL SWITCHING). In the third example, three languages alternate at multiple points within each sentence, sometimes within the same word. For example, the first sentence starts with a word which has a Zulu **prefix** attached to an English **stem** and **suffix** (➔ 5), followed by a complete word in Zulu, then another mixed Zulu-English word, three completely English words straddling a clause boundary (➔ 8), another Zulu word, and finally two words in Afrikaans.

All three examples were used in the sources we took them from to illustrate the general phenomenon known as multilingual **code-switching**, although some linguists make a distinction between multilingual code-switching proper, in which languages are alternated in the same turn but are kept separate, as in (1), and multilingual CODE-MIXING, where elements of one language are used within, or blended with, elements of the other language (examples 2 and 3 respectively).

Activity 16.4

Here are some of our own anecdotes about situations in which speakers have mixed languages. Consider each one and decide what's going on. Do you think they are examples of code-switching, code-mixing, or something else?

1   An English traveller recalls being surprised during a car journey from Germany to France when a garage attendant did not understand her question. Later she realized that she had put French verb inflections onto German verb stems.
2   A German/English bilingual recalls talking in her childhood about 'butterlings' – a fusion of the English word *butterfly* and the German word *Schmetterling*.
3   The same bilingual reported confusion in a business meeting when she said 'Das habe ich schon gementioned'.
4   A very excited three-year-old English/French bilingual child showed her 'new shoes blue' to her English father.
5   The same child then ran to tell her French mother in French that 'Papa aime mes nouveaux bleus souliers' (instead of the expected 'nouveaux souliers bleus')

It is sometimes difficult to distinguish multilingual code-switching at the word level from **borrowing**, the historical process through which one language assimilates words from another language (➔ 17, 18; R2.7). But there are no watertight borders when languages come into contact, either within or between individuals. For example, there must have been a phase in the history of English when bilingual speakers of Old English and Norman French were occasionally using the French word *boeuf* in English sentences. The subsequent assimilation of this word as English *beef* must have been a gradual process, so what started as code-switching ended as borrowing.

For those early scholars and many contemporary commentators who approach circumstantial bilingualism from a deficit perspective, multilingual code-switching is evidence of lack of competence: speakers switch languages because they don't have the ability to proceed in the original language. From such a perspective, multilingual code-switching is unsystematic, and can happen at arbitrary points in an utterance. The evidence strongly suggests that this is not the case: code-switching appears to be constrained by general organizing principles which are independent of particular languages (e.g. Myers-Scotton 1993) or which arise automatically from the interaction of the grammars involved (MacSwann 2004). For example, in Table 16.1 the Farsi words in sentence (2) appear in the right order for Farsi within the **noun phrase**, and the noun phrase itself is in the right English order with respect to the English verb of which it is direct object (➜ 7.5.3).

Finally, multilingual code-switching is not (only) the result of speakers being unable to find the expression they need fast enough in the language they start out speaking. On some occasions switching will occur to compensate for the speaker's lack of, or difficulty accessing, appropriate resources. But also, it can represent, among other things:

- an accommodation strategy, to enhance hearers' understanding (for instance when they are more familiar with a topic in one of their two languages, e.g. work issues)
- cases of increasing rapport, when strangers meet and shift to a common language they were initially unaware that they shared
- a marker of status, to indicate higher education levels (e.g. switching to English by Cantonese speakers in Hong Kong to get better service in a restaurant)
- a detachment strategy, to voice issues which might cause more emotional stress in the dominant language (Altarriba and Morier 2004: 258–261)
- a group identity/solidarity marker, for example the mixing of Turkish with a majority European language by immigrant children in the host country (Backus 2004: 700–711).

See Baker (2011: 107–110) for a list of thirteen social and communicative causes and functions of multilingual code-switching.

16.4.2 Language choice

The linguistic choices we make, some conscious, some unconscious, are influenced, and sometimes determined, by social factors such as the situation we are participating in, the other people involved and their relation to us, the meanings we are making and expressing, and our own personal histories and identities (➜ R3.1). Multilingual individuals choose between their languages depending on factors like these. It may depend on custom and practice throughout the duration of a friendship or on patterns set in childhood, where maybe one language is used in the home and another for all interactions outside the home (common in sequential bilinguals). Or it may simply depend on how fluent the interlocutors are in the relevant languages. We have seen in the last couple of sections that multilinguals deploy their language resources adaptably and creatively, in tandem or separately, according to context.

For many simultaneous and early sequential bilinguals, this linguistic resourcefulness is established very early on, in the family. Very often it is affected by deliberate choices made by both parents and children. The following is an account of a bilingual family by Martin Rhys from Wales, from a BBC series forming part of the Language in the National Curriculum project (LINC Coordinators 1992: 303–304):

In a bilingual family like mine, the language we speak to each other is very much part of the relationship between us.

[...] Both my mother's and father's families were entirely Welsh speaking – by that I mean my father and mother would have been brought up speaking only Welsh at home. English would have been acquired from school and people outside the family.

Oddly enough, though, my parents speak English to each other. They met when both were working on the railways during the war, and it seems that English was the language of the workplace. It also became the language of courtship, and then marriage.

Both speak Welsh to my grandmother, who has lived with them since the death of my grandfather.

They also brought me up speaking Welsh. Like them, my first taste of English was very much as a second language.

My wife Marianne, however, comes from the north west of England. Our children, Steffan and Lowri, have been brought up from the start speaking both Welsh and English. Marianne speaks English to them – I speak Welsh. They speak English to each other – that was their choice.

Although Marianne had come to understand Welsh perfectly, the patterns (see Figure 16.3) were pretty much set. In Rhys's words: 'The language is part of the relationship. To change one could mean changing the other.'

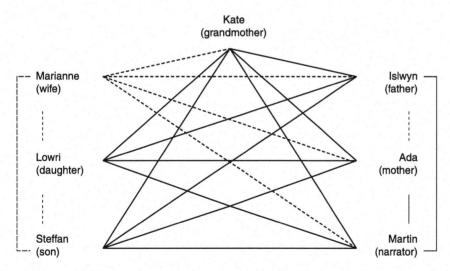

Key: bold lines = Welsh; dotted lines = English

Figure 16.3 Language use in a bilingual family. Adapted from LINC Coordinators (1992: 304)

Activity 16.5 🔑

Marta, a Greek Cypriot teacher of English, was asked which language she used with different members of her family. In her response, what different reasons does she identify for choosing which language to use?

> It depends who I am talking to. I mean with my sisters, if I ring them up I speak in English. If I ring my mother up, I speak Cypriot … Because I've just got used to speaking English with my sisters … If we are all together, I think we just hop from one language to the other. Maybe with my older sisters I tend to speak more Greek because their Greek is better whereas with my younger sister who hardly speaks any Greek it is more natural to speak in English. With my parents … sometimes we might say something in English but it sounds unnatural…. If we talk about the home for example, kitchen language, then I am much more comfortable with Greek language because obviously we've been exchanging comments with my mother and we've always spoken Greek so it's easier and maybe if I discuss education or teaching English then maybe I feel more comfortable speaking English.

16.5 SOCIETAL MULTILINGUALISM

We have concentrated so far on individual multilinguals, but as the last examples demonstrate, the use of more than one language is of course a feature of groups of individuals, from families like Rhys's and Marta's to groups of nations like the European Union. In this section we bridge the gap between individual and larger societies, introducing the important concept of diglossia, and then go on to discuss multilingualism at state and multi-state levels.

16.5.1 Diglossia

The term **diglossia** (from the Greek word for 'bilingual' ➔ 12, 13.3.5) was coined by Ferguson (1959) to refer to situations in which two or more language varieties are used systematically within a community for distinct social situations and purposes. Ferguson's work was extended by Fishman (2000 [1967]) to, in the words of Hoffmann (1991: 167), 'include different dialects, vernaculars or classical varieties, as well as distinct languages – so long as they are functionally differentiated'. Crystal (1997: 43) defines *diglossia* as 'a language situation in which markedly divergent varieties, each with its own set of social functions, coexist as standards throughout a community'. In a diglossic situation, linguists recognize one language or variety as the 'H' variety (for *high*) and the other as 'L' (for *low*). H is the prestigious one. It is used in formal contexts such as business, the courts and education. L is the non-prestigious one used in more informal circumstances – at home among the family and between friends. Examples often cited (Ferguson 1959; Hoffman 1991; Romaine 1989; Holmes 2001) include: Switzerland, where H is Standard

German and L the various dialects of Swiss German; the Middle East, where H is classical Arabic and L the local varieties of the different Arab nations; or Paraguay, where Spanish is used as H and the indigenous language Guaraní as L. Bilingual individuals in diglossic countries thus have bilingual communicative competence of the sort alluded to by Grosjean (2008): H and L coexist and complement each other in the speaker's mind, in the same way that jumping and running skills coexist and complement each other in the hurdler.

Activity 16.6

Consider Marta's account below (from later in the conversation used in Activity 16.5) of the use of different varieties in Cyprus. To what extent might this be seen as a diglossic situation? How does it compare with the situation in your own country or region, where there may be various dialects and a standard variety used in formal writing and other contexts?

> If a Cypriot speaks to a Greek in the dialect, the Greeks won't understand a thing. However, a Cypriot can communicate with a Greek through the standard language because the language of education is standard Greek. All our literature is written in the standard Greek language. We've got some Cypriot dialect written down but it's difficult to read because the writers have had to make a sort of letter combination in order to represent the Cypriot sounds which are not usually Greek combinations. And there is some literature in the dialect. The dialect is usually used in the family and it would sound very strange should we use the mainland language among the family or friends. Sometimes people try to use the mainland language among a circle of friends – they are usually laughed at because they sound very pompous … . With colleagues we usually speak the dialect. However, if I go, for example, to a government office I will start off speaking the mainland language or something that resembles the mainland language and then maybe revert back to the Cypriot dialect.

16.5.2 State multilingualism

During the Middle Ages, up until the time of the Renaissance, national languages were *talked* but not much *talked about*. Certainly the elites would be aware that the way they talked in their city or tribe or kingdom distinguished them from others, but there was little awareness of how language could project the power of dominant groups. The realization that language could be used as a tool to centralize royal authority in emerging states ultimately led to the currently widespread belief in the naturalness of 'one language, one nation' (➔ 18.7 for English). A key moment in the development of this idea was when Cardinal Richelieu founded in 1635 the *Académie Française*, to 'fix' one form of French as the only language of the (actually multilingual) French state. This is an early example of **language policy and planning** (the process of making decisions and choices about language use), at the level of the state.

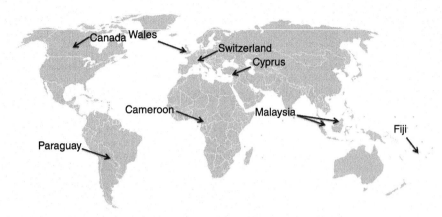

Figure 16.4 The location of some of the multilingual states mentioned in this chapter

Recently, language policy and planning has been harnessed to enhance linguistic diversity rather than reduce it. For example, Welsh is recouping its status in the principality of Wales after centuries of suppression by governments based in London, largely because of official support from the recently established devolved government in the capital, Cardiff. Figures from the 2001 UK census and a 2004 survey conducted by the Welsh Language Board reveal a significant increase in the numbers of Welsh speakers compared with the 1991 census (Welsh Language Board 2003, 2006). Here are some of the major findings:

- In Wales as a whole, 21.7 per cent of the population are able to speak Welsh, according to the 2004 survey, compared with 20.8 per cent in the 2001 census and 18.7 per cent in the 1991 census.
- Sixty-two per cent use Welsh on a daily basis, according to the 2004 survey.
- The largest segment of the population to speak Welsh is the children (40.8 per cent of children aged between five and 15 according to the 2001 census).

Whilst variation in use across Wales is notable, the presence of the language is immediately perceptible when you cross the border from England. Welsh is a major part of the linguistic landscape: it accompanies English on all road signs, is available along with English in the provision of services, both public and private (including healthcare), and is a well-established medium for artistic expression. It is now fully protected and promoted by legislation, following the model that has long existed in Canada to protect and promote the rights of French and English speakers there. The most recent legislation to strengthen Welsh in Wales is the *Welsh Language (Wales) Measure* 2011, which reaffirms the official status of Welsh in Wales and provides for the creation of a Welsh Language Commissioner, to 'promote and facilitate the use of the Welsh language' (Welsh Language Measure 2011).

16.6 TWO CASE STUDIES

We end our discussion of multilingualism with two case studies of multilingual states. Case studies can serve various purposes: they can act as models for your own research (see the activities at the end of this chapter) and they can provide interesting contextualized information about your object of study. As you read them, notice how the historical context informs and, in many ways, explains the current situation and also how different the situation in one country can be from that in another – even though both are considered multilingual. Whilst the two case studies are only brief, they do indicate the kind of information that you need to search for to carry out any of the activities which follow. Such information can be gleaned from good encyclopaedias, with print or online resources on the relevant country, and on world languages in general, to provide greater depth. To find relevant detail for the following case studies, we typed 'official languages in [name of country]' into a search engine and found a wealth of interesting and relevant information to follow up.

16.6.1 Cameroon

The historical context

Before any Europeans arrived in what is now the Republic of Cameroon, the region was inhabited by many different groups, each with their own language and customs. It is thought by some researchers that the now dominant Bantu family of languages had its origins in the borderlands between Cameroon and Nigeria (Collins 1993). Islam had spread from North Africa into the northern parts of Cameroon with the invasions of the Fula people in the late eighteenth century. There is still a significant number of Muslims in the northern areas. The Fula were in constant conflict with the indigenous kingdom of Mandara, speakers of an Afro-Asiatic language of the same name, until the region came under European control at the end of the nineteenth century.

The Portuguese were the first of the European powers to arrive, in the late fifteenth century, and there is a story that the name of the country derives from the arriving sailors' shouts of *camarões* ('shrimp') in their amazement at the size of the giant shrimp widely available. For the next 400 years, Cameroon's history, like that of most of the countries of West Africa, was intimately bound up with the slave trade and its aftermath. Missionaries also played a significant role in the development of the country. The Germans established a protectorate over the area in 1884 and were instrumental in developing a railway network and an education system. After the First World War, the country was divided between the French and the British in an arrangement subsequently confirmed by the United Nations after the Second World War. The French had control of the larger eastern part of the country and the British two smaller parts in the west. After a referendum in 1961, the northern part of West Cameroon chose to join Nigeria and the southern part of West Cameroon opted to join East Cameroon as a single country.

The current language situation

Each of the groups in Cameroon has their own language and there are now over 270 languages in use throughout the country, according to *Ethnologue* (Lewis 2009). As we have seen, one effective way of forging nationhood is through the declaration and promotion of a national language. In Cameroon, however, to choose between the colonial languages was not going to be practical, given the equal balance between them. So there are two

Ethnologue is a compendium of the world's languages maintained and published (in print and online) by the missionary organization *SIL International* → W16.2

official languages: English and French. Wolf (2001: 152) claims that to the best of his knowledge 'Cameroon is the only African state with two official languages which are geographically distributed and, beside Rwanda, the only one with English and French as joint official languages'. He also argues (2001: 217) that 'to speak of bilingualism may be an understatement … and *multilingualism* may characterise the situation better'. It is clear that educated speakers in what was formerly French Cameroon still tend to use French (to be *Francophone*) rather than English, and those in the former British Cameroon tend to use English (to be *Anglophone*). Wolf quotes at length (2001: 219), from Spreda's then unpublished thesis, a description of a typical day of language use for a male Anglophone Cameroonian. In this account, quoted below, PE is used as an abbreviation for Pidgin English (➔ 18.6), widely spoken throughout Cameroon and West Africa as a lingua franca (➔ 18.7).

> The educated urban West Cameroonian is multilingual, usually speaking at least three languages in the course of a day. As marriages are generally intra-ethnic, the language of the home is usually the language of the ethnic background. With other Cameroonians of the same background and education he will speak the common indigenous language, often with some code-switching. With anglophone Cameroonians of another ethnic background he will speak either Educated Cameroonian English or Cameroonian Pidgin English, depending on the situation. PE will be used with someone with little education but also as a language of intimacy with those of a similar educational background, for example in the teachers' common room in a school. Should he be resident in the francophone area of Cameroon, he will usually speak French with those of comparable educational background, and in every day business in shops and in public transport, French is also necessary.

From this account, it appears that choice of language remains with the individual based on his/her perception of their interlocutor. Social issues such as intimacy, respect, educational background and language purpose will all inform the decision about which language to use. Wolf comments (2001: 221) that 'bilingualism does not exist in an all-or-nothing manner' and he quotes research from others to show that, in Cameroon, English–French bilingualism can 'range from near perfect bilingualism to near-zero bilingualism'. It is important to note that the English part of the English–French bilingualism is itself a continuum from Pidgin English through to Standard Cameroonian English, which has many features of American English (➔ 18). The presence of American English features may well stem from a period of history when many of the teachers in Anglophone Cameroon secondary schools were US Peace Corps volunteers.

Within Cameroon, both French and English have equal status in law, but whether this equality extends to actual language use is debatable: do all Francophone Cameroonians use English to the same extent as Anglophone Cameroonians use French? Kouega (2002: 112) doubts this and wonders whether 'what has been going on in the country since Reunification some forty years ago has not been a one-way expansion of bilingualism, with speakers of English operating increasingly or fully in French, but their French-speaking counterparts remaining largely monolingual'. The situation in Cameroon is interesting because, if Kouega is right, the use of English does not seem to be increasing within the country and that is in sharp contrast to the position of English in many other parts of the world (➔18).

Finally, what of the role of Cameroon's indigenous languages? Although Fulfulde is still used as a language of wider communication in the Muslim north, the indigenous languages are generally restricted to oral interaction in the family and local community. Primary education is either in English or French (with most secondary schools now bilingual English and French). The fact that there is no first language education for many Cameroonians, and that most do not progress to secondary school, means not only that they have less ability to participate in national life, but also that most indigenous languages are now in danger of disappearing for good. One study (cited in Echu 2004) suggests that over 30 per cent of teenagers in the capital, Yaoundé, cannot speak an indigenous language at all. This is an example of subtractive bilingual education leading to **language shift**, and maybe **language death**. The following case study, on Fiji, contrasts with Cameroon quite dramatically in this regard.

16.6.2 Fiji

The historical context

Archaeological evidence shows that Fiji was first inhabited about 3,500 years ago, but we need not go so far back in history for developments relevant to the current bilingual situation. Up until European and Indian settlement in the nineteenth century, a number of different languages of the Austronesian language family were spoken on the island nation. Standard Fijian emerged from the eastern group, and is now spoken by most indigenous Fijians, but English and Standard Hindi are now the other official languages of the republic.

Tent (2001: 210–211) relates the history of the islands from colonial times and a summary of his account is presented here. In the early nineteenth century, the first non-indigenous inhabitants who introduced English to the islands were 'deserters, marooned sailors and runaway convicts' who 'settled and became beachcombers'. Commercial interest in the islands was increased by traders in *bêche-de-mer* (sea cucumber) and sandalwood, and then in 1835 the first missionaries arrived. With the establishment of churches and schools with Fijian as the medium of instruction there was, as yet, no imposition of English on the indigenous population. In the 1870s the earlier stability of the islands and their peoples was threatened by imperialist interests of France and the USA which inevitably led to internal political pressures. In 1874 Fiji became a Crown colony of Great Britain until 1970 when it gained independence.

The linguistic situation is complex and Tent (2001: 210–211) is the central source of information in what follows. In the early 1930s, English became 'the official language of instruction after class three' but 'Fijian was generally the medium of communication in the colonial administration' and 'was mandatory for British civil servants'. When some 60,000 Indian labourers were indentured (➔ 18.2) between 1879–1917, Hindi (and Urdu) arrived on the Fijian linguistic scene. Most of the labourers decided to stay when their period of indenture was over, and now Indo-Fijians represent around 37 per cent of the population (Fiji Islands Bureau of Statistics 2007). British civil servants were 'encouraged to learn Hindi' and by 1928 all were allowed to 'meet their language requirements

LANGUAGE SHIFT occurs when a society, more or less gradually or abruptly, adopts a new language, normally one associated with greater economic and political power and prestige. If the old language is not spoken elsewhere and the last speaker gives it up or dies, then LANGUAGE DEATH has occurred.

Linguistically, Hindi and Urdu are variants of the same language. The former is associated with Hindus, especially in India, and is written in a script called Devanagari. The latter is associated with Muslims, especially in Pakistan, and is written in a Persian variant of Arabic script.

in either Fijian or Hindi' (Siegel 1989 cited in Tent 2001: 211). At this time 'the use of English to communicate with Fijians and Indians was strongly discouraged by the authorities' but then a 'sudden influx of teachers from New Zealand' in the 1930s who 'did not know the local languages, were not keen to learn them or inclined to use any language other than English' led to English becoming the medium of instruction in the school system. At this stage, English started to gain prestige in the islands at the expense of the Fijian language and was 'promoted by the colonial authorities in the belief that it would serve as a "neutral" lingua franca allowing Fijians and Indo-Fijians to live together harmoniously' (➔ 18.7).

Activity 16.7

Why do you think the word *neutral* appears in "scare quotes" in the previous sentence?

Upon independence in 1970, the government decided on a policy in which initial schooling would be via Hindi or Fijian (representing the first language of most), with English introduced after three years as the medium of instruction for literacy development and all other subjects. The extent to which schools followed this policy is questionable, however, and doubt has been cast on the efficacy of the strategy, as the following section explains.

The current language situation

Although English remains the principal official language and major lingua franca, there has been a significant move away from English as the sole legitimate medium for engagement in national life. Following years of tensions between the dominant ethnic groups, the 1997 constitution provided for Fijian and Hindi to 'have equal status in the State' with English. But there is now increasing realization that the linguistic situation in Fiji is more complex than the apparently straightforward notion of a trilingual state suggests. For one thing, a total of ten currently spoken living languages are listed in *Ethnologue* for Fiji (Lewis 2009), distinguishing Western Fijian from Standard Fijian, and including other indigenous languages like Lauan and Rotuman spoken on island dependencies. Furthermore, the Standard Fijian and Standard Hindi used in schools are very different from the varieties spoken by most Fijians. Shameem (2002) points out that the reality is one of diglossia, and observes that the local 'L' varieties are so different from the standard varieties that in fact many speakers of Fiji Hindi adopt English for 'H' functions instead of Standard Hindi, which they have difficulty using (➔ 16.5.1).

There is considerable debate about whether greater protection should be given to the Fijian language. It is felt by many that recognition of language rights can play an important role in defusing the interethnic conflict that has characterized much of Fijian history since independence. A 2009 news item reports the views of Rajesh Chandra, the Vice-Chancellor of the country's main university, expressed at an event to celebrate World Hindi Day (Fijilive 2009):

'We [Indo-Fijians] are fortunate that due to our contact with India, the Hindi language is not facing any difficulty, Hindi literature is progressing in India; the popularity of Bollywood is further protecting Hindi and Indian culture.' [...] 'Fijian does not have all these opportunities. To promote and preserve Fijian, Fiji alone has to work hard.' Chandra said that with the fear among indigenous Fijians that their language may become extinct, 'it is our shared responsibility to help strengthen and preserve both these languages. The protection and preservation of the indigenous Fijian language will benefit the two ethnic groups by promoting unity and cohesion, thus creating a better future for all people of Fiji. [...].'

The current government is taking steps to protect and promote the Fijian language, creating an organization to fulfil this function, the *iTaukei Institute of Language and Culture*, and also 'rebranding' the indigenous language and ethnicity itself by replacing references to 'indigenous Fijian' with the indigenous term *iTaukei*.

16.8 SUMMARY

This chapter has explored multiple dimensions of multilingualism, in individuals, families, local communities, and nation states. We have emphasized how multilingual speakers' linguistic repertoires and behaviour respond to and exploit local communicative needs and opportunities, reflect group identities, and confer cognitive benefits. We have also discussed multilingualism in the context of educational policy and national language planning, providing extended case studies of two multilingual states. Taken as a whole, we think the account we have given demonstrates that far from being a curse, as in the biblical story of Babel, it is the positive message of the Pentecost story that most fittingly characterizes the role of multilingualism in today's globalized individuals and societies.

16.9 FURTHER ACTIVITIES

Activity 16.8

There are four national languages in Switzerland – German, French, Italian and Romansch – but only three have official language status: German, French and Italian. It is unlikely that any individual Swiss citizen is a balanced quadrilingual. The languages are largely divided regionally and the history of the country explains the geographical distribution of the language use across the country.

Language rights are written into the Swiss constitution together with provisions to ensure support in the relevant cantons for Romansch and Italian. However, despite the officially recognized and supported multilingualism, there are those who would argue that the country is no longer quadrilingual and that use of the official languages is fading with a preference developing for the use of English. In particular, there is concern about the continuing use of Romansch.

Using the case studies in 16.6 as a model, investigate the current linguistic situation in Switzerland. Here are some questions you might like to address:

- How many people speak each language?
- How many are monolingual, bilingual, trilingual or quadrilingual?
- Do the different kinds of mono- and multilingualism co-vary with canton, rural or urban context, age, education level, socioeconomic class, or other factor(s)?
- What language rights are legally protected? How?
- What measures are being taken to safeguard Romansch?
- What arguments are made for the promotion and protection of Romansch? (Do you agree with them? Why (not)?)

Activity 16.9

One of the most complex linguistic situations is currently to be found in South Africa, where language planning policies post-apartheid have had a clear political dimension. Start with the official websites for the government of South Africa to discover what languages are accorded official and/or national language status, how many other languages there are in use in the country, and why some languages were chosen for wider use and others not. Then see if you can track actual usage by investigating NGOs, blogs, discussion forums, university staff homepages, and other non-governmental Internet sites.

Other countries are also worth researching. Finland, Hong Kong, Israel, New Zealand, Papua New Guinea and the USA will all provide illuminating information about language policies and multilingual situations.

Activity 16.10

Within so-called monolingual countries there are increasingly large multilingual communities, such as Bradford, Manchester or London in the United Kingdom, New York and Los Angeles in the United States, Paris and Marseilles in France. Explore which languages are used in each city within daily interactions and try to explain how and why the language choices are made by those living in the city. Check local government websites to see what multilingual services might be offered.

This activity is not only possible in relation to large cities. One casual conversation with one of the authors' friends who lives in a village in North Yorkshire in the UK revealed many multilingual families living in village communities in the more rural areas of that apparently monolingual county. Choose a community (e.g. school, village, town, friendship group) and by interviewing community members, find out:

- how many languages are known and used in the community and by whom
- how frequently or regularly each language is used
- what percentage of the community uses which language(s)
- for what purpose individuals choose to use any one language of their repertoire.

COMMENTARY ON ACTIVITIES

O—ᴛ Remember that this symbol indicates that there is a commentary on the activity that you can find on the companion website at www.routledge.com/cw/merrison.

FURTHER READING and REFERENCES

Suggestions for further reading on the topics discussed in this chapter can be found on the companion website (www.routledge.com/cw/merrison).

Any piece of academic writing must always provide a list of publications to which reference has been made. Unusually and very unconventionally, this information is provided on the companion website (www.routledge.com/cw/merrison). Always ask your tutor about how you are to present references for any piece of work that you submit.

Chapter 17
History of English

Key Ideas in this Chapter

- Language changes all the time – even in relatively short time frames.
- Modern English has its roots in Middle English and Old English.
- What came before Old English?
- Many of the words that are used in every day English in the twenty-first century could be found in the earliest forms of the language.
- What do we mean when we talk of the history of a language?

Figure 17.1 Cool

Figure 17.2 Mouse

Look at these pictures and then do Activity 17.1 before you start reading the chapter.

Activity 17.1

For each word illustrated at the beginning of this chapter consider the following questions:

1 Do you use the word to mean the same thing every time you use it? Whether you use it to mean the same thing or not, what meanings do you express with each word?

2 Does the word mean the same thing for you and for your grandparents, your parents and your friends? How do their uses of each word differ from yours?

17.1 INTRODUCTION

What is history? The same events can be narrated in different ways depending on the writer's point of view. Milroy (➜ R2.5) considers how the story of English could have been told in other ways – in other words, the English language could have been given a different history.

For all its current status in the world (➜ 18), the English language is only about 1,500 years old and was pretty much confined to the British Isles until around 500 years ago; but it has changed enormously in that length of time. In this chapter we will consider the changes in English over time and we will work backwards from Modern English, which you know and use, to Old English which looks very different from Modern. Modern English (ModE) dates from about 1500AD. The period of Middle English (ME) is from 1100AD −1500AD and the forms of the language used between 450AD −1100AD are referred to as Old English (OE). All these dates are approximate, of course, and nobody would suggest that in a single given year the language changed radically; but the dates serve as useful staging posts in the development – or the history – of English.

One of the main purposes of this book is to consider the sheer variety of forms of English (➜ 12) now in the twenty-first century. That there is such variety poses a dilemma for teachers of English: which form(s) should children be taught in school and encouraged to use? Some people think that there was a "golden age" of English at the time of Shakespeare – and in the UK some education leaders argue that all children should be made to read his plays at school. Some even argue that children should use Shakespeare's writing as a model for their own. In the light of what you know about the English language in use, what position would you take in that debate? In the UK national press, you will frequently see letters to the editor bemoaning the changing use of **lexical items** (➜ 5) – such as those illustrated at the beginning of this chapter.

> ## Activity 17.2
>
> Ask your parents, your grandparents or older friends and acquaintances what changes in language they have noticed in their lifetimes.

ETYMOLOGY is the study of the history of words and their formation. Exploring such matters using online etymological dictionaries (e.g. Read Me! ➜ W17.1) may prove far more interesting and even entertaining than it might initially sound! Try using the Google Ngram viewer (W17.2).

As you will see later in this chapter, OE looks almost like a foreign language to anyone nowadays trying to read an OE text but there are still many words in use in the twenty-first century which date from that era. It is also true that many OE words have dropped out of regular use, such as kith, now obsolete other than in the compound noun phrase kith and kin (meaning one's friends and relations); churl used, if at all in ModE, only in its adjective form, churlish; or shrive now used almost exclusively in the name Shrove Tuesday; but many core words in ModE (e.g. he, man, live) do have OE roots. ME is more recognizable to the modern reader but there are still points where the meaning or the usage of a word has changed or where the syntax strikes the modern reader as non-standard. ModE is very familiar but it is still clear that the language has changed from the 1500s and the term Early Modern English is often given to the period from 1500–1700. In any text that you read, what proportion of the words do you think come from each of the major periods listed above? Just guess first of all and then check your estimate against what you find out when you do Activity 17.3.

Activity 17.3 🔑

Look up the words in the following paragraph in a good dictionary (➜ Read Me!) to find when each word was first recorded in the written language. This is the beginning of the first paragraph of *Northanger Abbey* by Jane Austen (1775–1817):

> No one who had ever seen Catherine Morland in her infancy, would have supposed her born to be an heroine. Her situation in life, the character of her father and mother; her own person and disposition, were all equally against her. Her father was a clergyman, without being neglected, or poor, and a very respectable man, though his name was Richard – and he had never been handsome. He had a considerable independence, besides two good livings – and he was not in the least addicted to locking up his daughters. Her mother was a woman of useful plain sense, with a good temper, and, what is more remarkable, with a good constitution.

17.2 MODERN ENGLISH (c.1500– PRESENT DAY)

Other chapters in this book provide a clear description of current Modern English. A reader of Jane Austen's or Charles Dickens' novels will not normally have problems in understanding their variety of English (➜ 12), other than where words have changed their meaning, as was apparent in the Austen text used in Activity 17.3. Readers may have difficulties where the authors are describing social customs that are no longer practised or may not understand a particular reference (to the name *Richard*, for example, in *Northanger Abbey* in Activity 17.3) but in such cases, the problem is not with the language but in our understanding of the cultural references. In this chapter, texts from the earlier period of Modern English will be considered, where the modern reader might have more difficulties with the language itself, not just with the ideas. In Act III, Scene 2 of *Hamlet* by William Shakespeare (1564–1616), the eponymous hero directs some visiting players (*actors in contemporary ModE*) on how they are to deliver the speech that Hamlet has written for them to insert into their play:

Hamlet:	Speak the speech, I pray you, as I pronounced it to you,
2	trippingly on the tongue. But if you mouth it as many of our
	players do, I had as lief the town crier spoke my lines. Nor do not
4	saw the air too much with your hand, thus. But use all gently. For in
	the very torrent, tempest, and, as I may say, whirlwind of your
6	passion, you must acquire and beget a temperance that may give it
	smoothness. O, it offends me to the soul to hear a robustious
8	periwig-pated fellow tear a passion to tatters, to very rags, to split
	the ears of the groundlings, who for the most part are capable of

10   nothing but inexplicable dumb shows and noise. I would have such
            a fellow whipped for o'erdoing Termagant. It out-Herods Herod.
12   Pray you avoid it.

Activity 17.4

Put Hamlet's speech into English appropriate for the twenty-first century before
you read the next paragraph.

No matter how you have rewritten or rephrased the speech, some **lexical** (➔ 5) changes
are predictable. It is most unlikely that you kept the word *lief* (L3 meaning 'rather' and used
with *have* to express preference) and it is described as obsolete in the Oxford English
Dictionary (OED). Similarly described in the OED as obsolete are *periwig* (L8 from the French
'perruque' meaning a wig) and *pated* (L8) which meant the top of the head in ME but which,
according to the OED, is 'not now in serious or dignified use'). Archaic according to the OED
is the word *robustious* (L7), though the later coinage of *rumbustious* is still in use, if relatively
rarely. *To split the ears* (L8–9) is perhaps less often used in this V + Cdo (➔ 7) form but it is
still heard, if indirectly, as a participial/**adjective** form, *ear-splitting*. *Groundlings* (L9), meaning
those who frequented the pit of the theatre, has its first appearance in *Hamlet* (OED) though
the same form is used to talk of small fish both before and after this theatrical meaning was
attached to the word. The use of *beget* (L6) is now limited to a religious register and *temperance*
(L6) was a dated word at the turn of the millennium – perhaps because in some Western
societies the idea itself is now dated and out of fashion. It is also unlikely that any rewriting
talked of having somebody whipped, unless they were using the word metaphorically
(➔ R2.6) as in many societies that would now be considered socially unacceptable.

It is not only the lexis that has changed, however. The double negative of *Nor do not saw
the air* (L3–4) is unlikely to have found its way into the rewriting of the speech if that
rewriting was into Standard British English. The double negative has been a stigmatized
form (though still frequently used in dialects (➔ 12)) since Lowth's Grammar of 1762
(Crystal 2003: 79). Shakespeare's use of the proper noun *Herod* (L11) as a verb (startlingly
and creatively innovative at the time of writing) will pass most modern readers by
completely and will almost certainly have been omitted from any rewriting as will the
reference to *Termagant*, an imaginary deity from medieval times.

Looking at the original scripts of Shakespeare's plays, there are clearly different spellings of the same word – indeed Shakespeare is known to have spelt his own name in
several different ways. Despite the earlier advent of the printing press, there was still some
time to go before the spelling of English became fixed and settled, though it is noticeable
that there are still variations in spelling and word forms. American English and British
English have some systematic differences in spelling such as *theatre*/*theater* or *colour*/*color* and
there are some variations in spelling according to meaning e.g. *programme*/*program*. Samuel
Johnson's dictionary, first published in 1755, is generally regarded as the first authoritative dictionary of the English Language in that it provides examples of usage as well as
definitions of meaning and the spelling of words.

'Verbing' nouns is a
frequent phenomenon in
language use: consider *to
diary* or *to transition* in
business-speak or *to medal*
or *to podium* in Olympic
Games-speak (this is called
CONVERSION ➔ 5.5.2). What
other examples have you
come across?

Despite some inaccuracies,
Ink and Incapability in the
third series of Blackadder
(BBC TV – available on
YouTube) provides an
entertaining insight into
how dictionaries might be
compiled and some food
for thought on how they
ought to be compiled.

17.3 MIDDLE ENGLISH c.1100–1500
17.3.1 Historical background

Whilst the language used by Shakespeare is different from that used in later centuries, it is much more familiar to modern ears than the language used by Chaucer (c.1343–1400) which will be considered shortly. In Shakespeare's language, as in many words in ModE, there are letters in the spelling that are not pronounced, as in *tongue* or *knight*. We know they were not pronounced from evidence such as rhymes in verse. In ME, however, almost every letter in a word was pronounced. There have constantly been changes in the pronunciation of English and such changes still occur (as in the current rise of so-called ESTUARY ENGLISH and the increasing use of the intervocalic glottal stop (➔10)). During the ME and early ModE period, there was a systematic sound shift in the long vowels of English, a shift now referred to as the 'great vowel shift' (GVS). Freeborn (1992: 128) explains that while there was 'variation between regional and social dialect speakers, … in time all the long vowels were either raised or became diphthongs'. An example might help: before GVS *mouse* (the vowel is now a diphthong ➔10.3) was pronounced the same as *moose*. Freeborn links this to the ModE writing system when he comments that, in English, the 'spelling system has never been altered to fit the changed pronunciations. Consequently, the sound of the short **vowels**, represented by the letters <a> <e> <i> <o> <u>, has remained more or less the same, while the sounds of the long vowels no longer match the letters' and this explains the different pronunciations of <oo> in, for example, *blood, good* and *food* (➔ 10).

Historically, this section on Middle English (1100–1500) must begin with the Norman invasion onto the south coast of England in 1066, in what is chronologically still the OE period. However, the effects of the Normans' arrival on the English language do not really manifest themselves until well into the twelfth century. Edward the Confessor had been on the English throne for 23 years, having retaken it from the Scandinavian kings and, on his death, the throne passed to Harold II who reigned for only ten months before his death in 1066 at the Battle of Hastings. In his reign, he had been beset by invasions from Scandinavia to the north of his kingdom and earlier invasions from France to the south. The political outcomes were serious but more important for the concerns of this book are the effects on the English language of this last invasion onto English soil.

17.3.2 The language of the period

The explosion of vocabulary as a result of the **borrowing** (➔ 16, 18, R2.7) of French words into English is one explanation for the number of near synonyms in Modern English: *big* (ME unknown origin perhaps from Scandinavian), *large* (ME from Old French (OF)) and *great* (OE); or *king* (OE) and *monarch* (ME from OF); *kingly* (OE) and *regal* and *royal* (both OF); *guard* (OF) and *ward* (OE).

With the arrival of the Norman king, William the Conqueror, it is hardly surprising that Norman French became the language of the English court and this continued for about two centuries. French therefore became the language of the aristocracy and the upper classes of the society of the time. Baugh and Cable assert that French 'was used in Parliament, in the law courts, in public negotiations generally' (2013: 130). However,

The inconsistency in ModE between phonetic and orthographic forms of English words can cause significant problems for many users of English and for second language learners in particular (➔ 15).

ESTUARY ENGLISH is spoken mostly in London and the surrounding southern counties of England. It is regarded by some as a new linguistic phenomenon and by others as an(other) example of an accent spreading from London to the surrounding areas and then even more widely.

While such synonyms do share essentially the same meaning, they are often used with slightly different connotations or in different contexts: for example what is the difference between *a big toe* and *a large toe*? Work through other examples that come to mind.

they also argue that 'English was widely known among all classes of people, though not necessarily by everyone' (2013: 133). The writers of the fourteenth century, among whom Baugh and Cable name Chaucer, Langland and Wycliffe, 'constitute a striking proof of the secure position the English language had attained' (2013: 150) by the end of that century. They argue (2013: 145) that by 'the fifteenth century the ability to speak French fluently seems to have been looked upon as an accomplishment' rather than as a necessity.

A social distinction between the use of French and English still appears, if indirectly, in Modern English. We keep *cows* (OE) and *pigs* (OE) in the *fields* (OE) but we eat *beef* (ME from OF) and *pork* (ME from OF) at the dining *table* (OE from OF and originally Latin). Similarly, we grow *potatoes* (ME from Spanish) in the fields, but rarely see potatoes by name on a menu: they are referred to in other ways often using French words to name the method of preparation e.g. *pommes de terre dauphinoises* or *pommes frites*. *Mansions* (ME from OF and originally Latin) and *houses* (OE) are lived in by people at different levels of society and such examples provide a clear indication of how words of French origin to some extent are still seen as privileged or preferred when compared with their OE near synonyms.

Mass production of written texts was unnecessary when the majority of the population could not read or write but the advent of the printing press (Caxton set up his first press in 1476) starts to settle the spelling of English. That the original spellings reflected the then current pronunciation of many words explains the apparently redundant letters in some modern spellings such as *though* or *knee* and also demonstrates how much the pronunciation of English has changed in the intervening centuries.

Wells-Cole (in Chaucer 1995: v) states that 'Chaucer is often regarded as the first English poet because he more or less turned the English language into an appropriate medium for poetry as his writing career progressed'. *The Canterbury Tales*, though incomplete at the time of Chaucer's death, is regarded as a masterpiece of English poetry largely because of the diversity of styles (➔ 8) found in the tales which are told by a group of fellow travellers during their pilgrimage from London to Canterbury. There is no manuscript still extant that is known to have been hand-written by Chaucer himself and so, as is the case for many ME and OE texts, there are various versions of the text. The Wife of Bath begins the *Prologue* of her tale thus (Chaucer 1995: 291):

To hear extracts from *The Canterbury Tales* and other OE and ME texts ➔ W17.3

1   'Experience, though noon auctoritee
2   Were in this world, were right y-nough to me
3   To speke of wo that is in mariage;
4   For, lordinges, sith I twelf yeer was of age,
5   Thonked be god that is eterne on lyve,
6   Housbondes at chirche-dore I have had fyve
7   For I so ofte have y-wedded be;
8   And alle were worthy men in hir degree.

Though most of this is comprehensible to the modern reader, there are still clear differences between this and later English writing. *The Canterbury Tales* is written in rhyming couplets, one feature that helps determine some of the pronunciation of ME. So, *mariage* and *age* (L3/L4), *lyve* and *fyve* (L5/L6) rhyme at the end of the lines as do the final vowel sounds in *auctoritee* and *me* (L1/L2). Noun plurals are mostly formed by adding the **suffix** {-s} and the irregular OE plural of *man* still remains in ModE (L8). *Yeer* when talking about age (L4) does not appear in the plural which may seem surprising until ModE phrases like *a five-year-old* are brought to mind. Verbs have a **prefix** (from OE) {y-/i-} on the past participle (L7) but what looks like the same **morpheme** in L2 is not prefixed to a verb – and is recognizable as an early spelling of *enough*. **Pronouns** are not the same as in ModE. *Hir* (L8) can only mean 'their'. *Alle* (L8) has a plural marker on it.

Now do Activity 17.5 before you read any further.

Activity 17.5 ⚷

The Wife of Bath's tale continues thus. Find examples of differences between Modern English as you know it and the text as presented here.

```
 9     But me was told certeyn, nat longe agon is,
10     That sith that Crist ne wente never but onis
11     To wedding in the Cane of Galilee,
12     That by the same ensample taughte he me
13     That I ne sholde wedded be but ones.
14      Herke eek, lo ! which a sharp word for the nones
15      Besyde a welle Jesus, god and man,
16     Spak in repreve of the Samaritan:
17     'Thou hast y-had fyve housbondes,' quod he,
18     'And thilke man, the which that hath now thee,
19     Is noght thyn housbond;' thus seyde he certeyn;
20     What that he mente ther-by, I can nat seyn;
21     But that I axe, why that the fifthe man
22     Was noon housbond to the Samaritan?
23     How manye myghte she have in mariage?
24     Yet herde I never tellen in myn age
25     Upon this nombre diffinicioun;
26     Men may devyne and glosen up and doun.
27     But wel I woot expres, with-oute lye,
28     God bad us for to wexe and multiplye;
29     That gentil text kan I wel understonde.
```

17.3.3 Middle English dialect boundaries

The dialect boundaries for ME (Figure 17.3) look very similar to broad dialect boundaries widely accepted in Modern English. Within the East Midlands dialect area, the **accent** spoken in the so-called "golden triangle" of London, Oxford and Cambridge provides the birthplace of Standard British English pronunciation (➔ 12.6), which has variously been labelled *Queen's English*, *BBC English* or *received pronunciation* (**RP**). Given that the three points of the triangle mark the two oldest seats of learning in England and the place of national government, it is perhaps hardly surprising that this accent developed into the prestigious accent. Crystal (2003: 365) claims that 'less

The Queen's English has changed markedly over her lifetime (➔12) and the BBC now encourages regional accents amongst its newsreaders. How helpful, therefore, are such labels as these when applied to the so-called prestige forms of English?

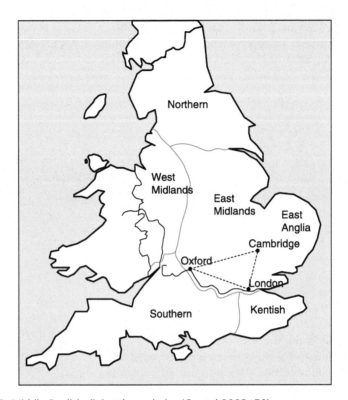

Figure 17.3 Middle English dialect boundaries (Crystal 2003: 50)

than 3% of the British people speak pure RP. Most educated people have developed an accent which is a mixture of RP and various regional characteristics – "modified RP", some call it'.

17.4 OLD ENGLISH c.450–1100
17.4.1 Historical background

Historically this period begins with the arrival of Angle, Saxon and Jute invaders from Germany in 449 after the withdrawal of the Roman armies. They came with the aim of dispossessing the Celts of their lands and they gradually pushed them to the west, towards what are now Wales and Cornwall. In time, the Anglo-Saxon kingdoms were formed by means of alliances between the local aristocrats or *eorlas* (from which the still-used title *earl* is derived) to improve resistance to invaders. The seven principal kingdoms that were finally established were Northumbria, Mercia, East Anglia, Kent, Essex, Sussex and Wessex and supremacy passed between them as the years passed. The OE dialect boundaries (Figure 17.4) can be linked to the borders between the kingdoms.

In the second half of this period in the eighth century, the Vikings invaded from Scandinavia. According to the *Anglo-Saxon Chronicle* (cited in Baugh and Cable 2013: 88),

Figure 17.4 Old English dialect boundaries (Crystal 2003: 28)

they arrived in 787 on the north-east coast of England and plundered the abbeys and monasteries, such as Lindisfarne and Jarrow. Later attacks were made on the coast of East Anglia and even the south coast of England: by the late 800s they were in charge of most of Eastern England. They turned to the west and were met by Alfred the Great and his armies and their incursions were halted. The Vikings were pushed back to a line roughly from Chester to London – and to the east of that line was known as the Danelaw as the people were subject to Danish law. Towards the end of the next century, there were further, more successful, incursions by the Danes onto the south-east coast of England and in the early 1000s there was a Danish king, King Canute, on the English throne for a period of about 20 years.

Such a summary does not indicate the number of Vikings who came and, even more importantly, who stayed, for whatever reasons, when their ships left to return home. The result of this is that there was also much peaceful interaction between the invaders and the indigenous population. They farmed neighbouring fields, they married each other and the incomers took part in local customs as well as introducing some traditions of their own. Inevitably, the two languages, which derive from the same branch of the Indo-European family (Germanic) started to influence each other and some of the features of OE which make it so different from any modern form of English came to be lost. The inflections (➔ 5) that appeared on nouns in OE began to disappear. The fact that there are now two very similar words in ModE, *shirt* and *skirt*, is due to the Viking influence: *shirt* comes from OE and *skirt* from Old Norse – and both words originally meant simply a garment.

17.4.2 The language of the period

In that eastern part of England which was ruled by the Danelaw, place names are frequently Scandinavian in origin. Near to York, its own name derived from the OE *Eoforwic*, the villages of Tholthorpe and Bishopthorpe both contain the Scandinavian Old Norse *thorpe* (village); Whitby and Helperby contain *by* (Old Norse (ON) for town). Kirkbymoorside contains *kirk* (ON church) and *by* with the OE *moor* (wasteland, marsh or mountain) and OE *side* (extending lengthways), a name (the town by/with the church on the side of the moor) which is both descriptive of itself and its location at the southern edge of the North York Moors. One might wonder whether the name itself is indicative of peaceful coexistence of two groups of people speaking different languages that were fast becoming merged.

Activity 17.6 0—ᴛ

Examine a map of the north-east part of England, the part of the country that was ruled by the Danelaw, and find examples of place-names with Scandinavian roots and of places with OE roots. Of particular interest will be those places where OE and Norse seem to have been merged in the name. A good dictionary will help you and Cameron (1996) will provide further information if needed.

Read the OE version of the Lord's Prayer (taken from Baugh and Cable 2013: 58) which is printed here and work out the meaning of the **clauses** (➔ 7). There are more modern versions of this central Christian prayer available on the Internet (put *Lord's Prayer* into a search engine to find other versions) which you could use if necessary to help you understand this OE version.

Fæder ūre,
þū þe eart on heofonum,
sī þīn nama gehālgod.
Tōbecume þīn rīce.
Gewurþe ðīn willa on eorðan swā swā on heofonum.
Ūrne gedæghwāmlīcan hlāf syle ūs tō dæg.
And forgyf ūs ūre gyltas, swā swā wē forgyfað ūrum gyltendum.
And ne gelǣd þū ūs on costnunge,
ac, ālȳs ūs of yfele. Sōþlīce.

To hear how this OE text sounds (➔ W17.4) or put *Old English Lord's Prayer* into a search engine and listen to one of the sound files that will be offered.

Graphology

The letters used in OE are not exactly the same as those used in ModE. The **consonant** letter forms that have now fallen out of use are <ð> (the letter was called *eth*; the form is now used as a phonetic symbol (➜ 10) and <þ> (called *thorn*) which represented both the sounds spelt in ModE with <th> (the OE characters were often used interchangeably though in later texts <þ> tended to appear at the beginning of words and <ð> at the end; they did not represent different pronunciations) and <ƿ> (called *wynn*) which represented the sound [w]. The letter <g> was sometimes written as <ᵹ>. The consonants <j>, <q>, <v>, and <z> do not appear in the OE alphabet. There were seven letters to represent vowels <a>, <e>, <i>, <o>, <u> and <y> which are still used but <æ> (called *ash*) no longer appears in ModE written text. The letter <y> is still used to represent vowel sounds in some ModE words such as *hymn* or *rhythm*.

Vocabulary

There were two words for the ModE *you*: *þû* (*thou*) for the second person singular (no longer used in ModE Standard English but still used in dialects (➜ 12)) and *ᵹê* (*ye*) for the plural form. Many modern function words (➜ 7) still in regular use in ModE are clearly evident. The OE forms for *our*, *on* and *and* are easily recognizable – though *on* might be translated in a modern version of the prayer in different ways. The OE word *rîce* (kingdom) is used as a bound morpheme in ModE in words like *bishopric* though it is no longer used as a free morpheme as here. The OE forms of many ModE words are easily found, for example, *heaven*, *guilt* and *today*. Other words are less closely related to any modern forms and have fallen out of use, though the meaning can still be discerned.

Vocabulary has to change over the centuries as there are new things to talk about (e.g. radios, televisions, computers). Identify some of the reasons why syntax and morphology also change over time.

Morphology

OE verbs are conjugated to agree with person and number (➜ 7) in the singular with the endings {-e}/{-(e)st}/{-(e)ð} for first, second and third person singular respectively, though in the plural a single form <að> was used with no variation for number. Some ModE dialect forms still use these inflections (➜ 7; ➜ 12).

OE nouns were masculine, feminine or neuter in grammatical gender. Nouns and pronouns were inflected for case (➜ 7) to show their function in the clause. Examples in this text include the second person singular pronoun, *þû* and *þin*, in nominative (as the subject of a clause ➜ 7) and genitive (possessive) case, respectively. Nouns are inflected to indicate case, *heofonum* and *gyltendum* being in dative case (Cio in a clause) and *constnunge* in accusative case (Cdo in a clause ➜ 7). Such inflections appear most noticeably in ModE within the pronoun system where the choice about which form of, for example, *I/me*, *he/him*, *we/us* to use in a sentence is determined by the role of the pronoun within the clause/sentence. The possessive case is still regularly marked in ModE nouns, as in, for example, *John's car*.

If a word consists of a single morpheme (e.g. *word*, *free*, or *guilt*, then that morpheme is a free morpheme. A bound morpheme such as {un} or {ing} can only appear in an English word if it is attached (bound) to another morpheme e.g. *unhappy, shining*.

Grammatical gender is a property of a noun and is displayed in the modifiers of any given noun. German has three grammatical genders: masculine e.g. *der Mond* (the moon), feminine e.g. *die Sonne* (the sun) and neutral, e.g. *das Land* (the land). Grammatical gender has nothing to do with meaning: in French the sun is grammatically masculine, *le soleil* and the moon grammatically feminine, *la lune*.

17.5 BEFORE OLD ENGLISH

This chapter has worked backwards through time to show how Modern English has emerged from its antecedent forms and it is quite possible for the quest to continue. Dictionary work for Activities 17.1 and 17.2 showed how the meaning of words in English have changed over the centuries and you will have noted as well how English words are derived from words in earlier languages as well as borrowing words from other contemporary languages. Latin and Greek as well as Old English have provided many words and **morphemes** now in use in Modern English, as a quick scan of any dictionary page will show.

Activity 17.7 0—⊤

1   Look at Table 1.2 on p. 15 for this activity. List words currently in use in Modern English which show that these ModE words could be seen as deriving from Latin or Greek. For example, the first morpheme in *hexagon*, a six-sided figure, comes from the Greek *hex*; the first morpheme in *sextuplets* from the Latin *sex*.

2   If Latin *novem* is number 9 and Latin *decem* number 10, why are they so clearly a morpheme in the months of November and December, respectively the eleventh and twelfth months of the modern calendar year?

Latin was also the origin of most of the words in Spanish, Italian and French. Metaphorically speaking, therefore, Latin can be seen as an ancestor of these languages and, indeed, it is often described as a parent language to them. In the same way that Latin can be seen as a parent language for French, Spanish and Italian, West Germanic can be considered a parent language for English, Dutch and German. The Scandinavian languages are also quite closely related (the same family metaphor being used) both to each other (with a parent language called North Germanic) and to the other descendants of Germanic. West Germanic and North Germanic are closely related and have a single parent, Germanic. The detail is complex but the principle of reconstructing the languages works and leads us to another question. If Latin or Germanic is the parent, what language is the grand-parent? The questioning can continue into the mists of the past (➜ 1). Family trees of language abound in various sources such as Crystal (2010), Fromkin, Rodman and Hyams (2011) or *Ethnologue* (Lewis 2009).

Whilst it is known that Latin and Ancient Greek were used in everyday life, languages from earlier periods still are more difficult to research. In the nineteenth century, linguists such as Jones, Grimm and Rask were convinced that the similarities between Sanskrit, Latin, Ancient Greek and the Germanic languages (into which family fits English) were too many to be pure coincidence (➜ 1). This is all very well and shows how a genealogy of the world's languages can be established but the question still remains of where language itself came from, a point that was considered briefly earlier (➜ 1) when comparing human language to other forms of communication as well as to animal language and communication systems.

17.6 SUMMARY

The English language has developed over a period of about 1,500 years from a highly inflected language with four cases and three grammatical genders to a morphologically simpler language with virtually no marked grammatical gender, few inflections for agreement of case and number on nouns and relatively few verb conjugations. The spelling system, however, seems relatively complicated. That can be explained by the earliest written forms of the language being set in relation to the pronunciation of the time, being maintained as originally devised and not changing in line with the changes in pronunciation. The lexicon of the language has developed continually throughout that period, as a result of invasions, contact with other languages, industrial and scientific inventions and it continues to expand in a process of perpetual language change.

17.7 FURTHER ACTIVITIES

Activity 17.8

Consider how the meaning and use of the following words has changed over the centuries by looking up the relevant entries in a good dictionary:

chronic	commute
nature	nice
queer	sophisticated
touch	wan

Activity 17.9

Chapter 16 starts its consideration of multilingualism by noting that different religions try to explain the diversity of languages in the world and specifically refers to the Christian stories of the Tower of Babel and the Pentecostal gift of languages. Using the accounts from the King James Bible (1611) provided here, show how the language in that version differs from Modern English. You may wish to compare the KJB version with other versions of the same texts.

The Tower of Babel (Genesis 11: 1, 6–9)

1   And the whole earth was of one language, and of one speech.
6   And the LORD said, Behold, the people is one, and they have all one language; and this they begin to do: and now nothing will be restrained from them, which they have imagined to do.
7   Go to, let us go down, and there confound their language, that they may not understand one another's speech.

8   So the LORD scattered them abroad from thence upon the face of all the earth: and they left off to build the city.

9   Therefore is the name of it called Babel; because the LORD did there confound the language of all the earth: and from thence did the LORD scatter them abroad upon the face of all the earth.

Pentecost (Acts 2: 4–8)

4   And they were all filled with the Holy Ghost, and began to speak with other tongues, as the Spirit gave them utterance.

5   And there were dwelling at Jerusalem Jews, devout men, out of every nation under heaven.

6   Now when this was noised abroad, the multitude came together, and were confounded, because that every man heard them speak in his own language.

7   And they were all amazed and marvelled, saying one to another, Behold, are not all these which speak Galilaeans?

8   And how hear we every man in our own tongue, wherein we were born?

COMMENTARY ON ACTIVITIES

O⎯ⲧ Remember that this symbol indicates that there is a commentary on the activity that you can find on the companion website at www.routledge.com/cw/merrison.

FURTHER READING and REFERENCES

Suggestions for further reading on the topics discussed in this chapter can be found on the companion website (www.routledge.com/cw/merrison).

Any piece of academic writing must always provide a list of publications to which reference has been made. Unusually and very unconventionally, this information is provided on the companion website (www.routledge.com/cw/merrison). Always ask your tutor about how you are to present references for any piece of work that you submit.

Chapter 18
World Englishes

Key Ideas in this Chapter

- English is a global lingua franca, with many more non-native speakers than native speakers.

- English spread to many parts of the world through British colonization, and has since become the principal international language of wider communication, largely due to US-led globalization.

- Users of English around the world can be classified into three groups: native speakers from the British Isles and colonies settled by them; second language speakers from the colonies formerly administered by the British; and foreign language learners and users from countries with no colonial connections with Britain.

- Native speaker Englishes broadly follow either British or American norms, whereas the 'New Englishes' of second language speakers are developing their own norms, influenced by the native languages of their users and by general processes of second language acquisition.

- English-based pidgin and creole languages have arisen when people have fused English with their native languages, rather than acquiring it as an additional language. This has occurred most often in trading contexts, especially the slave trade.

- English as a lingua franca (ELF) is the use of the language in communication between speakers of different native languages.

- Despite positive and negative attitudes towards the language and its different groups of users, the role of English as the only truly global language is assured for the foreseeable future, although it will continue to diversify as local speech communities make it their own.

18.1 INTRODUCTION

Imagine that linguists launched a satellite into orbit around the Earth to record the languages in which social interactions were taking place, and plotted occurrences of each language in use on a global map using a different colour for each one. The result would be a kaleidoscopic stippling on some parts of the planet's surface, where lots of different local languages were in use, alternating with large swathes of a single colour, where one language dominated whole regions. There would, for example, be a colourful cacophony of different tongues represented across Africa, India and South-east Asia. And there would be a great deal of monochrome uniformity over other regions, like Latin America, China, and Scandinavia, where local LINGUA FRANCAS (which ones?) would dominate conversation. But one hue would be visible in *all* parts of the world, sometimes at the expense of other languages, but very often in combination with them, and that would be the colour of English.

English is a LANGUAGE OF WIDER COMMUNICATION, along with Mandarin in China, Arabic in North Africa and the Middle East, Spanish in Latin America, Russian in Eastern Europe, Swahili in East Africa, and others. Like these languages, English has been adopted by (or imposed upon) users outside its original communities of speakers, and has either displaced the original languages of these speakers, leading to LANGUAGE SHIFT and (sometimes) LANGUAGE DEATH (➔ 16.6.1, 18.10), or has shared a space with them, leading to bilingualism (➔ 16) or in some cases the development of PIDGINS and CREOLES (➔ 18.6).

> A LINGUA FRANCA is a shared language used for communication between speakers of other languages.
>
> LANGUAGES OF WIDER COMMUNICATION serve as a lingua franca beyond the borders of the original speaker group.
>
> LANGUAGE SHIFT occurs when the primary language used by a community is displaced by another.

Activity 18.1 ⊙━🖘

If the language satellite's instruments were clever enough to detect whether the English in use was the interlocutor's native or non-native language, what do you think the proportions would be? Which parts of the globe might you expect each proportion to concentrate in? For this activity sketch your own blank map of the world to colour in, or if you are cartographically challenged, search for 'outline world map' on the Internet and print one off.

Over ten years ago, Graddol (1999) reported projections of change in speaker numbers according to which the number of non-native English speakers would probably be double that of native speakers by 2010, a figure that Crystal (2008) found conservative. Although we have no data on the frequency with which non-native speakers are using English on a daily basis along with the other languages they know, it wouldn't come as a surprise if we found that more than half of conversations in English at a given moment in time involved non-native speaker interlocutors. Graddol (2006) reported that in some contexts of use, like tourism, the proportion of interactions involving native speakers dwindles to 26 per cent, and that only 4 per cent of these are between two native speakers!

In most of the rest of this book, we conveniently side-step the issue of English outside the UK and USA. But in this chapter we go beyond the traditional borders of the English language, to look at native and non-native English around the globe. It is the central role of speakers of *other* languages that makes variety in English in the larger world particularly interesting, and merits its separate treatment outside the *Variety in Language* chapter (➔ 12). Inevitably, contact between English and other languages leads to substantial changes in its structure and use. So the kind of variety described in Chapter 12 is greatly compounded when English gets used regularly alongside other languages. And of course the personal factors and situational factors that we discussed there as causes of variation will be multiplied and deepened in the vastly different cultures around the world where English is now used.

Activity 18.2 🔑

Let's jump straight in with some data from a part of the world which has more speakers of English than the UK and USA combined. What follows is an extract from an Indian astrology website, showing a reader's question and an astrologer's response. Read the texts and try to identify as many ways as possible in which the language used is different from the way English is used by the authors of this book. Look for examples which reflect different choices of words and structures, differences in meaning and pragmatic effect, differences relating to who the writer is, and differences in the context or situation of writing and reading.

Respected Sir,

I was born on 18/09/1974 at 15:40 in New Delhi. For last ¾ years I am having lot of debts and financial loses. I have lost lot of money in medical expenditures, stock market, and theft. For many years in career there was no increase in income and promotion. Friends and Colleagues even those who were less qualified and skilled have gone far ahead of me. Current Situation is really very frustrating. Please advise some remedial measures so that the debts gets decreased and there is an increase in income, promotion. Thanks for your help

– Anonymous, New Delhi 12/14/07

[Response]

Let me try to find out the defects you have any in your chart. [...] Saturn is regarded as significator of Roga, diseases. Venus who is quite weak in shadabala, indicates disease/illness related with reproductive system. [...] Please check if you have a damaged (khandita) idol in your pooja or pooja is not being performed regularly. If this is so you need to perform visarjan of the damaged idol [or] if it is just neglected, you should get performed the pranapratishtha afresh for the idol. [...] Now, let us see when can you expect improvement in this condition. This period of Jup/Mars/Ketu is most critical period. [...] After July 2010, the dasha of Saturn will begin. The Sadesati would be there, however, if you learn lesson from the past and soften your ego, it would not be more troublesum. Don't go in for speculation or any other business where you have to make more compromise with the values and honesty. This is the only way to save from the wrath of Saturn. [...] Propitiate Ganeshji every day. He is VighnaHarta, surrender

> to him and seek for blessings. Chanting Ganesh Sankata nashan stotra 5 times
> daily would be very beneficial.
>
> May My Master Bless you & remove your Obstacles.

So where else is English used around the world, and what is happening to it in these diverse places? How did we arrive at this situation and what will happen next? Why are linguists concerned about such issues? Such questions are being asked by researchers in the burgeoning academic field known as *World Englishes*, and in this chapter we'll look at the answers some of the researchers are providing. We will also appreciate how the broader view of English they take leads to some potentially startling conclusions about English and about language in use more generally.

18.2 THE SPREAD OF ENGLISH

The English language is over a thousand years old (➜ 17) and in the last 50 years, 'a mere eye-blink in the history of a language' (Crystal 2003: 71), it has achieved a unique position in the world. How has this happened? In the fifteenth and sixteenth centuries, Europeans started to expand their horizons, both literally, by visiting lands new to the explorers at the time, and metaphorically, by creating new knowledge and new forms of expression (the Renaissance). The use of English was largely confined to the British Isles during this period, but Britain was expanding its influence abroad, as were other European powers, such as Spain, Portugal, France and the Netherlands. So before long Spanish, Portuguese, English, French and Dutch were being spoken in the Americas, the islands of the Caribbean, West Africa, the Indian subcontinent, and a little later in Polynesia and Australasia.

Individuals and groups left the British Isles for many reasons, some willingly and some unwillingly. Sir Walter Raleigh sailed to the New World in search of the fabled treasures of El Dorado, and later to colonize lands for Queen Elizabeth I. The Pilgrim Fathers left with the intention of finding a place where they could practise their religion as they wished to without the trappings and heavy rituals that they found unacceptable in the Anglican Church. Traders went from Britain to the west coast of Africa to transport slaves from there to the Caribbean and North American colonies, and they completed the triangle by returning to Britain with spices, tobacco, sugar, molasses and treacle (amongst other goods). Convicts were sent from Britain to Australia in an attempt to ensure that they would never return to the scenes of their crimes and they were soon followed by free settlers who chose to move to another land to improve their lot in life. All these people took English with them.

From the perspectives of the indigenous peoples of these lands, English must at first have seemed just one more strange and outlandish feature of the colonizers, along with their pink skin, deadly firepower, and even more deadly diseases. What happened afterwards depended on the way each colony developed. The British (and later American) authorities practised three basic kinds of colonization, which we can characterize according to what they did with the people of the colonized territory:

- They *displaced* the local population through large-scale settlement by British families (e.g. in Australia and what is now the USA). This led principally to the development of separate native speaker dialects of English.
- They *subjugated* the local population and administered the colony through a small military and civilian elite (e.g. in India and Kenya). As the local populations learnt English and passed it on to later generations, new non-native speaker varieties emerged.
- They *supplemented* the indigenous population with a workforce of slaves and/or later indentured labourers from elsewhere (e.g. in the Caribbean and Malaysia). This often led to great intermixing of English with local languages and those of the transplanted workers, often as English-based pidgins and, later, creoles.

Of course, these practices had been experienced or carried out by the colonizers' own ancestors in the British Isles after the Anglo-Saxon and Norman conquests, with similar linguistic consequences (➔ 17). From the fifth century, the British tribes were largely displaced by Germanic invaders in what is now England and the lowlands of Scotland, and the dialects they brought with them developed into what we now know as Old English. After 1066, the French of the conquerors merged with the Old English of the subjected indigenous population, and the result was Middle English, which we could view as a CREOLIZED variety of the two (➔ R2.5). Later, the English crown settled Scottish agricultural workers in what is now Northern Ireland, producing the distinctive Ulster Scots dialect. And later still many Irish and Scottish people were obliged or induced to emigrate to the settler colonies of North America and Australasia, thus influencing the shape of the new varieties that emerged there.

> A CREOLIZED variety is one that results from the fusion of two or more languages over a relatively short period of time, after passing through a pidgin stage.

Since the height of the British Empire at the end of the nineteenth century and the subsequent emergence of the USA as the first superpower in the twentieth century, English has also been exported to those countries that have no history of colonization by Britain. Thus, English eclipsed French as the international language of politics and diplomacy, and German as the language of science. Learners and users of English as a Foreign Language now make up the majority of English speakers, and their numbers continue to swell, from Europe to Asia (➔ R3.4). In other words, English has always been in contact with other languages, and it has always been bound up with and buffeted by the social and political events that occur when different peoples of unequal power encounter each other.

18.3 A TYPOLOGY OF ENGLISHES

The systematic study of how English is used outside its native-speaker 'homelands' has a surprisingly short history in linguistics. It is a mere forty years ago that Barbara Strang (1970: 17–18) first pointed out the essential difference between mother tongue speakers of English, those 'for whom English may not be quite the mother tongue, but who learnt it in early childhood, and lived in communities in which English has a special status [...]' and 'those throughout the world for whom English is a foreign language [...]'. Once recognized, the three-way distinction became quickly established. The three kinds of English are now referred to most commonly using the terminology of the 'Three Circles' model of Braj Kachru, the 'father' of World Englishes (Kachru 1985).

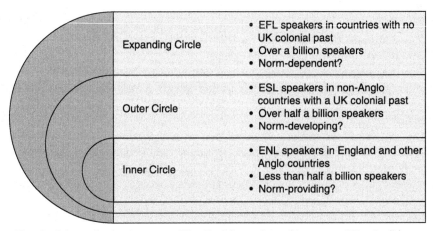

Key: EFL = English as a Foreign Language; ESL = English as a Second Language; ENL = English as a Native Language

Figure 18.1 Kachru's model of World Englishes. Reproduced with permission from Hall *et al.* 2011: 41)

The INTERNATIONAL CORPUS OF ENGLISH contains data on the following Inner and Outer Circle Englishes: Canada, East Africa, Great Britain, Hong Kong, India, Ireland, Jamaica, New Zealand, The Philippines, Singapore, Sri Lanka, and USA (➔ W18.2).

As you can see in Figure 18.1, native speaker Englishes are grouped in the INNER CIRCLE. In Kachru's original formulation, it was *nations* that were located in each circle, although it makes much more sense to locate individual *speakers* or *communities* there. England, for example, is home to many second and foreign language speakers of English and in the USA the proportion is much higher (➔ 15). In the OUTER CIRCLE are those speakers who use English on a regular basis in their daily lives because it has a major role to play in communication in the country they live in, often as an official language. These Englishes are the so-called 'New Englishes' of those postcolonial nations which were not subject to major settlement by British or US native speakers. Outnumbering both the Inner and Outer Circle together are the speakers of the EXPANDING CIRCLE, who have learnt English as a Foreign Language through the educational system and use it normally for communication with other non-native speakers with different language backgrounds from their own.

The question of norms is an entrenched one. It is deeply engrained in the minds of most learners and speakers of English that the UK and USA are the source of 'correct' versions, the models that should be taught and learned around the world. Certainly this is the case for most teachers and learners in the Expanding Circle, who are hence 'norm-dependent', looking to British or US tests like IELTS (International English Language Testing System) and TOEFL (Test of English as a Foreign Language) for validation of their knowledge of the language. But in the Outer Circle, English is becoming 'appropriated' after generations of usage and its continued importance in most former colonies, decades after independence. In a speech at Oxford University a few years ago, the Indian Prime Minister (Singh 2005) said:

Of all the legacies of the Raj, none is more important than the English language and the modern school system. That is, if you leave out cricket! Of course, people here may not recognize the language we speak, but let me assure you that it is English! In indigenizing English, as so many people have done in so many nations across the world, we have made the language our own. Our choice of prepositions may not always be the Queen's English; we might occasionally split the infinitive; and we may drop an article here and add an extra one there. [...] Today, English in India is seen as just another Indian language.

And as 'just another Indian language', it is developing its own norms, independently of Inner Circle influence.

18.4 NATIVE SPEAKER ENGLISHES

Activity 18.3 0⎯⊤

Among the native speaker Englishes, it is the differences between US and UK varieties that are perhaps most familiar, as seen in the small number of common words which have slightly different meanings for the users of each. What do the following words mean to you: *jumper, lift, hood, pavement, truck, pants, rocket, purse, bill*? Make your definitions as full and precise as possible.

The list of transatlantic lexical mismatches could go on for quite a while. Do you say *flat* or *apartment, fix* or *mend, tap* or *faucet, done* or *finished, cinema* or *movie theatre, powdered sugar* or *icing sugar, kind of* or *sort of, cling film* or *plastic wrap*? Your responses to these questions will help you to assess to what extent your use of English is British- or American-based. Strevens (1992: 33) represented the way English has spread round the world using the image of a family tree, with British English (BrEng) and American English (AmEng) as the two main branches of the English language family (see Figure 18.2). The usefulness of this distinction is now being questioned (see below), but the map shows clearly the number of descendants of British and American Englishes and their wide distribution throughout the world.

Do you use both of the forms in any of the above pairs? If you do, in what circumstances do you use each and why? The prevalence of AmEng is becoming so widespread that many British English speakers are not always aware that they are using American English forms. Spelling used to be a clear way of distinguishing between the two. A United States writer would use *labor, maneuver, criticize* or *theater* in preference to the British English spellings of *labour, manoeuvre, criticise* and *theatre*, but many British English writers have adopted some if not all of the North American spellings. North American English *aluminum* reflects the US pronunciation, as the British spelling *aluminium* reflects the British pronunciation. However, the fact that 'you say [təˈmɑːtəʊ], and I say [təˈmeɪɾoː]' (as in the well-known song) shows that the reverse can also be the case: the spelling, <tomato>, is the same, but the pronunciation differs (➔ 9, 10). This increasing lack of active awareness, however, is perhaps indicative of the emergence of a global variety of English, a point to which we return at the end of the chapter.

The playwright George Bernard Shaw, who offered suggestions on how to rationalize the spelling of English, is one of many who, it is said, have commented that the UK and

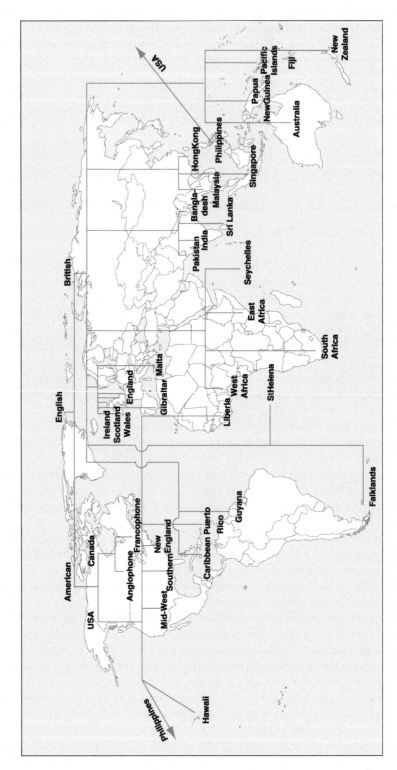

Figure 18.2 A family tree of World Englishes (Crystal 2003, based on Strevens 1992)

the US were 'two countries divided by a common language'. It is true that there can be times when the choices of words are confusing for somebody trying to work in both varieties, but the languages are, for the most part, mutually understandable. And the misunderstandings that *do* occur normally result in little more than entertaining anecdotes.

18.5 NEW ENGLISHES

'Nativeness' is seen by many as a rigid border at the outer reaches of 'non-standard' English (with 'Standard English', the only 'correct' version, at the centre). Beyond this border of nativeness the language is perceived to be only borrowed and often 'broken'. Hence, Australian English, Canadian English, and New Zealand English are viewed as legitimate national dialects alongside British and American English. But since the later colonizations by the UK and subsequently the USA, through which indigenous peoples were subjected to the far-away authority of London and Washington rather than effectively replaced by white settlers, 'New Englishes' have arisen, especially in Africa, South and South-east Asia, and the Caribbean. Unlike English as a native language (ENL) in the Inner Circle, these emerging Outer Circle varieties belong to non-native speakers, for whom English is a second language (ESL). The 'New Englishes' include Indian English in South Asia, Singapore English in South-east Asia, Nigerian English in West Africa, and Maltese English in Europe.

These 'New Englishes' are similar to ENL varieties in the way they evolve independently of the varieties they are descended from. Here are three examples from the lexical level. First, new varieties use productive processes from within English to expand their vocabulary, such as compounding (➔ 5): Zulu speakers of English, together with many other African and Asian English speakers, use the nominal compounds *cousin-brother* and *cousin-sister* to refer to the male and female offspring of their parents' siblings, reflecting local kinship beliefs. Similarly, prefixing builds new forms like Indian English *co-brother*, referring to one's wife's sister's husband (Mesthrie and Bhatt 2008: 112–113). Second, new varieties extend the meaning of words over time to serve or reflect local contexts: in India and East Africa the word *hotel* can now be used to refer to a public restaurant (i.e. a place to eat but not stay the night), and in Malaysian English the word *crocodile* can refer to a womanizer. Third, new varieties conserve forms which may be lost in older varieties: speakers in South Asia and Indian settlers in Cape Town still use *thrice* for 'three times', for example.

When English is decoupled from its native speakers, it undergoes changes which are different from those that occur when new dialects are formed (e.g. in York after the Anglo-Saxons arrived or New York after the English settled there). Two processes are especially significant in the shaping of non-native varieties:

- **cross-linguistic influence** from speakers' first languages (➔ 15.6.1)
- generalization and simplification through general processes of **Second Language Acquisition** (➔ 15.6)

Consider the absence of the phonemes /θ/ and /ð/ in Nigerian English, a feature shared by almost all New Englishes. Variation in the pronunciation of words using these sounds, e.g. in the phrase *think that*, is typical also of native speaker accents (➔ 9, 10). But the fact

The browsable Speech Accent Archive hosted by George Mason University contains samples of many native and non-native accents from around the world (➔ W18.3).

that Nigerian English uses /t/ and /d/ ('tink dat') *as well as* /s/ and /z/ ('sink zat') can be explained by the difference between the native African language phonologies of the two speaker types. Users of /t/ and /d/ take the phonemes from native languages like Igbo and Yoruba, whereas /s/ and /z/ come from languages like Hausa.

Vocabulary is also borrowed from local languages into English for local needs. The text in Activity 18.2 contains a lot of Hindi words relating to Hindu astrology and worship. For example, in the sentence 'you need to perform visarjan of the damaged idol', the Hindi word *visarjan* refers to ritual immersion. And aspects of the L1 grammar will also extend through into the New English L2. For example, speakers of Singapore English, like those of many New Englishes, do without the inflected tag questions used in most ENL varieties ('She is, isn't she?' *vs* 'We are, aren't we?' ➔ 7); instead, they use an 'X or not?' structure (Platt, Weber and Ho 1984: 130) inherited from the Chinese L1 of many of them (➔ R2.7):

L1 is the conventional abbreviation for 'first language' (the language or languages learned in early infancy) and L2 is used for 'second language' (the language or languages learned after the first).

- You come tomorrow, can or not? (*You can come tomorrow, can't you?*)
- All churches use the same, true or not? (*All churches use the same, don't they?*)

The New Englishes also exhibit generalization of ENL rules and the simplification of complex structures. Examples of generalization are:

- non-marking of third person singular verbs, e.g. *He go to school* from Philippines English (Mesthrie and Bhatt 2008: 66)
- making no distinction between count (➔ 7.3.1) and non-count nouns, e.g. *informations* and *an advice* in African Englishes (Kirkpatrick 2007: 174)

Examples of simplification include:

- reduction of **consonant clusters** (➔ 11) at the ends of words, e.g. [kol] for *cold* and [mɪs] for *missed* in Cameroon English (Mesthrie and Bhatt 2008: 128)
- use of invariant tags, e.g. *You are going home, isn't it?* in Indian English (Mesthrie and Bhatt 2008: 133), which is now appearing as *Innit?* in ENL in the UK, perhaps as a borrowing from London Jamaican.

Generalization and simplification can sometimes be explained by cross-linguistic influence (e.g. the Singapore English tag questions), but they are also the natural consequence of the general conditions in which second languages are acquired after infancy, where input is sparse and the learning process much more deliberate (➔ 15.6). These features also demonstrate the affinity between New Englishes and those creoles which arise as a blend between non-European languages and English. The main difference between the two is that New Englishes were originally acquired as second languages, whereas creoles arise from the mixture of two languages, originally as a pidgin (see the next section). Often we lack the necessary evidence to decide how a variety started: for example, in Kiesling's (2006) discussion of Aboriginal Australian English, he concludes '[...] the English vs. creole roots of this variety are now impossible to recover completely' (p. 80).

Activity 18.4 🔑

The following is a sample of Caribbean English from an email message in which the writer tells of the best moment of their life. Identify the specific features of this New English variety which mark it as different from the variety that you use (or another variety you are familiar with if it is the variety you use). Also, see if they reflect any of the processes affecting the development of New Englishes discussed in the chapter so far.

AS A YUTE GROWIN UP, MI ALWAYS HEAR DEM TALK 'BOUT GOD, 'BOUT HOW 'IM GOOD, AN HOW IM SEN' 'IM SON FI DEAD PON DI CROSS FI SAVE US FROM WI SIN. BUT MI NEVA UNDASTAN UNTIL MI START GET BIG AN' CAN REASON OUT T'INGS FI MI'SELF. MI WAS A TROUBLE MEKA IN SCHOOL SO EVRY BADY KNOW MI, MI FAMILY NEVA HAVE MUCH, BUT DAT NEVA REALLY BADDA MI CAUSE MI CUDA BEAR DI HUNGRY. ANYWAY, MI WASTE MOST A MY TIME A SCHOOL SO MI NEVA GET NUH SUBJEC' 'BOUT A YEAR AFTA MI LEF' SCHOOL MI GAA WAN CRUSADE DAT DI CHURCH DUNG DI ROAD DID A PUT ON, DI PASTA DID A TALK 'BOUT HELL AN FIRE AND ALLA DEM T'ING DEH. AT DI END A DI CRUSADE 'IM ASK IF NUH BADY WAAN GI DEM LIFE TO CHRIST AN' MI DID FEEL CONVICTED FI DWEET SO MI WALK UP AN' RIGHT DERE AND DEN MI AXEP' CHRIST AS MI PERSONAL LORD A SAVIOUR, DI ONLY REGRET I HAVE IS DAT I NEVA DWEET SOONA.

SO … DAT IS DI BEST MOMENT OF MY LIFE.

18.6 PIDGINS AND CREOLES

The slave trade of the seventeenth, eighteenth and nineteenth centuries was the abhorrent source of many of the English-based pidgin and creole languages which intrigue contemporary linguists. Slaves were forcibly removed from the west coast of Africa and taken across the Atlantic in appalling conditions. Different tribes, and therefore different languages, were mixed on the ships to reduce the chances of any attempt at insurrection on board. Inevitably and naturally, there was going to be some attempt to communicate between the slaves and such a situation forms rich linguistic soil for the development of a pidgin. Trade in goods other than people has also provided fertile territory for pidgins and creoles, as speakers of different languages needed quick and efficient ways to barter, buy and sell.

A PIDGIN language is a simplified contact language which develops to fulfil a particular purpose, for example, communication in the slave ships or for trade between peoples in South-east Asia. One of the widely-accepted etymologies for the word pidgin is that it was a reduced pronunciation form of the word business in South China pidgin. Mühlhäusler (1986: 1) offers other suggestions for the derivation of the word, as coming from a Chinese corruption of the Portuguese word ocupação (business) or from the Hebrew word pidjom (exchange, trade, redemption), or from Yago (an indigenous South American language spoken in an area colonized by Britain) in which pidian means 'people', or from a South Seas pronunciation of the English word beach (pronounced as 'beachee') which is where the language was typically used. Whilst this list of possible derivations is not definitive (as Mühlhäusler himself accepts), what is interesting is the number of possible sources from so many different languages world wide.

Pidgins arise where contact is too brief or infrequent for one group to find the opportunity to learn the native language of the other. They can thus be only temporary codes, falling into disuse as soon as the specific need disappears. On the slave ships, pidgin languages allowed the slaves to communicate with each other in a language that would not be understood by the ships' masters. Hong Kong, a profitable trading centre originally based on opium, silk, silver, tea and spices, is no longer using pidgin English for its multi-million dollar deals. But it does use its own variety of international English and the development from pidgin to international variety of English is worth noting.

CREOLE languages are pidgins which become permanent. A pidgin is inherently an L2, nobody's L1, but if children hear pidgin from their parents and others around them in infancy, they will develop it into a fully-fledged L1. At this point, it is called by linguists a *creole*, even if the distinction is not always made by the speakers themselves and those who interact with them. The West coast of Africa provides a clear example today (➔ 16.6.1). Many children in Nigeria, for example, are raised multilingually using the home language of their parents and a form of what is called Nigerian Pidgin English (also called simply Nigerian Pidgin or, more recently, Naijá) as a regional lingua franca. But this variety is being creolized. Schneider (2011: 142) reports that 'the number of its native speakers has been estimated to be as high as three to five million'. And there are efforts afoot to codify it so that it can better serve as a lingua franca for the region. Indeed, it now has its own academy, the *Naijá Langwej Akedemi*, which is devising a standardized spelling system among other projects (Esizimetor 2010).

Activity 18.5 🔑

Look at the example sentences below from Ofulue and Esizimetor's (n.d.) guidelines for spelling in Naijá (➔ W18.1). What can you deduce from the data about how the creole marks plural and possessive on nouns (➔ 5), and how its pronoun system works? (➔ 7)

1 Di bois we dem kach, polis tok se dem bi tif (*The boys that were caught, the police said they were thieves.*)
2 Jon-im pikin kom fo wi haus (*John's child came to our house.*)
3 Di lori draiva-dem na dem blok rod (*It is the lorry drivers who blocked the road.*)
4 Meri-im mama dé fo ospitul (*Mary's mother is in the hospital.*)
5 Di pikin-dem se dem neva chop (*The children said they have not eaten.*)
6 Di wimen we kom tode se dem go kom tumoro (*The women who came today said they would come tomorrow.*)

18.7 ENGLISH AS A LINGUA FRANCA

The case of Naijá and the *Naijá Langwej Akedemi* illustrates a significant dichotomy at the heart of World Englishes scholarship. On the one hand, scholars highlight the variability, hybridity and flexibility inherent in the language as it is used around the globe, but on the other hand they also recognize (and often lead) efforts to codify and standardize non-native speaker varieties. The approach is often described as pluricentric, as opposed to monocentric, to emphasize the fact that the English language can no longer be viewed as centred on England, as Japanese is centred on Japan or Icelandic is centred on Iceland. But the morpheme *–centric* in *pluricentric* still suggests that English has centres and peripheries, and these centres are still often defined in terms of standard national varieties. Even in the Expanding Circle, arguments have been made for the codification of characteristic 'national varieties' of English, such as China English (Hu 2005) or EuroEnglish (Modiano 2009). And yet the very nature of English as an *international* language is that it is used successfully in interactions between speakers of different first languages. As Kachru (2009: 176) writes:

> [I]n spite of various types of differences, we [...] communicate with each other – one user of English with the other, a Nigerian with an Indian, a Japanese with a German, a Kashmiri with a Tamil, a Bengali with a Singhalese, and a Singaporean with an American. It is in this broad sense of interlocutors that we have *one* language and *many* voices.

The kind of English usage Kachru is exemplifying here is ENGLISH AS A LINGUA FRANCA (known as ELF). Some scholars originally conceptualized ELF as a distinct set of forms, seeking to identify those that were optimal for teaching purposes (e.g. Jenkins 2002) and making a case for describing those most commonly used in successful ELF use (Seidlhofer 2001). Researchers' attention has recently turned to trying to understand the functions of ELF and the discourse and pragmatic strategies through which these functions are achieved (Seidlhofer 2011 provides an overview). This latter view shares much in common with the conversation analysis approach to interaction adopted in other chapters (especially ➔ 2).

The Vienna Oxford International Corpus of English (VOICE) contains around 120 hours of (mostly European) ELF interactions. It is freely accessible online (➔ W18.4).

The following is an example (from Cogo 2009: 262) of how non-native speakers of English typically make their ELF interactions work, despite their 'different voices'. Chako, a native speaker of Japanese, is asking Sila about variation in Sila's native language, Mandarin Chinese.

```
         1    CHAKO:   my    [specific interest in point
         2    SILA:          [yeah
         3    CHAKO:   when did language I mean ...
   →     4             because  [of revolution,
         5    SILA:             [mhm mhm
         6    CHAKO:   did language change?
         7    SILA:    yeah   [it's it changed
         8    CHAKO:          [specifically intentionally
   →     9    SILA:    because of revolution
        10             ↓(but it also changed from the
   →    11             beginning of the twentieth ce[ntury
        12    CHAKO:                                [yeah
```

Notice how in line 9 Sila repeats Chako's phrase 'because of revolution' (line 4) without the definite article *the* which an ENL speaker would use, even though in line 11 she uses it in 'the twentieth century'. In other transcripts of Sila's speech she also uses the definite article according to Inner Circle norms. According to Cogo's analysis, Sila omits the article in line 9 in order to align herself with her interlocutor and optimize the flow of the conversation. This is an example of ACCOMMODATION (➔ 13.4.4) at the grammatical level, whereby speakers change the way they use language to make it resemble the speech of their interlocutor (something that happens with native speakers as well, of course, at all levels from accent to vocabulary choice: an instance of claiming *common ground*).

ELF accommodation also involves *not using* features of your usual talk which are absent in the talk of your interlocutor. Crystal (2003: 186; ➔ R3.3), for example, refers to

> [p]eople who attend international conferences, or who write scripts for an international audience, or who are 'talking' on the Internet [...] consciously avoiding a word or phrase which [they] know is not going to be understood outside [their] own country, and of finding an alternative form of expression.

But of course this will depend on how aware you are of what's idiomatic and distinctive about the way you and your community talk. Research strongly suggests that monolingual speakers of ENL tend to be less aware than ELF users. In one study, Smith (1992) observes that:

> [n]ative speakers (from Britain and the United States) were not found to be the most easily understood, nor were they [...] found to be the best able to understand the different varieties of English. Being a native speaker does not seem to be as important as being fluent in English and familiar with several different national varieties.

One of us observed a case in point in a Covent Garden café in London a couple of years ago. A smartly-dressed young man entered and, although clearly hearing the markedly Eastern European accent of the person behind the counter, loudly ordered 'one of your *spuds*', and then responded rudely when the server hesitatingly reached for a salad instead of a baked potato (*spud* is an informal word for potato in the lexicons of many BrEng speakers). Of course, your awareness and tolerance of difference, and so consequently your willingness to make broader choices in the way you use English (➔ R3.1), will depend very much on your attitudes to its speakers and to (speakers of) other languages, an issue to which we now turn.

Accommodation is the process through which speakers change the way they talk (often for social reasons) to make it more like the way their interlocutors are talking.

18.8 ATTITUDES TO ENGLISH

Activity 18.6

What does the term *English* mean to you and to people in the communities you belong to (e.g. nation, region where you were born and currently live, university, online social network, sports club)? Is it a mother tongue? Is it a foreign language? Do you use English exclusively, or do you use other languages for some/many purposes? Would you say that you love English or have pride in it? Do you feel that its use is imposed on you? Are you happy to 'subvert' it or do you think you should respect its codified norms? And other languages you know?

Think about these questions carefully both from your own position and from the position of others in your communities before you read further in this unit.

Any one individual's or group's view of English will be informed by their personal or group experiences. A society's historical relation to Britain and the British or to the USA and Americans might affect how that society views ENL. Admission into the British Empire was not always seen everywhere as a good thing, and the USA's global economic and/or military might is not always and everywhere perceived as positive. Aboriginal peoples in Australia and Yupik peoples in Alaska, for example, could well see the English language as one form of oppression. The question is not always answered negatively, however. For example, millions of Chinese are learning English with great enthusiasm, seeing competence in English as one of the prime drivers in their modernization programmes. And many West Africans welcome English as an independent resource that can transcend local ethnic and linguistic rivalries, in the same way that Swahili, a local language of wider communication, does for East Africans.

Activity 18.7 🔑

It could be argued that a society's proverbs give some indication of their underlying attitudes. The following translated proverbs have all been taken from Alladina and Edwards (1991) with the language communities indicated in brackets:

- Your language [English] on our shoulders like a burden (Welsh Gwenallt).
- A people without their own language is only half a people (British Romani).
- Speech is wealth (Hausa).
- Anyone who does not love their own native language is disgustingly worse than a smelly fish (Filipino).

Consider what you think each proverb says about the importance of language to the community and then compare this with your own attitudes from Activity 18.6. You will also find it helpful to compare your own opinions with those of as wide a group of other people as possible.

When you've finished, try to find proverbs from your own culture and society which might indicate an attitude to (your) language(s), then search for one or two of them using a corpus or an Internet search engine to see who uses them, and in what contexts.

18.9 COUNTING ENGLISH SPEAKERS

The fact that people form strong attitudes about English and other languages suggests that they believe these languages to be real, separately countable phenomena, belonging to clearly defined communities of speakers who live within distinct national borders. And this is the working assumption of most linguists too. But World Englishes is making us more aware of the problems of such a monolithic approach to language(s). In this penultimate section of the chapter, we ask to what extent English and other languages can be delimited and counted.

According to *Ethnologue*, the compendium of languages most linguists accept as the most authoritative record (➔ W18.5), there are around 7,000 living languages spoken around the planet. In terms of speakers, Chinese is at the top, with 1.2 billion, followed by Spanish, at 329 million and then English an extremely close third, at 328 million (Lewis 2010). The fact that there are more Chinese and Spanish speakers than English speakers does not, however, undermine claims that English is the only *global* language, for three good reasons:

1   Chinese and Spanish are spoken widely in only limited regions of the world. Our language satellite (➔ 18.1) would detect significant numbers of Chinese conversations only in East and South-east Asia (Chinatowns in Western cities wouldn't show up from space!). And Spanish is largely restricted to Spain and the Americas. So the colours of Chinese and Spanish would be extremely dense on some areas of the globe, but give it a spin and they would largely disappear from view.

2   Many linguists argue that Chinese is not in fact a single language. *Ethnologue* treats it as a MACROLANGUAGE. Some varieties of Chinese are as different from each other as Spanish is from Portuguese or German is from Dutch.

3   If we counted international domains of use (e.g. banking, science, tourism, higher education, the media, social networking, popular music, aviation, diplomacy, aid work, etc.) we would see that English figures much more than any other language.

> A MACROLANGUAGE is a set of two or more closely related languages which are viewed by some people or in some contexts to be the same language (normally for non-linguistic reasons).

So if English is the only world language, does that mean that there are more *speakers of English* in the world than of any other language? That depends entirely on what counts as English and what counts as a *speaker* of English.

Activity 18.8 ⚿

Here is a line from four different language versions of the leaflet *Making the Scottish Parliament Work for You* (Scottish Parliament 2011a).

1   There are lots of ways to make your views known when there are issues you feel strongly about.

2   Tha iomadach dòigh gus do bheachdan a nochdadh nuair a tha faireachdainn làidir agad mu chùisean.

3   Istnieje wiele sposobów, w jakie ludzie moga przekazać swe opinie na temat spraw, które maja dla nich istotne znaczenie.

4   Ye hae mony weys tae mak yir views kent whan ye hae strang feelins aboot issues.

The first version is clearly English. Some readers might recognize the third as Polish. But probably the majority of readers outside of Scotland won't recognize the second version as Gaelic (though they might guess); and most will be puzzled by the fourth version, Scots, which developed independently of 'Standard British English', from the Northumbrian dialect of Old English (➔ 17).

Consider next the following clauses from the parliament's *Language Policy* (Scottish Parliament 2011b):

- When Gaelic is used in meetings of the Parliament and committee meetings, the Official Report incorporates the Gaelic text before the report of the English interpretation.
- When Scots is used in meetings of the Parliament and committee meetings, the Official Report incorporates that language in the body of the text.

Now discuss with a friend or acquaintance (preferably a Scottish one) your responses to the following questions:

1   On the basis of the small sample here, how different does Scots seem from English? (Use all the knowledge of linguistic description that you have accumulated in your study of the subject and from this book.)
2   On what different grounds, apart from purely descriptive linguistic ones, might one want to argue that Scots is a different language from English?
3   Why do you think Gaelic is treated differently from Scots in the Official Report?

Are speakers of Scots to be counted among speakers of English? If they can write Standard British English (which they must if they undergo public education in Scotland), are they therefore L2 or (additive) bilingual speakers (➔ 16)? And if Scots is a separate language, how about African American English, Indian English, Naijá or China English? Our discussion of World Englishes suggests that the borders between languages are extremely porous, and that the seemingly watertight distinction between native and non-native speaker is also perhaps equally leaky. Indeed, some linguists argue on the basis of this kind of evidence that languages as monolithic entities are really only convenient fictions, and that a 'plurilithic' view of English and other languages can more accurately reflect the practices of speakers around the world (Makoni and Pennycook 2007).

So, is English also the biggest language in terms of number of speakers? Well if we *do* count Englishes and English speakers in all their guises, native or non-native, a figure of two billion speakers is reasonable, according to Graddol (2006) and Crystal (2008). And this number is higher than Chinese and Spanish combined. But it really does depend on how you define a language and a speaker of it, a basic question that linguists still don't have a clear answer for.

18.10 THE FUTURE OF ENGLISH

At the beginning of this chapter we commented that the spread of English around the world has had (and is still having) different linguistic effects on the populations who came into contact with its speakers. In some cases there has been a wholesale shift to English, often resulting in the disappearance or marginalization of ancestral languages. Such is the case in anglophone North America and Australia, where rates of language death are extremely high and several are at severe risk of extinction. It is estimated that two languages are currently losing their very last speakers *every month*, and that by the end of the twenty-first century perhaps half the world's languages will be extinct (Krauss 1992). The spread of English has definitely contributed to this loss of language diversity, as part of what Phillipson (1992) controversially called 'linguistic imperialism'. But as we have seen, people in Outer and Expanding Circle contexts have also 'appropriated' English and fashioned it for their own purposes, adding it to or merging it with the other languages they know.

So what is the future for English in the world? Well, clearly many more people are going to learn it and it will be increasingly used as a lingua franca all over the planet. Despite the continued regional importance of Spanish in the Americas, Arabic in the Middle East and North Africa, Russian in the former Soviet Union, Chinese in East Asia, and Hindi in South Asia, it is unlikely that any of these will replace English any time soon. Ultimately, it is conceivable that Mandarin Chinese will become the language through which most of the world communicates, as a consequence of the inevitable rise of China and decline of the USA. And it's also possible that advances in automatic translation technology will render the differences between languages less important, leading to renewed international diversity in language use (see Hall *et al.* 2011, Chapter 10). But the numbers of English learners are still rising, and increasingly, around the world, English is being viewed by education departments as a basic skill rather than a foreign language: more like your maths or IT class than your Spanish or EFL lesson (Graddol 2006).

So the more interesting question is just what kind or kinds of English will be used in the future? One near certainty is that learners and users will not be prevented from forging their own versions of the language. Local versions of English (and pidgins and creoles in which English plays a role) will continue to develop, as the result of:

- deliberate choices by parents, learners, and users
- the sociocognitive processes involved in second language acquisition
- pressure for community cohesion and new possibilities for creating and expressing identities through social media.

Singapore provides a good example of this. Despite over ten years of government campaigns to promote 'Good English' (effectively 'Standard' Singapore English, very close to AmEng and BrEng), the colloquial version *Singlish* shows few signs of disappearing. Indeed, it appears to be an inevitable feature of the way speakers use the language in this multicultural and multiethnic, local and global city state (Alsagoff 2010; ➔ R2.7). But although local varieties will continue to diverge from each other as they are adapted for local purposes in local language ecologies, there will still be pressure to teach and learn a monolithic variety for international lingua franca communication, such as the *World Standard Spoken English* (WSSE) predicted by Crystal (2003; ➔ R3.3). The likelihood is that ENL varieties will lose their monopoly over English language teaching and testing, but that 'standard' varieties of BrEng and AmEng will retain their prestige (aided and abetted by government agencies, English testing bodies, and the major English language publishing houses). Where there is a difference between AmEng lexical usage and that of other varieties, it will probably be the AmEng alternant that dominates, as we saw earlier in the chapter. Variation in grammar (especially in the written modality) and in spelling is likely to diminish in favour of US conventions also. But spoken usage might resist these processes of homogenization for much longer. When our language satellite remaps English social interactions in 50 or 100 years time, it's likely that the colour of English will remain omnipresent, but in many different hues, and often striped or swirled with other colours. Will these different hues ultimately fade into different colours completely? Nobody knows.

Activity 18.9 0—⊤

Graddol (1997: 56) wondered whether Outer Circle speakers (in countries using English as L2) 'may bring new, non-native models of English … into competition with the older standard varieties' and thereby questioned whether the current supremacy of AmEng and BrEng will continue. Crystal (2003: 184) commented 'that some of the territories of the expanding circle … may be bending English to suit their purposes' and that 'local usages are emerging, and achieving a standard status within a region'. He also notes (2003: 188) that 'there is no reason for L2 features not to become part of WSSE'. How do you react to this possible state of affairs? How do you think education policy makers and English teachers from Kachru's three circles (Figure 18.2) might react? What implications does it have for English Language Teaching generally?

18.11 SUMMARY

English has been transformed from a collection of Germanic dialects spoken on a small island off the north-western coast of Europe into a language used all over the planet by perhaps a third of its population, for an astonishingly wide range of social purposes. From its very beginnings it has been changed by speakers of other languages. But this process was significantly accelerated by the spread of British and, later, US power, as well as by advances in technology and education, and the increased flow of goods, information and capital around the world, all using English as a principal medium. The result is on the one hand a vast number of different Englishes (some permanently entwined with other languages), and on the other hand the emergence of international ways of using English (which native speakers do not necessarily have an advantage with). The exciting fields of World Englishes and ELF are examining all these issues, and the results of their research reveal that the future of English is likely to be very complex, and is no longer in the hands solely of its native speakers.

18.12 FURTHER ACTIVITIES

Activity 18.10

Search on the Internet for speeches in English by three world leaders, each from a different circle in Kachru's model (Figure 18.2). The map in Figure 18.1 will give you an idea of countries and regions to look at for the Inner and Outer Circles. Using a similar portion of each speech (say five minutes), identify the differences and the similarities in the way the different speakers use the language.

Activity 18.11

From your own networks of friends and acquaintances, record a conversation between people who speak different international varieties of English and more than one L1 (try not to include more than one native speaker). Analyse examples of successful and unsuccessful ELF communication, using your knowledge of phonetics and phonology (➔ 9 and 10), grammar and lexicon (➔ 5, 7 and 8), semantics and pragmatics (➔ 3, 4 and 6), and conversation analysis (➔ 2).

Activity 18.12

As a follow-up to Activity 18.11, interview the friends and acquaintances who participated in the conversation (or others who you play it to) to find out their reactions to how English was being used, what effects this usage had on the flow of communication, and how their identities might account for their reactions.

COMMENTARY ON ACTIVITIES

O─╼ Remember that this symbol indicates that there is a commentary on the activity that you can find on the companion website at www.routledge.com/cw/merrison.

FURTHER READING and REFERENCES

Suggestions for further reading on the topics discussed in this chapter can be found on the companion website (www.routledge.com/cw/merrison).

Any piece of academic writing must always provide a list of publications to which reference has been made. Unusually and very unconventionally, this information is provided on the companion website (www.routledge.com/cw/merrison). Always ask your tutor about how you are to present references for any piece of work that you submit.

Epilogue

For last year's words belong to last year's language
And next year's words await another voice.

T.S. Eliot, Little Gidding II (1944: 65–66)

Glossary

accent   multi-faceted aspects of the pronunciation of a spoken linguistic form. It includes the choice of sounds used as segments (phonemes) as well as prosodic suprasegmentals.

active voice   see **voice** (ii).

adjacency pair   a sequential unit consisting of two communicative actions.

adjective   an open word class, whose members characteristically premodify nouns in a noun phrase or realize intensive complement in clause structure.

adjective phrase   a phrase with an adjective functioning as headword.

Adjunct   functions at clause level along with Subject, Finite, Predicator and Complement usually expressing a wide range of circumstantial meanings such as time, place, manner and reason.

adverb   an open word class, whose members characteristically premodify adjectives (e.g. _rather_ difficult) or realize the Adjunct slot in clause structure indicating a range of meanings such as time, place and manner, e.g. _They left_ _later_.

adverb phrase   a phrase with an adverb as headword.

affix   prefix or suffix.

allophone   a phonetic unit corresponding to a particular phoneme

ambiguous   having more than one interpretation.

antonymy   one kind of oppositeness, a semantic relationship between pairs of words which, when substituted for each other in sentences that are otherwise the same, yield only an entailment from an affirmative to a negative sentence, but not in the reverse direction. See **complementarity**.

aphasia   a brain condition in which language is disrupted independently of other cognitive functions.

articulator   the speech organs which move to produce speech sounds are the active articulators; the speech organs against which the active articulators move are the passive articulators.

aspect   a grammatical system indicating the duration of an action.

auxiliary verb   the primary auxiliary verbs (_do, be_ and _have_) indicate aspect or voice. In _Felicity is starting a new job_ and _Robert_ _has been_ _promoted_, the primary auxiliaries have been underlined. The modal auxiliary verbs (modal auxiliaries) are used to express a range of meanings relating to possibility, probability and obligation such as (modal auxiliary is underlined) _Kate_ _can_ _have three weeks leave_.

backchannel behaviour   short responses, such as 'mm' or 'aha', which provide feedback to the speaker.

borrowing   the use of words from one language in another, e.g. _le weekend_ (borrowed from English) appearing in a French utterance or _Zeitgeist_ (borrowed from German) or *haka* (borrowed from Maori appearing in an English one. There are many examples of borrowings in all languages.

cancellation   to reasonably deny an inference.

clause   appears above phrase in the hierarchy of rank and is typically analysed in terms of Subject, Finite, Predicator, Complement and Adjunct.

code   a set of arbitrary conventions for converting one system of signals into another.

code-mixing   using the rules of one language while speaking another.

code model   a model of language whereby a speaker simply says the words and a hearer simply decodes them to get the intended message.

code-switching   moving from one language to another in the course of a conversation.

coherence   relates to the meaning that a text is expressing and allows the reader to say 'This makes sense'. Chomsky's famous example *Colourless green ideas sleep furiously* shows that a sentence can be grammatical but not make sense – it is incoherent.

cohesion   the system of explicit links within a text to make the text hold together as the pronoun *she* does in this very short text: Ruth works very hard. <u>She</u> works very carefully as well.

co-hyponyms   the hyponyms under a given superordinate word.

communication   the transmission and reception of messages between two or more participants using any mode of communication; may or may not include the use of language.

communicative competence   what a person knows about the structure of the language(s) they speak (i.e. phonology, lexicon, morphology, grammar, semantics) and, importantly, how these structures are used appropriately in social contexts of use.

competence   what a native hearer-speaker of a given language knows about their language; what is stored in their brain about language.

Complement   functions with Subject, Finite, Predicator and Adjunct at clause level. There are three main types of complement: complement direct object *see* **direct object**, complement indirect object *see* **indirect object** and intensive complement *see* **intensive complement**.

complementarity (also called *binary antonymy***)**   a non-gradable semantic relationship between pairs of words, e.g. *wrapped* and *unwrapped*; when the words are used in sentences, entailments go both from affirmative to the corresponding negative sentences and from negative sentences to affirmatives; in the vocabulary of the language, the members of a pair of complementaries are treated as having no middle ground between them. See **antonymy**.

compound word   a word made by joining two (or more) words together, e.g. *newspaper*.

conjunction   the linking of words, phrases or clauses. Coordinating conjunctions (a closed word class, e.g. *and, but, or*) link elements of equal weight, e.g. *coffee or tea?* (where nouns are linked) or *the lion roared but the cat purred* (in which clauses are coordinated). Subordinating conjunctions (a closed word class, e.g. *after, although, because, whenever*) link elements of differing weight, e.g. *the lion roared while the cat purred* where a subordinate clause is inserted in the main clause, often but not always in the Adjunct slot.

consonant   a speech sound in which articulators typically come close together or form a complete closure. Consonants are typically peripheral in a syllable.

consonant cluster   a group of two or more consonants occurring next to each other in a word form or an utterance, with no vowels between them.

content words nouns, verbs, adjectives and adverbs; they carry the content of communications by making connections to the world outside of language. See **function word**.

context the complex totality of the situation in which an utterance is made, including aspects such as time, geographical location, cultural norms, social relationships between individuals, preceding linguistic material and so on.

Cooperative Principle (CP) the assumption that interlocutors are cooperative in their utterances (including being informative, truthful, relevant and clear).

corpus (plural **corpora**) a searchable database of authentic language use, normally containing very large numbers of words from different genres.

creole a pidgin which becomes acquired and used as a native language, and thus develops a full range of linguistic forms and functions.

cross-linguistic influence the process whereby the sounds, words, structures and discourse practices of one language (normally a person's first language) influence the learning and use of another language (normally a second language). Also known as *transfer*, and less positively, *interference*.

declarative one of three elements in the mood system; typically used for making statements. In declaratives, the Subject usually precedes the Finite (e.g. *Nick brought us a vegetarian pizza*).

deixis use of language which can only be understood in context, e.g. *I, here, yesterday* which can only be understood when the speaker or the time or place of utterance is known.

descriptive an approach to the study of language which objectively describes how it is actually used cf. **prescriptive**.

determiner a closed word class whose members typically come at the beginning of the noun phrase and determine the scope of the noun as in *each individual*, *all the time*, *some potatoes*. The word class includes the definite article (*the*) and the indefinite article (*a/an*).

dialect the term used when a form of language is distinct in matters of morphology, lexis, semantics or syntax.

diglossia the situation where two or more language varieties are used in different social domains and for different social functions where one language is perceived as the High (H) variety and the other as the Low (L) variety. Use of L in an H context could be seen as comical at the least and offensive at the worst.

diphthong a dynamic vowel that glides from one vowel quality to another within a single syllable (e.g. the *ow* in *wow!*)

direct illocution the illocution most directly indicated by the literal meaning of what is uttered. See **direct speech act**.

direct object (Cdo) one of three Complements, typically realized by a noun phrase and expressing the goal of a material process. (Cdo is underlined in *The students read the whole book*.)

direct speech act the speech act obtained when syntactic form and pragmatic function match.

entailment the conclusions (inferences) which are *guaranteed* to be true given the truth of an initial proposition. Attempting to cancel an entailment leads to contradiction.

entities people, things, places, events, times, tunes, ideas – indeed, whatever we can think and talk about.

face 'the positive social value a person effectively claims for himself' (Goffman 1967: 5 ➔ chapter 4).

field (of discourse)   subject matter, e.g. chemistry/linguistics/music.

finite   a verb form which is marked for tense (e.g. *saw, eats*). A verb form which is not marked for tense is non-finite (e.g. *taking, ridden*).

Finite   functions at the level of clause with Subject, Predicator, Complement and Adjunct and appears as the first verb in a finite verb group.

function word   a word which has little identifiable meaning and which is typically involved in grammatical work in the sentence. Auxiliary verbs, conjunctions, determiners, prepositions and pronouns are members of this class of words. Cf. **grammatical words**.

glottal stop   the plosive consonant articulated with the vocal folds, often associated with the regional variety of London English in words such as *letter* pronounced [lɛʔə].

grammar   the structure of a language. The term was traditionally used for sentence grammar (see **syntax)** and has more recently come to include text grammar.

grammatical words   *see* **function words**

h-dropping   omission of the consonant [h] particularly from initial position in a word.

hierarchy of rank   words in sentences are not usually all strung together on the same level; instead they are grouped into phrases which, in turn, are joined to make clauses, which may go together to make sentences and texts (*see* Figure 7.1).

homophone   words which sound the same even if spelt differently, e.g. *through* and *threw*.

hyponym   under a superordinate, a word with a more specific meaning, e.g. *chair* is a hyponym of the superordinate *seat*; the meaning of a hyponym is that of its superordinate plus some modifier(s), e.g. a *chair* is a 'seat with a back, for one person'.

illocutionary act (illocution)   the act (defined by social convention) which is performed when making an utterance, e.g. accusing, apologizing, asserting, boasting, congratulating and so on.

imperative   one of three elements in the mood system; typically used for giving instructions.

implicature   an implied inference derived through applying the Cooperative Principle.

indirect illocution   any illocution an utterance might have beyond the direct illocution.

indirect object (Cio)   one of three Complements, typically realized by a noun phrase and expressing the recipient or beneficiary of a material process. (Cio is underlined in *Richard bought* <u>*Kate*</u> *a new car.*)

indirect speech act   see **indirect illocution**.

inference   a conclusion worked out from information. See **entailment** and **implicature**.

inflection   the marking of grammatical information (e.g. tense and number) on content words, using affixes.

intensive complement (Cint)   one of three Complements typically realized by a noun phrase or an adjective phrase and expressing the quality or attribute in a relational process. (Cint is underlined in *Edinburgh is* <u>*the capital of Scotland*</u>.)

interlocutor   a participant taking part in the interaction.

interrogative   one of three elements in the mood system; typically used for asking questions.

interruption   an attempt to take the floor from the current speaker while they are still producing their turn constructional unit. Cf. **overlap**.

intonation   the movement of pitch during speech.

jargon   the technical words which belong to a particular subject area. The term is often used disparagingly ("Oh that is just jargon") by those who feel excluded from a discussion using such technical terms. See **technical words**.

language   the abstract system underlying the linguistic behaviour of a community based on conventions for the use of sounds or signs; considered by many to be an important part of what defines humans as human.

language death   the situation when the last native speaker of a language gives it up or dies.

language policy and planning   the process of making decisions about language use, often in educational or political contexts.

language shift   the process by which a society, more or less gradually or abruptly, adopts a new language, normally one associated with greater economic and political power and prestige.

lexical choice   choosing a unit of vocabulary.

lexical item   a unit of vocabulary.

lexical verb   not an auxiliary verb, underlined in *She has spoken*.

lexicon   an individual's mental store of words.

lingua franca   a bridge language used for communication between speakers of different first languages.

mental lexicon   the part of memory where a speaker's vocabulary is stored.

metalinguistic   language when it is being used to discuss and describe language itself, e.g. the terms *word, sound, sentence* are metalanguage words in English; includes all the technical linguistic terms used in this book.

minimal pair   words which differ by a single phoneme such as *peat* [pit] and *pat* [pat].

modal auxiliary   see **auxiliary verb**.

mode (of communication)   any one of the five senses (sight, sound, smell, touch or taste) through which communication can be effected. The main ones for language are visual (sign language and writing) and vocal-auditory (speech).

mode (of discourse)   medium of the language activity, e.g. written/spoken.

mood   a grammatical system including declarative, interrogative and imperative.

morpheme   the smallest meaningful unit that words are constructed from, e.g. the morphemes that make up *fire-eaters* are *fire, eat, -er* and *-s*.

morphology   the study of the structure of words. See **morpheme**.

neurolinguistics   the study of language and the brain, closely related to psycholinguistics, but focusing on the neural mechanisms underpinning language storage and processing.

non-finite   see **finite**.

non-verbal communication (NVC)   communication other than language, using any mode of communication.

noun   an open word class containing the subgroups count, non-count and proper noun.

noun phrase   a phrase with a noun or pronoun as headword.

overlap   simultaneous talk which does not violate the current speaker's turn often because it occurs near a possible transition relevance place. Cf. **interruption**.

passive voice   see **voice** (ii).

phoneme   a speech sound used distinctively in a language to make contrasts between words. See **minimal pairs**.

phoneme inventory   the selection of speech sounds a particular language employs from among all the phonetic resources available to humans.

phonetics   the study of speech sounds.

phonology   the study of pronunciation systems, concentrating on those speech sound contrasts in each language that make a significant difference in communication.

phrase   directly above word in the hierarchy of rank. Phrases are labelled according to the headword in the phrase and they themselves combine to form clauses.

pidgin   a simplified contact language with no native speakers which develops to fulfil a particular function, for example, trade.

pragmatics   the study of how interlocutors use their knowledge of a language to convey and interpret meanings. See **semantics**.

Predicator   all words other than Finite in a verb group.

prefix   a morpheme that is less than a freestanding word and which goes on to the beginnings of words.

preposition   a closed word class, e.g. *on, in, through, underneath* which typically combines with a noun phrase to create a prepositional phrase, e.g. *at the corner of the street*.

preposition(al) phrase   a phrase introduced by a preposition and completed by a noun phrase e.g. *over the table, after you*.

pre-request   a type of pre-sequence used to check that a subsequent request is not inappropriate.

prescriptive   an approach to the study of language which prescribes how language *should* be used. See **descriptive**.

pre-sequence   a sequence of turns built in orientation to a further upcoming sequence. Pre-sequences check that the necessary conditions for the subsequent sequence do in fact obtain. For example, if conditions are right, pre-announcements lead to announcements, pre-arrangements lead to arrangements, pre-closings lead to closings, pre-invitations lead to invitations, pre-requests lead to requests and so on.

pronoun   a closed word class, e.g. *I, him, that, each*. A pronoun stands in place of a noun phrase.

propositional meaning   the literal meaning of a piece of speech or writing, without involving context or outside knowledge.

psycholinguistics   the area of study concerned with language as a psychological phenomenon: its acquisition, mental representation, and processing. There is considerable overlap with neurolinguistics, the study of language and the brain.

rankshifted clause   functions as the Subject or Complement of a main clause or as a postmodifier in a noun phrase.

Received Pronunciation (RP)   the accent most often associated with standard British English; used as an index for describing other accents of English. It is sometimes also referred to as the Queen's English or BBC English.

reference   referring to an entity involves providing enough detail for the hearer/reader to successfully pick out whatever the speaker/writer is talking about (the referent).

referent   the entity in the real world to which a noun refers.

register   a combination of field, tenor and mode of discourse (sometimes known as 'genre').

relative clause   clause postmodifying head in noun phrase structure, e.g. *the house which Jack built*.

RP   see **Received Pronunciation**.

schwa: the common unstressed vowel found in the first syllable of *again* or the second syllable of *famous*.

Second Language Acquisition (SLA)   the learning of an additional language after the first language(s) acquired in infancy.

semantics   the study of meaning in language. In contrast to pragmatics, semantics focuses on the potential for meaning that comes from knowing a language, rather than how we interpret utterances in context.

sign languages   the natural languages of Deaf communities, articulated with the hands and face.

sociolinguistics   the branch of linguistics interested in the links between language and society.

speech act   when words perform some action beyond describing the world we say that they are performing a speech act.

standard language   the (often prestigious) dialect of a language associated with academic, government and religious settings, and with written and published material.

stem   the element of the word to which inflectional affixes can be added e.g. to the stem *eat* the inflections {-ing} and {-en} can be added; to the stem *dog* the plural inflection {-s} and the possessive inflection {- 's} can be added.

stress   extra prominence given to a syllable in terms of loudness, increase in pitch or increase in length.

stressed syllable   *see* **stress**

Subject   functions at clause level with Finite, Predicator, Complement and Adjunct. The Subject agrees with the finite verb in terms of number, e.g. *Ann speaks Italian fluently*.

substitution   (i) in syntax: a pro-form used for a previously mentioned element (substitution can be clausal, verbal or nominal); (ii) in child language: the use by young children of sounds that they already control in place of ones not yet mastered (e.g. [d] in place of the consonant [ð] needed for the beginning of the word *this*).

suffix   a morpheme that is less than a freestanding word and which goes on to the ends of words.

superordinate   a more general word, a cover term. See **hyponym**.

suprasegmentals   phonetic features which apply to more than one phonemic segment (such as pitch, stress and voice quality).

syllable   a phonological unit consisting of an obligatory nucleus, normally a vowel. Words contain one or more syllables.

synonymy/synonym   sameness of meaning of words; based on paraphrase between paired sentences differing only by the replacement of one word, e.g. *begin* and *commence* are synonyms.

syntax   the study of sentence making according to grammatical principles. Cf. **grammar**.

technical words   occur with relatively high frequency in texts on particular subjects and often have special meanings in the subject, e.g. *syntax* and *tenor* are technical words in language study. See **jargon**.

tenor (of discourse)   sometimes referred to as style, e.g. formal/informal.

text   a term for representations of both written and spoken language data.

transcript/transcription   a written representation of speech sounds using symbols.

transition relevance place   a place where it is relevant for there to be a transition (change) of speaker.

turn constructional unit   a unit of talk.

utterance   the physical production of linguistic behaviour.

variety   a term that covers both language and dialect, but is intended to be neutral between them.

verb   an open word class. English lexical verbs characteristically have five forms, most clearly seen in irregular verbs, e.g. *drive, drives, drove, driving, driven*.

verb group   a label for a group of words which consists only of auxiliary and lexical verbs (cf. second meaning given for verb phrase), e.g. *She might have been thinking about it*.

verb phrase   used in different ways in different approaches to grammar. It can be used to label (i) everything in the clause other than the grammatical subject of the clause or (ii) only the verb group.

vocabulary   the set of words that a language or variety has, or the set of all the words in a given language known to an individual person.

vocal folds   the two folds of tissue mainly composed of muscle which lie horizontally across the glottis and which vibrate to produce voice. Sometimes called vocal cords.

vocal tract   the airway which stretches from the lungs to the lips and nostrils, used in the production of speech.

voice   (i) in phonetics: the product of vocal fold vibration; (ii) in syntax: the system which allows choice about which participants in any process will be named and in what order. In active voice, the actor in the material process is named in the Subject slot, e.g. *Joyce played the piano*. When using the passive voice (auxiliary *be* + past participle) the speaker chooses as grammatical Subject of the clause a semantic role other than that of actor/doer of the process, e.g. *The piano was played by Joyce*.

voice quality   the characteristics defining an individual's speech as belonging to that individual. Can include qualities such as breathiness, speed of utterance, loudness etc.

voiced   sounds produced with vocal fold vibration.

voiceless   sounds produced without vocal fold vibration.

vowel   a speech sound during which articulators are not sufficiently close together to create friction. Vowels are typically central in a syllable.

word   a meaning, a pronunciation (optionally a spelling too) and a syntactic word class conventionally linked; e.g. learning the word *sandal* amounts to learning the linkage between 'ventilated shoe', [sændl], noun position in sentences and, optionally, the spelling <sandal> (instead of, for instance, <sandle>).

Index

THE INTERNATIONAL PHONETIC ALPHABET (revised to 1993, updated 1996)

CONSONANTS (PULMONIC)

	Bilabial	Labiodental	Dental	Alveolar	Postalveolar	Retroflex	Palatal	Velar	Uvular	Pharyngeal	Glottal
Plosive	p b			t d		ʈ ɖ	c ɟ	k g	q ɢ		ʔ
Nasal	m	ɱ		n		ɳ	ɲ	ŋ	N		
Trill	ʙ			r					R		
Tap or Flap				ɾ		ɽ					
Fricative	ɸ β	f v	θ ð	s z	ʃ ʒ	ʂ ʐ	ç ʝ	x ɣ	χ ʁ	ħ ʕ	h ɦ
Lateral fricative				ɬ ɮ							
Approximant		ʋ		ɹ		ɻ	j	ɰ			
Lateral approximant				l		ɭ	ʎ	L			

Where symbols appear in pairs, the one to the right represents a voiced consonant. Shaded areas denote articulations judged impossible.

CONSONANTS (NON-PULMONIC)

Clicks	Voiced implosives	Ejectives
⊙ Bilabial	ɓ Bilabial	' Examples:
ǀ Dental	ɗ Dental/alveolar	p' Bilabial
ǃ (Post)alveolar	ʄ Palatal	t' Dental/alveolar
ǂ Palatoalveolar	ɠ Velar	k' Velar
ǁ Alveolar lateral	ʛ Uvular	s' Alveolar fricative

OTHER SYMBOLS

ʍ Voiceless labial-velar fricative

w Voiced labial-velar approximant

ɥ Voiced labial-palatal approximant

ʜ Voiceless epiglottal fricative

ʢ Voiced epiglottal fricative

ʡ Epiglottal plosive

ɕ ʑ Alveolo-palatal fricatives

ɺ Alveolar lateral flap

ɧ Simultaneous ʃ and x

Affricates and double articulations can be represented by two symbols joined by a tie bar if necessary.   k͡p t͡s

VOWELS

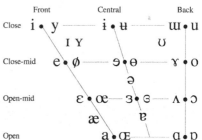

Where symbols appear in pairs, the one to the right represents a rounded vowel.

SUPRASEGMENTALS

ˈ	Primary stress
ˌ	Secondary stress
	ˌfoʊnəˈtɪʃən
ː	Long eː
ˑ	Half-long eˑ
˘	Extra-short ĕ
ǀ	Minor (foot) group
‖	Major (intonation) group
.	Syllable break ɹi.ækt
‿	Linking (absence of a break)

DIACRITICS

Diacritics may be placed above a symbol with a descender, e.g. ŋ̊

̥	Voiceless	n̥ d̥	̤	Breathy voiced	b̤ a̤	̪ Dental t̪ d̪
̬	Voiced	s̬ t̬	̰	Creaky voiced	b̰ a̰	̺ Apical t̺ d̺
ʰ	Aspirated	tʰ dʰ	̼	Linguolabial	t̼ d̼	̻ Laminal t̻ d̻
̹	More rounded	ɔ̹	ʷ	Labialized	tʷ dʷ	̃ Nasalized ẽ
̜	Less rounded	ɔ̜	ʲ	Palatalized	tʲ dʲ	ⁿ Nasal release dⁿ
̟	Advanced	u̟	ˠ	Velarized	tˠ dˠ	ˡ Lateral release dˡ
̠	Retracted	e̠	ˤ	Pharyngealized	tˤ dˤ	̚ No audible release d̚
̈	Centralized	ë	~	Velarized or pharyngealized	ɫ	
̽	Mid-centralized	e̽	̝	Raised	e̝ (ɹ̝ = voiced alveolar fricative)	
̩	Syllabic	n̩	̞	Lowered	e̞ (β̞ = voiced bilabial approximant)	
̯	Non-syllabic	e̯	̘	Advanced Tongue Root	e̘	
˞	Rhoticity	ɚ a˞	̙	Retracted Tongue Root	e̙	

TONES AND WORD ACCENTS

LEVEL			CONTOUR		
e̋ or	˥	Extra high	ě or	˩˥	Rising
é	˦	High	ê	˥˩	Falling
ē	˧	Mid	e᷄	˧˥	High rising
è	˨	Low	e᷅	˩˧	Low rising
ȅ	˩	Extra low	e᷈	˧˩˧	Rising-falling
↓		Downstep	↗		Global rise
↑		Upstep	↘		Global fall

© The International Phonetic Association